PRAISE FOR THE FIRST EDITION OF *THE ADVERTISING MANAGER'S HANDBOOK*

Thank you for creating the definitive Bible of advertising. I love your book.
—*Peter Brooks, Brooks Advertising, Lehi, UT*

Your practical approach to the subject has provided me with an invaluable tool I can use in my day-to-day business activity.
—*Shephard L. Mubiana, Advertising Consultant, Zambia*

I find many of the ideas helpful....
—*Peter Michael Murmer, Photographer, Albrightsville, PA*

SECOND EDITION

Advertising Manager's Handbook

ROBERT W. BLY

PRENTICE HALL

Library of Congress Cataloging-in-Publication Data

Bly, Robert W.
Advertising manager's handbook / Robert W. Bly — 2nd ed.
   p. cm.
   Includes bibliographical references and index.
   ISBN 0-13-757188-7(case). — ISBN-13-757196-8 (pbk.)
   1. Advertising—Management—Handbooks, manuals, etc.
2. Advertising—Handbooks, manuals, etc. I. Title.
HF5823.B364   1998
659.1'0973—dc21   98-29618
                                                          CIP

This publication is designed to provide accurate and authoritative information in
regard to the subject matter covered. It is sold with the understanding that the
publisher is not engaged in rendering legal, accounting, or other professional service.
If legal advice or other expert assistance is required, the services of a competent
professional person should be sought.

—From a Declaration of Principles jointly adopted by
a Committee of the American Bar Association and a Committee of Publishers and Associations.

Printed in the United States of America

10 9 8 7 6 5 4 3 2

ATTENTION: CORPORATIONS AND SCHOOLS

Prentice Hall books are available at quantity discounts with bulk purchase for educa-
tional, business, or sales promotional use. For information, please write to: Prentice
Hall Special Sales, 240 Frisch Court, Paramus, NJ 07652. Please supply: title of book,
ISBN number, quantity, how the book will be used, date needed.

ISBN 0-13-757188-7 (case)   ISBN 0-13-757196-8 (pbk.)

PRENTICE HALL
Paramus, NJ 07652
On the World Wide Web at http://www.phdirect.com

To Milt Pierce—Friend, Teacher, Colleague

PREFACE TO THE FIRST EDITION

This is a book for advertising managers and other people who are responsible for planning and managing their organizations' advertising programs. Whether your budget is $5,000 ... $50,000 ... $500,000 ... or $5 million, *The Advertising Manager's Handbook* can help you plan, implement, and manage an effective, successful advertising program—one that can get your message across, build your image, make your product famous in the marketplace, generate leads, build sales, motivate distributors, and achieve any other goal you desire.

Planning and managing an advertising program is a tough job. There are ad agencies, freelancers, and PR firms to help write the ads, place the feature stories, and crank out sales bulletins. There are HTML and Java programmers who can help program your Web site, and graphic artists who can design its pages. But there is little help available when it comes to sitting down and planning the year's activities. *The Advertising Manager's Handbook* was written to fill that gap.

The job of advertising manager is a balancing act. The ad manager must deal with and satisfy many people with diverse needs such as salespeople, product managers, brand managers, distributors, manufacturers' reps, vendors, the ad agency, freelancers, customers, prospects, and, of course, top management. I give advice on dealing with all of these folks.

The Advertising Manager's Handbook is short on theory, but long on practical, proven advice, information, and tools. I have been an ad manager for an industrial equipment manufacturer and an assistant marketing communications manager for an aerospace firm. As an independent advertising copywriter and consultant I have worked with more than 110 advertisers and their agencies writing, creating, and planning marketing communications programs. And I have talked with many more to gather additional information for this book.

While this book is designed to help small and medium-sized companies create sound, sensible, results-getting advertising, managers at larger firms will benefit from it, too. It is for full-time advertising managers as

viii   Preface to the First Edition

well as for managers who are responsible for advertising in addition to
their other tasks: marketing directors, sales managers, product managers,
brand managers, account executives, presidents, owners, and anyone else
who plays the role of ad manager, whether full- or part-time. Advertising
professionals who provide services to these managers—account executives
and planners, creative directors, market researchers, media planners and
buyers, copywriters, art directors, printers, list brokers, photographers,
space reps, ad agency owners, Web designers, and multimedia producers—
will also benefit.

The Advertising Manager's Handbook takes much of the guesswork
and coin flipping out of planning. The book presents a rational, step-by-
step approach based on proven advertising principles and practices. Easy-
to-follow discussions, advice, guidelines, checklists, and other tools help the
reader create an advertising plan for a company or division from scratch,
quickly and professionally.

Blank worksheets, designed to be easy to complete, guide the reader in formulating a plan based on your products, your markets, your strategies, and your selling methods. There are filled-in sample sheets to use as
examples. The worksheets can be photocopied and used over and over
again. In this way, the book continues to be a useful planning aid for many
years to come.

PREFACE TO THE SECOND EDITION

In the good old days you could write a business book, be done with it, and have it stay in print for 10 or 20 years and still be valid. No longer.

Electronic communication, personal computers, relational database software, the Internet, Web commerce, fax-on-demand, and new media are revolutionizing advertising, selling, and marketing at a breakneck pace. The first edition of *The Advertising Manager's Handbook* was written before these innovations came to light. This second edition includes an entire section on electronic marketing, and has been made even more timely by updating every chapter. The result is the revised and fully updated second edition you now hold in your hands.

HOW THE BOOK IS ORGANIZED

This handbook is organized in the following manner:

Part I—Planning gives you step-by-step instructions for creating your advertising plan. You'll learn how to define markets, set goals and objectives, create an advertising schedule and budget, and put a plan together. The role of the advertising manager in business is also addressed.

Part II—Tasks shows you how get the best results from the various types of marketing communications available to you, including print advertising, broadcast, sales promotions, trade shows, direct mail, brochures, catalogs, public relations, films and slide shows, newsletters, and house organs. You'll also learn what works (and what doesn't) in copy, graphic design, photography, illustration, printing, and audiovisual production.

Part III—Production is your guide to getting marketing communications materials organized, designed, written, and produced. Robert

Lauterborn, former corporate communications manager at International Paper, once described advertising management as quality control for marketing communications materials. Here you'll find the guidance you need to maintain that quality at a high level. You'll learn how to choose and work with an outside agency, and how to get the best from printers, photographers, freelancers, consultants, and other vendors and suppliers.

Part IV—Electronic Marketing talks about new and emerging marketing technologies, including database marketing, Internet direct mail, Web sites, data push, electronic commerce, CD-ROM and multimedia presentations, fax marketing, and more.

PART V—Management shows how to implement your plan successfully on a daily basis. You'll learn how to work with product managers and the sales force, how to sell your programs to top management, how to handle inquiries, and how to measure advertising results.

Appendices give you specific resources—publications, software, forms and model documents, organizations, and vendors—you may want to consult for assistance when implementing your advertising programs.

It is difficult to write a book of this length that is error free, and I'm certain some errors will be found. In particular, I have given special attention to making sure material used from other sources has been properly credited and permissions have been obtained. If I have not attributed material to its author properly, I apologize in advance. It was an error and not deliberate.

Also, many readers will disagree with some of the ideas presented here; others will feel important subject matter has been left out. If you have any questions, comments, corrections, ideas, suggestions, or complaints, let me know so we can correct the next edition accordingly. You can write to me at:

Bob Bly
22 E. Quackenbush Avenue
Dumont, NJ 07628
Office Phone 201-385-1220
E-mail: Rwbly@bly.com
Web site: www.bly.com

ACKNOWLEDGMENTS

I'd like to thank the hundreds of individuals and organizations who granted permission to reprint their work in this book. Although there are too many to list here, I've done my best to make sure they are given appropriate credit where their work is reprinted in the text. If I've missed anyone (and in a book this size, it's quite possible) my apologies!

Of these, I must single out Bob Donath of *Business Marketing* and Lee Rosen of B/PAA for generously granting permission to reprint articles, papers, and other research materials.

Special thanks go to Lansing Moore, Milt Pierce, Sig Rosenblum, Tom Quirck, and Terry C. Smith. When I was just starting out in advertising, they took the time to teach me what was going on and prevented me from making a total fool of myself and wasting my employer's money.

Thanks also go to my clients who have paid good money to put my ideas to the test on a daily basis. Although no one is successful all the time, together we've had far more successes than failures and have discovered the methods and techniques that this book is all about—that is, how to get better advertising results at lower cost.

I'd also like to thank my editors, Bette Schwartzberg, Tom Power, Sheck Cho, and Drew Dreeland for making this book much better than it was when it first crossed their desks. Thanks also to my publisher, Prentice Hall, for financing a project of this scope and magnitude, and to Rose Kernan for her excellent work on the design and production of the original edition of this book.

And of course, the greatest thanks to my wife, Amy Sprecher Bly, who makes it all possible and worthwhile.

CONTENTS

Part

PLANNING

I

Chapter **1**

ADVERTISING: ITS PLACE IN MODERN MARKETING

Several years ago, I received the following letter:

> Dear Bob:
>
> I produce in-house advertising for a manufacturer of
> concrete and metallurgical testing instruments and
> chrome chill rolls for the plastics industry. My respon-
> sibilities run the advertising gamut: concept; copy (I
> was a lit major); purchasing of printing, art, and pho-
> tography for direct mail, brochures, catalogs; media
> placement; trade show coordination; you name it.
>
> My question: Can you recommend the one best book that
> you know of on advertising? Or perhaps a small group of
> books that touch upon the subject....
>
> I have been in the business for about five years, which
> is just enough time to give me a real perspective on
> exactly how much I don't know and how much more I want
> to know.
>
> Thank you for your kind response.
>
> Sincerely,
>
> Daniel Gallio
> Advertising Coordinator
> Forney Incorporated
> Wampump, PA

It was mainly in response to Daniel's letter and inquiries from other people like him that I wrote the book you are now reading.

In order to make it useful to a broad range of businesses, I haven't limited the book to business-to-business advertisers (like Daniel) but offer proven principles, methods, and ideas that apply to all types of advertising, from retail to mail order, consumer products to high-tech, industrial to corporate. I have personally been involved in selling products ranging from industrial mixers and mainframe software to rental cars and vitamins.

Also, since Dan may be one of the few readers who advertises "chrome chill rolls," the ideas in the book apply universally to all products, all services, all types of businesses—manufacturers, wholesalers, retailers, distributors, and service organizations—and examples are drawn from a broad range of industries. You'll learn from a variety of selling situations: everything from selling office supplies by mail order, to increasing take-out orders for a gourmet foods store, to selling mainframe software to systems analysts and IS (Information Systems) managers. No matter what your business or industry, you'll profit from the information contained in this book.

WHAT MARKETING CAN DO FOR YOUR COMPANY

According to John Graham, a marketing consultant, there's a basic tension inside most companies that creates a corporate schizophrenia. It involves the conflicting forces of marketing, sales, and a company's goals and objectives.

These forces are pulling in two directions. At one moment, the message from the top is to gain a greater perspective, to think long term, and not to focus just on today. At almost the same time, the same voices are barking at the sales department to close more deals, to get the end-of-the-month figures up.

According to Graham, the message is clear: long-term thinking gets lip service, while this week's sales report gets attention.

While no company dares to abandon immediate sales in favor of a plan or program that will have long-term benefit, a way should be found to benefit from a marketing strategy that produces positive results over time. Is it possible to implement a long-term strategy and still have immediate sales?

The major problem facing businesses is the trend of peaks and valleys in sales. One month is great and the next is way off. Certain times of the year are outstanding, but at other times sales are slack.

Even more to the point are all the problems of reacting to competition, not being known as well as another company in the marketplace, and failing to be on the leading edge at the right moment.

The function of marketing is to deal with these ongoing, persistent issues head on. The goal is to create conditions such that there is a constant flow of sales, proper growth, and acceptance in the marketplace.

Marketing is no quick fix. There's no magic involved, no instant leap from the depths to the top of the heap. Marketing is a long-term investment in building a strong, enduring business.

What can marketing do for a company? Here are a dozen reasons why a consistent, cohesive, and unified marketing program best serves a company's needs.

1. Marketing establishes a company as a permanent player. Even though a business may be solid, it is the way it is perceived that makes the difference in sales. The most effective way to attract sales is to be viewed as an organization that has staying power. Customers and prospects are more interested in stability than in the past, and the competition is quick to take shots at a seemingly vulnerable rival. One of the roles of marketing is to shape or influence the way a company is perceived.

2. Marketing levels the playing field. Nothing guarantees that the field will ever be completely level. But it is possible to smooth out some of the hills and valleys so that the work is a little easier and more successful. Effective marketing gives a company that extra head of steam to continue charging down the field no matter what the other team is throwing at you.

3. Marketing helps avoid a constant crisis business environment. Many companies are victimized by a reactive posture. They never seem to set the direction; they are always doing damage control. A marketing program is designed to permit a business to take the initiative so that it can control its destiny and move in directions it chooses.

4. The goal of marketing is to provide a pull rather than a push. How often have you heard someone say, "Well, let's hit the street and get those sales up"? That's a short-term fix that doesn't fix anything—except this week's sales report. If a company is well known, respected, and trusted, sales come much easier.

5. Marketing builds enduring relationships with customers. While there are always those buyers who will jump ship for a penny, most customers are far more sophisticated today. They value relationships because they get better service in such a setting. Fewer and fewer companies are willing to sign on with vendors who are clearly only interested in "making a sale." They look for suppliers who are closer to being consultants than salespeople.

6. Marketing spotlights the customer. A marketing orientation forces a business to understand and cultivate the customer over a period of time. Marketing is not slipping a purchasing agent a pair of tickets to a Celtics game! With proper marketing, the customers recognize that a vendor is interested in their business—and that the partnership is there for the long term.

7. Marketing gives a company control over its image. In a day when everyone is bombarded with thousands and thousands of messages while trying to get the job done, there's little time for exhaustive analysis when it comes to suppliers. Evaluations—and eventually decisions—may well be based on instant (or at least quick) conclusions and imprecise impressions. Rightly or wrongly, we come to conclusions that stay with us. One of the primary functions of marketing is to "massage" those impressions to make sure they reflect the way a company wants to be portrayed and perceived.

8. Marketing aids in customer retention. We all love new customers. The latest sale produces excitement. But what about all those forgotten customers, the ones who just seem to fade away? They are the ones who conclude that no one cares or that it's only the "big accounts" that matter. Marketing recognizes that it is far more expensive to attract a new customer than it is to maintain or increase sales to existing customers.

9. Marketing helps increase sales to present customers. The greatest untapped source of new sales is a company's present customer base. The proof rests in the fact that customers say, "I didn't know you did that." One major home security company realized that it could increase its sales by 50 percent by upgrading and adding on to existing systems. Surveys showed that the company's customers did not know what was available! A primary function of marketing is to see to it that current customers know everything a business can do for them.

10. Marketing lets you attract the right customers. Many banks and insurance agencies are realizing that they have customers who are dead weight because they are unprofitable. In other words, they have the wrong customers. A marketing program lets a company steer its way to the right customers, the ones it can serve profitably. Marketing is a rifle approach; no shotguns here.

11. Marketing helps a business avoid wasting money. Even though marketing costs money, it is a disciplined approach to spending money because it depends on a plan, a program. An advertising shot here, a direct-mail piece there, an occasional news release, a quarterly newsletter that came out once—five years ago, all add up to wasted money, time, and effort. A consistent marketing program keeps it all together.

12. Most important of all, marketing allows a business to devote more of its energy to its real business. What does a construction company do? The answer is not constructing buildings. The smart builder creates efficiency, reduces costs, enhances productivity. A building is only a means to an end. What does F.A.O. Schwartz sell? According to the company's president, it's not toys. F.A.O. Schwartz sells fun. The widget mentality is dead, except that many in sales continue to peddle wonderful widgets. Marketing's aim is to help a business recognize and communicate how its products and services enhance the customer's life.

Pushing harder isn't the answer. Using the latest sales gimmick isn't the way to success. Making marketing a top priority is the best way for a business to ensure that it will be around for the long term. It is the commitment to the future that guarantees today's success.

WHERE MARKETING COMMUNICATIONS FITS INTO THE BUYING PROCESS

John Friedberg, of New York advertising agency Friedberg Feder, says buyers go through a six-step sequence to decide on a purchase:

1. *Credibility*—They must be convinced that the product, service, or company is reliable.

2. *Awareness*—If they don't know you and what you are selling, they won't consider it.

3. *Need*—People won't consider the purchase unless there is a real or perceived need.

4. *Evaluation*—The buyer tests, examines, and investigates the product to make an evaluation.

5. *Conviction*—The prospect becomes convinced that your product offers the best value for the price.

6. *Maintenance*—Once they've made the purchase you must reassure buyers that their decision was the right one.

Marketing communications can enhance the purchase process at every step, but it is especially effective in the earlier stages—steps one, two, and three.

AN UNCONVENTIONAL POINT OF VIEW

Although some of the conventional wisdom about advertising reflects sound thinking, much of it is misguided or out of date. When it comes to advertising practice, you will find that I am often a contrarian, holding opinions and views different from what others may tell you or what you may find in other texts.

My opinions and views are not based on personal bias or idiosyncrasy, but on tested, proven advertising results reflecting work on hundreds of projects for more than 110 clients nationwide. In each case, our objective was not to satisfy corporate committees or generate exciting creative work. (You'll find later that creativity for creativity's sake can be the greatest destroyer of advertising effectiveness.) Instead, we wanted to achieve immediate, specific, measurable sales results in a short period of time.

As a result, scattered throughout these pages you'll find hundreds of new ways to get better results out of your advertising. Even the "old pros" will find some gems here, proven but little-known techniques you can use to multiply the response and sales your advertising campaigns generate.

Why does your employer pay you to conduct an advertising and communications program for your company? Many advertising managers have difficulty answering that question. When asked by management, "What are we getting for our investment in advertising?" they stammer weakly about "building image" and "awareness" and "readership scores" and "brand preferences." The thought that their advertising actually has to sell something makes them uncomfortable, as if the crass, cold-blooded pursuit of a sale were something on a lower plane than the lofty art of creating beautiful printed pages with words and pictures. These advertising managers understand nothing about their jobs, and maybe they never will.

The amateur in advertising management is concerned solely with aesthetics, with creating an ad or brochure that is beautiful to look at, a pleasure to read, and a sure bet to win an award from the advertising industry.

The professional knows that the only reason to spend money in business is to make money. Claude Hopkins said it best: "The only purpose of advertising is to make sales. It is profitable or unprofitable according to its actual sales. It is not for general effect. It is not to keep your name before the people. It is not primarily to aid your other salesmen."

My answer to the question, "What is the purpose of advertising?" is the same as Claude Hopkins', only slightly modified. I put it this way:

The purpose of advertising is to sell or help sell your company's product or service.

The "help sell" part of this definition recognizes that a single ad or promotion may not do the entire selling job. Instead, it is part of an over-all promotional campaign or program whose single-minded goal is to generate the maximum sales possible at the lowest possible promotional cost.

"Too much advertising is aimed at mass entertainment," wrote John Egley in the *Business to Business Marketer* (August 1997, p. 2 and October 1997, p. 3). "That's not its proper mission. All you should be concerned about is having your advertising zeroed in on the product-related interests of potential buyers of your product. No one else matters. Not even your mother. Much advertising fails because it's based on delusions of grandeur. Contrary to what many advertisers think, they aren't the center of the universe and their target audience does have other interests besides forming fan clubs to collect and pore lovingly over their ads."

The headline from an article in the *Wall Street Journal* tells an all-too-common tale. "Nissan's ad campaign was a hit everywhere but in the showrooms," it proclaimed. "Critics gave boffo reviews to bizarre commercials; meanwhile, sales skidded."

You may have seen this campaign. The commercials all end with a brief shot of an elderly Asian man holding a sign and smiling knowingly. This is supposed to be Yukata Katayama, former head of Nissan U.S. operations.

The commercials started running in September 1996. According to the *Wall Street Journal* article, Nissan's U.S. sales fell 2.7 percent that month compared with the previous year. October 1996 sales fell 10.2 percent and November dropped 4.2 percent. The ad agency's response was that immediate sales weren't the goal; they had created "brand awareness." Nissan dealers, the *Journal* reported, hated the campaign because of its negative sales effect. The article concluded: "More than ever, agencies are scrambling to make ads that create a buzz but have little to do with the products their clients sell."

"The real creativity in good ... advertising comes well before an ad is designed," wrote Valerie Moul, Vice President, Godfrey Advertising, in *Business Marketing* magazine (September 1997). "It's about crafting a message that is relevant, compelling, and persuasive."

ADVERTISING *DOES* SELL

Direct marketers already know this fact. They can run an ad and measure the sales it produces and whether it is profitable to the penny.

"Advertising must change behavior, not just attitudes," wrote Lester Wunderman, considered by many the founder of direct marketing, in his book *Being Direct* (New York: Random House). "Favorable consumer attitudes go only part of the way to creating sales. It's also the consumer's accountable actions such as inquiries, product trials, purchases, and repurchases that create profits."

Retailers, too, can see immediate results from circulars, newspaper inserts, catalogs, and newspaper advertisements. Electronic cash registers linked to a central computer tell the store exactly what is sold each day and can track peaks and valleys in sales activity. Retail ad managers know by counting the take whether yesterday's ad helped boost this week's sales. Copywriter Bob Westenberg tells the joke about a jeweler who was asked whether his advertising got results and replied: "You bet! Last week we advertised for a night watchman ... and the next night we were robbed!"

Sole proprietors, self-employed professionals, and other entrepreneurial firms with a small number of employees also know that advertising sells. For them, it has to. If a home-based business spends $10,000 in marketing and gets no business as a result, it will quickly go out of business.

It's not only consumer advertising that is supposed to sell. Industrial advertising helps sell products and services, too. If you market primarily to business and industry, you will want to get a copy of an important research paper, the *ARFIABP Study on the Impact of Business Publications Advertising on Sales and Profits* (American Business Press, 675 Third Avenue, New York, NY 10017, 212-661-6360). This important piece of advertising research linking business advertising to sales is vital reading for every ad manager.

The study concludes:

- More advertising means more sales.
- More advertising can result in higher profits.
- Increased advertising frequency can also increase sales leads.
- It takes four to six months to see the results of an advertising program.
- An ad campaign can keep working for a full year and longer.
- Advertising can help build a dealer network; if the product is sold through dealers, it pays to advertise to both dealers and end users.
- Business publication advertising is effective for a wide range of products sold at a wide range of prices.

Lester Wunderman concludes: "The results of advertising are increasingly measurable; they must now become accountable. Advertising can't be just a contribution to goodwill—it must become an investment in profits. Advertising must be as relevant to each consumer as the product or service is. General advertising and more targeted direct marketing must both be part of a holistic communication strategy. Measurable results from media are what count."

SIX WAYS ADVERTISING CAN INCREASE YOUR SALES

1. Sell Direct. Some products can be sold directly from an ad or direct mail solicitation. This works best with products that have clearly defined benefits, are not available through local retail outlets, have some inherent degree of excitement, and are priced under $1,000. There are exceptions. Some mail order marketers offer higher-priced products. A recent gift catalog advertised a working two-person submarine for around $70,000! In 1997, Victoria's Secret offered a white satin Miracle Bra enhanced with 101 diamonds for $3 million. Mail order selling also works for supplies and other commodity items that can be grouped by category and offered in a catalog (office and computer supplies are good examples).

2. Generate Sales Leads. For the smaller firm with a limited budget, the best use of marketing communications is to generate immediate inquiries that can be converted to sales. This type of ad encourages responses by making a free offer of some type, usually a free booklet, free initial consultation, free estimate, free evaluation of a problem, or other free information. Generally scorned and overlooked by corporate ad managers, these inquiries, properly handled, can add tens of thousands, even hundreds of thousands, of dollars to your gross sales each year.

3. Educate Your Prospects. Advertising can communicate information about your product, your service, your business philosophy, your way of doing business, or your unique approach to solving the customer's problems. A typical example is an industrial manufacturer whose product is differentiated from the competition's because it uses a different engineering principle of operation. Advertising would highlight this key difference, explain why it was chosen and how it works, and stress the benefits of this type of construction (better performance, higher reliability, greater efficiency, lower operating costs, etc.) to the reader.

Service businesses are often successful with an even purer educational approach, in which advertising tells the reader about a subject in general, only glancingly referring to the firm's particular services. One successful ad for a collection agency used the headline, "Seven questions to ask before you hire a collection agency and one good answer to each." The copy was filled with facts about the methods and techniques used to collect more money from delinquent accounts. Readership was high because the ad presented valuable information of immediate use to the reader. Response was high because, by giving this information instead of a blatant sales pitch, the copy convinced readers that the advertiser was someone who could help them.

"Create an advertising curriculum that teaches as it sells ... a learning system that teaches one bit of information at a time," advises Wunderman. "Each advertising message can build on the learning of the previous one. It can teach consumers why your product is superior and why they should buy it."

4. Create Awareness. There are so many products, services, and ideas on the market today that a big part of your job may be simply to make people aware that you offer a particular solution to their problems. An example is Ed Werz, who as far as I know is the only consultant in my immediate geographic area specializing in postcard deck advertising.

Ed does not need to convince prospects that he is better than his competition, for he has no direct competitors. Ed's challenge is to make his prospects aware that a) postcard deck advertising works and is profitable; b) he is a recognized authority and expert in this type of marketing; and c) he is available for hire. His marketing concentrates on building awareness of his area of expertise and his ongoing consulting practice.

5. Establish Credibility. Madison Avenue talks lovingly of "building an image"; I prefer to think of it as "establishing credibility." Even if you offer a service or product that clearly is ideal for your prospect, he or she may not respond because the prospect may not know you and may never have heard of your company before. People have a built-in uneasiness about dealing with unknowns and prefer to buy from well-established firms; this is why for many years IBM PCs outsold cloned microcomputers that were equal or better in quality and lower in price.

Repeated advertising in select media can help build familiarity with your name and establish your identity. Free advertising publicity is even more effective at establishing you as the unchallenged authority in your field.

6. Keep Your Name in Front of the Public. Although Claude Hopkins said this isn't what advertising is for, in a way keeping your name in front of the public does help to stimulate sales from new buyers and especially among past customers. People who have inquired about your product in the past or have used your service once may quickly move on to other activities. Soon, all the time spent in making contact and selling yourself will be just a distant memory—a memory that can be stimulated into action and interest by renewed contact via marketing communications.

For example, after I gave a speech, a member of the audience approached me about doing some consulting work for his firm. We exchanged information and he promised an assignment, but no assignment came. Because I was busy, I let it go and did not pursue him. He faded from my memory, and I'm sure I did from his. But he had put me on his company's mailing list, and six months later I received a promotional mailing from them. I scribbled on the reply card, "Jim, I want to write your next mailing," and signed my name. Two days later he called and the assignment was mine. Even though he had my marketing materials, I had simply faded from his mind. Marketing helped revive that lead and make the sale.

CASE STUDY:
A FORTUNE 500 COMPANY SELLS ON THREE LEVELS

Table 1.1 outlines how one Fortune 500 corporation views its marketing communications activities. At the top of the pyramid, the corporate level, the mission is to promote the corporation as a whole to a diverse audience that includes business leaders, the financial community (e.g., investors, financial analysts), government (because this corporation's sales are primarily to federal agencies), opinion leaders, the community, academia, and the press. Print ads in business publications reach business leaders in corporate America. Television commercials bring the corporate message to a broader audience, which includes the general public as well as the business community.

Table 1-1. Marketing communications responsibilities.

	Mission	To This Audience	Through These Media	To Sell
Corporate	Sell the Corporation as a Corporation	Business Leaders Financial Influentials Government Opinion Leaders Community Academia Press	Television Business Publications Major Newspapers	Basic Strengths of the Corporation
Business Units	Present Capabilities for Markets/Industries	High-Level Decision Makers Planners/Engineers Financiers	General Business & Horizontal Industry Publications	Systems Capabilities Broad Product & Service Capabilities
Divisions	Inform Prospects of Available Products & Services	Specifiers Designers Purchasers Purchasing Influences	Vertical Publications Functional Publications	Specific Products & Services

Marketing Communications Channels

Advertising—Print, TV, Radio	Sales Training
Direct Mail	Product Information
Brochures	Co-op Advertising
Exhibits & Trade Shows	Point of Sale Displays & Demos
Meetings—Internal & External	Permanent Signs

This large corporation is divided into several major companies or business units. At the company level, the mission of marketing communications is to promote each company's capabilities to the specific markets and industries they serve. Here, the purpose of marketing communications is more specific; namely, it attempts to convince the company's target prospects (at the highest level of decision making) to do business with the company. Print ads, appearing in general business publications as well as industry-specific trade journals, tell readers what the company does, the types of products it sells, how it solves specific problems in the industry, and other reasons why the reader should buy from the company.

At the bottom of the pyramid is marketing communications created for specific divisions within each company. For example, one division might sell one product line to one industry, while another division sells another line of products to a different customer base. The mission of marketing communications is to generate sales of specific products and services by advertising to buyers (those who specify, recommend, or purchase the product) in specific trade publications. Ads feature specific products and include detailed discussions of features, specifications, and benefits. Web pages contain the specifications and facts buyers need to make a purchase decision, and sites with secure electronic commerce let buyers order right from the Web site.

For small and medium-sized firms, most of the advertising and marketing effort will be equivalent to the division level in the marketing communications responsibilities represented in Table 1.1. That is, it will be aimed at generating measurable increases in sales of specific products and services within a specific time frame, such as "to increase billable hours in my law practice by 20 percent and get 5 new retainer clients within 12 months."

USING THE CAST SYSTEM TO SELECT APPROPRIATE MARKETING COMMUNICATIONS TOOLS

What types of marketing communications activities can go into your promotional plan? You should already be familiar with most of these:

Audiovisual presentations

Brochures

Case histories

Catalogs

CD-ROMs

Classified ads

Direct mail

Directories

E-mail

Fax broadcasting

Magazine advertising

Newsletters

Newspaper advertising

Outdoor advertising

Point-of-purchase displays

Postcard decks

Publicity and public relations

Radio advertising

Referrals

Sales promotion

Sales representatives

Specialty advertising

Technical and business publications

Telemarketing

Television commercials

Testimonials

Trade show displays

Videos

Web sites

Yellow Pages

We could probably add to this list or expand some of these categories, but these are the basic marketing communications activities used by most companies to promote their businesses. Before you create any advertising schedule or marketing plan, sit down with this list for a few minutes and ask yourself: "Which of these techniques works best with my company ... in my industry ... with my type of product or service ... with the particular markets I am trying to reach?" The answer provides direction as to where to allocate most of your time, energy, effort, and budget.

George Black has outlined a system you can use to rank each marketing communications program according to how effective it is in your particular situation. His approach, called CAST (Comparative Analysis of Sales Tools), ranks each marketing tool on a scale of 1 to 5 in terms of its effectiveness in 11 basic categories. They are:

1. *Impact or impression*: The ability to get attention, to penetrate consciousness and be remembered.

2. *Size of audience or reach*: Ability to reach large numbers of prospects at the same time.

3. *Cost per contact*: Efficiency in reaching large numbers of prospective customers.

4. *Sales lead development*: Effectiveness in securing inquiries from the audience reached, usually measured in terms of cost per inquiry.

5. *Message control*: Ability to state and restate the message exactly the way you want to say it.

6. *Flexibility*: Facility for changing the message to fit the need or to overcome objections as they are raised.

7. *Timing control*: Ability to reach out to your prospects when you want to make the move, or when the buying action is imminent.

8. *Repetitive contact*: Suitability for repeating the message with effective frequency without wearing out your welcome.

9. *Reaction speed*: Capacity for sensing the prospect's reaction rapidly so that message changes can be made.

10. Credibility: Capacity for inspiring belief and acceptance.

11. Closing the sale: Effectiveness in getting the signature on the order.

Table 1.2 shows a CAST analysis matrix used by the Automatic Switch Company of Florham Park, New Jersey. All sales tools used by the firm—sales engineers, media advertising, reference publications, public relations and publicity, exhibitions and trade shows, catalogs and sales literature, direct mail, and telemarketing—were ranked on a scale of 1 to 5 in each of these 11 categories (1 = not very effective, 5 = extremely effective).

Table 1-2. CAST—Comparitive analysis of sales tools.

	Impact or Impression	Size of Audience	Cost Per Contact	Sales Leads	Message Control	Flexibility	Timing Control	Repetitive Contact	Reaction Speed	Credibility	Closing the Sale
Sales Engineer	5	2	1	3	4	5	5	2	5	5	5
Media Advertising	4	5	4	4	5	1	3	5	2	4	2
Reference Publications	2	4	4	3	5	1	3	3	1	2	1
Public Relations/Publicity	3	5	5	5	2	1	1	4	2	5	1
Exhibitions/Trade Shows	5	2	2	2	4	5	1	2	5	5	5
Catalogs/Literature	3	3	3	2	5	2	2	3	2	4	3
Direct Mail	4	4	3	4	5	3	3	4	3	3	3
Telemarketing	2	3	2	3	4	5	5	2	5	3	2

The matrix is useful because it shows, at a glance, what each marketing tool can and cannot do for your company. As seen in Table 1.2, public relations rated the maximum score (5) in several categories. It was found to be extremely effective in reaching a wide audience and generating a large volume of sales leads at low cost. In addition, public relations is more credible than media advertising or the company's own promotional literature. But public relations does not close sales (here it ranked 1, the lowest rating).

By comparison, the sales engineer is the person who goes in and gets the order. However, sales engineers can call on only so many people per day, and sending them around is expensive, so they ranked low in terms of size of audience and cost per contact. Also, sales engineers did not rank highly in terms of generating sales leads. This is not surprising, because salespeople tend to be more comfortable calling on current accounts rather than prospecting for new business.

You can readily see the logic in this system and adapt it to your own situation. Which marketing communications activities give you what you need in terms of leads, cost, credibility, flexibility, timing, and other factors important to you? The CAST system can help you make a logical, informed decision about which marketing activities deserve the bulk of your attention and budget.

Although far from scientific, CAST does force you to view marketing decisions quantitatively rather than from pure gut instinct.

THE AD MANAGER'S ROLE

At a speech given before the New York chapter of the Business/Professional Advertising Association (B/PAA), Robert Lauterborn, then corporate advertising manager for International Paper, described the advertising manager's job as one of "quality control for marketing communications." When Lauterborn's young son realized his dad's company produced the famous "Power of the Printed Word" corporate ad campaign, he asked his father about his involvement. Did he write it? No. Design it? No. Come up with the idea? Not all by himself, no. Then what, Dad? Lauterborn thought for a moment and replied, "I made sure it came out right."

A few years ago, a group representing several facets of advertising met in Toronto, Ontario to discuss the changes they foresaw in the position of advertising executives 20 years in the future. Here is how some of these experts predicted the role of ad manager will change in the early years of the twenty-first century:

I think good advertising managers in the future will be doing exactly what they are doing today, and have done in the past: producing excellent communications. The only things that may change are some of the tools and the level of sophistication of some of the means that we use to get our messages across in the future.

True communicators must sensitize their principles to the needs of a varied audience, and must educate that audience in the true worth of the company or the goods and services that they are prepared to deliver. This also means that the traditional role of the advertiser will change to fill that need, rather than as the creator of product or service awareness and of persuasion to use.

With the product line we make, I feel that it's critical that the advertising department become involved very heavily into technical aspects, as well as the advertising of the product. Without good technical backup to install or work a product like ours, consumers are not going to enjoy it. I feel that advertising a product like ours will get heavily into the technical aspect, in terms of the way the manuals are graphically illustrated and produced. The communications techniques and tools that improve that will help to sell particular products.

In my opinion, the future of the ad manager as a distinct species is about the same as the peregrine falcon. The ad manager will live in crevices in the corporate structure. As far as the future of an advertising department, I think its name will change. Advertising as a distinct function will disappear; it will probably be called "communications." I think it is likely to assume a corporate importance equivalent to finance, production, and manufacturing within the next sixteen years. Advertising people will be primarily intuitive, planning, and development and production. Policy and strategy will be done on a higher level of communications responsibility.

In many small to medium-sized organizations, the title advertising manager is a misnomer. The title has been inappropriately bestowed upon individuals whose only real role was to provide a clerical link between the company, its agency, and the media. Often, to the detriment of the company, this person is used as a buffer between the client and advertising professionals. This individual has survived by reverting totally to secretarial clerical duties. On the other hand, we have the true advertising manager, newly employed by medium- to large-sized companies. More often than not, this person has had at least some formal training, and is usually fairly conversant with the company's marketing objectives. Unfortunately, to the detriment of the entire industry, many of these people, often highly qualified, particularly in the United States, have become the victims of recession.

The advertising director must become a consultant to his or her own company, telling the marketing people where the markets are, why they're there, why they're profitable to that particular sector. I think it's no longer a simple job of just buying space and making sure that colors match and that sort of thing, because that task is being run outside. If the ad person wishes to grow, it's going to have to be on an international plane, because our competition is that way.

I think the title is going to change from advertising manager to marketing services manager, which will encompass a lot more than just pretty pictures and advertising media. The media, I think, will encompass more marketing support, in terms of helping a marketing manager and a product manager, and how to sell the product. So I think it's not going to be the advertising manager, per se. I think it's going to be marketing services, and it seems to be a trend these days with more companies, to call that person a marketing services manager, as opposed to advertising manager.

We have the opportunity to get in on other things, like public affairs consulting. We're not just producers of advertising and promotion items. We perform a consultative role to senior management on many things having to do with communications directed toward employees and the outside world. We have a public relations group in the company, and we work hand-in-glove with them. We like to think we're the people who understand and see opportunities first.

Advertising is going to have to be seen as significant. At the moment, it's something that's convenient. If you can't get anybody else to do it, the ad department will handle it. That kind of attitude has gone by the board. We can't afford it any more.

Today's advertising managers, marketing communications managers, or marketing services or support managers are much more than ad makers or printing supervisors or premium orderers; they are consultants to their companies, advising marketing, sales, and top management on the best way to increase sales and boost profits through effective use of advertising, publicity, and promotional techniques. Ad agencies also will make the switch from order takers to trusted advisors. As one of the previously quoted business consultants observed, "Advertising agencies are going to become more consultative, rather than executional. I believe they will become very professional and they are going to be much more expensive."

Equipped with personal computers and desktop publishing software, many businesspeople who are not marketing professionals regularly turn out their own brochures, bulletins, newsletters, and other marketing communications. Another role advertising managers may find themselves playing is instructor, trainer, and consultant to managers who intend to produce all or some of their communications on their own, without assistance from the marketing department. You might be called upon to edit copy already written by an engineer, critique a Web site put up by product managers, or add flare to a data sheet layout a manager did on her own desktop system. My advice is: Don't fight it; get used to it.

As a freelance copywriter, for example, in addition to offering copywriting of marketing documents, I have for several years also offered a "copy critique" service for clients who want to write their own copy but have it checked by a professional copywriter before sending it out. For a fee much less than my normal fee to write the copy from scratch, I critique their work and make suggestions for improvement.

Other trends affecting marketing communications professionals are downsizing and outsourcing. AT&T announced the layoff of 40,000 employees. IBM recently offered early retirement or layoff to 60,000 people, and after the Burroughs/Sperry merger, Unisys fired 50,000. Between 1979 and 1992, corporate America fired a total of 4.4 million people. The result is a large market of unemployed managers and professionals, many of them former marketing communications staff.

Many of those people are turning to some form of freelancing or consulting within the advertising field. They offer services ranging from copywriting and strategic planning to Web site design and database consulting. Manpower, the world's biggest staffing agency, now employs 1.5 million people. According to the National Association of Temporary and Staffing Services (NATSS), 21 percent of temp workers in the U.S. can be classified as "professional and technical." A Coopers & Lybrand survey shows that in 1996, 81 percent of America's fastest-growing companies hired temporary, part-time, or contract employees. Dun & Bradstreet Information Services reports that 40 percent of small businesses outsource at least one function.

More and more advertising and marketing professionals are becoming self-employed, many as an alternative to being unemployed. In 1992, the *Wall Street Journal* reported that over 10 million Americans worked in their own unincorporated businesses. *Occupational Outlook Quarterly* estimates that more than 15 million workers are self-employed, with 3 million owning incorporated businesses. During the past decade, more than 700,000 workers made the transition from corporate employment to self-employment.

The growing popularity and accessibility of the Internet has also affected the advertising industry. More than 60 million people worldwide use the Internet, and more than 17 million Americans browse the World Wide Web at least once a week. There are 7 million home pages on the Web, many of them sponsored by freelancer consultants and small consulting firms. Internet communication, networking, and job postings will result in increased business for consultants and may reduce both selling costs and the sales cycle.

In addition, for the first time in history, it is unnecessary to commit a marketing document to print in order to make it accessible to prospects, salespeople, and customers. Print-oriented ad agencies and design firms have lost business as some marketers have opted to publish select documents only on the Internet or on a company intranet without producing a printed version. More common, however, is the creation of marketing documents in both Internet and printed form.

WHAT COMMUNICATIONS CAN—AND CAN'T—DO FOR A BUSINESS

Paul Sherrington, Chairman Emeritus of the Business Marketing Association, made the following comments on the role of marketing communications in the modern business world. They are reprinted here with his permission:

> Flipping through a few old notebooks the other day, it was interesting to revisit the hot topics in communications ten, fifteen, twenty years ago. Moving fast forward to today, it's remarkable how much and how fast things changed.
>
> New media channels, the ways smart marketers now build their communications mixes, the rapidly evolving role of agencies, the shrinking size and shape of corporate staffs, the emergence of highly specialized vendors, and many other outcomes from the revolution in our business can be seen with the naked eye.
>
> Even the most constant issue over the years, the struggle to justify communications in a business-to-business environment, has taken on a new face. Old articles talked about the need for "selling *your* budget to management," or "Why $1.8 million is really better than $1.7 million," or whatever might have been appropriate given the size and scale of your business or client.
>
> Today, the game is much more severe. It may involve working to sell *any* budget to management. At the very least, there's often a struggle not to swallow inappropriate, force-fed objectives and measurements. Compounding the problem, in many cases, are some very real divisions among former allies in marketing, sales, and communications. After all, who gets what size piece of a smaller pie?
>
> Why do this stuff? It's scary. People who confuse all communications with direct response seem to be everywhere. You know the type. And you cringe when the question comes: "How much will sales increase if we run that ad?"
>
> Yeah, right. If every ad generated a traceable three-dollar return for every dollar spent, I guess there would be no limit to communications budgets. Spend fifty million dollars and increase revenue by a hundred and fifty million. Soon, you'd be up to a billion dollars in communications and the bottom line jumping three billion.
>
> Life should be so simple. Actually, communicators probably have created a lot of problems for themselves by over-promising what can be delivered in the real world. Maybe we've started believing the hype from awards entries. You know the drill: "Running this spiffy new ad three times resulted in a sales leap of eighty-four million dollars"—or something equally absurd.
>
> But probably the biggest problem is that we're dealing with a lot of fish out of water. Often these days, propeller heads, bean counters, and other non-marketing types occupy marketing chairs. If you're lucky, you might get a salesperson who at least knows the value of brochures and won't want to quantify results from an ad in the first two days. But not too many of them are around anymore, either.

Down the road in Atlanta, we have one of the most sophisticated marketers on the planet. I'm thinking of Coke. They're so good they even turned a "classic" disaster a decade ago into roaring success—almost overnight. Somehow, I don't picture them running a few television spots on Wednesday night and lining up Thursday waiting for the phones to ring with people wanting to order a can of Coke.

I don't buy a car every time I see a Ford, Chevy, or Toyota commercial. That would even be true if someone someday did a truly great car ad (though Saturn did a few years ago and have at least assured themselves they will be on my list next time I shop). I doubt a great mailer from a CPA firm would cause a company to go out and fire its auditors, or that an Internet page from a company that designs power plants will generate three start orders in the southeast in a week.

Too bad too many think communications should accomplish feats akin to the above. But back to reality. Paid communications can do a lot for an organization—ranging far beyond what can be immediately measured. To be sure, public relations must be part of the mix. But the primary focus here is on budget justification. And budget battles typically focus on every other form of marketing communications.

So why pay bucks to communicate? Here are a couple of dozen reasons off the top of my head:

1. It's management's voice—you can say exactly what needs to be said.

2. You can target very select audiences.

3. Communication lowers the cost of selling.

4. It's critical to building stronger brands and stronger brands are critical to bottom-line success.

5. In many cases, communication is the only way to reach hidden buying influences.

6. You can outmaneuver the competition—flooding channels on a given date with a product launch or major announcement.

7. Communication makes the initial contact and is often the first thing a prospect knows about a business.

8. You can efficiently create primary desirability—the big benefit when someone responds to an ad, mailer, or electronic message without a direct sales prompt.

9. You can build a "reason-why-to-buy" case and provide all kinds of evidence relating to value—something especially important to sophisticated marketers selling differentiated products and services.

10. It's a way to microsegment audiences smartly—reaching different titles with specialized messages and thereby preconditioning buying influences.

11. Communication can repeatedly ask for the order without being obtrusive.

12. It's by far the best way to provide detailed specifications.

13. You can search out unsuspected prospects.

14. With all the tools available today, communication allows you to make thousands, even millions, of calls simultaneously.

15. It's about the only way to open closed doors, especially in reaching people who won't talk to your sales rep and who tried and rejected earlier versions of your product or service.

16. You can efficiently introduce a new product or service, speed acceptance, and keep current customers sold.

17. Communication is a clear signal about long-term commitment to an industry and your own customers and prospects.

18. It helps open new markets.

19. You can test various types of appeals.

20. Communications are critical to relationship management.

21. Ongoing programs establish and maintain the prestige not only of your company but of its products and services as well.

22. It's a way to stimulate sales channels—VARs, independent contractors, trade outlets, et cetera.

23. Communications are essential to positioning and gaining share of mind awaiting the day a purchase decision will be made.

24. And, by the way, communications can generate sales leads—if sales leads are the goal.

Of course, my premise is that communications can do only so much for a business. It can't:

- sell a bad product or service—twice;

- create demand for overpriced or otherwise noncompetitive products or services;

- work overnight or on a one-shot basis;

- deliver results when tactics are not integrated (Using a sales-only or an advertising-only program is the equivalent of sending in the Marines without air cover.);

- do the selling job alone (Business marketing usually depends upon the sales force to close deals.);

- push seasonal products or services out of season;

- move poorly distributed products;

- sell products or services to people having no use for them;

- prop up a weak sales force;

- accomplish anything if poorly conceived, written, or produced.

So just what can you promise that communications will do for your company or client? It depends on the premise.

What does the program seek to accomplish? What are its goals? What can realistically be done?

If sales leads for a new product are what's needed, measuring effectiveness is easy. But leads converted to sales are not the only reason to communicate.

A company needs to communicate qualitatively and quantitatively if it values the industry it serves; values its customers; seeks to lure its prospects; believes it has a real message to put forth in the marketplace; wants to compete (because most others in your industry are wearing down the resistance of your customers every day); and understands that sales effectiveness does not happen in an information vacuum.

Those seeking to shrink can expedite the process by *not* communicating and signaling their industry, customers, and prospects that they're clueless about the future; are shriveling and can't afford to maintain ongoing dialogues; and are really planning exit strategies rather than new products and services.

Marketing in the New Millennium

Rick Kean, director of the Business Marketing Association, a trade group of business-to-business marketers, sees the future challenges to the professional communicator as follows:

> More and more companies have decided to carve out the recovery in their profit margins by frenetic cost-cutting and restructuring, reengineering, or whatever euphemism you choose for "layoffs." Now the gains are coming harder again and the margins are narrowing. A lot of companies have gotten the best lift they can from cost reduction, so what will fuel the next ratchet upward? Will it be faster growth, more volume, or more cuts?
>
> Some time ago Peter Drucker, writing about the downsizing phenomenon in the *Wall Street Journal*, said, "for a short time, costs are likely to go down and profits and share prices will go up. But a year or so later each company will be no better off than it was before and then it will surely announce another layoff."
>
> If he's right, marketing could indeed be in trouble. Not long ago, marketing was seen as the engine propelling business forward. It was understood that marketing played a key role in a company's success. Today, marketing departments around the world are struggling with diminished stature and thinning ranks, as layoffs target those who cannot justify their contribution to corporate profits.
>
> Bain & Company consultant Frederick Reichheld maintains that the status of the marketing profession has been diminished for one simple reason: It has failed to keep pace with advances in other disciplines within the company, and has not defined for itself a meaningful and measurable role critical to the mission of the company. He suggests that finance jumped ahead of marketing by innovating new capital structures, using powerful advances in information systems and discovering leveraged buyouts because of the strong influence of Wall Street and the need to maximize returns each quarter. Manufacturing rediscovered and applied total quality management principles and created innovative vendor partnerships.
>
> In short, people in other disciplines within the company were learning to think like marketers and were using marketing concepts and marketing information to make better decisions. Traditional boundaries have disappeared as marketing permeates the organization. So marketing isn't so much in trouble as it is changing, and business marketers had better change with it.
>
> Gan Avery, who is a past chairman of the Business Marketing Association and the manager of Marketing and Planning for the Automotive Controls Division of Eaton Corporation, has put together a list of ten things marketers can do to survive and prosper in this changing business marketing world.

1. Assume or exhibit team leadership skill. Since cross-functional teaming is proliferating, building teams is a display of management competence as well as a visual recognition of the new management priorities. The key is to recognize that stand-alone "experts" in narrow tactical skills are not what's needed in leaner, flatter organizations.

2. Take broader responsibilities. Seek out opportunities to broaden your role. Don't wait for an invitation to become part of the company's strategic planning process. Remember, too, that lack of involvement can give the appearance of lack of commitment.

3. Build relationships. Alliances both within and outside the company will be an asset in developing a better understanding of the changes that may be to come, and for benchmarking your own experiences against those of others. This could be particularly important in determining appropriate career moves.

4. Be a good listener. You can't rely on your knowledge and experiences to guide you in these uncharted waters. You can learn cross-functionally from others inside your company, and certainly from those with experiences in other organizations and industries.

5. Capture a broader perspective. Keep an open mind to the issues that extend beyond your own core competencies. Recognize the limitations of a narrow perspective and seek opportunities to expand beyond it. According to an advertisement from the American Institute of Chemical Engineers, you will have an average of seven jobs in your lifetime. Do you have the skills to handle the next one?

6. Educate yourself. Continually educate yourself in other marketing skills so that you're positioned to take on new responsibilities as they become available and so you'll be recognized as capable of accepting those broader roles. In expanding your knowledge you'll create your own opportunities and open new doors.

7. Rely on outside experts. Use outside experts and partners to pick up responsibilities that go beyond your in-house capabilities. In the flatter organization there will be skills lost. Take stock of the departmental strengths and weaknesses and use outside partners to reinforce your weak areas.

8. Create your own credibility. Continually demonstrate the value of your performance through as many objective measurable ways as possible. Create the logical links between your efforts and objectives and the corporation's strategic objectives.

9. Educate upper management. You can't afford to be an idle observer in times of change. Many routine marketing activities uncover information that is often valued by upper management, like research results and competitive intelligence. Pass it on.

10. Get involved. The burden of your personal achievement and advancement are yours and yours alone. Through access to information, proven ideas, and interaction with your peers, you will learn and grow.

SEVEN COMMON MARKETING COMMUNICATIONS MISTAKES ... AND HOW TO AVOID THEM

Entrepreneur Laura Rodriguez-Archilla has identified seven costly marketing mistakes and techniques you can use to avoid them (these were written by her and are reprinted with permission):

Mistake Number 1—Your copy focuses primarily on you and not your prospect.

Look at your marketing piece. Who is the primary subject of the document? Is it you or is it your prospect? If you're like many marketers, you probably assume that ads are supposed to promote and describe your company and the products and services you offer.

Wrong! You fail the test! In the increasingly competitive 1990s prospects always want to know, before anything else, "What's in it for me?" when they read or hear any type of marketing message. Don't succumb to the worn-out Mohammed Ali tactic of proclaiming "I'm the greatest" and expect that the customers will just come if you provide them with enough facts about why you're the greatest. Yes, talk about your service or product—but **only in terms of the prospects' needs and goals**, i.e., what they seek to achieve.

Your marketing document should decisively move your prospects toward taking advantage of your product or service because they instantly realize it will help them achieve their specific, vital objectives.

CHECKLIST FOR AVOIDING MISTAKE NUMBER 1:

❑ Advertising has been defined as "salesmanship in print." Successful salespeople capture their prospects' attention and interest and engage them in an active dialog by asking the right questions, identifying their needs, and clearly demonstrating how what they are selling meets those needs.

To create maximum-results marketing communications, check to see how often you use "You" when discussing how your product or service will meet your prospects' objectives. Using "you" establishes familiarity and actively engages your prospects.

❑ Does your copy clearly identify who, *specifically*, is your target prospect? Right now I'm looking at a print ad for a learning center that helps students improve their academic performance. The headline reads, "Don't Wait! Help Your Child Now." "Help my child with what?" I asked myself after reading this ad. I didn't quickly grasp who this ad was targeting. Was it for parents whose children have drug or alcohol addictions? No, it is targeting parents whose children are failing or doing poorly in school. By not clearly identifying this target audience and snagging their attention right away, the ad undoubtedly loses many prospects.

❑ Carefully scrutinize your marketing documents. Delete any details that fail to tell your prospects what they have to gain by using your product or service.

Mistake Number 2—You lead with features rather than benefits and you lack a benefit-oriented headline.

Many marketers focus more attention on the features or descriptive facts of their products than on the benefits their products or services offer.

Worse still, many marketers fail to include any benefits in their marketing communications!

A large display ad that recently appeared in a newspaper for attorneys and other legal professionals read simply, "Quorum provides specialized legal document management services, including: consulting, document review, image scanning and OCR, high-speed photocopying, document coding, etc."

Nowhere in this ad can you find any statement of benefits—of what the attorneys or their firms can expect to gain, specifically, by using these services. Quorum further claims it is celebrating "30 years of excellence"—excellence in what? Touting the company's feature of 30 years of experience without clearly linking it to how prospects will benefit means little. Does their 30 years of experience represent a host of clearly definable advantages or do they merely have one year of experience 30 times? We're not told.

Furthermore, the ad's attempt at a headline, "Blending tomorrow's technology with the tradition of quality," is nebulous, communicates no obvious benefit, and fails to stimulate interest in reading any further. A powerful, effective headline acts as "the ad for the ad." A headline needs to arrest the prospect's attention, state a major benefit she seeks, and give her a reason for reading the rest of the document.

Contrast Quorum's weak, ineffectual ad with a phenomenally successful ad for a woman's dress that appeared in a daily newspaper. The headline for this ad read, "Double-Knit Dress that is a **wardrobe in itself**." The three words, "wardrobe in itself," immediately honed in on a major benefit that the dress offered—its exceptional versatility. Consequently, it riveted the attention of many budget-conscious women seeking a multipurpose outfit. Only after the major benefit was powerfully communicated were details presented about the dress's numerous features: color, material, neckline, etc.

CHECKLIST FOR AVOIDING MISTAKE NUMBER 2:

❑ Does your marketing document have a headline? If not, create one.
❑ Does the headline promise the targeted prospect a key benefit? If not, review your product or service. Select a *leading* benefit and create a headline that highlights it.
❑ Identify the other benefits your product or service offers, present them clearly, and follow by discussing distinctive product or service features.

Mistake Number 3—You fail to provide a meaningful incentive or call to action.

Prints ads and direct mail pieces are designed to produce an immediate sale and should include a strong incentive to prompt the prospect to call or buy from you right away. Even materials such as trade and feature articles, promotional newsletters, annual reports, informational booklets, how-to articles, and case histories that are usually designed to build relationships with prospects and clients over time should offer an incentive or call to action. In any case incentives should move prospects at least one step closer to buying from you, as soon as they are ready, rather than from your competition.

Surprisingly, too few business include any incentive or call to action in their marketing communications!

What kind of incentive should you use? It should be meaningful and distinguish you from your competition. If you're a contractor (painter, plumber, electrician, etc.) who offers free estimates, that incentive alone will probably not be very compelling since everyone in those trades offers free estimates. Free estimates are expected. A painting contractor in Mississippi tried to attract new customers by distributing thousands of fliers advertising his painting services. One reason his effort failed was that he relied on the overused "free estimate" that did not distinguish him from his competition.

What is also critical about using incentives is that your prospect should understand what she has to gain now by taking advantage of the incentive. These days people are so inundated with freebies (free booklets, free consultations, etc.) and so starved for time that they have become jaded by stand-alone free offers that don't provide something of unique, practical, and immediate value.

Incentives should also relate to and be consistent with the specific type of benefits offered by your product or service—not merely tossed in as an afterthought.

Recently a discount long-distance telecommunications company approached me for copywriting advice. The company was already using an incentive in its direct mail piece. It offered a choice of any one of three free reports that the prospect would receive after switching to this long-distance carrier.

Given that the direct mail piece was targeting residential consumers interested in saving money on their long-distance telephone bills, the incentive was weak. The free reports being offered were "Uncle Sam's Free Giveaways for Seniors," "Government Guide to Free Giveaways," and the "Entrepreneur's Guide to Free Giveaways." There's no clear link here between these reports, which list free giveaways for at least two distinct audiences (seniors and entrepreneurs), and the cost-savings service being promoted to residential customers.

It would be more effective to offer residential consumers information about other cost-saving strategies via free reports with titles like "Five Easy Ways to Slash Your Electricity Bills by 20% a Month Now!" or "Seven Things You Need to Know to Save Money on Your Next Mortgage." Such reports would likely prompt a greater response because they are consistent with the cost-savings service already being marketed.

CHECKLIST FOR AVOIDING MISTAKE NUMBER 3:

❑ Have you remembered to offer an incentive or call to action in your marketing piece? If not, create one!

❏ Is this incentive or call to action meaningful to your prospect? Does it offer something of distinct, practical value that is not offered by all your competitors?

❏ Does your incentive lead your prospect a step closer to ultimately buying from you? Ideally, your incentive should provide just enough value to motivate the prospect to want even more from you, either now or soon.

Mistake Number 4—You use jargon that makes it difficult for your prospect to understand your offer.

Unless you sell products or services to people who share your industry expertise (e.g., a computer hardware and software company selling upgrades directly to computer systems integrators or analysts) and who might question your credibility if you don't at least sprinkle your marketing documents with technical terminology, avoid alienating and losing potential customers by using industry jargon in your marketing documents.

The Quorum ad I discussed earlier commits this mistake in a big way. Quorum is presumably selling legal document management systems to law firms. Even though they don't identify their target prospects, it's probably safe to assume Quorum's target audience comprises office managers and the managing partners of law firms. Neither group typically has a very high level of technical expertise. However, in its ad, Quorum lists its services to include "OCR, document coding, image scanning, electronic repository management, etc." Such terms are likely to be Greek to the typical office manager or managing law partner, particularly if they are not defined or explained further in any way—which they aren't in this ad.

I was baffled by jargon when trying to compare several Internet service providers last year. Having only a scant understanding of the Internet, I became completely confused when reading or, to be more accurate, attempting to read the literature I received, which was replete with technical terms. I had no idea what the technical specifications meant and how they related to the result I was after—to connect with more prospects and to serve current clients more efficiently by setting up an Internet home page.

The service provider I ultimately chose distilled all I needed and wanted to know in simple, lay terms. They made it very clear how they could help me achieve my objective. They also provided enough information to validate their technical capabilities without making my head spin with Internet jargon.

CHECKLIST FOR AVOIDING MISTAKE NUMBER 4:

❏ Remember who your prospects are. Ask yourself, "What do they most need to know and understand about how my product or service will help them reach their goals?"

❑ Translate all your technical gobbledygook into clear, lay terms that specify the benefits your prospects seek. For example, managing partners at a law firm are not really interested in reading technical terms that describe the amazing speed of a computer system designed to store and retrieve legal documents. All they want to know is how this feature will generate more billable time for the firm. For such a client it would be more effective to explain that by using this computer system, all legal documents required for any case will be stored and retrieved much more rapidly. Consequently, the firm's attorneys will have more time to take on additional clients and billings and profits will rise.

❑ Read through your entire marketing piece. Can anyone with a high school education and no training in your field understand it? Answer this honestly.

Mistake Number 5—You fail to use the "pain or fear" principle.

As personal power expert Tony Robbins explains in many of his seminars, we human beings are motivated to action out of either seeking pleasure or avoiding pain. He vividly illustrates, however, many situations in which our motivation to avoid loss or pain far exceeds our interest in gaining pleasure. Robbins emphasizes that most of us will do more to make sure no one steals $1,000 from us than to take whatever action is necessary to make $1,000.

Powerful marketing communications not only underscore benefits, but also tell prospects in clear, specific, believable language what pain and how much pain they will avoid by taking immediate advantage of the offered product or service. Unfortunately, too few businesses use this effective strategy.

Although the ad I discussed earlier for a learning center that helps academically troubled students uses the headline, "Parents—Don't Wait— Help Your Child Now," it doesn't delineate exactly what kind of pain the parents could avoid by taking immediate action. Parents whose children are failing in school may have had this problem for a year or two and may already feel resigned or inured to it. The ad fails to alert the parents about what additional pain they and their children will suffer if they do nothing now to eliminate the problem.

The ad should stir up more pain in the targeted parents by describing how inaction could cement their children's sense of helplessness and hopelessness forever. These children could get stuck in a vicious, inextricable cycle of failure that would jeopardize their lives as adults. The ad could then present specific details about how the learning center's programs can alleviate or eliminate the pain before it is too late.

CHECKLIST FOR AVOIDING MISTAKE NUMBER 5:

❑ Identify what pain your prospects suffer that your product or service eliminates or alleviates.

❑ Describe that pain in your document. Alert the prospect to its severity. Be as graphic and precise as possible.

❑ Explain the additional negative consequences that can occur if the prospect fails to act immediately.

❑ Describe exactly how your product or service eliminates the pain—how quickly, how easily, what is involved, and long-term versus short-term results.

Mistake Number 6—Your written presentation is vague, dull, and lacking enthusiasm.

Do you remember the last time you listened to a public speaker who had some important, even exciting information to share but quickly lost your attention because of a phlegmatic, monotone delivery and vague examples? It's no mystery that clarity, enthusiasm, and specific examples to which the audience can relate are crucial for effective public speaking. They are also critical for and can be adapted to developing compelling marketing messages communicated in print.

Yet many businesses continue to create marketing materials that are as vague, dull, and unenthusiastic as the Quorum ad for legal document management services. To start, the Quorum ad doesn't even identify who it is addressing. We just deduce this since the ad appears in a newspaper for attorneys and other legal professionals.

Second, although Quorum's service may be excellent and might help law firms become much more productive and profitable, this benefit is not conveyed in its yawn-inducing headline. The jargon-filled laundry list of services that follows offers no specific examples of success to arouse the prospect's interest. No attempt is made at communicating Quorum's message with any enthusiasm apart from its banal claim of celebrating "30 Years of Excellence." As valuable as Quorum's service may be, the firm is probably losing qualified prospects in droves.

CHECKLIST FOR AVOIDING MISTAKE NUMBER 6:

❑ Have you made it crystal clear to whom you are talking? Do your target prospects immediately recognize that you are speaking to them? As master copywriter Dr. Jeffrey Lant says (paraphrased) in his excellent book, *Cash Copy*, "to speak to everyone is to speak to no one."

In the case of the learning center ad discussed earlier, the headline should have been rewritten from the vague "Parents—Don't Wait!" to a more precise "Parents, Don't Wait! You Can Help Your Child Succeed in School Now!"

❑ Do you enthusiastically present the benefits of your product or service by using vivid language and concrete examples of success that your prospects can relate to and get excited about? To illustrate, the ad for the academic learning center could be enlivened and stir more interest by enthusiastically presenting data to show by how much its students increase their grade averages and over what period of time.

Mistake Number 7—You are striving to be too clever, creative, or different.

Clever, creative, and attention-getting copy and graphics may catch a prospect's eye. But, if they are merely slick gimmicks and don't direct a prospect to the specific benefits you offer and move the prospect closer to taking advantage of your product or service, they fail at great expense!

Some advertisers go beyond trying to be merely clever or creative. Because of their substantial advertising budgets, many large companies can afford to spend millions on image building and media recognition. A few years ago, a clothing designer regularly jolted the advertising community by placing large ads focusing on highly controversial social issues such as AIDS or depicting provocative scenes viewed as profane by many audiences. Although such ads may have brought that company considerable media attention, I would wager that they have succeeded in their business despite the notoriety of their ads, not because of it. Don't make the same mistake by striving to be "different" in your marketing communications. You can't afford it.

CHECKLIST FOR AVOIDING MISTAKE NUMBER 7:

❑ Imagine yourself to be your prospect and ask yourself, "What is the primary message here? Do I grasp it immediately?" If you can't answer these questions adequately, revise your copy.

❑ Does every component of your marketing piece enhance your message and relate directly to it? Or, do you have Chagall-like figures floating across the page or poetic phrases dropped here and there that make your piece look or sound interesting or different but don't reinforce your key message? Remember, however clever and creative you may be with words and graphics, your purpose is not to entertain—it's always to show your prospect how you can serve him or her.

FINAL ADVICE

None of Laura's ideas are new or esoteric. For years, the most successful advertising and marketing professionals have created clear, compelling, and effective marketing communications by taking a practical, systematic approach that includes the principles discussed here. There's no need to reinvent the wheel—just be sure you use it!

Chapter

DEFINING YOUR PRODUCT

THE PRODUCT **DOES** MATTER

When I first started writing advertising copy, I naively thought that if I did my job well enough, people would buy the product being advertised, regardless of what it was or whether they wanted it.

Many people share this attitude. Many advertising managers labor under the misconception that if you make the advertising good enough, it can sell anything to anybody. They believe that advertising forces people to buy products they don't want, don't need, and don't like. They believe that advertising has some magic, almost hypnotic power to make the masses do the advertiser's bidding.

This is nonsense. If you need convincing, try the following test: Send a catalog offering gourmet steaks and other meats for sale, by mail, to a mailing list of vegetarians and to a list of animal rights activists. How many orders do you think you will receive? You know the answer: precious few.

Now, send that identical mailing to a list of subscribers to gourmet magazines, and another to a list of people who have previously bought steaks and meats through the mail (such as can probably be rented from Omaha Meats, a company that sells steaks as business premiums). Note the staggering increase in response to this second mailing. Yet we have not changed one word of copy or altered the design one bit.

Why was the first mailing a bomb and the second mailing a success? Simple. In the first case, we were mailing to a market that we had good reason to believe would abhor our proposition. In the second case, we were mailing to a market that already has a desire for what we are selling.

Thus, matching the right product to the right market is at least as important to advertising success as brilliant copy, layout, and concepts. In fact, as you will see, it is actually much more important. You need to have

31

a product that people want and a way to reach that audience with your offer if your advertising is to have any chance of success.

"The power, the force, the overwhelming urge to own that makes advertising work, comes from the market itself, and not from the copy," writes advertising genius Eugene Schwartz. "Copy cannot create desire for a product. It can only take the hopes, dreams, fears, and desires that already exist in the hearts of millions of people, and focus those already existing desires onto a particular product. This is the copywriter's task: not to create this mass desire but to channel and direct it."

Don Hauptman, a New York–based direct response copywriter, adds: "Don't try to change behavior. It's time-consuming, expensive, and often futile. It's usually wise to capitalize on existing motivations. In other words, preach to the converted. Unless you have an unlimited budget, avoid products and services that require the buyer to be educated or radically transformed."

In a recent Dilbert cartoon, a marketing communications person asks Dilbert to define the important features of a new product. "We have higher prices, stale technology, fewer features, and it's hard to use," says Dilbert. "Can you work with that?" The marketing person replies: "Suddenly, I don't feel so bad that we won't be using recycled paper to print the brochure."

Be aware of the importance of the product, the market, and the kind of fit that exists between them. Then tailor your copy to bring them even closer together. Recognizing that advertising channels the prospect's desires for the benefits your product provides rather than creating those desires is a distinguishing characteristic that separates amateurs from professionals.

You see this in the behavior of advertising agencies all the time. The amateurs are the ones who, quite frankly, do not know what they are doing, become excited at the prospect of doing any assignment (perhaps because they are sitting around waiting for one), and jump in immediately with an ad that, in the most clever and artistic way, dramatizes what the client says is important about the product. They do not stop to question: a) whether the potential buyers really want such a product in the first place; or b) if they do want it, whether what the advertiser says is the main selling point will actually move people to action.

Many advertising agencies today are repositioning themselves as being in the business of marketing communications consultation, not advertising. Before they will sit down and write an ad, they ask questions: "What is the product we are selling?" "How do we know people will buy it?" "How do we know which sales points, product features, or benefits—the reasons why people would buy this product—to stress in advertising?" "Should we be advertising, or selling through some other method?"

START WITH THE PROSPECT, NOT THE PRODUCT

In planning any marketing campaign, "start with the prospect, not the product," advises Don Hauptman. "Avoid superlatives and brag-and-boast language. Wherever possible, incorporate anecdotes, testimonials, success stories, and other believable elements of human interest." As Hauptman has told many audiences during his speeches, successful advertising addresses the prospect's concerns, not the advertiser's. Thus, if you are selling telephone systems, your ads and sales letters should talk about the prospect's telephone bill, not how many years your company has been in business. Features and facts may be of some interest, but they are secondary compared with the benefits (lower phone bills, better telephone service) the prospect gets from the system.

Unfortunately, advertising people are often called into the picture after the product has been developed, the prices set, the sales and support strategies written, and the marketing plan completed. What they find are products and services that don't meet the needs of the customer and are not prospect-centered. Management fails to realize that the advertising department cannot simply "make up" copy points as they go along, lie (although some advertisers do), or sell a product that does not deliver to customers the value they want.

The solution? Managers responsible for product, sales, and marketing planning should consult with the advertising manager earlier in the game rather than later. Although advertising managers are not product development experts, they often have a lot of good, creative ideas on how to design, package, and sell products. Advertising managers can create much better advertising if they have input into the benefits and value that are built into the product at its inception or that can be added as product changes and marketing plans are adjusted along the way.

As an advertising manager, you should be an insistent voice for adding value to the services your company markets, packaging products that give customers the benefits they need, and setting prices, guarantees, contracts, and offers that provide your buyers with tremendous incentive to choose your firm over the competition.

Do not be afraid to push for the product and service improvements you need to sell the product to your prospects and customers. Copywriters will tell you that most of their big success stories came from writing ads or mailings for products that were already winners; very rarely does a freelance copywriter achieve dramatic sales breakthroughs for a product that is inherently a dog.

SIX STEPS TO UNDERSTANDING AND DEFINING THE PRODUCTS YOU SELL

To be an effective advertising manager, you must have a clear understanding of what your company sells, who they sell it to, and why people buy it.

"Who they sell it to," or the market itself, is covered in Chapter 3. For now, concentrate on "what your company sells" and "why people buy it."

There are six essential steps to understanding your product and its appeal to the market:

1. Define your core business.
2. Define the specific product, product line, or system you are selling.
3. Determine how much of a need there is for the product.
4. Understand the consumer's decision-making process.
5. Understand why the consumer buys your type of product.
6. Come up with the right package.

Let's take a look at each of these six steps in a bit more detail.

Step 1: Define Your Core Business

Companies flounder and get confused when they start acquiring and selling products and product lines that are unrelated and not tied together with a common thread or theme. A jumble of product offerings is more difficult and more expensive to promote than a group of clearly related products and services providing an umbrella package of benefits to a well-defined audience. My test is that if you can't put all your products and services together and sell them in a catalog, you probably shouldn't be selling those that don't fit in the catalog in the first place.

According to marketing consultant Carolyn Hosken, asking the question "What business are you really in?" is the first and most critical step in successful marketing. In her special report, *Four Steps to Dramatic Business Growth*, Hosken observes:

> To market your products or services effectively, first you have to know what business you are in. This sounds obvious, but consider that in the early part of this century, the major railroad companies missed a superb opportunity because they had a very limited answer to this question. They thought they were in the railroad business. Had the railroad companies understood that they were really in the transportation business, they could have founded and owned the airlines.
>
> Another way of looking at this question is to identify the general category of service your company provides. Your company's specific products or services are the means for this more general service to be delivered.
>
> Take the example presented by a vice president of a large, well-known company that sells sporting and entertainment event tickets through an extensive system of outlets. He outlined difficulties his company was experiencing in designing a new ticket-handling computer system, and the impact of that on the business.
>
> The problem was not the computer system, but rather that the company thought it was in the ticket selling business. In fact, it was really in the business of providing the public with convenient access to entertainment and sporting events. This insight, if acted upon, would have a major impact on the new computer system's design and potentially on the company's whole way of doing business.

Many companies struggle to define exactly what business they are in or should be in. The immediate impact of making this decision is its effect on the overall direction of advertising campaigns, including slogans, product packaging, major themes, and copy approach.

An industrial firm manufactures ultrafiltration systems for specific markets including water treatment, food and dairy, and chemical processing. One day, the marketing manager, ad manager, and product managers got together to come up with a new slogan for the firm, a "tag line" that would position and define the company's function in a single pithy statement that could be used in advertising and sales literature, appearing under the company logo in these materials.

One product manager suggested, "The leader in ultrafiltration systems." After all, that was the company's business, and they were specialists, so why not get to the point?

The advertising manager objected. What if the company should start selling related equipment or technology? They were already getting into reverse osmosis systems and were looking at other filtration products to add to their line. No, the leader in ultrafiltration was clearly limiting. How about, "The leader in ultrafiltration, reverse osmosis, and filtration technology?"

Too wordy, complained the marketing manager. We have to look at the big picture. What do filters do? They separate solids from liquids. How about, "The leader in separation technology?"

"Too vague," the other managers replied. Separation could mean anything from separating the wheat from the chaff or rocks from wood in a pulp mill wood yard. But ultrafiltration is a highly specialized separation technology used to remove ultrasmall particles from liquid using a unique membrane process.

Suffice it to say, this went on for hours and the problem was never resolved. To this day, the company does not have a slogan or tag line.

Try this exercise with your own company. Can you summarize your business activity in a single line that is specific enough that it highlights your unique nature and service, yet broad enough that it doesn't keep you from branching off into new products and markets? If you can, you are lucky. You have a business that is logically organized and thus easy to define.

Red Flag: If you can't find an appropriate slogan, watch out. This may indicate trouble in putting together a cohesive advertising and promotion program down the line.

Step 2: Define the Specific Product, Product Line, or System You Are Selling

A product has many components, including:

- the name of the product
- the packaging
- the physical product itself: its weight, dimensions, color, design, and features

- the benefits the customer gets from having the product
- the perceived value of the product
- the variety of different models, colors, and features available
- options and accessories available
- warranty or guarantee policy
- price
- ease and method of purchase
- method of delivery or distribution
- speed of delivery
- service and support
- reputation of the company

You should list the specific information under each of these categories for your product before you begin to write your advertising. Also, rank each of these categories on a scale of 1 to 5. A "1" means you are weak in this category and shouldn't stress it in your advertising. It also indicates a possible opportunity for improvement. A "5" indicates strength in the category, a strength that can be capitalized on in promotional material. An example is shown in Figure 2.1. (Note: As an example I have chosen a product I sell via mail order. It is a manual that tells freelance writers how to increase their income and make money writing for commercial clients.) For your own product, use the blank ranking sheet (Figure 2.2).

Realize that a product is not just a lump of material put together in a certain design. Rather, it is the sum of the attributes that make up its identity. For example, an IBM PC is not just a collection of circuit boards that perform certain functions; other companies offer nearly identical machines at substantially lower prices.

When people buy an IBM or Compaq PC for thousands of dollars instead of a clone for half the price, they are buying other elements of the product, including IBM's superior service, IBM's size and presence in the computer marketplace, and the comfort of knowing that if something goes wrong IBM will take care of it. People who tell me that IBM ads sell the company or IBM's excellence in service sell the product are wrong; what they don't understand is that the company and IBM's excellence in service are part of the product. They are the factors that sway many buyers in favor of IBM.

The perceived value of a product is inherent not just in the physical item but also in the attributes listed earlier. Service, support, the company selling the product, packaging, and price all have an effect on how desirable your product is to consumers. The more desirable the product, the greater the response to your ads and other promotions.

Consider the selling of information in the form of books, cassette programs, and other information media. You'd think that the more information the product offered, the higher the price would be. Not so.

Figure 2.1. Sample product definition and description ranking sheet.

1 = weak; don't stress this aspect in promotion

5 = strong; stress in advertising

NA = not applicable

Name of product: *Secrets of a Freelance Writer* (paperback book)

Category	Comment	Ranking
Packaging	None; mailed in plain envelope.	NA
Description	6" x 9" trade paperback. Attractively designed.	3
	Typeset, not typewritten. Lengthy: 297 pages (longer than most mail order books selling for comparable prices).	
Benefits	Strong sales appeal: The book gives complete step-by-step plan detailing how the reader, a freelance writer or would-be writer, can earn $100,000+ a year without leaving home. Appeals to people who want to make money and be self-employed.	5
Perceived value	High. Readers consistently praise the book for its accuracy, comprehensiveness, good quality of information, and inspirational/motivational style of writing. Note: Plenty of testimonials available for use in ad copy.	5
Models	Paperback book with 6 audiocassettes.	1
Options/accessories	NA	
Guarantee	30-day money back guarantee.	3
Price	$492, similar to other products of this type.	1
Ease and method of purchase	Order via direct mail. Must send check or money order. No CODs. No telephone or credit card orders. No bill-me option.	1
Method of delivery	Book shipped via 4th class book rate.	1
Speed of delivery	All orders shipped same day received.	2
Service, support	Consulting services available.	1
Reputation of the seller	Author has good credentials in the field:18 years of experience as freelance writer, 37 published books, 110 clients.	4

Example: *Let's compare a book with an audiocassette. A 300-page trade paperback might sell for $12; such a book contains over 100,000 words of information. Because we have been conditioned by bookstores, we expect to pay a low price for a paperback despite its content.*

Audiocassettes, on the other hand, typically sell for $10 to $15 per cassette, yet a one-hour cassette selling for the same price as the book contains approximately 9,000 words—less than one-tenth of the information in the book.

Why does the cassette sell for more than the book? Because cassettes have a higher perceived value than books. If you are experienced at

Figure 2.2. Product definition and description ranking sheet.

1 = weak; don't stress this aspect in promotion
5 = strong; stress in advertising
NA = not applicable

Name of product: _____

Category	Comment	Ranking
Packaging	_____	_____
Description	_____	_____
Benefits	1. _____	_____
	2. _____	_____
	3. _____	_____
Features	1. _____	_____
	2. _____	_____
	3. _____	_____
Perceived value	_____	_____
Models, colors, & special features available	_____	_____
Options/accessories	_____	_____
Warranty/guarantee policy	_____	_____
Price	_____	_____
Ease and method of purchase	_____	_____
Method of delivery or distribution	_____	_____
Speed of delivery	_____	_____
Service and support	_____	_____
Reputation of the seller	_____	_____

Note: Fill in the correct information for your product or service.

selling information, especially by mail, you know that the package of several cassettes and a printed workbook together in an album usually sells for more than the sum of what the cassettes and book would sell for separately! It sounds crazy, but customers perceive that they are getting a "program" (a more complete instructional course than either books or cassettes provide by themselves) and are willing to pay a premium for it.

Beginning marketers are amazed to discover that the lowest price does not ensure the greatest sales. Again, perceived value is the reason. If something is sold inexpensively, then consumers think that it must be cheap. Wouldn't you hesitate to go to a doctor who charged $12 a visit if every other doctor in your community charged $45? Naturally, you'd be suspicious of the low price, fearing that something must be wrong with the $12 doctor. Price is part of your product and is linked, with the other factors listed, to perceived value.

Other Considerations in Defining Your Product

Here are some other issues that come up in defining the product that your firm will advertise, promote, and sell:

Product vs. system. Some companies believe they are offering their prospects a complete system for handling the prospect's application rather than an individual product.

Example: When personal computers became popular in the early 1980s, many small firms flourished by integrating and marketing computer systems aimed at serving the data processing needs of specific types of companies and industries. These systems sellers were in contrast to other companies that merely sold hardware (PC manufacturers) or software (programmers). They found that many small and medium-sized firms didn't want to bother putting all the pieces together and were happy to pay a premium for a systems approach that would solve their problems once and for all.

Product vs. product line. An important decision to be made by marketing and advertising management is whether to sell a specific product as opposed to a product line or group of products.

Example: Let's say you were given the assignment of doing retail advertising for a local bank offering home mortgages. After studying the competition, you discover that most of your mortgages are fairly similar to the competition's. You also discover that your fixed rate mortgage is a slightly better value (a quarter of a percent lower annual rate; 2 points versus 2.25 for the next best competitor) than the competition but only for a 15-year borrowing period. (At 30 years, you are slightly more expensive.) How would you write the ad?

You reply, "I'd write an ad featuring our low interest rate, low points, 15-year fixed rate mortgage." Okay, but keep in mind two factors: First, your mortgage is only slightly better than the competition's, so potential homebuyers may not be excited about it, especially if they don't know your bank or live far away. Second, not everyone wants that specific mortgage. Some prefer adjustable rates. Others want a 30-year borrowing period instead of 15 years. Some may be happy to pay higher points if the interest rate is lower, or pay lower points in exchange for a slightly higher borrowing rate. This being the case, perhaps your advertising theme should be freedom and flexibility, or the broadest range of home mortgages to meet your customers' specific needs. Or, you may want to stress convenience, or location, or number of branch offices, or help in filling out the paperwork.

There is no single right answer, but these are the kinds of strategic questions that should be asked before you write your headline or a single line of copy.

Deciding whether to feature a single product or a product line in your advertising isn't always a simple matter. Here are a few guidelines that may help:

- If you have one product that is your biggest seller and the clear leader in your product line, feature that product in your ad.
- If you have one major product and many smaller products that are sold as add-ons or extras to the main product, sell the major product first in ads, then offer the follow-up products in a catalog or series of product mailings.
- If potential customers have a strong preference for one or two of your products, feature these products in your ads.
- If sales of different products are about equal, and customers do not have a strong preference for one product against the others, sell your product line.
- If you do not know which product best meets the customer's needs, and the customer is in a better position to make this determination than you are, sell your product line.
- If you are mailing to customers who are proven shoppers (e.g., catalog buyers), sell your product line.

Sell the solution, not the product. In many selling situations, you will have two different types of buyers:

1. Those who know the specific product they want to buy and are comparison shopping to get the best source or deal:
2. Those who have a specific problem but do not know that your product can solve it (they may not even be aware that your product exists).

A living example of this can be seen at gift counters during Christmas season at department stores across America. Some shoppers—those in the first category—have a detailed, specific list of gifts and will buy because your brand is either best or cheapest or simply because you have the product available. In the second category are shoppers with a specific problem: that of finding the right gifts for friends and relatives. They know they need something for Uncle Frank, who has particular likes and dislikes, but they don't know exactly what to buy.

This is an ideal opportunity for the store to gain additional sales through friendly, helpful sales clerks who can help the shopper solve his or her problems by asking the right questions about the gift recipient and then suggesting items that might be appropriate. Unfortunately, America's stores are filled with indifferent and uncaring sales clerks who rarely bother to make this extra effort, and so millions or perhaps billions of additional sales are lost each year.

How does this relate to advertising? If you have a number of products and services, you might offer to use those products and services and your own expertise to solve the consumers' problems rather than "sell" them on a specific product or product line.

Example: One insurance firm offered a free analysis of the consumer's current insurance policies. Instead of advertising a specific policy or plan, this company would send a representative to sit down with you and review your current coverage to make sure it was adequate. If you were underinsured or lacking in insurance in any vital area, the representative would try to solve your problem by selling you the appropriate insurance, thus meeting your needs while making sales for the company.

I do not know what the representative would do if you had too much insurance, but the right thing would be to tell you so you could reduce coverage and save on premiums ... even if it was on one of their own policies. Yes, they would lose some revenue in the short run, but they would gain a loyal customer whose lifetime purchases would far exceed that small cancellation.

Consultative selling. This term became hot during the 1980s. Consultative selling is an extension of the problem-solving type of selling discussed previously. In dealing with clients, salespeople act as consultants, asking questions that help pinpoint the specific nature of the client's problem and how the company's product or service can solve it. The benefit is that the salesperson and the company become trusted advisors, not peddlers, who are seen in a helping rather than a high-pressure role.

A good example of this can be seen in ad agencies as they pitch your account. The product salespeople are the agencies that push their portfolio in your face and try to dazzle you by showing their creative work. The consultative sellers are those who focus on you, your company, your products, your customers, and your marketing problems.

If your firm does consultative selling, can you feature this to your advantage in advertising? Instead of merely putting a brochure in the mail, can you offer free advice, information, or other help to the prospect? This type of helpful attitude, reflected in copy, makes the ad far more powerful.

Step 3: Determine How Much of a Need There Is for the Product

According to Jerry Buchanan, publisher of *TOWERS Club Newsletter*, the secret to business success is simple: "Learn what it is your customer wants and needs, and then develop different plans to see that your company offers it better and cheaper than your competition."

How much the customer wants or needs your product will be a major factor, perhaps the major factor that determines whether your advertising succeeds or fails.

Newsletter publisher Stephen Sahlein has written: "There are two answers to the question, 'What succeeds in newsletters?' The wrong answer is 'need to know' information.... The right answer is 'want to know' information.... Base your sales campaign on market wants, not product strengths."

Substitute "product" or "service" for the "newsletter" and you have a pretty good answer to the question, "What do people buy?" At the very least, your product should be something they need; if they don't need it, you'll have a tough time convincing them to buy it. But even better than selling a needed product is offering a product that people want.

Let's say you are selling a product I need. The problem is, I may not realize I need the product. Or perhaps, in the back of my mind, I know I need it but, like most people, I don't always do what is good for me and am not eager to part with my hard-earned dollars just to "do the right thing." You can sell me, but your task is a formidable one: to convince me that I need your product and that I should spend my money to fulfill this need.

But if you have something I want, then your task has suddenly become much, much easier, because people love to spend money on things they desire. If I want your product, simply telling me that you have it may be sufficient to get me to buy. You might have to sell me on buying your product instead of the competition's, but not on acquiring some product of this type; because it's something I want, I've already sold myself.

Example: One local medical equipment manufacturer designed a revolutionary new heart monitor that can provide doctors with much more information about heart performance during surgery than conventional cardiac monitors can. But doctors are basically satisfied with the conventional monitors and don't perceive the need for the information the new monitor provides, even though study after study proves its usefulness in improving patient care and surgery success rates. This company may be able to overcome this marketing barrier, introduce its new product successfully, and save lives with it, but they face a huge obstacle. The problem is that they are trying to sell the market something that the market doesn't even realize it needs, rather than something the market both realizes it needs and also wants.

Many companies in this situation speak hopefully of educating the market or creating a market for a great product. This is an ambitious undertaking and enormously expensive. If you are the leader in your field, a giant in your industry, or just enormously wealthy, you may succeed at it. But the average advertiser, or even the larger-than-average firm, simply cannot afford to educate the market and then sell its specific product. It's much better to offer a product your prospects already desire and use your advertising budget to channel their desire toward buying your specific offering.

If people do not want your product but do need it, the question becomes, "How badly do they need it?" Marketing consultant Dan Piro talks about intensity of need; the more intense the need for your product, the more likely your marketing and sales campaign is to succeed. If the intensity of need is low—if your product doesn't solve some important problem or fulfill a major desire—your chances of success are slim. If your product solves a pressing problem not being addressed by the competition, you do have a chance to successfully sell your prospects, even if they aren't yet beating down the door to buy what you are selling.

Knowing whether your prospects want or need your product, and how much they need it, is the third essential step to understanding your product and how to market it.

Step 4: Understand the Consumer's Decision-Making Process

A long-standing argument among advertising copywriters is whether copy should appeal to consumers based on a rational, logical point of view or should seek to move people on an emotional basis, from the heart.

Dick Vaughn, research director at Foote, Cone & Belding, realized that it's really not a case of emotional appeals versus logical appeals. Rather, some product purchases involve rational buying decisions, others are for emotional reasons, and others are made for a combination of the two.

At the same time, he realized that the buying process for some products (stereos, for example) involved a lot of thought and consumer involvement, while other product purchases (staples, paper clips, etc.) are more casual and require little thought or agonizing over selection on the part of the buyer.

Vaughn came up with a simple psychological grid (Figure 2.3) on which the forces behind consumer purchases can be plotted. He called it the FCB Grid, after his ad agency, Foote, Cone & Belding. The x axis (horizontal) measures whether consumers evaluate the decision to purchase the product intellectually (think) or emotionally (feel). The y axis (vertical) measures whether consumers consider the purchase decision relatively important or major (high involvement) or unimportant (low involvement). Once a product is plotted, you have a reference point on which to base your advertising.

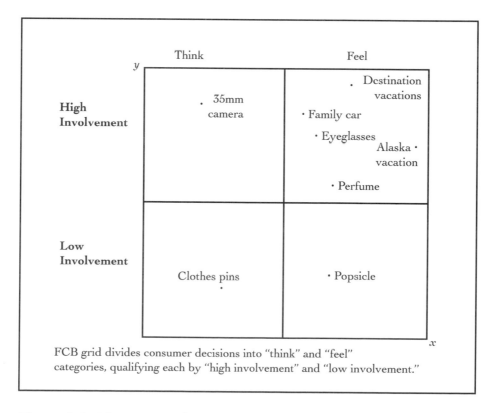

FCB grid divides consumer decisions into "think" and "feel" categories, qualifying each by "high involvement" and "low involvement."

Figure 2.3. The FCB grid.

Example: Consumers respond to perfume emotionally and become highly involved in the decision-making process. Clothespins, by comparison, are a low involvement product with no emotion attached to a purchase. A 35mm camera is a high involvement product, but unlike perfume purchasing, a camera purchase involves a highly rational decision-making process.

What does this tell us about the advertising? Perfume commercials should probably be dramatic and emotional and feature people. Camera ads should show the product, give details about operation, features, benefits, and performance, and perhaps provide a comparison between the advertiser's camera and the competition's. People could not care less about which brand of clothespin they use and aren't going to spend even 10 seconds thinking about it.

Take floppy disks as another example. When personal computing began to explode in the mid to late 1980s, floppy disk manufacturers did heavy advertising to business and consumer users. Then the advertising of floppy disks slowed to a trickle. Why?

Consumers, it seemed, just didn't care about floppy disks and didn't want to spend time reading ads explaining why floppy disk brand A would protect data better and last longer than brand X. Plotted on the FCB grid, floppy disks would be in lower left corner: although the purchase decision is rational and nonemotional, involvement is low, almost nonexistent. Personal computer users don't seem to pay much attention to floppy disks at all and generally buy whatever their retail store or mail order supplier carries. If you are a floppy disk manufacturer, you should probably forget about consumer advertising and concentrate on getting mail order catalogs and computer stores to carry your product.

Plotting your own product on the FCB grid takes only a few seconds and can help enormously when formulating advertising strategy. Seeing the position of your product in the grid brings the advertising challenge sharply into focus.

Step 5: Understand Why Consumers Buy Your Type of Product

As shown in Figure 2.4, there is a hierarchy of reasons why the consumer buys the type of product or service you are selling. From the bottom of the pyramid to the top, these reasons include:

- features
- advantages
- benefits
- ultimate benefits

Let's look at each of these in more detail.

Features. Features are the factual description of what you're selling. For example, rack and pinion steering and gas-cushioned shock absorbers are features

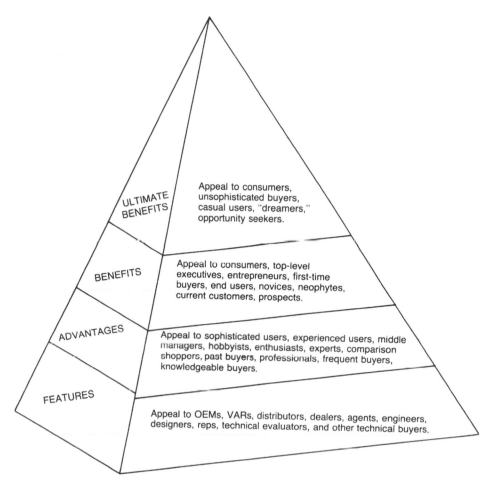

ULTIMATE BENEFITS — Appeal to consumers, unsophisticated buyers, casual users, "dreamers," opportunity seekers.

BENEFITS — Appeal to consumers, top-level executives, entrepreneurs, first-time buyers, end users, novices, neophytes, current customers, prospects.

ADVANTAGES — Appeal to sophisticated users, experienced users, middle managers, hobbyists, enthusiasts, experts, comparison shoppers, past buyers, professionals, frequent buyers, knowledgeable buyers.

FEATURES — Appeal to OEMs, VARs, distributors, dealers, agents, engineers, designers, reps, technical evaluators, and other technical buyers.

Figure 2.4. Why customers buy a product or service.

of a car. A 12-inch amber CRT display is a feature of a personal computer. A changeable outgoing message cassette tape is a feature of a telephone answering machine. You get the idea.

Although benefits are the most important reasons why people buy your product, keep in mind that there are many customers whose decision-making process hinges on whether you offer a particular feature or set of features. For example, many readers of seminar promotions make the decision to register based on one or two of the specific items mentioned in the course outline printed in the seminar brochure.

In certain markets, features can be equal to or even more important than benefits. One such situation is selling products to original equipment manufacturers (OEMS) and value added resellers (VARs), companies that buy your product and incorporate it into a larger product or system that they then resell to the end user or consumer. These companies are primarily concerned with getting performance characteristics and technical specifications compatible with their own designs, and they look for specific features rather than the benefits these features give the end user.

Note that manufacturers, engineers, and other technically oriented buyers are also more concerned with features than benefits. If you look at advertising in the semiconductor field, for example, you'll notice that ads typically devote a large portion of the space to listing product specifications.

Most books on the subject of copywriting tell you never to put features in your ads, and that every feature must be transformed into a benefit. I disagree. Sometimes, listing a feature alone is more powerful. For example, in many book ads you read the line "22 weeks on *The NY Times* best-seller list!" (This copy is usually highlighted in a burst or banner.) This is clearly a feature. The benefit is the implication that, if the book is so popular and liked by so many people, you will like it also. Yet, I would not state this explicitly in the ad; I'd let the feature speak for itself. Why? Because the benefit is so obvious that to spell it out is unnecessary and may also be ineffective: Prospects who prefer best-sellers know why they like them and don't need to be told. If other people reading the ad aren't swayed by popular opinion, telling them that they should read the book because a million other people have bought it isn't going to convince them.

Advantages. Power brakes and steering are features of a car. The ability to stop on a dime or make a sharp turn are the advantages those features give you. Preventing accidents and saving lives are the benefits you get from having the advantages derived from the features.

In a telecommunications network designed for banks, brokerage houses, and other financial applications, a statistical multiplexer provides a feature that automatically switches to a redundant route in case of line failure. The advantage is instant switchover with no interruption in service or loss of data. The benefit is that you avoid losing thousands or millions of dollars per hour by preventing down time.

Remember: Although benefits are usually the key elements to stress in your advertising, advantages are important to many buyers. These include buffs, hobbyists, enthusiasts, experts, technical buyers, and others who are sophisticated and knowledgeable about your product. In many cases, these people know of the benefits your products provide and don't need to be sold on them. Their buying process is driven by comparing the advantages and disadvantages of your product against the competition's. A comparison chart, showing point by point that your product offers more advantages, is very effective in selling to this audience. A sample is shown in Table 2.1.

Table 2.1. Product comparison chart.

Product	All-Aluminum Construction	Thermostat Control	Modular Design
Widget A	Yes	Yes	Yes
Widget B	No	Yes	No
Widget C	No	No	No
Widget D	Yes	Yes	No

Benefits. A benefit is what the customer gains by purchasing and using your product. If you sell a daily planning diary for executives, the benefit might be that it saves time, helps you organize your day better, or helps you keep projects on track and meet your deadlines.

"One of the rules of good copy is: Don't talk about yourself," says copywriter Sig Rosenblum. "Don't tell the reader what you did, what you achieved, what you like or don't like. That's not important to him. What's important to him is what he likes, what he needs, what he wants." Or, as Dr. Jeffrey Lant puts it, "Benefits answer the prospect's question, 'What's in it for me?'"

Example: Independent consultants, working at home or from a small rented office, do not buy personal computers per se; they buy the benefits they get from the computer. These benefits might include saving time, reducing paperwork, easier access to important documents, ability to communicate with clients electronically, more efficient research through on-line databases, improved communications, better-looking documents, and so on.

Benefits, always important, dominate copy when you are writing ads aimed at consumers, end users, executives, entrepreneurs, current customers, financial types, and other nontechnical buyers. For example, entrepreneurs buying a telephone system are almost wholly concerned about benefits, while a telecommunications engineer working for a large bank might be more concerned about the technical features.

Ultimate benefits. An ultimate benefit, expressed in the broadest terms, is the overall, key benefit the buyer derives from the product.

Example: Suppose you are selling a seminar aimed at teaching manufacturer's representatives, insurance agents, stockbrokers, and other commissioned salespeople how to sell more effectively. The feature of your seminar is that it teaches them proven techniques for increasing their sales. The advantage is that it reveals sales secrets not taught in other seminars, and thus it is more effective. The benefit is that it increases their sales, thus allowing them to earn more money. The ultimate benefit is that they can become rich beyond their dreams, earn millions of dollars in a few years, and retire to the Bahamas at an early age to live a life of luxury.

Although the ultimate benefit holds the most promise, its statement often lacks the focus and specificity of more product-specific benefits. It's nice to say that your sales seminar will make customers rich beyond their dreams, but used alone, this isn't specific enough to gain the prospect's attention or to make your message sound credible. You've got to add more product-specific benefits to give "meat" to your message and highlight the uniqueness of your product or service. For the selling seminar, additional benefits might include:

- eliminating fear of making cold calls
- increasing your sales conversion ratio
- qualifying prospects before you visit them

- increasing your income by \$20,000 a year or more
- raising your gross sales by 10 percent a year

Balancing features, advantages, benefits, and ultimate benefits. Many experts will tell you to stress benefits and forget about features. But, as you have seen, certain audiences (for example, engineers, OEMs, VARs, dealers, distributors, agents, wholesalers, technical buyers, hobbyists, and many others) are concerned with technical features and advantages, not just benefits or ultimate benefits.

Whether your copy will primarily stress features or benefits or will give equal weight to both depends on your audience and their decision-making processes. Table 2.2 provides a guide that may be helpful in finding the right balance.

Table 2.2. Balancing features and benefits.

Audience	Copy Contents: Features vs. Benefits (percentage)	
	Features & Advantages	*Benefits & Ultimate Benefits*
Consumers, end users, current customers, prospects, first-time buyers, novices, neophytes, high-level business executives, entrepreneurs	10–15%	85–90%
Experienced users, frequent buyers, middle management, professionals, hobbyists, enthusiasts, experts, and other knowledgeable buyers	25–30%	70–75%
OEMs, VARs, remanufacturers, rebuilders, dealers, distributors, agents, reps, engineers, technical professionals, designers, process experts, and other technical buyers	50–75%	25–50%

Step 6: Come Up with the Right Package

The sixth and final step in understanding your product as it relates to advertising and promotion is to package the product in such a way that it has the greatest appeal and desirability to the consumer. The more appeal the product has, the easier and less expensive it will be to generate interest and sales through advertising, publicity, and other marketing communications vehicles.

Packaging refers not only to the container or box (although this is part of it) but to a number of factors involved in the way the product is presented and offered to the buyer. These factors include:

- unit of sale (Is the product sold by the gross, dozen, half-dozen, or individual unit?)
- price
- discounts and other special price-off deals available
- warranty and guarantee terms and periods
- accessories, parts, and supplies included (For example, if you are selling a flashlight, does it come with a battery?)
- physical packaging design, construction, and copy on box, package, or label
- method of distribution (mail order, wholesale, retail, and so on)
- service and support

Example: One of my clients sells a satellite telecommunications system. As part of installing it, buyers must get a telephone line connecting their offices to my client's facility. Although my client cannot provide this line directly (since he is not a telephone company), he does tell prospective buyers, "Although we cannot install this line for you, we will call your local telephone company and make the arrangements for you to get it, and we won't charge you for doing so." Thus, there is a service element packaged and included in the overall price of the product.

As a rule of thumb, it is usually better to offer the customer greater value at a higher price than less value at a lower price, although it is possible to load up your product package with so many extras that the price you must charge customers to make a profit makes your product unaffordable. Most people appreciate extra service and value and are willing to pay for it.

Example: Many people buying a new car accept dealer financing on the spot, even though they might possibly get a lower rate or better value if they comparison shopped from other sources (banks, primarily) or took out a home equity loan. They prefer the convenience of getting the loan on the spot and driving the car out of the showroom with the details taken care of.

Add value to your package.

Some business writers call the practice of creating a package with extra value added marketing. It is practiced by firms who realize their customers want more value and are willing to pay for it rather than save a few pennies by buying the economy or stripped-down version. Even buyers with little money want the best, and the barrier to a sale is often not their lack of desire for your product but rather their inability to pay for it.

As an advertising consultant, I constantly advise my clients about how they can increase sales by offering more value in their packages, and I recommend that you, as advertising manager, do the same. Often, a minor adjustment in the package, for example, extending the warranty from 90 days to 12 months or offering free home delivery, can cause a dramatic increase in advertising and sales results.

Example: One successful entrepreneur who added value to his package is Dr. Gary Blake, director of the Communication Workshop, a management consulting firm offering communications seminars to businesses. Blake is a successful independent trainer, and he charges handsomely for his seminars. Occasionally, a prospect balks at paying a high fee for a short seminar. One concern is that, once the seminar is over, the managers will not be able to maintain a steady improvement in communications skills.

Blake's solution was to offer his training clients a Business Writing Hotline. The deal is that anyone who has taken the seminar can call the hotline to ask follow-up questions or consult with Blake and his staff on a communications problem. There is no charge, as the cost is included in the fee for the training program.

By including the hotline as part of his training package, Blake increased the value offered to his clients and thus boosted his own sales, with little time, effort, or expense. Although the hotline is a big attraction to potential clients and helps overcome a lot of sales resistance, only a small percentage of attendees actually take advantage of the free service, so the hotline is not a big drain on Blake's time.

Red Flag: A not-so-good alternative is to charge a nominal fee for hotline calls, as some software companies do. This lowers the perception of your product and company and makes buyers of expensive services or software feel that you are overcharging. It's better to work it into the overall package and get the expense covered by charging a slightly higher total price.

How can you add value to your company's product or service? Here are 14 practical tips:

1. If you are selling a product, include select parts, accessories, or attachments with the purchase of the product. Not all parts and accessories need be included, just the ones your buyers want most.

2. If your product has parts or supplies that need to be replaced periodically, include the first replacement part or batch of supplies free with purchase.

3. If there is a monthly subscription fee for your product or service, give the customer the first month's use free as a bonus for subscribing.

4. If you perform a service, guarantee performance or results.

5. Include a hotline number the buyer can call to get help, ask questions, or make complaints. A toll-free number is best but not mandatory.

6. If you perform a service, remind the prospect by mail or telephone when it is time to perform the service again. Many dentists do this with a telephone call and a postcard. If your gutter cleaner and chimney sweep did the same, you might not forget to call them when it is time for a cleaning.

7. Send your customers or clients a free newsletter or magazine.

8. Extend the guarantee or warranty. If your competitors offer a 90-day warranty on parts and labor, offer an unconditional one-year warranty. If your competitor has a 30-day money back guarantee, offer a 90-day money back guarantee.

9. Accept credit card and bill-me orders.

10. Allow customers to order round the clock. Make sure your telephone never goes unanswered. At the very least, install a telephone answering machine or voice mail system, or hire an answering service to take messages during off hours. An amazing number of companies, both large and small, don't do this.

11. Offer faster response to service requests than your competition. If your competitor sends a service person within 24 hours, you should send someone within 4 hours.

12. Explain what you are doing and the value of your methods to the client or customer. For example, if you offer a service rebuilding equipment, describe the painstaking process by which your technicians remove, examine, and replace all worn parts. Point out that each system is tested and retested six times. Communication helps create the perception of value in the customer's mind. This is something that can be accomplished through the use of print advertising, direct mail, and sales literature.

13. Make a list of things that your competitors (and other companies) do to you that you don't like. Then, make sure you don't commit these sins when serving your own customers.

14. Give prospects your personal pledge that, if something is not to their liking, you will make it right. Stick to that promise.

"Service is not an afterthought; it is one of the primary reasons we are in business," writes Bruce D. Smith, president of Network Equipment Technologies. "It is the concept of providing value added to our customers at all times. A truly customer-driven vendor has to consider himself in partnership with his customers."

The value-added approach is eloquently summed up by entrepreneur Russ von Hoelscher. "Don't cheat or take advantage of your customer; you'll be the loser. Instead, win success by giving your customers their money's worth. And if you really want great success, give your customers more than their money's worth."

Key Point for Success: Make sure your company adopts this value-added, customer-centered philosophy in its dealings. If you don't, all the clever advertising in the world won't save you from marketing failure.

Chapter

3

DEFINING YOUR MARKETS

THE HIDDEN MARKET

Most advertising and marketing people are so involved in pursuing their known market that they ignore other markets almost completely. Yet these markets are potentially larger and could become a major source of profits.

By the hidden market, we mean all the sales controlled by all the buyers and specifiers you are not now in direct contact with. These include:

- people who have never heard of your company;
- people who have heard of you but know little about you;
- former customers and prospects;
- people who have a need for a product but no source.

Note that salespeople tend to call on customers and accounts they already know. Word of mouth and referrals can generate new business, but slowly. Advertising and marketing communications provide the most effective means of reaching markets that you are not now selling to, or that you are selling to but in which you do not have the market share you desire.

At any moment, people who are not now buying from you are eagerly looking for a new source of products and services for a variety of reasons:

- Some are new to your market. These include companies building new plants, new companies, companies that have just moved to your area, new distributors, overseas buyers, companies with new needs caused by changes in legislation (EPA, OSHA, etc.), and buyers with new needs caused by a decision to buy a product or service outside instead of producing it in-house.

- Some are dissatisfied with their current source because of personality clashes, price increases, delivery and service problems, unsatisfactory product quality, or failure to meet the customer's needs in some other way.

- Some have emergency needs because a current supplier can't deliver, discontinues selling a product, or goes out of business.

- Some are buyers looking for a second source to guarantee uninterrupted supply or eliminate their dependence on their current supplier.

- Some are current customers who don't realize that you also make other products that they need. Most customers don't know the full product line of their current suppliers. Mailing them a catalog and keeping them informed through a series of mailings will solve this problem.

- Some are your former customers. Former customers may not be buying from you simply because they forgot about you, can't find you, or lost your telephone number, or because you moved or changed your name.

- Some are price shopping and need other sources to give them competitive bids.

- Some are prospects you solicited in the past but who didn't buy from you. They may not have bought for any of a number of reasons. Perhaps your product or service was not right for them then, but is now. Or maybe they didn't have a need for a new supplier when your salesperson called them, but now they are looking. Or maybe the person in charge didn't like your personality, but he or she has moved on, and the new person is open to doing business. Or perhaps your sales representative gave up too soon.

Note that, according to Thomas Publishing, 80 percent of sales to business and industry are made on the fifth call, but only 10 percent of salespeople call more than three times.

For whatever reason, there are many people who are not in touch with you through personal selling but are potential customers or clients for your product or service. At a relatively low cost per contact, advertising can reach into, uncover, and activate exciting and profitable new markets for any business.

"Advertising digs prospects out of the woodwork," explains ad agency owner Bob Pallace. "It finds new business in the boondocks where salespeople don't reach. Salespeople usually concentrate their time calling on current accounts and don't like to prospect for new business. Advertising gets you into places you would never have thought of going."

There are dozens, perhaps even hundreds, of markets and submarkets for your product or service, and you cannot possibly reach all of them and sell to them effectively, because the total market is larger than your budget for communicating with them. For this reason, you must select which markets are most important to you and concentrate the bulk of your effort and money in reaching these key target markets.

WHAT IS A TARGET MARKET?

A target market is a group of potential buyers for your product or your service; members of the group have certain geographic, demographic, psychographic, and other characteristics in common that set them apart as a distinct market.

For example, doctors are often targeted as a separate and distinct market by financial services firms and other marketers because doctors are high-income individuals with lots of money to spend. Doctors are actually a subgroup of a larger consumer market, the "affluent consumer"—college educated, professional, residing in major metropolitan and suburban areas, with household incomes of $50,000 or more.

The marketplace can be segmented into distinct target markets by age, income, occupation, lifestyle, avocation, industry, geography, or any other characteristic that distinguishes the buying habits and patterns of a consumer or business prospect. Specific markets include writers, teachers, suburbanites, city dwellers, homeowners, car drivers, home-based businesses, corporate managers, engineers, accountants, nurses, vegetarians, pet owners, credit card holders, do-it-yourselfers, Macintosh users, IBM PC users, hospitals, manufacturers, lawyers, married couples, singles, retirees, people over 50, parents, investors, opportunity seekers, book buyers, sports and fitness enthusiasts, left-handed people, VCR owners, camcorder owners, compact disc player owners, skiers, boat owners, Manhattanites, hospital administrators, gas station owners, and women. There are literally hundreds of other categories that can be broken down into thousands of subcategories.

WHY TARGET?

One of the keys to marketing and advertising success is not to treat all prospects uniformly as a single mass market, but to identify key target markets and tailor advertising campaigns to the specific needs, concerns, and problems of each type of potential buyer. Doing this is essential for two reasons:

1. It allows you to reach your prospects with a meaningful message a sufficient number of times in order to generate the desired sales result. On a budget of $50,000, your firm could not even begin to reach all consumers or business prospects in the United States or advertise your product on national television. But you could send letters or run ads reaching all the physicians in group practices in Maryland, if that was one of your target markets. Target marketing takes an overwhelming prospect base and cuts it down to manageable size.

2. Targeting improves the quality and effectiveness of communication, because it allows you to tailor a message that precisely meets the needs and concerns of the potential buyer.

Example: If you are doing a mass market ad campaign to sell a facsimile machine, you are limited to describing the features of your machine or the general benefits of facsimile use. But if you target a specific market—say, self-employed people working at home—you can write copy that speaks to their needs and problems. For example:

```
A Fax for Your Home Office—Only $550 Complete

If you work at home, you know that more and more of
your clients, vendors, and colleagues want to be able
to communicate with you by fax. You know you need one.
But the price may be holding you back.

Other fax machines are expensive because they are
designed for big corporations that can afford them.
But now BizCom Inc. introduces the HOMEFAX 100, the
first facsimile machine designed specifically for self-
employed professionals and others who work out of
their homes.

To begin with, HOMEFAX 100 is priced at an affordable
$550. It can send and receive a fax as efficiently as
any machine on the market. But it isn't loaded with a
lot of unnecessary "extras" that drive up the price of
corporate machines. Maybe the Fortune 500 can afford to
spend $2,500 on a fax; but with one or two people in
your office, you can't.

Another big plus of the HOMEFAX 100 is that it saves
space in your already cramped spare bedroom, garage, or
basement office, measuring a compact 12 x 9 inches. We
eliminated the feed and output trays so the fax can fit
easily on your desk or on a bookshelf.

Although we've saved money by trimming features, HOME-
FAX 100 still does everything you need a fax to do:
Send a page in 25 seconds, receive a fax in 30 seconds
per page, and store in memory the fax numbers of up to
20 of your most frequently dialed clients and other
numbers.

We can deliver and have the fax working in your office
today or tomorrow. For more information, visit our
store in midtown Manhattan or call the tollfree number
below.

[ logo, address, telephone]
```

SEVEN WAYS TO TARGET ADVERTISING TO A SPECIFIC MARKET

1. Identify your target audience in the headline of your ad, the cover of your brochure, or the outer envelope teaser of your direct mail package.

Examples:

Headline	Target Audience
"We're looking for people to write children's books"	Aspiring writers
"A message to all charter security policyholders..."	Policyholders
"Attention: C programmers"	Computer programmers
"An important announcement for entrepreneurs"	Small business owners

2. Show pictures of people, equipment, and events related to the reader's industry or interests. Example: In a brochure aimed at farmers, show silos, tractors, fields of wheat, farmers meeting at the general store.

3. Use facts and statistics that demonstrate your knowledge of the reader's interests, hobbies, problems, or needs. Example: "Trucking company executives: With insurance costs rising 50 percent or more, rising premiums can easily add 4 to 5 cents operating costs per mile and substantially eat into your already shrinking profit margins. But now there's a program that can reduce premiums and hold the line on rising operating costs...."

4. Write copy that sounds the way your prospect talks. Jargon is acceptable; if not overused, it is effective in showing readers that you speak their language. For example, don't be afraid to use terms like CICS, abend, and MVS when writing to systems analysts who are familiar with this language.

5. Begin your copy by talking about issues and concerns that are foremost in the reader's mind. Show that you know the problems of this particular group of buyers and understand their needs.

6. When you give examples, case histories, or testimonials, make sure they are from customers in the same target market group as the person reading your copy. Example: Bankers do not relate well to examples from manufacturing; they want to read about how you have helped other banks with your product or service.

7. Demonstrate your extensive experience in serving this target market by citing facts such as:

- number of customers you serve who are in the same group or field as the reader;
- case histories and success stories;
- news coverage and publicity in specialized publications serving the target market;
- memberships in their trade associations and professional societies.

Tip: If you are actively pursuing a certain market, join the trade associations serving that market. Not only does this give you a credential you can mention in your sales literature, but it gives you access to valuable membership directories and mailing lists for marketing purposes.

HOW TO DETERMINE WHETHER A
PARTICULAR MARKET IS WORTH PURSUING

A question you must ask before committing advertising dollars to pursue any specific market is whether the market is worth pursuing. Does it offer enough sales potential to justify a small- or large-scale advertising campaign? The following checklist will help you decide:

❑ *Size.* Is the market large enough to be worth pursuing? The real question is whether it's large enough for *you* to pursue. Many small companies are successful selling to niche markets (small, vertical target markets) that their larger competitors can't be bothered with.

Example: Computer systems integrators who design turnkey computer systems for specific industries such as liquor stores, real estate agents, and accounting firms.

Tip: If the market is not large enough to support a trade journal or other specialized publication catering to its members, then it is probably not large enough (or easy enough to reach) to be worthy of a sales effort. An exception would be the availability of a specialized mailing list to reach a significant portion of the market or an association membership directory that can be converted into a mailing list.

❑ *Reachability.* To reach the market cost-effectively, there must be a readily available publication, mailing list, or association. If such media outlets do not exist, mounting an affordable advertising campaign will be next to impossible. Aside from giving up on the market, you have two other options:

1. Compile your own prospect list. This is difficult and expensive, but feasible in some cases. The cost of compiling such a list can range from $2 to $4 per name or more, as opposed to 5 to 15 cents per name for renting names from existing lists.

2. Use a shotgun approach. Instead of placing targeted advertising messages in narrow vertical media, advertise in general publications and hope that enough members of your target audience respond to make it cost-effective.

Example: The late Howard Shenson, a California-based consultant, offered a seminar on how to become a successful independent consultant. The seminar targeted professional people who, dissatisfied with corporate life (or suddenly out of a job), were considering new careers as self-employed consultants. Since there are no magazines aimed at this group, Shenson ran his seminar ads in daily newspapers, reasoning that would-be consultants, like other business professionals, read the newspaper. This type of advertising was successful for Shenson, despite the enormous wasted circulation (perhaps 99.9 percent of the newspaper's readers were not candidates for the seminar).

❑ *Profit Potential.* Ideally, you want to target those markets that not only have a desire or need for your product but can afford to pay for it, too. For example, although both medical doctors and freelance writers have a need for financial products and services, financial marketers devote a lot of effort advertising to doctors and very little to writers. The reason is that the average doctor makes a lot of money, while most writers earn only a modest income.

❏ *Authority.* Advertising should attract those groups of buyers who not only want and can afford your product but have the authority to buy it, as well.

Example: Much of the advertising in the home furnishings field is directed at women rather than men. In many households the purchase of a rug, wallpaper, or bathroom fixture is a joint decision. For example, married men usually do not make such a purchase without the approval of their wives. Advertisers don't target married men because they do not have the authority to buy without their wives' approval. Other examples include cereal advertising aimed at adults as well as children (because children do not make the purchase without parental approval) and industrial advertising that targets the CEO as well as the middle manager (because the middle manager cannot authorize the capital expenditure required without the CEO's approval).

❏ *Desire.* You have the best chance of success when the people in the target market not only need your product but also want the product.

Building the Customer Profile

Once you identify one or more target markets for your product or service, you need to develop an in-depth customer profile of each group you target, advises management consultant Carolyn M. Hosken.

The profile for business-to-business customers will include criteria such as:

- industry or type of business,
- geographic location,
- annual sales,
- job title and name of contact person,
- job function or department within the firm,
- number of employees in the firm, and
- types of products purchased.

One system of specifying industry or type of business is the Standard Industrial Code, or SIC. The SIC was developed by the U.S. government and U.S. businesses to classify virtually all economic activity. This system uses codes to group various types of businesses according to category and subcategory.

Standard Industrial Codes appear in the *SIC Manual*, published annually by the U.S. Government Printing Office. For more information, write to the Superintendent of Documents, Washington, D.C. 20402-9325. To order using Visa or Mastercard, call 202-783-3238.

Dun & Bradstreet assigns each company in its database of 11 million American businesses a primary SIC code based on the activity that generates the most revenue, and assigns up to five secondary SIC codes representing the firm's other sources of revenue. A gas station would have a primary SIC code of 5541. But it might also have a secondary code of 5499 (miscellaneous food stores), 5993 (tobacco stores and stands), or 5994 (news dealers and newsstands) if those products are sold on the premises.

In addition to SIC codes, prospects in business databases can be selected by job title, number of employees, revenues, products purchased, or zip code.

The profile for a consumer market includes criteria such as:

- age
- location
- income level
- vocation
- family status (single, married, divorced, widowed)
- family size (number of children)
- age of children
- interests or concerns
- ethnic background
- religion
- level of education
- sex
- ZIP code
- hobbies or other interests

These days, an increasing number of consumer marketers are targeting children as a separate market. According to *USA Today* (March 31, 1997, p. 7B), children younger than 12 years old in this country spend $17 billion of their allowance on products each year. In addition, children influence how their families spend $167 billion annually on vacations, home computers, and schools.

If you have children, you already know that children respond to different marketing appeals than their parents do. For example, children want to go to Burger King to get the latest free toy being offered. When I was a child, I nagged my parents to buy whatever cereal had the prize in the box I wanted that week. Children today are predisposed to buying merchandise based on their favorite movies and TV shows.

Example of Customer Profile: Consider the New Jersey accounting firm that chose to target specific Middlesex and Monmouth County businesses with sales volume between $250,000 and $5 million. Their "Desirable Customer Profile" appears as Figure 3.1.

Tip: Be as specific as possible in developing your own Customer Profile. The more specific you are about the people you wish to do business with, the easier it will be to find them. Just as important, says Hosken, you will have more satisfying customer relationships because they will be with people you have chosen to do business with.

Figure 3.1. Desirable customer profile—Example: accounting firm.

A desirable client is one who:

1. Has business volume of $250,000 to $350,000 minimum up to about $5 million in gross sales (up to the level at which an in-house controller is brought on board).

2. Is in one of a wide variety of businesses such as retail, wholesale, construction, manufacturing, restaurants, etc. (specific by SIC code).

3. Will generate a minimum of $3,000 a year in billings.

4. Requires services on a monthly basis (preferable), or at least on a quarterly basis.

5. Is reasonable to deal with and knowledgeable concerning the business.

6. Pays at the time of service (or pays invoices on time).

7. Falls into one of two categories:

    • Can be handled efficiently and profitably by the firm's staff and current computer system; or

    • Is sufficiently complex, entrepreneurial, and lucrative to require the personal attention of the firm's senior partner.

8. Is located within 30 to 40 minutes' driving time of the office or can be handled primarily through the mail.

HOW TO FIND AND IDENTIFY TARGET MARKETS

How do you uncover and discover the target markets that are best for your product or service? Here are some ways to go about it:

1. First, start with what you know—the logical and obvious markets for your product or service. There must be some potential markets you have in mind; otherwise, you wouldn't have created the product or service in the first place.

2. Look for markets that are similar to but slightly different from your current markets. Your current product, service, and marketing efforts can probably be tailored to the new market with minimal effort. For example, if you are selling collection services to record clubs, what about targeting book clubs?

3. Check your competition. Keep tabs on their advertising and promotion. Read their brochures. Their marketing efforts will reveal the markets they are selling to—markets you may want to compete for or, conversely, avoid.

4. Talk with people who are not competitors but sell related products or services to the same markets you do. Ask them what new markets they are planning to explore. Perhaps you can even team up as partners in approaching this new base of prospects.

5. Read industry trade publications for news of your competitors' sales efforts and advertising campaigns. In their desire to show off to the trade, your unwise competitors will frequently (and unwittingly) reveal their new marketing strategies to the world and to you.

6. Examine your sales records. Do they suggest patterns—clusters of sales made to buyers who can logically be grouped by one or more common characteristics to form a reachable target market?

7. Ask for more information about your prospects when you take an order. For example, get their age, sex, telephone number, areas of interest, etc.

Tip: Many warranty cards that manufacturers ask buyers to complete and mail back are, in reality, mini marketing surveys that reveal information on consumer lifestyle, buying habits, demographics, and income. Include such a mail-back survey when you ship your product or render your service. Study the information you have collected on your buyers. Do the data suggest markets where you should concentrate the bulk of your promotional effort?

8. Ask your salespeople which markets you should emphasize in your advertising. If salespeople are successful in selling to a market where you don't do much promotion, perhaps you should consider supporting their efforts with more aggressive marketing communications.

Figure 3.2. Desirable customer profile.

For: _____
(your company name)

Selling: _____
(your product or service)

A desirable client/customer is one who:

1. _____

2. _____

3. _____

4. _____

5. _____

6. _____

7. _____

8. _____

Please complete one Customer Profile for each target market you wish to reach.

9. In a creative brainstorming session, try to come up with as many possible new markets as you can. Then evaluate the list to see which, if any, are worth further consideration.

Brainstorming Tip: Try to come up with as many new applications of your product or service as you can ... even off-the-wall ideas. Often, new applications in turn suggest new uses and new markets.

10. Study your customer list. Which customers are your best customers—the ones who buy the most, are easiest to reach, and give you the most pleasure to deal with? You may find that all the best customers fall into one or more clearly identifiable target markets to which you have not been actively marketing.

11. Make a commitment to find and test one or two new markets a year.

BRAINSTORMING IS THE KEY

Using the techniques just listed, it is usually a simple matter to come up with a rich variety of key target markets for virtually any business. Here are three examples of target markets as defined for various types of businesses.

1. Business: A home-based word processing service.

Target markets: All businesses within 30 to 40 minutes' driving time of your home.

Special target markets: Companies that need a lot of typing but do not have large support staffs.

Examples: Lawyers, writers, consultants, home inspectors.

Other potential markets: Screenwriters (if you live in LA), students who need typing for term papers (a good market if you live in a college town), graduate students (thesis typing).

Idea: Accept assignments by fax and deliver copy in electronic form via modem to extend your service beyond your immediate geographic vicinity.

2. Business: Freelance proofreader.

Markets: Advertising agencies, pharmaceutical companies, law offices, publishers, corporations (especially those with in-house publication departments), secretarial services.

Secondary market: Getting work on a subcontract basis through temp agencies.

Suggestion: If ad agencies are a good market, what about PR firms?

3. Business: Window washers.

Markets: Building owners and managers, schools, local municipalities, office complexes, corporations, residential customers, apartment superintendents.

Idea: Franchise your operation to individuals outside your own immediate area.

RANKING TARGET MARKET POTENTIAL

List at least half a dozen target markets you could be selling to but are not now reaching with your advertising and promotion. Now that you've identified your target markets, rank them on a Target Market Rating Sheet (see Figure 3.3).

1. Write down all the target markets you've identified in the left column of the Target Marketing Rating Sheet.

2. In the middle column, jot down which products and services you intend to offer to each market, along with any other comments about the market and its potential.

3. In the right column, rank each market on a scale of 1 to 5.

5 = Best market (ideal fit with product or service, good profit potential, easy to reach, large size, market has a strong need and desire for the benefit your product or service offers).

4 = Good market, but not quite as strong as a 5.

3 = So-so market. Mix of pros and cons (e.g., market has a need for your product but is not aware of the need, or market is a good fit for your product but is difficult to reach).

2 = Marginal market. Questionable whether it's worth pursuing.

1 = Long shot. Would be nice if we could get them, but not worthy of any major advertising effort except as an experiment.

4. When we discuss planning in a later chapter, you will find that I advocate creating a separate advertising plan for each market rather than lumping them all into one large, clumsy, unwieldy, and unreadable document.

Figure 3.3. Target market rating sheet.

	TARGET MARKET	PRODUCT OR SERVICE OFFERED	RATING
1.			
2.			
3.			
4.			
5.			
6.			
7.			
8.			
9.			
10.			

When planning your advertising activities, start with all the target markets ranked 5 on your Rating Sheet. If there is money remaining in the budget, start creating programs for the 4 markets, the 3 markets, and so on.

Tip: Because budgets are finite, your advertising will probably cover the 5 and 4 target markets and perhaps some of the 3 markets. It is unlikely that you will be able to spend much, if anything, on the 1 and 2 markets.

FIVE TARGET MARKETING TECHNIQUES

Stan Rapp and Tom Collins have suggested five more excellent techniques for targeting your market in their audiocassette program, *Maxi-Marketing*.

1. *Fishing.* "This is when you let your hook down and wait for your prospect to grab it." Essentially, this is the technique of identifying your target market (or their interests) in the headline of your ad. Example: An ad aimed at getting consumers to change brands uses the headline, "ATTENTION: Loving Care Users! L'Oréal wants to change the way you color your hair for FREE."

2. *Mining.* "Here you dig in where you know there's a rich vein of prospects." This means advertising to obvious markets in obvious media (e.g., run an ad selling yacht rope in a yachting magazine).

3. *Panning.* "Sift through a database of prospects using selection factors to separate pure gold prospects." For example, when renting a mailing list, don't rent the entire list but select only those prospects that are likely candidates for your offer. When I rent the *Writer's Digest* subscriber list to promote my seminar on becoming a published author, I rent only the names in my state, because people will not travel hundreds of miles for a $100 seminar.

4. *Building.* You can build your own database by collecting names produced by inquiries in response to direct response ads, publicity, and 800 number TV commercials.

5. *Spelunking.* This is another term for niche marketing in which you find a new and untapped market for an old product. A good example is Ben Gay, which was once thought of as an "old person's" product for alleviating the pains and aches of arthritis. New television commercials repositioned the product for young, active people (the health spa crowd) as a pre-exercise rub-in to loosen muscles.

COLD MARKETING VS. DATABASE MARKETING

Up until now, you have been segmenting your market or universe (the total population of people who might conceivably buy your product) by special interest groups. As an example, if you sell office furniture, you might have three target markets: office managers at corporations, home-based businesses, and interior decorators and office designers.

As exciting as it is to reach new markets and get new customers, the greatest profit potential lies in your existing database of customers and prospects. Unfortunately, this is an area most companies ignore.

Example: A local firm offering a repair service for hospital equipment spent 98 percent of its budget on mailings to rented lists, print advertising, and other promotions aimed at generating sales leads. Analysis of their advertising program showed that the average closing ratio (conversion of leads to sales) was 15 percent. Yet, when they instituted a campaign aimed at getting past customers to buy again, the success rate was an astonishing 80 percent! Once they realized this, they shifted a portion of their budget to building, maintaining, and marketing to their customer/prospect database.

"Use direct response advertising and other lead-generating techniques to build inquiry files," advises marketing consultant Ken Morris. "While only a percentage of these may translate into direct orders immediately, you can start to build a database of your affinity groups and down the line, repeated promotions to this database will yield ten times the order conversion rate as opposed to rented lists."

Are your current customers and prospects really a separate target market? Yes, because they have a different awareness of your product, a different perception of your firm, and a different relationship with you than any other group you deal with. As such, they should be treated as a distinct target market covered by a deliberate, well-thought-out communications program. Because your existing accounts are more responsive to messages from your company than cold prospects are, such a program can achieve much higher sales results than traditional advertising, and with a far smaller budget.

BUILDING THE DATABASE BY GOING UP THE LOYALTY LADDER

All advertising and marketing essentially seeks to turn strangers into prospects, prospects into buyers, and buyers into repeat buyers (known as customers or clients). The loyalty ladder (Figure 3.4) illustrates this concept. As explained by Murray Raphel in his column in *Direct Marketing* magazine, the hierarchy on this ladder, starting from the bottom, is as follows:

* *Suspect—your total universe.* This includes everyone who could possibly buy your product or service. This list is expensive to advertise to. Suspects, also known as cold prospects, are the target markets who could buy your product or service but have not yet demonstrated any interest in doing so.

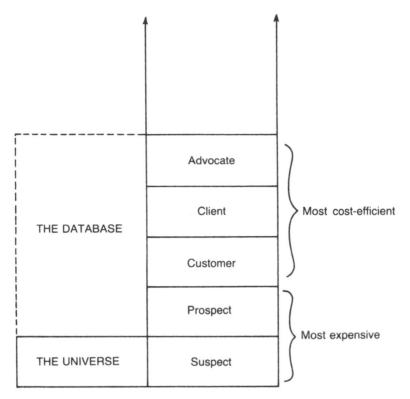

Figure 3.4. The loyalty ladder.

- *Prospect—someone who has heard about you but hasn't come to buy anything from you.* The prospect has either inquired about your product or service or at the very least has been exposed to (and remembers) some of your advertising and sales messages. Note: If a prospect has made a direct inquiry about your product or service by requesting more information in response to an ad or mailing, you can capture the prospect's name for your database, allowing you to contact him or her repeatedly until he or she does buy.

- *Customer—someone who has bought from you once (spent at least $1 with you).* This group can be customers of yours and also customers of your competitor. Warning: In many businesses, someone who has bought once is not really considered a customer, because a single purchase is more like a test or trial than an indication of satisfaction with your firm. For example, in mail order marketing, mailing lists of multi-buyers (buyers who have ordered two or more times from the same source) are priced at a premium, because experience proves that someone who has made multiple purchases is twice as likely to respond to a mail order offer as someone who bought only once.

- *Client—a customer who buys multiple services from you and with whom you have a strong ongoing, almost contractual relationship.* At this point, clients are moving to the upper rungs of the loyalty ladder. A relationship has been established, and clients are beginning to build loyalty to you and your company.

- *Advocate—someone who buys everything you sell.* Advocates are so happy with what they are buying from you that they become disciples. An advocate is someone who brings customers to you. When new people come to town and are looking to buy a particular product, an advocate brings them directly to you and says, "I want you to take care of these folks the same way you take care of me."

DON'T OVERLOOK THE GOVERNMENT MARKETPLACE

In determining target markets, most small to medium-sized businesses concentrate on the obvious commercial and consumer marketplaces in front of them and ignore a large and potentially lucrative source of additional revenue: the government.

The government buys over $691 billion of products and services each year, but the procurement responsibility is highly decentralized. In the federal government alone, there are more than 15,000 individual authorities responsible for major purchases, with tens of thousands more in regional, state, county, and municipal governments. The challenge is to identify those buying authorities who have specific needs and budgets for the types of services you sell, then contact them individually to request that they include your company on their bid lists.

In most cases, the individual buying authorities will grant your request to be included. Often they're required by law to open their doors wide to every company asking for the opportunity to bid. Many government projects have set-asides requiring that a portion of all purchases be made from small and minority-owned businesses. This practice is designed to encourage competition and fairness.

The bidding process is highly structured and fairly involved, with many bid questionnaires running to dozens of pages and requiring supporting documentation, a factor that discourages many smaller firms from participating in these markets. But the huge size of the sales potential can make competing for government business extremely worthwhile.

Targeting the Government Market

Even though the government tries to make itself accessible to potential suppliers, the number of government departments and buying authorities is so large and diverse that considerable effort is required to locate them. Usually, government employees are helpful and accommodating, but expect a long series of referrals before you get through to the right people in the right departments. Some of this can be accomplished by phone, but you'll find personal visits far more productive. Based on the experience of companies enjoying strong sales to the government, here are some suggestions on how to get started selling to the three basic government markets: federal, state, and local.

SELLING TO THE FEDERAL GOVERNMENT

- For any widely used products and consumable supplies, the General Services Administration is the logical place to start. In many product categories, the GSA produces standard catalogs through which government employees can order your product (up to limited dollar amounts) without a bid or separate contract.

- The federal publication *Commerce Business Daily* regularly carries notices of bid opportunities. For a subscription, write to the U.S. Government Printing Office, Washington, D.C. 20402.

- Each federal agency and major department has specialists who can give you information about the principal buying authorities in their jurisdictions. They can also give you referrals to the specific buying authorities and locations that interest you most.

- If yours is a small business, the Small Business Administration can help. Start with the local SBA office in your area.

- Also, visit the offices of your local congressional representative. More than likely, they will have staff members assigned to helping area businesses.

SELLING TO STATE GOVERNMENTS

- In your own state, begin with your local congressional representatives or senators. Their offices can give you referrals and perhaps introductions to the important buying authorities in your state government.

- In other states, start by identifying the state agency that coordinates purchases, if there is one. Otherwise, contact the state agency that coordinates budgets.

For a complete listing of more than 13,000 state agencies and state officials, including names, addresses, and phone numbers, consult the *National Directory of State Agencies*, published by Cambridge Information Group, 7200 Wisconsin Avenue, Bethesda, MD 20814, 800-227-3052 or 301-961-3052.

SELLING TO LOCAL GOVERNMENTS

- The Comptroller's office or the Mayor's office will point you in the right direction. Frequently, local governments centralize their buying activities, which makes your search easier.

RESOURCE

A good guide to government mailing lists on the federal, state, and local levels is the *Guide to Gale Lists: Carrol Government Lists*, available free from Gale Research, Dept. 77748, Detroit, MI 48277-0748, 800-877-GALE.

This publication describes numerous government mailing lists, including legislators, White House officials, mayors, city council members, government executives, contractors, and more.

HOW TO AVOID THE MOST COMMON MISTAKE WHEN TARGETING MARKETS

The most common mistake companies make when launching a marketing program is to treat all their customers as a single group to which they sell the same products, make the same offers, and talk in the same language.

In most instances, your target market can be profitably subdivided into a number of submarkets, each of which represents a group of potential buyers with different needs, different concerns, different problems, and varying levels of purchasing power. The successful advertiser recognizes this fact and creates separate promotional campaigns aimed at the key interests and concerns of each submarket.

Example: Let's say you are a marketing executive for an airline. Your responsibility is promoting flights to Florida. When asked to define your market, you might initially respond, "People who fly to Florida or will fly to Florida in the near future."

But is this definition sufficiently detailed for meaningful marketing? Let's consider some of the submarkets within this group:

1. *Business travelers.* The large density of corporations, conference centers, and conference facilities at Florida hotels results in a lot of businesspeople flying to Florida. This segment of the market is concerned with comfort, extras (such as fax machines or telephones available on board the aircraft), roominess (space to spread out and work), special class available for business flyers, frequent flyer programs (so they can get free trips for personal use), and frequency of schedule (so they can arrive and leave at their convenience). The business flyer is not price sensitive, because the company is picking up the tab.

2. *The Disney market.* A large percentage of air travelers to Florida are people visiting Disney's Magic Kingdom and Epcot Center. Mostly families, they are often on a budget. Their concerns are price, low or free fares for young children, and seasonal discounts. One strategy that might work is advertising special low rates for Orlando (the Disney location).

3. *Condominium owners.* A growing group of people is buying vacation condominiums in Florida. Vacation homeowners are likely to travel to Florida several times a year. One approach might be to offer a frequent flyer discount or a discount if the traveler prepays for a coupon book of round-trip tickets in advance. The benefits of prepayment are a discount over the regular fare plus the ability to lock in the current low rate.

4. *Retirees.* Florida is a favorite spot for retirees. One resident recently commented, "Florida consists of a minority population of people in their

twenties, working for 'oranges and sunshine' wages, serving hand and foot a majority population of people over 55." How about advertising an "over 50" discount for this market?

5. *Families visiting family.* As more and more people retire to Florida, more and more families—adult children with their own children—are making annual pilgrimages to visit mother and father in their retirement condominium developments. How about a special discount for families visiting families?

These submarkets and strategies were developed off the cuff in about five minutes. Spend an hour or two now thinking about your own markets. How can you subdivide them into target markets? What messages, strategies, approaches, and offers would appeal to these groups?

As a rule of thumb, the more narrow your target markets and the more tightly focused your advertising message is to the specific needs of these narrow vertical markets, the better your advertising results will be in terms of awareness, inquiries, and sales. Target marketing generates a higher response rate.

Chapter

HOW TO SET YOUR ADVERTISING BUDGET

4

According to the Competitive Media Reporting and Publishing Information Bureau, the number one advertiser for the period August 1995 to July 1996 was General Motors, spending $1.63 billion. Procter & Gamble was the second biggest ad spender, at $1.58 billion. Phillip Morris was third, spending $1.3 billion a year.

Coca-Cola was number 38 on the list of the nation's biggest advertisers, spending almost $300 million a year. Discount broker Charles Schwab spent $60.5 million, while CompUSA spent slightly over $56 million. The number 200 firm on the list, the BMW AG Auto Dealers Association, spent $47.5 million during this period. Campbell's Soup, at number 61, spent $173 million.

Your budget is probably a lot smaller. In a 1996 survey of its members, the Business Marketing Association found that 48 percent of the advertisers responding had budgets of over $1 million. Only 15 percent had advertising budgets over $5 million.

The advertising manager faced with the task of setting an annual advertising budget is challenged to answer a number of key questions. Among them are:

- What percentage of the marketing budget should be spent on advertising as opposed to other marketing programs (e.g., sales training, sales commissions, trade show displays, franchises, dealer incentives, coupons, point of purchase displays, etc.)? Often, increasing the budget for advertising means cutting somewhere else, and in some cases the money may indeed be best spent elsewhere. Contrary to what some in the field practice, successful ad managers do not fight for every penny to be given to advertising. Instead, they seek only what they need to get the job done—no more, no less. Nevertheless, with today's rising media,

71

printing, and production costs, the problem is frequently too little money rather than too much money.

- How much money (in dollar amount) should be spent on marketing communications this year?

- Of that budget, how should it be allocated? How much for space ads versus direct mail versus telemarketing versus radio and television?

- How should the spending be paced? Should it be spent evenly throughout the year or should the bulk of the money be spent at certain times?

- How much will individual items (the January newspaper supplement, the March circular) in the ad budgets cost? Answering this question requires the ability to make somewhat accurate estimates based on little data or specifics about each project, an ability that develops with experience and time spent on the job.

To answer some of these questions, let us see what others are doing and examine some methods you can use to determine your own budget.

DETERMINING HOW MUCH TO SPEND ON MARKETING COMMUNICATIONS

McGraw-Hill surveyed 535 sales managers and received responses from 284. These sales managers' responses are summarized in Table 4.1, showing budget allocation in key marketing areas.

The first column indicates actual budget allocations. The second column indicates how they would allocate the budget if given a 25 percent budget increase. Note that the sales managers now spend most of their budget on salespeople and only a small percentage on advertising and promotion, but say that they would spend more on advertising and promotion if they had more money for it. (Percentage columns may not add up to 100 percent due to rounding.)

Business Marketing magazine performed a similar survey among top business-to-business marketers. The survey, summarized in Table 4.2, revealed how the communications budget was spread among more than a dozen areas.

Table 4.1. Marketing tools used by sales managers.

Tool	Current Budget	Imaginary Budget (25% Higher)
Salespeople	60%	42%
Advertising/promotion	17%	30%
Company catalogs/directories	8%	9%
Trade shows	7%	8%
Direct mail	4%	9%
Other	3%	3%

Table 4.2. The average budget picture of top business marketers.

Communications Tool	% of Budget
Media	31%
Literature	24%
Trade shows	11%
Direct mail	8%
Ad production	5%
Sales promotion	5%
Public relations	4%
Inquiry fulfillment	2%
Market research	2%
Telemarketing	2%
Point of purchase	1%
Other	5%
TOTAL:	100%

Table 4.3. Industrial marketing communications budget breakdown.

Communications Tools	% of Budget Spent
Print advertising	36.3%
Exhibits and trade shows	19.9%
Catalogs/directories	13.6%
Literature, deals, coupons, point of purchase	9.9%
Direct mail	7.5%
Dealer and distributor aids	5.3%
Public relations and publicity	4.8%
Radio/TV/billboards	1.9%

The McGraw-Hill Laboratory of Advertising Performance surveyed 382 marketing managers in major industrial companies. The results are summarized in Table 4.3.

What about the marketing communications and advertising budget based on a percentage of sales? Research Report #8015.8 from the McGraw-Hill Laboratory of Advertising Performance indicates that marketing communications costs average 1.73 percent of sales among major industrial companies. According to *How to Promote Your Own Business* (Gary Blake, New American Library, 1983), most small businesses spend between 1 and 3 percent of sales on advertising, while large consumer companies such as General Motors, Carter Wallace, Revlon, Pepsico, and Procter & Gamble have advertising budgets ranging from less than 1 percent of sales to more than 30 percent, with 2 to 10 percent being typical.

Table 4.4. Advertising budget as a percentage of sales.

Industry	Advertising Budget as a Percentage of Sales
Advertising agencies	0.1%
Agricultural production, crops	2.9%
Air courier services	2.1%
Air transportation, certified	1.8%
Aircraft and parts	0.5%
Auto dealers, gas stations	0.5%
Auto rental and leasing	2.9%
Auto repair services and garages	4.0%
Bakery products	1.9%
Book publishers	3.8%
Business services	5.3%
Catalog showrooms	3.7%
Chemicals (wholesale)	3.5%
Coating and engraving services	2.6%
Computer program and software services	3.5%
Communications and signaling devices	4.1%
Commercial printing	1.2%
Computer equipment	1.9%
Computer stores	1.0%
Computers, micro	5.1%
Connectors	1.2%
Construction, special trade	9.8%
Dairy products	4.9%
Data processing services	1.2%
Detective and protective services	0.2%
Drugs	4.4%
Educational services	5.0%
Electric appliances, wholesale	0.8%
Electric lighting	1.1%
Electronic components	2.3%
Engines and turbines	1.8%
Engineering, architect, survey services	0.8%
Farm machinery and equipment	1.6%
Financial services	0.7%
Food	7.3%
Freight forwarding	3.6%
Hardware, wholesale	6.4%
Health services	3.3%
Hospitals	5.8%
Hotels	0.4%
Industrial controls	1.7%
Industrial machinery and equipment, wholesale	2.0%
Insurance agents and brokers	0.6%
Lumber, wholesale	2.2%
Machine tools	2.0%

Table 4.4. (*Cont.*)

Industry	Advertising Budget as a Percentage of Sales
Material handling equipment	1.0%
Medical laboratories	0.9%
Metalworking equipment	5.4%
Management consulting	1.8%
Motor vehicle parts and accessories	1.6%
Motors and generators	1.0%
Musical instruments	3.3%
Newspapers	3.9%
Office automation systems	2.3%
Office furniture	1.4%
Optical instruments and lenses	1.5%
Outpatient care facilities	1.1%
Paint, varnish, and lacquer	3.1%
Paper and paper products	3.8%
Personal services	3.7%
PR services	1.8%
Office supplies	5.2%
Photofinishing laboratories	1.8%
Photographic equipment and supplies	3.2%
Plastics, resins, elastomers	1.6%
Pollution control machinery	0.8%
Prefabricated metal buildings	0.7%
Pumps	1.2%
Real estate agencies	2.8%
Savings & loan associations	0.7%
Securities & commodities brokers	3.8%
Semiconductors	1.2%
Ship and boat building and repair	2.3%
Soaps and detergents	7.6%
Telephone communications (wire, radio)	1.9%
Textile mill products	1.1%
Tires and inner tubes	3.1%
Training equipment and simulators	1.6%
Valves	1.0%

Business Marketing magazine has published advertising-to-sales ratios for a variety of different industries, shown in Table 4.4.

Dana K. Cassell lists the advertising budget-to-sales ratios for a variety of retail businesses in Table 4.5.

Again, the advertising budgets for most small retail businesses and chains fall in the range of 1 to 3 percent of sales.

Table 4.5. Ad budget as a percentage of sales for retail businesses.

Type of Store	Advertising Budget as Percentage of Sales
Appliance, radio, TV dealers	2.3%
Auto accessory and parts stores	0.9%
Bookstores	1.7%
Camera stores	0.8%
Children's and infants' wear stores	1.4%
Cocktail lounges	0.9%
Department stores	2.8%
Discount stores	2.4%
Drugstores	1.5%
Florists	2.1%
Food chains	1.1%
Furniture chains	5.0%
Gas stations	0.8%
Gift and novelty stores	1.4%
Hardware stores	1.6%
Home centers	1.3%
Jewelry stores	4.4%
Liquor stores	0.9%
Lumber and building materials dealers	0.5%
Meat markets	0.6%
Men's wear stores	2.9%
Music stores	1.8%
Office supply dealers	0.8%
Paint, glass, and wallpaper stores	1.3%
Photographic studios and supply shops	2.4%
Restaurants	0.8%
Shoe stores	1.9%
Specialty stores	3.0%
Sporting goods stores	3.5%
Tire dealers	2.2%
Variety stores	1.5%

HOW TO DETERMINE YOUR ANNUAL ADVERTISING BUDGET

How much should you spend on advertising this year? There is no right answer, no precise, scientific formula that you can plug into a calculator and say to the boss, "See, this is exactly how much we have to spend to reach our sales objectives!"

There are standard formulas that represent seven different methods of determining the advertising budget. We will review these formulas here; then I will present a method that is a combination of two of the formulas and that I think makes the most sense. Use any method or combination of methods you are comfortable with.

Formula 1: Percentage of Sales

The most widely used method of establishing an advertising budget is to base it on a percentage of sales. Advertising is as much a business expense as, say, the cost of labor, and thus should be related to the quantity of goods sold.

The percentage of sales method avoids some of the problems that result from using profits as a base. For example, if profits in a period are low, it might not be the fault of advertising; material costs might be higher. By using the percentage of sales method, you keep your advertising in a consistent relationship to your sales volume, which is primarily what your advertising should be affecting.

You can select the percentage figure to use (e.g., 1 percent, 2 percent, 2.5 percent) by finding out what other businesses in your line of work are doing. These percentages are fairly consistent within a given category of business.

It's fairly easy to find out this ratio of advertising expense to sales in your industry. You can check trade magazines and associations or consult Census Bureau and Internal Revenue Service reports as well as reports published by financial institutions, such as Dun & Bradstreet, Inc., 99 Church Street, New York, NY 10007. Some of the tables in this chapter may also prove helpful.

Knowing the ratio for your industry tells you whether you are spending more or less than your competitors. But remember, these industry averages are not gospel. Your particular situation may dictate that you spend more or less than the average. Average may not be good enough for you. You may want to out-advertise your competitors and be willing to cut into short-term profits to do so. Growth requires investment.

No ad manager should be bound to any single method for determining an advertising budget. It's helpful to use the percentage of sales method because it's quick and easy. It ensures that your advertising budget isn't way out of proportion for your business. It's a sound method for stable markets. But if you want to expand your market share, you'll probably have to use a larger percentage of sales than the industry average.

Your budget can be determined as a percentage of past sales, of estimated future sales, or as a combination of the two:

- *Past sales.* Your budget can be a percentage of last year's sales or an average of a number of years in the immediate past. Consider, though, that changes in economic conditions can make your figure too high or too low.

- *Estimated future sales.* You can calculate your advertising budget as a percentage of anticipated sales for next year. The most common pitfall of this method is an optimistic assumption that your business will continue to grow. You must always keep general business trends in mind, especially if there's a chance of a slump, and hardheadedly assess the directions in your industry and in your own operation. Note that when launching a new product, the advertising budget must, naturally, be calculated based on a percentage of future sales, since the new product has no sales record.

- *Past sales and estimated future sales.* The middle ground between an often conservative appraisal based on last year's sales and a usually too optimistic assessment of next year's sales is to combine both. It's a more realistic method during periods of changing economic conditions. It allows you to analyze trends and results thoughtfully and to set advertising expenditures with a little more assurance of accuracy.

Formula 2: Unit of Sales

In the unit of sales method, you set aside a fixed sum for each unit to be sold, based on your experience and trade knowledge of how much advertising it takes to sell each unit. That is, if it takes two cents' worth of advertising to sell a case of canned vegetables and you want to move 100,000 cases, you will probably plan to spend $2,000 on advertising them. Does it cost X dollars to sell a refrigerator? Then you'll probably have to budget 1,000 times X if you plan to sell a thousand refrigerators. You are simply basing your budget on unit of sales rather than dollar amounts of sales.

Some people consider this method just a variation of percentage of sales. However, unit of sales lets you make a closer estimate of what you should plan to spend for maximum effect, because it's based on what experience tells you it takes to sell an actual unit, rather than an overall percentage of your gross sales.

The unit of sales method is particularly useful in fields where the amount of product available is limited by outside factors, such as the weather's effect on crops. If that's the situation for your business, first estimate how many units or cases will be available to you. Then, advertise only as much as experience tells you it takes to sell them. Thus, if you have a pretty good idea ahead of time how many units will be available, you should have minimal waste in your advertising costs.

This method is also suited for specialty goods, such as washing machines and automobiles; however, it's difficult to apply when you have many different kinds of products to advertise and must divide your advertising among these products. The unit of sales method is not very useful in sporadic or irregular markets.

The unit of sales method can be helpful when selling durable goods of high value, such as television sets and VCRs, or goods of small unit value, such as toilet paper and flashlights. It is not a valid approach to setting a budget for a service business.

Formula 3: Objective and Task

The most difficult method for determining an advertising budget is the objective and task approach. Yet it's the most accurate and best accomplishes what all budgets should: It relates the dollar appropriation to the marketing task to be accomplished under usual conditions.

To establish your budget by this method, you need a coordinated marketing program with specific objectives (see Chapter 5) based on a thorough survey of your markets and their potential.

While the percentage of sales method determines how much you'll spend without much consideration of what you want to accomplish, the task method establishes what you must do to meet your objectives. Only then do you calculate costs. You set specific objectives, determine what media best reach your target market, and then estimate how much it will cost to run the number and types of advertisements you think it will take to get the results you want. You repeat this process for each objective. When you total these costs, you have your projected budget.

You may find that you cannot afford to advertise as much as you would like. It's a good idea, therefore, to rank your objectives. As with the other methods, be prepared to change your plan to reflect reality and to fit the resources you have available.

Formula 4: Historical

The easiest way to set a promotion budget is to base it on what you have spent historically. Typically, companies take last year's budget and add 10 percent for inflation to come up with this year's budget.

The advantages of this method are its simplicity and the fact that management, especially financial management, finds it so acceptable. Few chief financial officers will make any objection to an ad budget presented this way unless sales and profits have fallen off dramatically or the economy is bad.

The disadvantage of this method is that it doesn't accurately reflect your goals, objectives, economic factors, market conditions, or current plans. Also, it is possible that the previous year's budget upon which the historical method is based was not sensible. In this case, the historical method simply repeats a bad business decision over and over again.

Formula 5: Match the Competition

This is a reactive method whereby management spends money in reaction to what it perceives the competition is spending. Clients often call me wanting to place expensive ads in publications we have previously determined were undesirable. When I ask why the change of heart, the answer is always, "Because [name of competitor] has an ad there and I want a bigger one [or one the same size]." This is a poor reason to run an ad and rarely provides the desired results.

Formula 6: All You Can Afford

With the all you can afford method, you first appropriate money for essential operating and capital expenses, such as new equipment, materials, inventory, supplies, labor, insurance, rent, and so on. Whatever is left over is spent on marketing.

This technique is dangerous for companies that are limited in growth potential or want to deliberately remain a certain size; the danger is that it can generate more business than the company can handle. The company has no choice but to "waste" the sales interest generated by the advertising, turning down the business it cannot handle. Thus, sales remain flat while profits actually decrease because of the extra money spent on unnecessary promotion. Since most companies must expand under a mode of controlled growth, the all you can afford method is rarely sensible.

The only the all you can afford method makes sense is in situations when the following three conditions are met:

- You can handle all the business and as many sales or inquiries as your advertising can generate.

- Money spent on advertising generates an immediate and measurable return in excess of its cost. That is, a dollar spent on advertising yields at least $1.30 (and preferably $1.50 to $2 or more) in net revenue.

- The threat of competitors moving in to copycat your marketing or product provides pressure to capture the market as soon as possible before competitors can follow suit.

Successful mail order operators often use the all you can afford method. When test ads prove profitable, they immediately put the profits generated into more ads on a larger scale. When these pay off, that money goes into still more advertising, for as long as it is profitable and before competitors can knock off the product or ad generating the revenue. Fad and craze businesses also use this method since they too must quickly grab all the sales they can before imitators and competitors take away their customers.

Formula 7: Seat-of-the-Pants Method

The seventh method of setting the advertising budget is not to set one, that is, to "feel" your way along on a month-by-month basis without any formal plan, to step up marketing efforts when you see an opportunity, and to pull back when you are flush with business or, conversely, when spending money is tight.

Advertising professionals and consultants quite naturally hate this method and think anyone who uses it is a boob. Perhaps I should agree. But the fact is, I have several entrepreneurial clients who operate this way and are tremendously successful; many have become millionaires through their current businesses. I know this approach cannot work when the entrepreneurial firm grows, becomes more complex, and forms into a larger corporation with departments and specialists and structure and multiple layers of management. But for the smaller entrepreneurial firm, whose guiding force is an entrepreneur with superior marketing instincts, seat-of-the-pants advertising management can and does work, much to the chagrin of consultants like myself.

ONE SENSIBLE SOLUTION

While you are free to use any of these seven methods in selecting a dollar amount for your annual advertising expenditure, I use a method that combines several of the other methods and, I think, makes the most sense:

1. First, use the percentage of sales method to set an upper and lower limit on your budget. For example, let's say in your industry it is typical to spend between 1 and 2 percent of sales on advertising and promotion, and that your sales are $10 million a year. Your advertising budget would be between $100,000 and $200,000.

2. Now step back and take an objective look at the competitive environment, the marketplace, and your own operation. You might set your budget at the upper end of the range if:

- the competition is doing heavy advertising and promotion;
- your markets are expanding;
- favorable economic considerations are causing a general rise in consumer spending; or
- you are introducing a hot new product.

On the other hand, you might set your advertising budget at the lower end of the range if:

- there is little competition or the competition is inactive in marketing or promotion, and you have all the sales you want without heavy marketing effort;
- your markets are contracting or shrinking;
- a decline in the economy has had an adverse impact on consumer spending;
- your operating costs have risen to the point that it is essential that you make cuts in spending; or
- you are introducing no new products and instead have a line of older products that are steady but reliable sellers.

3. Now that you have evaluated the sales environment and have established a budget range, allocate money to complete specific tasks that will achieve your planned objectives (the task and objective method).

Example: How do you allocate money to specific tasks that will achieve a planned objective? Let's say you run a graphic design studio and your objective is to get six new accounts. You know from past experience that doing a direct mail promotion costs you $1,000 per thousand pieces mailed, that you get a 6 percent response rate (60 inquiries per thousand pieces mailed), and that one-tenth of the prospects making inquiries become clients. Therefore, to get six new clients (one-tenth of 60), you need to mail 1,000 direct mail pieces, and you would budget $1,000.

ADDITIONAL BUDGET-SETTING GUIDELINES

Here are ten additional factors to consider when determining your advertising budget. These guidelines are based on a thorough study of the marketing activities of more than 1,000 businesses producing capital goods, raw and semi-finished materials, components, and supplies. The study was performed by the Strategic Planning Institute (SPI) of Cambridge, MA.

1. The higher your company's market share, the more you should spend on advertising. Market share is the single most important determinant of absolute marketing expenditure. For example, SPI found that a company with a 30 percent market share is likely to spend three times as much on advertising as a company with a 9 percent market share.

2. Companies launching new products have to spend more on advertising than companies with mature or old products. Introducing many new products to the market dramatically increases your advertising expenditures. In fact, the new product innovator will spend more than twice as much on advertising and promotion as a business with few new products.

A corollary of this rule is that the higher the level of new product activity in the market, the higher will be the marketing expenditures of all companies in that market. The reason is that high levels of new product activity in a market increase advertising expenditures significantly as competitors inform potential customers of features and benefits of their offerings and maneuver for superior market share positions.

3. Fast-growing markets typically require higher ad expenditure. In rapidly growing markets, businesses must spend substantially more than in mature markets where buyers know all the suppliers and have relatively well-established relationships. As an example, compare the marketing dollars being spent on promoting laptop computer notebooks against the amount spent to promote staplers.

In many cases, the fast-growth market may be new and innovative, and the product's features may not yet be well known to potential customers. A special effort is then needed to educate them and overcome buying resistance caused by skepticism, high switching costs, or sheer inertia. This effort translates into higher marketing expenditures.

The relationship between the rate of market growth and the level of advertising expenditures is illustrated in Table 4.6.

4. Advertising expenditures are higher when a large amount of your plant's production capacity is underused. When production capacity is available, marketing expenditure increases. In particular, firms with a large fixed asset base cannot afford to have production idled. They turn to advertising and promotion in order to load capacity. Businesses require lower advertising expenditures as production capacity fills up. Generating demand without adequate capacity may result in dissatisfied customers.

Table 4.6. Advertising expenditures as a function of growth rate.

Rate of Market Growth	Annual Percentage Market Growth	Advertising Expenditures per $1,000 Market Sales
No growth	0.0–0.9%	$0.95
Slow growth	1.0–4.9%	$0.95
Moderate growth	5.0%–11.9%	$1.20
Rapid growth	12.0% and up	$1.30

Table 4.7. Advertising expenditures as a function of how busy the company is.

% Capacity Utilized	Media Advertising and Sales Promotion per $1,000 of Market Sales
under 65%	$3.60
65–74.9%	$2.80
75–84.9%	$2.90
over 85%	$2.50

Sometimes a business that wishes to enter a new market or capitalize on market growth will build production capacity in anticipation of demand. In this case, its managers tend to spend advertising dollars readily to make fixed investment productive and to capture market share.

The relationship between advertising expenditures and capacity utilization as found by SPI is illustrated in Table 4.7.

5. High levels of advertising and promotion are required for low-ticket items. Advertising expenditures decline as purchase amounts rise. A business whose end users typically buy in amounts of less than $100 spends nearly twice the amount on advertising and three times as much on sales promotion than a business that sells large-ticket items costing $100,000 per unit.

What accounts for this? It may be that high-ticket items are more likely to be customized and price insensitive when performance is at stake, while low-ticket items are more frequently standardized, price sensitive, and likely to be pushed through channels by discounting and other promotional practices. Also, high-ticket items are purchased less frequently, and for that reason demand a less constant persuasive sales effort.

But perhaps the greatest factor at work here is that businesses selling large-ticket items can market them directly to a few large customers, while businesses selling small-ticket products must push them through wholesale and multilevel distribution channels. Some industries realize huge economies of scale by focusing on a few large customers.

Table 4.8. Advertising expenditures as a function of price of product.

Cost of Item	Media Advertising and Sales Promotion per $1,000 of Sales
less than $100	$5.00
$100–$999	$3.60
$1,000–$9,999	$3.20
$10,000–$99,999	$2.80
$100,000 and over	$1.80

The relationship between purchase price of an item and advertising expenditures is shown in Table 4.8.

6. The less your product represents as a percentage of the customer's total purchases, the greater the advertising and sales promotion expenditures. SPI's research revealed a strong relationship between the amount a customer purchases of a given product and the level of advertising required to sell that product. Take business products, for example. A business product that represents less than 1 percent of the buyer's total purchases requires a 31 percent greater level of advertising than a product that represents 10 percent of the customer's total purchases.

What's the reason? A good guess is that the frequently purchased product, because it is so frequently ordered, is foremost in the prospects' minds, and so they don't need advertising to remind them about it. The product that is bought only once in a while, on the other hand, is rarely thought about, so advertising is needed to remind the prospect and provide a buying source when the need for the product does arise.

7. Products at both the low and high ends of the price range (discount products and premium products) require higher ad expenditures. The conventional wisdom in marketing is that you must support a premium price position in the market with aggressive advertising and sales promotion. This is needed to convince the customer that the quality of the product translates into superior value for the premium price.

However, SPI research revealed that products with discount pricing may also require more marketing support than do products priced "average" in their category. Perhaps extra effort is needed to convince the customer that the function for which the product is bought will be delivered but at a better price. SPI found that discount-priced products required approximately 39 percent greater advertising and promotion expenditure than the average-priced products, while premium-priced products required 72 percent greater advertising and promotion expenditure than the product of average price in its category.

8. High-quality products typically require higher advertising expenditures. The relationship SPI found between relative product quality

(as measured by a variety of product and service attributes) and media advertising and sales promotion expenditures is shown in Table 4.9.

A corollary of factors 7 and 8 is that businesses that have high relative product quality but provide greater value to the customer through lower relative pricing can spend less on advertising. This is obviously a trade-off between pricing and advertising expenditures. The business that provides a more favorable price-to-performance ratio (charges less for premium quality) can afford to spend less than its competitor that offers the same high quality but wants to charge a premium price for it.

Also, a business that, through marketing communications, positions its product as the premium product in the marketplace must spend two to three times as much on advertising as its competition to create and maintain that position. However, SPI found that businesses that have established a premium product position typically hold the number one share in their markets.

9. Broad product lines typically require higher advertising expenditures. An additional dimension of product positioning and business strategy is the breadth of product line relative to competitors. Experience indicates that manufacturers with broad product lines support their sales forces with aggressive advertising and promotion. SPI research showed that companies with broad product lines spent an average of 71 percent more on advertising and promotion than companies with narrow product lines.

10. Standard or off-the-shelf products require higher levels of advertising expenditure than custom products. Customized products require less marketing support than standardized ones. The reason is that, when products must be produced to the customer's specifications, the cost of switching suppliers may be high and alternative sources may not be readily available. Quality may be important, and the customer may be reluctant to leave a reliable supplier.

Markets for standardized products, on the other hand, are more susceptible to product substitution. Purchase decisions are more likely to be affected by price and less influenced by personal relationships with the supplier. As a result, greater marketing support is required to communi-

Table 4.9. Advertising expenditures as a function of product quality.

Relative Product Quality Rating	Media Advertising and Sales Promotion Expenditures per $1,000 of Market Sales
Poor quality (lowest rating)	$1.50
Fair	$1.80
Average	$2.10
Good	$2.60
Excellent	$3.40

cate product and company benefits. SPI found that companies supplying standard products spent, on average, 60 percent more on advertising and promotion than companies that provide customized products tailored to the buyer's specifications.

WHAT THINGS COST

To complete your budgeting, you have to know what things cost. Therefore, when budgeting, it helps to have at hand a list of the typical projects that will be paid for by the budget along with an approximate dollar figure or range of what they cost.

You can put this list of estimated fees together yourself, based on experience and what you have paid in the past. Or you can ask the vendors you will be using—ad agencies, PR firms, Web designers—to provide rough estimates for typical projects such as ads, Web sites, or product brochures.

In 1997, the Business Marketing Association surveyed 325 advertising professionals to determine project costs. Results were as follows:

10-minute video	$15,400
Trade show exhibit	$55,068
60-page catalog	$70,848
12-page brochure	$32,288
Logo design	$ 6,240
Full-page, full-color ad	$11,685
Fractional black and white ad	$ 1,457
Four-color annual report	$99,612
Direct mail program	$41,808
Planning session	$ 3,336
Advertising specialty items	$ 55

These are averages and are not definitive. Prices for such services, as freelance copywriter Sig Rosenblum notes, "are all over the lot." Recently I got quotes from two graphic artists in the New York area to design a direct mail package. One wanted $6,000; the other charged $1,500. I don't urge people to buy just based on price; I just want you to realize that items in your budget can be gotten for a wide range of prices.

ADVERTISING BUDGETING: A PANEL DISCUSSION

A panel of members of the Business/Professional Advertising Association met in Houston to discuss advertising budgeting. Included in the panel were two ad agency presidents, the marketing communications manager of a major industrial firm, the assistant to the president of public affairs and advertising of another firm, and the director of marketing communications for a major industrial company.

The format of the meeting called for a moderator who posed key questions to the panel. Each member answered the question and the panel discussed various aspects of the answer.

The first key question posed to the panel was, "What are the major problems with budgeting for a company or client advertising program?" The panel identified these four key difficulties:

First, the person with the power to approve budgets often lacks appreciation of the value of advertising investment; he or she is oriented in another direction.

Second, the budgets are the first item subject to change in business conditions. Worse, they are cut arbitrarily because the budget cutters do not understand the function of advertising.

Third, clients are unwilling to do benchmark studies (discussed in Chapter 5) to measure what the advertising is trying to accomplish as a guide to setting realistic budgets to accomplish each objective.

Fourth, the panel mentioned the inability to forecast with any degree of accuracy. Advertising should be tied to a profit plan or marketing plan. Once approved by management, the budget is an integral part of that plan and is changed only if the plan itself changes.

The second question addressed by the panel covered the fact that management often has difficulty understanding advertising and setting objectives for it. Panel members discussed aspects of this problem and agreed that most managers who control budgets have a low level of appreciation for what advertising can do or how much it costs. Management is not the only culpable factor; ad agency people often arbitrarily raise or lower budgets without reference to objectives of a campaign or program.

The third question addressed by the panel was, "Just what elements of communications make up a budget?" One panelist listed media, media production, direct mail, trade shows, audiovisual programs, and literature—everything except public relations. Another commented, "We include every single thing that has to do with the public, except when salespeople take prospects to lunch."

The fourth question involved approval of budgets by top management. In corporations, advertising executives tend to report to upper management echelons. In ad agencies, however, there are problems reaching those levels. Often programs and budgets must be given to the advertising manager, who then makes another presentation to top management. "We lose control completely," one agency president commented. Whether the budget survives often depends on the skill of the advertising manager.

Another element in the survival of the ad budget is the orientation of the top executive. Executives who come from the accounting side are less interested and informed. Those who come from the sales side understand more fully the role of advertising.

Marketing communications and ad agency executives alike have become adept at planning overestimation of budgets. Some have "slush funds" built up over long time periods to take care of unplanned necessities. One equated budgeting with selling a home. "You'd be absolutely crazy to start out asking the price you expected to get," he declared. To some degree, replied another panelist, all budgeting is hypothetical. It is the best estimate of needs at the moment, which is then etched in stone and must be lived with.

The fifth question involved budget control. Three panelists use a log or job number system to track what has been spent on individual projects and elements within those projects. Each phase or element is assigned a number within the overall job number. The final expenditure can then be compared to the estimate or allocation for that project and over- or under-spending can be determined.

How do panelists present their budgets for approval? Answers ranged from, "I just send it to the president" to creating elaborate multiprojector slide presentations. A simple narrative explaining what is going to be done and how much it will cost represents one end of the scale. A full and frank, point-by-point discussion with top management represents the other end.

Panelists provided the following advice on how to be a good budgeting manager:

- Develop the ability to delegate. Delegate various aspects of budgeting to your internal and agency people. From the data they generate, you can make a rational budget.
- Find out where you are, so you can tell where you want to go.
- Question each item in last year's budget. Was it effective? Do you need it? Do you need more money?
- Set definite objectives and spend what you have to in order to reach them.
- View advertising as an investment, not a cost. Allocate funds the same way you would for adding another salesperson or buying another piece of equipment.
- Treat advertising as if it were that salesperson or piece of equipment. Justify its cost. Track its results.

ALLOCATING THE BUDGET FOR MAXIMUM RESULTS

Once you have determined the total dollar amount you can spend on advertising and promotion, you must allocate it among the many tasks, markets, products, and divisions within your company that need these resources. Allocation may be by one or more of the following categories:

- *Division.* Large corporations have numerous divisions, each with its separate advertising goals and objectives. The first step is to allocate the corporate budget, dividing it between the various divisions. How do you do this? Each division should come up with a divisional budget figure based on the methods outlined in this chapter. The corporate advertising manager evaluates these for accuracy, then allocates the gross budget among the divisions according to their needs.

- *Departments*. In the largest corporations, some divisions may be organized in subdivisions or departments, each with its own marketing activities and objectives. Again, come up with a budget figure for the division based on the methods outlined above, then allocate the budget among the individual departments based on this analysis of needs.

- *Product*. More likely than allocating among departments is the probability that a division will have to share its budget among a number of different products it sells. Each product manager should propose an advertising and promotion budget for his or her product, justifying it with calculations based on the methods outlined in this chapter. Then the division manager allocates a share of the overall budget to each product based on the product manager's analysis of how much money is needed to achieve the marketing objectives.

- *Product line*. If product managers are responsible for a large number of products rather than individual products, each product manager's annual advertising budget can be allocated for the entire line rather than for individual products, especially if the company markets the products as a line rather than as individual elements.

- *Market*. Some companies organize their marketing efforts by market rather than by product and should allocate the budget accordingly.

- *Media*. Most companies like to have a sense of where and how advertising dollars are being spent. You may want to set your budget so that specific percentages are spent on various media: so much for direct mail, so much for trade shows, so much for magazine ads, etc.

- *Month*. When creating your advertising plan, keep in mind that in your business some months may be better sales months than others, and you may want to allocate your budget accordingly. Many business-to-business marketers cut back on advertising in the summer and during the Christmas holidays but spend heavily in January and February, when most prospects begin spending their annual budgets for acquiring new products, and in September, when many prospects are planning their expenditures for the coming year. Mail order catalog and gift marketers, on the other hand, spend heavily in November and December because most of their sales are made in the Christmas season.

   Tip: The forms reproduced as Figures 4.1, 4.2, 4.3, and 4.4 will be most helpful in allocating your budget by media and month. You can photocopy these forms and do a separate budget breakdown for each product, product line, and division. You can also do an overall budget worksheet for the entire corporation, if you wish.

Figure 4.1. Sample annual advertising budget.

Month	Total	Magazines	Newspaper	TV	Radio	Direct Mail	PR
January							
February							
March							
April							
May							
June							
July							
August							
September							
October							
November							
December							
Total							

Figure 4.2. Sample annual advertising budget (filled out).

Month	Total	Magazines	Newspaper	TV	Radio	Direct Mail	PR
January	250	150	50	50		100	
February	250	150	50	50			100
March	250	150	50	50		100	
April	300	150	75	100			75
May	250	150	50	150			
June	200	150	100	50			
July	250	150	50	50		100	
August	450	150	100	150			150
September	600	150	100	150			300
October	300	150	150	100			
November	400	150	100	100		150	
December	500	150	200	200			50
Total	$4,000	$1,800	$1,075	$1,200		$450	$675

Figure 4.3. 19_____ Advertising Media Program and Budget
Advertising Budget $_____

Media	Annual Expenditures	Frequency	Ad Size
Print:			
Newspaper			
1)			
2)			
3)			
Consumer Magazine			
1)			
2)			
3)			
Trade Publications			
1)			
2)			
3)			
Radio:			
AM			
1)			
2)			
3)			
FM			
1)			
2)			
3)			
Television			
1)			
2)			
3)			
Specialty			
1)			
2)			
3)			
Direct Mail			
1)			
2)			
3)			
Point-of-Purchase			
1)			
2)			
3)			
Co-op			

Figure 4.3. (*Cont.*)

Media	Annual Expenditures	Frequency	Ad Size
Co-op			
1)			
2)			
3)			
Other			
1)			
2)			
3)			

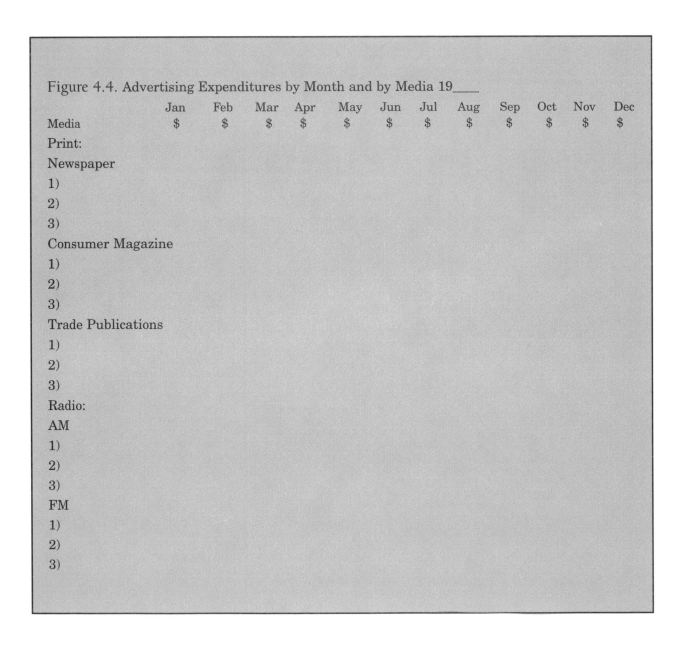

Figure 4.4. Advertising Expenditures by Month and by Media 19____

Media	Jan $	Feb $	Mar $	Apr $	May $	Jun $	Jul $	Aug $	Sep $	Oct $	Nov $	Dec $
Print:												
Newspaper												
1)												
2)												
3)												
Consumer Magazine												
1)												
2)												
3)												
Trade Publications												
1)												
2)												
3)												
Radio:												
AM												
1)												
2)												
3)												
FM												
1)												
2)												
3)												

Figure 4.4. (*Cont.*)

Media	Jan $	Feb $	Mar $	Apr $	May $	Jun $	Jul $	Aug $	Sep $	Oct $	Nov $	Dec $
Television												
1)												
2)												
3)												
Specialty												
1)												
2)												
3)												
Direct Mail												
1)												
2)												
3)												
Point-of-Purchase												
1)												
2)												
3)												
Co-op												
1)												
2)												
3)												
Other												
1)												
2)												
3)												

TEN TIPS FOR MAKING YOUR ADVERTISING BUDGET GO EVEN FURTHER

Here are ten ways to get more out of your advertising dollars—without detracting from the quality and quantity of your ads and promotions. In some cases, these ideas can even *enhance* the effectiveness of your marketing efforts.

1. Use your ads for more than just space advertising

Ads are expensive to produce and expensive to run. But there are ways of getting your advertising message in your prospect's hands at a fraction of the cost of space advertising.

The least expensive is to order an ample supply of reprints and distribute them to customers and prospects every chance you get. When you send literature in response to an inquiry, include a copy of the ad in the package. This reminds prospects of the reason they responded in the first place and reinforces the original message.

Distribute ads internally to other departments—engineering, production, sales, customer service, and R&D—to keep them up to date on your latest marketing and promotional efforts. Make sure your salespeople receive an extra supply of reprints and are encouraged to include a reprint when they write to or visit their customers.

Turn the ad into a product data sheet by adding technical specifications and additional product information to the back of the ad reprint. This eliminates the expense of creating a new layout from scratch, and it makes good advertising sense because the reader gets double exposure to your advertising message.

Ad reprints can be used as inexpensive direct mail pieces. You can mail the reprints along with a reply card and a sales letter. Unlike the ad, which is cast in concrete, the letter is easily and inexpensively tailored to specific markets and customer groups.

If you've created a series of ads for the same product or product line, publish bound reprints of the ads as a product brochure. This tactic increases prospect exposure to the series and is less expensive than producing a brand new brochure.

If your ads provide valuable information of a general nature, you can offer reprints as free educational material to companies in your industry. Or, if the ad presents a striking visual, you can offer reprints that are suitable for framing.

Reuse your ads again and again. You will save money—and increase response rates—in the process.

2. If something works, stick with it

Too many marketers scrap their old ads and create new ones because they're bored with their current campaigns.

That's a waste. You shouldn't create new ads or promotions if your existing ones are still accurate and effective. You should run your ads for as long as your customers read and react to them.

How long can ads continue to get results? The Ludlow Corp. ran an ad for its erosion-preventing Soil Saver mesh 41 times in the same journal. After 11 years it pulled more inquiries per issue than when it was first published in 1966.

If a concept still has selling power but the ad contains dated information, update the existing ad—don't throw it out and start from scratch. This approach isn't fun for the ad manager or the agency, but it does save money.

3. Don't overpresent yourself

A strange thing happens to industrial advertisers when they get a little extra money in the ad budget: They see fancy four-color brochures, gold embossed mailers, and fat annual reports like the ones produced by Fortune 500 firms. Then they say, "This stuff sure looks great. Why don't we do some brochures like this?"

That's a mistake. The look, tone, and image of your promotions should be dictated by your product and your market, not by what other companies in other businesses put out.

Producing literature that's too fancy for its purpose and its audience is a waste of money. It can even *hurt* sales—your prospects will look at your overdone literature and wonder whether you really understand your market and its needs.

4. Use modular product literature

One common advertising problem is determining how to promote a single product to many small, diverse markets. Each market has different needs and will buy the product for different reasons. But on your budget, you can't afford to create a separate brochure for each of these tiny market segments.

The solution is modular literature. This is a basic brochure layout that has sections capable of being tailored to meet specific market needs.

After all, most sections of the brochure—technical specifications, service, company background, product operation, product features—will be the same regardless of the audience. Only a few sections, such as benefits of the product to the user and typical applications, need to be tailored to specific readers.

In a modular layout, standard sections remain the same, but new copy can be typeset and stripped in for each market-specific section of the brochure. In this way, you can create many different market-specific pieces of literature for the same product using the same basic layout, mechanicals, artwork, and plates. Significant savings in time and money will result.

5. Use article reprints as supplementary literature

Ad managers are constantly bombarded by requests for "incidental" pieces of product literature. Engineers want data sheets explaining some minor technical feature in great detail. Reps selling to small, specialized markets want special literature geared to their particular audience. Each company salesperson wants support literature that fits his or her individual sales pitch. But the ad budget can only handle the major pieces of product literature. Not enough time or money exists to satisfy everybody's requests for custom literature.

The solution is to use article reprints as supplementary sales literature. Rather than spending a bundle producing highly technical or application-specific pieces, have your sales and technical staff write articles on these special topics. Then place the articles with the appropriate journals.

Article reprints can be used as inexpensive literature and carry more credibility than self-produced promotional pieces. You don't pay for typesetting or production of the article. Best of all, the article is free advertising for your firm.

6. Explore inexpensive alternatives for generating leads

Many smaller firms judge ad effectiveness solely by the number of leads generated. They are not concerned with building image or recognition; they simply count bingo-card inquiries.

If that describes your approach to advertising, perhaps you shouldn't be advertising in the first place. Not that lead generating isn't a legitimate use of space advertising. But if leads are all you're after, there are cheaper ways to get them.

New-product releases lead the list as the most economical method of generating leads. Once, for less than $100, I wrote, printed, and distributed a new-product release to a hundred trade journals. Within six months, the release had been picked up by 35 magazines and generated 2,500 bingo-card inquiries.

The second-best inquiry generator is the direct-action postcard pack. You can write and typeset your own postcard for less than $200. Running the card in a trade journal's postcard pack generally costs from $800 to $1,200. But that same $800 to $1,200 would probably buy only a sixth or a third of a page in the magazine.

I've seen a single postcard mailing pull nearly 500 inquiries; you'd have a hard time doing that with the average one-third page ad.

7. Don't overbook outside creative talent

Hire freelancers and consultants whose credentials—and fees—fit the job and the budget.

Top advertising photographers, for example, get $1,000 a day or more. This may be worth the fee for a corporate ad running in *Forbes* or *Business Week*. But it's overkill for the employee newsletter or a publicity shot. Many competent photographers can shoot a good black and white publicity photo for $200 or even less.

When you hire consultants, writers, artists, or photographers, you should look for someone whose level of expertise and cost fit the task at hand.

8. Do it yourself

Routine tasks, such as mailing publicity releases, duplicating slides, or retyping media schedules can be done cheaper in-house than outside. Save the expensive agency or consultant for tasks that really require their expertise.

Even if you don't have an in-house advertising department, consider hiring a full-time administrative assistant to handle the detail work involved in managing your company's advertising. This is a more economical solution than farming administrative work out to the agency or doing it yourself.

9. Get the most out of existing art, photography, and copy

Photos, illustrations, layouts, and even copy created for one promotion can often be lifted and reused in other pieces to significantly reduce creative costs. For example, copy created for a corporate image ad can be used as the introduction to the annual report.

Also, you can save rough layouts, thumbnail sketches, headlines, and concepts rejected for one project and use them in future ads, mailings, and promotions.

10. Pay vendors on time

You'll save money by taking advantage of discounts and avoiding late charges when you pay vendor invoices on time. You'll also gain goodwill that can result in better service and fairer prices in the future.

Chapter

5

THE MARKETING COMMUNICATIONS PLAN

KEY CONSIDERATIONS IN WRITING A COMMUNICATIONS PLAN

In previous chapters we have addressed the key elements that go into the advertising planning process. These include:

- the elements of the marketing communications mix—the advertising and sales promotion tools available to use in your program;
- the products you are selling, the markets you are selling them to, and the wants, needs, and desires of those target prospects;
- the objectives of your advertising campaign—what you want it to accomplish; and
- the budget, or the amount of money you can spend in pursuit of these objectives.

Having confronted these issues and identified the appropriate information, you now are faced with the task of putting it all into in a written advertising plan. The questions you may be asking at this point include:

- Do I even need a written or formal communications plan?
- If I decide to write a plan, how do I go about it?
- What is the proper format for such a plan?

Let's first address the question of whether a plan is needed. Next, we'll look at the process to use in creating the advertising plan. Finally, we'll study a sample marketing communications plan, so you can get an idea of the format.

DO YOU NEED A COMMUNICATIONS ADVERTISING PLAN?

Conventional wisdom dictates that anyone writing a text on advertising management would answer this question with a hearty, "Of course!" But experience teaches that the real-world answer is closer to, "Maybe."

Whether to create a written communications plan depends, in part, on your corporate culture and the nature of your company management. Is your management formal or informal? Do they tend to operate from written plans or by the seat of the pants? Are they planning oriented, or do they react on a day-by-day basis to challenges and problems as they arise? If your management is reactive rather than proactive, a written plan may do nothing more than gather dust on the shelves. If your management is more structured, a written plan may be a well-appreciated tool that is used both to conduct marketing communications activities and to evaluate the results.

In a random, nationwide survey of more than 430 marketing communications managers and senior executives, *Business Marketing* magazine found that 80 percent of companies whose marketing communications programs were successful and exceeded expectations had a written plan. In the weeks prior to the creation of the annual communications budget, the marketing communications managers at these firms met with senior executives to arrive at mutually agreed-upon objectives for their company's marketing communications programs and a plan to accomplish these objectives.

Among the senior executives surveyed, 91 percent who had a marketing communications plan incorporated this plan into their company's strategic business plan. Of the executives who did not have a communications plan, 79 percent wanted to have a communications plan in the future. Further, 52 percent of planning-oriented executives expected a new marketing communications program to produce results in three months or less. The methods they used to measure the results are summarized in Table 5.1.

Table 5.1. How companies measure advertising results.

Measurement Method	Percentage of Companies with Successful Marketing Communications Programs Using This Method
Relating communications activities to sales or profits	39%
Number of leads generated	28%
Ad benchmark/readership studies	13%
Company awareness research	12%
Sales force feedback	12%

Table 5.2. How ad managers communicate with senior management.

Communications Method	Percent of Marketing Communications Managers Using This Method
Sales meeting presentations	24%
Written reports	22%
Meetings scheduled with boss	14%
Discussions over lunch, coffee, or drinks	10%
Periodic newsletter	8%
Phone calls	8%

Table 5.3. Promotional tools favored by marketing communications managers.

Tool	Percentage Using This Tool
Brochures	97%
Trade shows	97%
Media ads	94%
Inquiry management	91%
Public relations	86%
Direct mail	77%
Communications planning	73%
Audiovisual	71%
Communications research	63%
Telemarketing	57%

Marketing communications managers at companies running successful ad and promotion programs make sure they regularly communicate the progress and results of their programs to senior management. The methods by which they communicate with management are listed in Table 5.2.

Finally, marketing communications managers at companies with successful advertising and promotion programs tend to make full use of the broad range of marketing communications tools available to them, as shown in Table 5.3.

The *Business Marketing* report concludes: "The moral? With markets becoming more fragmented and the buying decision getting more complex, communications planning is essential."

THE PLANNING PROCESS

Advertising planning is not a complex or specialized procedure. Mostly, it's common sense. It consists of sitting down and thinking about what your marketing problem is and how to solve it, then developing those thoughts more fully on paper. The best communications plan is simply a discussion on paper, in narrative form, of the problems facing the company, the objectives that must be met, and your proposed solutions (the advertising).

Ray Jutkins, of Nelson Panullo Jutkins Direct Marketing in Santa Monica, CA, provides the following framework for creating an effective advertising and marketing communications plan. His outline, which is reprinted with his permission, covers the areas of information essential to establish a marketing communications plan that is effective, efficient, and highly targeted.

The Eight-Point Market Action Plan

1. Clearly state your **objectives** for your particular program.

- Projected total sales revenue, short- and long-term?
- Projected sales revenue by individual product?
- What is the target cost per lead?
- What is the target cost per sales close?
- What is your geographic sales pattern? Locally? Regionally? Throughout the country?
- Is there a seasonal pattern that should be addressed?
- Are there any legal or other marketing restrictions?
- What is the industry history?
- What is your corporate history?
- What is the previous sales trend or direction?
- Is the trend the same today as in the past?
- What is the advertising and marketing history? Did it meet your objectives, fall short, or surpasss the plan?

2. Define a **timetable** to accomplish specific objectives.

- By quarter, what objectives do you wish to reach?
- What is your national advertising schedule?
- How does the fiscal year or calendar year affect your scheduling?

3. Establish a **budget** to meet your objectives within a time frame.

- What is your budget history?
- Where have you invested your advertising and marketing dollars in the recent past?
- Where do you see the major emphasis for next year's budget?
- What is your prime competitor's share of the market compared to yours?

- How much do they invest to maintain that share? How do they spend it?
- What is your total advertising budget?
- How is the budget allocated by quarter? By month?
- Is the budget available on an accelerated schedule, if necessary, to meet seasonal or unusual opportunities?

4. Clearly identify your target market **audience.**

- What is the size of the market for your product line?
- How can that market be expanded?
- How can it be exploited?
- Is your product marketed to particular segments of the community?
- Can you clearly identify those segments?
- Does research define the measurable characteristics of the prospective customer?
- Who are your current customers?
- How many of them are there?
- Do they share any common characteristics?
- What do the current customers buy?
- For how long do they remain customers?
- What additional products and services can they be sold?
- Does the profile of your current customer meet the profile of your potential customer?
- If not, what is the profile of your best prospect?

5. Create and define your **offer**.

- Who is your competition and what are they offering?
- What are your unique selling propositions?
- What are the unique selling propositions of your competitors?
- What are your weaknesses? Your competitors' weaknesses?
- How does your price compare with the competition—competitive, discount, or premium?
- Is an incentive or premium desired or needed to capture sales?
- How does the customer benefit from using your product?
- What benefits do you offer prospects?
- What does market research say about the position of your product?
- Can this position be improved or redirected?
- How can you communicate this new position to your audience?

6. Set direction for your **creative** approach—the copy and art.

- What is the best way to articulate your product positioning, features, and benefits?

- How do they differ from the competition?
- Are buying incentives desired or needed?
- What buying incentives should be used? When?
- How do you present these incentives to gain a call to action?
- How many steps should there be in the sales cycle? One? Two? Three?
- In what vehicles should your message be communicated? Ads? Brochures? Telephone? Broadcast? Direct mail?
- How do demographic and psychographic data on the market affect the creative approach?

7. Select **media**.

- Which media are best suited for communicating your product benefits?
- Which media are best suited for motivating your prospects to action?
- Which media will best reach your target audience?
- Can the medium be used effectively for direct response marketing?
- Is the product to be marketed geographically? If so, what are the boundaries of the medium?
- Can the medium selected be used regionally? Nationally?
- Are there seasonal variations in expected response levels that will affect media scheduling?
- Will scheduling be affected by other activities within the company, such as special promotions, trade show exhibits, or industry events (major conferences or conventions)?
- In print media, how much space is needed to present the offer?
- In broadcast media, how much time is required to sell the offer, present the product, and maximize response?
- What media mix will produce the desired sales volume results, within the budget parameters and the time frame, and meet your marketing criteria?
- What is the relative cost efficiency and response potential of each medium?
- Within a particular medium, which vehicles will reach your target audience most effectively and efficiently?
- What response must be generated to achieve the target cost per inquiry and cost per sales close?
- In magazine space, is the editorial environment compatible with your product? Is other advertising or marketing in the publication compatible with your company?
- Where is the competition advertising?

- Is there a duplication of audience between the various media selected? If so, can one medium (or several) be safely eliminated with no decline in sales results?
- Does the overall schedule achieve the desired level of frequency?
- What percentage of promotional effort is being devoted to your current customer base?

8. **Analyze** the results. There are four key points to establishing a good evaluation. You want to know:

- What worked?
- What did not work?
- Why?
- What are you going to do about it, now that you know what worked and what did not?

Here are some specific things to look for when analyzing specific ads, promotions, or media:

- response level,
- cost per response,
- cost per order, and
- sales generated per dollar spent on advertising.

Additional factors to consider:

- How valuable are "new" customers?
- Do they buy additional products and services? How long do they remain customers?
- Which media produce the greatest number of high-value new customers?
- Which creative offer, approach, or format produced the most cost-efficient response and additional business?

CASE HISTORY: MARKETING COMMUNICATIONS PLAN FOR A SERVICE FIRM

The following is the actual planning process used to create a working marketing communications plan for a firm selling highly specialized business services. All references to the nature of the service and the market being served have been deleted and the dollar figures and the names of various media have been changed to protect the identity of the firm.

Note that this is only one of many formats that can be used. You can follow any format you please. The main thing is to keep the plan simple, write in plain English, and explain the rationale or thinking behind each item in the plan so you can sell it to management.

Sample Marketing Communications Plan for a Service Company

A. Cover Letter

The first page is a cover letter or letter of transmittal. This simply tells the reader what is attached and what to keep in mind while reading and evaluating the material.

Here is a typical letter of transmittal:

```
Mr. George Smith
President
ABC Company
Anytown, USA

Dear Mr. Smith:

Here is the preliminary marketing plan for ABC Company.
It covers marketing activities for 19XX.

The important thing to remember is that this is a work-
ing plan that should be adjusted to fit the current
situation, not a commandment etched in stone. If some-
thing works well and is profitable for us, we should do
more of the same even if it's not on the plan. If some-
thing is unprofitable, we should drop it even though we
scheduled more of it for later in the year.

Sincerely,

Your Name, Advertising Management Consultant
```

B. Introduction

Here, in plain, simple language, summarize your overall sales goal. Sometimes this is stated as an image or position the company wants to achieve. In this case, because the goal was to increase sales of the service, specific numbers were used to show exactly where the company is and where it should go:

```
Introduction

Our goal is to increase sales by 35 percent over the
next 12 months.

A 35 percent increase would mean annual revenues
increasing from $10 million in 19XX, to $14 million in
19XX—$4 million more in sales per year.

At average revenues of $10,000 per order, we would need
to go from 1,000 orders per year to 1,400 orders per
year—or from 19 to 27 orders per week.

As our profit margin on these sales is approximately 50
percent, this sales increase will result in an addition-
al $2 million in profits for the coming calendar year.
```

C. Objectives

In this section we list specific objectives that will contribute toward achieving the overall sales goal. The service firm, ABC Company, offers a variety of services, some profitable, some marginal. The communications plan must indicate whether the money will be spent expanding the sales of already proven services or trying to boost sales for poorly performing areas. Generally, the better strategy is to support your winners with the most advertising dollars and not spend on products or services that are not marketable.

Here is the Objectives section of the plan for ABC Company.

```
Objectives of the Program
```

1. Most of our time and effort will go toward promoting our two most profitable services, Service A and Service B. At least three-quarters of the budget will go toward increasing sales of these services.

2. Approximately 20 percent of our budget, time, and effort will be spent marketing our new service, Service C. Although not a big seller in the past, new market conditions indicate that this could be a big profit center, accounting for up to 20 percent of revenues within the next 3 to 5 years.

3. Our main goal is to increase sales by generating high-quality leads that result in quotations that, in turn, result in a sale.

4. Image building, or keeping our name before the marketplace, is a secondary concern and will not be our primary objective.

5. Based on our analysis of past marketing activities, our average cost to generate a sales lead is $95. Therefore, any promotion that falls significantly below this mark is cost-effective, while any promotion that brings in leads at an inquiry cost of over $100 will have to be examined closely. (This assumes a good quality lead, of course.)

D. Market Analysis

The market analysis section typically contains:

- a description of the different markets for the product or service;
- the share of the market held by you and by your competitors;
- numbers indicating the size of each market and whether the market is expanding or contracting; and
- comments on the buying habits of the market and the best way to sell to each particular group of prospects.

In the case of the sample marketing communications plan, ABC Company sells all its services to a single market. There is no analysis of market share because ABC Company is the only major vendor providing special services to this market. Here is an excerpt from the plan:

```
Market Analysis

We estimate that there are 15,000 firms in the United
States that own one or more XYZ machines requiring our
repair, maintenance, and support services. Each prospect
owns an average of four machines, for a total market of
60,000 machines in operation.

We estimate that of these machines:

• x percent are new and still under manufacturer's war-
  ranty;
• x percent are relatively new and under extended war-
  ranty or a manufacturer's service plan;
• x percent are serviced by in-house technicians (repre-
  senting the larger firms that are able to maintain
  such technical personnel on staff); and
• x percent are serviced by other sources, such as
  small independent service firms.

This leaves 40 percent of the machines, or 24,000
machines, requiring service.

Since the reliability of this type of equipment is such
that service is required only once a year, then 1/52nd
of these 24,000 units, or 461 machines, are in need of
service in any given week.

With a current level of 19 orders per week, we are ser-
vicing only 4 percent of this market. An increase to a
6 percent market share will give us our target volume
of 27 orders per week.

Why, with so little competition, is our market share so
small? We know that these are the primary reasons:

• Most machine owners do not make repairs, but continue
  to operate machines that are not working at peak
  efficiency without being aware of the degree of wear
  and inefficiency they face.
• Manufacturers encourage frequent trade-in and replace-
  ment of machines rather than repair, and offer
  attractive terms that prompt most customers to keep
  replacing machines every few years, before the need
  for our service is perceived as serious.
```

E. Overview of Marketing Communications Campaign

Before getting into the details of what ads will be created and where they will run, give an overview of what marketing communications tools have been selected to achieve the sales objective. From the sample plan:

Overview of the Marketing Campaign

Aside from creating a new catalog, the bulk of our effort will be in generating leads and inquiries via direct mail.

We will also use PR activities to supplement direct mail and enhance our image.

Advertising, not proven successful in generating quality leads or a high volume of sales, will be reduced; however, we will continue a limited schedule in a few select publications.

Another key addition to our program will be database marketing—continued contacting of our database customers and prospects. Based on last year's results in this area, database marketing may be our most profitable activity.

F. Marketing Communications Plan and Schedule

The next and largest part of the marketing communications plan is a breakdown of the specific activities that make up the program.

Some planners use oversize worksheets that organize activities by calendar month. Large plans may even require separate worksheets for each month. Other planners use separate worksheets for each product or product line.

You can use any format that works for you and that clearly shows people what you are doing and why you are doing it. One technique is to create a separate plan for each product line or group of related services and break it down by specific marketing communications tools, with one section relating direct mail activities, the next section giving the print media schedule, the third section showing trade show activity, and so on.

In the case of the sample plan for ABC Company, there is only one schedule, since all services are related and are sold to the same group of buyers. Here is the sample plan:

Marketing Communications Plan

Direct Mail Activities:

We will do three major mailings of approximately 10,000 to 20,000 pieces each.

Mailings will be done in late March or April, June, and September.

The mailing package will consist of a cover letter, the color service flier, and a reply card. Letters mailed to XYZ machine owners will be tailored to four titles:

• Plant engineer
• Purchasing agent
• Maintenance engineer
• Vice President of Operations

We will key and test a variety of list sources, including rented lists (Edith Roman catalog), subscription lists, and compiled lists (i.e., lists we input from directories and other information sources).

Among the lists to be tested:

XYZ Machine Buyers—42,950
Purchasing Today subscriber list—12,504
Plant Engineering subscriber list—20,585
Buyer List: ABC Ball Bearing Co.—15,390 (Note: These are special ball bearings used in the repair of XYZ machines.)
Plastics Expo trade show attendee list—10,338
American Society of Maintenance Managers membership list—4,980

Cost of the mailing is approximately $500 per thousand, $15,000 for 30,000 pieces and $30,000 for 60,000 pieces.

We will experiment with different letters and offers. Our first letter should probably offer the Free Machine Evaluation, since this has been our most successful offer to date.

Catalog:

We are currently producing a new catalog to replace the existing catalog. The new piece is designed to graphically enhance our image, contain up-to-date information on our services, and position us as the leader in the field.

We estimate producing an initial run of 20,000 catalogs. Cost: $ _____

Premium:

We will develop a leave-behind premium for our salespeople to leave on the prospect's desk after a sales call. (Premium will also be suitable for mailing.)

Cost: approximately $2 to $4 per unit, depending on quantity ordered.

Publicity Releases:

Publicity releases get us exposure we cannot afford to buy with ad dollars and also generate a high volume of leads at extremely low cost.

Here is our schedule for mailing publicity releases:

March—Background release on our company (to Ohio business publications and business sections of Ohio newspapers)
May—New literature release on updated catalog
July—Release on "How to maintain XYZ machines"

September—Release on preventive maintenance program
November—Release on how to perform your own machine inspection

Additional publicity:

• *Plant Engineering* article on "10 ways to improve XYZ machine performance"

Press releases allow us to reach readers of numerous publications, far more than we could afford to advertise in. These include:

• engineering publications,
• plant publications, and
• purchasing publications.

Cost for printing and mailing or distribution of two-page press release to approximately 500 contacts: $224 plus postage.

For five releases, this comes to a total of $1,120.

Database Marketing:

Database marketing is defined as promotions aimed at our existing list of current customers, past customers (who are now inactive), and prospects (sales leads).

First, we will expand our database to include all of the following:

• Current customers;
• Customers who bought from us in the past but are not now using our services;
• Inquiries and leads from the past 3 years in paper file system (must be converted to computer database);
• In addition, we will automatically capture and add to the database the names of people who respond to an ad, a mailer, our catalog, or any other promotion.

Next, we will contact this database at least three times during the year using a series of letter mailings:

• April/May—Mail a sales letter introducing our new catalog (which will be enclosed).
• August—Mail promotion featuring rebuilding service and sale of rebuilt XYZ machines. Possible offer: "Old customer" discount.
• October—Mail promotion on our Preventive Maintenance and Service contracts. Objective: Get inactive but satisfied customers to reestablish their relationship with us. Get current customers to sign up for regular service.

Note: Experience proves that marketing to a database of existing customers and prospects will yield up to 10 times the response of mailings aimed at cold (rented and compiled) prospect lists.

Cost: No outside printing or production costs if the database mailings are handled in-house.

Postcard Decks:

XYZ Machine Owners Card Deck (sponsored by manufacturers co-op)
Date: April
Circulation: 75,000
Cost: $1,950

Plant Engineering Deck
Date: Spring
Circulation: 29,704
Cost: $1,305

McKnight (owners of *Purchasing News*)
Date: July
Circulation: 15,000
Cost: $1,200

Advertising Schedule:

Purchasing World

Ad: "How to save money on XYZ machine maintenance"

Our current ad is a 2/3 standard page. Size is 10" deep by 4 9/16" wide. Cost per insertion is $3,100 (2X rate).

We will condense the current ad (and eliminate coupon).
New size: 1/4 standard page.
Size is 3/8" wide by 4 7/8" deep.
Cost per insertion (2X rate): $ 1,130.

We will run the ad in February (already inserted) and again in September. Total cost: $2,260

Note: September is a special issue for the World Purchasing Show

Shop Floor Machine Care:

Current ad: "Your single source for XYZ machine care"
Our current ad is a 2/3-page standard (4 1/2 X 10")
2X rate is $1,775 per insertion.

We will condense (and eliminate coupon) to reduce ad size.
New size: 1/4 page square (3 3/8 X 4 7/8")
Cost: $750 per insertion

We will run the ad in August and October. Total Cost: $1,500.

G. Schedule and Costs

The final section is an appendix consisting of worksheets showing the entire advertising and promotion schedule and associated costs. These may be written in narrative form, table form, or using scheduling sheets. You may use the forms provided in Chapter 4.

Additional Tips on Creating the Advertising Plan

1. Most companies have calendar year plans running from January to December of a given year.

2. If you have a calendar year plan that begins with January of the coming year, the best time to begin planning is September of this year. Try to get the budget approved by October or November, but certainly no later than December.

3. The tendency when making cost estimates is to underestimate so that the budget can be stretched to cover more items. But it's better to allocate your budget based on an honest estimate of costs so you can more realistically determine what you can afford and what you cannot afford.

4. Establish a contingency fund as a separate line item in the budget. This fund covers unexpected expenditures (e.g., management decides they want a 16-page brochure instead of a 12-page brochure), uncertainties in cost estimates, and the unavoidable rise in media and production costs. This fund should be 5 to 10 percent of the total budget.

5. Create a separate advertising plan for each product (or, if you sell one product, for each market). Each product deserves and needs its own well-thought-out marketing strategy.

6. If you have to sell the ideas, concepts, and items in the plan to senior management, put into the plan as much narrative text for explanation and support of your ideas as is required. Think of the plan not just as a budget or a schedule but as a selling document. If it doesn't sell management on your ideas, it won't be approved.

7. To make accurate cost estimates of line items on the budget, go to two or three vendors, describe the generic type of project, and ask for rough or ballpark estimates of the cost. Do this until you have a pretty good idea of what a typical ad, brochure, or any other promotion will cost so that you can simply plug this rough figure into the budget as necessary.

8. Realize that vendors can't and won't be held to estimates made off the cuff based on rough descriptions of a project. Although such estimates are vital for putting down some numbers in your plan and vendors are happy to cooperate, the actual estimate cannot be made accurately unless detailed specifications for the specific project are in hand. Caution: Vendors, like advertising managers, tend to underestimate when giving ballpark figures.

9. Put a paragraph in your plan that says something along these lines: "Of course, this is a preliminary plan only, not a rigid schedule etched in stone. The key to success will be flexibility to react and respond to changing market conditions and sales opportunities." This says to senior management, in effect, "Just because we have a written plan doesn't mean we have to follow it to the letter or can't make changes in midstream if a new strategy is called for." Be flexible.

10. You will have to determine your basic marketing communications and sales objectives by yourself or by working with the sales managers, marketing managers, product managers, and brand managers in your company. No outsider can do it for you. However, you can rely on your agency for support and advice on planning advertising concepts and media schedules. Take advantage of their expertise by making them part of the planning process early on.

Part II

TASKS

Chapter

MAGAZINE ADS

SPECIALIZED MAGAZINES FOR SPECIALIZED MARKETS

According to Louis Rukeyser's *Business Almanac*, the first magazine ad in America appeared in Ben Franklin's *General Magazine* in 1741. While magazines and magazine advertising continue to flourish, the age of the general magazine is just about over. They have been largely replaced by specialized magazines catering to narrower and narrower target audiences with highly specialized interests.

For example, while computer magazines were once a specialty in themselves, now the field is so highly specialized that there are separate magazines for people using IBM personal computers versus Apple Macintosh computers. The current volume of *Bacon's Publicity Checker*, a directory of magazines, lists more than 7,000 weekly and monthly trade journals and consumer magazines published annually in the United States. The publications are grouped into more than 600 categories, ranging from abrasives and accessory merchandising to yachting and youth magazines. Some of the titles include *Hog Farm Management, Sludge Newsletter, Toxic Materials, Valve Magazine, Hydrocarbon Processing, Export Today, Candy Wholesaler*, and the *American Journal of Sports Medicine*. Circulations range from less than 10,000 to over a million.

According to a report in the January 1989 issue of *Direct Marketing* magazine, approximately $6.1 billion was spent by national advertisers in 1988 on magazine advertising, up 8 percent from the previous year. This represents approximately 9 percent of the total national media budget of $66 billion. Advertisers spent more on network TV ($9.4 billion) and direct mail ($21.2 billion); less on cable TV ($0.9 billion), network radio ($0.4 billion), and newspaper advertising ($3.6 billion).

Table 6.1. Degree of targeting by industry or specialization.

Key: 1 = broadly targeted, horizontal media, aimed at mass market
        5 = highly focused, vertical media, aimed at narrow audience with specialized inter-
             ests

Marketing Tool	Degree of Targeting
Newspaper advertising	1
Magazine advertising	4
Broadcast advertising	1
Cable TV advertising	4
Network radio	2
Spot (local) radio	3
Billboards	1
Transit advertising	1
Catalogs	5
Direct mail	5
Postcard decks	4
Publicity and public relations	3
Telemarketing	4
Trade shows	4

MAGAZINES ARE MORE TARGETED

What is the main difference between magazine advertising and newspaper advertising? Actually, there are several differences, including frequency (newspapers are published daily or weekly, while magazines are published weekly or monthly), quality of reproduction (newspapers are black ink on newsprint, while most magazines offer four-color reproduction on glossy coated stock), and size (most newspapers are tabloids, while most magazines are 7 by 10 inches).

But the most critical difference is that newspapers target their audiences geographically (by city or region), while magazines target by industry, job, or type of interest. In this regard, magazines are more like cable television, which has many small channels aimed at special interest audiences and covering narrow topics, while newspaper advertising is more like broadcast television, targeting a mass audience. This is summed up in Table 6.1.

HOW TO ADVERTISE IN DIFFERENT TYPES OF MAGAZINES

There was a time when magazines, like newspapers, catered to a general, mass audience. Publications such as *Life* and the *Saturday Evening Post* carried a broad spectrum of reading material designed to cater to all tastes, and they were read primarily for entertainment, not for information.

Today, all that has changed. Although magazines still entertain us, the secondary goal of informing the reader on a topic of special interest has become more predominant and in many cases, the information content of the publication is actually more important to the reader than whether the articles are entertaining. This trend is illustrated in Table 6.2.

As a rule of thumb, the following apply:

- Scholarly and scientific journals are written almost 100 percent to educate and inform. Professionals turn to them for reference and hard data.

- Business and trade journals are written primarily to educate and inform but must have some entertainment value or at least be interesting to read.

- Hobbyist and special interest magazines are written primarily to educate and inform, but they are informing the reader about something that entertains him or her (a hobby or other interest).

- Consumer and general interest magazines are written primarily to entertain. They are read for pleasure but must also contain useful information the reader can use in his or her life.

- News magazines are written both to inform and to entertain. They inform but do not educate (in the "how-to" sense of the word).

The advertising approach should be tailored to the editorial environment of the magazine. Therefore, the following rules of thumb, while not definitive, at least provide a starting point for creating a magazine ad:

- Ads for scholarly and scientific journals are typically fact-filled and statistical in nature. They have a serious, almost scholarly tone and seek to establish credibility by revealing important information. Copy does

Table 6.2. Information vs. entertaining in magazines.

These Magazines are Written Primarily to Entertain	These Magazines are Written Primarily to Inform
M	Forbes
GQ	Business Week
Omni	Scientific American
Reader's Digest	Writer's Digest
Life	American Photographer
Smithsonian	Science News
Cosmopolitan	Civil Engineering
Playboy	Plastics World
Penthouse	Publisher's Weekly
Esquire	Engineering Analysis
Glamour	Popular Science
Sports Illustrated	Software News

not take a hard sell approach but instead seeks to sway the reader by presenting the facts.

- Ads for business and trade journals are more promotional and less rational and objective than scientific journal ads. The ads communicate in a dramatic, forceful manner the key benefits of a specific product, rather than simply discussing technical information about a product or issue.
- Ads for hobbyist and special interest magazines are written for the enthusiast and must reflect a high degree of enthusiasm about the particular hobby or field. Copy must show an insider's understanding of and empathy with the particular issues or activities being promoted. Copy contains details and jargon to demonstrate to the reader that the advertiser is knowledgeable in the field.
- Ads for consumer and general interest magazines have to work even harder to grab attention and quickly orient readers toward thinking about a particular product or problem they were not thinking of before. Strong benefit-oriented or curiosity-arousing headlines and dramatic visual concepts with strong human interest and appeal work well here.
- Ads for news magazines are similar to those for consumer and general interest magazines in that they must work hardest to grab the attention of a prospect whose mind is on something other than the topic of the ad.

These rules are summarized in Table 6.3.

Table 6.3. Basic magazine advertising approaches.

Type of Publication	Editorial Environment	Advertising Approach
Scholarly and scientific	High-level, professional, accurate, information-heavy.	Factual, rational, educational. No hype or hard sell. Presents important technical data or news in the field.
Business magazines and trade journals	Informational, straightforward, informative, but lighter tone than scholarly publications.	Promotional and sales-oriented. Stresses product benefit or company image. Approach may be either straightforward or imaginative.
Hobbyist and special interest publications	Combines how-to advice and information with enthusiasm for subject. Entertains as it educates.	Ads must establish empathy with readers, mirroring their enthusiasm for the subject matter. Long copy works because readers have strong interest in products related to their field.

Table 6.3. (*Cont.*)

Type of Publication	Editorial Environment	Advertising Approach
Consumer and general interest publications	Entertainment. Articles are a blend of profiles, human interest stories, service, and general interest items.	Dramatic approaches designed to grab attention. Visually oriented. Stress benefits and solutions to people's problems or appeals to core desires.
News magazines	Information and education. Keep readers current on local, national, and world affairs.	Same as for consumer magazines.

THE FOUR BASIC TYPES OF ADS

There are four basic types of magazine ads:

1. Awareness ads
2. Image ads
3. Inquiry ads
4. Mail order ads

Before examining the specifics of the four basic magazine ads, you must realize that, although an ad may have characteristics belonging to several categories, to be successful the ad should have only one primary goal and fall clearly into one of these basic categories. For instance, although you might want the ad to build product awareness (category 1) and generate inquiries (category 3), you should decide before creating the ad whether the primary goal is to create awareness or generate inquiries.

Remember that a magazine ad is a limited medium with limited space. Even a costly full-page magazine ad only provides 7 by 10 inches of space in which to get your message across. You weaken your ad's effectiveness when you try to accomplish too many goals or communicate too many sales points.

The successful ad should have one primary goal. It should be written and designed to communicate one basic message, theme, or sales appeal, although secondary themes or points may be included to support the primary message and make it credible.

Let's take a closer look at the four basic types of ads.

Category 1: Awareness Ads

As the name implies, an awareness ad creates awareness of a particular product, product benefit, product feature, or brand name. Most consumer advertising falls under this category. The ad is not designed to generate direct sales or inquiries for the product. Rather, through frequent repetition of the ad, the message being communicated about the product sinks into the consciousness of the American public.

The desired result is to have consumers think of your brand first when they think about the generic product category or the need it fills. In business-to-business advertising, the desired result is to instill in the business buyer awareness of your brand or company name, or to get buyers to believe in the superiority of your product.

Figure 6.1, an ad for GE/RCA/INTERSIL semiconductors, is a good example of an awareness ad. The ad features a MOSFET, which is a specialized type of semiconductor, and specifically "rugged" MOSFETs, which are devices designed to withstand higher currents and voltages. The purpose of the ad is to communicate that, while many manufacturers claim ruggedness in their MOSFETs, only GE/RCA/INTERSIL provides a MOSFET that is truly rugged and able to give users the protection and performance they need.

If you read electronics publications, you know that most semiconductor ads consist merely of a picture of the product against a white background and a table of technical specifications. The GE/RCA/INTERSIL ad, by comparison, uses a more dramatic concept to demonstrate that only GE/RCA rugged MOSFETS have been proven reliable through extensive testing.

The illustration, a familiar image of the mad scientist at work, gets across the point of testing in a visually interesting, eye-catching fashion. The headline is both relevant and clever (note the word play, in which the device is referred to as a "creation" in keeping with the Dr. Frankenstein motif of the drawing).

The ad concludes with a toll-free number, but unlike a direct response ad, there is no coupon, no address, no offer of a free catalog or data book or brochure. The real purpose of this ad is not to generate inquiries but to communicate a single message: that GE/RCA MOSFETs are proven the most rugged. This is the mission of the awareness advertisement.

Category 2: Image Ads

An image ad makes an overall statement about the firm, its products, and its way of doing business. In consumer advertising, the goal may be simply to create awareness and recall of the advertiser's name, product, or business philosophy in the reader's mind. The campaign, "GE: We Bring Good Things to Light," is an example. The commercials and ads don't discuss specific products or features; they simply get across the point that General Electric provides the lighting America needs to live and enjoy life.

In business-to-business advertising, the purpose of an image ad is not just to create an awareness or impression of a company but to create a comfort zone, a feeling that the company is reliable, well established, and reputable. In short, the goal is to make the prospect more inclined to do business with the firm.

Virtually all corporate advertising falls into the category of image advertising. For examples, simply flip through any recent issue of *Forbes*,

There's an easier way to make sure it's rugged.

Order GE/RCA Rugged MOSFETs, the only ones with an "R" on the label. Because the wrong device can ruin your creation.

Two years ago an independent testing company compared GE Ruggedized MOSFETs with all leading competitive units. The results were even better than we expected.

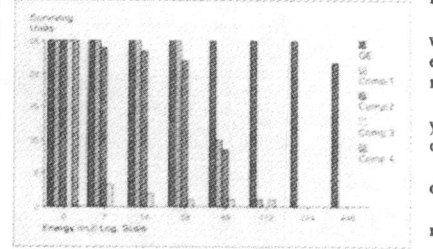

In this test conducted by Associated Testing Laboratories, Inc., the ruggedness of 25 GE IRF-series MOSFETs was compared with 25 devices from each of four competitors. As you can see, the GE parts significantly outperformed the others.

Today, the situation is different.

Because our MOSFETs are more than *twice as rugged* as they were then. Yet our ruggedized MOSFETs cost no more than competitors' standard MOSFETs.

A powerful combination.

We've achieved this by combining the rugged technology of GE products with the outstanding manufacturing, quality control and cost-effectiveness of RCA power MOSFETs. So we can bring you the best line of rugged PowerFETs in the industry.

And the benefits are considerable.

Why you need Rugged FETs.

Our Rugged MOSFETs are fast. But they're not fragile.

They're designed, tested and *guaranteed* to withstand a specified level of circuit-induced electrical stress in breakdown avalanche mode.

When you design with our Rugged devices, you can eliminate zener diodes, snubbers and other costly circuitry.

So you save money. And by simplifying your design, you improve system reliability.

Just as important, these devices give you a margin of error.

Because you can never be sure when your system will be subjected to voltages beyond what you expected.

And if you're designing for applications that routinely have to handle surges and transient voltages, these devices are perfect.

A wide selection of drop-ins.

We have more than 200 parts in distributor stock. And they're drop-in replacements for virtually any N-channel devices.

So why take chances, when you can improve your system performance and reliability at no added cost?

For more information, contact your local GE Solid State sales office or distributor. Or call toll-free 800-443-7364, extension 28.

In Europe, call: Brussels, (02) 246-21-11; Paris, (1) 39-46-57-99; London, (276) 66-59-11; Milano, (2) 82-291; Munich, (089) 63813-0; Stockholm (08) 793-9500.

GE/RCA/INTERSIL
SEMICONDUCTORS

123 Figure 6.1. Sample awareness ad.

Fortune, or *Business Week.* The pages are filled with ads espousing some company philosophy or corporate point of view or the firm's history, track record, or recent accomplishments.

Most of these ads are, frankly, ineffective and of little interest to readers. Because they are advertiser-centered instead of client-centered, they contain messages that may fascinate management but mean little or nothing to the company's customers and prospects.

Liberal use of the words "leader," "leadership," or "quality" are sure signs of this type of ad. So are four-color, two-page spreads in which 100 percent of the space is taken up by a painting, sculpture, or other abstract artwork, with the remainder of the space containing one or two lines of faintly reproduced copy set in an unreadable 7-point type.

Breakthroughs in this field are rare, but they do happen. One of the most famous is the popular "Power of the Printed Word" series from International Paper Company. Figure 6.2 displays one ad from the series. According to Robert F. Lauterborn, director of corporate advertising for International Paper, the purpose of these ads was to "prove that we were committed to the paper business by dealing with one of its most nagging long-term concerns—the ability and propensity of young people to read and write as well as they need to, to cope in this age of increasing competition. We decided to actually help young people to read and write and communicate better. But we had commercial motivations. If young people read and write better, they'll read and write more. Then our customers will sell more books, magazines, and newspapers, and International Paper will sell them more paper."

Instead of talking about International Paper's commitment to the printed word, this ad demonstrates that commitment by providing information to help young (and not so young) readers. International Paper is only mentioned in a box on the second page of the two-page spread. The ad campaign has been tremendously popular and successful, with International Paper receiving 1,000 requests for reprints per day.

The lesson to be learned is to respect your readers' intelligence, whether your ad is an image, awareness, or direct response piece. Prospects respond positively to useful information, helpful guidance, and true claims. They have good noses for sniffing out phoniness and resent being lied to or "sold."

Category 3: Inquiry Ads

Inquiry ads are designed to generate responses. An inquiry ad not only grabs attention and communicates a message but also creates a desire to know more about the product and motivates the prospect to ask for that additional information.

Figure 6.3 is a good example of an inquiry ad. Its aspects include:

1. The headline and visual dramatize a key benefit ("stop burglary").

2. Subheads and long copy present a logical sales argument and give reasons why the reader should be interested in the product.

How to write a business letter

Some thoughts from Malcolm Forbes
President and Editor-in-Chief of Forbes Magazine

International Paper asked Malcolm Forbes to share what he's learned about writing a good business letter. (And who can argue with a guy named Forbes about getting the most out of business letters?)

A good business letter can get you a job interview.

Get you off the hook.

Or get you money.

It's totally asinine to blow your chances of getting whatever you want—with a business letter that turns people off instead of turning them on.

The best place to learn to write is in school. If you're still there, pick your teachers' brains.

If not, big deal. I learned to ride a motorcycle at 50 and fly balloons at 52. It's never too late to learn.

Over 10,000 business letters come across my desk every year. They seem to fall into three categories: stultifying if not stupid, mundane (most of them), and first rate (rare). Here's the approach I've found that separates the winners from the losers (most of it's just good common sense)—it starts *before* you write your letter:

Know what you want

If you don't, write it down—in one sentence. "I want to get an interview within the next two weeks." That simple.

List the major points you want to get across—it'll keep you on course.

If you're answering a letter, check the points that need answering and keep the letter in front of you while you write. This way you won't forget anything—*that* would cause another round of letters.

And for goodness' sake, answer promptly if you're going to answer at all. Don't sit on a letter—*that* invites the person on the other end to sit on whatever you want from him.

Plunge right in

Call him by name—not "Dear Sir, Madam, or Ms." "Dear Mr. Chrisanthopoulos"—and be sure to spell it right. That'll get him (thus, you) off to a good start.

(Usually, you can get his name just by phoning his company—or from a business directory in your nearest library.)

Tell what your letter is about in the first paragraph. One or two sentences. Don't keep your reader guessing or he might file your letter away—even before he finishes it.

In the round file.

If you're answering a letter, refer to the date it was written. So the reader won't waste time hunting for it.

People who read business letters are as human as thee and me. Reading a letter shouldn't be a chore—*reward* the reader for the time he gives you.

Write so he'll enjoy it

Write the letter from his point of view—what's in it for him?

Beat him to the draw—surprise him by answering the questions and objections he might have.

Be positive—he'll be more receptive to what you have to say.

Be nice. Contrary to the cliche, genuinely nice guys most often finish first or very near it. I admit it's not easy when you've got a gripe. To be agreeable while disagreeing—that's an art.

Be natural—write the way you talk. Imagine him sitting in front of you—what would you say to him?

Business jargon too often is cold, stiff, unnatural.

Suppose I came up to you and said, "I acknowledge receipt of your letter and I beg to thank you." You'd think, "Huh? You're putting me on."

The acid test—read your letter out loud when you're done. You might get a shock—but you'll know for sure if it sounds natural.

Don't be cute or flippant. The reader won't take you seriously. This doesn't mean you've got to be dull. You prefer your letter to knock 'em dead rather than bore 'em to death.

Three points to remember:

Have a sense of humor. That's refreshing *anywhere*—a nice surprise

"Be natural. 'Imagine him sitting in front of you—what would you say to him?'"

in a business letter.

Be specific. If I tell you there's a new fuel that could save gasoline, you might not believe me. But suppose I tell you this:

"Gasahol"—10% alcohol, 90% gasoline—works as well as straight gasoline. Since you can make alcohol from grain or corn stalks, wood or wood waste, coal—even garbage, it's worth some real follow-through.

Now you've got something to sink your teeth into.

Lean heavier on nouns and verbs, lighter on adjectives. Use the active voice instead of the passive. Your writing will have more guts.

Which of these is stronger? Active voice: "I kicked out my money manager." Or, passive voice: "My money manager was kicked out by me." (By the way, neither is true. My son, Malcolm Jr., manages most Forbes money—he's a brilliant moneyman.)

Give it the best you've got

When you don't want something enough to make the effort, making an effort is a waste.

Make your letter look appetizing—or you'll strike out before you even get to bat. Type it—on good-quality 8½" x 11" stationery. Keep it neat. And use paragraphing that makes it easier to read.

Keep your letter short—to one page, if possible. Keep your paragraphs short. After all, who's going to benefit if your letter is quick and easy to read?

You.

For emphasis, underline impor-
tant words. And sometimes indent sentences as well as paragraphs.

Like this. See how well it works? (But save it for something special.)

Make it perfect. No typos, no misspellings, no factual errors. If you're sloppy and let mistakes slip by, the person reading your letter will think you don't know better or don't care. Do you?

Be crystal clear. You won't get what you're after if your reader doesn't get the message.

Use good English. If you're still in school, take all the English and writing courses you can. The way you write and speak can really help you—or hurt.

If you're not in school (even if you are), get the little 71-page gem by Strunk & White, *Elements of Style.* It's in paperback. It's fun to read and loaded with tips on good English and good writing.

Don't put on airs.

Pretense invariably impresses only the pretender.

Don't exaggerate. Even once. Your reader will suspect everything else you write.

Distinguish opinions from facts. Your opinions may be the best in the world. But they're not gospel. You owe it to your reader to let him know which is which. He'll appreciate it and he'll admire you. The dumbest people I know are those who Know It All.

Be honest. It'll get you further in the long run. If you're

"I learned to ride a motorcycle at 50 and fly balloons at 52. It's never too late to learn anything."

found out. (The latter, not speaking from experience.)

Edit ruthlessly. Somebody has said that words are like inflated money—the more of them that you use, the less each one is worth. Right on. Go through your entire letter just as many times as it takes. Search out and annihilate all unnecessary words, and sentences—even entire paragraphs.

"Don't exaggerate. Even once. Your reader will suspect everything else you write."

Sum it up and get out

The last paragraph should tell the reader exactly what you want him to do—or what you're going to do. Short and sweet. "May I have an appointment? Next Monday, the 16th, I'll call your secretary to see when it'll be most convenient for you."

Close with something simple like, "Sincerely." And for heaven's sake sign legibly. The biggest ego trip I know is a completely illegible signature.

Good luck.

I hope you get what you're after.

Sincerely,

Malcolm S. Forbes

Figure 6.2. Sample image ad.

125

Figure 6.3. Sample inquiry ad.

126

3. There is a specific offer the reader can send for, in this case, a free information kit including a booklet titled "6 Things Burglars Know That You Should Know Too."

4. The title of the free booklet further fuels the reader's desire to obtain the information. (People seek inside information, hence the appeal of "things burglars know." The phrase "6 Things" is effective because people wonder what the six things are.)

5. A toll-free number is provided for response. The offer to call the number appears twice: once in the headline and once above the coupon.

6. The advertiser provides a coupon the reader can use to request the information by mail.

Remember that the primary objective of the inquiry ad is to generate sales leads, not to communicate a message, build awareness, or establish an image. Thus, let's say you sell widgets and your firm offers a broader line of widgets than any other supplier. Further, you have a 48-page catalog that lists and describes all the widgets available and tells how to select the right widget for a particular application.

The headline for an awareness ad might be, "XYZ Company: Your Single Source for Widgets." The visual might show a huge pile of widgets or endless rows of storage bins containing widgets of every shape and color. The copy explains that XYZ Company stocks more widgets than any other firm and can meet all the buyer's widget needs.

The headline for an inquiry ad might read, "Yours Free—The XYZ Company Guide to Widget Selection." The visual would be a picture of your catalog, which is offered free to anyone who responds to the ad. The copy stresses the catalog: its broad line of widgets, clear illustrations, and selection tips.

Category 4: Mail Order Ads

A mail order ad is a response ad that asks for an order instead of an inquiry. In a mail order ad, there is no free information or brochure to ask for, no salesperson to answer questions or give advice. Instead, the reader must send a check or money order or provide credit card information to receive the product being advertised.

Therefore, the mail order ad has the toughest selling job. It must not only make the reader want the product so much that the reader will part with money on the spot to buy the product sight unseen, but it must also overcome and answer any possible objections or questions the reader might have, because there is no salesperson or brochure to provide those answers. The ad must also contain complete instructions for ordering, such as whether credit cards are accepted, how much the product costs, sales tax, quantity discounts, and so on.

TEN RULES FOR CREATING EFFECTIVE MAGAZINE ADVERTISING

Through long years of experience, advertisers and advertising agencies have uncovered some basic principles of sound advertising strategy, copywriting, and design. Following these suggestions won't guarantee a winner, but it will prevent you from making costly mistakes that could destroy the selling power of a potentially lucrative ad. The following discussion presents the ten rules.

1. The Right Product for the Right Audience

The first step is to make sure you are advertising a product that is potentially useful to the people reading your advertisement. This seems a bit simple and obvious, yet, many clients believe that a great ad can sell anything to anyone. They are wrong. For example, no advertisement, no matter how powerfully written, will convince vegetarians to have a steak dinner at your new restaurant. But if persuasively worded, your ad might entice them to try your salad bar.

Charles Inlander of the People's Medical Society is a master at finding the right product for the right audience. His ad, "Do you recognize the seven early warning signs of high blood pressure?" (see Figure 6.4), sold more than 20,000 copies of a $4.95 book on blood pressure when it ran approximately ten times in *Prevention Magazine* over a three-year period. "First, you select your topic," said Inlander, explaining the secret of his advertising success; "then you must find the right place to advertise. It's important to pinpoint a magazine whose readers are the right prospects for what you are selling." In other words, choose the right product for the right audience.

2. The Importance of the Headline

Next to the selection of subject matter and the placement of your ad in the proper publication in which it will reach the right prospects for your product, the headline is the most important ad element.

The main purpose of the headline is to grab readers' attention and make them stop long enough to notice and start reading your ad. You can achieve this in several ways. For example, here's an attention-grabbing headline from an ad published in a local newspaper:

IMPORTANT NEWS FOR WOMEN WITH FLAT OR THINNING HAIR

This headline is effective in gaining the attention of the prospect for two reasons: 1) It promises important news, and 2) it identifies the prospect for the service (women with flat or thinning hair). Incidentally, this ad persuades more than 1,200 readers a month to clip a coupon and send for a free brochure on a hair conditioning procedure.

3. The Visual Must Work with the Headline

The ad should be illustrated with a photograph or drawing that visually gets across the main idea communicated in the headline.

Do You Recognize the Seven Early Warning Signs of High Blood Pressure?

1.
2.
3.
4.
5.
6.
7.

That's right. There are no signs. No symptoms. And no cure.

One out of every four Americans has high blood pressure. Yet only half these people know it.

You may be one of them.

If you are over forty, you owe it to yourself to have your blood pressure checked. But that isn't enough. You also need to know the facts about "hypertension."

Fortunately, you can get those facts more easily now than ever before...from a new publication by Bob Rodale's *People's Medical Society*. It's called ***Blood Pressure: Questions You Have...Answers You Need***. And it's a book that just might save your life.

Could You Answer These 3 Questions If Your Life Depended On It?

1. What kind of exercise can lower your blood pressure...and what kind can actually make it worse?

In general, exercise is good for hypertension. But some forms of exercise are downright dangerous. Do you know which ones? You'll find the answer on page 15.

2. What common nutrient can bring your blood pressure down?

If you think controlling blood pressure is only a matter of eliminating certain foods from your diet, you'll be happy to know there are some tasty foods you should actually be eating more of. Turn to page 22 to find out which ones.

3. What happens if high blood pressure is not treated?

A 35-year-old man with untreated high blood pressure could lower his life expectancy by 16 years. Like the scores of other alarming facts in this book, better to be surprised now than later.

Don't Die Young Just Because You Didn't Know The Facts

In 1981, nearly a million Americans died of heart attacks, strokes or related diseases. How many of these deaths could have been avoided if people had simply taken the time to learn the facts about high blood pressure? Hypertension cannot be cured. But it can be controlled. More important, it can be prevented. ***Blood Pressure: Questions You Have...Answers You Need*** will show you how.

Just Published... By The People's Medical Society

There's no technical "mumbo-jumbo" here, no lecturing and no nagging. Just straight talk from your friends at *The People's Medical Society*—the non-profit group founded by Bob Rodale to help Americans get better medical care.

At only $4.95, the first printing is bound to go fast. So please, place your order today. Just fill out the coupon below and send it with $4.95 to:

The People's Medical Society
14 East Minor Street, Suite 100
Emmaus, Pennsylvania 18049

☐ Yes, I want to know how to control high blood pressure. Please send me this life-saving guide right away. I enclose $4.95.

Name ____________________

Address ____________________

City ____________________

State ____________ Zip ____________ PNAJ

Figure 6.4. People's Medical Society ad.

Together, the headline and visual should get the gist of your sales pitch across to the reader. "Every good ad should be able to stand as a poster," writes Alastair Crompton. "The reader should never have to dip into the small print in order to understand the point of the story."

Often, simple visuals are the best visuals. "We tested two different mail order ads selling a collector's reproduction of a watch originally manufactured in the 1920s," said Will Stone of the Hamilton Watch Company. "One ad used a large, dramatic photo showing the watch against a plain background. The other visual had less emphasis on the product and focused on a scene depicting the 'roaring twenties' period during which the watch was originally made. It showed flappers and a 1920s car. The ad with the straight product photo, product as hero, generated three times as many sales as the other version."

As a general rule, simple visuals that show the product or illustrate some aspect of its use are better than far-out, creative concepts that can actually hide what you are selling, thus reducing the ad's selling power.

4. The Lead Paragraph Expands on the Theme of the Headline

The lead must instantly follow up on the idea expressed in the headline. For instance, if the headline asks a burning question, the lead should immediately answer it. The promises made to the reader in the headline (e.g., "Learn the secret to richer, moister chocolate cake") must be fulfilled in the first few paragraphs of copy. Otherwise, the reader feels disappointed and turns the page.

Here is an example of how this works. This is from an ad selling a business opportunity:

```
Quit Your Job or Start Part-Time

Chimney Sweeps Are Urgently Needed Now!

My name is Tom Risch. I'm going to show you how to make
$200 a day saving people from dangerous chimney fires....
```

Do not waste the reader's time with a warm-up paragraph. Instead, go straight to the heart of the matter. In editing a first draft, the first question to ask yourself is, "Can I eliminate my first paragraph and start with my second or third paragraph?" Eight times out of ten, you can, and the copy is strengthened as a result.

5. The Layout Draws the Reader into the Ad

This is something that cannot be described in words but is experienced visually. Right now, take a minute or two to flip through the ads in any magazine you have handy. Some seem friendly. Some seem inviting. Some seem to draw your eye to the page, and make reading a pleasure. This is the type of layout you want to use in your own ads. Avoid layouts that make the ad hard to read or that discourage readers from even trying.

One key point to keep in mind is that your ad should have a focal point—a central dominant visual element that draws the reader's eye into the page. This is usually the headline or the visual. (I often prefer to make it the headline, since a good headline can usually communicate more effectively than a picture.) But it might also be the coupon, or perhaps the lead paragraph of copy. When there are two or more equally prominent visuals competing for the eye's attention, readers become confused and don't know where to "enter" your ad and start reading. Always make one element larger and more prominent than the others.

6. The Body Copy Supports and Expands upon the Idea Presented in the Headline and Lead Paragraph of Copy

What facts should be included in your body copy? Which should be left out? The decision is made by listing all the key points and then determining which are strongest and will best convince the reader to respond to your advertisement.

Start by listing all the features of your products and the benefits people get from each feature. For instance, a feature of an air conditioner is that its Energy Efficiency Rating is 9.2; the benefit is a lower electric bill.

After making a complete list of features and benefits, list them in order of importance. Then begin your body copy with the most important benefit. Go down the list until you run out of room. Now you've written copy that highlights the most important reasons to buy the product, given the limitations of the space your ad allows for description.

7. Be Specific

The most common mistake in advertising today is lazy copy—copy written by copywriters who were too lazy to take the time to learn about their audience and understand the features and benefits of their product (the reasons why someone would want to buy it).

Good advertising is effective largely because it is specific. There are two advantages to being specific. First, it gives customers the information they need before they will make a buying decision. Second, it creates believability. As Claude Hopkins points out, people are more likely to believe a specific, factual claim than a boast, superlative, or generalization.

Does this mean ad copy should be a litany of facts and figures? No. But the copywriter's best weapon is the selective use of facts to support the sales pitch.

8. Start with the Prospect, Not the Product

This may sound like a contradiction, but it's not. Your ad must be packed with information about the product. But the information must be important to readers: information that they will find interesting or fascinating; information that will answer their questions, satisfy their curiosity, or cause them to believe the claims you make. In short, include imformation that will convince readers to buy your product.

The readers' own concerns—their needs, desires, fears, and problems—are more important to them than your product, your company, your goals. Good advertising copy, as Dr. Jeffrey Lant points out, is "client centered." It focuses on the prospects and how your product solves their problems, not on you, your company, or how the product was invented or is made.

For instance, instead of saying, "We have more than 50 service centers nationwide," translate that fact into a reader benefit: "You'll be assured of prompt, courteous service and fast delivery of replacement parts from one of our 50 service centers located nationwide." Don't say "energy efficient" when you can say "cuts your summer electric bills in half."

The real star of your ad is the reader. Your product is second and is only of concern in that it relates to a need, desire, or problem readers have or a benefit they want. Your company is a distant third (the least important element of your copy) and is only of concern as a way of reassuring those prospects who want to do business with a well-known firm that has a good reputation and is financially stable.

9. Write in a Clear, Simple, Natural Conversational Style

According to *Business Marketing* magazine's Copy Chasers, a panel of judges who regularly critique advertising in a monthly column, good ad copy should sound like "one friend talking to another."

This is good advice. Copy should not be pompous, remote, aloof, or written in corporatese. It shouldn't strive to be poetic, creative, or imaginative. The most effective copy is written in a plain, simple, conversational style, the way a sincere person talks who wants to help or advise you.

In a sense, Madison Avenue has created an accepted style for ad copy that all the big agencies now use. This style is the type of copy that seems to deliberately remind you that you are reading an ad. Avoid this type of slick lingo.

10. Decide What You Want the Reader to Do Next

Here are three easy steps for turning your ad into a response-generating marketing tool. First, decide what type of response you want, the action you want the reader to take. Do you want your prospect to phone you? Write to you? Clip a coupon and mail it back to you? Do you want the reader to visit your store? Request a copy of your catalog or sales brochure? Set up an appointment to see a salesperson? Test drive your product? Order your product directly from the ad? Decide what you want the reader to do.

Next, tell the reader to do it. The last few paragraphs of your copy should spell out the action you want readers to take and give them reasons to take it. For instance:

```
Just clip the coupon or call our toll-free number now
and we'll send you this policy FREE without obligation
as a special introduction to Employment Guide.
```

```
So why not call 1-800-FINE4WD for a dealer convenient
to you?

Just send in the card [or the coupon] and have some fun
with your first issue. Then pay us after you've taken a
look.

And send for Display Masters' invaluable FREE booklet on
Point of Purchase Marketing, "33 Ways to Better
Displays: What Every Marketing Executive Should Know
about Point of Purchase Displays in Today's Market."
```

Third, give the reader a mechanism for responding, emphasize this mechanism in your ad layout, and simplify the process of making contact with you.

In print advertising, this is accomplished through use of a toll-free phone number (usually printed in large type to bring attention to it) or by including a coupon in the ad. Some magazines also allow you to insert a reply card, which is bound into the magazine and appears opposite your ad. This is expensive but can dramatically increase the number of replies, multiplying returns by a factor of two to four or more.

Even if your ad is not primarily a response ad (and with rare exceptions, it is hard to understand why you wouldn't want a response), you should still make it easy for your readers to get in touch should they want to do business with you. This means always including an address and telephone number.

Recently, I saw a television commercial for Lilco (a Long Island utility) offering a free booklet on electricity. The ad informed viewers that they could get the booklet by calling their local Lilco office, but no phone number was mentioned in the commercial! This represents a response-killing mentality that many advertisers embrace and that I will never understand. Why make it difficult for people to get in touch with you or to order your product? It doesn't make sense.

THE MOST COMMONLY ASKED QUESTIONS ABOUT MAGAZINE ADVERTISING

Here are some of the questions clients and seminar attendees frequently ask me about magazine advertising.

Q: There are a dozen or so publications covering my industry. Should I advertise in all of them, a few of them, or just one?

A: Generally it's best to advertise only in the two or three leading publications in any one industry. You know which ones these are, or you can find out by asking your customers what they read. Magazines that are not in the top two or three in a category generally deliver a poorer quality circulation and are not worth considering unless the price makes them a real bargain. If you only have money to advertise in one publication, choose the top one in your industry.

Q: How do I know how much duplication of circulation there is among the magazines in which I advertise?

A: You don't. Unlike mailing lists, which can be run through a computer to remove duplicate names, magazine subscriber bases do overlap, and there's nothing you can do about it. This is another reason why you should advertise only in the top two or three publications in any given field. If you put more magazines on the media schedule you will probably end up duplicating a lot of the readership, resulting in wasted ad dollars.

Q: Is it better to run a small ad several times or one big ad once?

A: If you have to choose between frequency and size, choose frequency. It is generally more effective to run a quarter-page ad in three or four issues of a monthly magazine than to run a full-page ad once a year. Many subscribers do not read every issue of a magazine, so frequency gives them more chances to come across your ad.

Q: What size ad is best?

A: If money is no object, a one-page ad is the best buy. Two-page spreads are not cost-effective. According to one study reported in The New York Times, *two-page ads get only 30 percent more readership than one-page ads, but the cost is twice as much.*

If money is a consideration and you must run smaller ads, I think the following units are all good sizes: 1/4-page, 1/3-page, and 1/2-page. For the price of a 2/3-page ad in most publications, you may as well run a full page. One-sixth of a page or less is generally not enough room to tell your story.

Q: What position is best on the page?

A: A right-hand page is better than a left-hand page. A page facing editorial matter (articles) is better than a page facing another ad. (A two-page spread with both pages containing ads only is called an ad well.)

For a fractional ad, being on the outside edge of the page is better than being against the center of the magazine (the gutter where the magazine is stapled or glued together). Top of the page is better than bottom of the page. The worst position for a fractional ad is to be surrounded by other ads. It's better to be on the outer edge of the page and next to editorial content.

Q: What is the best position in a magazine?

A: The preferred positions are, in order, the inside front cover, outside back cover, inside back cover, and the page facing the contents page. The more toward the front of the magazine, the better.

However, Martin Schrader, publisher of Harper's Bazaar, *says: "I've always believed that a good ad will be seen and a bad ad will be ignored. A good ad will pull. A bad one won't. Recent research by*

Starch again proves, for example, that there's virtually no difference between left- and right-hand pages, and inside positions are as good as outside."

Q: How can I get these preferred positions?

A: Some of them, such as the front and back covers, are sold at premium prices. You can ask for others and will generally get them if they are available.

Q: Should we run a reader service card with our ad?

A: A reader service card, or bingo card, is a postcard bound into the magazine. The postcard contains a series of numbers, with numbers on the postcard keyed to different numbers appearing in various ads. Typically, these reader service numbers are imprinted on your ad by the magazine and read, "For more information, circle Reader Service No. XXX."

The reader service card provides a fast, convenient way for readers to request information from advertisers. They simply circle all the numbers on the card corresponding to the ads they want to respond to. They then mail the postcard to the magazine, which in turn forwards the requests to the various advertisers.

Should you include a reader service card number in your ad? The reason in favor of this is that it increases response rates and makes it easy for your prospect to get in touch with you. The reason against it is that many advertisers think bingo card inquiries are of low quality.

Unless responding to inquiries is a tremendous burden for you, I recommend you include a reader service card number, at least in your initial ads. If the quality of replies is poor, you might then test dropping the number to see if the ad still generates enough responses to pay off.

Q: Can I take my own photographs or draw my own pictures for use in my ad?

A: No. The reader is accustomed to quality and expects the appearance of your ad to match the quality of other ads and of the magazine's editorial layouts. Poor-quality photos and crude, amateur drawings detract from your ad more than they enhance it. Leave drawing and photo taking to the professionals.

Q: Must I illustrate my ad with drawings or photography?

A: No. All-copy ads are extremely effective. Why? I'm not certain. Perhaps it's because readers perceive that all-copy ads are closer to editorial material (which they think is valuable) than advertising (which they think is full of hype). At any rate, I have written numerous all-copy ads for clients that outperformed fancier, elaborately conceived and illustrated visual concepts. Another advantage of all-copy ads is that they are inexpensive to produce. I have had them *done by desktop publishing services for as little as $250, including design and laser original.*

Q: Most of the ads I see are color. Are black and white ads effective anymore?

A: Yes, for the same reason that all-copy ads work: Readers perceive them as reading matter rather than promotional hype. Most of the ads I create for clients are black and white, and they work well.

Q: Does running an ad in four colors pay off?

A: Four-color ads allow you to reproduce photographs and other artwork in full color through the process of color separations. Whether or not you need four colors depends on your product. Is it something that is more enticing or appealing when shown in color, such as food, clothing, cosmetics, jewelry, home furnishings, or travel destinations? Or is it something that doesn't benefit from a full-color treatment, such as a book, a consulting service, or a piece of machinery? If the appeal is aesthetic, or if some facet of the product is demonstrated most realistically in color, then color may pay off. Otherwise, I don't think it does.

Some will disagree with me, however. McGraw-Hill's Laboratory of Advertising Performance, a respected and widely read research service dealing with advertising effectiveness, has run numerous studies that show that a) the trend to run four-color ads instead of black and white is on the rise and b) four-color ads are more effective.

One study concludes that four-color ads gain approximately 40 percent higher readership yet cost only 30 percent more than black and white. A similar study focusing on medical journal advertising found that color ads were seen by 31 percent more doctors and read by 33 percent more doctors than black and white ads. A third study of ads published in Business Week *showed that color ads were remembered by 39 percent more readers than black and white ads.*

Q: What about adding a second color to a black and white ad?

A: A far less costly alternative to a four-color ad is a two-color ad. A two-color ad is a black and white ad with a second color (usually blue but also red, yellow, or green) added to highlight headlines, subheads, blocks of copy, or other graphic elements. In a two-color ad, full-color photo reproduction is not possible; however, you can use the second color to throw a tint over the photos. Generally, the cost of buying space is increased 15 percent if you add a second color.

My feeling is that using a second color simply for the sake of having an extra color and avoiding black and white hurts the ad more than it helps. The color is usually added as an afterthought, thrown over a logo or photo in a slapdash sort of way, without any real purpose or effect in mind. I see no evidence that two-color ads outpull black and white ads, although one report has shown a 7 percent increase in people being able to remember an ad in two colors versus black and white.

I would use color only if it fit or logically dramatized some key selling point, for example, yellow on the cover of a Yellow Pages *directory, red in the symbol for the Red Cross, or blue for Blue Cross and Blue Shield.*

Q: Do coupons in ads really increase response rates?

*A: Yes. A coupon will get you at least 20 percent more inquiries and possibly up to double the leads your ad would generate without a coupon. Why do they work? I think it's because they visually say to the reader, "This a direct response ad, not an awareness ad. That means you will get something **free** if you stop and look at the ad and read the coupon." So the reader feels compelled to see what you are giving away, and those who actually have an interest in your proposition stop long enough to read and respond to your message.*

Q: Do I need a toll-free number?

A: Toll-free numbers do increase response rates for much the same reasons that coupons do. The 800 number visually clues readers that you are running a response ad through which they can get something if they call. So readers pause to find out what you are offering.

Must you have a toll-free number? Absolutely not. A regular phone number will do fine; many, many people will still call you. A toll-free number increases response rates, but you can still get good phone response without it. If most of your advertising is direct response, however, a toll-free number is a definite advantage in that it makes it easier for the reader to respond.

In consumer advertising, where the cost of making the telephone call may be a significant barrier that prevents your prospect from picking up the telephone, toll-free numbers are even more important. You don't need one if your ads are primarily to build image or awareness or if your advertising is local. However, if you want to generate inquiries or mail order sales on a nationwide basis, a toll-free number can boost response rates anywhere from 10 to 30 percent or more. Companies with toll-free numbers report that as much as 50 percent or more of inquiries and orders are made by telephone. Consumers especially appreciate the cost savings and convenience.

Q: Is there a certain proper word length for headlines?

A: A headline should be as long as it needs to be to get your point across. However, if you can say the same thing in fewer words, do so. Short, pithy headlines are more memorable and can be set in larger type to attract more attention. A long headline can be broken up into two or even three subheads to increase readability.

Q: *How many words are in a typical ad?*

A: *That's hard to answer because no ad is typical. In some of the slick, Madison Avenue–type ads, the copy may consist only of a head-line, a slogan, and the advertiser's name. For example, the ads for Absolut vodka have just a two-word headline (Absolut whatever) and a visual.*

However, as a rule of thumb, I'd say that the following holds true as a guide for word length:

Type of Ad	Number of Words in Full-Page Ad
Image or awareness	100–150
Inquiry	150–300
Mail order	500–800

Q: *What size type should the body copy be set in?*

A: *Body copy should be set in the same type size as or slightly larger type than the editorial matter of a publication. Usually the point size for an ad is 9 or 10, with 8-point being the minimum and 12-point the maximum. Note: A point is equal to 1/72nd of an inch.*

Q: *How many times can I repeat my ad before I need a new ad?*

A: *Experience shows that ads can run for a long time without losing their potency. In most cases, advertisers get tired of their ads and replace them with new ads sooner than is necessary.*

Several studies support the claim for greater ad longevity. One report showed that ads repeated during a three-year campaign were seen and noticed as well on their last appearance as on their first appear-ance, and readership scores declined only 7 percent. Some of the ads were repeated up to five times during this period. Another study of 50 different ads repeated in 4 to 7 issues of a business publication showed that reader interest levels either remained the same or actu-ally increased with each repetition. In other studies performed by the Laboratory of Advertising Performance, one ad continued to pull high levels of inquiries after 8 insertions and another after 41 inser-tions over a period of 11 years.

The exception to this rule is full-page mail order ads, whose first insertion generally pulls the most orders, with orders dropping off between 10 and 50 percent on subsequent insertions. However, small display and classified mail order ads can pull profitably for years with no decrease in response.

The answer to the question, then, is that you can continue to run the ad until the response rate drops off sharply (and this can be months or years) or until the message it contains is no longer current or accu-rate.

Q: *Is it necessary for my ad to have a catchy slogan or tag line?*

A: *No. Most slogans are superficial and meaningless and only detract from the ad. Unless you are lucky enough to come up with a brilliant slogan, omit the slogan or tag line altogether.*

Q: *Is it important that all my ads have a consistent look and graphic design?*

A: *While it isn't mandatory, I think having a uniform look and appearance enhances a series of ads and makes the ads more memorable. If you find a style and stick with it, readers gradually begin to recognize your style and know when an ad is from your company even before they have read the headline or looked at the logo. At the very least, you can use the same style typography in all your ads, even if the designs are not identical.*

Q: *What are some of the things I can do to increase ad response?*

A: *Here is a partial list:*

- *Ask for action.*
- *Offer a free booklet or brochure.*
- *Show a picture of your free brochure or booklet.*
- *Include a toll-free number.*
- *Include a coupon.*
- *Offer a free gift or bonus for prompt response.*
- *Offer a free estimate, consultation, diagnosis, evaluation, or other free service.*
- *Use a reader service card number.*

Q: *I see some ads with postcards bound into the magazine opposite the ad. Does this technique increase response rates?*

A: *Yes. Typically an ad with a bound-in postcard generates two to five times as many responses as the ad with no postcard. But it is costly.*

SPECIAL TIPS FOR FRACTIONAL ADS

A fractional ad is any ad that is smaller than a full page but larger than a classified or classified display. Typical fractions are 1/12, 1/6, 1/4, 1/3, 1/2, and 2/3 of a page.

Although most of what is written about advertising in books and the trade press deals with full-page ads and two-page spreads, and most of the ads that win awards are full-size ads, fractionals are more difficult to write and to design. The fractional ad competes with the big ads. It asks for attention from the same audience, must communicate the same message, and must demonstrate and describe similar products. Yet it must do all this in a smaller space. It's difficult to do well and is seldom appreciated by clients.

Here are some techniques for making small ads stand out and generate more responses:

1. Take full advantage of the medium. Acknowledge that the space is limited, and work within those limitations. The best example of this is the fractional ad by the brilliant entrepreneur who wrote the headline, "Do you read small ads like this one?" Don't try to scale down a full-page ad and cram it into a 5-inch by 5-inch box. Instead, start with the small box and find creative ways to fill it.

2. Put a dashed border around the ad. This creates the feeling and appearance of a coupon which, in turn, stimulates response. It is an inexpensive and easy way to make your ad stand out on the page. And it works every time, because not one advertiser in 1,000 knows this simple technique.

3. In the closing paragraph of your copy, say, "To receive more information, clip this ad and mail it with your business card to [address]." Many business prospects will follow your directions and respond in this way.

4. Use simple visuals. A fractional ad has no room for developing a complex visual concept. Visuals should be straightforward: Photos of the product, cutaway drawings showing how the product works, and sketches of applications are best. Clip art (books of stock line drawings) can work well here.

5. In the bottom right corner of the ad, next to your closing paragraph, show a small picture of your brochure, catalog, or other free information the reader can send for. It almost always increases response.

6. Use short headlines. For example, instead of "How to Stop Liquid Waste," write "Stop Liquid Waste." By cutting words, you free up space and can set the headline in larger type or have more room for body copy or visuals. For fractional ads, short, pithy headlines in large, boldface type work best. For example, if you are selling boilers and have room for only one word in the headline, it should read, "Boilers."

7. Cut the fat out of your body copy. Short ads have to be less conversational and talky, more telegraphic and clipped in style. Put in the essential points and cut out all the transitions, fluff copy, and unnecessary phrases. One way to accomplish this is to use numbered or bulleted points.

8. If you have a lot to say, consider a series of ads rather than a single ad. For example, let's say you are advertising an air freight delivery service. Your service is the best because it is the fastest, most reliable, and most economical. You could get all that across in a full-page ad, but it's too much to say in a quarter-page ad.

The solution is to create a series of three quarter-page ads, one on speed, one on reliability, and one pushing cost savings. You could even create continuity by putting a kicker (small line of copy) above the headline that reads, "Number [1,2,3] in a series." This actually increases readership because it makes the ad seem important and people will look for the other ads in the series.

9. A common technique for making small ads more noticeable and dramatic is to set the entire ad in reverse type. Don't do it. Body copy set in white type against a black background is often difficult to read.

10. Always specify the best position (right-hand page, right-hand side of page, top of page) in your insertion orders. You might get it if you ask, but you will rarely get it if you don't ask.

According to Cahner's Advertising Research (Report No. 210.93), the favorite response mechanism of buyers with an immediate need is to call an advertiser's toll-free number—62 percent of buyers surveyed listed this as their number one preference. Web response is growing, with 20 percent of buyers with an immediate need saying they liked to go to the advertiser's Web site. Thirty-five percent prefer to call a sales rep.

But many prospects have a future rather than an immediate need. The Cahner's survey found that 66 percent of buyers with a future need liked to circle the reader service card number the ad is keyed with. A large percentage of these prospects with non-immediate needs, 29 percent, favor calling the toll-free number.

WRITING CLASSIFIED ADS

Do not ignore classified ads. They can be powerhouses as response generators. A classified ad will generate inquiries and orders at far less cost than a large display ad. Unfortunately, the overall response will be lower so you can rarely depend on classified ads alone.

A big plus of classified ads is that they are inexpensive to run and inexpensive to produce. There are no fees for illustration, photography, typography, or layout. You simply send your copy to the magazine and they take care of the rest.

Because I am not an expert classified ad writer, I turn to successful mail order entrepreneur Joe Barnes for advice on the topic. Here are some of his guidelines on the subject, reprinted from his Special Report and from personal letters he has sent me over the years:

1. Certain key words and phrases attract the most attention and generate the greatest number of replies. They include Free, How To, Amazing, Sell, Easy, Make Money, Save, New, and You. Try to use any of these words as the first words in your classifieds. Many readers run their fingers down a column of small classifieds until stopped by the appeal of the first word.

2. Be brief. Avoid using more words than are necessary. In classifieds, you pay for each word, so why use two or three words when one will convey the same message?

For instance, don't say You Can Make Extra Money (five words) when Make Extra Money (three words) will accomplish the same thing. Another way to save words is to use figures rather than words, for example, $500 (one word) instead of five hundred dollars (three words). Instead of

Westinghouse Electric Corporation (three words) use Westinghouse (one word). Instead of Commercial and Residential (three words) use Commercial/Residential (two words).

3. Avoid abbreviating words in classified ads. Spell them out in full to prevent confusion. The cost is the same; no money is saved by abbreviating. For example, write Government, not Gov't.

4. Be honest with your prospects. Be specific enough in your ad to attract a large percentage of qualified prospects. The number of inquiries is not a measure of success. You want inquiries that have a reasonable chance of being turned into sales.

5. Place your ad only in those publications where you find others advertising similar products or services, especially if you recognize ads that have appeared time and time again in previous issues. Fish where the fish are biting. Others have tested the waters and found them to be productive.

6. Avoid, or at least be extremely cautious about, placing ads in cheap little ad sheets. A so-called low price of $12 to $20 becomes expensive if no results are achieved. Far too many times these sheets are circulated primarily to other advertisers and to worthless name lists. You have no way of verifying how many were actually mailed. Stick to the big circulation magazines. You will be way ahead.

7. An exception to this is if you are selling a specialty item, such as rare guns. Then, advertise in a specialty magazine aimed at this market, such as *Gun World*.

8. Answer all inquiries. Those who send postcards or scribbled messages may turn out to be some of your best repeat customers.

9. Key each ad in each magazine. Then keep accurate records so you can determine which ads produce the best results. For example, Dept. WD means the ad ran in *Writer's Digest*.

10. Classified ads have one use: to generate inquiries. They are useless for image building or awareness and are not cost-effective for selling directly any item over $5. The typical offer is more information on the product, usually phrased as "free information," "free details," or "free brochure."

THE 61 MOST COMMON MAGAZINE ADVERTISING MISTAKES AND HOW TO AVOID THEM

Here are 61 of the most common mistakes made in designing, writing, and placing magazine advertisements.

Headlines

Mistake No. 1: You don't have a headline.

Headlines are a must. They grab attention. They tease readers with promises. They summarize your message and give readers the reason to order. Without a headline, your ad is weak.

Mistake No. 2: Your company name is the headline.

Readers respond to benefit headlines. "What's in it for me?" is their primary concern. Put your company name at the bottom of the ad. At the top, it distracts readers from the benefit headline.

Mistake No. 3: You don't promise the main benefit.

Selling headlines promise the major benefit.

Why? Because readers must be convinced that it's worthwhile to read your ad, and only major benefits have that kind of convincing power. Some weak headlines: 1) your company name (not really a benefit); 2) your company is number one (Who cares? What's in it for the reader?); 3) you've been in business for ten years (Yes, and...?). Tell how you'll improve the readers' lives or they won't read the rest of your ad.

Mistake No. 4: Your headline is too logical.

Appeals to emotion consistently outpull appeals to logic. Wrong: "Team Basketball Action for Your Computer" (logical). Right: "Jump into the Big Leagues with CompuTex" (emotional). Don't just don't state facts. Dig for the emotion behind them.

Mistake No. 5: You use a one-word headline.

Current styles notwithstanding, one word can't possibly do the work of three or more. I have yet to see an effective one-word headline.

Mistake No. 6: You use the name of your product as the headline.

Not enough information. Besides, where's the benefit?

Body Copy

Mistake No. 7: You're not selling the reader.

Your copy implies that the reader is three-quarters sold. All you have to do is describe your product or service and the reader will order. Result? Readers aren't motivated.

Instead, address the skeptical prospects. You have their momentary attention, but they're resistant. Communicate your enthusiasm, your strong belief, your willingness to satisfy. That gives your message the edge it needs.

Mistake No. 8: Your copy is not reader oriented.

Don't write about your product or service. Write about readers and how your product or service will benefit them.

Wrong: "Cannot be compared to any other peripheral." Right: "Easy to use; no software required."

Mistake No. 9: Your body copy begins with a description of your company.

You've hooked readers with an intriguing headline. Now keep them hooked by elaborating on the benefit you promised in the headline. Forceful, believable promises keep readers from abandoning your ad.

Mistake No. 10: You don't convert features to benefits.

Features disclose product or service facts. Benefits show what's in it for the reader. Converted features turn facts into benefits. Feature: Tough. Benefit: Lasts a long time. Converted feature: Tough enough to last a full year.

Mistake No. 11: Your message is not focused.

Readers can digest only one offer at a time. Don't distract them with brief notes about other offers, even if they are related to your present offer.

Mistake No. 12: You lie to readers.

Never claim your product or service is lowest in cost unless it is. If it is, think of a unique and believable way to express it, for example, "If you can find a lower price, we'll refund twice the difference, plus send you a free set of six diskettes."

Mistake No. 13: You mention price before benefits.

Imagine this sales pitch from an encyclopedia salesman: "The price is $595. Now let me tell you about it." Feel a little resistance, do you? So will your reader unless you present benefits first.

Mistake No. 14: You don't tell readers how much they save by buying now.

You're having a sale and you mention the sale price. Readers know the regular price and can add, so why point out the obvious? Because precise figures make the savings more real. Remember, you are writing to the skeptical prospect.

Mistake No. 15: You don't prove you are number one.

Because everybody does it from time to time, claiming you're number one often increases reader resistance to your message. If you are number one, show it with a professional quality, four-color ad that makes competitors drool. Nobody will believe you're number one if your ad doesn't prove it.

Mistake No. 16: Your subheadlines don't sell.

Promise a benefit in every subheadline, for example, "Save $12 Now." Good subheadlines make a strong message more potent.

Mistake No. 17: You don't include any testimonials.

Testimonials give your offer credibility. Use names, titles, and occupations. Also, be specific and realistic, and avoid superlatives; they usually sound artificial.

Wrong: "The best package I ever saw." Right: "The graphics are sharp and the color is excellent."

Mistake No. 18: You attack the wrong competitor.

If you're number 5, don't go after number 4; attack some weakness in number 1, such as the fact that your guarantee is better (assuming it is). Many readers identify with the underdog. If you're number 1, never mention competitors. To do so is to elevate them to your level in the reader's mind.

Mistake No. 19: You don't mention who your product or service is for.

Even if it's obvious, readers need to be reassured that your product or service is specifically for them. Name the occupational level ("For office managers") or tap into an emotional need ("For people who hate wasting time").

Mistake No. 20: You don't have a guarantee.

Guarantees build confidence in your offer. They are so important that you should highlight them visually with a border, underlining, or bold lettering. The stronger your guarantee the better, as long as the wording rings true.

Mistake No. 21: Your close is weak.

Close forcefully. Readers respond well to firm directions. Avoid questions. Tell readers to order now!

Mistake No. 22: You don't add a clincher.

You have a clincher when you connect some desired emotional response with ordering, for example: "Avoid the discomfort of eyestrain. Send for Clear Writer today!"

Mistake No. 23: You don't stress your order preference.

If readers can either fill out an order form or order by phone, and you prefer one over the other, tell them several times in your copy. When you mention the two ways together, mention the preferred method first ("Phone in now or mail the order form"). In addition, highlight the preferred method visually with large, bold type, or show a picture of a phone to indicate you want phone orders.

Style

Mistake No. 24: You use long, complicated sentences.

Short sentences are easy to read. They lessen reader resistance to your message. Long, complicated sentences turn readers off, as do long paragraphs.

Mistake No. 25: Your tone is too formal.

The most effective copy is conversational, as if you were speaking face to face with a single reader. Don't talk down to readers. Treat them as equals.

Visuals

Mistake No. 26: You lack a provocative visual idea.

Your ad needs a dramatic visual to help readers absorb and remember your message. Without that idea, your ad lacks impact.

Mistake No. 27: The visual features your product when something else would be better.

To be effective, your visual must be related to the main benefit. If your main benefit is time savings, feature a stopwatch instead of your product. Include the product as a secondary element, or put it in a smaller photo somewhere else in the ad.

Mistake No. 28: You don't use people in your visual.

Photos with people pull better than photos without them.

Also, a person doing something works better than a person standing passively. The activity encourages action by readers.

Mistake No. 29: In a computer ad, your screen simulations just fill space.

Use simulations to demonstrate a benefit. Make sure they are clear and clean-looking.

Mistake No. 30: Your visuals don't have captions.

Captions multiply the powers of your visuals. Never miss an opportunity to convey some important message to readers.

Mistake No. 31: You don't highlight your toll-free number.

Make it easy for readers to say yes to your offer. Add emphasis by making the number larger than surrounding copy, or use color, or surround it with a lot of white space to make it look more important.

Mistake No. 32: You don't use graphic emphasis devices.

These devices direct readers' eyes to key parts of your message. They include: underlining or circling key words, bullets, indenting paragraphs, subheadings, and parentheses.

Mistake No. 33: You don't include a visual of your product.

Use a photo of your product to heighten readers' identification when they see it in a store. Show it as readers will see it at the point of purchase.

Mistake No. 34: You use a drawing rather than a photo.

Photos outpull drawings, because readers respond better to the realism conveyed by photos.

Mistake No. 35: Your photo is too small.

The impact is greater with a large photo. Ideally your headline, copy, and photo should each take one-third of the ad space.

Mistake No. 36: Your company logo is prominent.

Readers don't care about your company logo. It's an ego builder, and it doesn't belong in selling ads.

Logos, however, may belong in image ads. If you insist on using your logo, put it at the bottom of the ad with your company name.

Mistake No. 37: Your black and white photo looks washed out.

Photos are just as important as copy. Use a professional photographer and approve all photos before the ad is completed.

Mistake No. 38: The quality of your black and white photos is inconsistent.

To readers, that means your company is not reliable. When composing an ad, have all photos done at the same time by the same photographer.

Color

Mistake No. 39: You use too much reverse copy.

Use reverse copy—white letters on a dark background—in moderation. Reverse ads stand out, but more than 100 words in reverse makes your copy less readable.

Mistake No. 40: Your colors are not functional.

Colors are functional when they highlight important parts of your ad. Don't use color merely as background. Feature your toll-free number, your guarantee, your headline, or all three.

Mistake No. 41: You're number one, but you're running a black and white ad.

If you're number one, go with a four-color ad. Otherwise, if a competitor gets a professional four-color ad, they'll look like number one and steal your customers. The extra cost is worth it.

Mistake No. 42: You use weak colors.

Strong colors draw out positive emotions from readers. Dark red, dark blue, dark green, dark brown, and black are the strong colors. Pastel colors make your message seem weak and ineffective, even if readers can't say why.

Mistake No. 43: Your headline is not visually forceful.

Use thick, black letters or another strong color. Avoid scriptlike letters that make your message appear weak.

Layout

Mistake No. 44: Your ad is cluttered.

Cluttered ads increase reader resistance. Devote one portion each to headline, copy, photo, and order form (when appropriate). Don't insert copy about other products and services just to fill up space.

Mistake No. 45: Your layout is symmetrical.

Balance can work against you. You don't want the left side of your ad completely balanced with the right side. You want things out of kilter a bit, with more ad components on one side or the other. It doesn't matter which side. The out-of-kilter ad stimulates reader action.

Mistake No. 46: Some of your copy slants at a 45-degree angle.

The reader has to do more mental work when copy slants at any angle. One big word at 90 degrees is okay, but blocks of body copy should be horizontal.

Mistake No. 47: Your headline gets hung up in the gutter, where two pages meet.

In a two-page ad, put your headline entirely on the left page. You'll avoid getting part of your message stuck in the gutter and rendered unreadable. You'll also avoid a headline that doesn't line up from one page to the next.

Order Form

Mistake No. 48: Your order form begins with price information.

Price information creates reader resistance. Make it easy to respond: Use a brief version of your main benefit as an order form headline.

Mistake No. 49: You don't include an verbal order form.

Don't tell readers to "Write your name and address" on a piece of paper to mail in. Do the work for them by providing a coupon.

Mistake No. 50: Your order form is not a selling device.

Sell on your order form. Offer a savings for ordering more now. Offer dollars off for a response within 10 days. Keep readers motivated.

Mistake No. 51: Readers have to do some figuring on your order form.

Never ask readers to do arithmetic. Some of the most sophisticated mathematicians can't do simple arithmetic. Others think it's too much trouble. Arithmetic kills sales. Either do the arithmetic for readers or rearrange your offer.

Mistake No. 52: You don't key your ad.

When you place two or more of the same ad, put an extra number, letter, or suite number in your address to indicate the origin of the response. The next time you place ads, you'll know where to focus your dollars.

Mistake No. 53: Your address marks you as an amateur.

Don't use a post office box. Get a street address. Even if you have a post office box, use the street address, then substitute a suite number for your post office box number. Image sells.

Type

Mistake No. 54: You use sans serif type for your body copy.

Sans serif type is lettering without the little feet on the bottoms of certain letters. Serif type gets a better response because it's more readable. Sans serif is okay in headlines and short blocks of copy, but for more than 100 words, use serif type.

Mistake No. 55: Your body copy is too small.

The ideal point size is 10 to 12. That results in the highest readability for your body copy. Point sizes outside that range slow readers down, making them read unnaturally.

Mistake No. 56: You use more than one typeface in your ad.

When you do that, your ad looks cheap. Use a consistent typeface throughout. Headlines can be in another typeface if you desire.

Placement

Mistake No. 57: Your ad is visually dominated by another ad on the same page.

Avoid this by becoming the dominant advertiser. If your ad is black and white, ask that no color ad be placed on the same page. Or ask for the dominant position—top half of the page. For a quarter-page ad, ask for the top right-hand side of a right-hand page, the ultimate dominant position when you don't have a full-page ad.

Mistake No. 58: You forget to watch your backside.

The advertiser behind your ad has an order form that needs to be clipped. Once that's done, your message is ruined.

When you place your ad, ask that no coupon ad be on your backside.

Mistake No. 59: You copy a competitor's style.

The first company out with a style or a marketing idea tends to gobble up the lion's share of the business. Don't be in awe of a competitor because it's bigger than you. Set your own trends.

Mistake No. 60: You're butting heads with the competition.

Most multiproduct ads look alike. Don't be one of the gang. Instead, make a niche for yourself. For example, become known as the modem company. Readers prefer specialists.

Mistake No. 61: You become a slave to these rules.

Don't let these rules become a straitjacket. It's okay to violate them when you know how. If you can think of a message so compelling that it grabs attention and pulls well, go for it. With practice, you'll know when you have a winner.

COPY CHASER RULES

1. Use high visual magnetism.

On average, only a small number of ads in any issue of a magazine will capture the attention of any one reader. Some ads will be passed by because the subject matter is of no concern. But others, even though they may have something to offer, fail the very first test of stopping the reader who is scanning the pages.

Ads perish right at the start because, at one extreme, they just lie there on the page, flat and gray; and at the other extreme, they are cluttered, noisy, and hard to read.

An ad should be constructed so a single component dominates the area—a picture, the headline, or the text (but not the company name or logo).

Obviously, the more pertinent the picture, the more arresting the headline, the more informative the copy appears to be, the better.

2. Select the right audience.

Often, an ad is the first meeting place of two parties who are looking for each other. So there should be something in the ad that at first glance will enable readers to identify it as a source of information relating to *their* interests—a problem they have or an opportunity they will welcome. This is done with either a picture, a headline, or preferably both. The ad should immediately say to the reader, "Hey, this is for you."

3. Invite the reader into the scene.

Within the framework of the layout, the art director's job is to visualize, illuminate, and dramatize the selling proposition. The art director must consider that the type of job a reader has dictates the selection of the illustrative material. Design engineers work with drawings; construction engineers like to see products at work; chemical engineers are comfortable with flow charts; managers relate to pictures of people, and so on.

4. Promise a reward.

An ad will survive the qualifying round only if readers are given reason to expect they will learn something of value. A brag-and-boast headline, a generalization, or an advertising platitude will turn readers off before they get to the message.

The reward can be explicit or implicit and can even be stated negatively, in the form of a warning of a possible loss. The promise should be specific.

5. Back up the promise.

To make the promise believable, the ad must provide hard evidence that the claim is valid. Sometimes, a description of the product's design or operating characteristics will be enough to support the claim.

Comparisons with competition can be convincing. Case histories make the reward appear attainable. Best of all are testimonials: "They say" advertising carries more weight than "We say" advertising.

6. Present the sequence logically.

The job of the art director is to organize the parts of an ad so that there is an unmistakable entry point (the single dominant component referred to earlier) and the reader is guided through the material in a sequence consistent with the logical development of the selling proposition.

7. Talk person to person.

Copy is more persuasive when it speaks to the reader as individuals, as if one friend were telling another friend about a good thing.

Terms should be the terms of the reader's business, not the advertiser's business. But more than that, the writing style should be simple:

Short words, short sentences, short paragraphs, active rather than passive voice, no clichés, frequent use of the personal pronoun "you."

8. Make copy easy to read.

Text type should be no smaller than 9 points. It should appear in black ink on white. It should stand clear of interference from any other part of the ad. Column width should not be more than half of the width of the ad.

9. Emphasize the service.

Many business-to-business advertisers insist that the company name or logo be the biggest thing in the ad, that the company name appear in the headline, that it be set in boldface wherever it appears in the copy. That's too much.

An ad should make readers want to buy, or at least consider buying, before telling them where to buy.

10. Reflect company character.

A company's advertising represents its best opportunity—better than the sales force—to portray the company's personality, the things that will make the company liked, respected, and admired.

Messy ads tend to indicate a messy company. Brag-and-boast ads suggest the company is *maker*-oriented, not *user*-oriented. Whatever it is, personality should be consistent over time and across the spectrum of corporate structure and product lines.

Chapter

7
NEWSPAPER ADVERTISING

NEWSPAPERS VS. MAGAZINES

What are the differences between newspaper advertising and magazine advertising?

Newspapers are published more frequently than magazines.

Newspapers are published daily or weekly, as opposed to weekly or monthly for magazines. The advantage to newspapers is that you can get ads into print more quickly and even target ads for specific days of the week. For example, to get an ad in the June issue of a monthly magazine, you must reserve the space by May (or even April for some publications). But the newspaper ad you create today can be in the paper tomorrow. (Note: The sources for most of the newspaper industry figures quoted here are *Facts about Newspapers*, published by the American Newspaper Publishers Association, and reprinted with permission of McCann Erickson Inc. and the Newspaper Advertising Bureau, Inc.; and *Key Facts: Newspapers, Consumers, Advertising*, published by the Newspaper Advertising Bureau, Inc. and reprinted with permission.)

Newspaper ads have greater size flexibility.

Magazines generally have only a half dozen fixed units of space (full page, 1/2 page, 1/4 page, 2/3 page, 1/3 page, 1/6 page).

Newspaper space is sold by the column inch and can be any size that fits your message and budget. An ad that is two column inches, for instance, is one column wide by two inches deep. A-six-column inch ad might be one column wide by six inches deep, or it could be two columns wide by three inches deep.

A specialized system of measuring and selling newspaper and advertising space, the Standard Advertising Unit system (SAU), was introduced on July 1, 1984. It has been endorsed by the Newspaper Advertising Bureau and the American Newspaper Publishers Association, and practically every daily newspaper in the United States accepts it.

Standard newspapers, called broadsheets, have printed pages 13 inches wide with a depth ranging from 21 inches to 22 1/2 inches. Each column is 2 1/16 inches wide. Measurement and billing of advertising are based on the standard column inch. *The New York Times* is an example of a broadsheet. Broadsheets are typically folded horizontally across the middle for easier handling while reading.

Newspapers with a smaller page size are called tabloids. A full tabloid page is usually 14 inches deep. The width varies from 9 3/8 inches (called a short cut-off) to 10 13/16 inches (a long cut-off). The *New York Daily News* is an example of a tabloid.

Most tabloids use a 5-column format with the same column width as broadsheets. The SAU chart, reproduced as Figure 7.1, depicts the Standard Advertising Units available on a single page. Table 7.1 shows column-inch equivalents and Standard Advertising Unit options for fractional parts of broadsheet and tabloid pages.

Figure 7.1. The Expanded SAU Standard Advertising Unit System.

Depth in Inches	1 COL 2.76	2 COL 4	3 COL 66.76	1 COL 2.6	5 COL 106.6	6 COL 13
FD	1×FD	2×FD	3×FD	4×FD	5×FD	6×FD
	1×18	2×18	3×18	4×18	5×18	6×18
	1×15.75	1×15.75	3×15.75	4×15.75	5×15.75	
	1×14	2×14	3×14	4×14	5×14	6×14
	1×13	2×13	3×13	4×13	5×13	
	1×10.5	2×10.5	3×10.5	4×10.5	5×10.5	6×10.5
	1×7	2×7	3×7	4×7	5×7	6×7
	1×5.25	2×5.25	3×5.25	4×5.25		
	1×3.5	2×3.5				
	1×3	2×3				
	1×2	2×2				
	1×1.5					
	1×1					

1 Column 2 1/16 Double truck 26 3/4

2 Columns 4 1/4 There are four suggested double truck sizes: 13×10.5, 13×14, 13×18, 13×FD. FD = full depth (21 inches).

3 Columns 6 7/6

4 Columns 8 5/8

5 Columns 10 13/16

6 columns 13

Table 7.1. Fractional pages: column-inch equivalents, with standard advertising unit options.

Broadsheet	Tabloid
Full page = 126 column inches 6×21 (full depth) Two-thirds page = 84 column inches 4×21 (full depth) 6×14	Full page = 70 column inches 5×14 Four-fifths page = 56 column inches 4×14
Half page = 63 column inches 3×21 (full depth) 4×15.75 6×10.5	Three-fifths page = 42 column inches 3×14 4×10.5
One-third page = 42 column inches 2×21 (full depth) 3×14 4×10.5 6×7	Half page = 35 column inches 5×7
Quarter page = 31.5 inches 2×15.75 3×10.5	Two-fifths page = 28 column inches 2×14 4×7
One-sixth page = 21 column inches 1×21 (full depth) 2×10.5 3×7 4×5.25	One-fifth page = 14 column inches 1×14 2×7 One-tenth page = 7 column inches 1×7 2×3.5

While magazines target audiences by industry or special interest, newspapers target geographically.

There are some national newspapers (*USA Today* is the largest), but the majority of newspapers are regional. For this reason, newspaper advertising is popular with retailers and service firms offering goods and services to local rather than national markets. In fact, most newspapers offer a lower advertising rate to local advertisers than to companies with out-of-town addresses. (Retail and mail order advertisers also get a lower rate.)

Newspaper ads cost less to produce.

Production costs for a full-page, four-color magazine ad can run as high as $11,000 or more if a professional advertising agency and photographer are employed. But most newspaper ads are copy with simple line art and can be produced much less expensively. Newspapers will even set your ad into type for you (called pubset) at no cost, if you desire.

"The daily newspaper is a unique advertising medium that readers value as a useful source for many kinds of information," notes the Newspaper Advertising Bureau. "The most common way of reading the paper is to start with the front page and go through the issue page by page, scanning it for articles and ads that look interesting. Readers know the difference between editorial content and advertising, but in practice they don't pay much attention to this distinction.

"Interest in newspaper ads is highly correlated with buying interest, with 87 percent of 'hot' prospects for a particular product being interested in ads dealing with that product. This close link between prospect status and interest in advertising may seem self-evident, but it does not necessarily hold for other media in which advertisers depend on novelty, humor, or celebrity presenters to attract the consumers' attention."

What types of ads get the highest readership in newspapers? According to the Newspaper Advertising Bureau, 58 percent of newspaper readers read supermarket ads, 57 percent read store ads for clothing, 50 percent turn to newspaper advertising to see what movies are playing, 43 percent look for jobs in the help wanted ads, and 31 percent scan the real estate classifieds.

There are 1,645 daily newspapers and 7,498 weekly newspapers published in the United States. The average circulation of these newspapers is 62.8 million for the dailies and 51.7 million for the weeklies.

Seventy-two percent read the Sunday paper. The typical daily newspaper reader spends an average of 44 minutes per day reading one or more newspapers. The average newspaper is made up of 60 percent ads and 40 percent articles.

My own sense of it is that, while still strong, newspaper readership is on the decline. Few of the people I know read a daily paper. A recent Roper poll shows that 69 percent of Americans prefer to get their news from TV versus only 37 percent from newspapers. The average American household watches 50 hours of TV a week. In 1980, 62.2 million newspapers were sold each day. In 1995, that figure had dropped to 59.3 million, a decline of 4.8 percent in 15 years. During the same period, the number of daily newspapers in America dropped from 1,743 to 1,548—a decline of 11 percent.

On the other hand, I suspect that more people are spending more time with the Sunday newspaper than ever before. A cover story in *Direct Marketing*, "The Cocooning of America," told of the phenomenon in which people are "cocooning or holing up at home with the spouse, kids, and trays of gourmet junk food to watch videotapes." My observations indicate there is much truth to this, and obviously staying home all day with the Sunday *Times* is part of it. But this is all personal opinion, and does not reflect research of the Newspaper Advertising Bureau. Daily newspapers are published in 1,526 U.S. cities. One hundred ten cities have two or more daily newspapers. Table 7.2 lists the 20 largest U.S. daily newspapers and their circulation (approximate).

Most important, newspaper advertising works. Results show that, on average, newspaper advertising triples sales volume for items advertised at cut prices and doubles sales for items advertised at regular prices.

Table 7.2. 20 largest U.S. daily newspapers.

Newspaper	Circulation
Wall Street Journal	1,852,863
USA Today	1,800,000
Los Angeles Times	1,242,864
New York Times	1,150,000
Washington Post	810,000
New York Daily News	754,043
Chicago Tribune	741,345
New York Post	644,738
Detroit Free Press	626,434
San Francisco Chronicle	559,527
Chicago Sun-Times	537,780
Boston Globe	516,981
Philadelphia Inquirer	515,523
Newsday	512,419
Newark Star-Ledger	485,362
Detroit News	481,766
Miami Herald	444,581
Houston Chronicle	439,574
Cleveland Plain Dealer	432,449
Denver Post	413,343

TYPES OF NEWSPAPERS

There are five basic types of newspapers you can advertise in.

Daily

Standard Rate & Data Service says that a paper must be issued at least four times a week to be considered a daily newspaper. Some dailies are published in the morning; others in the evening. Others have both a morning and an evening edition. According to retail advertising consultant Dana Cassell, morning papers are more business oriented, with more hard news. They tend to be bought at newsstands and read on the way to work or in the office. Evening editions are more family oriented, containing more human-interest features, which are read at leisure by parents as well as older children.

Sunday Editions

According to the American Newspaper Publishers Association, 820 U.S. papers have Sunday editions. Sunday editions reach people on a day when they have the most time for leisure reading.

Supermarket Tabloids

These are sold primarily at supermarket checkout counters and cater to a mass audience. They include the *Globe*, the *Star*, the *National Enquirer*, and the *National Examiner*. These papers are good media for mail order advertising. (Other good mail order papers include *Grit, Cappers Weekly, Moneysworth*, and the *Spotlight*.)

Weeklies

These include town, county, neighborhood, and other local and regional papers. Although most ads are from small local firms, these papers can also prove effective for national advertisers, especially those with regional branches. Also under this category are the penny savers and shoppers distributed free to local residents, plus religious and ethnic publications. Cassell reports that ads with coupons generate a much higher return in penny savers and other weeklies than in daily newspapers.

Sections

Daily newspapers are divided into sections and features that offer special benefits to advertisers. A section is an entire section of a paper devoted to a specific topic, such as business or lifestyle. A feature can be either a page, several pages within a section, or even a single regular column or article devoted to a specific topic. For example, the weekday editions of the *New York Times* have a book "page," which is actually a single book review surrounded by ads for books (occasionally there are other feature articles covering books). The *Times* also has an advertising "page" that centers around the advertising column.

The section or feature is to newspaper advertising what the special issue is to magazine advertising: an opportunity to run your ad in an editorially compatible environment, that is, surrounded by articles dealing with the same topic as the ads. The benefit is that readers turning to these sections or features are more likely to be interested in your proposition.

A 1987 survey of newspapers has enabled the Newspaper Advertising Bureau to supply a computerized list of newspapers that regularly carry a specific section or feature. A partial list of the topics these sections and features cover follows.

SECTIONS

- Business, Finance
- Entertainment
- Fashion
- Food
- Home
- Lifestyle, Women
- Science
- Sports
- TV, Radio
- Travel

FEATURES

- Advice on personal finance
- Astrology
- Beauty
- Best food buys
- Books
- Business, financial
- Career advice
- College
- Computers
- Diet, nutrition
- Fashion, men
- Fashion, women
- Fashion, teenage
- Games and puzzles
- Gardening
- Health and medical
- Home repair, building
- Home furnishings
- Movie timetable
- Music, records, tapes
- Op Ed page
- Outdoors: camping, etc.
- Personal advice
- Pets
- Physical fitness
- Real estate
- Recipes
- Religion
- Science
- Stamps, coins
- Theater
- Travel and resort
- Videotape reviews
- Wine

If you operate a local winery, it would pay to advertise your free wine tastings and winery tours in the food section or on the wine page rather than in the business, sports, or home furnishings sections. Another good place to feature your ad would be on a things-to-do page or local calendar of events.

THE BASICS OF NEWSPAPER ADVERTISING

An Interview with Eric Linker, Senior Vice President of Advertising, *The New York Times*

To get the full story on effective newspaper advertising, I turned to Eric Linker, who is Senior Vice President of Advertising for *The New York Times* and has been in newspaper advertising for 14 years.

Q: *What types of firms should consider newspaper advertising?*

A: There is probably no advertiser who should not at least consider newspaper advertising.

Retailers make up one big category. Another is advertising managers for a brand or product that has local retail support or distribution through retail outlets.

If you look at where newspapers get their advertising revenue, a high percentage is from retail outlets, specialty stores, department stores, chains, supermarkets, and convenience stores. The second-biggest source is classified advertising: recruitment, help wanted, real estate, automotive, merchandise, business opportunities, auctions. Those are all classified areas. The lowest percentage of advertising revenues, and The New York Times *is an exception here, is revenues from national advertising: liquor, tobacco, airlines, financial services, amusement, entertainment.*

Corporate advertising companies trying to reach specific constituencies or to persuade or give a point of view on their company's direction or product mix are key sources of revenue for The New York Times, *the* Wall Street Journal, *and other influential and important media. And there are other types of corporate or image newspaper advertising: cause and appeal; opinion; associations or organizations voicing an opinion on public issues. Mobil invented "advocacy advertising" and has been running for 17 years on* The New York Times *Op Ed page every Thursday.*

Q: *Is there any type of firm that should not advertise in newspapers?*

A: From a brand standpoint, many soft drink people and beer advertisers are not predisposed to newspapers. Packaged goods advertisers (i.e., national food products) use newspapers selectively. We are not a big part of the media mix for them. And when they use newspapers, it's for sales promotion inserts and coupons rather than brand advertising.

Q: *How should the ad manager plan newspaper advertising and what are the specific advantages newspapers offer over other media?*

A: If you are the client, the first thing you want to do is look at objectives. If you work with an agency, you set the direction, and the agency comes to agreement. You need to determine what the compe-

tition is doing, the demographics of target markets, your trading or geographic zone, and how much you are willing to spend.

Once these questions are answered, then you must say, "How can I best communicate this message?" Look at the values of each of the media. In newspapers, immediacy, impact, local audience, ability to distribute by town, zip code, or county, and short lead time are the major advantages. Also, newspapers have an upscaleness to them. The audience has a better education and income than, say, TV viewers.

Once you have made a decision to use newspapers, now determine the type of ad you will run: Display or classified? Will you use a coupon? Graphics? Photography? What size will the ad be? What day of the week will the ad run? How often? Which months? Is your business seasonal? Will ads be tied into announcements of specific product sales or new product announcements? Will newspaper advertising support other media?

Another key issue is position. The position you get is somewhat dependent on frequency and volume—how much you spend. The paper will be more flexible about where you run if you are a bigger advertiser. Once position is determined, other key factors are frequency, size, and days of the week.

Q: How is newspaper space sold?

A: Newspaper advertising is generally sold on a column-inch basis. We also have Standard Advertising Units of various sizes defined by the Newspaper Advertising Bureau.

Q: How do you determine the cost of advertising?

A: By rate cards. You can buy space contracts based on frequency, size, and number of pages run. The more lines or inches or pages you run in a year, the greater your volume discount.

Make sure you understand what rates are available and get the best possible discount available based on the investment you will make. All rates are published. The New York Times has 14 rate cards for different advertiser categories: retail, beverage, tobacco, transportation, national food advertisers. Within a given category, each advertiser gets the same rate. Discounts are based on annual spending. This enables us to offer advertisers an incentive to invest more in advertising.

Q: What is the difference between a volume discount and a frequency discount?

A: Volume is based on number of pages; frequency is based on how often you run. Volume and frequency discounts can be mixed. They might even be interchangeable.

Q: What happens if you don't run as many ads as you contracted for?

A: An advertising contract with a newspaper is not a legal contract in the strict sense of being forced to hold to it. If you do not run that lineage, we just bill you at the higher rate.

Q: What happens if you spend more on advertising than contracted for?

A: Within the calendar year, we change the contract to get you the appropriate rate and the highest discount possible.

Q: How does an advertiser determine which section of the paper to advertise in?

A: We get hundreds of ads every day. Positioning of these individual ads is based on the size of the paper, the type of ads we run, and the requests we get. If you never used our paper before, the sales rep takes you through its makeup. In most cases, retailers run in the front of the first section of the paper.

Then, based on how many advertising units or inches you might run per day, there are theme sections offering opportunities within their pages. Positioning is really predicated on the type of advertiser, how much you run, and the type of news hole we have. News is made up around ads.

If you don't have a major budget, the key is: Where in the newspaper can an ad the size you are going to run get the highest amount of exposure? The sales rep can help. Frequency dictates level of exposure: the more you run, the better your opportunities for good positions. Premium positions can be bought by paying more; for example, top, outside, or even a designated page can be bought as long as it is not already taken up by a major full-page advertiser.

Q: Is it better to be near the front of a particular section, in the middle, or toward the back?

A: Newspapers do readership studies on how their particular papers are read, and it is almost common sense that folks who look through a paper will at least notice most pages. There is a high level of readership on national and local news. But if you are interested in business, advertise in the business section. Overall, you run in the main news section.

Many times, an up-front position does have a better chance for better readership. But if an ad is not creative and does not hold attention, someone with a strategic position and solid creativity could get a better response and readership score.

Q: Is there a position on the page that is best?

A: Premium positions are the top of the page and the outer edge of the page. When people do not have big budgets, they buy these posi-

tions and end up with greater exposure. It translates into better response rates.

Q: How do you get the best position?

A: *Sales reps can help here. They understand the marketplace of the newspaper, what positions are most appropriate, what is available. Smaller advertisers must judiciously use their space and positions.*

Q: How do you determine what size ad to use?

A: *What kind of reach and frequency do you want? It depends on your creative approach. If you feel you need a dominant halftone, strong headline, and intrusive copy, then I think it dictates a certain size. I've seen people use one word or no words on a page. Yet I've seen a whole page of type. There are as many techniques as there are pages in the newspaper.*

Thousands of ads run daily. If you think about all those transactions, and that a person in Long Island put a four-line classified ad in a one-hundred-plus page real estate section and sold a home from that ad, you realize it's pretty remarkable. People who read papers preselect their reading. It is targeted, and newspapers are a utilitarian product. People read based on their needs.

Now, if you are a store or brand manager, your objectives differ from those of the home seller running a classified. You are doing business every week, every day of the week. Your needs are different. So creativity and merchandise and prices and image become important.

Q: What's the best frequency for newspaper advertising? Daily? Twice a week? Weekly?

A: *Frequency is based on budget. If you have a store, and your budget is finite, and you do the most business on weekends, then advertise on Wednesday or Thursday in the living and home sections. This catches your customers as they are planning for the weekend. But newspapers are read five days a week. And some smart marketers use other days effectively.*

Q: Which is more important—frequency or size?

A: *Size is sometimes more important, based on the message. I think there is a minimum size, and it depends on how tight your objectives are and what you want your ads to deliver, not only to consumers but to other audiences as well.*

Q: For how long can an ad run before the response rate drops off and the advertiser must change it or run a completely new ad?

A: *Those with the least patience are the people who create. Some consumer ad campaigns—the Prudential Rock, the Marlboro Man— have been with us for years. When to change your ad? It depends on the desired freshness of creative approach, which is based on your own sales cycle or product development cycle.*

If you are a retailer, you want to move merchandise, so you run ads every day of the week to move product out of the store. If you are an image advertiser, you run the same ad in the same position to give people more information about your store or product. Most retailers change their ads every week based on merchandise and pricing.

Q: How do I know whether I should be running in the Sunday edition or during the week?

A: In many markets, Sunday is still the primary day, the one day of tranquillity. In dual-income households, Sunday is the one day that people are together and can make buying decisions. Also, it's a day when more attention can be given to the newspaper. Many newspapers offer Sunday sections that are actually delivered in advance, on Saturday or even Friday. Sunday can be a primary advertising day for retailers who can come back with a few ads during the week to carry them through a cycle of seven days.

Q: Are some months better than others in terms of when to run newspaper ads?

A: The Newspaper Advertising Bureau has done an analysis on merchandise sales cycles. White sales sell better in January. Furs and swimsuits are also seasonal. But seasonal trends change. Some products that were once seasonal are now sold by people all the time.

Q: Does adding a second color enhance the effectiveness of an ad?

A: Most research indicates that when color is introduced into an ad, the readership of the ad is enhanced. Color becomes a benefit.

Q: Do you prefer to pubset or have the advertiser send in a camera-ready mechanical?

A: The New York Times encourages camera-ready art. Many other papers pubset [i.e., set the advertiser's copy into type]. We do a degree of that, but most material is camera ready.

Q: Should advertisers advertise only in the large local daily, or should weeklies, shoppers, and penny savers also be part of the program?

A: I think that, based on budget or reach, the first thing to consider in running your ad is the editorial environment. How does it rub off on advertising? If you want just a quick hit for a limited number of people, smaller weeklies and shoppers may suffice.

But if you need credibility and have the money, associate yourself with a well-written product where the news is gathered on a daily basis. Most major daily advertisers look to the more sophisticated papers. But at the same time, there is no denying the market trend toward highly segmented papers that reach individual counties or towns, or even certain streets within a city. Advertisers today want to know what specific households the paper is going to and learn as much about each person in each household as possible.

The majority of newspaper dollars today are spent with major market papers, even though smaller regionals and weeklies represent a strong alternative. In response to this competition, most major papers are looking to become more user friendly, with relevant editorial content to help busy people and more emphasis on news features as well as hard news.

For the intelligent individual looking for analysis and points of view, there is no substitute for newspapers. The time spent reading a quality paper versus a shopping sheet or penny saver is an advantage we offer. Yet there is no denying that these weeklies and shoppers proliferate and offer segmentation that advertisers are looking for.

Q: Do you do P.I. [per inquiry] deals or sell remnant space [unpurchased ad space] at a discount?

A: We have standby space. It is what the name indicates: The ad is put on standby and inserted when the space becomes available.

We don't offer it on a regular basis, and we insert standby ads only as needed to make up sections or balance them out. They must fit specific size requirements. And the advertiser has no control of timing, which destroys the advantage of immediacy. Standby space at The New York Times *is available for 30 to 50 percent off our regular published rates.*

Q: What is your policy for make-goods [free rerun of an ad if the quality of reproduction is poor or some other mistake is made]?

A: Each paper has its own policies. It's really a customer service issue that's difficult to standardize. With a metro paper running 70,000 copies an hour on high-speed presses, sometimes the tints or reproductions are not going to be as good as in a magazine, which is on a higher-gloss paper and prints using a different printing process. When an ad is questioned, we evaluate the damage and determine what type of credit is indicated.

Q: What about cooperative advertising in which manufacturers pay for a portion of the retailer's ad if the retailer features the manufacturer's product? Is the newspaper itself an active participant or is that all done between the manufacturer and the retailer?

A: Co-op advertising is a multibillion dollar business and a way in which manufacturers can move product by having multiple distributors contribute to the advertising. It is also a way for retailers to garner dollars from their manufacturer based on amount of units purchased.

Most major newspapers have specific structures to deal with co-op advertising. I would suggest finding out who the co-op manager is at your newspaper. He or she can help bring together more dollars from the manufacturer by uncovering opportunities for the retailer.

Q: What elements make for an effective newspaper ad?

A: There are some basics: a strong headline or an arresting art display that leads people to want to read it; strong copy; intrusive artwork. The best copywriters in the world are retail copywriters.

Q: Does it help to have an ad agency in terms of getting better quality ads or saving money on space?

A: Whether you use an agency depends on your needs, your budget, and whether you require all the services an agency provides. When you choose an agency, work with one that shares your outlook and philosophy on advertising.

Q: Do you give the 15 percent agency discount on space to advertisers who place their own ads through in-house ad agencies? If so, what qualifies an in-house ad department as an official agency?

A: Agencies get the 15 percent commission. You don't get the commission if you are an advertiser. An in-house agency must have more than one account or we don't give them an agency discount.

Q: If I want my ad to run on Wednesday, when must I get it to the paper?

A: By Tuesday afternoon. Twenty-four hours is standard lead time.

Q: What are some of the most common mistakes you see advertisers make?

A: Advertisers do not spend enough time analyzing how they should be using newspapers to best advantage, not enough time planning. Also, advertisers do not use enough frequency to build a brand or image or develop responses.

Pay close attention to creativity. You need good creativity to sell your product and present to the reader what your product really represents. That is a real trick.

Q: How are newspapers changing the way they work with advertisers?

A: Primarily by focusing more on marketing. Newspapers will now work with you to design marketing plans. More newspapers are doing it more and more, developing partnerships with advertisers to help them plan their strategic positions, frequency, and media schedules. This goes way beyond the traditional role of just selling an ad.

Advertisers are also using newspapers as information sources on markets, customers, product purchasing habits, advertising performance, trends, techniques, consumer behavior, and so on. the Newspaper Advertising Bureau and the American Newspaper Publishers Association can also be helpful in this regard.

Computers are also revolutionizing advertising in many ways, with such advances as computer makeup and composition of newspaper pages and desktop publishing. Two interesting developments are the Ad Sat system for transmitting photo-engraved artwork via satellite and remote entry computer systems for classifieds.

INCREASING THE RESPONSE TO YOUR NEWSPAPER ADS

What kind of response do you want your ads to produce? Some advertisers want direct mail order and telephone sales of their product. Others want to induce the consumer to come to their places of business, such as a retailer who uses advertising to increase store traffic.

Whatever you are selling and however you are selling it, you probably want some kind of immediate, measurable response. Mike Pavlish, one of the top copywriters in the United States, offers the following tips for improving your advertising response rate:

1. Make a low-priced sample or trial offer. The less it costs the buyer, the better your response rate. For example, test a 3-month subscription at $30 against a 12-month subscription at $120.
2. Offer a no-risk money-back guarantee. Make it good for at least 30 days. Feature the guarantee prominently in your ad.
3. Offer a bill-me-later option.
4. Accept Visa and MasterCard.
5. Don't state that you wait for checks to clear.
6. Include a toll-free order number.
7. Offer a free bonus or two with the order. Give it a price for high value perception.
8. Offer a free trial.
9. Make your price sound like a bargain. Compare it to something else to show the true value. For example: "For the price of a night on the town that lasts only one night, you'll have a self-motivating tool that'll increase your income for a lifetime."
10. Test various offer presentations. For example, test "buy one, get one free" against "50 percent off."
11. Make your offer good for a limited time only. State a specific time limit or deadline date in the copy.
12. Write your headline to state your biggest customer benefit.
13. Use a benefit-loaded subhead under the main headline.

14. Get the word "Free" into your headline or subhead.

15. Offer something for free—either a free gift with purchase or a free booklet or brochure with inquiry.

16. Say "No salesperson will visit you" or "No salesperson will call you," if one won't.

17. Use a coupon.

18. Don't talk about your company unless a customer benefit is in the same sentence.

19. Indent each paragraph three to five spaces for easier reading. This subconsciously gets the reader into the paragraph, which is what you want to do.

20. Improve your guarantee. The less risk your customers perceive they are taking, the higher your response rate.

21. Make a better, hard-to-resist offer.

22. Test different media. Key your ads so you know which publication did best.

23. Put yourself in the reader's shoes. What benefit would you want the most? Stress that in your copy forcefully.

24. Include specific testimonials.

25. Leave plenty of white space around all your advertising. This eliminates the cluttered, cramped, hard-to-read look.

26. Have your headline set in big, bold type. The more the headline jumps out at readers with a big benefit they want, the easier the advertising will appear to read. As a rule of thumb, your headline can take up to one-fourth of the space in the ad.

27. Keep sentences and paragraphs short. As a rule, no paragraph should be more than five lines. No sentence should be more than 20 words. You should also use an occasional very short paragraph. This will break up the monotony of all paragraphs being the same size.

28. Underline, capitalize, or italicize a few key words or statements. The key is not to overdo it, but to make the advertising look more exciting and easy to read. It also emphasizes the particular word or phrase being underlined.

29. List benefits using bullets, check marks, asterisks, or numbers. It makes the ad look much easier to read.

30. Use subheads. Using subheads is a very effective method for making advertising easier to read. They also allow you to make an easy transition from one selling point to another.

HOW TO MEASURE RESPONSE

Newspaper advertising (all advertising, for that matter) elicits only two types of response: qualitative and quantitative. Qualitative responses are more difficult to measure. They represent the shaping of attitudes in the marketplace; how people feel about your business, your store, your professional services. Quantitative responses are easier to measure. They represent the number of coupons returned, the number of sales rung up, the number of new patients brought in.

Many advertisers believe the latter is more important than the former. In truth, both types of response contribute to the success of any advertising program. But for planning purposes, it is more reasonable to characterize qualitative responses as part of your strategic efforts, and quantitative responses as your tactical methods.

There are two elements to consider in measuring responses. First is the accumulation of data, and second is the interpretation of that data—the translation of raw information into useful, practical information that gives you sales figures and helps you formulate future plans and direction.

The accumulation procedures will depend primarily on the nature of your enterprise and on what style of advertising you utilize. For our purposes, there are only five kinds of newspaper advertising. These are:

1. the single- or multiproduct ad,
2. the single- or multiservice ad,
3. the direct-selling ad,
4. the announcement ad, and
5. the image-building ad.

Of these, only the first three provide a clear-cut foundation for gathering quantitative responses. The remaining two are more likely to evoke qualitative responses. To complicate matters, some ads may be more accurately described as a combination of two or more ad types. It is helpful at the outset, therefore, to know precisely why you are advertising and what types of response you wish to achieve, and then choose the simplest ad type to reach your tactical objective.

Strategically, you may wish to measure all advertising on a broad calendar front; that is, set aside a quarterly (or annual) advertising budget, and not be overly concerned about each insertion's success quotient. Some advertisers adopt this procedure to eliminate the day-to-day problems of data gathering, interpretation, and cost accounting. But since all responses are valueless without comparative data, a manager may find himself or herself looking only at last year's figures to see if this year's sales are any better.

For small-space advertisers (with comparatively small budgets), it's best to conduct quantitative research on a per-ad or per-campaign basis. The management value behind this more detailed undertaking warrants the effort. It enables you to see if an ad has paid for itself. It gives you an accurate historical record so that you can repeat a successful ad next week or next year to see if you can achieve the same results (with little more invested in production). Finally, it gives you some minimal data on ad positioning and how it may or may not have affected response. (This information may help you in persuading your newspaper to respond more favorably to your specific position requests.)

The size of some enterprises may make it logistically impractical to secure detailed sales response figures (although many chain operations have installed sophisticated reporting devices that can give managers nearly hour-by-hour results). Multimedia promotions for the same products or services make it nearly impossible to determine which medium was responsible for which sales. (You can alter your record keeping accordingly, if you wish, to include gross media costs.)

The performance system suggested here, then, is primarily for measuring specific responses to a specific newspaper ad. It's a single-medium system. The system assigns a share of your space costs to corporate advertising, i.e., the pure value of promoting your enterprise, or getting your name out in front of the public. We must presume that this investment in general exposure will boost total annual sales, including sales of products or services not advertised.

Note: Some managers make it a practice to record mark-downs as advertising expenses. This may be done to satisfy some weird accounting procedure; we're interested primarily in whether or not the ad paid for itself. Mark-downs will simply reduce the gross return on investment. But managers hope, of course, that the increase in volume that results from this price-cutting tactic will more than offset the reductions, or at least speed up the return.

Inherent in the system are three parts:

Part I: The collection of response data

This will depend on your own operations. In some circumstances, the cash register will record the information needed; in other situations, copies of sales slips will have to be examined. For smaller operations, a clipboard at the sales counter that holds a report form can be used, or a pad of colored paper ballots with a shoe box ballot holder can be installed. The amount and type of data collected will vary.

For example, in addition to sales figures, you may want to learn additional facts. Although this system attributes all sales to advertising effectiveness (and correctly so), you may want to know which customers are new. Building new business is the only way to offset normal attrition, replacing customers lost through moves, deaths, and other unhappy reasons, and it's the only sure way to increase gross sales. You will also want to know the value of collateral sales. These should be reported and included in the payback calculations. Because of the brief shelf life of newspapers, sales figures should be assessed no more than 72 hours after an ad runs; this term can be shortened, of course, to coincide with the published end date of a particular sale. In all instances, staff cooperation is imperative. Employees should understand why they are collecting this information—that it will help management to establish valid, more cost-effective advertising and marketing policies and thus increase total sales. A healthy company is a good company to work for.

Part 2: The collection of advertising data

You will need to know 1) the cost of advertising space, 2) the cost of advertising production, and 3) any rebates due to co-op advertising contributions or newspaper credits. (These are dollar value figures.) But in addition, you will want to record for later interpretation 1) the position of your ad within the newspaper, 2) weather conditions on the day the ad ran and for the two days following, and 3) any extenuating circumstances, such as staff out sick, running out of the advertised item, etc.

The formula for determining advertising investment is:

Cost of Ad Space + Production Costs – 15% for Corporate
Advertising – Any Co-op Credits = $ Total Investment

Part 3: Information storage and evaluation

By totaling up gross profits from the sale of the advertised item, and any collateral sales too, and subtracting the cost of the space and production, minus 15 percent for Corporate Advertising value, and minus any co-op funds or credits, you should have a fair idea of the return on your investment.

A good ROI is 20 percent. Few retailers achieve that level consistently. There are special instances when you may show far more than that amount. Averaging a 15 percent ROI across the year is good business. Keep in mind that a good advertising campaign will give you collateral benefits that are not easily measurable: for example, new customers attracted to the operation who may continue to be patrons even for unadvertised goods or services; improving your commercial standing or presence in the community; fortifying your position vis-à-vis your competition; and building credibility for subsequent advertising. Because these additional benefits are difficult to measure, yet undeniably result in increased sales, some value has to be assigned to them. We group these peripheral factors under the heading of Corporate Advertising, and assume that at least 15 percent of any insertion can be charged off to this effort.

Collect at least two copies of each insertion. One ad gets cut out of its page and placed in a scrapbook with response and evaluation data attached. The other ad is filed intact (the whole page) so you can refer to it later if you need to argue with the paper for better position, or to more accurately compare the returns from the same ad, run at different times of the year, with substantially different sales results. If you run the same ad three times in a row (either daily or on alternate days) you need mount only one insertion in the scrapbook, indicating all three insertion dates. But keep full tearsheets of all the ads in your file for possible future reference.

To summarize, the formula for gathering sales data is:

(No. of Units Sold Each Day for 3 Days × Gross Profit Earned on Each
Unit) + Gross Profit Earned on Collateral Sales = $ Gross Profit

Subtract one total from the other (hopefully Sales from Investment) to determine return on investment, or ROI. Express the difference as a percentage of the investment. Example: If gross profits equal $2,000 and the investment equals $1,500, then the ROI is $500, or 30 percent. By using the decimal system as the common denominator for expressing sales results, you will have a more practical formula for comparing results between different campaigns.

This formula, with appropriate modifications, can be used to measure the advertising responses for single- and multiproduct ads, single- and multiservice ads, and direct-sell ads. Of these, the direct-sell ad (taking orders for a specific item or items by mail or by phone) is obviously the easiest to measure.

As a rule of thumb, however (because you eliminate the possibility of accumulating collateral sales benefits), a higher profit margin is recommended for items sold through the mail. Most direct selling entrepreneurs use a 100 to 300 percent markup formula; for example, an item that costs $20 should be sold for $40 to $60 to help ensure a reasonable ROI. In those instances when there is no retail establishment, do not deduct the 15 percent allowance for Corporate Advertising. Direct selling must be its own sole support. Remember also to include any costs for shipping if the item sold is postpaid.

This measurement system forces management to take a hard look at profitability, particularly where services are sold. Generally, services are a product of time. If it costs the company 2 person hours to clean and check a furnace @ $20 per hour, and the service is advertised for $60, the gross profit is $60 minus $40, or $20. The question is, how many of those service calls, at a gross profit of $20 each, will have to be sold to make the ad pay for itself? If, however, you're trying to open the door to annual fuel oil deliveries at the same time, then that becomes your collateral sale.

Obviously, the 72-hour measuring term must be abandoned in this case, so you can include the anticipated seasonal gross from the collateral sale. This figure could easily surpass the service sale, and should enter into the decision-making analysis when establishing your annual advertising budget.

Some service costs or profits are not so easily calculated. In the banking industry, for example, although bankers are prone to call their services "products" (checking accounts, savings certificates, etc.), chances are the customer does not perceive them this way. The customer wants a checking account service; the financial institution, utilizing historical data, must determine how much is in the average checking account balance and how much gross profit the institution can expect to derive from that balance within a 12-month period.

In this case, the profit yield cannot be measured in 72 hours (although the number of sales can). There remains the possibility of cross-selling new or existing customers into collateral services. (This effort has become so important to larger institutions that they have installed software systems that profile each customer, listing the services, balances, etc. that accrue during each customer's tenure.)

(Number of Checking Accounts Opened Each Day for 3 Days × the
Anticipated Gross Profit from Each Account) + Any Anticipated Gross
Profits from Collateral Sales = $ Gross Profit

The formula for determining advertising costs, however, would be
unchanged, except that there would be little opportunity for any supplier
co-op funds:

Cost of Ad Space + Production Costs – 15% for
Corporate Advertising = Cost of Advertising

This assumes profits that may never materialize. That may discourage some financial advertisers, but our intent here is threefold: 1) to
somehow get a handle on the effectiveness of small-space newspaper
advertising as a marketing tool, 2) to sensitize financial marketers to the
disparity in profit potential inherent in different financial services, and 3)
to reconfirm the importance of cross-selling services to both new and existing customers. Indeed, each customer should become a profit center;
nobody's going to get rich just renting safety deposit boxes.

Two types of ads—announcement ads and image ads—are far more
difficult to measure quantitatively. Although these types of newspaper
advertising are not designed to get an immediate return on investment,
they should become a part of each advertiser's campaign budget.

As with financial advertising, medical services require cost-account-
ing methods, too, to determine the potential annual value for each new
patient subscriber. Thus, on the average, if each new patient can be expected to yield $200 in gross profit within a 12-month period, then it is that fig-
ure that is used for calculating ROI.

One way to insure at least a partial, immediate ROI is to combine
an announcement or image ad with product or service sales. In this
instance, the 15 percent ratio set aside for Corporate Advertising would be
increased proportionately. Thus, if half the ad space were devoted to an
announcement of new walk-in clinic hours, for example, then 65 percent of
the cost (50 percent plus the existing 15 percent) should be subtracted
from the space and production costs for calculating the ROI.

Physicians may want to adopt two sets of gross profit ratings, one
for individual patients, male and female, and another for families. This
data can be refined even further by age (statistically, a married woman of
childbearing age may be worth more to a clinic in the next 12 months than
a single, 20-year-old male).

In any case, patient retention is imperative. Natural attrition will
account for 10 to 20 percent patient loss in any year, depending in part on
the characteristic mobility of community residents. Acquiring new patients
(as in any business or practice) is good for the financial health of the clinic or medical office.

One more word about image advertising: My own inclination is to
abstain from running direct product or service promotions in combination
with an image program. If you've committed your enterprise to an image
newspaper campaign, chalk the whole expense up to Corporate Advertising.

Then, if you can, put your ear to the ground and your nose to the grindstone and your finger on the pulse of the market. In that position you may be able to elicit some qualitative feedback to help justify the expense.

Naturally, you will have some objective in mind before undertaking an image campaign (improved awareness levels, change in management or customer policies, etc.). Your curiosity may require benchmark surveys, taken before and after the campaign, to determine if you have successfully altered any attitudes in the marketplace. You may discover that, with clever direction, you can accomplish the same attitude changes with product or service advertising and thus reap the benefits of direct sales, too.

CHECKLIST FOR NEWSPAPER ADVERTISING

- ❏ *Merchandise.* Does the ad offer merchandise having wide appeal, special features, price appeal, and timeliness?

- ❏ *Medium.* Is a newspaper the best medium for the ad, or would another medium such as direct mail, radio, or television be more appropriate?

- ❏ *Location.* Is the ad situated in the best spot in the paper (in both section and page location)?

- ❏ *Size.* Is the ad large enough to do the job expected of it? Does it omit important details, or is it overcrowded with nonessential information?

- ❏ *Headline.* Does the headline express the major single idea about the merchandise advertised? The headline should be an informative statement, not simply a label. Example: "Sturdy shoes for active boys, specially priced at $12.95" is better than "Boys' shoes, $12.95."

- ❏ *Illustration.* Does the illustration (if one is used) express the idea the headline conveys?

- ❏ *Merchandise Information.* Does the copy give the basic facts about the goods, or does it leave out information that would be important to the reader?

- ❏ *Layout.* Does the arrangement of the parts of the ad and the use of white space make the ad easy to read? Does it stimulate the reader to look at all the contents of the ad?

- ❏ *Human Interest.* Does the ad appeal to the customers' wants and wishes through illustration, headline, and copy?

- ❏ *"You" Attitude.* Is the ad written and presented from the customer's point of view and with the customer's interests clearly in mind, or from the advertiser's viewpoint?

- ❏ *Believability.* To the objective, nonpartisan reader, does the ad ring true, or does it perhaps sound exaggerated or somewhat phony?

- ❏ *Typeface.* Does the ad use a distinctive typeface, different from those of competitors?

❑ *Spur to Action.* Does the ad stimulate prompt action through devices such as use of a coupon, statement of limited quantities, or announcement of a specific time period for the promotion or impending event?

❑ *Sponsor Identification.* Does the ad use a specially prepared signature cut that is always associated with the store and that identifies it at a glance? Also, does it always include the following institutional details: store location, hours open, telephone number, location of advertising goods, and whether phone and mail orders are accepted?

RESOURCES

* For a more detailed discussion of newspaper advertising, read *How to Create Small Space Newspaper Advertising That Works*, by Ken Eichenbaum. For sales information, write to Unicorn Publishing Group, 4100 W. River Lane, Milwaukee, WI 53209, or telephone 414-354-5440.

* The Newspaper Advertising Bureau is a valuable resource for information on newspaper advertising and publishing, offering numerous books, seminars, slide presentations, newsletters, booklets, and special reports. For a free copy of their catalog, write: Newspaper Advertising Bureau, Inc., 1180 Avenue of the Americas, New York, NY 10036; or phone: 212-921-5080.

* Another good information resource for advertisers is the American Newspaper Publishers Association, Box 17407 Dulles Airport, Washington, D.C. 20041, 703-648-1000. Ask for *Facts about Newspapers* and a free publications list.

GLOSSARY OF COMMON NEWSPAPER TERMS

AD/SAT. The Satellite Network for Advertising Delivery provides high-resolution facsimile transmission of newspaper advertising, by satellite, in minutes.

Broadsheet. A standard or large-size newspaper. In July 1984, most broadsheet dailies adopted a uniform, 13-inch printed page width and a full depth of from 21 inches to 22 1/2 inches.

City zone. The corporate city limit, plus adjoining areas in cases of heavily populated areas, as designated by the Audit Bureau of Circulation (ABC).

Color scanner. Electronic equipment that automatically produces separations for ROP process (or full) color.

Column inch. Space measurement one column wide and one inch deep.

Double truck. Two facing pages used for a single unbroken advertisement. Also called a two-page spread.

Facsimile transmission. The electronic transmission of a page image (usually to printing plants at other sites).

Front-end system. A total computer system for text entry, editing, formatting, and billing, for editorial, display advertising, and classified advertising.

Pagination system. A computerized makeup system for composing whole pages of type, line art, and halftones.

Penetration. For a given newspaper within a specified area, the ratio of circulation to households; the newspaper equivalent of a household rating in broadcast.

ROP (Run-of-Paper). ROP is a term generally applied to ads that appear on a newspaper page (as distinguished from inserts or preprints).

Scotch double truck. A single unbroken advertisement on two facing pages bordered by one full column of editorial content on each of its vertical sides and by shallow columns of editorial across the top.

Tabloid. A newspaper with a smaller page size than a broadsheet. A full tabloid page is usually 14 inches deep. The width varies from 9 3/8 inches (short cut-off) to 10 13/16 inches (long cut-off).

Chapter

$EVALUATING$ AND $BUYING$ $MEDIA$

8

MAKING MEDIA DECISIONS

At this point, you have probably made some decision as to whether you will use print advertising and, if so, what percentage of your budget will be allocated to space advertising, what products will be advertised, and how frequently you will run your ads.

The next tasks are to evaluate and select the specific publications where your ads will run and to plan an exact schedule of the dates your ads will run.

Two concepts that are important in evaluating various media opportunities are cost per thousand analysis and frequency–reach balance. These concepts help establish a price–value relationship between media and opportunities.

COST PER THOUSAND

When media opportunities are compared, it is often confusing to determine which one offers the best value. For example, suppose an advertiser is considering two newspapers to carry advertising. Both newspapers cover the market, but they have different costs and circulations, as is shown in Table 8.1.

Table 8.1. Comparison of advertising expense in two newspapers.

Newspaper	Cost of Ad	Circulation
Newspaper A	$100	25,000
Newspaper B	$200	60,000

Which paper offers the best deal? At first glance, you might say Newspaper A, because the ad costs half as much as Newspaper B. But wait a minute. Newspaper B has 35,000 more readers. How do you balance cost with readership? The answer is to compare the two media on a cost per thousand basis, abbreviated as CPM. Simply stated, cost per thousand is the unit of price of media. It is the cost of advertising (in dollars) that the advertiser pays per one thousand individuals reached by the medium.

Cost per thousand is calculated using this formula:

$$CPM = \frac{Cost\ of\ Media}{Circulation\ of\ Media} \times 1000$$

To solve the example problem:

CPM for A = 100/25,000 X 1,000 = $4.00
CPM for B = 200/60,000 X 1,000 = $3.33

When you advertise in Newspaper B, you pay only $3.33 to reach 1,000 readers as opposed to $4.00 to reach 1,000 readers in Newspaper A. Moreover, Newspaper B reaches a greater audience. From this perspective, Newspaper B is the better media buy.

Cost per thousand analysis helps to provide a common comparison point for evaluating media vehicles, regardless of the size of the vehicle or its cost. Although cost per thousand analysis provides a comparison of the cost and relative audience of media vehicles, it does not evaluate the effectiveness of the vehicles. Also, it can be misleading to presume the most cost-efficient media will be the one that is best read or that generates the most response.

For this reason, caution is suggested in comparing different media vehicles strictly on a cost per thousand basis. The best use of cost per thousand analysis is to compare similar media vehicles (e.g., two local newspapers) as opposed to completely different media vehicles (e.g., radio station WXYR against daily newspaper the *Podunk Courier*).

Tip: When calculating cost per thousand, be sure to divide the cost of the media by the circulation of the medium rather than the readership. Circulation is the actual number of copies distributed. But most media sales reps quote a readership figure, which is the circulation (number of copies) multiplied by the number of people reading each copy—the "pass along" factor (so named because the primary subscriber passes a copy of the magazine or newspaper along to others in the household or office).

While circulation figures for most publications are scrupulously audited by independent auditing organizations, pass-along figures are frequently subject to exaggerated claims. Therefore, readership figures can be misleading and overstated. Circulation figures are more likely to be accurate, and all CPM calculations should be based on circulation.

REACH AND FREQUENCY

When comparing advertising programs it is important to select the most effective balance of reach and frequency. Reach and frequency are two terms used to describe the overall delivery of an advertising program. Reach is the number of individuals exposed to at least one advertising message over a period of time. If a media plan covers four out of five people in the target market, it has a reach of 80 percent (4 divided by 5). The formula for calculating reach is:

$$\text{Reach} = \frac{\text{Number of People Exposed to Advertising}}{\text{Total Number of People in Target Market}} \times 100$$

Frequency is the average number of times an individual is exposed to a message. If four people see six of your messages, the frequency is 1.5 (6 divided by 4). The formula for calculating frequency is:

$$\text{Frequency} = \frac{\text{Number of Times Message Is Repeated}}{\text{Number of People Seeing Your Message}}$$

Although they are separate concepts, frequency and reach are interrelated. Consider this hypothetical situation as an example. An advertiser who uses magazines for an advertising program has two options:

1. Run the ad one time in five different magazines.
2. Run the ad five times in one magazine.

Assuming both options have the same cost, it's easy to see that option 1 emphasizes reach while option 2 emphasizes frequency.

A major cause of failure in advertising programs is insufficient frequency. It is far more effective to reduce the reach of an advertising campaign, that is, to narrow the target audience and add frequency, than to reduce frequency and add reach.

Example: Let's say you are a leasing company. Your business is to buy and lease large capital equipment to businesses that want to expand their operations but don't want to tie up capital by buying equipment outright. Leasing enables them to get the machinery they need without a large capital expenditure.

Assume that your geographic market is confined to your home state, that there are 100,000 potential prospects for your service, and that you have a promotion budget of $50,000. This might, if you count your pennies carefully, allow you to do one mailing to all the potential buyers. If they happen not to need leasing that day, they'll ignore you. They may hesitate to do business with you because they haven't heard of you. Your campaign bombs because you've gone for reach (quantity) instead of frequency (quality).

The solution? Target a specific industry, for example, plastics manufacturers that need expensive extruders and injection molding machines. You discover that there are 1,000 plastics manufacturers in your state. Now your $50,000 allows you to use a mix of direct mail, telephone follow-up, print advertising, and trade show promotion to get your message to these folks on a monthly basis. Not only that, but the message can be more tailored to their needs (e.g., copy can talk about providing "injection molders and extruders," not just the vague term, "equipment").

The result? By increasing frequency, you dramatically increase the likelihood that your message will reach prospects at a time when they need or are considering the benefit your service provides. The repetition of the message will build awareness of your company and its reputation in the prospects' minds, so even if they don't have your material in front of them on the day they decide to look into equipment leasing, your name will come instantly to mind and they will call you to initiate a discussion.

HOW TO SELECT AND EVALUATE PRINT MEDIA

In this two-step process, you will:

1. determine which magazines and newspapers are possible candidates for advertising;

2. evaluate each publication and select those you will advertise in.

The indispensable advertiser's guide to print media is *Standard Rate and Data Service*, 3004 Glenview Road, Wilmette, IL 60091, 800-323-4588. The first three volumes list virtually all newspapers and magazines that accept paid advertising, including 1,800 newspapers, 4,800 business and trade journals, 400 farm publications, and 1,600 consumer magazines. Listings give basic facts about the advertising policies of each publication, such as advertising rates, space units available, circulation, and the name of the advertising director. The fourth volume lists 8,500 radio stations, and the fifth lists 970 TV stations that run paid commercials.

All five books are published monthly and are available on an annual subscription basis (combined annual subscription fee for all three volumes covering print media is over $1,000). The main branch of your local library should have copies.

Tip: Want to get your own set of *SRDS* for free? Most ad agencies subscribe; because new editions are issued monthly, they probably throw out last month's set each time new books arrive. Ask your ad agency (or, if you don't have one, a friend or colleague who works at an ad agency) to give you the books instead of throwing them out. For your purposes, having an *SRDS* that's a few months old is no handicap, because you'll be contacting all publications for updated rates and schedules anyway before you commit to advertising.

Go through *SRDS* and select those publications that are likely candidates for your media schedule. For magazines, these would be publications covering your readers' industry, hobby, or specialized area of interest. For newspapers, these would typically be papers serving your target geographic market area.

Next, call or write to all likely candidates and request that they send you a sample issue, rate card, and media kit. These are sent free to legitimate potential advertisers, and there is no obligation to advertise. However, the salespeople will ask for your phone number so they can call back and sell you on their publication. That's okay; they're in business to make money, not give out free sample issues.

You will use these materials to evaluate the publication and make your media selection. For large-scale advertising campaigns, media selection is a massive, complex task so specialized that most ad agencies have people called media planners to provide advice and guidance to your clients.

Tip: If you are using an ad agency, take advantage of their media planning expertise. While the setting of overall marketing objectives and creation of a business or marketing plan is best done primarily in-house by the advertiser with some assistance from outside consultants, media planning and buying are usually best done by the ad agency.

Typically, the agency creates a first draft of the media schedule (based on a thorough understanding of your objectives) and submits it to the client for review. The client leans heavily on the agency's familiarity with the media and their overall greater expertise in the area of media planning.

However, clients are often aware of insider publications (typically newsletters, association bulletins, specialized journals, or small regional publications) that agencies are unaware of, and clients may have good arguments why these should be added to the media schedule. The agency goes back and then submits a final plan based on the client's input into the first draft schedule.

While the expert advice of an agency media planner or outside advertising or media consultant is frequently beneficial, small to medium-sized advertisers—especially those in specialized markets where the number of publications is few and the relative merit of each journal is well known—should be able to make their own media selections without help. This is done by talking to people (your own staff, customers, prospects), through market research (surveys and questions asking prospects and customers which publications they read), by reading *SRDS*, and by studying the media kits you have sent for.

Inside the Media Kit

How do you evaluate media? There is no magic formula. Both CPM and reach-frequency analyses are helpful. But they are just two means of comparison, not the final word.

Numbers are helpful, but they are not the entire story. An analysis of readership, ad response rates, and circulation figures may clearly indicate that Publication X is the most cost-efficient media buy and reaches the greatest number of target prospects. But what if the articles are lousy, the magazine is a joke, and no one in the industry reads the thing? There is no known formula that takes this into account, yet it is one of the most important factors in media selection. Suppose you received a stack of media kits in the mail. Let's open one and go through the contents. Here is what you will find:

Sample Issue

One of the most important items to study is the sample issue. As stated earlier, the quality of the magazine is of key importance. Some things to consider as you thumb through the sample issue are:

Amount of advertising. What is the ratio of editorial content (articles) to advertising? In an informal survey of business magazine publishers, Howard Sawyer found that a mix of 40 percent editorial and 60 percent advertising was considered ideal by most of the publishers he spoke with.

Too few ads means a financially unhealthy publication and a medium that other advertisers have not found effective (or a medium that is new and unproven and therefore considered high-risk, low-potential by most of your fellow advertisers).

If there are too many ads, the magazine is closer to a shopper than a legitimate journal and may not be read or respected by your prospects. Also, your ad runs the risk of being lost in the shuffle.

Placement of advertising. Should ads face editorial content? Are there many ad wells (two-page spreads where each facing page contains an advertisement)? Ad wells are undesirable because people skip over them. Is there a directory section in the back where small classifieds and display classifieds can be placed inexpensively? This is sometimes a good way to check the pulling power of a publication at a low cost before committing to larger space.

Quality of editorial content. Are the articles real news and information or promotional fluff? Is the technical level sufficient or too superficial for your audience? If it's a newspaper, does it provide adequate local coverage? (Newspaper buyers want to see news of people and events close to home.) Are there special sections in which your ad would get extra notice?

Editorial schedule. Are there one or more special issues or theme issues on topics related to your product? Many advertisers prefer to run ads in special issues where the editorial environment is related to the proposition in their ad.

Tip: Compile an annual special issues schedule that lists, by month, all the special issues published by all the magazines covering your field. This can be done by incorporating the editorial schedules from the various media kits into a summary report. Advertising and publicity activities can then be planned to take maximum advantage of the special issue coverage.

Graphic quality. Our society is on the way to becoming less word-oriented and more visually oriented. Does the publication have an attractive layout, readable typography, and eye-catching photos and illustrations that draw readers into the pages? Is color advertising available?

Editorial opportunities. Are there "new literature" sections that could feature a publicity release on your product? Would it be possible for someone at your company to contribute an article, article series, or even a regular column to the magazine? A mix of editorial content and advertising supporting your product is more effective than advertising alone.

Paid vs. controlled subscriptions. Paid means that people pay to receive the magazine. Controlled means the magazine is distributed free to readers who qualify; to qualify, they must complete a questionnaire (called a qualification card) indicating their position, industry, type of firm, and job activities.

Whether there is any difference in advertising effectiveness between paid and controlled circulation publications is a subject of never-ending and inconclusive debate. The paid publications argue that their product is more valuable because people pay for it, and that controlled circulation magazines are worthless—so worthless that the publishers have to give them away.

The controlled circulation publications point out that, while anyone can buy a subscription to the paid magazine, the controlled circulation publication picks and chooses its circulation, distributing only to those who qualify and denying subscriptions to the rest. This ensures a readership that has the characteristics the advertiser desires. Also, because the controlled publications aggressively offer free subscriptions to everyone in the industry, they claim more complete coverage than paid journals, which generally are read by a smaller percentage of people in any given market.

Current advertisers. Who else is advertising in the magazine? Beware of publications with no ads from other companies selling products similar to yours. Usually, if a publication is a good medium for your type of product, at least one or more of your competitors will already have discovered it and will be advertising in it. The late copywriter Paul Bringe put it this way: Fish where the fish are biting.

Audit Statement. The audit statement (also called the publisher's statement) is an official confirmation of the publication's circulation. To be official, the audit statement must be approved and certified by an independent auditing organization. The two major auditing organizations are the Audit Bureau of Circulations (ABC) and the Business Publications Audit of Circulations (BPA). The ABC and BPA audit statements are printed in black ink on colored paper and have the seal of the certifying organization on the first page.

The presence of an audit statement allows you to accept the magazine's circulation claims with a high degree of certainty, while the lack of an audit statement makes the figure somewhat suspect. Many advertisers have a standing rule against advertising in any unaudited publication. Another use of the audit statement is that it allows you to perform a more refined CPM calculation based on your specific target market rather than just gross circulation. For example, if an ad in Magazine X costs $1,000 and the circulation is 20,000, CPM is $50. But is it really?

Suppose you are interested in reaching only Chief Financial Officers, but not CEOs or other executives. You check Magazine X's audit statement and find the following circulation breakdown: 2,500 subscribers are Chief Financial Officers, 2,500 are Chief Executive Officers, 5,000 are Chief Operating Officers, and 10,000 are Plant Managers. As far as reaching your target market is concerned, the CPM of this publication is $1,000 divided by 2,500 CFOs (the 7,500 CEOs and COOs are of no interest and represent wasted circulation). This refined CPM is $1,000/2,500 × 1,000, or $400.

You compare this with another magazine, Magazine Y. An ad also costs $1,000 here, but the circulation is only 3,000. However, all 3,000 subscribers are CFOs. The CPM, as it relates to reaching CFOs, is $1,000/3,000 × 1,000, or $333, making Magazine Y the better buy even though its circulation is less than one-third of its competitor's.

Rate Card. The rate card is a price list for advertising. To calculate CPM, you divide the advertising space costs listed in the rate card by the circulation figures listed in the audit statement. The rate card contains the prices for all space units (full page, half page, etc.), physical dimensions of these units (width and depth), frequency discounts, mechanical requirements, charge for special positions, closing dates (dates by which the insertion order and the film or mechanical of your ad must be received), publication schedule, terms, shipping instructions, and charges for color.

Your main interest in evaluating the rate card is calculating CPM, comparing the CPM with similar publications, and determining whether the publication is a good value and whether you can afford the space. Some publications might have a low CPM but such a high overall space rate that they are simply beyond your budget. In this case, you would opt for publications with smaller circulations, choosing frequency instead of reach.

Editorial calendar. For each issue, the editorial calendar provides a partial list of proposed articles as well as the themes or topics of any special issues. Advertisers generally check the editorial calendar for three things:

1. Special or theme issues with topics complementary to their advertising.

2. Issues showcasing a particular trade show or convention that the advertiser is participating in or deems important.

3. Issues with bonus distribution, meaning distribution of extra copies beyond the circulation listed in the audit statement. Typically, these are distributed at trade shows or conventions.

Special issue notices. Many publishers print monthly fliers or bulletins highlighting the editorial features of the next issue in which advertising space is available. When an advertiser or agency receives a media kit, the current month's notice is included.

The person requesting the media kit may also be placed on a mailing list to automatically receive notices announcing each monthly issue's editorial content and slant. This is an effective marketing strategy for the publication: The advertiser gets the notice, sees there is an article relating to its product or service, and decides on that basis to place an ad in that particular issue.

Editorial profile. This is a narrative description, usually on a single sheet of paper, intended to communicate the position the publication holds within its industry. For example, the editorial profile of *Folio* begins by stating that *Folio* is the "magazine for magazine management" and is written for "executives in the magazine publishing industry." The editorial profile defines the purpose, audience, slant, and style of the publication. It may be stated briefly in the rate card and expanded upon in a number of glossy advertising pieces and brochures contained within the media kit.

The editorial profile is important because it describes the type of environment in which your ad will appear. If you are selling a home study course on how to fix your own car, would a magazine called *Popular Science* be a good place to advertise? You can't tell just by the title. But read the editorial profile, and you learn that *Popular Science* is indeed a good choice because it is written for the same do-it-yourselfer to whom your course would appeal. On the other hand, if *Popular Science* were an academic journal, a course on fixing cars would not be appropriate for its readership.

Reader or subscriber studies. These are surveys performed by the magazine (or by an independent research firm on behalf of the magazine). They are designed to create a profile of the average reader (buying habits, job title, interests, likes, dislikes, demographic characteristics, etc.) so that advertisers can see whether the magazine readership matches the characteristics of the target prospect.

There are basically two types of studies:

1. The first is an in-depth profile of the readership, going into all the items described above. *Folio* magazine's subscriber study, for example, tells:

- Average length of time reader has been in the magazine business (the industry covered by *Folio* is magazine publishing).
- Average budget each reader controls.
- Amount of time spent reading each issue.
- Types of products and services purchased.
- Pass-along readership (number of other people reading the subscriber's copy of the magazine).
- Responsiveness to ads (whether readers take action as a result of reading ads in the magazine).

Obviously, this type of information is helpful in formulating advertising plans. For example, if you are selling widgets and the study reveals that only 2.5 percent of the readership is involved in widgets, the magazine is not the right medium for your widget ad.

2. The second type of study makes a direct comparison with competitive magazines in the same field. For example, if there are three major magazines in an industry—Magazines A, B. and C—Magazine A might do a study comparing readership, circulation, or popularity and reputation of the three magazines. This is sometimes called a preference study and labeled as such in the media kit.

Frankly, these direct comparisons are of only limited value. Rather than shedding light on pure information useful to advertisers, these studies are designed deliberately to promote and push Magazine A over its competitors. The proof is that, in reviewing hundreds of media kits, I have never found a competitive study in a media kit that did not claim 100 percent superiority for the magazine publishing the study. Comparison studies are promotional, not objective or informational, and should be read as such.

Insertion Order. More and more media kits contain order forms called insertion orders or advertising orders. To reserve space in the magazine, you simply complete the insertion order and mail or fax it back to the publication.

Years ago, media kits did not contain order forms because most advertising was placed by agencies, and the agencies all have their own standard, preprinted insertion order forms. Today, a growing number of advertisers are not using agencies, but instead buy creative services à la carte from freelancers, consultants, design studios, and other independent sources and do their own media buying. Lacking a standard insertion order, these advertisers appreciate the ease and convenience of being provided with the necessary form. The magazines include insertion orders in their media kits because it means more sales and they recognize that advertisers often place their own space orders.

Some Questions to Ask When Evaluating Media
As you look over the media kit and sample issue, ask yourself:

- Is the audience of the media vehicle appropriate for your advertising campaign? (Does the medium reach your target market?)

- Relative to the available media, does this particular medium provide a large audience at comparatively low cost?

- Can the media vehicle be effective in communicating the sales message?

- Is this a good publication? Is it well-written and attractively designed and do people in the field read and respect it?

- Is there the right mixture of ads and articles (anywhere from 40:60 to 60:40)? If there are few ads, why is this? If the publication is mostly ads, what does this say about how well it is read?

- Do most of the readers fit the profile of your target market? Or is there a lot of wasted circulation (e.g., readers who are not prospects for your product or service)?

- Is there a publication that is less well-known but more targeted toward your specific target prospect (i.e., a more vertical publication)?

- Should you be advertising in horizontal publications, verticals, or both? (Horizontal media aim at broad audiences. Vertical magazines target specific, narrow, special-interest readerships.)

- Is the cost of an ad affordable? If not, are there publications with less reach (smaller circulation) that are in line with your budget?

- Does the magazine provide alternative media for reaching its subscribership? (These can include directories, catalogs, postcard decks, and new publicity releases or opportunities for editorial contributions.) If so, would it be better to use a combination of these rather than just a schedule of the more costly ads?

- Does the magazine have a readership card service for inquiries? This may be important if generating a high quantity of leads is your goal.

- Does the publication offer readership studies? Some publications offer free ad readership studies to advertisers who advertise in certain issues. These are useful if you want to know how effective your ads are but don't have the budget to conduct your own study.

- What is the CPM (cost per thousand)? How does it compare with the other top publications in the field? If it is significantly higher, is this magazine really worth the extra money?

- Have you surveyed your customers and prospects to find out what they read? If so, is this magazine at the top of their list? If not, why not?

- Does the publisher stick strictly with the published rate card or are they negotiable? Some are, and it would be foolish not to take advantage of every price break you can get.

- Do your competitors advertise in this publication? If not, why not? Have they tested it and found it unproductive? Rarely will you find a suitable publication that is truly an undiscovered gem.

- Is the publication audited? If not, how can you be sure that the circulation and readership figures quoted in promotional literature are accurate?

- Is the publication so unique, highly specialized, narrowly targeted, well respected, or inexpensive that you should test some ads even if the numbers indicate that you should pass?

- Are there special issues or features that would make a good editorial tie-in with your ad? If so, can you get news coverage or feature placement for some editorial content on your company or product to complement your advertising?

- Are there regional editions? Some of the larger national magazines sell advertising confined to a particular geographic region of the country (e.g., east, west, north, south). The advantage is that you pay a lower rate because your ads are limited to a particular market. This is beneficial to advertisers who want to save money and target their markets geographically.

- Have you advertised in this publication in the past? If so, did it pay?

- Can you afford to test the publication? That is, can you afford to risk the price of some ads to find out whether the publication will work or not? If you have no extra money to spare, forget tests and put this year's ad dollars into proven media.

- Are you being forced by management to advertise in a publication for subjective reasons? Many executives do not understand advertising and insist on having a nice color ad in Magazine X because they think it's prestigious, or they insist on an ad in a society's newsletter because they think it is important to "pay their dues." If you are forced into making media selection based on subjective criteria rather than thoughtful analysis, tell your management you agree to do so—provided these insertions can be listed separately on the advertising schedule under the heading "Charity Cases/Dues Paying," because that's exactly what they are. Make it clear that you cannot be held accountable for the productivity of ad space purchased on anything other than rational analysis of media.

- If you are an ad agency or consultant, ask yourself: "Does the client have superior knowledge of this publication—knowledge that enables me to validly add the medium to the client's media schedule despite the fact that it falls short in my own analysis?" Sometimes a publication or other medium is better than the numbers indicate, and clients know that it's good because they are more in touch than the agency or consultant with what people are reading, watching, or listening to in a particular market.

A Recap: 12 Steps to Better Media Selection

1. Determine your total advertising budget.

2. Select the marketing communications tools you will use to promote your product (e.g., magazine ads, direct mail, postcard decks).

3. List the marketing communications tools you will not use (e.g., television commercials, radio, billboards).

4. Allocate your total budget among the marketing communications tools you have selected. For example, if your budget is $100,000 and you allocate 50 percent to magazine advertising, 30 percent to direct mail, and 20 percent to public relations, your budget for magazine advertising is $50,000.

5. Take the first item in your budget (e.g., magazine advertising) and make a list of all possible publications (or mailing lists, or channels, etc.) you might advertise in. Use *SRDS* as your reference.

6. Get media kits for all the publications.

7. Analyze each publication using the guidelines discussed in this chapter.

8. List, in order of preference, the publications worth advertising in. Eliminate those that are poor or marginal.

9. Determine the desired frequency—the number of times you want to advertise—as well as the size of the ad you need.

10. Multiply the frequency by the cost of the ad space. For example, your ad is a full page in four colors. The cost per insertion in Magazine A is

$4,000. You want to run six times. Total cost is $6 \times \$4,000 = \$24,000$. This leaves a budget of $26,000 ($50,000 − $24,000) for the remaining publications on your list.

11. Go to the second most important publication on your list and repeat step 10. If you have money left over, go to the third publication on your list, the fourth, and so on, until you have used up the allotted budget for this particular communications medium.

12. Repeat this procedure for other media (i.e., newspaper ads, directory ads, etc.) called for in your advertising plan.

More Media Selection Tips for Specific Media

Magazines. Magazines are useful in targeting specific audiences, such as teenagers, travelers, fashion-conscious men and women, retirees, and many others. Magazines also provide access to various geographic markets. National magazines are distributed nationally, but there are also local or regional magazines that are ideal for an advertiser whose business is limited geographically.

Magazines have a much longer life than newspapers. According to research, magazines are kept an average of four to six months after their original sale. Thus, magazines will continue to generate readership and exposure for some time.

Also, magazines have much longer lead times. Generally, magazines require reservations and advertising materials at least one month prior to the intended issue date. Advertisers who require timely and constantly changing messages find magazines difficult to use because of this. It is important to analyze circulation by examining the magazine's audit statement; most reputable magazines are audited. Readership studies are also helpful in defining the demographics and purchasing habits of a magazine's readers.

Newspapers. Besides reaching a large audience, newspapers have two other desirable characteristics. First, newspapers convey a sense of immediacy. The contents are extremely timely, and newspapers are usually read the same day they are published. Second, advertising in newspapers is usually welcomed by readers. Unlike other media where advertising is sometimes considered interruptive or annoying, many newspaper readers actually search out advertisements. The biggest drawback to newspaper advertising is competition from other ads. Any single issue is likely to have pages and pages of advertising. Fractional ads must compete with other ads on the same page.

Because newspapers have large print runs and appear daily, they often suffer from poor reproduction. Time deadlines and budget restrictions prevent newspapers from equaling the reproduction quality of photographs and illustrations found in magazines. As a result, simple line drawings are usually the best illustrations for use in newspapers.

When buying newspaper advertising, keep in mind two important factors: the circulation and the size of the ad. The cost of newspaper advertising is based mainly on these two factors. It is important to examine and evaluate a newspaper's circulation. First, compare the total circulation of several newspapers. Most large newspapers have their circulation audited annually by an independent organization. Once an audit is completed, the newspaper will publish a sworn audit statement, which is the official estimate of circulation for a given year.

In addition, newspaper audit statements break down circulation geographically. For a given newspaper, the audit statement reveals the different areas in which the paper is sold and the quantity sold in each area. This information is essential in analyzing the total circulation of paper against the desired geographic circulation.

Using the optimal size ad in the newspaper is critical for success. Even though the size of an ad is most often governed by budget and communications needs, it is also important to be at parity with your competitors. If both you and your competitor advertise in the same paper, and your competitor uses a larger ad, it is likely that your competitor will receive more readership unless your creative effort is clearly superior in its attention-getting power.

Similar to frequent flyer programs offered by airlines, newspapers give rate discounts to frequent advertisers. These discounts depend on individual newspaper policy, but most newspapers publish a rate card detailing all discounts and other terms of advertising. In summary, use the newspapers that provide the highest desired circulation at the lowest cost with the least waste.

Outdoor Advertising. Outdoor advertising is available in a variety of forms: traditional billboards along roadsides; placards in mass transit vehicles; posters in airports and train stations. Outdoor advertising offers tremendous exposure opportunities because the signs are placed in strategic locations where thousands of people see them daily.

As a result, outdoor advertising can be expensive. Although the cost can be justified for some advertisers in terms of potential audience and high efficiency, outdoor advertising is unaffordable for many others.

The biggest drawback to outdoor advertising is the limitation of message content. A typical exposure to an outdoor advertisement ranges from a few seconds to perhaps ten seconds. Thus, advertising content is limited to just one or two simple thoughts.

The location of outdoor media is the key factor in selection. Do you want a marketwide program, or one limited to a particular neighborhood? Review all of the proposed locations of an outdoor medium.

Be sure each location is well maintained and offers an unobstructed view of your potential advertisement. Once the advertising is placed and actually running, be sure that your ads will be checked and receive prompt attention if damaged. In subway and bus advertising, the use of "take-ones" (bunches of detachable reply forms attached to the signage) can dramatically increase response rates.

Directories. Directory advertising is completely different from most other advertising media. Directories are used by people who are ready to buy.

Although other media deliver readers, viewers, or listeners, directories deliver strictly buyers. Because directories are published annually, advertisers are unable to change or modify their messages often.

As with any print vehicle, coverage of the marketplace is important. Be sure your entire marketplace is covered by the intended directory with minimal waste. To ensure the success of an advertising program, try to meet your competition head-on. Look at your competitors. What sections do they advertise in? What size ad do they use?

Directories are a source of information for buyers. People who use directories need specific information to complete their buying decision and frequently make decisions based on information in the directories. Therefore, you should include as much information as possible in your directory ad, making sure all key points are listed.

Television. Television is one of the most effective media vehicles. Because television presents sight, sound, and motion, commercials closely represent personalized selling. Additionally, television can reach tremendous numbers of people. Nearly every home in the country has at least one television set. The average household watches over seven hours of TV per day.

Although television has wide appeal, advertisers can target their messages to specific audiences. Most TV stations subscribe to research studies on viewing habits, which they share with advertisers. With this information, advertisers can limit their buys to the specific time periods or programs most likely to contact their target audiences. In addition, the use of cable TV, even in local markets, can add selectivity in targeting advertising messages.

Television's biggest drawback is cost. TV costs are based on two factors: the size of the audience and the relative demand for TV time.

Because the most popular shows attract the largest audiences, advertising during these shows is most expensive. Likewise, a high demand for television time will also increase price. Also, the cost of producing a single 30-second television commercial can easily exceed $40,000 if done by a professional ad agency or TV production house. For most small to medium-sized advertisers, television is not affordable.

Television advertising must be simple and brief. Commercials are usually only 30 seconds long, and advertisers must present their messages within this time limit. Consequently, commercials are limited to easily understood ideas and only one or two sales points per commercial. To buy television time, contact the sales department of a TV station and ask for a proposal based on your target audience, length of commercial time, and the dollar portion of your total advertising budget allotted to television. Check the station's coverage map to determine if your market will be reached or if many of the people watching represent wasted viewership.

Compare proposals from competing stations and use rating information to determine the most efficient value. Additionally, refer to competitive proposals to negotiate with high-priced stations.

Finally, consider the timing of your commercials throughout a schedule. Be sure your commercials will not always be shown at the same time during the same program. Your chances of success are better if you present your commercials at different times during several different TV programs.

Radio. Radio and television are closely related, yet radio has its own advantages and disadvantages. Advertising costs, as with TV, are based on the size of the audience and the demand for advertising. But radio generally costs far less than television.

Radio is a fairly targeted medium, more so than outdoor advertising but less so than direct mail. By selecting appropriate stations and time periods, advertisers can reach specific audiences.

For example, radio stations that concentrate their programming on top hits tend to attract teens and young adults. Also, because listeners are loyal and tend to listen to the same shows and stations day after day, radio is an excellent medium for building recognition through frequency.

Unlike television, radio commercials can be simple and inexpensive to produce. By using on-air announcers to read your commercials, you eliminate production costs. Some radio stations will even assist you in writing the script or will do it for you at no charge.

Radio's most obvious drawback is its lack of visual qualities. Also, because there are so many stations to choose from, especially in large cities, selecting the best station can be difficult. Another concern with radio is its broadcast coverage. Depending on the power of the radio station's transmitter, exposure within the market may be insufficient. Or, if the transmitter is powerful, it may broadcast far beyond your immediate geographic market, which means wasted listenership.

Remember two factors when buying radio time. First, summer is a popular time for radio advertising, and you should expect to pay more from June through September. Second, radio commercials are usually 30 or 60 seconds long. Generally, a 30-second commercial is priced at 80 percent of the cost of a 60-second commercial.

Otherwise, radio time is purchased like television time. You contact the sales department of a radio station and ask for a proposal based on your target audience, length of schedule, and budget. Also, ask for the ratings of the radio station for your target audience. Large stations subscribe to radio research services and can share this information at no charge. Consult the coverage map and double check that the radio station can be clearly heard throughout your intended market area.

Be sure to compare proposals from different stations and negotiate prices with the stations. The goal of your purchase is to use radio stations that provide maximum ratings and market coverage for the lowest cost.

HOW TO TAKE 17 PERCENT OFF YOUR ADVERTISING COST

There is an easy way to save 17 percent on the advertisements you place in major newspapers and magazines. Mail order dealers, as well as many other businesses, have been using this secret for years. What you need to do is to set up your own **in-house advertising agency**. This is a lot easier than it sounds, it's perfectly legal, and you don't even need to know anything about advertising.

First, think up a name for your "advertising agency" that is totally different from your current business name. Don't connect the two. This is done to convince the publications you are advertising with that the "agency" is a legitimately different business. Next, get letterhead stationery made up with your advertising agency's name on the top. You will use this stationery for your insertion orders. Insertion orders are simply the order blanks that ad agencies use to tell the publications what ad is being placed, how many issues are being paid for, any preferred placement, etc. If you look in any stationery or office supply store, you should be able to find a standard insertion form. Take note of what information is on the form, and make yours up to look similar.

Then, when you place an ad, send your camera-ready artwork along with the insertion order. Remember, your insertion order must say it's from your ad agency, not your other business. Send them in with your payment.

Wait, how do you save 17 percent? Well, it's standard practice for publications to allow a 15 percent discount to advertising agencies. This is the primary way ad agencies make money. The other 2 percent? Another standard practice is to discount 2 percent when payment is received with the insertion order. So, when you figure the cost of the ad, deduct 17 percent and send the remainder.

A bonus to this approach is that, after a few times of sending the payment with your order, the publication will probably offer you payment terms. This can stretch from 30 to even 90 days. You won't get the 2 percent discount, but you'll still get the 15 percent, and you can hold onto your money longer.

KEYING YOUR ADS TO TRACK RESPONSES

Advertising smartly means you must keep track of which publications draw the most responses, as well as which ad copy is best. This can be done by keying your ads. A key is the identification code you use in your ad. It shows you which publication, date, and ad copy brought in the response. Keying your ads is simple to do, and can be done in a few different ways. Keying your ads means that you place a code of some sort in your address so that when people write and order something from you, you will know immediately where they saw your ad.

Keep a record of the name and address of every publisher you send an advertisement to. Record the date you sent the ad and the date you received a checking record—the code you used—so you can immediately identify where it came from.

The easiest and most common way to key your ads is to attach the key code to your address. For example, if your address is 555 Easy St., your keyed address might be 555 Easy St., Dept. IOP-8. Dept. IOP-8 is the key, and could signify *Income Opportunities*, August issue. If your address is

123 Anytown St., it could become 123 Anytown St., Suite A for one publication and Suite B for another. The post office will still deliver your mail to 123 Anytown St. Of course, if you live in an apartment complex and there are apartment numbers you could turn 111 Johnson, Apt. A into 111 Johnson, Apt. A-1 for one publication and Apt. A-2 for another. Post office box addresses are also simple. Turn P.O. Box 585 into P.O. Box 585, Dept. A-1 for one publication and Dept. A-2 for another.

People sometimes even change their names on the ad for keying purposes. You might see the name "Harriet's Recipe Book" instead of Harriet Ranger. Harriet might also use "Harriet's Cookbook" or even "Harriet's Solution to Stress" on her ads relating to these products. Use your own imagination and pretty soon, keying your ads will be a normal part of your life. Be sure to keep track (on your Record Sheet) of how many responses you receive from each publication.

The addition of the key to your address should not pose problems for the post office, but it's still a good idea to contact your postmaster. Show him or her the keys you intend to use and ask for an opinion. The postmaster will know which formats will be disruptive to delivery.

If you use the phone for responses, you can put a Department Number in your ad, and instruct the customer to ask for the department when calling. You or your phone operators would then take note of the codes and use them to tally your responses.

Finally, a good way to check which of your mailings or flyers are succeeding is to use different colors of paper. For example, if you're testing three different mailing lists, use three different colored papers, one for each list. You can then tell instantly when you receive order blanks which list the responses come from.

After three months, look over your Record Sheet (see Appendix C) and get rid of the publications that didn't do well. You'll go broke if you spend $10 per month on a 2-inch ad if you only receive $1 back in orders. After a while you'll be able to see where it pays you to advertise your particular product, and then you can send in larger ads to those publications. Never stop using this method and you'll never stop getting orders in your mailbox. It's a win–win situation for everybody!

Be sure to keep a list of your key codes and what they correspond to. By doing this, you can tell which publications are worth continuing your ads in, which should be canceled, and which ad copy should be used. This will allow you to pour your ad funds into the most worthwhile places, and reap the benefits!

TAKING CREDIT CARD ORDERS

You can greatly increase your orders by accepting credit cards for payment. It's easy and convenient for the customers, and that makes it more likely that they will order. The only problem is that it's hard for a business, especially a small mail order business, to gain the ability to accept credit cards. Banks are very reluctant to authorize credit card acceptance, mainly because they have been burned too many times by fraudulent businesses. So many businesses go on accepting only checks or money orders for payment, and miss out on the added sales they would get using credit cards. There is a way, though, for businesses that can't get bank authorization to accept credit cards.

The easiest way to get a merchant account is to work with an Independent Sales Organization (ISO), which acts as an intermediary between small businesses and banks. The ISO will charge an additional fee for each transaction, so you will be paying a bit more than the standard percentage charged for credit card transactions. There will also be an application fee. Here are the typical charges to expect, as of this writing:

Application fees—usually these range from $95 to $400—may or may not be refundable. When you are accepted, the ISO will offer you a point of sale terminal via purchase or lease. This is the terminal you use to process the charge and check for fraudulent numbers. If you get merchant status direct from a bank, the POS will run several hundred dollars. If you are working through an ISO, prices will range from $400 to as high as $1500! You can usually lease the terminal, though, at an average of $45 per month. The best thing to do is to find an ISO that will provide computer software that can be used in place of a terminal. This usually costs only around $150.

Concerning service fees, banks charge between 2 and 5 percent for processing a credit card purchase. An ISO's charge is higher, usually 3 to 7 percent. In addition, ISOs usually charge a per-transaction fee of 20 to 25 cents, and a monthly statement fee of $5 to $10.

Why all these fees? The ISOs only want to work with legitimate businesses and ones that will stay with them for a long period of time. If a business can afford these fees, they are considered less of a risk. Thus, the important thing to do is to shop around for an ISO. Get as much information as you can about each ISO you are considering, and read it thoroughly. Look for hidden charges and unreasonable requirements.

Here is a list of some of the ISOs you may want to consider. This is not an endorsement of any or all of them; they are simply the most prominent ones.

- Bancard, Inc., 1233 Sherman Drive, Longmont, CO 80501, 800-666-7575
- Data Capture Systems, 231 Quincy St., Rapid City, SD 57701, 605-341-6461
- Electronic Bankcard Systems, 2554 Lincoln Blvd., Suite 1088, Marina Del Rey, CA 90291, 213-827-5772
- Gold Coast Bankcard Center, Ft. Lauderdale, FL, 305-492-0303
- Harbridge Merchant Services, 681 Andersen Dr., 4th Flr., Bldg. 6, Pittsburgh, PA 15220, 412-937-1272
- Teleflora Creditline, 12233 West Olympic Blvd., Los Angeles, CA 90064, 800-325-4849
- U.S. Merchant Services, 775 Park Avenue, Huntington, NY 11743, 516-427-9700

All of these services will require you to fill out an application. Be 100 percent truthful about everything on the application and don't let the representative talk you into including any false information. If the banks affiliated with the ISO you use were to find out that any information on your application was false, you would probably be canceled immediately and your business name and address would go on a no-service list that would prevent you from being able to accept credit cards for a indefinite period of time. Don't let this happen to you. Most of the ISOs out there are legitimate, but there are a few that may put down spurious information, rather than lose the fees they'd receive. Be sure to look everything over twice. If you do, you'll probably find an ISO that will work with you to expand your business through the acceptance of credit cards.

HOW TO AVOID COMMON ADVERTISING MISTAKES

Advertising isn't hard to do. You prepare an advertisement or write a classified ad to sell your product or generate requests to send people more information. Most people make mistakes in advertising either through their inability to write effective ad copy or by sending ads to be published in the wrong publications. Here are some pointers to follow.

Writing Effective Copy

Never try to sell anything costing more than $5 in a small display ad or a classified ad. You don't have enough room to tell people everything they need to know to entice them to order.

Instead, you need to employ the Two-Step method of advertising. Request the reader to send you $1 or four first-class postage stamps for more information. When they respond, you will send them a brochure, flyer, order form, and cover letter so they can place an order for the product.

Now that pricing is out of the way, let's talk about writing your ad copy. The best way to learn how is to read the ads other people have written. Don't copy them word for word, but use them as a guide to write your own ads. Once you get the hang of it, you'll be writing effective ad copy just as well as the pros.

Placing Your Ad in the Right Publication

Although this may sound a little silly and you might think it is only common sense to consider this, people often overlook this aspect when choosing the publication they will be advertising in. Instead, they look for the lowest price for the amount of circulation they receive. Unfortunately, this does not work well. Even though you need to look for good deals that make it easy on your pocketbook, you will be throwing money away if you don't prequalify the publication you choose. One way of prequalifying the publication is to send for a sample copy. Most publishers will send samples free of charge for the asking. If you are a mail order marketer and don't know of any mail order publications, just write to Glenn Bridgeman, P.O. Box 10150, Terra Bella CA 93270, or William Lee, Rt. 1, Box 10790, Madisonville TN 37354 and ask them to send you some. (Be sure to enclose $1 or four first-class postage stamps with your request to offset postage costs.) If you tell them you are new to mail order and are interested in publications to advertise in, you certainly will find the $1 is well spent because both of these publishers are very reputable, honest, and helpful.

Study the publication to see what products other people are advertising and how they are advertising them. Contact some of the people who sell items similar to your own with the hope of networking with them. You would be surprised how much free publicity you can get just from corresponding, calling, and networking with others.

Once you locate a publication you want to advertise in, give it a try for three months. If you get no response or only a few orders, try another publication. There are millions of them and eventually you will hit the right target market that will be interested in what you have to sell.

Advertising in More Than One Publication

Just because you locate the target market of people who are interested in purchasing your product there is no reason you can't advertise in more than one publication. In fact, if you don't, your ad will become stale. If the same people continue to see your ad every month they will probably get tired of looking at it. Besides, if they wanted the product they would have ordered it by now. Don't tire them out! Alternate different size ads and get rid of ones that don't work well. Leave your ad running as long as it brings in orders for you but also advertise in 5,10, 20, or 50 other publications to generate a steady stream of orders and to reach more people.

Tabloids versus Adsheets

Many people question whether it's better to advertise in tabloids or adsheets. People will try to sell you information on the best day to mail and the best time of the year to advertise. They think they have it down to a science and will try to convince you to use their methods.

However, there are no set rules that can be employed by everyone, because there is a wide variety of ways to approach various products. If you sell travel services and believe a report that tells you not to advertise during the summer months, you'll go broke. Summer is the travel industry's biggest money-making season!

Don't get hung up on specific statistics reported by people who claim to be expert researchers. There is no other way to determine what is best for you than to try it yourself and see what works. You are the person in control of your business and you are where the buck stops. Take advantage of your authority and try every angle you can think of until you determine what's best for your company's product or service.

Tabloids are fantastic advertising vehicles and adsheets are too. Sometimes people think a one-inch camera-ready ad gets lost in a tabloid filled with hundreds of them. This may be true in some circumstances and not true in others. Do you look at one-inch ads in tabloids? Of course you do. You scan the pages and your attention is directed to one or two on the page that catch your eye. Ask yourself why they caught your eye. Was it because the ads were placed in a specific area on the page? Was it because of the headline or the word "free"?

Classified ads sometimes work well in tabloids and adsheets and sometimes they don't. Look in the back of the *Globe* or the *Enquirer*. Don't they have page after page of classified ads? If nobody was reading and responding to the ads, the advertisers wouldn't continue submitting them. So evidently, people **do** read classified ads—even if there are hundreds of them. Test the waters and do what works best for you.

Chapter 9

SCHEDULING YOUR ADVERTISING PROGRAM

WHEN SHOULD ADVERTISING BE SCHEDULED?

In previous chapters, we learned how to develop an overall advertising plan and select the specific media in which our advertising will run. The next step is to develop a schedule that outlines the precise days, weeks, or months and the specific issues in each medium in which our advertising will be placed, in other words, the timing of the campaign.

"Timing in advertising also has a profound effect on its success," notes Michael F. Walsh of Ketchum Communications. "Some products can be advertised and sold all year, while others can be advertised and sold during specific seasons. Advertisers should take advantage of seasonal trends. For example, the Christmas season accounts for up to 25 percent of some business' yearly sales.

"In addition, special events such as grand openings, new product introductions, and special promotions need appropriate advertising. Companies should schedule advertising to match these events. An effective advertising campaign is targeted to a specific audience in a specific place at a specific time. Knowing the objectives of who, where, and when in advance improves the advertising program's success."

Table 9.1 lists some common products and services along with the season when sales are greatest and hence the most effort should be put toward advertising.

Although most businesses have seasonal peaks and valleys, few are wholly dependent on a particular season for total sales. For this reason, advertising needs to be scheduled to ensure a steady stream of business throughout the year. It may be more concentrated in some months than others; some months it may be absent altogether; but frequency must be planned for and maintained. That is, you must deliberately determine how many times to communicate with your target audiences and when.

Table 9.1. Seasonal trends for common products and services.

Product / Service	Best Time to Promote and Advertise
Lawn care service	Spring (March to June); early summer
Air conditioners	Late spring; all summer
Storm doors and windows	When weather turns cold (fall; winter)
Home improvements (general)	Spring
Firewood	Fall
Mail order gift catalogs	Christmas season (October to December)
Greeting cards	Christmas season
Business gifts	Christmas season
Business-to-business products and services (general)	January–May; September–mid-November
Back-to-school products (clothing, supplies)	Labor Day
Flags	Memorial Day, Fourth of July
Weight loss centers; health spas; diet products	Spring (in preparation for bathing suit season)
Home insulation	Fall
Gardening tools; supplies; flowers	Spring (but bulbs in fall)
Self-improvement/home study materials	September; January
Seminars (business and general public)	September–mid-November; January–May
Landscaping service	Spring
Swimming pools	Spring and summer
Ski resorts	Winter
Florida or Caribbean vacations	Fall, winter, spring
Resume service	March to June (graduation time)

What kind of advertising schedule is required to meet this need? The answer is the Rule of Seven, a concept invented by marketing consultant and author Dr. Jeffrey Lant. Let's take a look at this idea in detail.

DEFINITION OF THE RULE OF SEVEN

The Rule of Seven basically says that if you want prospects to take action and buy what you are selling, you must connect with them a minimum of seven times within an 18-month period. Then and only then can you reasonably expect prospects to know what you can do for them and get them to take action on their own behalf.

The Rule of Seven begins with the simple premise that most people don't take action the first time they become aware of a product or service. There are several reasons for this:

- They have other commitments.
- They forget about it.
- They don't have time.
- They don't have a pressing need for what you are selling right now.

- They mean to take action but somehow "never get around to it." (Translation: You have not provided sufficient motivation or urgency for them to act now.)
- They have qualms about the value of the product or service.
- They have qualms about the reputation of the seller.
- They hesitate because of the expense.
- They know they will probably be seeing your ad or getting your mailings again and therefore can always make a buying decision later on.
- They don't pay attention to your ad, read your copy, or understand what your product is and what it can do for them.
- They already have what you are selling.
- They already buy from someone else and are satisfied with that supplier.

Most people really don't pay that much attention to advertising. Part of the reason is that the average prospect is bombarded with 2,500 to 7,500 advertising messages each week. We have all become adept at screening out the noise of these intrusions.

PUTTING THE RULE OF SEVEN TO WORK

To overcome the prospect's indifference, disinterest, and plain lack of attention, you must repeat your message over and over again until it sinks in or the prospect finally takes notice.

To do this, says Dr. Lant, you must connect with your prospect at least seven times within a year and a half. Each communication with your prospect must clearly convey that you understand the prospect's problem and have something that can solve it. Also, each communication must reach the same person again and again.

What does this mean? First, it suggests that all your marketing must be rigorously customer centered, focusing exclusively on prospects and their needs, not you and your offer. Second, you must connect again and again with the same prospect: namely, the prospect you know has the problem you can solve. Your objective is to make a permanent impact on individuals so that they know, must know, that you exist, that you understand their problems, and that you can solve them expeditiously.

If you want your marketing to work, you must target the people who have the problem your product or service can solve. You must connect with them a minimum of seven times in 18 months, using the following kinds of vehicles (this is a partial list):

- Free publicity via radio, television, newspapers, magazines, and newsletters.
- Workshops and seminars sponsored by trade associations catering to your prospects.
- Telemarketing.

- Direct mail.
- Catalogs.
- Postcard decks.
- Paid advertising.

Note that the Rule of Seven does not require that all seven contacts with your prospect be in the same medium. For example, you do not have to run seven ads. Instead, you can run three ads, send out two mailings, and telephone your prospect twice to connect the required seven times.

According to Dr. Lant, the steps required to successfully apply the Rule of Seven are as follows:

1. Identify a compact body of prospects.
2. Identify, in advance of using them, all the means of reaching these prospects.
3. Ensure that you have the necessary skills and resources to use these marketing communications tools effectively.
4. Select at least seven means of connecting with the same group of prospects within an 18-month period.

A SAMPLE RULE OF SEVEN PLAN

There are literally thousands of seven-step plans that might enable you to connect with your prospects in ways that convince them to take action and buy what you are selling. Here is a sample from Dr. Lant:

First Contact. Write a problem-solving article for your trade association's publication. Conclude the article with information about the problem you solve and how the buyer can reach you. Make sure you include your name, address, and telephone number.

Second Contact. Arrange to make a presentation at the trade association's annual meeting. So that all the people attending this meeting are aware of you, ask to have your sales brochures or other marketing materials placed in the registration packets of everyone attending.

Give each person attending your session a questionnaire, letting them tell you what problems they want to solve in their businesses. All questions should be geared to the kinds of products and services you sell. Thus, if you are selling widgets, one question might be, "Which models of widgets do you have the most difficulty getting delivered on short notice?"

If people in your audience answer this question, follow up by promising swift delivery on the models they indicate.

Third Contact. Follow up on all the people in your session with either a letter or a phone call to find out how you can be of service. This includes those who returned the questionnaire as well as those who did not.

Fourth Contact. Speak with next year's workshop planner about your session. The time to begin planning next year's presentation is the minute you have finished this year's successful presentation.

Fifth Contact. Rent the mailing list of the association (whose members should now have some idea of who you are). Send a direct mail package to the list, including complete information on your products and services and how they can be ordered.

Sixth Contact. Follow up in 90 days with a second mailing.

Seventh Contact. At the same time, arrange to have a second article by you published in the association's publication. This should reach them at about the same time your mailing does (preferably a few days beforehand).

Key point: Seven contacts are the minimum required in the 18-month period to ensure that prospects are really getting your message. If you think and plan systematically, you will soon exceed the minimum. The more frequently you contact prospects above the minimum seven times, the better. Most marketers agree that you cannot communicate with your prospects and customers too often. Budget, time, and energy are usually the limiting factors.

TIPS TO MAKE THE RULE OF SEVEN WORK

1. Write down your Rule of Seven schedule. The trick to successfully using the Rule of Seven is to first identify all the marketing gambits you could use to reach the same body of prospects. Then ascertain whether these are really available to you. For instance, perhaps you want to place an article in an association's newsletter, but upon checking you discover they do not accept contributions from non-members. This bit of information will inevitably influence what you can do.

Once you've discovered that an alternative is available, however, close on it. If the publication can print your article, write to the editor and propose the article, so that you soon learn whether you can count on publication of the article as one of your seven connections with this group of prospects. If the editor does not want the article, you will need to find another alternative.

2. Always select an inexpensive alternative over an expensive one. Thus, before buying a paid ad, see whether you can get free publicity.

Tip: Think creatively. Swap an article for an ad. Then use the ad in a different issue or in another publication reaching the same audience. Instead of using direct mail, see whether your information can get to the same people as a package or invoice stuffer or through some other ride-along offer. These formats are invariably less expensive than stand-alone direct mail packages.

3. Make sure every gambit you use enables the prospect to connect with you directly. Thus, each must contain your name, address, and telephone number. If you accept credit cards, add this information, too. Finally, if you have a catalog or free brochure, mention its availability. In short, each marketing gambit must tell the reader how to reach you and what to ask for.

4. Plan completely and far in advance. Write down the minimum of seven marketing gambits you need in the 18-month time period and make sure each of them is available to you.

As you complete one of these gambits, begin exploring the possibility of another that will place you in touch with the same group of prospects. If you wish to maintain your competitive edge, you must always have a gambit in place and a series of additional contacts ready to connect you with your prospects in the future.

MEDIA SCHEDULING

There are countless media scheduling options. If you can dream it up, it can be done. There is certainly no right or wrong way. Two things that will obviously affect what schedule you choose are season and budget. If you're introducing a new product, your schedule will be different than if you're in a maintenance period.

The eight common methods for scheduling media, as illustrated in Figure 9.1, are:

1. *Steady*. You are visible an equal amount every month—a steady, continuing, and ongoing schedule. Very, very few marketers do this, except for those conducting corporate image campaigns.

2. *Alternating even*. The same as steady, except you advertise every other month rather than 12 times a year. A few do this, usually in print and broadcast efforts.

3. *Alternating staggered*. This is an every other month effort that builds up, drops back, and then builds again. This could be a good schedule if you have two very identifiable selling seasons, say, one at Christmastime, another in the spring.

4. *Flighting*. You advertise heavily and constantly for a period, then drop your ads altogether, then get back in again. Many times this is done on radio, usually for short periods of time: six weeks in, six out, and six back again. It can also work in newspapers and direct mail: in the marketplace every few weeks for several months, then out, followed by a heavy repeat schedule.

5. *Pulsing*. Pulsing is similar to flighting, except that during the slow periods you merely cut back on advertising rather than drop it altogether. The pattern is: a heavy program, followed by a lighter one, and then heavy again. Print and broadcast are typical tools to use for pulsing campaigns. Sometimes the telephone is included to support the heavy time.

6. *Seasonal*. This is just what it says: You run ads steadily as your season approaches, and you don't advertise the rest of the time. This is common among marketers who have a single, super-heavy season.

7. *Teaser step-up.* This is similar to the seasonal method, except as the season approaches, advertising starts small, then gradually builds each month until it is greatest at the peak of your sales season. This is also a typical schedule for many in direct marketing, particularly those with consumer mail order products.

8. *Step-down.* This is the opposite of step-up. The two can go together. Use step-up to lead to your heavy season, and then keep the season going with a step-down: a lesser campaign, but nevertheless a presence. Step-down gradually decreases advertising after the peak sales period until it vanishes during your dead months.

As Ray Jutkins points out, "There are really no 'principles of scheduling.' Direct mail is different from print and broadcast. Business-to-business schedules will be different from consumer schedules. Financial service products have a different timetable for promotion from consumables. Previous experience, common sense, and your budget will many times dictate your schedule."

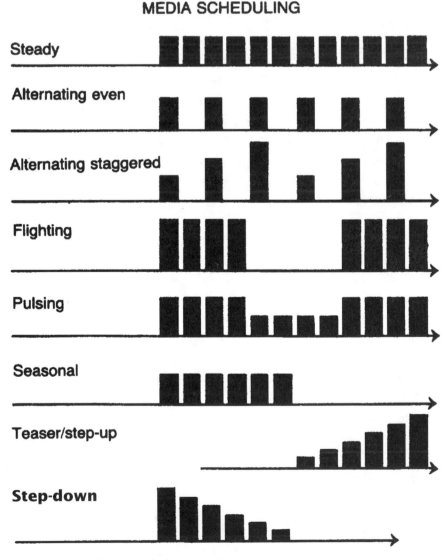

Figure 9.1. Eight methods for scheduling media.

MORE RULES OF SCHEDULING

1. If sales are seasonal, schedule ad appearances accordingly. Remember that your move on the market should be made well in advance of the buying season.

2. December and the summer months are not such poor months in which to advertise as is generally suspected. In fact, one Laboratory of Advertising Performance study of inquiry response for a manufacturer showed July to be consistently the peak of the year, with August above average in some years. In another LAP study, one publication found that inquiries in August are about average, better than September and October, and that December pulls better than either May or June.

The fact that many advertisers do stay out of summer issues means that the remaining advertisers have all the better opportunity. Studies have shown that any one ad has a better chance of readership in a thin issue than a thick one. So you have a chance of getting more for your advertising money in the less popular months.

3. Begin a new campaign at the start of your selling season (which is not necessarily the start of the market's buying season), not in January when your new advertising budget year is most likely to begin. Most new advertising campaigns are kicked off at the start of the new budget year, but most sales campaigns start with enthusiasm the highest early in the fall. The intelligent practice is to coordinate advertising with the rise of sales activity, which usually occurs following a vacation period.

4. Prepare ads as far in advance of publication as you feel safe in doing. This gives you a chance to distribute reprints of the campaign to salespeople, distributors, dealers, and customers well ahead of appearances in the magazines. Nothing makes a salesperson feel so foolish as to have a customer refer to an ad the salesperson has not yet seen.

5. Allow creative and mechanical departments plenty of time to prepare the ad. Ten weeks is a recommended minimum. That is, the background facts should be in the copywriter's possession ten weeks before the first closing date. This may appear to be a long period of time, but it allows ample time for copy, design, approval, production, and unforeseen delays.

COMMONLY ASKED SCHEDULING QUESTIONS AND ANSWERS

Q: *What is the right method for scheduling an ad campaign?*

A: As Ray Jutkins pointed out earlier in this chapter, there are no "principles of scheduling," no correct method or formula. Experience, objectives, seasonal patterns, and market conditions are the key factors in determining a schedule.

Q: *Is it better to run small ads many times or big ads fewer times?*

A: Obviously, the most desirable alternative is to run the big ad many times, but with a limited budget that's not usually possible.

The answer is that you have to strike a balance. You must run your ads frequently enough so that they make an impression upon your audience (the Rule of Seven). Yet they must be large enough to contain all the key information you want to communicate.

However, if you have to choose between size and frequency, go for frequency. Repetition is a key factor in communications success, and an ad that is twice as large is not necessarily twice as cost-efficient.

Q: What is the minimum number of times I should run my ad in a publication?

A: A rule widely quoted by advertising agency experts is that to have any impact, you must run not fewer than six times in a monthly magazine. But according to Dr. Lant's Rule of Seven, the key consideration is not the number of times a specific ad is repeated in a particular publication, but rather the number of times the same message is communicated to the same audience in various formats. The Rule of Seven says this should be a minimum of seven times in 18 months.

By making your ad a direct response ad, you can get an immediate measure of whether running the ad in a particular publication is generating the desired results. When you are unsure of a publication and you have a full-page ad, run it once. Then wait to see what type of response you get. If it's good, expand the schedule. If it stinks, don't continue. If it's marginal, proceed with caution. If you are sure of the publication but have a limited budget, it's better to run a 1/4 or 1/3 page ad three times than a full-page ad once, given those two alternatives for the same space dollars.

Q: Is there a danger of running an ad so often that readers tire of it?

A: Yes, but this danger can be minimized by monitoring response (or readership, if that's how you measure). Continue to run the ad according to whatever schedule you set until response begins to drop off. At that point, consider creating a new ad or rerunning an old ad.

A drop-off in response indicates that at this point the majority of prospects have seen your ad and those who are going to respond already have. A new ad featuring a different appeal can lift response because it intrigues prospects who were indifferent or unmotivated by the previous ad's content.

Research studies from the McGraw-Hill Laboratory of Advertising Performance show that good ads can continue to generate a high level of readership and response with no appreciable drop-off after numerous repeat insertions. For example, the report summarized in Figure 9.2 tells of a full-page, four-color ad running in Architectural Record, *a monthly publication. The results show that the fifth insertion pulled almost double the number of inquiries from the first insertion, but the thirteenth insertion pulled 12 percent less response than the original insertion.*

Laboratory of Advertising Performance/McGraw-Hill Research

13 Repeat Ads Continue to Draw Inquiries With Each Insertion

The Mineral Panels Division of Manville Corporation ran the same full-page, four-color ad 13 times in ARCHITECTURAL RECORD between July 1986 and October 1987. Five times throughout the campaign, repeated insertions generated more inquiries than the initial insertion in July.

Further, throughout the advertising campaign, the same ad continued to draw inquiries for each repeated insertion. Production costs involved in creating a new ad were saved.

McGraw-Hill Research kept records of inquiries received for each insertion. The number of inquiries generated from the initial insertion was indexed at 100, and indices were calculated for the number of inquiries pulled from each subsequent insertion.

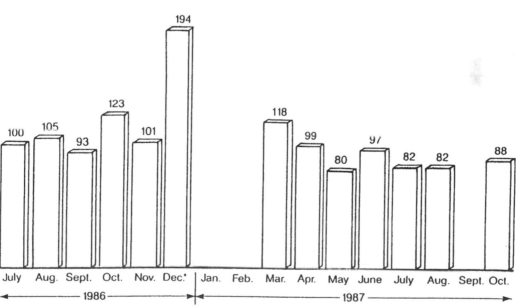

Inquiries Generated from a Repeated Ad In A Monthly Publication

Index

Source: McGraw-Hill Research

*Annual New Products Issue

Figure 9.2. Report summary.

207

Q: How do I resolve scheduling conflicts between ads for my different product lines?

A: Obviously, if the ads appeal to different markets and appear in different media, there is no problem. The question arises when a company has two or more products or product lines that overlap in the target market. If two different products from two different divisions are advertised in the same magazine, how should the schedules be balanced?

All else being equal, the ads should appear in different issues rather than the same issue, for purposes of increasing frequency and repetition of the advertiser's name and logo. However, this may not always be possible. For example, the product managers of the two divisions may both want to run in the May issue, either because it's a special issue or because May marks the beginning of their busy season. If this is the case, you can run multiple ads on consecutive right hand pages. This creates almost a mini-catalog for your company while avoiding ad wells (two facing pages, both with ads). Designing the ads with similar typefaces and layout styles further reinforces the company image and enhances recognition.

Q: How do I find the peak selling periods for my industry?

A: Experience is the best teacher; any salesperson or other executive who has been with your company or in your industry for more than a couple of years knows the answer to this one. However, if there is no one you can ask, then observe the activities of your competitors. A flurry of colorful catalogs in your mailbox during the holiday season makes it quite clear when you, as a catalog marketer of consumer gift items, should be mailing.

Books on selling specific types of products or services also help point the way. In his book, How to Market and Promote Seminars, Howard Shenson reveals the best and worst months for promoting public seminars. Russ von Hoelscher gives similar information on the best and worst months to run mail order ads selling books in How You Can Make a Fortune Selling Information by Mail. Similar information may be available in books on how to market and sell other types of products and services.

Q: Should different marketing gambits (e.g., direct mail, telephone solicitation, publicity, paid advertising) reach my prospects at the same time, or should these communications be spread out evenly over the months?

A: There is no right answer. It depends on your situation. If you want a steady flow of inquiries, a steady pattern would be best, with a different marketing gambit reaching your audience every month. January might be an ad, February a mailing, March a phone call, April a sales visit, and so on.

On the other hand, if your business is seasonal, you might use the flighting or pulsing patterns shown in Figure 9.1. This means that some months you would bombard your prospects with ads, mailings, articles, phone calls, TV commercials, and so on. Other months you would send them nothing or just do a little advertising.

As you experiment, you'll learn which combinations work best. Again, there are no rules. Different people have different experiences.

For example, consider the combination of paid advertising and publicity. Many people say that if you can get an article you've written published in a trade magazine, you should run your ad in a different issue to increase frequency and give readers two months to catch your message instead of one.

My experience is to the contrary. I suggest that you run your ad in the same issue your article appears in. Why? Because people reading your article will want to know more about you, your company, and your product, and will want to get in touch with you. The article builds interest, while the ad provides the address and telephone number needed for taking immediate action based on that initial interest.

Q: Any special tips for scheduling advertising for a new product?

A: Only that the schedule will naturally be more heavily weighted at the beginning, in order to make a splash when the product is introduced. As Figure 9.1 demonstrates, the flighting, pulsing, or a combination of step-up and step-down patterns fit this requirement.

Q: Are special issues really worthwhile?

A: We touched on this in Chapter 8, and you may want to refer to that discussion.

As for my observations and opinion:

- I have seen no hard data indicating that ads in special issues get higher readership or response, or that special issue advertising is more effective in any way.

- On the other hand, many clients have told me that they feel special issues do pay off and that they get greater readership for their ads. I do know that, while not all special issues are of equal value, certain special issues of certain publications are read more, discussed more, and kept longer, which surely extends the useful life of any ads in these issues.

- I see absolutely no evidence that advertising in special issues is any less effective than regular issues. Because the cost of the space is usually the same, I therefore see no harm in accommodating an advertiser who prefers placement in a special issue over an ordinary issue.

- On the other hand, I do not believe you should run an ad simply for the sake of being included in a special issue. They are not as important or critical as the publishers make them out to be. As Scotty Sawyer notes in *Business-to-Business Marketing*, "The argument to the effect that it is disastrous to be 'missing' from any one issue is a thin one. It's difficult enough to get an ad noticed without worrying about its absence being noticed."

RESOURCE

The Annual National Media Congress is a yearly conference on the subject of media, media buying, media planning, and scheduling. For registration information contact: National Media Congress, Marketing and Media Education, 49 East 21st Street, 6th Floor, New York, NY 10010-6213, 212-505-2350.

Chapter

10
YELLOW PAGES AND DIRECTORY ADVERTISING

SHOULD YOU ADVERTISE IN THE YELLOW PAGES?

Should you advertise in the Yellow Pages? The answer to that question is not terribly complex. Basically, you should advertise if you are in a type of business where similar companies get all, most, or at least a significant portion of their business from Yellow Pages advertising.

This is determined from your own knowledge of the business, your own buying habits as a consumer, and by checking the Yellow Pages to see if your competitors are there and, if so, whether they have small listings or large display ads.

Yellow Pages advertising is an ideal medium for local service businesses and retailers who serve residents of a particular area. Examples include insurance agents, home remodelers, plumbers, restaurants, limousine services, taxi companies, roofers, tree surgeons, aluminum siding contractors, house painters, landscapers, nurseries, hairdressers, barbers, rent-a-car companies, auto mechanics, and dozens of other businesses. Ask yourself: "When people find themselves in need of my type of service or product, are they likely to turn to the Yellow Pages for sources?" If the answer is "yes," Yellow Pages advertising is probably a good bet for you.

Then turn to the Yellow Pages. See if your competitors are there with big ads. Check old copies you have of last year's book. Go back two years, if you can. If the same companies in your field have been running large ads for years, you will know it has been successful for them and would probably work for you, too.

Nowadays, many phone companies offer a separate volume of business-to-business Yellow Pages for local service companies and distributors that sell to local businesses. Advertisers in these books include advertising agencies, accounting firms, commercial banks, data processing service bureaus, computer consultants, software vendors, office supply dealers, office furniture outlets, public relations firms, graphic design studios, printers, and so on. Again, whether to advertise is determined by checking what the competition is doing but also by asking, "How favorably does this medium compare with the other means at my disposal for selling my service?"

Many business-to-business advertisers prefer not to advertise in the Yellow Pages or, if they do, to have a small ad or listing only. They feel the money is better spent on advertising in industry directories and trade publications.

THE YELLOW PAGES ARE DIFFERENT

The difference between ads in the Yellow Pages or other directories and ads in newspapers or magazines is as follows:

People reading newspapers and magazines are reading articles for information or entertainment, and they tend to pass over the ads. (The average consumer reads only four ads in a magazine). Therefore, to be effective, a newspaper or magazine ad must forcefully grab the reader's attention through a novel, interesting, or powerful presentation—a fascinating photo, a distinctive layout, a compelling headline.

But when people turn to the Yellow Pages they are prime prospects, ready to buy and looking for a supplier. They do not have to be persuaded to buy your type of product or service; they merely have to be persuaded to buy from you instead of from your competitors.

THE TROUBLE WITH THE YELLOW PAGES

Richard A. Gajewski is president of Directory & Advertising Consultants, a Williamsville, NJ firm specializing in Yellow Pages advertising.

Writing in the *Insurance Advocate*, Gajewski says the major mistake companies make is spending too much on Yellow Pages advertising, not too little.

"More than $11 billion a year is spent on Yellow Pages advertising, and I have found that as many as seven out of ten businesses are often sold on spending more than is needed to get the job done," writes Gajewski. "I have found that some companies spend twice as much as is necessary."

Gajewski lists the following reasons for this overspending:

* Lack of planning.
* Too little information.
* Decisions made in a hurry because sales reps from the Yellow Pages approach advertisers as space deadlines are about to close.
* Confusion with respect to the different listings, sizes, colors, positions, package deals, and especially the multiplying numbers of competing directories within each geographic area.

- Ad rates increasing faster than company revenue.
- Sales reps trying to sell more space than is needed to earn greater commissions.

The solution? "Do some thinking about how much you spend, how it affects your business, and whether some of that money could be used in other media," advises Gajewski.

STARTING YOUR PROGRAM

If you are already in business and have not been advertising in the Yellow Pages (or have been advertising, but not in a major way), then obviously Yellow Pages advertising does not mean life or death to your company. If you think more Yellow Pages advertising might be beneficial, my advice is to test, but slowly.

If you have no listing, start with a regular listing, a boldface listing, or a one-inch listing. If that generates positive results, gradually step up in size, taking a slightly larger ad each year. Keep track of all inquiries (almost all will be by telephone) generated by your Yellow Pages ad. Calculate the cost per inquiry by dividing the dollar amount spent on the ad space by the number of inquiries.

At first, running bigger ads will generate more inquiries. But at some point, running a bigger ad may cost you more money but not generate more business. Or, it may generate only a few more inquiries, thus raising the cost per inquiry substantially. At this point, you know you have reached the optimum size and should not take a bigger ad.

Also keep track of the cost per inquiry compared with other media. If the Yellow Pages cost per inquiry is competitive or slightly higher but brings in a lot of new business, keep the ad. On the other hand, if Yellow Pages advertising has a much higher cost per inquiry than other media and it does not bring good prospects to your door, drop it.

One small advantage of Yellow Pages advertising is that it is automatic. That is, you place your ad once and then forget about it; the ad runs throughout the year. With a direct mail program, on the other hand, a lot of time and effort go into planning, creating, and preparing the mailings. So if the two media produce equal results, the Yellow Pages gives you an edge because it takes a minimum of your time and attention.

TEN POWERFUL TECHNIQUES FOR IMPROVING YOUR YELLOW PAGES ADS

1. Use an identifying graphic. An identifying graphic is a simple illustration that immediately identifies the product or service being sold. If you run a limousine service, show a picture of a limousine. If you deliver flowers, show a hand holding flowers or the florist's delivery van. If your competitors do not use visuals (and many Yellow Pages ads do not), this graphic device will draw the reader's eye toward your ad first.

2. Highlight the phone number. Put the phone number in large type. Even if you include an address, 99 percent of your Yellow Pages inquiries will be via telephone. Any ad has only three-tenths of a second to catch the reader's attention or lose it. If you force readers to search for the telephone number—the information they want—they will give up and go to the next ad. People are busier today and more in a hurry than ever. The number should instantly pop off the page. Putting it in a box or highlighting it with some graphic device (sketch of telephone, arrow, etc.) also helps.

3. Position your ad toward the front. Unfortunately, the Yellow Pages are organized alphabetically and you cannot violate this order even by paying for a premium position. Many companies that depend on Yellow Pages advertising name themselves A-Plus or AAA simply to get at the front of their section. I'm not saying you necessarily want to do that, but it is something to consider.

4. List everything you sell. Another proven technique is to list everything you sell in your ad. One New Jersey insurance agent begins his Yellow Pages ad with the headline, "Insurance," and then goes on to list more than 30 different types of items he insures. He reasons that if he is the only agent to list snowmobiles in his ad, anyone turning to the Yellow Pages with a snowmobile to insure will be hooked by the ad. As a result, his small 2-column by 2 1/2-inch ad generates one or two phone calls every single business day of the year.

5. List your locations. People looking in the Yellow Pages want someone near them.

Let's say there are two plumbers. Plumber A's ad says,"We are located in Town A but serve all of Alphabet County." Plumber B's ad simply lists "Town A, Town B, Town C, Town D, Town E" under the telephone number. If people living in Town D need a plumber, who will they call first? That's right, Plumber B, because the ad creates the perception that Plumber B is local, and people would rather deal with a local company than a distant one. Somehow we think that, if the firm is local, they will charge less because they travel a shorter distance to reach us. Also, if there is a problem, it will be easier to get them back to correct it.

Our perception is that Plumber A has to travel far to reach us. Even if the company doesn't explicitly charge a travel fee, the time spent on the road will somehow be reflected in the invoice. Also, they will be less eager to come back if there's a problem because it costs them more in time.

In your Yellow Pages ad, make yourself look as local, nearby, and accessible as possible. All else being equal, consumers want to buy from the company nearest to them.

6. Include complete addresses. If space allows, put in your full street address, not just the town. Also include copy that identifies your precise location (e.g., "between Fifth and Sixth Avenues off Veteran's Circle").

Consumers are afraid of dealing with fly-by-night companies. They prefer to deal with a long-established, large firm with roots in the community and a proven track record of success rather than an individual who works out of the back of a pickup truck. A real street address says that you, too, must be real.

Along these lines, you might also include a sketch or photo of your building, especially if you are advertising in local (town or county versus multicounty) Yellow Pages and the building is well known or recognizable. This would be silly in a national ad, but locally, people feel comforted if they see a building they've driven by. The natural response is, "Oh yes, I know them."

7. Include your hours. People want you to be accessible. They want to know when they can reach you. So put your hours in your ad.

The ideal for a service firm is a company that can be reached 24 hours a day. If you are available 24 hours or have a separate phone number for evening or emergency service, put it in the ad and let people know they can reach you 24 hours a day, 7 days a week. If you are not available round the clock and your competitors advertise 24-hour service, consider adding it.

I also believe that a person should be able to call your company any time of the day or night and be able to leave a message rather than have the phone ring with no one picking up. I strongly recommend a night answering service or telephone answering machine for all businesses. Your fax machine should also have its own dedicated line and operate 24 hours a day, 7 days a week.

8. Highlight a free offer: free estimate, free analysis, free inspection, free design, free consultation. If you have a free offer, stress it in the ad. Use the word "Free." Put it on a separate line in large, bold type.

In many businesses, you must visit the consumer's home to give a price quotation. You have to go there to measure, inspect, examine, and determine what is involved with the job and what the cost will be. While you are there, you also sell the prospect on using your service.

Instead of viewing this as a sales call or a mandatory step in the selling process, consider it a free service to the consumer and emphasize it in your ad. Surprisingly, some of your competitors do not offer this for free but charge some nominal sum. You will get more inquiries and more opportunities to quote on jobs if you advertise a free estimate or other free offer in your Yellow Pages ad.

9. Put in licensing, bonding, and other technical credentials. People want to deal with a firm that is legitimate, and they are afraid that you may not be qualified to do the work or may not be properly licensed, bonded, or insured. Assuming you have the proper licensing, bonding, insurance, and permits, mention these in your ads, either in general terms ("licensed and insured") or in specifics ("NJ DEP License No. 44956"). Another credibility builder is to list the number of years you have been in business, especially if it is five years or longer.

10. State your unique selling proposition. Use a slogan, tag line, headline, or copy line that sums up the nature of your business and what you offer. Examples:

- "The largest variety of birds in Bergen County"
- "Specialists in plastic surgery of the nose"
- "The faucet specialists"
- "Professional resumes that work"
- "World's largest pool builder—from the simple to the sensational"

If you do something specialized, stress this in your tag line. For example, if you specialize in installing flat roofs, say "The flat roof specialists." People who are looking for what you sell, namely, a flat roof, will call you first before calling any of the others who merely advertise general roofing services.

OTHER OPTIONS

The Yellow Pages are not the only directories available. There are thousands of other directories aimed at business, institutional, and even some consumer markets.

Basically, there are two types of directories: vertical market directories (those aimed at specific industries) and general purpose directories (including the Yellow Pages, the *Thomas Register*, and others aimed at national or local audiences without regard to industry).

There are distinct vertical market directories for virtually any industry, discipline, or SIC code (Standard Industrial Classification). If a significant portion of your sales potential is in one market, the industry directory may be worth considering. An example is the *Red Book*, or *National Directory of Advertising Agencies*. Another is *Chemical Engineering Catalog*.

As for general directories, there are three basic types:

- Traditional industrial directories (such as the *Thomas Register*) that cover industrial products and services on a national or regional basis. Thomas Publishing, publisher of the *Thomas Register*, now sells a series of state directories of manufacturers.

- A growing number of business-to-business directories that cover not only manufacturers but services, computers, telecommunications—everything a business needs.

- The phone companies' Yellow Pages.

Which type of directory and which specific books or combination of books is right for you? That depends on the type of customer you serve (business, consumer, both), your geographic marketing area (local, regional, or national), and what you are selling. One way to determine the answer is to compare the profile of your customer base with the circulation profile of each directory. You'll also want to compare directories for ease of use, how actively the directory is promoted and distributed to users, completeness, reputation, distribution, subscriber costs, and, of course, advertising rates.

USAGE OF YELLOW PAGES AND INDUSTRIAL DIRECTORIES

According to Bell Atlantic, 61.5 percent of all American adults use the Yellow Pages at their place of business. Usage for individuals in professional and managerial positions was even higher: 70 percent, according to a study by Simmons Market Research Bureau.

Another national study, conducted by Audits and Surveys Company, polled a random sampling of 6,000 individuals representing a base of 458,943 buyers at manufacturing companies with from one to 1,000 or more employees. The study concluded that nine out of ten buyers use the Yellow Pages and initiate a phone call, letter, or visit as a result.

Directories and the Yellow Pages work well for business-to-business marketing, because in business-to-business, 97 percent of purchases result from buyer initiative (the buyer actively seeking a source) rather than seller initiative (the seller actively soliciting business), according to a survey of 900 business executives conducted by Business Marketing Services for *Thomas Register of American Manufacturers*.

According to this survey, a buyer typically looks at four potential suppliers before making a purchase: two new sources and two sources with which the company has previous experience. The survey revealed that 54 percent of the new sources are selected from industrial directories and guides by the buyer, 24 percent from the efforts of a salesperson calling on the company, 44 percent from a direct mail piece or magazine ad, and 18 percent from other sources.

In addition, 42 percent of the sources the company had previous experience with were also selected from directories, even though there was already an existing relationship between buyer and seller. Fifty-five percent of the contact with known vendors was made through salespeople, with the rest from magazine ads, direct mail, and other sources.

Business and industry buyers at all levels use directories. A high percentage of them use directories when they are ready to buy or when they need a new supplier. Prospects turning to your directory ad need a product but are not locked into a particular vendor. Indeed, a study by Burke Marketing Research of business and industrial buyers who used the Yellow Pages showed that 83 percent had no specific company in mind when they turned to the book.

Another growing trend is for companies to make purchases from local vendors rather than distant firms, when possible. According to research done for Illinois Bell among business-to-business directory users in the Chicago area, 76 percent of respondents with buying influence make more than half of their purchases in the metropolitan area.

These buyers also use directories frequently. The Illinois Bell study indicates that 91 percent of the buyers use directories at least once a month and 76 percent use them weekly.

EIGHT POWERFUL IDEAS FOR IMPROVING BUSINESS AND INDUSTRIAL DIRECTORY ADVERTISING

1. The bigger your ad, the more you get noticed. Every directory is crammed with thousands of ads and listings. An ordinary listing has little chance of being noticed. By using a boldface listing or display ad, you can increase effectiveness over a regular listing in the ways shown in Table 10.1.

As you can see, a one-column ad is 193 times more likely to be noticed and read than a regular listing.

2. Be complete. Industrial and business prospects want complete information, including product illustrations, brand names, types, sizes, specifications, tolerances, service policies, special capabilities, availability, delivery, company name, location, and telephone number. Remember, the person browsing through a directory wants to buy and is actively looking for a source. The more information you can provide, the more reasons for that buyer to respond to your ad. Make sure all information is accurate and up to date, paying special attention to trademarks, logos, product brand names, and telephone and fax numbers.

3. Consider color. In directories that offer it, using a second color in your ad is often worthwhile. According to the McGraw-Hill Laboratory of Advertising Performance, two-color ads earn a 60 percent better readership score than black-and-white ads. Color can be used to command attention, highlight important features and information, and even add a sense of urgency.

4. Make the layout clear and readable. Although directory ads typically contain many more elements than magazine ads, the layout should still be clear and readable, not cluttered. According to the Burke Marketing Research, 25 percent of directory users say they prefer ads with superior layout and design.

Table 10.1. Increased effectiveness of larger directory ads.

Type of Ad	Effectiveness Improvement vs. Regular Listing
Boldface listing	3:1
One-inch ad	9:1
1/4-column ad	13:1
1/2-column ad	64:1
1-column ad	193:1

5. Use co-op dollars. If you're involved in sales or distribution of products for other manufacturers, ask if they will sponsor your directory ad with co-op dollars. This can reduce your out-of-pocket costs by up to 50 percent.

6. Choose your categories carefully. Designing an ad program for a large, multiproduct general directory can be confusing. Often, there is more than one classification under which your ad could logically be placed. What do you do?

Make a list of all classifications pertinent to your business. Be sure to list every conceivable category under which a prospect might look to find you. List and number these categories in order of priority. Then determine the number and size of ads needed to do the job.

For example, there are five categories under which your product would fit. Two are the main categories; the other three are secondary. One solution would be to take large display ads in the two main sections and one-inch ads or boldface listings in the three secondary sections. Include a line with your one-inch ads or boldface listings that refers readers to your larger display ads in the other sections.

7. Study the competition. Directories are highly competitive environments in which you are literally guaranteed of being surrounded by your fiercest competitors. It pays to carefully study what the competition is up to and to respond accordingly. If you can afford to beat your competition by taking the biggest ad on the page, do so. If you can't, you'll have to rely on creativity to make your ad stand out. For instance, if your competitors don't offer free estimates, put "Free Estimates" in big, bold type or in a starburst in your ad. If your competitors don't feature a full product line, advertise the broadest line. You get the point.

8. Measure responses. Track and measure carefully both mail and phone response to your directory ads. Keep a record not only of inquiries generated but of how many of those inquiries were converted to sales and what the dollar amounts of the sales were. Directory ads are designed not to build image but to generate hard inquiries that result in serious prospects and new business. You should judge the success of directory advertising by the number of inquiries and the volume of sales produced.

CREATING MULTIPAGE CATALOG INSERTS FOR INDUSTRY DIRECTORIES AND BUYER'S GUIDES

When we say "catalog," most of us think of the kind you distribute or mail to customers and prospects. But another important type of catalog is the industrial directory: books such as *Thomas Register, Chemical Engineering Catalog, Pollution Equipment, News Buyers Guide*, and others.

Many companies find that inserting multipage ads (ranging from 2 to 16 pages and more) in these directories is the most productive catalog promotion they can use. But writing these inserts (as they are referred to in these directories) is different from writing freestanding catalog copy. These tips will help you produce effective inserts.

1. **Space is at a premium.** You pay for your insert as you would for space advertising: Each additional page increases the cost of the space by the directory's page rate. To run your regular catalog might take your entire ad budget for the year. So you've got to *condense your catalog* to an affordable number of pages.

Rarely is there space to solicit direct order by mail. Instead, *concentrate on stressing product benefits and superior service* so your insert will generate leads by phone. Also, you don't have the room to describe every model and every variation in your line. Instead, *highlight your best products in abbreviated fashion.*

2. **Generate leads.** This type of insert, like a Yellow Pages ad, is primarily designed to get the prospect to respond with a phone call and say, "This looks like it might meet my needs. Tell me more."

Make it easy for the prospect to respond. Highlight your toll-free number throughout the copy, at least once on every page. List regional offices and sales reps and their phone numbers (many people prefer to call locally). Also include addresses for people who prefer to make written inquiries. Give more than one phone extension so the reader won't get a busy signal. Label products clearly so the reader knows what to ask for. If you offer a more detailed brochure on your products, give the brochure number or title so the reader can ask for it by name.

3. **Skip the "cover."** Though brochures and other kinds of inserts use the front cover as a graphic and image-building device (and sometimes leave the back cover bare except for a logo), such a design tactic is a waste of money in a bound-in directory insert. *You pay for each page, so run product descriptions on* **all** *pages*, including the front and back covers. Don't waste a single inch of costly space. You'll have plenty of competition in these directories.

4. **Consider the competition.** Your insert competes with all other inserts in the directory (or at least with inserts selling similar products), so it pays to make yours stand out.

The best way to do this is with headlines and subheads that speak directly of the *benefits* of the products, what those products can do for the reader. Most directory inserts are poorly written: They consist of dry recitations of technical specifications and grainy black-and-white photos of the products against drop-cloth backgrounds. *Make yours exciting.* Show how the reader will come out ahead by doing business with you. Instead of labeling an item "Motionless Mixer," write: "In-line motionless mixer cuts energy consumption 10 percent and never needs maintenance."

5. **Grab their eyes.** The layout should be simple but also bold, crisp, and attractive. Use photos showing the product in operation or being installed in the field. Big headlines and subheads help tell the story and move the reader's eye along the page. Short paragraphs and a clean typeface make the copy more readable. Make your page a pleasure to look at and to read.

6. **Write in directory style.** A Yellow Pages or other directory ad is different from a magazine ad. The magazine ad must rely on a clever headline and visual to stop a reader who may not be thinking of the product. In a directory, the reader is actively looking for what your ad is selling. *The effective directory ad is one that gives readers what they are looking for.*

So it is with the insert. When readers pick up the industrial directory, they have a specific need in mind. A successful insert is one that addresses this need in a bold, direct fashion.

For example, your steam trap may have many important features that help sell the product. But experience has taught you that when people are ready to buy, their main concern is fast delivery. Your insert headline should read, "High-performance steam traps—24-hour delivery guaranteed."

7. **Focus on product features, not catalog utility.** Elsewhere I have stressed the benefits of making your catalog more valuable by including useful technical information in it. This turns your catalog into a technical reference work that the reader is inclined to keep around.

But this doesn't apply to the directory insert. The insert is bound into a directory that the reader has paid for and has every intention of keeping until next year's edition is available. So including general advice and information is a waste of space. Instead, concentrate on describing and selling your products.

8. **The insert on its own.** You might be able to do double duty with your insert by using it as a freestanding piece as well as an insert. If you plan on doing this, think about how this affects design and copy. Can the insert stand on its own as is? Will you need to add a cover, additional copy, or an order form? How expensive will these changes be? Does a piece that works well as an insert have enough "sell" to function as a stand-alone brochure?

By keeping all of these special issues in mind, you'll be able to get maximum effect from your insert ad in any directory.

ADVERTISING IN INDUSTRIAL DIRECTORIES PAYS OFF

If you can't afford a multipage buyer's guide insert, you can still advertise profitably in these directories with a space ad that's only a fraction of a page. Here are some pointers to keep in mind when planning these ads.

1. **Bigger is better.** According to a study by the Thomas Publishing Company, the biggest ad on the page in the *Thomas Register* pulls 40 times more response than a standard listing. Even a boldfaced listing pulls double the response of a regular listing. So the bigger the ad, the better.

2. **Is one big ad better than many small ones?** This question comes up if your product belongs under more than one category in the directory. The answer is to have the biggest ad you can in the category where people are most likely to look for your product. Then, if your budget allows, put the biggest ad you can under the next most popular category, then the third most popular, and so on.

Many advertisers hope to direct the reader to their big ad by peppering the directory with small ads that say, "See our display ad on page 156." Unfortunately, readers are lazy and seldom bother to turn to page 156. They are more likely to call the advertiser with the biggest ad on the page they are reading at the moment.

3. **Be first.** Ads in the front of a particular section of the directory are more likely to be read than ads in the middle or the back, so it pays to put your ad up front. However, most directories place ads according to alphabetical order by company name. Unless you're willing to change your company name from Zenon Tubing to A-Plus Tubes, you'll be stuck at the back. (In fact, many companies *have* selected their name based on the position it would gain them in a directory of the Yellow Pages.) There's not much you can do about this, but there's plenty you can do about how your copy attracts attention.

4. **Telegraph the headline.** In a magazine ad, you must rely on a clever, attention-getting headline to stop a reader who's not necessarily looking for what you are selling. You *make* the reader interested. But a reader who turns to an industrial directory is actively looking for a specific product or for a solution to a problem. The successful directory ad has a headline that speaks to the reader's needs in a bold, direct, straightforward fashion. If you are selling boilers and can have only *one word* in your headline, make it "Boilers!" in 72-point type.

5. **Highlight the reader's immediate concern.** Your experience has revealed what your customers' main concerns are when they're close to ordering your product. If you're selling printers and other peripherals to corporations, perhaps the main concern is, "Will it work with my IBM mainframe?" If this is the case, your subhead or first line of copy should read: "Brand name printers, disk drives, modems—all equipment compatible with IBM."

6. **Make secondary features immediately clear.** The reader also has other concerns that the copy must immediately address—or else the reader will drift to the next ad.

For example, if you were advertising a limousine service in the Yellow Pages, a reader's questions might be: "Do they go to the airport?" "How much do they cost?" "Can you reserve a ride in advance?" "Do they have 24-hour service?" "What kind of car do they send?" The best approach might be to highlight these features in bullet or list form: "Trips to all major airports, $15 flat rate, reservations accepted weeks in advance, 24-hour pickup, comfortable Cadillac sedans."

7. **Complete information can help sell.** Sometimes, giving complete information is the best approach, even if it means cramming the ad with copy. One insurance agent reasoned that people looking for insurance would be most likely to respond to an ad mentioning the specific type of insurance they want: homeowners', life, motorcycle, mobile home, yacht, etc. Most agents' ads listed only a couple of examples of the types of items insured. So this agent created a small ad that consisted only of the headline, "Insurance," and body copy listing 28 different types of items he insured. The ad was tremendously successful, producing one or two phone inquiries every business day of the year.

8. **Highlight the fine print.** Some features that seem minor at the start of the sales cycle become major concerns when you're close to the sale. When people pick up a directory, they're moving rapidly from prospect to customer. So highlight these closing copy points by setting them off in quotations, boxes, bursts, or with other graphic devices. Typical features to highlight include: "20-year guarantee," "free estimates," "24-hour service," "fully licensed," "bonded," "fully insured," "custom jobs handled," and "meets military specifications."

9. **Make it easy to respond by phone or mail.** Print your phone number in larger type so it leaps out at the reader. Don't make the reader search for the phone number or address. Use a toll-free number if you have one. Include more than one extension so the reader won't get a busy signal. But don't design the ad as a coupon. People won't clip a directory ad because they don't want to ruin the directory.

Chapter

11
TELEVISION COMMERCIALS

In his book, *How to Produce an Effective Television Commercial*, Hooper White states, "The television commercial...a combination of sight and sound that moves to impart fact or evoke emotion...is one of the most potent selling tools ever forged." The *Handbook of Advertising Management*, edited by Roger Barton, says "Television is the closest thing to the ideal salesman—a real person available within our current media environment. It moves, it talks, it demonstrates, it is in the home." According to Coopers & Lybrand, U.S. advertisers spent $13.7 billion on broadcast advertising on TV networks and $6.6 billion on cable TV advertising in 1996 (as reported in *Business News*, November 17, 1997).

Not surprisingly, then, the television commercial is one of the most popular selling tools used by advertisers today. The viewing public is now bombarded with 320,000 commercials per year, up 20 percent from 1985. More importantly, according to the Television Bureau of Advertising, Inc., adults rate TV advertising as the most authoritative, most believable, and most influential of the advertising media. Many of the larger full-service advertising agencies derive as much as 70 percent of their billings from television commercials.

When should you consider making broadcast advertising a part of your marketing mix? If you work for a large consumer products company, the broad reach provided by television advertising may well be worth the high cost of producing a commercial (anywhere from $10,000 to well over $1,000,000), not to mention the cost of airtime.

For many small companies, television advertising is automatically dismissed because of the high cost. But as David Ogilvy writes in *Ogilvy on Advertising*, "Inexpensive commercials can be highly effective if they come directly to the point and offer something of genuine interest."

WHEN BUSINESS-TO-BUSINESS ADVERTISERS CAN BENEFIT FROM TV

For small business-to-business advertisers to benefit from TV advertising, according to Jeffrey W. Kaumeyer, vice president and group manager at Hammond Farrell Inc., a New York City advertising agency, these conditions must be met:

1. Your prospects must be concentrated geographically. Unless you're an IBM or Xerox, you probably can't afford to take 30 seconds during prime time television at $200,000, at least not frequently enough to achieve concentration and continuity. But if your prospects are concentrated in a regional area, a 30-second spot on a top-rated news program in that area may cost as little as $200 or $300. While a similar spot in New York City may cost $3,500, it's still an efficient buy on a cost-per-thousand basis.

2. Even if you can afford a nationwide broadcast of your television commercial and have potential customers scattered throughout the country, you must balance the prospects reached with the vast number of nonprospects who will also receive your message and the cost of production and airtime. That's why cable television, with its segmented audiences, has gained a strong foothold with advertisers against "the big three" networks.

3. You must be willing to have your sales pitch boiled down to one simple, compelling message. Your message should be simple because there is time for only about 65 words in a 30-second spot. Also, "as with your other ads, your sales proposition should be single-minded and worthwhile," says Kaumeyer.

4. Because your TV spot has to compete with about 3,000 other advertising messages daily for your prospect's attention, you need to appeal to the human, emotional side of your prospect.

5. Television must be complemented by the other more basic components in a complete marketing communications plan. A media mix adds impact to a plan. A combination of TV and print is more effective than either one alone. Publicity plus TV plus print is even better. Therefore, says Kaumeyer, a business marketer should not consider TV as its only medium. Don't expect any one form of advertising to do the whole selling job. But TV can turn the spotlight on your company.

6. Before you go ahead with a commercial, be sure you have the appropriate sales training and inquiry handling procedures in place. Aim for consistency with your other advertising messages, too. For television to be effective, it should reinforce the overall selling theme that is featured in your print ads and radio commercials.

MAKING YOUR TV COMMERCIAL STAND OUT AND SELL

The average household spends more than seven hours a day watching television. Since the public's attention is already captured by television, the challenge to advertisers is not to get prospects to turn on the commercials but rather to prevent them from tuning them out.

"On a mass consumer goods level," writes Herschell Gordon Lewis in *How to Make Your Advertising Twice as Effective at Half the Cost*, "a product can't achieve high visibility without television. But no other mechanical invention in history is so capable of emptying pocketbooks, bringing peculiar results in which competitors are helped as much as you are, or building the advertiser's ego if not his business."

To avoid wasting your money, you have to know what works and what doesn't in TV advertising. With the increasing clutter of TV commercials, fueled by the growing number of 15-second spots, how do you make your commercial get noticed and succeed at selling your product or service? Here are some tips from experts:

1. First, remember that television is a visual medium, something even as esteemed an authority as David Ogilvy admits to mistakenly ignoring in the early days of TV advertising. In *Confessions of an Advertising Man*, he writes, "You must make your pictures tell the story; what you show is more important than what you say. Words and pictures must work together, reinforcing each other."

2. Use verbal exclamations that trigger the viewer's interest. Words such as new, amazing, revolutionary, and incredible still work if they truthfully describe a product or product innovation.

3. Provide information about the product so that prospects can make a judgment about buying it. True potential buyers want information, and without it they may feel cheated.

4. Follow David Ogilvy's dictum of repeating the name of the product "ad nauseum" throughout the commercial, and show it at least once. Show the package or product itself. "Make your product the hero of the commercial," Ogilvy advises. Be sure to use the name of the product within the first 10 seconds.

5. Don't mention your competitors. If you do, you take the risk that viewers will think your commercial promoted your competitor's product.

6. Stick to one or two points. If you try to make too many points, you'll wind up not making any as far as the viewer is concerned.

7. Use close-ups of the product so that, when people remember your commercial, they'll remember what it was advertising.

8. Use a strong opener. If you don't have an attention-getting, dramatic opener, viewers won't stick around long enough to find out anything more.

9. Sound effects that relate to the product, such as coffee percolating or eggs frying, will enhance emotional appeal.

10. Use an on-screen actor rather than a voice-over for narration.

11. If you offer a money back guarantee, stress it. Alvin Eicoff, a pioneer in television direct response techniques, writes in his autobiography, *Or*

Your Money Back, "there is no more powerful sales tool than a money back guarantee. It bridges the credibility gap. It can be the offer that persuades undecided viewers to try your product. It's especially important in overcoming buying resistance when a product seems to be too good to be true."

12. Supers increase sales. Spell out your message in type and superimpose it over the visual. Reinforce the message by having an actor read it while it's being spelled out.

NINE TYPES OF COMMERCIALS THAT WORK BEST

According to David Ogilvy in *Ogilvy on Advertising*, research and experience show that nine types of commercials are above average in their ability to change people's brand preference:

1. Humor. At one time, well-known advertising men like Ogilvy and Claude Hopkins held fast to the belief that humor didn't sell. But studies of changes in brand preference today indicate that humor can sell. Be forewarned that writing humor is difficult, however, and few copywriters can do it well.

2. Slice of life. This widely used format features a real-life setting in which one person explains to another why he or she should use the particular product. The commercial is essentially a playlet that establishes a problem, introduces the product that will solve the problem, and ends with the product being used to solve the problem.

While this format is often disdained by copywriters because it has a tendency to seem corny, research shows it is effective in increasing sales for large manufacturers of soaps, detergents, and other packaged goods.

3. Testimonials. These commercials depict a loyal user of the product defending it and, in the process, describing its merits. Alternatively, such commercials show real people being introduced to a product and discovering that they like it. Such commercials work best when the users do not know they are being filmed.

4. Demonstrations or problem–solution commercials. These show how well your product can perform. Adman Alvin Eicoff believes this is the most effective TV commercial you can make if you can set forth a problem, explain a solution, and then demonstrate why your product offers the best solution. It's even better if you can make your product show how to solve a really tough problem, such as a car wax shining up an old, battered car or a laundry detergent getting out grease. Such demonstrations carry added impact.

5. The stand-up presenter (also called a talking head). Agencies don't generally like these commercials, which consist solely of a presenter describing the virtues of a product, because they think they're not creative enough. But this type of commercial is above average in changing brand preference.

Good casting and good direction are the keys to making it work. Hooper White writes, "This approach works best when the product needs a human being to demonstrate it or when you want the mesmerizing effect of a forthright salesperson talking to a potential customer."

6. Characters who become identified with a product over the course of several years, such as Josephine the Plumber for Comet and Rosie the Waitress for Bounty Paper Towels, become the living symbol of the product. They are often featured in the slice-of-life playlet format. If the characters are relevant to your product, they can be above average in changing audience brand preference.

7. Reason why. Give viewers a rational reason why your product is superior, and you'll increase sales. Remember when freeze-dried coffee was first introduced? It was advertised as being better than regular instant because the flavor was quickly "locked in" during the freezing process. Explaining the advantages of freeze drying convinced many viewers to try the new coffee.

8. News. "Products, like human beings, attract the most attention when they are first born," writes Ogilvy. So if a product is new, play it up. If you can come up with new uses for an old product, so much the better. By telling consumers that an open box of baking soda would keep their refrigerators smelling sweet, Arm & Hammer rang up millions of new sales.

9. Appealing to the emotions can be as effective as any rational appeal, but people also need a rational excuse to justify their emotional decisions. Beer and wine cooler commercials, car commercials, and food commercials typically play off viewers' emotions, such as nostalgia or the desire for enjoyment, adventure, love, status, or respect.

White writes, "Often, commercial ideas can be expressed nonverbally by using an emotional combination of pictures and music. This is an interesting approach, particularly if your idea would benefit from emotional responses."

Ogilvy lists three types of commercials that do not work well: the celebrity testimonial, musical vignettes, and cartoons or animation. The first two entertain but they usually don't sell. Too often, viewers remember the celebrity and not the product or worse, think the celebrity was pitching a competitor's product. Cartoons reduce credibility when used to pitch products to adults. However, there are cases when animation can be effective in selling a product or service, such as in showing the effect of a fertilizer on a lawn's root system, for instance.

WHAT LENGTH SHOULD YOUR COMMERCIAL BE?

Currently, you can purchase television commercials in the following lengths: 10 seconds, 15 seconds, 20 seconds, 30 seconds, 45 seconds, 60 seconds, 90 seconds, and 120 seconds. Infomercials are typically 30 minutes. The length will affect not only the cost of airtime, but also production costs.

To determine the length of the commercial, you must decide how much time it will take to sell your product or service.

Advertisers and ad agencies have long debated over what length commercial is the most effective. For instance, Alvin Eicoff writes, "Generally, between one and two minutes is necessary to do an effective selling job. An even more compelling reason for advertisers to create longer commercials is the isolation factor theory: It stipulates that if you can obtain sole possession of a commercial break, you can greatly increase the motivational power of your commercial." He compares the clustering of 30-second commercials to "having four salesmen confronting you at once, with no time to absorb one sales pitch before the next one starts."

Indeed, research studies show that, although viewers don't time commercials, they are more irritated when many commercials occur in a row than when one or two longer commercials are back to back. Corporations such as Hallmark, Kraft Foods, and IBM sponsor specials so that they can achieve isolation of longer commercials within the shows. In fact, the "big three" networks' concern over the high cost of programming, coupled with advertisers' desire for more quality programming in which to advertise, is leading to a resurgence in fully sponsored programs.

On the other hand, 30-second commercials have long been the most popular choice of advertisers. But since 15-second commercial spots became widely available in 1985, they have been steadily gaining in popularity. Fifteen-second spots accounted for 10 percent of total network commercials in 1985, but for 36 percent of network commercials by the end of 1988.

The fact that 15-second spots cost half as much as 30-second spots in network airtime, while reaching the same number of viewers, is largely the reason for this popularity. Whether they have the same impact as a 30-second commercial is debatable, however. Early recall studies in the mid-1980s showed the average 15-second spot to be about two-thirds as effective as a 30-second spot. But since 1985, there has been a slight, yet consistent, drop in commercial recall.

Although there is less time to get your message across, if your primary objective is frequency to reinforce a brand name or your company name to prospects who already are familiar with you, a 15-second spot can represent the ideal buy.

While the advent of 15-second commercials has helped smaller and lower-budget advertisers break into TV advertising, as an advertiser you should be aware that the growth in 15-second spots is a cause of concern to many television sales executives, advertisers, and ad agencies, who worry that this "clutter" will further alienate a declining network television audience. To limit the number of 15-second spots, television executives are already discussing raising their prices from 50 percent to 65 percent of the cost of airing a 30-second commercial.

In addition, local stations already charge a premium for the 15-second spot, at 75 percent of the airtime cost of a 30-second spot. They also limit the availability of the shorter units and subject them to preemption by 30-second spots.

One last tip on selecting commercial length: When planning your commercial, think not only in terms of your present campaign but what you might want to show in the future. Many companies run shorter versions of their 60-second or 30-second spots to build frequency. But if you're planning to run a 15-second or 30-second spot now, you may want to shoot extra footage at the same time for running longer commercials later. This can be done at much less cost now when sets, crew, cast, and equipment are already in place, than if you later decide to produce a new, longer commercial. Most of the extra work will fall to the creative team, who will have to draw up another script and storyboard expanding on the shorter commercial.

RELY ON REPETITION

Overall, repetition of your commercial message counts more toward increasing sales than does length. "One of the most effective ways to advertise is through repetition, and advertisers can reach TV's many audiences often because people spend so much time viewing," reports the Television Bureau of Advertising.

Longevity is another aspect of frequency. Rosser Reeves long ago pointed out, "If you find something that works, keep it on the air until it doesn't work any more." Also remember that you will get tired of your commercial long before your audience does. Changing commercials that still pull wastes your company's money.

When and how often you run your commercial depends on your budget, your product's sales cycle, the commercial's message (a retail commercial advertising an upcoming sale obviously won't run for very long), and the market you are targeting (if you're a business-to-business marketer targeting executives, you won't run your commercial during the day). Many advertisers start out a campaign with 60-second commercials, and then switch to a higher-frequency schedule of 30-second spots, reasoning that viewers won't perceive the switch to the shorter commercial (proven by research to be true) but will connect the 30-second message with the 60-second one.

According to Herschell Gordon Lewis, if you want to stretch your budget, an ideal period in which to buy commercial time is the 10:30 or 11:30 P.M. movie. Husbands and wives both watch, and audience size compares favorably to cost.

In both network and spot television (television time bought market by market), prime time costs by far the most money. Early evening news comes in second highest in airtime cost on the network side, and late news holds that rank in spot television. But late evening (the time period during which the late movie runs) is only slightly more expensive than daytime, the cheapest period of the day in which to buy time. In 1989, the cost per 30 seconds of a late evening commercial came to $26,400 on network television. Meantime, the average cost of a 30-second commercial during prime time is $109,400 on network television. Considering that the audience for the late evening commercial is roughly one-third of that watching the prime-time commercial, but that the late evening price is less than one-quarter of the prime-time price, late evening is the more efficient buy from a cost-per-thousand standpoint.

Writes Lewis, "No one pays the one-time [commercial] rate. And only beginners try to buy 60-second spots between 7:00 and 10:00 in the evening on network affiliated stations, because those are reserved for program sponsors." Rate cards (published in *Television Rates & Data*) mean very little, since time buyers negotiate for discounts and special deals. For the savvy buyer, ten spots can end up costing less than five. The inroads made by cable TV and syndicated shows in attracting advertisers have made network and local stations more willing to cut deals and tailor a varied package of buys to the advertiser's needs. Discount time buying companies are one way to buy time cheaply; another is to use an ad agency familiar with buying TV time.

PRODUCING THE TV COMMERCIAL

Advertisers interested in broadcast advertising usually work with an ad agency. "The making of a commercial is a three-way partnership between agency, client, and director," points out John Lyons in *Guts: Advertising from the Inside Out*. Production typically involves a director, camera operator, actors, editor, electricians, prop people, stylists, makeup people, and sound engineers. Careful preproduction planning well in advance of shooting the commercial is essential to avoid costly changes and overtime during filming.

If you are limited in terms of how much you can spend on the commercial, be sure your ad agency knows your budget. You don't want to end up with a multi-actor extravaganza shot in numerous locations that costs $500,000 when you were budgeting on $100,000.

Choosing the Commercial Idea

The first step in the production process is coming up with a good idea for the commercial, one that will fit into your overall marketing plan for the product or service, with the goal of building public awareness and increasing sales. The idea should be strong enough on its own not to depend on jazzy production techniques to make it work. White writes, "The best commercial ideas are those that are strong enough conceptually to become campaigns, rather than one-shot commercials."

Such repeatability can develop out of presenting a copy claim in the same unique way in each commercial; using an unusual technique, such as music, casting, or editing style, to identify the idea throughout the series; or following a theme that sets your products apart from the competition in the same way throughout a campaign. For example, if all of your competitors are emphasizing low cost, you might focus on reliability or fast service.

One effective commercial can be the prototype for a series that runs for years. Other commercials may run for only 13 weeks. If you can come up with a long-running commercial that increases sales, you can not only save money on new creative strategy costs every few months but also strengthen the overall impact of your advertising through quick customer recognition and loyalty.

The Review Process

After an internal agency review and revisions, the commercial idea is presented to the advertiser on a storyboard, which consists of multi-frame illustrations of the action that will take place in the commercial. The storyboard also contains the copy to be spoken or superimposed throughout the commercial. A storyboard for a 30-second commercial has between 8 and 16 frames, and each must be part of a logical sequence. If you are not happy with the storyboard or some element of it, this is the time to speak up. Be specific about what you don't like, but try not to take an adversarial tack with the agency staff. Remember, both you, the advertising manager, and your ad agency have the same goal: to produce the best advertising for your product.

Hooper White offers these other tips, directed at agency creative staff but useful to anyone reviewing a commercial idea:

- Unless you can describe the thrust of your commercial in one or two sentences, it's probably too complicated.

- Keep your commercial simple and direct. Develop the ability to be exact, brief, and to the point.

- Think in terms of sight and sound combinations that will verbalize and illustrate your idea.

- Try to visualize your prospective customers and produce a commercial that will make them receptive to your selling message.

- Learn to think and plan within budgetary restrictions.

As ad manager, you can help your ad agency do its job better by informing your account executive of your company's marketing strategy, budget, target markets, and which features or benefits you and company management feel are your product's strongest selling points. You should provide the account executive ahead of time with everything needed to make the commercial idea and the presentation meet your key criteria. By helping your ad agency know as much as possible about your product and your marketing goals, you increase the chance that they will create a mutually pleasing commercial the first time around, saving your company time and money.

Choosing a Production House and Director

Once the advertising agency producer receives approved storyboards from the advertiser, he or she must then obtain bids from commercial production houses. Usually bids are requested from three houses and then reviewed with the advertiser. The agency generally makes the recommendation as to which production house to hire. The recommendation may not be based on the lowest bid, since the choice of a director is often critical and a more expensive director may well be worth the additional cost.

On the other hand, a top-notch director may not be as available to spend time with you and the agency on casting and other important pre-production decisions. So you'll need to weigh cost and availability against the director's talent (as judged from past work and reputation), flexibility, and personality as well as your own needs in order to make a decision.

Be aware that directors have their own styles and specialties. Some are good at putting together humorous commercials, others are better at slice-of-life commercials. Some prefer the excitement and uncertainty of on-location shooting, others like the control of filming on a sound stage. Look for a director who knows that the ultimate job is solving a marketing problem and selling a product, albeit in an entertaining manner. Good directors take the time to ask questions about the product and its target audience.

Tape or Film?

Videotape lends a real "live" quality to a commercial and is faster to handle in postproduction. Unlike film, it can be played back immediately after takes on production day, allowing the director to make quick decisions about whether to reshoot a scene. On the other hand, film offers deeper color and texture and more choices in optical effects. Your agency and producer will make the decision about which to use and can fill you in on the advantages of using each for your specific commercial (although almost no one uses film anymore).

Casting

Casting for the commercial will begin during the bidding process. Although casting is really the province of the agency and production house, you should approve the casting specifications before casting begins. Casting specifications include a profile of the type of person to be used in the commercial including age, physical description, and personality. After the agency and director make their selection, you will be asked for approval.

In *How to Get the Best Advertising from Your Agency*, Nancy L. Salz suggests you ask the following questions in judging casting:

- Is the casting believable and convincing?
- Does the individual fit the specifications agreed to?
- Do you feel yourself respond as the actor is reading?

If you cannot make a judgment and don't feel strongly negative about the casting, trust the instincts of your agency and director, who have seen a lot of talent and have good eyes for who's right in what type of commercial.

Preproduction Meeting

This is where all the details of the final production are determined. The meeting should be held several days before the actual shooting, in case you wish to make changes in casting, set design, location, or anything else. Many agencies and production companies hold preproduction meetings without the client but, since it's your money that's being spent, it's wise to take the time to attend. Your presence and answers to questions can help prevent problems and extra expense on shooting day or in postproduction. However, the agency person in charge of the production should run the meeting.

A strict agenda should be followed in the preproduction meeting, which may involve agency creative staff, the director, producer, production assistant, casting director, set designer, stylist, and sometimes the cameraperson, if special lighting effects are required. During this meeting, final details regarding the commercial are discussed, such as set or location, props, music, casting, production schedule, and clothing or food styling.

This is the time to discuss alternate casting choices, specific camera angles, extra shots, product handling and delivery, and essentially all the details that might come up during actual production and cause cost over-runs. Both cast and crew are usually unionized and their costs are fixed. If you go into overtime during shooting, you can end up spending thousands of dollars extra for their time on the set.

Since food or clothes stylists, set designers, camerapersons, and other production staff charge for their meeting time, invite them to show up at a specific time and limit their participation to a scheduled time slot. This will not only keep expenses down, but will help prevent wandering from the prepared agenda, so that the meeting stays on track and does not run unnecessarily long.

Production Day

In New York or Hollywood, your commercial's production crew will probably number at least 15 people. This is because of union requirements that require a different person to handle each of the many responsibilities on a shoot. Your crew will probably be members of IATSE (the International Alliance of Theatrical Stage Employees) or of NABET (the National Association of Broadcast Electrical Technicians).

On the set, your role will be to make sure everything is filmed as approved by your management on the storyboard. While new shots and camera angles can be added for possible editing into the commercial during the postproduction phase, the commercial must also be filmed as agreed upon in preproduction. If you have any questions or concerns during production, you should relay them to the agency producer, who serves as liaison with the director. The agency producer may be the copywriter, art director, or someone else from the agency, but it is up to him or her to get the answers to your questions and solve any problems with the director. This chain of command is designed to keep the production running smoothly.

Keep your eye on what is happening in front of the camera, so that any problems can be resolved while there's still time to act on them. If you say that something isn't correct, be prepared to explain why. On the other hand, be aware that directors and actors need time to get things right. First shots usually aren't final takes, so don't panic if the actor doesn't read the lines correctly at first.

Your other responsibility will be to make sure the product is shown, handled, and used correctly.

Postproduction Editing

The dailies (unedited film footage) are usually viewed the day after shooting. The set has not yet been taken down so, if reshooting is necessary, the cost will be minimized.

Although the advertiser does not usually have a representative present for this screening, you can ask to see these preliminary results of the shoot. Usually the director, editor, script clerk, agency producer, and sometimes the agency writer or art director will view the dailies. The purpose is to make sure all necessary footage has been shot and developed, decide if any retakes are necessary, and give the editor an opportunity to note comments from the director and others about the effectiveness of certain scenes.

If you do attend this screening, be forewarned that the scenes you will see will not yet have been corrected for balanced lighting or color from take to take, and any special effects, dissolves, or supers will not be incorporated at this stage. The scenes will probably not be in chronological sequence, and words spoken at the start and end of the takes by the director and crew will not be edited out yet.

After this initial screening, or in some cases once the director has done an initial editing, the film or tape is given to the editorial house that has been selected to do the finish work. A 30-second dialogue commercial shot in 35mm film typically has 3,000 feet of film. A commercial that has many scenes to be edited to an existing soundtrack may require as much as 16,000 feet of film. The editor's job is to reduce that to 45 feet (about 720 frames of film) for the finished commercial!

At some time during the editing process, you or your ad agency will have an opportunity to review either a rough cut or "answer print," the first composite film print struck from the negative that shows whether color and quality are acceptable for the commercial. This is the time when you can make editing changes without great expense. By the way, if the editor needs to cut dialogue either to fit the commercial's time limitations or to make it flow more smoothly, he or she must seek approval from your ad agency.

Whether your commercial was shot on film or tape, it will be finished and made color-perfect by transferring to tape. This is the point at which opticals are inserted, audio tracks are mixed, and the commercial is finished. You and your management will then be asked to give final approval before duplicate tapes are made and shipped to the television stations.

PRODUCING JOINT-VENTURE COMMERCIALS AND INFOMERCIALS

Financing is a common roadblock for most start-up businesses, particularly if the business involves direct response television, which people outside the industry often perceive as an extremely high risk. Infomercials, a relatively new form of marketing, have their share of critics who consider their stability to be suspect. Because of this and the general volatility of television advertising, conventional financing is often out of the question. Start-up businesses and individual entrepreneurs often seek friends and family members to provide seed capital for infomercial production and test marketing.

A simple infomercial with no celebrities, elaborate props, or post-production effects may cost anywhere from $10,000 to $15,000 to shoot and edit in 3/4 inch U-Matic format. Add to this another $10,000 to $15,000 for TV airtime, and you should estimate a minimum cost of $20,000 to reasonably launch an infomercial on your own.

Infomercial Marketing Companies (IMCs)

These are among the best sources for financing for two primary reasons: 1) they are familiar with the industry and have available funds, and 2) their hands-on involvement with your campaign provides expertise. Here are some points to consider if you are thinking about using an IMC:

Airtime inventory. The strength of IMCs lies in their huge inventory of excellent TV airtime available for half-hour paid programs. Most of these companies buy huge blocks of strategic (early evenings and weekends) airtime from most major cable networks.

Quality production. Most IMCs have their own production facilities. Those that don't usually have access to the best production houses in the country. These production capabilities are usually combined with talent agencies that enable them to negotiate the best rates for celebrities.

Management. The third benefit to using an IMC is its experience in managing infomercial campaigns. If a major IMC takes on your product, your campaign is likely be handled by experienced managers.

Proven products only. Two major constraints are normally imposed by IMCs. One has to do with your product; IMCs do not take on every product that comes their way. Presenting your product to an IMC is similar to an author selling a manuscript to a major publishing firm. Your product must pass a set of litmus tests before the IMC will consider risking its dollars on your product. If you have only a prototype of your product, it may be more difficult to sell to an IMC. If the IMC does buy it, they usually want to get involved with the actual manufacturing of your product.

Conversely, if your product has been successfully sold in some other form of direct response marketing, or if you have already produced and test marketed some version of your infomercial and have impressive sales performance numbers, IMCs will be more receptive. Furthermore, having numbers to substantiate your offer will give you negotiating leverage.

Control. Some entrepreneurs hesitate to deal with an IMC because of the control factor, both financial and creative. Without any numbers to back your projections, your figures are mere speculation. As a newcomer to the business, you will not have the leverage to dictate financial terms nor will you have a free hand in determining how your product should be presented.

As with most other business, the leverage goes to the party with the most to offer. If you are new in the business and have an unproven product, you do not have the luxury of shopping around for the best offer. On the other hand, if you have a proven product, particularly one that has been test marketed via an infomercial, you can compare offers and negotiate the best terms.

Open deal. There is no set structure for financial terms between entrepreneurs and IMCs. Each company has a formula for structuring a deal, which may vary from one product to the next. You will be better off focusing your evaluation on two factors: 1) how much money you stand to make based on their projections; 2) how much time it will take for you to make your first dollar.

Needless to say, where profit projections are concerned, IMCs tend to be conservative. When your objective is to convince them that your product will make them a lot of money, the IMC will naturally argue the opposite. Therefore, when evaluating an offer, consider your own projections objectively while viewing the IMC's figures as being pessimistic.

Going upscale. To provide leverage for dealing with major IMCs, entrepreneurs commonly launch their own small-scale infomercial campaigns to produce performance figures favorable for negotiation.

The strategy usually follows this sequence:

1. Produce a simple infomercial to test market your product.
2. Buy airtime in a number of secondary markets and track the results.
3. Present your product and your test market numbers to an IMC.

```
A major infomercial company can rev up your sales at an
accelerated pace you may not be able to afford on your
own.
```

With a heftier production budget and a huge inventory of prime infomercial airtime, an IMC can do wonders for your campaign. You can reshoot your basic infomercial to feature celebrities and give your new infomercial a glossy look. With the expanded access to better TV airtime, your sales can soar at a rate you may have been unable to produce on your own.

TYPES OF TELEVISION MEDIA BUYS

To appreciate the true value of a particular media buy, we have grouped TV stations into three categories and analyzed their rates based on their comparative coverage. The three categories are:

National. These TV stations are either cable networks or national super-stations. (To illustrate, we'll use Nickelodeon at 1:30 A.M. on weekdays, which costs $12,500.)

Primary. These are local broadcast TV stations in major cities with at least one million TV homes. (We'll use WPGH, the Fox affiliate in Pittsburgh, at 1:30 A.M. on weekdays, which costs $900.)

Secondary. These are local broadcast TV stations in smaller or secondary cities, usually with fewer than 500,000 TV homes. (We'll use WWAT, an independent in Columbus, Ohio at 1:30 A.M. on weekdays, which costs $150.)

Charting comparative rates and effective reach of each station yields the following:

TV Group		CPM*	Rate	TV Homes
Nationals	0.20	$12,500		63 million
Primary	0.75	$ 900		1.2 million
Secondary	0.43	$ 150		350,000

* The acronym CPM stands for Cost Per Thousand (M stands for mil, Latin for thousand). Based on the preceding table, if all the potential viewers being reached by each respective station were watching that station at that time, it would cost you 20 cents to reach every 1,000 viewers watching a widely subscribed cable network, 75 cents per 1,000 viewers for a primary station, and 43 cents per 1,000 viewers in a secondary market.

Although it seems obvious that you may want to split your media buys between the national and secondary markets, often this is not possible. Here are some of the reasons:

• Airtime on national stations is hard to come by. Fewer than 20 cable networks and superstations fall into this category, and most available infomercial time has already been purchased or is controlled by major media brokers and infomercial production houses.

• In the test market stage, it is unwise to invest a lot of money in national media buys. It is better to spread your budget over a string of secondary markets to get a better feel for viewer feedback.

• Finding good secondary markets involves a fair amount of research. It is best to deal with media brokers who specialize in this category.

Testing. Always test media on an OTO (one-time-only) basis. Even Fortune 500 companies with multimillion-dollar budgets always test their products and the media where they are placed. No one can accurately predict the outcome of an untested campaign. Lay out a sensible test campaign and evaluate the results accordingly.

To do it yourself, secondary markets with airtime rates between $150 and $400 offer ideal, low-risk vehicles for test marketing your infomercial. Although TV stations in secondary markets do not generally offer the best CPM (compare to nationwide cable channels), they charge the lowest entry fees required to get a fair "let-the-market-decide" type of evaluation for an infomercial.

Approval. As soon as the first draft of your infomercial is complete, make several copies and send one to each station you are considering. But before you send any tape for approval, contact the station to confirm that they have available airtime. The approval process can take anywhere from a day to a month, depending on who you know and the overall attitude at that station.

Media brokers. Media brokers are independent companies that sell airtime for stations nationwide. Stations pay these brokers a commission based on the cost of airtime purchased. Brokers come in all shapes and sizes, depending on the type of TV stations they represent and their volume of business. In some cases, brokers who buy a lot of media have better pricing leverage. Therefore, two brokers may have different rates for the same time slot at the same station.

Brokers work like one-stop shops for TV airtime across the country. If you want to buy airtime outside your state, a broker will come in handy, giving you vital information about TV stations in different markets. Brokers are particularly helpful when you're buying airtime on a network affiliate (ABC, CBS, NBC, Fox), a cable network (ESPN, A&E, CNN), or a superstation (WGN or WOR). Brokers give you access to as many stations in as many regions as you want, but you only have to deal with one person, saving you the hassle of negotiating with each station individually.

However, if you are buying airtime from stations in your city or in a geographic area that you're familiar with, using a broker may hurt rather than help. For example, if the station you want to use does not recognize your broker, that broker may try to convince you to advertise on a different station that will pay a commission. Likewise, a media broker may cost you more if you are buying large quantities of airtime. By placing your order as a direct account, you can negotiate a rebate on the portion of the fee that the station would otherwise pay a broker.

Targeting by ZIP code. If your media buy is sensitive to demographics, one method of buying will deliver precision, especially if you buy from cable service companies on a local basis.

From Beverly Hills to the Bronx, expanding your geographic exposure is as easy as qualifying the socioeconomic profiles of your audience. Marketers now use ZIP codes to identify the geographic distribution of their potential viewers. As markets become more segmented, a new method of categorizing American neighborhoods is gaining ground.

In *The Clustering of America*, author Michael J. Weiss dissects different lifestyles in contemporary America based on the U.S. Postal

Service's Zone Improvement Plan, better known as ZIP codes. Weiss explains that your ZIP code, which actually represents the community where you live, reveals a lot about the people who live within its boundaries. The five digits of your ZIP code are now being used to tell marketers the kinds of magazines you read, what you eat for breakfast, and the brand of toothpaste you are likely to use. Marketers are even using ZIP codes to decide which celebrity to use in their advertising. (From *The Clustering of America*, Michael J. Weiss; Perennial, Harper & Row, New York; ISBN 0-06-091599-4; $10.95.)

BUYING TV TIME ON COST PER ORDER

If your media buys are to be based on any single common denominator that monitors performance, it should be Cost Per Order (CPO). In direct response television, the bottom line is your CPO—how much it costs you to generate one sale or one inquiry.

The lower your CPO, the higher your profits. Remember, with DRTV, media buying has nothing to do with programming or demographics. It is strictly a numbers game. The fewer dollars you spend to reach your viewers, the better your CPO.

CPO should generally be under 50 percent of selling price. To determine your CPO, simply divide your airtime cost by the number of orders you generated from that single airing of your infomercial. This amount should be less than 50 percent of your selling price.

Performance ratio. Performance ratio is a percentage derived from dividing your CPO by your selling price, or by dividing your total sales revenue by your total media cost. Although the maximum CPO should be 50 percent of your selling price, few advertisers consider 50 percent to be acceptable. Ideally, your CPO should be 20 percent of your selling price, which means you should receive $5 for every dollar you invest in media.

For example, if $1,000 worth of airtime produces 50 sales, your CPO is $20, which means it cost you $20 in media time to sell one unit of your product.

- If your selling price is $40, your CPO is 50 percent of your selling price ($20 divided by $40), a 1 to 2 ratio.

- If your selling price is $60, your CPO is 33 percent of your selling price ($20 divided by $60), a 1 to 3 ratio.

- If your selling price is $100, your CPO is 20 percent of your selling price ($20 divided by $100), a 1 to 5 ratio. This means that for every dollar you invest in media time, you're getting $5 back.

Monitoring and evaluation. The success or failure of an infomercial can be determined by one or two airings. If the first airing produces marginal results, you may want to give it a second shot for comparison. If the second airing is equally disappointing, go back to the drawing board.

Immediately evaluate the performance of each airing, preferably the morning after. Although orders may continue to straggle in two or three days after an infomercial is aired, each airing's performance can largely be determined by evaluating it within 12 hours.

EACH AIRING MUST BE PROFITABLE, NO IFS, AND, OR BUTS. YOUR ONLY OTHER CONCERN SHOULD BE TO COMPARE THE CPO AND RATIO OF ONE MEDIA BUY TO THE NEXT. Infomercials are not like regular programs, which can build viewership with an increase in frequency. If your infomercial does not deliver a profitable return after one or two airings, it probably never will.

Furthermore, if after one or two airings, your infomercial proves profitable, your next task is to develop a media plan that will increase those profits. By selecting stations, time slots, and air dates that will produce the lowest CPOs, you can dramatically increase your profit ratio.

From an economic standpoint, media buying is the most important stage in your commercial or infomercial project because it involves the largest chunk of your budget. How you buy your TV airtime dictates the profitability of your direct response campaign. If you buy wisely, you can make a fortune. Buy poorly, and you can lose a fortune.

Our discussion of media buying is based on half-hour infomercials. Unless specified otherwise, figures, stats, and examples used in this chapter are for half-hour, sales generation infomercials. Besides actual media buying, product fulfillment and other activities generally associated with the media stage of your infomercial campaign will be considered.

When the American TV viewing market was being served by only three or four stations—ABC, CBS, NBC, and in some cities, an independent station—behavioral and social patterns were mainstream and demographic diversity was not an issue. Viewing patterns were, therefore, quite similar everywhere. Back then, media buying was relatively easy.

Now the reverse is true. With cable service, satellite programming, low power and full power broadcasting, the route to today's TV audiences is more complicated and difficult to follow. Today, the TV viewing public is divided into over 200 markets, each with 20 to 30 channels to choose from.

Fortunately, television retailing pioneers have paved part of the way for us, making it possible to identify certain media buying styles that work well for infomercials.

For example, those who cultivated DRTV have proven to us that buying late-night TV time is cost effective. Since late night airtime costs less, it delivers one of the lowest cost per order, or CPO, figures obtained, enabling marketers to break even with fewer orders.

There are three types of commercial TV stations, distinguished by how their programming is delivered to the public.

Broadcast

These TV stations use the airwaves to transmit their programs over a specific geographic area. By design, all broadcast stations are local, to the extent the power of their antennas transmit their signals to TV viewers. Some broadcast TV channels are also carried by the local cable service in the station's primary broadcast area.

Based on their transmitting power, there are two types of broadcast TV stations: 1) low power stations, usually operating on UHF frequencies;

and 2) full power stations, those you usually get as channels 2 through 13 if you don't have cable. These depend on your antenna to pick up the TV signals.

Based on how they are owned, managed, or operated, TV stations can be either independents or network affiliates, more often called network channels.

The four recognized broadcast TV networks in the U.S. are ABC, CBS, NBC, and Fox. It is difficult, if not impossible, to acquire TV airtime on any of these networks. With the possible exception of Ross Perot's half-hour paid announcements during his 1992 presidential election bid, no half-hour paid programs are aired on the broadcast network level. On the local level, however, networks have different policies regarding paid programming.

Cable

These are TV stations whose programming is delivered exclusively through a cable system, meaning that homes without cable service have no way of watching these channels. Since these stations send their signals to different cable service companies across the country, they are also referred to as networks. The extent of the coverage of any cable network depends entirely on the number of local cable service companies carrying its programming. The following are the ten most widely distributed basic cable networks. Figures are as of March, 1993, represented in total million households.

Cable TV Stations

	Stations
Cable News Network	CNN,66
Cable News & Business	CNBC, 65
USA Network	USA, 65
Video Hits	VH1, 64
Nickelodeon	NIK, 63
Lifetime	LIFE, 61
Headline News	HLN, 61
Entertainment Sports	ESPN, 61
Discovery	DSC, 61
Music Television	MTV, 61

Superstations

A superstation is a local broadcast station whose programming is being received by cable markets outside its primary broadcast area. Without the cable aspect of their coverage, they are nothing more than local broadcast TV stations. Without the broadcast aspect of their coverage, they are strictly cable channels. Superstations are either regional or national in their coverage.

A regional superstation has its programming carried by cable companies within the same state or region where the superstation operates. Examples include WPIX in Florida and KTVT in Texas.

A national superstation has its programming carried by cable companies in more than one state. The three major national superstations are TNT, WOR, and WGN.

Georgia-based TNT, part of the Turner Broadcasting Group, is known for programming dominated by its extensive collection of old movies. TBS also has strict guidelines on direct response programming and rarely accepts paid programs. WOR and WGN have a more enterprising position with regard to their airtime. They have an extensive market coverage and their rates are competitive.

Superstations

Superstation	Subscribers
WWOR	35 million
WWGN	42 million
WPIX	12 million
KTVT	4 million

Television, both broadcast and cable, reaches over 93 million homes in over 200 major U.S. markets. Some 63 million homes have cable service. The ten largest TV markets in the U.S., with a total of 26.6 million homes (28 percent of all viewing homes), are:

TV Markets

TV Market	TV Households (Millions)	Percent of Homes with Cable
New York	7.0	58
Los Angeles	5.0	57
Chicago	3.1	77
Philadelphia	2.7	70
San Francisco	2.2	64
Boston	2.1	71
Washington, D.C.	1.7	57
Dallas–Ft. Worth	1.7	47
Detroit	1.7	59
Houston	1.5	50

THE BEST WAY TO SHOOT YOUR TV COMMERCIAL OR INFOMERCIAL

You can write your own script and direct the actual shooting of your infomercial, but you should never shoot and edit your own infomercial unless you have all the necessary equipment and know-how. Home systems simply do not work. Never shoot your infomercial with a camcorder. It will never get aired!

Production

Production takes place in two stages: the actual shoot and postproduction.

The Shoot

During the actual shooting stage, all the footage that will form part of your infomercial is shot. Your responsibilities should focus on selecting and hiring the camera crew. After all the footage is shot, you enter the postproduction phase. That is the time to edit your infomercial, taking out the bad cuts and putting all the good shots into one coherent presentation, adding music and special effects, and more. During that stage, you will be responsible for selecting and hiring a postproduction facility with the right editing system and a competent editor.

Hiring the same company to shoot your infomercial and then do all the editing and postproduction work makes sense for three reasons:

1. The postproduction people are already familiar with your project and how it was shot.

2. Rates are usually cheaper for a packaged deal.

3. If you worry about confidentiality, you'll only have one supplier to worry about.

Choosing a Tape Format. If you have the money and demand the highest quality, shoot your infomercial on film rather than on videotape. You will have more flexibility and the highest quality postproduction effects available. Keep in mind, however, that a film project can cost as much as ten times more than an infomercial shot on videotape. For this reason, nearly 95 percent of all infomercials are taped.

Chances are that the production company you hire will try to convince you that the best tape format to shoot is the one they have in their studio. Those who use Beta will tell you Beta is the best. Those who use 8mm will tell you about the miracles it can do. If you shop around, you are likely to hear the advantages and disadvantages of every format there is. Here's a sample:

1. Betacam. This is currently the favored video format because it delivers the highest video resolution. Since Beta equipment is expensive, expect to pay more to shoot in this format. The popularity of Beta mastering tapes is disturbing, since no TV stations require Beta as an actual broadcast copy tape. All in all the Beta format is overrated because it is not used at the television stations themselves. (Average daily rental cost of a BetaCam with camera crew: $995.)

2. 3/4-Inch U-Matic. If you want basic broadcast quality at a good price, use 3/4 inch U-Matic. You can shoot and edit without having to change formats, and you can make same-format dubbed copies of your finished master for broadcast copy. (Average daily rental with camera crew: $495.)

3. *S-VHS.* This is a higher grade VHS with 400-line resolution. Although not particularly recommended as a finished format, it works perfectly for non-sensitive outdoor shoots. If you're shooting testimonials from different locations, S-VHS will provide portability and acceptable quality. (Average daily rental with camera crew: $295.)

4. *Hi-8.* Some production outfits build their systems around the 3-chip Hi-8 camera format. In spite of its impressive specifications, Hi-8 has inherent shortcomings. Unless you want a home video effect for authenticity purposes, you should avoid this format at all costs.

5. *1-Inch.* Whereas all the previous formats are in cassette form, 1-inch tapes come in reel form. Since most cameras and editing systems are not built around the 1-inch format, it is never used for production. One-inch tapes are used primarily for broadcast copy. Whether you shoot your infomercial in Beta, U-Matic, or S-VHS format, you may need to dub your finished master into a 1-inch copy for airing on some TV stations. (Average cost of 1-inch dub copy: $100.)

Finished Length. From the first frame to the last, your infomercial should be 28 minutes and 30 seconds long. Your first frame should actually be the standard disclaimer stating that "this is a paid program" from your company. Your last frame should state that "the preceding was a paid program" presented by your company.

Postproduction

This is the part of the production process in which you create the tone of your infomercial, so we'll review what's involved. This portion of the production process is usually considered the editing stage, although it involves much more than just editing your footage. Text, graphics, background music, and video and audio effects are all added during postproduction. How you cut, fade out, insert, roll, and merge one scene with the next lends to the overall tempo of your show. This is when you can run wild with animation, 3D graphics, split screens, multiple screen images, and much more. With today's technology, your infomercial's ultimate look is limited only by your imagination and your budget.

Desktop Level. For rock-bottom, basic postproduction work, you can use a studio with a system built around a desktop video system. Popular desktop brands like Video Toasters and Matrox will give you basic broadcast quality. (Average rate: $75 per hour.) Integrated simultaneously in a variety of ways, these systems use a wide assortment of effects. Although some companies using desktop-level video editing systems have A-B roll capability, most postproduction houses with this capability use more sophisticated, top of the line editing systems. (Average rate: $125 per hour.)

Nonlinear. This is the future of postproduction. It is called nonlinear because your program is edited without using a tape. Instead, the hard drives of a computer store and manipulate the images you've shot. The system is highly digital and usually comes loaded with effects. Because it edits at the speed of a digital hard drive, your work is finished faster and with more creative flair. (Average rate: $250 per hour.)

Special Production Tips for Infomercials

The right format is at the heart of every infomercial project. To begin with, the show is usually a half-hour in length, and there will be significant expenses for production. Your production costs, the way you present your information, the pacing of your show, and its ability to keep the audience glued to the TV depend on your infomercial's format.

For two examples, Time-Life produced its "Rock 'N Roll of the '60s" infomercial as a music video documentary hosted by a disc jockey who presents a succession of music videos from a broadcast control booth. Psychic Friends Network made its infomercial, a talk show hosted by Dionne Warwick, before a live audience.

There is no such thing as the one most effective format. Shoot your infomercial in a format that best demonstrates the benefits of your product. Having a roomful of people with serious bald spots may not be the most aesthetically pleasing sight on television. However, it was certainly the most effective way for Ron Popiel to introduce his GLH Formula, a baldness treatment.

If you're having trouble deciding between different formats, watching some of the most popular regular TV programs may offer some interesting clues. One thing to think about is what your viewers are accustomed to watching on television today. One example of popular programming is tabloid-type programs like "A Current Affair," "Rescue 911," and "Hard Copy." These shows present investigative segments that explore subjects in an exciting and entertaining manner.

Once you've established your primary objective and decided on a format, it's time to write your infomercial. Unless you're an experienced writer who can create a fast-paced, well staged, logically arranged audiovisual presentation, don't even try writing your infomercial. Instead, prepare an outline for a script writer. Explain what your product is, its uses, its benefits, and its economic value.

If you think you possess the inherent talent to pen your own presentation, keep the following points in mind:

Keep selling. Every word must draw blood. You're not there to look cute or impress your competitors with how creative you are. Focus on the product. Never stop selling. Remember, if the TV viewer does not reach out for the phone to place an order, the infomercial didn't work.

Keep it interesting. With the availability of remote control, your infomercial must be engaging. You may have a potentially good product, but if you cannot hold the viewer's attention, the remote control is your worst enemy.

Use block scripting. An infomercial is divided into several smaller segments that are usually repeated within the half-hour show. This is a result of infomercial writers using block scripting (also known as pocket scripting) for an infomercial.

As a rule of thumb, to keep an infomercial interesting, something entertaining and informative must be happening every 60 seconds. When preparing your outline, think of a channel hopper accidentally landing on your infomercial at any given part. You have about 60 seconds to give this viewer an idea of what you're selling and grab interest. If you fail to keep that viewer's attention, you've lost a potential sale. A fast-paced script will keep your viewers watching.

Scripting checklist. Decide which of the following elements will make up the core of your presentation. These ingredients will influence the style of your show and the manner in which your product will be presented to your TV audience.

- Testimonials. This format presents satisfied customers talking about their successful experiences with your product. You can have actual product endorsers, or you can hire paid performers to do dramatized endorsements.

- Interviews. If you choose to include this format in your infomercial, you must decide whether the interview will be a panel (with a moderator) or one-on-one (an interviewer with one guest at a time). Will the interview be in a studio or on location?

- Celebrity endorsements. A celebrity can add credibility and recognition to your product. A familiar face can make channel hoppers stop and watch your infomercial. Effectively done, using a celebrity can be a wise investment.

- Case histories. A product with a demonstrable before-and-after effect, such as diet plans, cosmetics, and fitness products, can provide a compelling argument for your product.

- Demonstrations. If your product's primary selling features are convenience and ease of use, you must capitalize on product demonstration as the backbone of your presentation.

Ordering information. This segment usually last 30 to 45 seconds. This portion of the infomercial tells the viewer the product's price and the accessories, tie-in items, bonuses, and refund guarantees that come with each order. It shows how the product is packaged and gives the phone number for ordering. It can be integrated into the DRTV spot or presented independently.

DRTV Spot. This is usually a 2-minute spot that summarizes vital points about your product and the ordering procedure. To emphasize important points, most effective DRTV spots use footage lifted from the infomercial itself. The spot should be repeated at least three times within the infomercial.

USING YOUR PRODUCTS AS PROPS IN A
MOVIE OR TV SHOW

Casual advertising is one of the most effective ways to present your product to the market. By placing your products as props in movies or TV shows, you gain exposure to a wide audience base, and with some implied level of endorsement.

When Clark Kent spooned Cheerios into his mouth in the movie *Superman*, it was not because the director or the writers found it essential or entertaining. It was the result of negotiations between the film's producers and General Mills.

To advertise your product this way, it is essential to hire a broker who specializes in placing products in movies and TV shows. For movies, brokers work out the details of placing your product in a film and guarantee that the product will be used in a very positive way. For TV exposure, the most common uses are game shows on which your product can be given away as a prize or mentioned as a prize sponsor. (Dramatic or comedy TV shows, including series and soaps, generally refuse to take casuals because of the conflict it may create with regular sponsors of the show.)

Cost. Movie casuals can cost around $25,000. Of course, the price varies depending on the stars of the film, the length of time the product will be on screen, and the products' identifiable role in the movie.

Brokers. Associated Fil Promotions, 10100 Santa Monica Blvd., Los Angeles, CA 90067; Donald Degnan Co., 400 Madison Ave., New York, NY 10017.

RESOURCES

This chapter covers the basics of commercial production. Far more comprehensive information on all aspects of television production can be found in *How to Produce an Effective TV Commercial* by Hooper White, published by Crain Books in Chicago. For an in-depth discussion of how to work with your advertising agency to produce effective TV commercials, radio, and print advertising, read *How to Get the Best Advertising from Your Agency* by Nancy L. Sale, published by Dow Jones-Irwin. More detailed information on buying television time can be found in Herschell Gordon Lewis' book, *How to Make Your Advertising Twice as Effective at Half the Cost*. For more details about choosing a director and the director's role in making the commercial a success, see John Lyon's book, *GUTS: Advertising from the Inside Out* (New York, NY: AMACOM).

Finally, for up-to-date comparisons of broadcast versus other media costs, demographics, and basic facts on TV advertising, contact the Television Bureau of Advertising, Inc., 477 Madison Avenue, New York, NY 10022, 212-486-1111.

Chapter 12

RADIO ADVERTISING

BASIC FACTS ABOUT RADIO ADVERTISING

Almost everyone in the United States listens to radio, but most people don't think of radio listening as an activity. They just do it. Radio listening is a natural activity of just about everyone's lives as revealed in a study by Research and Forecasts, Inc., a New York research firm.

"During the pretest of our questionnaire, most people had difficulty thinking about radio as a leisure-time activity," notes John Crothers Pollock, president of the firm. "Radio is so closely integrated with all the other activities people pursue—brushing their teeth, driving to work, walking down the street. Radio, rather than a leisure activity, is an integrated activity. It is so universal as to be indistinguishable from other aspects of daily concern."

Here are some additional facts about radio and radio advertising from the Radio Advertising Bureau in New York City:

- Radio reaches 77 percent of all consumers daily and 95 percent of all consumers weekly.

- The average consumer spends almost 5 hours a day reading, listening to, and watching media. Of this time, 44 percent is spent listening to radio versus 41 percent watching TV and 15 percent reading newspapers and magazines.

- Among adults age 18 or older, 82 percent listen to the radio while they drive.

- Radio generates immediate purchases, more so than other media. More consumers buy products within one hour of hearing a radio commercial than within one hour of seeing a TV commercial or reading an ad.

- Retailers are the largest users of radio advertising. In 1995, retailers spent $343 million on radio advertising. The top radio advertiser in the U.S. is Sears, spending more than $71 million a year.

- Companies offering business and consumer services were the second biggest radio advertisers, spending almost $245 million in 1995. AT&T was the biggest advertiser in this category, spending almost $60 million.

- In 1995, radio ad revenue from national spots was $1.92 billion; local revenues were $9.1 billion. While the cost per thousand of media in general increased 71 percent over the past decade, the cost per thousand rose the least of any major media, only 31 percent.

- Consumers spend 85 percent of their time with ear-oriented media such as radio and TV, but spend only 15 percent of their time with such eye-oriented media as newspapers and magazines. Yet advertisers spend 45 percent of their dollars on ear media (broadcast) and 55 percent on eye media (print). In a study by the PreTesting Company, 84 percent of radio listeners could recall commercial messages they heard during a 15-minute radio program.

Although radio listening may be an integrated rather than a separate activity, there is little doubt that it has a powerful impact on society. "Nothing treats the spoken word better than radio," observes Phillip Dusenberry, vice chairman and executive creative director of REDO, one of the nation's largest advertising agencies. "Nothing caresses and massages the language or brings such sweet poetry to the consumer. Radio speaks with one thing that attracts writers to the profession in the first place: words. Powerful, moving, and persuasive, the creative opportunities we have in radio are fantastic. It's wonderful indoors and the greatest outdoor medium in the world. At REDO, radio helps sell Old Milwaukee beer by the carload, radio goes full throttle for Dodge, it puts Black and Decker tools in millions of homes, it sells Campbell's Chunky Soup, and brings good things to life at GE."

Even former president of the United States Ronald Reagan said, "In its flexibility and immediacy, radio is unsurpassed as a communications tool."

TAPPING INTO THE RADIO AUDIENCE

Radio reaches 94.8 percent of people 12 years and older every week. If your customers are men age 18 and older, then radio reaches 95.5 percent of them every day. It also reaches 93.1 percent of women 18 and older daily. Radio is everywhere. It goes places other media cannot. The time lapse between the exposure to the advertising message and the response is the fastest with radio: 2 hours for a radio commercial against 3 1/2 hours for television, 3-3/4 hours for newspapers, and 4 hours for magazines. Radio has the fastest rate of return.

Radio sales are in the billions, reaching millions of consumers every day. The average family owns 5.5 radios. In the Los Angeles market alone, that totals approximately 25 million radios. National statistics reveal that

Americans purchase more radios than any other consumer electronics item, including stereos.

Radios can be found in every room of the house: 58 percent of households have a radio in the bedroom, 50 percent in kitchens, 67 percent in living rooms, 22 percent in studies and dens, and 9 percent in dining rooms. Plus, radios can be found in bathrooms, garages, patios, and pool areas.

Adults spend 45 percent of their media time with TV, 39 percent with radio, 10 percent with newspapers, and 5 percent with magazines. Among high-income adults, media time is divided as follows: 44 percent radio, 39 percent TV, 13 percent newspapers, and 7 percent magazines.

Dr. Elizabeth Loftus of the University of Washington commented on a recent study from Northwestern University: "This study shows that if you try to convince people about a product (the one in the study was shampoo), and you do it with a verbal message, people are much more persuaded about the product. They like it better and want to buy more than if you accompany those verbal messages with pictures. The verbal message alone seems to create in people's minds more of a positive feeling from the product."

Further studies show that the selective quality of radio has produced loyal listeners. This assures advertisers of a consistent audience of the type of listener that the radio campaign is designed to attract. Most large manufacturers have co-op advertising programs for radio through which the manufacturer reimburses the local advertiser—a supermarket, retailer, or other distributor—for a portion of the advertising expenditures.

EIGHT ADVANTAGES OF RADIO VERSUS OTHER MEDIA

1. *Economy.* Radio commercials are inexpensive to produce because the listener's imagination—and not a costly photographer or video production house—provides the picture. Radio time also has a lower cost per thousand than newspapers, magazines, or television.

2. *Selectivity.* Radio offers a wide selection of program formats, each catering to a specific segment of the population (various types of formats are listed later in this chapter).

3. *Penetration.* Radio reaches nearly 99 percent of the consumer market.

4. *Mobility.* Radio can reach customers just about everywhere, even at the point of sale.

5. *Immediacy.* Advertisers can change their messages quickly and easily. They can get new commercials on the air rapidly. A commercial can be written and taped or read live literally the same day, if necessary.

6. *Flexibility.* Radio enables advertisers to talk to customers during the time of day and in an environment most likely to induce a selling response.

7. *Intrusiveness.* Radio advertising can pervade a listener's mind, even when interest doesn't exist. Radio can and often does invade the mind of a preoccupied listener, forcefully delivering a commercial message.

8. *Audience.* Radio can reach virtually any segment of the consumer market, including people who don't frequently read newspapers (teens, for example). It reaches newspaper readers who don't read the retailer's ads because they are not regular customers. It reaches prospects for your business whose names are not on the mailing lists you rent or who don't read unsolicited mail. Radio gives you the ability to pinpoint your target audience by demographics, psychographics, and geography.

Recent studies show that approximately one in five American adults is functionally illiterate. Only TV and radio can reach this vast audience; newspapers, magazines, and direct mail cannot.

RADIO AS A DIRECT RESPONSE MEDIUM

Radio traditionally has not been an effective advertising medium for direct response advertisers and local firms desiring immediate leads or sales from their commercials. The reason is that the most effective time to advertise on radio is drive time, during the rush hour when people are commuting to and from work. The problem is that people normally cannot call the toll-free number given in your radio commercial if they are in their cars.

According to James R. Rosenfield, chairman of Rosenfield/Vinson advertising agency, the growth in cellular phones is changing that. "Radio will be the great new direct marketing medium of the 1990s," writes Rosenfield in his special report, *Direct Marketing in the 1990s.* He notes that the price of car phones is rapidly decreasing, making them affordable. Rosenfield also states that car phones will be used most extensively by upscale professionals and managers, a prime target market.

"There's a co-factor here: the worsening traffic situation everywhere in the world," observes Rosenfield. People stuck in traffic have time on their hands. They will listen to and respond to radio commercials. He advises direct response advertisers to buy drive time commercials in areas with a high number of cellular phones and heavy traffic.

In addition, Rosenfield predicts radio will become a more powerful direct response medium in the home, as well. The reason has to do with demographics, he says. Already, 25 percent of American households consist of one person living alone. With the demise of the traditional nuclear family and the growing population of the aged, that number will increase.

"Lonely people keep the radio on for company, and lonely people call 800 numbers because they need stimulation and interaction," says Rosenfield. He also notes that elderly people sleep less and less well, so there will be more opportunity for direct response radio advertising at odd hours. Rosenfield advises that advertisers should buy non-drive-time commercials in areas with a large population of older people or single family households.

RADIO COMMERCIALS: ENTERING THE THEATER OF THE MIND

While most radio commercials seem to be the spontaneous ramblings of a disc jockey, they really aren't. They are well-planned marketing presentations designed to make sales when other media can't.

Radio is different. It appeals directly to the listener, one on one. Not even television, with its talking heads, can do that. The reason is that radio is still, in the mind of the listener, live. Television, on the other hand, is canned. The viewer knows it...or, at least, believes it. What they see on TV is not real, but a recording either on film or videotape. What they hear on radio they perceive as being live.

"Radio reaches more people, more often, than any other medium," says radio advertising expert, copywriter, and announcer Grey Smith. "It is powerful. Radio is word-of-mouth advertising amplified a thousandfold. It's the stuff that makes people laugh, cry, chuckle, and dream. Radio advertising stretches the listener's imagination. Television limits you to a twenty-one-inch screen. Radio has no limits at all."

No other medium, save theater, can stir the imagination as radio can. Stan Freberg, one of advertising's most creative copywriters, gives us an exceptional example of its power: "Okay, people, now when I give the cue, I want the seven-hundred-foot mountain of whipped cream to roll into Lake Michigan, which has been drained and filled with hot chocolate. The Royal Canadian Air Force will fly overhead and drop a ten-ton maraschino cherry into the whipped cream, to the cheering of twenty-five thousand extras."

On radio, producing this commercial is a piece of cake. On television, it's a multimillion-dollar nightmare.

No matter what selling approach you use, be it humor, spokesperson, slice of life, or news, radio still commands the most dynamic marketing approach available to an advertiser, large or small.

WRITING FOR RADIO: WHERE IMAGINATION TAKES CONTROL

While paid radio commercials are the predominant means of marketing communications during any given time period, there are other types of radio spots that need to be mentioned because they also play an important role in marketing products, services, events, and people.

These other forms include public service announcements (PSA) that can be produced by an advertiser; interviews with key personnel of a business, service organization, or government agency; news clips for general distribution; and other recorded or "live" content.

The most common lengths for radio commercials are 30 and 60 seconds, although 10- and 15-second spots, plus sponsorships, are available.

A 60-second commercial is actually 59 seconds long, and a 30-second commercial is 29 seconds. There's a reason for this: That one second is used by disc jockeys or engineers to start the next commercial so that a commercial starts and ends within a 60- or 30-second time period. Unlike most other media, in radio, time is of value. Once it's gone, it's gone. If commercial time isn't used, the radio station loses the revenue forever.

Radio advertising, even for a small local advertiser, should not be run without a master copy platform. This is a single document that guides the radio copywriters in what they are going to write about. It gives direction to the copy and the commercials. Under the best conditions, a radio campaign should be developed by someone who understands both radio as a medium and advertising campaign development. The copy platform might spell out such things as:

- what the product is,
- features and benefits,
- which benefits should be highlighted in the copy,
- which features must be mentioned (e.g., hours of operation, location),
- positioning or image the commercial must convey,
- sales goals and marketing objectives of the radio ad campaign, and
- tone (e.g., humor, no humor, etc.).

With a master copy platform in hand, you are ready to write the radio commercial. Radio copy is written in ALL CAPITAL LETTERS. Numbers, like 555-1212, are always spelled out: FIVE-FIVE-FIVE, ONE-TWO-ONE-TWO. If a word or phrase is hard to pronounce, it is written out phonetically. Radio copy is always double spaced, no exceptions. There are 20 lines of copy to the commercial minute; 10 lines of copy in a 30-second commercial; 5 lines of copy in a 15-second commercial; and 3 lines of copy in a 10-second spot.

Radio copy is typed with a wide margin on the left. There is usually a line that goes down the page, with small numbers from 1 to 20, double spaced, next to the line. To the left of the numbers is usually an inch of space. This area is used for sound effects (SFX) directions and announcer (ANN) cues. ANN cues are used when there is more than one person performing in the commercial.

There are three critical parts of a radio commercial:

1. name of product or service;
2. price; and
3. location.

The location can include any or all of the following: address, directions, or telephone number.

Which part is most important? It depends on what you are selling. If you are selling the product, then price and location are given less attention. If you are pushing a store sale, price is the key factor. The copywriter decides by reviewing the master copy platform.

A wise old radio station sales manager was once asked what makes for a successful radio commercial. He replied: "Name, name, name, name, name, name." In a 60-second spot, you should mention the name of the product at least six times. To the average copywriter or advertiser, this may appear redundant, but it is not. "One of the best name-recognition radio spots I've ever written mentioned the name 26 times in 60 seconds," said Grey Smith.

When stressing location instead of product name, mention the location three times, not six times, in a 60-second spot. The same goes for telephone numbers. Why? Because the address, directions, and phone number take longer to say than a product name, so you have less time for repetition.

Trick of the Trade: When mentioning telephone numbers, refer your listener to the white pages instead of the yellow pages of the phone book. If you mention the yellow pages, your listener will turn to your category in the directory and be exposed to your competitors' ads as well as your own. You don't want to promote their advertising at your expense. Better to make the consumer remember your name and find it in the white pages.

There are as many ways to begin a commercial as there are products and services to sell, but there are several elements that must be included to make the spot work. First, the commercial must have a hook. If you don't catch listeners in the first 10 seconds, you won't catch them in the remaining 49. Second, you must include the necessary information: product name, where to buy it, price (if important), and address and telephone number, if required. Third, you must ask for the order. Ask your customer to buy. Even institutional commercials that are only intended to spread goodwill and the company name are asking people to buy something, if only a concept.

The fourth and last element to be considered carefully is the emotional mood or approach that you intend to use to grab and keep the listener's attention. You can be friendly, festive, dignified, exciting, mysterious, humorous, melancholy, romantic, sentimental, quiet, provocative, extravagant, and outrageous—to name just a few. Choosing the right mood is important. The only one to be cautious about is humor. Humor doesn't always work; even if the commercial is good, things are funny only when they are fresh.

All the remaining particulars like secondary announcers, sound effects, music, and jingles will be determined by the unique selling position of your product or service as defined in your master copy platform.

When you finish writing your 20 lines of copy, read it aloud. Copy that looks structurally good on paper won't sound natural when spoken. It will be stuffy. The spoken language isn't delivered in perfect, complete sentences. It's more like sentence fragments. Write the copy the way you speak (but take out all the *ums*, *uhs*, and *you knows*). If you have trouble writing conversationally, record your ideas into a tape recorder, then have a transcript made of the tape. Read the transcript aloud. You'll immediately recognize the difference between spoken and written copy.

FOURTEEN PROVEN RADIO COPYWRITING TECHNIQUES

1. Stretch the listener's imagination. Voices and sounds can evoke pictures in the mind. Take your listeners somewhere they've never been before, or better yet, somewhere they're dying to go.

2. Listen for a memorable sound or a distinctive voice, a jingle, anything that will make your message stand out.

3. Present one idea. Be direct and clear or your message may become subject to distractions.

4. Select your customer quickly. Get the attention of your customer fast. Flag them down before they have a chance to change stations.

5. State your product or service and promise early. Radio spots that do so get higher awareness ratings. Be sure to repeat the product name at least six times in a one-minute commercial.

6. Capitalize on local events. Tie in with fads, fashion, news events, weather, or holidays.

7. Music helps. It's great for reaching teenagers who prefer the "now sounds." Good jingles are remembered for years. But keep the music simple. Don't let it overpower the selling message in the words.

8. Ask listeners to take action. You can't make a sale unless you ask for the order. Don't be afraid to ask the customer to try your product or service today.

9. Use the strength of radio personalities. They have steady listeners. Have them deliver the radio spot live. Many disc jockeys and show hosts have a strong hold on their audiences.

10. Have more than one spot ready for broadcast. Radio is a high-frequency medium. You need to have variety in your sales message. You will also have to refresh your pool of spots so you don't bore your listeners.

11. Special messages geared to special groups do very well. It pays to design radio spots for ethnic groups and even produce them in that group's language (e.g., in Spanish for Hispanic marketing).

12. Use radio for special promotions. A holiday sale, a grand opening, an anniversary sale, and a "this week only" promotion all work well on radio.

13. Don't evaluate radio copy by reading a typed radio script. The spoken word is different from the printed word. In a newspaper ad, consumers can always go back and reread if they miss part of your message. In radio, if your customers miss part of the message, they can't go back and hear it again.

   Your copywriter should read the commercial to you or have a demo made to approximate the finished commercial. Judge your radio commercials in context. Just as you would ask to see your print ad as it would appear in a magazine or newspaper, ask to hear your radio commercial inside several minutes of actual programming.

14. Get help if you need it. You can write the spots yourself, but if you are not an expert in radio advertising, get help from a professional who has experience in the field. Many freelance copywriters specialize in different types of media. Find one who has a strong radio background. If you decide to use radio station personnel to write and produce your spot, it might be wise to get a second opinion on your demo before you schedule air time.

PRODUCING THE RADIO SPOT

Of all the production processes—print advertising, television, direct mail, etc.—radio is the easiest to understand. It's usually the quickest and least expensive, too, if you have all the proper equipment available to you.

The simplest form of delivery is, of course, live. You simply provide the script to the radio station, and their announcers read it during their shows. If the announcer has a strong audience, then listeners perceive that their beloved announcer or program host is endorsing your product.

A good example is the popular New York radio show "What's Your Problem?" with Bernard Meltzer on WOR-AM. Meltzer has a large and faithful audience who practically worship the ground he walks on, and an advertiser would be foolish to submit a canned commercial and pass up the opportunity to have "Uncle Bernie" personally praise its product. Many talk show and news station announcers contribute to sales success simply from the fact that they are plugging the product or service.

Often, these live spots are recorded so they can be played at any time during the play schedule. At KABC TalkRadio, for instance, Michael Jackson records many of his spots. But they sound live when played during his show. Only when he's on vacation or not doing his air shift do you notice that he's not delivering the spot live.

Radio spots are recorded on reel-to-reel audio tape. Most production companies and radio stations use the highest quality tape available so production quality can be equal to or better than that of the record industry.

Once your radio copy is finished, and if it is not designed to be read on-air by the announcer or show host, then you need to find talent. This involves rounding up audition tapes of available announcers and music groups. An audition tape is a collection of previous commercials the announcer or music group has done.

Sometimes announcers provide a demo tape of them reading your specific commercial. There may be a small fee for this, but it allows you to get a good idea of how the finished commercial will sound, with the announcer reading it minus any special effects.

Note that there are many agencies and copywriters who say they can do radio, but few who actually have substantial radio experience. Listening to audition or demo tapes can help separate the pros from the amateurs. (Don't even consider hiring someone who does not have an audition tape of sample commercials.)

Make sure the spots you hear are ones you are familiar with. Then, call other radio advertisers and check their results. Find out if they're happy and if they are making sales from their radio spots.

When you've chosen your talent, you are ready to go into recording. You may rent a professional recording studio or opt to use the radio station's production booth. The spot can be recorded all at once, in sequence, or it can be recorded in segments, to be mixed together later by an audio engineer.

When the commercial is "in the can" (recorded and finished), copies are made for distribution. These are called dubs. If you buy more than one radio station, you must send a dub to each.

Before you buy airtime, test the finished commercial on an audience. Find out if it works. Find out if the major elements—product, price, address, and the like—are remembered by listeners.

CHOOSING THE RIGHT RADIO STATION

This is probably the most difficult portion of radio advertising. You cannot begin to select stations unless you know exactly who your customers are. When you know their demographics, then you need to find out what kind of radio station they listen to and at what times.

There are all kinds of stations out there, each broadcasting to a fragmented audience. These include:

- Adult contemporary (AOR)
- Middle of the road
- News
- Talk
- Rock
- Country-western
- Jazz
- Classical
- Top 40
- Easy listening
- Progressive rock
- Ethnic
- Variety
- Educational
- Religious

There are more, and it breaks down even further: You can choose either AM or FM. Currently, FM enjoys the largest audience.

In the end, choose the radio station or stations that reach your customers. To find out specifics about each station, call and request their media kits. Stick with the demographics—age, sex, income, education, employment, residence—so you can target your customer. The more narrowly you can target your customer, the better your chances of selling to him or her.

BUYING AIRTIME

You cannot guess about the purchase of airtime. You must know when your customer is listening. It's impossible to survey each and every customer and potential customer, of course. But there are some things you can determine based on your demographic research.

You'll know, for example, if they commute to work, are working mothers, are teenagers, etc. You'll know what periods of the day they listen to radio and what stations they prefer.

If your customer drives to and from work, then drive times are the best buy. Drivers are a relatively attentive audience. Research proves that drivers recall commercial messages better than home listeners. Radio is the perfect medium for selling car products and services (e.g., cellular telephones, muffler shops, used cars).

If your customer listens to radio at home or in the office, midday spots are good buys. Many radio stations have audience participation promotions during working hours, so there is active listening throughout the day. Other customers don't like television and listen to special radio programming at night.

Spot radio is broken down into different daytime parts or day parts. The premium times are 6 to 9 A.M. (usually designated as AAA time, which is the most expensive); 9 A.M. to 3 A.M. (midday, which is known as AA time, the second most expensive); 3 to 6 A.M. (also AAA time); 6 A.M. to midnight (A time); and midnight to 6 A.M. (B time).

Of the two drive times (morning or evening commutes), morning is better. For the most part, radio listenership is greatest between 6 A.M. and 6 P.M. After 6 P.M., listening drops off substantially, probably due to the competition from television, which has news at 6 P.M. and begins prime time programming at 8 P.M.

Mondays through Thursdays are the best days on radio, unless something special is happening on Friday or the weekend. Airtime on the weekends is usually charged differently from weekdays. Tuesdays are usually the best days, followed by Wednesday and Thursday, then Monday. Fridays are last; no one knows why.

Find out when your consumer is listening, then buy that day part.

EVALUATING RADIO STATIONS

The first thing you need to evaluate a radio station is a rate card. It comes with the media kit you requested from the station. The rate card is crowded with numbers, broken up into day parts. The number you see for any given day part is what a single spot costs when played during that time of day. If you order a specific time, say 3:15 P.M., it will cost you a premium. The standard radio media buy is ROS (run of schedule). ROS means the station will guarantee your spot to be aired between certain hours in a specific day part but does not schedule an exact time.

There are also different rates for different length spots. Every rate is based on the 60-second spot. Usually a 30-second spot costs 75 percent of a 60-second spot. A 15-second spot costs 50 percent of a 60-second spot, and a 10-second spot costs around 45 percent of a 60-second spot.

There are a number of ways to buy radio time. You can buy spots one at a time, in a package, or in bulk. The more spots you commit to, the cheaper each minute becomes.

If you are going into radio for the short run, stick to the package deal, unless your budget allows you to buy bulk. Bulk usually means over 1,000 spots during a schedule year. If you buy bulk and decide to back out of your contract, then the spots you actually ran will be prorated back to premium rates.

If you are serious about selling products by radio, one spot an hour won't do it. Neither will two or three. You will need to run at least six spots an hour to have an effect during a short-run campaign. Twelve an hour borders on too much. Eight an hour is about right for really pushing a sale or special item.

Example: Let's say you are having a weekend sale at your business. What would your schedule be like? You are selling furniture at 50 to 80 percent off original prices to get rid of the old and make room for the new designs. You want to push the sale hard for two weeks and you've got a reasonable budget to do it with.

A good schedule would be as follows:

First week: ROS, Tuesday through Friday, four spots an hour during morning drive, four spots an hour during middays (to hit people who are at home), four spots an hour during afternoon drive, and three spots an hour from 9 A.M. to 3 P.M. on weekends.

Second week: ROS, Tuesday through Thursday, eight spots an hour morning and afternoon drive, six spots an hour middays. Friday, eight spots an hour, morning drive. Saturday, six spots an hour, 9 A.M. to 3 P.M., and Sunday, 9 A.M. to 12 noon. That should move everything out of your store by Sunday evening, if your prices are too good to pass up.

HOW TO GET THE BEST RATES

Account executives won't admit this unless you ask, but rates for radio time are negotiable. Push for the best rate. Make sure you get your rates protected if there is a future rate increase in the works. National advertisers pay more than local. Remember that if your account executive helps you plan a successful radio campaign, it means he or she will get good commissions from your account for a long time to come. If the campaign doesn't work, he or she loses a valuable advertiser—you.

TRACKING THE RESULTS

Despite the popular notion that radio generates instant sales, there are times when it doesn't produce the desired results. Like any other advertising medium, it takes time to build a relationship with your audience. Customer trust is hard to gain. It simply takes time—time to develop familiarity, time to build confidence, time to track results.

This is not to say that under certain conditions it won't work. Take a weekend sale, for example. If you have the right product or service and you are offering it at a low price, then you will get a certain number of immediate sales. But over the long haul, radio takes time to develop if you want to be able to measure your success and increase sales.

Tracking radio advertising is different from tracking other types of advertising. If you do print advertising, customers will often bring the ads to your place of business. People like to cut out ads from newspapers and magazines or save fliers they get in the mail. But how do you cut out a radio ad? A lot of people say it can't be done, but it can. Creativity is the key.

One advertiser recently ran a "coupon ad" on the radio! Part of the 60-second spot was dedicated to instructing the listener how to draw an official coupon. It worked. After the ad had been running for several weeks, the coupons began coming in. It took time to generate responses because listeners had to be convinced that this was an honest offer for a service.

Once the offer took hold, the advertiser maintained it. Just as in other media, you have to maintain consistency in your radio advertising.

RADIO VERSUS PRINT MEDIA

"Compared to print advertising, radio is dirt cheap," states Grey Smith.

Let's compare the circulation of a newspaper against the audience of a radio station. Say you live in a city of 500,000. The city's biggest newspaper has a paid circulation of 200,000 with additional street and newsstand sales of 50,000 per day. You want your ad to reach as many adults as possible.

A quarter-page ad, positioned in the upper right corner of the first available page, costs $1,000 for a one-time run. The cost per thousand is $25, which means for each 1,000 people the ad is supposed to reach, you pay $25.

The broadcast of the biggest radio station reaches all 500,000 residents. You can be fairly certain that each household has at least one radio; in fact, the national average for the number of radios per household in the United States is almost six.

Of the 500,000 potential customers, 80 percent are in the 18 to 65 age group, the customers you want to reach. This gives you a listener base of 400,000. Say a 60-second radio spot costs $100 during drive time (6 A.M. to 10 A.M. or 3 P.M. to 7 P.M.). Just to keep the cost of advertising the same, you spend $1,000 with the radio station. That's ten 60-second spots.

When the first spot runs, you make a maximum of 400,000 impressions. But let's be less optimistic. Say the radio station has only a 50 percent market share in your town (two other stations have the other 50 percent). So you have made 200,000 impressions, about 50,000 fewer than the newspaper. But you've only spent one-tenth the amount. When all ten commercials have run, you've made 2 million impressions (ten impressions each on 200,000 potential customers). That's eight times what you got with one newspaper ad for the same budget.

Granted, newspapers stay around longer than one day. The ad can also be cut out and saved. But in a newspaper, it's easy to intentionally skip over a particular ad or even not notice it in the first place, because so many ads compete for a reader's attention in each two-page spread.

On the radio, as on television, a listener is exposed to only one ad at a time. So unless they stop listening to the radio altogether, all listeners must listen to the commercials. They can't be avoided.

RESOURCE

For more information on radio advertising, contact the Radio Advertising Bureau, 2261 Madison Avenue, 23rd floor, New York, NY 10016, 212-681-7200.

Most of the material in this chapter was provided by the late Grey Smith, and I am grateful for his help and cooperation.

Chapter 13

SALES BROCHURES

We live in an age of entrepreneurism. Hundreds of thousands of new companies are started each year, most of them sole proprietorships run by one or two people; many of them are operated out of a garage, den, or spare bedroom using a post office box for a business address.

This boom in entrepreneurism solves some problems, but it creates problems, too. For example, it's easier to form or dissolve a company today than ever before. As a result, while the number of legitimate firms is on the rise, there is also a growing number of fly-by-night organizations popping up. This makes consumers wary. They're more cautious, more skeptical about doing business with an unfamiliar firm. You have to prove that you're legitimate before they'll take the next step with you.

Brochures can go a long way toward establishing credibility and gaining consumer trust and acceptance. After all, anyone can spend $50 for business cards, letterhead, and an impressive sounding name. But, reasons the consumer, a brochure distinguishes you as a "real company."

According to a study by Thomas Publishing, 90 percent of business and industrial buyers will not do business with a company that does not have some form of company or product literature to submit for inclusion in the buyer's purchasing files.

I know this to be true from experience. A firm for which I worked as advertising manager lost a $300,000 sale on a new type of industrial equipment because we did not have a sales brochure or data sheet on the product. It was not enough to submit a typewritten proposal. A brochure was needed to convince the buyer that the product was indeed real and proven.

Many firms cannot afford TV advertising or full-page magazine ads, but almost every firm has some sort of brochure. According to an article in the *Kodak Print Media Gazette* (Volume 3, Number 1), the fastest-growing market segment of the printing industry is marketing and promotion support materials—in other words, brochures.

What, aside from establishing credibility, can a brochure do for you? A brochure can inform prospects about your offer and educate them about your product or service. It can build an image and position your company in the marketplace. A brochure can sell (or help sell) your product by presenting its key benefits to prospects and convincing them to acquire the product.

Most products and services have a multistep sales cycle, meaning that a number of different steps occur before the sale is closed. The steps occur in sequence, and the function of marketing communications and sales is to persuade the prospect to take the next step, and the next, and the next, until the final step (the sale) is made. The function of the brochure in these cases is not to sell directly but to convince the prospect to take the next step in the buying process.

For instance, the sales cycle for a widget-making machine might be:

1. Prospect sees ad in widget trade journal.
2. Prospect responds to ad and requests literature.
3. Prospect receives and reads literature.
4. Prospect contacts company and requests salesperson to visit.
5. Salesperson visits prospect and makes initial presentation.
6. Prospect reviews presentation materials with top management.
7. Salesperson invited back for second presentation to management team.
8. Salesperson makes second presentation.
9. Prospect organization reviews second presentation and makes decision to proceed.
10. Prospect organization requests formal proposal and price quotation.
11. Seller submits proposal and price quotation.
12. Prospect places order.

A brochure or series of brochures may be used at different stages in the sales cycle to move the prospect forward to the next step. For instance, an introductory brochure presented at Step 3 must be persuasive enough in its presentation of benefits to convince the prospect to move forward and take Step 4, which involves asking the sales rep to make a presentation. During the visit, the salesperson may leave behind a more detailed brochure at Step 5, either to reinforce and repeat the points made in the oral presentation or to answer any questions the prospect might have. This material must be comprehensive and powerful enough to get the prospect to go to Steps 6 and 7. Do you see anywhere else in this sales cycle where a brochure or other persuasive marketing document might come in handy?

Another important but much overlooked function of sales brochures is not just to attract the right prospects but to screen out undesired inquiries. Sending a salesperson to visit each potential client or customer who calls is impractical because of the time and cost involved. So instead of spending hours of time and hundreds of dollars of the company's money on a visit to a questionable sales lead, we send a brochure in the mail. Total cost: $1 to $5, depending on the complexity and elaborateness of the package.

Ideally, the brochure is written so that it attracts the right prospects while screening out the wrong prospects. For example, if you offer a consulting service, perhaps you get many leads from small businesses who waste your time on the phone but cannot afford your fees. A line in the copy such as "Minimum consulting fee: $1,200" would give legitimate prospects some idea of initial cost while discouraging those who cannot spend this much from calling.

FIVE BASIC USES FOR SALES BROCHURES

There are five basic situations for which brochures are created:

Leave-Behind

As the name implies, a leave-behind is a piece of sales literature you leave with a prospect. For example, a person who sells vacuum cleaners door to door might have a booklet or brochure to leave behind with people who don't have time to talk or aren't convinced on the first visit. Any service company that gives free estimates—an exterminator, a home improvement contractor, a landscape designer—might leave behind an informative or promotional sales piece to reinforce the advantages the firm offers or simply give the prospect a way to get back in touch.

The leave-behind typically repeats and expands upon the salesperson's pitch. It can also be designed to answer questions the prospect may have. In business-to-business marketing, the leave-behind brochure may have to be reviewed by several executives within the firm, so you should either leave behind extra copies or design the brochure so it can be photocopied easily. This means using standard page sizes, no complex fold-outs, and color schemes that reproduce well on an office copier (dark ink on light paper).

Make sure your leave-behind has your name, address, and telephone number so the prospect can contact you. If you sell through dealers or distributors, leave a space for them to imprint their logo, address, and phone number or to attach self-stick address labels.

Inquiry Fulfillment

Inquiry fulfillment material is the brochure and other literature you send to prospects who request more information about your company. These inquiries can be generated from a variety of sources, including ads, direct mail, publicity, and word of mouth.

There are four basic requirements for good inquiry fulfillment brochures:

1. The brochure should have an attractive title that implies value. "Product guide" is a better title than "catalog." "Information kit" is better than "spec sheets" (unless prospects are hungry for spec sheets). "15 Ways

XYZ Company Can Cut Your Telecommunications Cost" is better than "XYZ Company: The Leader in Telecommunications Equipment."

Give your piece an enticing title that can be featured in print advertising to get more people to want it and send for it. One sure way to increase response to your ads or mailings is to offer the free booklet in your copy. Instead of just ending with your logo and address, say, "The tax-saving benefits of this new bond are described in a free, informative pamphlet, 'How to Invest Profitably in Municipal Bonds.' To receive your copy without cost or obligation, write to us today." People will send for it because the title makes them think it contains useful information, not just sales talk.

2. The brochure must be informative. The person requested the brochure not to be entertained but because he or she wanted more information on the product or service being advertised. The brochure must provide the information the prospect wants, or the prospect will be disappointed.

3. It is not enough for the brochure merely to present the facts; it must also persuade. The copy should present the product features and benefits in such a way that it convinces the prospect that he or she should have, indeed must have, the product being promoted.

4. Having created a desire for the product, the brochure must spell out the next step in the buying process and tell the reader to take it. Not only must you tell your prospect to take action, you should also provide a strong incentive for the prospect to take action now rather than later, because a delayed decision usually means no decision, which means no sale for you.

Your inquiry fulfillment package should ideally provide a response mechanism that the prospect can use to take this next step. For example, one company had a standard questionnaire every salesperson used when talking with prospects over the phone. Only by getting answers to the questions could the salesperson work up an exact price quotation. They improved response to their brochure by binding the questionnaire into the next printing and adding copy that asked the prospect to tear out, fill in, and mail the completed questionnaire to the company after reading the brochure. Many did. On order forms today, you should add a line that reads, "For faster service, simply complete this questionnaire and fax it to [fax number]." About 10 percent of prospects will send the completed form back by fax.

When planning your inquiry fulfillment package, think of it as a package, not just a brochure. An effective inquiry package includes:

- the brochure—the information the prospect asked for;
- a cover letter—to acknowledge the prospect's interest, stress key sales points, and encourage a response;
- a reply mechanism—typically a reply card, questionnaire, sheet, or other form the prospect can complete and mail back to request more information or place an order; and
- an outer envelope—to carry the whole package.

Some marketers are fond of pocket folders used to contain the various elements of the package. I prefer to mail them loose so that they fall out and separate when the envelope is opened. This forces the prospect to at least glance at each element before throwing it away, giving you multiple opportunities to grab attention. A single folder is easier to rip up and throw away in a single motion.

Tip: The outer envelope of an inquiry fulfillment package should always be imprinted or rubber stamped with this phrase: "Here is the Information You Requested." Without this label, the prospect or a secretary might mistake the package for unsolicited direct mail and throw it away, even though it was requested.

Point of Sale

A point of sale brochure is a brochure that is made available to prospects at your place of business. They are also called rack brochures because they are typically displayed in literature racks or cases. The two most common examples are bank brochures and travel brochures displayed in travel agencies.

The key requirement of a rack brochure is that it have an interesting, attention-grabbing cover. People who stop and glance at literature displays often are not thinking about your products or services but may be browsing or just passing time.

A cover that stops the reader, with either a striking graphic or a powerful headline, can get the person to stop, lift the brochure out of the rack, read the headline, and, if effective, turn the page to see what's inside. For instance, if you are advertising a health spa or weight loss program, a color photograph of attractive women and men working out in exercise clothes or bathing suits will draw people's eyes to the cover and get them to pick up the brochure. (Yes, sex still sells.)

Sales Tool

Some, but not most, literature pieces are designed as sales aids. That is, they are created to be used by salespeople as aids during presentations to prospects.

Sometimes these are designed in formats similar to regular brochures. The piece may do double duty as both a sales aid and a leave-behind. However, if the primary function is as a sales aid, the brochure should contain more visuals (charts, diagrams, tables) and less copy, and what copy there is should probably be in bulleted lists or some other easy-to-scan format.

If the piece is designed solely as a presentation aid, you might go to a flip chart format, with each page covering one major point (in a headline and visual) with two or three copy points (in bullet form) to support the main idea. Or, you can use three-ring binders containing a variety of sales materials that can be customized to fit the individual salesperson's presentation. These are known as sales kits. A sales kit for an aluminum siding salesperson, for example, might contain photos of homes the company has sided, a list of references, and actual samples of the different siding materials in a variety of sizes, colors, and finishes.

Direct Mail

The fifth category of brochure is those used in direct mail, specifically in mass mailings sent in bulk to rented prospect names on commercially available mailing lists.

These brochures are typically folded rather than stapled, glued, or bound, and are designed to be read quickly rather than kept and referred to for long periods of time. There is an old saying in direct mail: "The letter sells, the brochure tells." The role of the direct mail brochure is to repeat the key sales points stressed in the letter, support these sales points with more detailed information, and display drawings, photos, and other visuals that illustrate the key selling points.

When designing a direct mail brochure, pay particular attention to the panels readers see first when they initially remove the brochure from the envelope. Make these bold and attractive with enticing headlines and graphics that lure the prospect inside. For example, the outer panels may present a series of related copy lines, each leading the reader deeper into the piece. The inner panels are usually reserved for heavier copy and a more detailed explanation.

Many companies desire a single brochure that can be used both in direct mail and in inquiry fulfillment. This creates a problem. If you send your brochure to prospects in the cold mailing, it makes no sense to have them respond and ask for the piece they already have. The direct mail brochure should hit the highlights only and be more promotional, while the inquiry fulfillment brochure should be more detailed and discuss product features and benefits in greater depth.

PLANNING YOUR BROCHURE

There are 12 key considerations in planning any sales brochure:

1. Objective or sales goal

2. Type of literature needed

3. Topic

4. Content

5. Audience

6. Sales appeals

7. Image

8. Sales cycle

9. Competition

10. Format

11. Budget

12. Schedule

These 12 aspects, taken in sequence, provide a logical platform for planning the production of a brochure, catalog, flier, pamphlet, booklet, or any other printed promotion piece. Make photocopies of the blank Literature Specification Sheet (Figure 13.1) and fill out a new sheet for each project. Give a copy of the completed sheet to your agency, copywriter, and other vendors as part of your background briefing for the assignment.

Let's take a closer look at each step in the process.

Step 1: Determine Your Objective

The most common telephone call I get is from a client telling me, "We need a new brochure." My response is always the same: "Why?" What is the purpose of the brochure? What is it supposed to accomplish? If you can't give a firm answer to this question, maybe you don't really need a brochure after all.

Example: One prospective client answered the question by saying, "I am bidding on a big job for a major phone company and as part of the proposal they require me to submit a company brochure. I don't have one; that's why I need one." This is a legitimate answer, and at least the client is spending hard-earned money on expensive copy, design, and printing services for a purpose: to win a major contract.

If you don't really know what results you want from your brochure, the chances of the brochure generating any specific results for you are slim. Your first step is to define your objective. Use the Literature Specification Sheet, Figure 13.1, to select one or more objectives for your project. (Note: The steps described in the text correspond to the numbered steps on the Specification Sheet.)

Figure 13.1. Literature Specification Sheet.

1. Objectives of the brochure (check all that are appropriate)
    - ❏ Provide product information to customers
    - ❏ Educate new prospects
    - ❏ Build corporate image
    - ❏ Establish credibility of your organization or product
    - ❏ Sell the product directly through the mail
    - ❏ Help salespeople get appointments
    - ❏ Help salespeople make presentations
    - ❏ Help close the sale
    - ❏ Support dealers, distributors, agents, and sales reps
    - ❏ Add value to the product
    - ❏ Enhance the effectiveness of direct mail promotions
    - ❏ Leave behind with customers as a reminder
    - ❏ Respond to inquiries
    - ❏ Hand out at trade shows, fairs, conventions

Figure 13.1. (*Cont.*)

- ❑ Display at point of purchase
- ❑ Serve as reference material for employees, vendors, the press, investors
- ❑ Disseminate news
- ❑ Announce new products and product improvements
- ❑ Highlight new applications for existing products
- ❑ Train and educate new employees
- ❑ Recruit new employees
- ❑ Provide useful information to the public
- ❑ Answer the prospect's questions
- ❑ Generate new business leads
- ❑ Qualify your company to be on a customer's approved vendor list
- ❑ Other (describe):

2. The type of literature needed (check one):
   - ❑ Annual report
   - ❑ Booklet
   - ❑ Brochure
   - ❑ Case history
   - ❑ Catalog
   - ❑ Circular
   - ❑ Data sheet
   - ❑ Flier
   - ❑ Invoice stuffer
   - ❑ Newsletter
   - ❑ Poster
   - ❑ Other (describe):

3. Topic
   a) What is the subject matter of the brochure? (Describe the product, service, program, or organization being promoted.)
   b) What is the theme or central message (if any)?

4. Content
   a) Is there an outline of the main points and secondary points that must be included in the brochure and the order in which they should be presented?
   b) Is the outline thorough and complete? Does it cover all points?
   c) What is the source of this information? Have you provided the copywriter with the necessary background documents?
   d) What facts are missing? What additional research (if any) is required?

5. Audience
   a) Geographic location
   b) Income level

Figure 13.1. (*Cont.*)

    c) Family status (married? single? children? divorced or widowed?)

    d) Industry

    e) Job title/function

    f) Education

    g) Politics

    h) Religion/ethnic background

    i) Age

    j) Concerns (reasons why they might be interested in your product or service or organization)

    k) Buying habits/purchasing authority

    l) General description of the target audience (in your own words)

6. Sales appeals

    a) What is the key sales appeal of the product?

    b) What are the supporting or secondary sales points?

7. Image

    What image do you want your literature to convey to the reader?

8. Sales cycle

    ❏ How does the brochure fit into your sales cycle? (Check all that apply.)

    ❏ Generate leads

    ❏ Answer initial inquiries

    ❏ Provide more detailed information to qualified buyers

    ❏ Establish confidence in the company and its products

    ❏ Provide detailed product information

    ❏ Answer questions frequently asked by prospects

    ❏ Reinforce sales message for prospect ready to buy

    ❏ Support salespeople during presentation

    ❏ Close the sale

    ❏ Other (describe)

9. Competition

    What images and sales appeals do competitors' brochures stress?

Competitor	Image	Key Sales Appeals
_____	_____	_____
_____	_____	_____
_____	_____	_____
_____	_____	_____

10. Format

    a) Approximate number of words

    b) Number of color photos

Figure 13.1. (*Cont.*)

c) Number of black and white photos

d) Number and types of illustrations and other visuals (describe)

e) Number of pages

f) Page size: ❏ 8 1/2 x 11"   ❏ 7 x 10"   ❏ 6 x 9"   ❏ 5 1/2 x 8-1/2"   ❏ 4 x 9"
❏ Other:

g) Method of folding or binding (describe)

h) Number of colors used in printing: ❏ 1 color   ❏ 2 color   ❏ 4 color process
❏ Other

i) Type of paper (weight, finish, texture, color)

11. Budget

Use the worksheet below to estimate cost.

Task	Cost
Copywriting	_____
Photography	_____
Illustration	_____
Design and layout	_____
Typesetting	_____
Mechanicals (paste-up)	_____
Printing	_____
TOTAL	$_____
Number of copies to be printed	_____
Cost per copy	_____

12. Schedule

How long will it take to produce?

Task	Number of days to complete
Copy	_____
Copy review	_____
Copy rewrite	_____
Design	_____
Design review	_____
Design revision	_____
Typesetting	_____
Photography and illustration	_____
Mechanicals	_____
Delays, mistakes	_____
Printing	_____
Total	_____

Step 2: Determine the Type of Literature You Need

What type of sales literature do you need? A brochure is best for presenting a single product, while a catalog is more appropriate for presenting a line of related products. If you simply want to keep in touch with your clients and potential clients on a regular basis, you might consider a newsletter format, mailed quarterly. You can use Table 13.1 as a guide to choosing the type of literature format that's appropriate for your application.

Step 3: Choose Your Topic

What is the subject matter of the brochure? Is it about your service, or does it deal with the problem your service addresses? If the purpose is to present your company's capabilities, what percentage of the brochure is devoted to descriptions of specific services as opposed to a general discussion of your firm and its good points? If it's about a single product, shouldn't you at least mention your other products, or would that confuse the reader?

You must determine the exact subject matter of your brochure and then stick with it. If you vacillate on this point, there will be nothing but confusion and disagreements between you and your ad agency or copywriter.

As a rule of thumb, the most effective brochures typically deal with one topic and one topic only. Other topics, products, or services should be covered in other brochures.

In most cases, the topic is a specific product or service. You might have one brochure on Product A, a second covering Product B, a third describing Product C, and so on. But you might also write brochures in which the topic is a specific audience or market and its needs, rather than a product.

Example: Let's say one of your big markets is the chemical industry, and they are large purchasers of Products A, B, F, and P. You might do a separate brochure titled, "[name of product category] for the Chemical Industry." The outline of the brochure might be:

1. The chemical industry has special needs.
2. [Name of company] specializes in meeting these needs.
3. We have a line of [type of product] tailored to these needs.
4. They include Product A, Product B, Product F, and Product P [with descriptions and benefits of each].

It is important for you, the advertising manager, to clarify and agree on the topic internally before hiring outside copy, art, and creative services to create the piece. Changing the core topic and subject matter once the project has started involves enormous additional charges for revisions and change of direction, charges you want to avoid.

Tip: An easy way to get consensus on the creative and marketing direction of a project is to fill out a Literature Specification Sheet for each piece you are doing. You can make blank forms by photocopying Figure 13.1.

Table 13-1. Types of sales literature

Use this...	To do this...
Annual report	Gain status
	Establish credibility
	Build an upscale image
	Tell your corporate story
	Communicate financial data
Booklet	Give a quick overview
	Answer questions via a Q&A format
	Disseminate information
	Build your image as the expert in your field
Brochure	Describe and sell products and services
	Provide prospects with the information they requested
	Introduce, position, or establish your product or company in the marketplace
Case history	Overcome skepticism
	Sell your product to a specific market or for a specific application
	Build the prospect's comfort level
	Show how your product can solve a specific problem
Catalog	Sell a line of products
	Let customers know what other products you offer
	Help buyers find and select products they need
	Generate additional revenue by informing buyers of one product that you have many other related products of interest to them
Circular	Promote sales and specials
	Distribute price-off coupons
	Increase retail store traffic
Data sheet	Answer buyers' questions
	Give complete information about a product
	List specifications
	Satisfy the information requirements of the technical buyer or specifier
Flier	Promote your business on a local level
	Get your name around
	Announce an event
	Get new literature out quickly
Invoice stuffer	Reinforce a sales message
	Get additional sales at low promotional cost
	Get your message to all customers
Newsletter	Build awareness of your company with a specific group of prospects over a period of time
	Make announcements
	Distribute miscellaneous bits and pieces of information that don't warrant their own fliers, brochures, or mailings
	Disseminate news
	Highlight recent developments
Poster	Make your message stand out from the crowd
	Get the prospect's attention
	Keep your name in front of the buyer

Step 4: Outline the Exact Content of the Brochure

Once you have determined the topic, you need to define exactly what will be covered in the brochure. Just as a book author writes a chapter-by-chapter table of contents as a guide to what will go in the book, you may want to create an outline, either rough or detailed, of the key points that must be covered in the brochure.

Basically, there are three types of brochures: product brochures, service brochures, and corporate or capabilities brochures. A product brochure describes and sells a tangible product, such as equipment, hardware, or systems. A service brochure describes the services a firm performs for clients. A capabilities brochure presents a broad outline of a corporation—its history, abilities, strengths, products, services, and activities.

The sample outlines in Figure 13.2 provide a starting point for outlining your own brochures in each of these categories. Use these samples to stimulate your thinking and to make sure all important points are covered in any outline you write.

Step 5: Determine Your Audience

A brochure, or any piece of promotional copy, can be effective only if it is written with a specific reader in mind. The more narrowly focused the market, the better. "There is often a need to look at the broad audience and break it into segments," writes Charles A. Moldenhauer in communications briefings. "Once this is done, it may be possible to identify different positionings for each segment."

Why don't more companies have separate brochures for each target market? Cost is the main factor. Some markets may be too small to justify the cost and expense of creating a separate brochure. In other markets, you may not be sure that the market is right for you, and so you don't want to incur major marketing expenses until you've demonstrated success.

What are the alternatives to doing a separate brochure for each market? One technique is to compartmentalize, a term invented by Steve Isaac, president of the Stenrich Group, a direct marketing consulting firm. In a compartmentalized brochure, you have a section listing all the various markets and, underneath them, a bulleted list of the different benefits the product offers to each of these groups.

A second technique is to keep most of the brochure the same but simply tailor the cover and perhaps the opening page. A good way to create strong affinity with the reader is to identify the reader on the cover, either visually or in copy.

Example: Let's say you sell compressors. One brochure cover might read, "Compressors for the chemical industry," with an illustration of a chemical plant. Using essentially the same inside layout and text, you create a second cover showing a paper mill and change the headline to read, "Compressors for the pulp and paper industry." Now the chemical industry prospects who receive the first brochure will think your compressor was designed especially and solely for them, and the papermakers receiving

Figure 13.2. Sample brochure outlines.

Product Brochure

  I.   Introduction—a capsule description of what the product is and why the reader should be interested in it.

 II.   Benefits—a list of reasons why the customer should buy the product.

III.   Features—highlights of important features that set the product apart from the competition.

 IV.   How It Works—a description of how the product works and what it can do. This section can include the results of any tests that demonstrate the product's superiority.

  V.   Types of Users (Markets)—This section describes special markets the product is designed for and, if appropriate, specific benefits it offers each market. This section can also include lists of users as well as testimonials from satisfied clients.

 VI.   Applications—descriptions of the various applications in which the product can be used.

VII.   Product Availability—models, sizes, materials, colors, finishes, options, accessories, and all the variations in which the product can be ordered. This section can also include charts, graphs, formulas, tables, or other guidelines to aid the reader in product sizing and selection.

VIII. Pricing—information on what the product costs, including prices for accessories, various models and sizes, quantity discounts, and shipping. Often published as a separate price list so as not to date the brochure.

 IX.   Technical Specifications—electrical requirements, power consumption, resistance to moisture, temperature range, operating conditions, cleaning methods, storage conditions, safety warnings, product life, and other characteristics and limitations of the product.

  X.   Q&A Section—frequently asked questions about the product and their answers; a good place to include miscellaneous information that doesn't fit logically under the other sections.

 XI.   Company Description—a brief biography of the manufacturer, written to show the reader that the product is backed by a solid, reputable organization that will be in business for the long haul.

XII.   Product Support—information on delivery, installation, training, maintenance, service, warranty, and guarantee.

XIII. The Next Step—instructions telling the readers what you want them to do next or how to place an order.

Service Brochure

  I.   Introduction—a listing of the services offered, types of clients handled, and the reasons why the reader should be interested in your services.

 II.   Services Offered—detailed descriptions of the various services offered by the firm and how they satisfy client needs.

III.   Benefits—describing what readers will gain from establishing a relationship with the service firm and why they should engage your firm instead of the competition.

 IV.   Background Information—a discussion of the problems the service is designed to solve. This section can offer generic advice on how to evaluate the problem and how to select professional help. Such free information adds to the value of the brochure and encourages readers to keep your literature.

Figure 13.2. (*Cont.*)

    V.   Methodology—an outline of the service firm's method of doing business with clients.

   VI.   Client List—a list of well-known people or organizations who have used the firm's services.

  VII.   Testimonials-endorsements from select clients, usually written in the client's own words and attributed to a specific person or organization.

 VIII.   Fees and Terms—describing the fees for each service and the terms and method of payment required. This section includes whatever guarantee the service firm offers its clients.

   IX.   Biographical Information—capsule biographies highlighting the credentials and expertise of key employees plus an overall capsule biography of the firm.

    X.   The Next Step—instructions on what the customer should do next if he or she is interested in hiring the firm or learning more about its services.

Corporate Brochure

     I.   The Business (or businesses) the company is engaged in.

    II.   Corporate Structure—parent company, subsidiaries, divisions, departments, branch offices, overseas affiliates, etc.

   III.   Locations—addresses and phone numbers of all offices, branches, agents, and representatives.

   IV.   Major Corporate Officers—names, titles, photos.

    V.   History—brief corporate biography.

   VI.   Plants and Other Facilities.

  VII.   Geographical Coverage.

 VIII.   Major Markets the Company Sells To.

   IX.   Distribution Systems.

    X.   Sales—annual for this year and growth over the past 5 to 10 years.

   XI.   Ranking in Its Industry compared with the competition.

  XII.   Extent of Stock Distribution.

 XIII.   Earnings and dividend records.

 XIV.   Number of Employees.

  XV.   Employee Benefits.

 XVI.   Noteworthy Employees—scientists, vendors, and well-known authorities, for example.

 XVII.   Inventions and technological firsts.

XVIII.   Significant Achievements.

 XIX.   R&D—current research and development activities.

  XX.   QC—quality control and assurance practices and programs.

 XXI.   Environment—actions with respect to preserving the environment.

 XXII.   Contributions—to art, welfare, public service, community, etc.

XXIII.   Awards.

XXIV.   Policies.

 XXV.   Future Plans, goals, objectives.

designed especially and solely for them, and the papermakers receiving the second brochure will have the same impression.

A third technique is the modular brochure. In this format, the main brochure is a four- or six-page folder with a pocket. Folder copy presents a broad overview of the firm or product. Insert sheets, stored in the pocket, highlight specific topics and can be added or removed to tailor the brochure to the needs and interests of individual prospects.

People want products and services tailored to their needs. They want to perceive that your service is customized for them. A brochure clearly written and aimed at a specific, narrow market segment creates this perception. So be sure to identify your audience, then write and design the piece with them in mind. To further pinpoint your audience, fill out Section 5 in the Literature Specification Sheet (Figure 13.1.)

Step 6: Identify Key Sales Appeals

What is the most important benefit your product offers the audience—the most compelling reason why they should buy it? Identify this benefit and stress it on your cover and in your first few paragraphs of copy. Do not save your best points for a strong close or bury them in the middle of the piece. The reader may never get that far. Instead, determine the one, two, or three most important points and draw attention to them right away. To do this, make the title of your brochure the name of the product, then highlight the two or three key sales points in big, bold bulleted lines directly underneath.

One way to determine the main message or key point is to telephone half a dozen or so potential prospects and ask them, "What is the biggest problem you have in your business (or your life) right now?" If you can tailor your copy to address this concern and then show how your product can alleviate the problem, you'll have a winner of a brochure.

Step 7: Determine the Image You Want Your Brochure to Convey

The first thing a brochure conveys, even before it is opened and read, is an impression or an image. A glossy, slick, beautifully designed and expensively printed color brochure, just by virtue of the production values, creates an image of stability, excellence, quality, even elegance. A typewritten flier, hand-illustrated and run off on cheap paper on an office copier, creates a very different image.

This is not to say that every brochure must be lavish. Rather, the tone of your copy, the style of design, and the quality of the paper and reproduction should be appropriate to your market and your product. Don't overpresent. A black and white flier or an inexpensive two-color pamphlet may be totally appropriate for your audience and offer.

Example: One firm's brochure is elaborate. In fact, it is bound by an imitation leather cover complete with gold tassel. The paper is of the finest quality. The headlines are in finely penned calligraphy. Unfortunately, this firm sells rat poison to warehouse managers who want to get rid of rodents eating their inventory! The brochure is too elegant for the product and market. Not only does this waste money, but it sends a message to the reader that you are not really in touch with your market. Don't overpresent. Most companies spend too much on production, not too little.

A good graphic artist can create a piece that looks more expensive than it actually is. One technique for achieving this look is judicious selection of ink and paper colors.

Traditionally, we think of a one-color print job (the least expensive method) as black ink on white paper, but it need not be. One designer created an elegant look by printing in maroon ink on gray paper—a color scheme that has been widely imitated. By using screens or bendays, you can achieve varying shades of the same color using only one color ink. If you are printing a circular or flier in black ink, you might choose a brightly colored stock such as salmon, blue, yellow, or gold instead of white.

Choice of type style can also have a major effect on the image your brochure conveys. An elegant or classy typeface may not cost any more than a cheap-looking one. Graphic artists are responsible for the selection, but use your own taste to evaluate their choices.

Step 8: Determine Where in Your Sales Cycle the Brochure Fits

As we've discussed, the purpose of the brochure is not to do the whole selling job, but simply to move the prospect one step along in the sales cycle, from point A to point B, from E to F, etc. To accomplish this, you must first clearly write out your step-by-step sales cycle, then decide where in this cycle your brochure fits and which particular step it is designed to persuade the reader to take. Content, copy, and level of technical detail are all dependent on this.

Example: Let's say you are selling personal computers. A prospect who is first shopping doesn't want to be overwhelmed with technical details. The brochure probably should concentrate on what your computer can do for the prospect and whether it is designed for his or her needs.

After shopping around and doing a lot of reading, prospects will be more knowledgeable. At the point when they are ready to buy, their questions are probably a lot more technical (e.g., How much RAM does your computer have compared with the competition's? What microprocessor do you use? How many expansion slots are there?). For these prospects, a data sheet flier with a lot of technical specs clearly laid out would be more appropriate. The point is that technical content and depth are dependent on which stage in the sales cycle the prospect has reached.

TWO RULES OF THUMB

1. The closer the prospect is to making a purchase decision, the more information your brochure must contain.

2. The more technically oriented the prospect is, the more detail the brochure should contain. "Upper management people are interested in the viability of the company with which they will be doing business and in general sales information," writes Rick Austin in *Computers & Electronics Marketing*. "Technical experts are most interested in specifications and 'blood and guts' product information. Middle managers need a little salesmanship, a little hand-holding, and more technical information than upper management but not quite as much as technical experts."

Step 9: Evaluate the Competition

Your brochure may fail to stand out from the crowd if it is too much like the competition's. Do your competitors' brochures stress a certain sales point? Perhaps you can grab the prospect's interest by highlighting a benefit that others do not stress or discuss. Are your competitors all using full-size, 8 1/2 × 11 or 7 × 10 brochures? Be different and make yours 5 1/2 × 8 1/2. Are they printing in blues, reds, and browns? Make yours orange.

The Sameness Syndrome is a danger in industries where companies tend to copy each other, with all advertisers using essentially the same style, format, and approach. After a while, your brochure begins to blur in the readers' minds and they cannot distinguish your piece from the 30 other promotions they have received from similar companies. A good example of this is the seminar business, which is flooded with look-alike 11 × 17-inch, two-color self-mailers.

Advertisers copy one another and stick with standard formats because these formats are proven to work. But the advertiser who develops a new format that works will be that much more successful, because the format will be distinctive and unique. Be aware of your competitors' brochures and try to be different, if you can.

Step 10: Design the Format

Format includes such factors as page size, number of pages, folding or binding method, color schemes, design scheme, and graphic style. For example:

- Will you have a lot of copy on each page or will you use a spare effect with lots of white space?
- Will you use many photos to communicate information, or will you use only a few large, artistic photos for dramatic impact?
- Will the brochure be plain or colorful?
- Will it be full-size or designed to fit in a standard #10 business envelope?
- Will it be made from a single sheet of paper (with pages created through folding) or will you print on several sheets of paper and bind them together?

Most direct mail and rack brochures are made by folding a letter or legal size sheet of paper into six or eight oblong panels. Most inquiry fulfillment and leave-behind brochures use larger 7 × 10 or 8 1/2 × 11 pages.

Once you have selected a size and format, make a dummy. This is a model or mock-up of the finished piece created by cutting, folding, and taping together sheets of paper. The dummy is the same size, has the same number of pages, and folds and opens in the same manner as your final piece. With a dummy in hand, you can better determine how much room you have for copy and where each section of copy will go.

TWO TIPS

1. Make the dummy from the same stock on which you intend to print the finished piece, then weigh it. This tells you the exact weight of your proposed brochure, which you can use to determine postage costs for mailing.

2. Use standard size brochures: 7 × 10, 8 1/2 × 11, 6 × 9, or 4 × 9. Odd-size brochures may require custom envelopes for mailing, and printing special envelopes is expensive. European brochures, printed with 8 1/2 × 14 pages, do not fit in standard American letter-size files.

Step 11: Determine the Budget

The easiest way to make a rough guess at a project budget is to base it on past experience. If you've done other brochures, you know roughly what you can expect to pay for a small, folded, all-copy, two-color pamphlet or a large, glossy color piece with original photography and artwork. If you haven't done brochures before, get estimates from the various vendors involved—copywriter, photographer, illustrator, artist, typesetter, printer, color separator—and work up an estimate using Section 11 in the Literature Specification Sheet (Figure 13.1).

Tip: One way to reduce the cost per copy is to print more copies. The largest expense is in preparing the copy and artwork for the printer and in making the printing films or plates and running the first copy. To print more copies is not that much more expensive than to print only a few.

For example, if your total cost is $5,000 and you print 1,000 brochures, the unit cost is $5.00 per brochure. A print run of 5,000 might only cost an additional $900, or a total of $5,900, which brings the unit cost down to $1.18 per brochure, a number that's a lot easier to sell to management.

Step 12: Set Your Production Schedule

As a rule of thumb, allow three months for the production of a brochure from the initial conceptual planning and development to receipt of the finished pieces from the printer. This is roughly one month for internal concept development and review plus two months for outside vendors (copywriter, artists, printers) to do their work. On four-color jobs, allow an extra two to four weeks for color separations and corrections.

You can use Section 12 in the Literature Specification Sheet (Figure 13.1) to determine the schedule for any project. Note that it is frequently possible to do multiple steps simultaneously to save time. For example, if you know what photos you want, you can have the photographer doing the photo shoot while the copywriter works on the copy.

THE 24 MOST COMMON BROCHURE MISTAKES

According to Nat Starr, a graphics consultant specializing in brochures for professionals and businesses, these are the 24 most common mistakes advertisers make when producing their brochures:

1. The cover fails to identify its contents and its relevance to the reader.

2. Long words, long sentences, long paragraphs, buzzwords, and jargon make the text difficult to read and understand.

3. The text fails to list all the benefits.

4. Benefits are listed sequentially in one long paragraph rather than set in a bulleted column for easy reading. Thus, many are overlooked by the reader.

5. The text fails to ask for the order or demand some action at the end.

6. The contents are not organized sequentially so as to deliver an effective sales message that will involve and persuade the reader (i.e., building your case).

7. The designer failed to include line illustrations and charts or other graphic elements necessary to clarify and reinforce the descriptive text.

8. Photographs are too large, too small, washed out, or dark and blotchy.

9. Text is set in typefaces that are too small, too bold or too light, too masculine or feminine, too whimsical or industrial, too cute or powerful.

10. Typeset line length is too long for good readability.

11. Large blocks of italic type and reverse type are hard to read.

12. Headlines are not set in type large enough and bold enough to provide good contrast with the text type.

13. Headlines are not written so that the reader will get the gist of the message just by reading the heads.

14. Solid, uninterrupted pages of text type are hard to read and don't get read in their entirety.

15. Insufficient contrast between text type and the area on which it is printed. Example: small, medium red type overprinted on a green tint block (almost impossible to read).

16. Not enough contrast between colors used. One should be dark, the other light, for good balance in the layout.

17. Too many colors used indiscriminately with no attempt to balance them in the layout.

18. Insufficient white space to separate the various elements of the layout; everything jammed together and hard to read.

19. Large bubbles of white space inside the layout (too distracting to the eye).

20. Brochure sent as a self-mailer (without an envelope). Virtually guarantees worse results.

21. Too many inserts in a pocket-size brochure that is inconvenient to handle and store.

22. Information unclear (or missing) as to how or where to get additional information or order the product or service.

23. Failure to make it easy for the customer to buy by not providing easy terms, 30-day free trial, credit card acceptance, etc.

24. Paying too much for printing. Experienced graphics people can help you find many ways to slash your production, printing, and lettershop costs.

12 POWERFUL IDEAS FOR IMPROVING YOUR SALES BROCHURES

Richard H. Hill, vice president of High Technology at Alexander Marketing Services of Grand Rapids, MI, offers the following tips and ideas on how to improve the selling power of your next sales brochure:

1. Show test results that confirm that your product or service performs as you say it does.

2. Use case histories showing the successful application of your product or service.

3. Provide sample calculations of cost savings or other benefits.

4. Compare your product with the competition's, feature by feature.

5. Compare your product or service with the buyer's alternative of doing nothing and sticking with old ways. That's a particularly strong approach for new, advanced technology products.

6. Provide useful information about the application of your product or service that is not readily available. This can earn your brochure the status of a reference work, keeping it in use by the prospect.

7. Present points logically. Outline a progressive presentation that answers the buyers' probable questions in the order they would ask them.

8. Design the piece so that it presents one major topic per spread or page.

9. Don't cram too much material into the first page or spread. It must be very inviting if you're going to get your prospect started on your message.

10. For longer brochures, consider using an index or table of contents to direct prospects to the right section.

11. Try to include at least one photograph of your product in your literature. This is particularly important for a new product. Using drawings instead of photos with a new product can imply that you haven't really made any of them yet.

12. Use tables and graphs to support your claims and present the properties of your products. They are far better choices for presenting quantitative data than body copy. There is nothing like a string of numbers and units in a paragraph of body copy to slow down the transfer of information.

FINAL CHECK

Use the checklist presented in Figure 13.3 to check new brochures for quality and accuracy before printing. Also use it to analyze existing pieces and determine which ones need to be redone.

Figure 13.3. Brochure analysis. (Reprinted with permission of Nat Starr Associates.)

General Information

1. Is the information accurate?

2. Do you offer any service not shown in the brochure?

3. Are your address and phone number correct?

4. Do you have a toll-free 800 number, and is it correct?

5. Is your logo correctly reproduced?

6. Is your bio current and sufficiently comprehensive?

7. Have you added any new service since printing the brochure?

8. Is your list of clients valid and current?

9. Does your description of services and products correspond to other forms of advertising or promotion you may have published?

10. Is information presented in a logical sequence?

Physical Appearance

1. Are the photos current, clear, and appropriate?

2. Do action photos look real or posed?

3. Are photos used effectively in the layout?

4. Is type style up to date and easy to read?

5. Is type broken up frequently by white space, to present information in short bursts?

6. Is type in headlines large enough to attract the reader's eye?

7. Do headlines and subheads convey the gist of your message?

8. Are words, sentences, and paragraphs short?

9. When sentences contain more than one or two ideas, are the ideas visually separated as in this sentence?

Figure 13.3. (*Cont.*)

10. Is there sufficient white space and is it used properly?

11. Is a second color of ink used?

12. Should your brochure use two color (inks) or four?

13. Are the proper colors used?

14. Has the proper type of paper been used?

15. Is the printing quality acceptable?

16. Can the format (size and shape) be physically stored in a file folder?

Selling Ability

1. Does the brochure clearly and immediately define what you do?

2. Do you use a byline (tag line, slogan) that positions you in your market?

3. Is the proper information highlighted?

4. Does it zero in on the prospect's needs?

5. In the first ten seconds does it give the recipient a compelling reason for reading it?

6. Are the selling benefits clear to the prospect?

7. Are your selling features easy to find?

8. Does your brochure project the current corporate image?

9. Does it state who the audience is?

10. Does it state why the prospect should buy from you?

11. Does it avoid flowery language with too many superlatives?

12. Does it use active verbs and picturesque language, with ideas stated succinctly?

13. Have you used sufficient testimonials?

14. Have testimonials been properly edited?

15. Does the brochure ask for the order?

CREATING EFFECTIVE SALES BROCHURES FOR TECHNOLOGY PRODUCTS

To find out what determines whether product literature falls in the Success or Failure category, I spoke with several communications managers at high-tech firms and the agencies who produce their literature.

The experts disagree more than they agree, but several general principles surface. Chief among them is that high-tech brochures need to contain *more* information about the product, not less. Yet everyone I spoke with said the brochures should be written by professional copywriters who understand the importance of stressing product benefits, and not by engineers—despite the difficulties of educating ad people about technical subjects.

To Terry C. Smith, communications manager at Westinghouse Defense and Electronic Systems Center in Baltimore, MD, content—or the lack of it—is what separates a winner from a loser among sales brochures aimed at the high-tech market. "The biggest single thing that improved our brochures was making sure they had enough content, so readers would go away thinking they learned something," says Smith, whose department is responsible for producing sales brochures to promote the various electronic defense systems marketed by Westinghouse. "At one time, our brochures were glossy, pretty things without much meat. But now, when prospects finish reading one of our brochures, they feel their time has been well spent."

Smith draws an analogy to automobile sales literature. "Take a look at a Saab brochure," he says. "The Saab brochure has 60 pages or so, with maybe 30 cutaways giving detailed technical information. A Chevrolet brochure, on the other hand, has less information, and the photos show mostly exterior shots—glamour shots. We feel a technical brochure should be more like the Saab brochure. Instead of trying to sell with a shallow presentation, a good brochure should inform and educate the reader."

According to Smith, who has produced more than 500 pieces of sales literature in a career spanning over three decades, a brochure describing a technical product should tell the reader what the product is, what it does, and how it works. He teaches his staff writers to describe technical products on three levels: functions, features, and benefits.

"A function is what something does," Smith explains. "A feature is the technical 'gee-whiz' that allows the equipment to perform a specific function. And a benefit tells what the payoff is in terms of time and money saved or improved performance."

In Smith's mind, the brochure writer—not the technician—is ultimately responsible for the accuracy of content. "I tell writers that if you pick something up from another source, use it in your brochure and find out later that it's incorrect or outdated, *you* are responsible for the error," he says. "The minute you use a drawing or specification, it becomes yours. The brochure writer should become knowledgeable enough about the subject to suspect something is wrong, or at least know when to check with an expert."

Although Smith advocates a heavy technical content, he concedes that many people won't read long copy. The solution, he says, is to use visuals to communicate information and concepts. "The average reader spends more time looking at pictures and captions than at text, so use a lot of visuals, and write informative captions," he advises. "However, the full text must also be there to tell the complete story for readers who want the detail."

Smith and his department strive for new ways to use visuals. In one sales brochure for the F-16 fighter aircraft's radar system, an artist proposed a block diagram to describe the system. One of Smith's writers improved on this by using photos of the actual components instead of blocks with labels.

What types of visuals are appropriate for a high-tech brochure? "Of course, show your product," Smith says. "But if your product is part of a larger system, show the system too. The system—not the component—is what turns the customer on. In our F-16 radar brochure, we show the entire aircraft, not just our radar."

The bottom line, according to Smith, is that technical customers need to be educated about the products they buy, and they look favorably upon manufacturers who provide this information. Smith says the professional technical communicator should be constantly thinking of creative ways to use information as a marketing tool.

"One of the most popular promotions we ever did, a weapons chronology wall chart, was originally published as a diagram buried in an obscure technical report," Smith recalls. "All we did was recognize it as valuable information a prospect might enjoy having, then dress it up, produce it, and make it available to our customers. Not a day goes by when we don't get at least one request for our wall chart. It's a good example of sales literature that works."

Like Terry Smith, Dick Hill agrees that brochures need to be informative. The secret of success, says Hill, is knowing how to organize key sales points in a logical sequence and clearly communicate them to key prospects.

He should know. As vice president of technology for Alexander Marketing Services, a Grand Rapids, MI-based business-to-business advertising agency, Hill has created brochures for such clients as Irwin International, a manufacturer of Winchester disk drives; Knowledgeware, a software firm; and Dow Chemical.

"One of my pet peeves is the practice of starting a brochure with a company's history or philosophy," he says. "Buyers are looking for products that fit their applications and needs. Their interest in the company itself varies with the situation, but is nearly always secondary."

Ideally, a brochure should be organized like a good sales pitch, Hill says.

"Follow the approach a good salesperson would use," he says. "First qualify the prospect, then generate interest, then go through the features and benefits, then give details about selections and models. Try to learn the logical sequence the buyer goes through in making a decision. Then follow that sequence in organizing your sales brochure."

Unlike engineering reports, which are often written as one continuous stream of thought, brochures should be organized according to pages or two-page spreads, Hill says. He recommends that each major topic should be given its own page or spread.

Engineers and other technical readers respond favorably to this type of approach. Says Hill: "Technical readers are logical people, and they like their information presented in a clear, logical format."

The first step, he says, is to help readers determine whether reading the brochure is worth their time. "Up front, you have to convey key benefits or where the product fits into the reader's application," he explains. "People won't read through the whole brochure to find out whether they're interested."

One favorite Hill technique is to segment sales brochures, creating separate pieces of literature for each market or application and identifying that market or application right on the cover. He also advocates adding some helpful technical tips or other service information to sales brochures, to turn them into semi-reference pieces that people will read and save.

One problem with technical brochures is the varying backgrounds of the readers. Some readers need greater education and will read your brochure from cover to cover. Others may be more knowledgeable, or may lack the time to wade through a lot of copy. Hill says the ideal sales brochure is one that accommodates both types of readers.

His recommendation: Use clear, informative subheads on each page. "The subheads should be written and arranged in such a way that the casual reader skimming the heads and subheads will get the gist of your story," he says. "Copy then becomes supporting evidence for readers who want more depth or detail." If he thinks a few readers may need basic background information on a subject, he includes short backgrounder articles in sidebars sprinkled throughout the brochure.

Although Hill has a technical background, he has very definite prejudices against company engineers writing their own sales literature. "Many companies rely on their own engineering staff to write about their products, and only involve an outside agency to dress up their literature," he says. "I think this is a mistake. While the company's engineers certainly understand the products, they don't know how to write. They don't understand the buying process, and they are addicted to long sentences and jargon that both hurt readability. High-tech companies should use an ad agency staffed by people with technical backgrounds."

What about the complaint that nontechnical people oversimplify when writing about technical products? Says Hill: "As long as the information is there, you have an obligation to make it as clear as possible."

In an article in the *Business to Business Marketer* (August 1997), John C. Schmidt, marketing communications manager for Lucent Technologies, says there are two common mistakes high-tech companies make in their brochures. The first is becoming too preoccupied with promoting its newest technology. "Customers aren't always looking for new technology," Schmidt warns. "They may prefer products that protect investments they've already made. They may not want to gamble on something new and untested."

The second common brochure mistake is emphasizing the company itself—background, history, and so on—rather than being customer-focused. He says the reader's number one concern is how you can help solve a problem that exists now.

BROCHURES AS DIRECT RESPONSE TOOLS

Unlike many ad managers I talked with in doing this book, New York City–based marketing consultant and seminar leader Chip Chapin couldn't care less whether others consider his brochures beautiful. "All I care about," Chapin says, "is whether people respond to it."

A former national director of Evelyn Wood Reading Dynamics, Chapin's approach is to turn every sales brochure into a direct marketing tool, something that produces a concrete, measurable response. "The purpose of a sales brochure is not just to disseminate information," he says. "You'd go broke handing out that type of brochure. And brochures should not be primarily for building image, either. Magazine ads can do that. I believe the purpose of a brochure is to generate a response on the part of the reader—to get the reader to take the next step in the buying process."

In contrast to those who speak of the need for painstaking attention to graphic design, Chapin believes such details are relatively unimportant. "A lot of companies get their egos involved in brochures," he says. "The result is brochures that get prettier and prettier. Marketing people tend to fall in love with 'pretty.' Companies are so involved with their product that they become more concerned with image than with what their customers want.

"What really matters is marketing strategy, not whether you use blue or red, or which photo you select. These are only tactics. Gorgeousness is immaterial. All the tactics in the world may get you only 10 percent more response. But a change in strategy can increase response 50 to 100 percent or more."

Chapin distinguishes four basic types of high-tech brochures: the presentation piece (used by salespeople as a visual aid), the leave-behind, the rack piece, and brochures used in direct mail.

"The presentation aid only needs an outline of the product features, since the salesperson can elaborate on the benefits in person," Chapin explains. "But, because the other types of brochures are read by the prospect without the presence of a live salesperson, they must be 'salespeople in print,' presenting all the benefits and telling the full story."

Chapin criticizes spec sheets and rack brochures that merely list technical features and product descriptions. "Your customers don't buy products," he warns. "They buy benefits—what the product *does*, not what it is."

Chapin believes copy, not design, should be the dominant element in any product brochure. He feels the writer, not the artist, should call the creative shots. "The writer should do a rough sketch showing where the elements go, then hand it over to an artist for tighter execution," he says.

Chapin scoffs at the notion that people won't read long copy. "It's the nonprospects that hate long copy," he explains. "Prospects are the ones who want the information and always say 'Give me more.' You need enough copy so the well-qualified prospect will do what you want—become a buyer."

He says prospects will read brochures as long as the brochures are relevant to their interests. "People talk about a glut of advertising messages," he says, "but the only glut is caused by irrelevance. Take the guy who is into backpacking. If he gets a catalog from Eddie Bauer and another from L.L. Bean, he'll read both, because he's interested. The way to break through the clutter is by being relevant to the customer's needs."

GUIDELINES FOR CREATING CORPORATE CAPABILITIES BROCHURES

"Every company should have a corporate brochure," advised Howard G. "Scotty" Sawyer in his book, *Business-to-Business Advertising*. "A small company in order to become better known, a big company in order to give a clear picture of what it has probably become, in the course of growing, a complicated and confused situation."

Each year, thousands of companies follow Sawyer's sensible advice. But unfortunately, the end result leaves much to be desired. Pick up any firm's corporate capabilities brochure and you're likely to find a brag-and-boast document that puffs the corporate ego but fails to provide useful information to the prospect...a document that's heavy on superlatives and light on specifics...in short, a document written for the advertiser, not the potential customer.

To understand why most corporate literature is so bad—and how yours can be better—it helps to know what the corporate capabilities brochure is, and what it is intended to accomplish.

First, you should remember that a brochure—or any single marketing document—cannot do the whole job of selling your company for you. Your sales success depends on the sum of all your sales and marketing activities, plus the quality of your products, service, and people. It will not be determined simply by what you say in a brochure that people may glance at for only a few minutes.

With that in mind, here are four things that corporate literature can do for you, and do well:

- **Save time.** If people don't know your company, you may find yourself reciting your corporate mission, charter, and purpose over and over to new prospects, new people at client companies, new vendors, and new employees. By putting this corporate background on paper, you can save time and quickly communicate who you are and what you do.

  Think about whether your target market really needs to know about your firm before they buy your product or service. If you run a messenger service in New York City, you probably don't need a corporate brochure. But if you sell mainframe computers, you probably do.

- **Establish credibility.** Hundreds of thousands of small firms will be started this year and hundreds of thousands will close their doors. For that reason, prospects are cautious about placing important business in the hands of unknown vendors. A brochure goes a long way toward establishing credibility.

  "Anyone can spend $50 to have letterhead and business cards printed up," an entrepreneur once told me. "But a brochure says to your client, "Hey, this is a real company!"

The week I started freelancing, a frantic owner of a small company approached me and said he needed a corporate brochure in a hurry—within three days, if possible. Why the urgent deadline? "We pitched a big contract," he explained, "and the buyer now tells us that our proposal must include a corporate brochure. If we don't get one by Thursday, we lose the contract."

Out of curiosity, I asked how many copies he needed by Thursday. "Oh, just the one," he replied.

That isn't the way to go about getting a brochure produced, of course. But it does show that, in some situations, having a company brochure can mean the difference between getting the contract and losing the sale.

- **Generate more business.** By highlighting all of your problem-solving activities in a single marketing document, the capabilities brochure helps generate additional sales. Customers who buy one of your products read it and say, "Hey, I didn't know you also made *purple* widgets! Can you give me a quote for 5,000 units?"

  By presenting the full spectrum of your capabilities at a glance, the corporate brochure can pull additional sales from current buyers and also help open new accounts. A company that's well-known in one area may be obscure in another, even though it has an excellent product or service to offer. The corporate brochure is an ideal forum for highlighting your obscure products and capabilities. You can give prominent mention to those products or services in your brochure, or even cover them in a separate section for added emphasis.

- **Get your message across.** The corporate brochure is effective for communicating a single message convincingly and forcefully.

  A large electronics manufacturer once hired me to write an elaborate corporate brochure on one of its smaller divisions. I was surprised to learn about the large budget. It seemed way out of proportion, considering the division's modest sales. But, the client told me, "There have been rumors in the industry that we are planning to abandon this product line. That isn't so. The purpose of this brochure is to get the message out that the company is in this technology for the long haul. We are deliberately making the brochure expensive and elaborate, so that people will realize that we wouldn't be investing so much money in a brochure unless we were really serious about this business." His logic made sense.

On the flip side, here are two things a corporate brochure *cannot* do well:

- **Transmit a lot of information.** Because corporate literature gets low readership, your corporate brochure is not the place to tell a detailed product story. Separate product brochures should be used for selling individual items. Specific factual references should be incorporated into the corporate brochure, but only to explain or build credibility for the central message you want to communicate.

- **Build image.** A corporate brochure can enhance your image, but won't build it single-handedly. Image is a perception prospects and customers have of your firm based on all contacts with your firm, both personal and through advertising and promotion. A single brochure, soon filed or forgotten, can add a touch of class or comfort, but it will not change the reader's perception of you overnight.

If you really want to change your image, the place to start is with the quality of your product and the courtesy of your service. The executives at many companies say they want their brochure to portray an image of being helpful and friendly. But too often, those are the same firms that have the rudest receptionists, the most indifferent salespeople, and the least helpful customer service departments.

Image is a reflection of reality, and a brochure can only reaffirm what prospects believe about you, not contradict what their real-life experience has been.

FOUR QUESTIONS

Now that we understand what a brochure can and cannot do, let's look at the four basic factors that will help make your company's brochure an effective marketing tool. Too often, executives slap together a brochure without asking:

"What's the brochure's purpose?" The overwhelming majority of corporate brochures have no visible purpose or mission. They simply present information and reproduce attractive photographs.

The key to success is to start with an objective. I recently wrote a brochure for a firm that performs civil engineering service to municipal clients. I asked the president why he needed such a brochure in the first place.

He replied: "An elected official who has to decide which engineering firm should handle a municipal project needs to be confident about making the right decision and that the decision can be logically defended in case something goes wrong. The purpose of our brochure is to provide that person a comfort level, knowing he or she will not be criticized for selecting us and can defend the decision."

That type of clearly defined objective is a prerequisite for producing any successful marketing document, including the corporate brochure.

"What information will show prospects how our company can solve their problems?" In another assignment, a chemical company asked me to write a brochure describing the capabilities of its glass coatings division. "We want this brochure to be an idea stimulator," the client explained. "Any readers with an application that we might be able to handle should, after reading this brochure, come away with the impression that we can solve their problem for them."

Problem solving is what 99 percent of all business products and services are about. As Bob Donath, editor of *Business Marketing*, points out: "Your readers are looking for solutions to their problems, not information on your people or your company." Yet too many corporate brochures talk only about the firm's excellent staff or reputation or years in business, never showing what the firm can do for the reader. That's a mistake.

"How can we make the brochure inviting to readers?" Corporate brochures typically get low readership. Engineers, executives, and other business buyers have mentally trained themselves to study product documents but ignore corporate capabilities brochures, which they perceive as self serving and not containing useful information.

- Once you understand that the reader is not sitting around waiting to read your new company brochure, you can overcome that built-in lack of interest by designing the piece accordingly.
- Use descriptive headlines and subheads so the person who just skims the headings can get the gist of your story.
- Break the copy up into very short sections, each with its own subhead. Short paragraphs and sections get better readership than long blocks of text.
- Use plenty of photos.
- Whenever possible, put material in a table, graph, or chart rather than in body copy.
- Include an informative caption with every visual. Captions get greater readership than body copy.

"Isn't it best to base the brochure on copy, not design?" Many art directors will disagree with this point. But doesn't it make sense to let form follow content instead of force-fitting copy to fit a design? (Most artist's comps, created before copy is written, are drawn to dazzle the client rather than communicate the material to the reader.)

TEN TIPS

Having said all that, here are ten tips for creating more effective corporate documents:

1. Start with a strategy. What's the purpose of this brochure? What should the reader come away with after reading it? Do we even need a corporate brochure? Those are the questions you must answer before the first word of copy is written. Too often, those questions are never even asked.

2. Collect all pertinent data. Facts are what make your message believable and hold the reader's interest. Without the facts at their fingertips, even the best corporate writers cannot produce an interesting document.

Gather all the background material on the company (or division) that is the subject of your brochure. Some of the materials that will help your agency or writer include:

- sales brochures on all products or services that your brochure will discuss;
- previous corporate brochures;

- annual reports for the last three years;
- copies of employee magazines, company newsletters, customer bulletins, and other such periodicals your company has published within the last 12 months;
- copies of all press releases your firm produced this year;
- tear sheets of all currently running advertisements;
- copies of major articles about the company, press clippings, and executive speeches;
- scripts of corporate videos, films, and similar presentations.

Collect about ten times as much material as you think will be needed. Although reading all of it is time-consuming, you never know when a certain fact or statistic will illuminate your message. A competent writer will study all your information.

3. Fill in the gaps. Determine areas of information not covered by the written materials. Arrange interviews between your writer and company staff members who can fill in the missing details. Tell the writer who will be interviewed, what that person's role is and the purpose of the interview—the nature of the information that must be uncovered during the meeting.

4. Chicken or the egg? What comes first—the outline or the layout? Since you know my bias toward copy first, you know I'm going to say it's the outline.

Is an outline always necessary? Not for very short brochures, or brochures describing small organizations with just a few products, services, or departments. It's also not needed when the company already has a clear vision of the direction and content of the piece.

But for large organizations, companies with a large number of divisions and product lines, or in cases when no one seems certain what should be included in the brochure, an outline is helpful. Use the standard format of Roman numerals and letters (IA, IB, IIA, IIB, IIC). That shows the reviewer what facts will be included and how the material will be organized.

Helpful Hint: If you've deliberately left out certain topics or facts discussed in preliminary meetings, you might type them up on a separate sheet in alphabetical order and attach the list to your outline. Preface the list with a short introduction that says, "Here are topics not included on the outline. If you think they should be in the brochure, just add to the appropriate section to the outline." That eliminates the panic managers feel when they think you have omitted a topic because you were ignorant of it, when in reality, you made a deliberate decision not to include it.

5. Assemble visual materials. Go through your photo files and assemble a collection of existing visuals that can be used in your new brochure.

One of the biggest expenses for corporate literature is photography. Often, however, many of the scheduled shots already exist in someone's files, unknown to the person coordinating the brochure! A little digging can save you the expense of duplicating photographs already shot and paid for.

Walk around the company and ask permission to go through the files of those people who keep the best photos. Check existing brochures and other literature for visuals that can be lifted, and track down the originals.

Helpful Hint: If you or your writer will be interviewing people to gather information, always ask them for visuals to illustrate the points they are making. Even a rough chart or diagram drawn on a sheet of paper can easily and inexpensively be turned into a piece of artwork that enhances your document. Ask people to show, not just tell.

6. Tone tips. Another decision to make is about the tone and style of your brochure's copy. Should it be serious and corporate? Light and breezy? Friendly? Humorous? High-tech?

Actually, all good copy—whether corporate or promotional—should be simple, direct, and easy to read. My advice is to just write it in a clear, natural, conversational style, much as you would a business letter or an ad.

Don't try to achieve a deliberate style, which will only sound phony and alert readers that they're reading copy rather than a message from one human being to another. Above all, avoid the brag-and-boast style that pervades so much corporate literature.

7. Just the facts. The selective use of specific factual information is the key to producing a corporate brochure that is both interesting and believable. Here's an example, the opening paragraphs from a corporate brochure for RKW Standardbred Associates:

> From British Columbia to Florida's Gold Coast, from southern California to tranquil Prince Edward Island, the Standardbred horse racing and breeding industry is a multibillion-dollar business and part of the third largest spectator sport in North America.
>
> In 1986, attendance at harness tracks totaled just under 26 million people. These people wagered slightly less than 5.2 billion dollars on more than 57 thousand different horses that raced for 511 million dollars in purses.

The lazy copywriter would have been content to begin: "Horse racing and breeding is a big business in America. And RKW Standardbred Associates is proud to be a part of it." Which opening do you think is more interesting to read?

8. Future vs. present. Another question that must be resolved is: Should the brochure talk about our company as it is now or about how we will be (or want to be) in the future? Should we focus on our current business or on our goals, dreams, plans, and ambitions?

Readers distrust brochures that spend more time gazing into crystal balls than they do discussing the hard realities of today's marketplace. At the same time, what better place to share your plans with your customers than in a corporate brochure?

The solution is to write a brochure that's firmly grounded in today's reality but also takes a brief peek into the future. As a rule of thumb, I recommend that 80 to 85 percent of your brochure should focus on current products and services, while 15 to 20 percent should discuss future products, goals, and directions that are likely to come to fruition within the next three years or so.

9. Build in a response device. The back page of your brochure should include the address and phone number of your headquarters and all branch and regional offices, including those overseas. After reading your brochure, the prospect may want to contact you, and I find it absurd that so many corporate brochures and annual reports don't include any address or phone number.

In addition, you should include a reply card (either loose or bound in) that the reader can send in to receive a detailed bulletin on any product or service mentioned in your corporate brochure.

Many people tell me they think a reply card is inappropriate because the corporate brochure is for building image, not making sales. Even so, some readers will have an immediate need for a product or service described in your literature. Why deny yourself a sale by making it hard for those folks to reach you?

10. Distribute the brochure widely. Many people also tell me that they limit the distribution of their corporate brochure, treating it much like the holy grail. "After all," they note, "it's expensive."

But as anyone familiar with production knows, the real cost comes from printing Copy Number One. After that, ordering another 5,000 or 10,000 is really a minimal expense compared with what it took to get that first copy off the press.

According to Scotty Sawyer, the people who should receive your new brochure include employees, distributors, dealers, suppliers, customers, prospects, community business groups, local banks, elected officials, shareholders, financial analysts, and trade journal editors. So, why not print up a few extra copies, and get your message out?

Chapter

A catalog is a comprehensive directory describing all the products a company sells. "Resting on the table in a farm, suburban or city home, the catalog functions like a one-stop shopping center," writes Julien Elfenbein in his book, *Business Letters and Communications*. Rural dwellers have always been avid catalog buyers because, unlike suburban and urban families, they do not have access to a vast quantity of convenient nearby stores and malls. It is logical for them to do more shopping through the mails.

According to Lauren R. Januz, a printed catalog consists of illustrations, descriptions, selling copy, and prices of multiple products presented in a format that permits easy handling, filing, and reference. Januz notes that the catalog may be as simple as a single sheet of paper printed on both sides, or as complex as hundreds of pages bound to form the big, heavy, expensive catalogs. The prices might be on the same page as the merchandise descriptions or they might be printed on a separate insert mailed with the catalog.

"This season, well beyond the merchandise, everything about a catalog's design, printing, and mailing is devised to make you want to buy," writes Margaret Webb Pressler (*Record*, December 7, 1997, page A-7). In the first nine months of 1997, according to the Commerce Department, mail order sales rose 9.3 percent to $49 billion versus a 4.1 percent gain for total retail sales (excluding automobiles).

The difference between a brochure and a catalog is that brochures typically describe a single product in detail, while catalogs cover more products in less detail. The brochure promotes an individual item; the catalog provides a single source of information on your company's entire product line. A brochure is narrowly focused; a catalog is comprehensive in the breadth of products offered.

Catalogs have several uses. By inserting a catalog in the shipping envelope or box when you pack and ship products ordered by customers, you educate those customers about other products you offer that may be of interest to them. Catalogs can also be mailed separately to your customer list one or more times a year to remind those customers of your existence and get them to buy more from you.

To expand your catalog sales, you can mail the catalog unsolicited to potential buyers whose names you rent from mailing list brokers. You can offer your catalog, either at no cost or for a nominal fee, in small print ads. Be sure to fulfill requests for your catalog promptly; according to a study by Thomas Publishing, 43 percent of all catalogs sent in answer to requests arrive too late to make the sale. Catalogs should be mailed within 48 hours after you receive the inquiry.

Catalogs can also be distributed at retail outlets, either as point of sale buying guides or to stimulate mail order sales for those shoppers who would rather buy at home than in a store. The Sharper Image is one of several marketers that actively distributes a mail order catalog at its retail outlets. In some stores, you can simply pick up a catalog from a rack or counter. Other stores mail the catalog to shoppers who complete and mail a coupon at the sales counter (the purpose of this strategy is to capture the shopper's name and address for future mailings).

The variety in the production of catalogs is truly amazing. Some advertisers, especially those whose products must be depicted in full and natural color, send committees of top executives to the printing plant as the catalogs roll off the press so proofs can be checked and rechecked and color corrections made at every step to ensure quality. At the other end of the spectrum, small marketers often type their first catalog sheets themselves and run them off on office copiers.

Some catalog companies use elaborate color photography and glossy paper to sell their merchandise. Others prefer illustrations and print on cheaper grades of newsprint stock. Dr. Jeffrey Lant, one of the top catalog entrepreneurs in the country, produces a lengthy catalog that is all copy with not a single picture, and it is enormously successful.

Styles also vary enormously, and successful catalogers have developed their winning formulas only over time and through trial and experience. Drew Kaplan's DAK catalog is famous for its long copy approach with a full page or even two pages devoted to each high-tech electronic gadget he sells. When you read his copy, you realize that he is truly in love with his products, having tried each and every gizmo himself before recommending it to his band of loyal buyers.

By contrast, Harry & David's Bear Creek catalog takes a homey approach and is loaded with gorgeous color photos of their fruits, cakes, and pies, with copy so compelling that even mundane foods like pears or grapes seem a gourmet delight. A great catalog like DAK or Bear Creek transcends mere sales savvy; its arrival becomes a welcome event on a par with receiving one's favorite magazine or a gift in the mail. You not only buy from it; you look forward to receiving it.

Most catalogs are direct response tools encouraging the recipient to order immediately by completing and mailing an order form or calling a toll-free number to place a credit card order. Many catalogs, such as those used by bathroom accessory or power tool manufacturers, are designed as in-store sales tools: They are kept at sales counters where shoppers can browse through and select the items they want. The advantage of such a catalog is that it can display every item the manufacturer offers, while the hardware store or home improvement center, with its limited space, can afford to display only a few items from each company. A few catalogs, like IBM's PC Guide, don't generate sales directly but instead give buyers a preview of the merchandise so they know what to ask for when visiting the store.

The early catalog giants, such as Sears, made their success with general interest catalogs offering the convenience of buying a broad range of consumer goods by mail. Today the trend is toward specialized catalogs. One specialized catalog contains nothing but fireplace products: kindling, screens, and other implements not easy to buy at stores. Another, Wolferman's, specializes in English muffin gift packs.

A large number of orders placed through certain catalogs are purchased as gifts rather than for personal consumption by the consumer. Mail order catalogs offer a wonderfully convenient means of sending gifts at holiday time, because they eliminate the need to shop, wrap the gifts, and mail them to distant friends and relatives. Order forms in gift catalogs have spaces where the customer can write in the names and addresses of people who will be receiving the gifts so the catalog house can mail directly to the recipient. The order form should also leave room for a personalized message from your customer that your order clerks will write on a card and enclose with the gift.

Although catalogs are nearly infinite in their variety, they can be separated into three basic categories:

- Consumer catalogs
- Mini-catalogs
- Industrial catalogs

Let's take a closer look at how to develop each type.

HOW TO CREATE A CONSUMER CATALOG

As the name implies, a consumer catalog offers merchandise to consumers. Products offered include clothing, videotapes, compact discs, books, food, wine and spirits, coffee, toys and games, gardening products, and furniture. There is even a catalog offering items specifically designed for left-handed people!

Sandi Lifschitz, president of Copy Creations in New York City, offers the following tips for creating successful consumer catalogs:

1. Know who you are. More formally, position your company in the catalog marketplace. There's a lot of soul-searching and objectivity involved. Consulting with a marketing specialist is extremely beneficial.

2. Get involved with your customers. Discover who they are. This goes beyond studying demographics. Keep up with their lifestyles and needs. Pay attention to their requests and comments. Most importantly, listen to their problems and learn from them; they often give the best direction. That's how a good merchandiser becomes a great cataloger.

3. Practice creative merchandising. Learn all about your industry and everything you are going to sell. Study the merchandise and the markets. Keep up with the trends. This may sound academic, but it makes a big difference. Merchandising is the key to all catalog sales.

Product promotion today, fashion in particular, takes on many moods and definitions. Introduce a new accessory. Show the latest footwear even if you're not selling it. This tells the customer you understand the total picture, you really know what's happening.

Take a basic item and interpret what meaning it has for the customer. For example, a white polyester blouse adds a great finishing touch to a business suit...has wonderful versatility (because it's white)...and is an ideal travel item because it never needs ironing. This one product creates lots of "selling mileage" and fills many needs at the same time.

4. Go beyond the benefits. Catalog copy has to communicate to touch an emotion, fulfill a need, initiate an impulse, or stir a fantasy. Never underestimate the mind of the consumer. Vulnerable? Maybe. Gullible? Sometimes. But consumers are more knowledgeable and aware than ever before. You have to be ten steps ahead of your customer at all times.

5. Create a mood and keep it going. Don't just produce that fabulous cover. Whether a theme or a season, illustrate it throughout the catalog, talk about it in the copy. Make readers feel good as they turn the pages of your catalog. You want them to look forward to receiving the next one.

Ready to wear and home fashion catalogs stimulate impulse buying. Commercial product catalogs take on another aspect. A reader holds onto them; they become reference material and don't change as frequently.

Copy versus Art

The most prevalent opinion in marketing is that the visual takes first place when you're selling a product, and the verbal takes over when you're selling a service. Many have seen the reverse work well too. The fact is: Both the visual and the verbal are important.

You're especially lucky when you find a good rapport between artist and writer. A naturally visual copywriter has a great advantage because he or she *sees* the words on the page, almost "writing the layout." A less visual writer might do best working directly from a layout.

The artist who understands that the layout must "work" for the merchandise being advertised as well as look great is a real treasure. The ideal situation is for the artist and writer to work together on a project, but that's not always possible due to tight schedules.

Use Specifics

Don't leave the customer with questions in mind. Answer them in advance:

- How tall is the table lamp?
- How many paper cups are in the package?
- Are the earrings post or clip-on?
- How do S, M, L, and XL translate into numbered size ranges?

Give all the facts. If you don't know them, take the time to find out. If necessary, use or wear the product yourself. Showing that you care about every detail can turn customer indifference into enthusiasm, as well as ensure customer satisfaction.

Make It Believable

Someone once said, "There's a cynic in all of us." If anything can make cynicism surface, it's advertising that makes unrealistic claims or promises.

Make sure your merchandise is readily available. Nothing irritates customers more than being told the item is sold out when they call to order the same day they receive the catalog.

Believability means merchandise that is true to your photographs. Make sure that red is not magenta. Don't show a cubic zirconia ring that looks the size of the Hope diamond when it's really the size of the head of a pin. Or qualify it by saying, "Illustrations enlarged to show details."

Have you ever ordered a piece of furniture that was "easy to assemble"? It's more like a wrestling match, unless you're a carpenter. Why not just say, "Assembly required," instead of "Easy to assemble"? It's honest without being antagonistic.

Make It Easy to Order

If the KISS theory (Keep It Simple, Stupid) applies anywhere, it's on the order form. What a painful task to even look at some of them, let alone try to fill them out, unless you're an accountant who likes to shop. Don't intimidate readers. At least give them the option of going to the phone (preferably to dial an 800 number) and offer them the assistance of a pleasant customer service representative (difficult to find, but they are out there).

Mail order merchandisers report that having an 800 number and accepting major credit cards can increase orders by 30 percent, and that 50 percent or more of people ordering use the telephone rather than mail the order form. Why? First, because it's easier, less complex, faster, and more convenient. Second, if buyers are puzzled or have questions, they want to call you to get answers before they order. They can't do that if you don't take phone calls.

Tip: Put your toll-free number in bold type in a box on every page of the catalog to make it stand out. The easier you make it to order, the more orders you will get.

In a recent mailing, the Franklin Mint offered a collector's ring selling for hundreds of dollars. What obstacle is there to ordering? Many people do not know their ring sizes. The solution? Franklin Mint enclosed a handy but simple measuring guide (a series of circles printed on a strip of white paper) that readers could use to determine their ring sizes in seconds. This is the type of thing you should be doing to make it as easy as possible for your customers to order.

Fulfill Orders Correctly and Promptly

Fulfillment success establishes your credibility and instills confidence in your customers. Customers judge you by how quickly you ship, especially on the initial order.

Don't make promises you can't keep, but ship all orders as quickly as possible, preferably within 24 to 48 hours of receipt. If you can't ship the item right away, at least send a card that acknowledges the order and specifies when the customer can expect to receive the goods.

The Customer Is King or Queen

Keep in mind the importance of a close relationship between cataloger and consumer. Your consumer catalog is a motivator—an image-building tool to excite the customer into buying specific merchandise. Let your customers know you are catering to them. Make them feel they are important. That's what direct selling is all about.

Brandel Communications, a direct marketing firm, says the following items can improve response to mail order catalogs:

- Products that are useful, interesting, attractive, and with easily perceived value.
- Prices that are as low as possible. However, higher prices can be charged when the merchandise can't be found elsewhere or when convenience outweighs cost.
- Products with a common theme. Mail order people should appeal to a particular interest group or specific lifestyle (for example, L.L. Bean's outstanding catalog of outdoor-oriented products).
- Merchandise that's artfully displayed. Color isn't necessary. Factual descriptions are.
- Testimonials from satisfied customers.
- An order blank that is easy to fill out according to simple instructions and that is printed in a type style that is easy to read.
- A toll-free service for phone orders.

HOW TO CREATE A SUCCESSFUL MINI-CATALOG

In contrast to the large, full-color mail order catalog on glossy stock is the less fanciful, more functional mini-catalog. "If you sell many related products and services, but not enough to justify a large, fancy catalog, a self-mailer mini-catalog of between two and eight pages may work well for you," says copywriter Mike Pavlish. "The mini-catalog makes it easier for the reader to grasp everything you sell; tends to be saved more and longer for reference, therefore generating more orders; and simplifies your advertising program. Instead of having to send out several different and often confusing pieces, all you'll have to do is send out one piece: your mini-catalog."

Here are Pavlish's suggestions for writing an effective mini-catalog:

1. Use a sales letter on the first or second page. It should give the main benefits readers will obtain by responding, encourage them to read the catalog now, and motivate them to order immediately.

2. Keep it organized, simple, and easy to read. Of course, this applies to all advertising, but it's especially important for a mini-catalog because readers see more copy at one time. You don't want to overwhelm or confuse them. Border the different products so they are clearly separated from each other. Use short, snappy copy blocks throughout the catalog to build interest, maintain attention, and push for action.

3. Make it easy to order. Leave plenty of room for an order blank section the reader can use to order by mail. If you intend to use the mini-catalog as a self-mailer, design it so the customer's mailing label is affixed to the reverse side of the order coupon. This way, when the customer clips and mails back the coupon, you get the label back. This enables you to determine which mailing list pulled the most orders.

4. Use a second color only for the most important points. Be careful not to overuse the second color (if you use two colors) to the point that it loses effectiveness. The best places to use a second color are: sales letter headline and signature, product name, product benefit, ordering information.

"Once you have a winning mini-catalog, keep sending it to your prospects and customers," Pavlish suggests. "The beauty of the mini-catalog is that it's your all-in-one sales piece for both prospects and customers. Instead of spending time developing new mailings, you can keep mailing the same catalog to your list for as long as it pays out."

Figure 14.1 shows two pages of a sample mini-catalog, my Writer's Profit Catalog selling special reports, books, and audiocassettes aimed at teaching freelance writers how to make more money. This four-page catalog is printed in black ink on two sides of two 8 1/2 × 11" sheets of paper. (Actually, I duplicate them on my office copier.) I use a brightly colored stock, either canary yellow or gold.

HOW TO CREATE AN INDUSTRIAL CATALOG

An industrial or commercial catalog sells products to business buyers. Some of these offer commercial items such as office furniture, computer software, or office supplies. Others feature ball bearings, machine components, nuts and bolts, and a wide range of industrial products used in factories and manufacturing operations.

Writer's Profit Catalog™

Reports, books, and other information resources that help you get clients, gain confidence, and increase your writing income!

600-Series Reports

These special reports tell how to earn $100,000 or more as a freelance commercial writer—expanding on the material in Secrets of a Freelance Writer. Each report is 8–10 pages.

601 Tips for Beginners: How To Get Started in High-Profit Writing™

What if you have no experience, no portfolio, and no contacts? You can still get into high-profit writing quickly...but your strategy will differ somewhat from experienced writers. This report outlines methods beginners can use to hide, overcome, and even exploit their novice status including: How to generate lucrative business, regardless of your credentials...tips for writing sales letters that get clients to hire you...types of clients that hire beginners...how to create a winning portfolio of sample copy. $7

602 How To Set Your Fees...and Get Paid What You're Worth!

An in-depth discussion and explanation of how to determine, set, negotiate, and get your fees. Includes a survey of what top, intermediate, and novice freelancers are now charging for ads, press release copy, and many other typical assignments. If you're not earning at least $500 per day, you need this report! $7

603 How To Make $100,000 a Year As a Direct Mail Writer

Direct mail/direct response is one of the better-paying areas for freelance writers. This report tells what's going on in the direct mail industry today, how to break in, what the top writers are charging, how to get lucrative direct mail copy assignments. Find out why Bill Jayme gets paid $10,000 for writing a sales letter—and how you can, too. $7

604 How To Turn Dead Time Into Extra Profits

Every freelance writer will have periods when business is slow. This report tells how to use that "dead time" productively instead of sitting around and getting depressed. You'll also learn a simple technique that can prevent slow periods and virtually ensure a steady stream of work. $7

605 How To Double Your Freelance Writing Income—This Year!

Most writers don't have a business plan that projects cash flow. This report shows how to estimate your annual income based on your current fees, type of work you do, and how busy you are. Once I show you how much money you can expect to earn this year, I'll then tell you how to double that amount (no matter how much it may be). To do this, I charge only $7. Fair enough? $7

606 Bob Bly's Promo Package

This is the sales package I send to clients who request information on my freelance writing services. Estimating conservatively, I can confidently say it has generated at least $750,000 in direct sales of my freelance copywriting services and added 75 top companies to my ever-growing client list. If I were to write such a package for you as a client, my fee would be $3,000. Now it's yours for only $7. $7

607 How To Overcome Problems When Working With Clients

What do you do when a client doesn't like your copy, or won't pay your bill, or has an unreasonable deadline? What happens when an assignment turns out to be much more work than you bargained for—and you want to tell the client you are going to have to charge more than you originally quoted? How do you tell a current client that you have to raise your fees, or charge more than his budget for a particular project, or that you can't (or won't) handle his next assignment because you are too busy? In 11 years of freelancing I've been in just about every tough situation you can imagine...and in this report, I give you proven strategies for tackling each problem head-on with success. $7

608 Successful Moonlighting: How To Earn an Extra $2,000 a Month Freelancing Part-Time

Let's say you want to break into freelance commercial writing but can't (or won't) give up your current full-time job. Well, you can still make $2,000 a month or more in commercial freelance writing—as a moonlighter! What are the options for commercial writing on a part-time (evenings and weekends) basis? What are the limitations on the projects you can accept (e.g., you can't leave your office or talk with freelance clients during the day)? This report tells you how to avoid complications and earn a comfortable second income writing copy for local and national clients in your spare time. $7

609 Freelancing in a Recession

Is your business hurting right now? Are things too slow? This timely report provides 12 proven, practical strategies for surviving (and even prospering) in a recession, soft economy, or during a business downturn—12 action steps you can take to get more business *now!* $7

610 Government Markets for Writers

The U.S. government, with hundreds of agencies and 34,000 offices nationwide, spends approximately $14 billion a year on writing and editorial services. Most of this writing is done under contract by private organizations and often by individuals. This special report by Herman Holtz explains how to successfully find, bid for, and win government contracts for high-paying freelance writing assignments. $7

611 How To Make Money Writing Speeches

Freelance writers can make $1,000 to $3,000 or more for writing a 20-minute speech. In this report, veteran speechwriter Richard Armstrong reveals the secrets of how to succeed in the lucrative speechwriting market including: how much to charge...where the clients are...how to get assignments...how to research and write an effective speech...and much, much more. $7

612 How To Make Money Writing Annual Reports

Freelance writers are paid $8,000 to $10,000 and up for writing annual reports for major corporations. This report reveals how to break into this lucrative market including: who hires freelance annual report writers; how to reach them; what to charge; how to write annual reports; how to get an assignment even if you have never done any annual report writing before. $7

BBL   10

Figure 14.1.

Writer's Profit Catalog™

700-Series

These reports are longer and more in-depth than the 200 and 600-series, averaging 30 to 50 pages or more. They are written by experts and tell you exactly what you must do to achieve the objective stated in the title of each report.

701 How You Can Make Big Money Writing Magazine Articles—NOW!

The traditional "one-shot," query letter approach to magazine writing won't make you rich. This report shows how to establish *long-term* relationships with editors who give you a steady stream of lucrative, ongoing assignments. Written by Steve Manning, author of 1,000 published articles, the report also includes Steve's proven 5-step article-writing formula, guaranteed to increase your output 10 to 50 percent or more. $19

702 How You Can Make $50,000 or More as a Freelance Copy Editor or Proofreader

Most proofreaders and copy editors barely earn a living. But some are making $1,000 a week or more. Learn how to set up and run a copy editing or proofreading business from your home that grosses $40,000 to $50,000 a year! Author Steve Manning's eye-opening report also includes complete instructions on how to properly edit and proofread manuscripts. $19

200-Series Reports

Want to write books, magazine articles, or other nonfiction material? These reports reveal the secrets of how to get your writing published. Most are from my popular Saturday seminar, "How to Become a Published Author"—which won't be repeated again for at least 2 years (so you can only get the information here). Reports are 5–12 pages.

201 Publish Your Way To Profits!

If you know something, one way to profit from that knowledge is to package it as a self-published book or special report—and sell it via mail order, distributors, and through other channels. My own self-published series of Special Reports brings in thousands of extra dollars in income a year—with virtually no effort. If you've ever had the urge to self-publish…or are just thinking about it…you need the information contained in this report. Written by Brooks Owen. $7

202 How To Get a Good Literary Agent To Represent You.

Once you have a good book idea and a proposal for it, you need to find an agent who can sell your book to a publisher and get the best deal for you. Fewer and fewer publishing houses nowadays will even consider a proposal unless it is submitted by a recognized literary agent. But where do you find agents? What's the best way to contact them? How can you get them to take you seriously? What should you look for in an agent—and what kind of results can you expect once an agent takes you on as a client? This report will answer these questions and help you get the agent you need. $7

203 How To Write Winning Query Letters.

Students at my writing seminars are amazed when I tell them that (with a few exceptions) sending a finished article to an editor who didn't ask to see it can actually prevent you from making the sale. Editors want to see a query first—and your ability to write persuasive queries will, in large part, determine whether you become a published and prolific magazine writer. This report shows you: How to write successful query letters…how to produce queries that make the editor think you've done a lot of research (even if you haven't!)…plus numerous sample query letters you can follow and adapt to suit your needs. $7

204 How To Make Money In the Public Seminar Business.

Giving seminars (on writing, publishing, communication, or any topic you choose) is an excellent way for you, the writer, to cash in on your ability to inform, entertain, educate, and communicate. Profits, in many cases, can exceed $1,000 per day, and you can even present seminars in your spare time (Saturdays and evenings) if you hold a regular 9-to-5 job. This report serves as the perfect introduction for writers who think they might want to make money in the public seminar business. You'll learn the steps to take—and the mistakes to avoid. $7

205 How To Write a Winning Book Proposal

If you want to sell your book to a publishing house and become a published author, you must learn to write effective book proposals. This is easy if (a) you know the steps involved in writing such a proposal, and (b) you have a sample book proposal you can "copy" and use as a model in developing your own proposal. My information-packed report fills both those needs. It teaches you step-by-step how to write a winning book proposal, and each section is followed by an excerpt from an actual book proposal. Once you have this report in hand you'll be able to easily and quickly translate any idea into a solid proposal ready to submit to agents and publishers. $7

206 $50,000 A Year Through Self-Syndication

This report provides step-by-step instructions on how to make money as a nationally syndicated columnist. It tells how to sell through major feature syndicates (King, United Features) as well as how to market your columns to newspapers and magazines directly. Written by Herman Holtz. $7

Full Length Books (300-Series)

300 Get Paid to Write Your Book

The definitive work on how to write a nonfiction book and sell it—for a nice advance—to a major New York publishing company. Topics include: coming up with book ideas, evaluating the market potential of your book, how to write a successful book proposal, how to get a literary agent to represent you, selling your book to publishers, and negotiating your advance and royalties. (NOTE: This book includes the complete text of Special Reports 202 and 205.)

Oversize paperback, 100 pages $22

301 The Copywriter's Handbook

While *Secrets of a Freelance Writer* tells you how to run your copywriting business, *The Copywriter's Handbook* tells you how to write effective copy for ads, brochures, catalogs, direct mail, press releases, TV and radio commercials, newsletters, speeches, and other projects your clients need. "I don't know a single copywriter whose work would not be improved by reading this book," says David Ogilvy, founder of Ogilvy & Mather. "And that includes me."

Trade paperback, 353 pages $15

Figure 14.1. (*Cont.*)

Writer's Profit Catalog™

**302 Secrets of a Freelance Writer:
       How To Make $85,000 a Year**

Do you want to make a *lot* of money through freelance writing? There are dozens of high-paying commercial writing projects and clients in your own backyard—yours for the asking. Step by step, this book reveals how you can make $85,000 to $125,000 a year or more writing ads, brochures, and promotional materials for local and national clients.

Trade paperback, 274 pages $13

**302-A Secrets of a Freelance Writer:
         Book II: The Graduate Course**

This money-making manual picks up where *Secrets of a Freelance Writer* left off, presenting dozens of strategies for earning $100,000 to $150,000 a year or more as a freelance commercial writer. Topics include: What to do when the client says, "Your fee is too high"...how to get clients to pay you to attend meetings with them...what to say when following up on prospect inquiries...contracts for freelance writers...how to say "no" without blowing the client away...and much, much more.

Oversize manual, 50 pages $19

**303 Advertising Freelancers:
       The New Lure of Freelancing**

Everything about this promising work style as told by successful copywriters and art directors—and their clients, companies, and ad agencies. Read how dozens of independent-spirited creative people left the security of salaried jobs to control their own careers. Read, too, about the companies and ad agencies who hire freelancers: why they prefer to work with them, what they look for, how they approve the work, what they pay for it. Written by Ed Buxton and Sue Fulton.

Trade paperback, 114 pages $22

305 The Elements of Technical Writing

Freelance and contract technical writers can earn $25 to $80 an hour writing manuals, proposals, specifications, and other technical documents. And here's the style guide you need to handle such assignments with confidence. Covers use of numbers, units of measure, equations, technical terms, symbols, and other special concerns of technical writing.

Hardcover, 140 pages $20

306 Creative Careers: Real Jobs in Glamour Fields

A job-hunter's guide to ten of today's most exciting industries including travel, theater, photography, motion pictures, publishing, music, finance, gourmet foods, television, and advertising.

Trade paperback, 334 pages $12

**307 Create the Perfect Sales Piece:
       A Do-It-Yourself Guide To Producing Brochures,
       Catalogs, Fliers, and Pamphlets**

You can make $50,000 or more per year writing sales materials for clients. This book provides the step-by-step instructions you need to successfully research, outline, and write sales brochures, booklets, fliers, pamphlets, annual reports, catalogs, and many other lucrative assignments.

Trade paperback, 242 pages $20

311 How To Make Money Writing Technical Manuals

John Lancaster's clear, informed, well-thought-out book spells out everything you need to know about making money writing technical manuals. You learn who the clients are...how to find business...how to determine what to charge the client... contracts, advances, and payment schedules...submitting your

bills and getting them paid...and much, much more.

Oversize paperback, 41 pages $31

**312 Turbocharge Your Writing:
       The Vitale Instant Writing Method**

A 7-step formula for effective writing. I find it especially helpful when I'm faced with a difficult or intimidating writing assignment or am just having trouble getting started. This book by Joe Vitale is like a gem—small but valuable.

Paperback, 23 pages $5

313 How To Promote Your Own Business

A practical, do-it-yourself guide to advertising, publicity, and promotion for the small-business manager or owner. Lots of good marketing advice for promoting your own freelance writing business or the products and services sold by your clients.

Trade paperback, 241 pages $13

**315 Selling Your Services: Proven Strategies for
       Getting Clients to Hire You**

If you sell professional, personal, consulting, trade, technical, freelance, or any other kind of service, this book will give you the information you need to get large numbers of prospects to call you, convince those prospects to hire you at the fees you want, and dramatically increase the sales of your services.

Hardcover, 349 pages $27

316 The Elements of Business Writing

The Elements of Business Writing presents the basic rules of business writing in a concise, easy-to-use handbook organized along the lines of Strunk and White's classic book, *The Elements of Style.*

Hardcover, 144 pages $20

317 Business-to-Business Direct Marketing

This book shows you how to improve results from business-to-business marketing communications including ads, direct mail, PR, brochures, catalogs, postcard decks, and more. Also identifies and explains the 7 critical differences between business-to-business and consumer marketing.

Hardcover, 267 pages $42

318 Targeted Public Relations

A no-nonsense guide to achieving maximum visibility, press coverage, leads, and sales from public relations done on a limited budget.

Hardcover, approx. 220 pages $25

319 Keeping Clients Satisfied

In today's economy, clients and customers want it better, they want it cheaper, and they want it *yesterday!* This book shows you the customer service techniques necessary to satisfying and retaining clients in this new competitive marketplace.

Hardcover, approx. 250 pages $27

320 Technical Writer's Freelancing Guide

A complete and authoritative guide to the lucrative form of freelancing known as *contract work,* in which freelancers are hired by companies to do technical writing—at a high hourly rate and for an extended period of time—working at the company's facilities (similar to being a high-paid "temp"). Written by Peter Kent.

Trade paperback, 160 oversize pages $15

Live Seminars With Bob Bly
"How to Make $85,000 a Year As a Freelance Writer" and "How to Become a Published Author."
For more information, call The Learning Annex at (212) 570-6500.

Figure 14.1. (*Cont.*)

Writer's Profit Catalog™

321 Make Money Writing Newsletters

A complete guide on how to make big money writing promotional newsletters for local and national businesses. Author Elaine Floyd's ideas and tips are based on 5 years of operating her own newsletter production company with annual sales of $250,000.
Oversized paperback, 138 pages $32

322 Ghostwriting: How To Get Into the Business

Want to make big money ghostwriting books for celebrities, corporations, and individuals? This book tells how. Written by Eva Shaw.
Trade paperback, 185 pages $10

325 The Ultimate Unauthorized Star Trek Quiz Book

More than 750 trivia questions to test your "Trekpertise." Covers the Star Trek movies, TV shows, and novels.
Trade paperback, 162 pages $11

326 Power-Packed Direct Mail

Complete, easy-to-follow instructions on how to increase direct mail response rates. Covers planning, offers, mailing lists, testing, copy, design, formats, personalizations, and more.
Hardcover, 349 pages $27

Audio Cassette Programs (800-Series)

801 Secrets of a Freelance Writer: How to Make $85,000 a Year

This audio cassette program is packed with my latest information and newest ideas on how to make $85,000 to $100,000 a year or more as a freelance writer in today's competitive marketplace. The program was professionally recorded "live" at my full-day Learning Annex seminars, now given in New York City just one or two times a year.
Six 1-hour cassettes $49

802 10 Magic Steps to Freelance Writing Success

Presents the 10 essential steps every writer must take to make the leap to an annual income of $100,000 or more and consistently maintain (or increase) that income, year after year.
Single cassette $12

803 How to Boost Your Direct Mail Response Rates

Proven techniques for dramatically increasing your direct mail response rates. Includes rules for testing, target marketing strategies, offers, list selection, design, copy, mistakes to avoid…and much, much more.
Single cassette $12

804 Sixteen Secrets of Successful Small Business Promotion

How to use low-cost/no-cost advertising, marketing, sales promotion, and public relations techniques to build your business. Learn how to: Gain credibility through public speaking. Generate thousands of leads using simple press releases. Get big results from tiny ads. And more.
Single cassette $12

805 Selling Your Services in a Soft Economy

How to successfully sell and market your freelance writing services in a recession or soft economy.
Single cassette $12

812 The Motivating Sequence

A proven, easy-to-follow 5-step formula for writing more persuasive sales letters, billing series, ads, mailers, and more.
Single cassette $12

814 Get Paid to Write Your Book

How to write a nonfiction book and sell it for a $5,000 to $15,000 advance to a major NY publisher. Covers book proposals, literary agents, royalties, book contracts, and much more.
Six cassettes $59

Videos (900-Series)

901 How to Get Your Nonfiction book Published

This video, filmed live at Barnes & Noble, outlines the 5 main criteria by which publishers decide whether to accept or reject ideas for nonfiction books…and tells you how to satisfy each of the 5 requirements in your proposal to them. Also included: 10 proven techniques for generating saleable book ideas.
60-minute video, VHS format $24

Clip this coupon and mail it with your payment. (You may photocopy it, if you wish.)

Items you wish to order (indicate item #'s): _____ _____ _____ _____

_____ _____ _____ _____ _____

_____ _____ _____ _____ _____

_____ _____ _____ _____ _____

_____ _____ _____ _____ _____

Name _____ Phone # _____

Address _____

City _____ State _____ Zip _____

Enclose money order, cash, or check (payable to "Bob Bly") for appropriate amount. NJ residents add 6% sales tax. Canadian residents add $2 (U.S. dollars) per order. 30-day money-back guarantee on all books and cassettes. All items guaranteed to please. **Please allow 2–4 weeks for delivery.**

❑ Please rush my materials. I've enclosed an extra $1 per book (300-series) and 50¢ per tape or report (200, 600, 700, and 800-series) for first-class delivery.

MAIL TO: Bob Bly, 22 E. Quackenbush Avenue, Dumont, NJ 07628   BBL-601.10

Figure 14.1. (*Cont.*)

Although industrial catalogs are often "drier" than colorful consumer catalogs, they are not just technical specifications or information bound into a book. They must sell the prospect on benefits—either the specific product benefits or the benefits of choosing the catalog company as a supplier versus other firms offering similar products.

Industrial catalogs must also make buyers' jobs easier by giving them the technical data and specifications they need to order the correct product for an application. Graphs, guides, tables, and other devices that simplify the selection process are critical. If your products are compatible with and can be substituted for similar products made by other firms, for example, include a table showing which model numbers from your line can be substituted (or dropped in) for specific model numbers of your competition.

According to research from the Thomas Publishing Company, there are three reasons why industrial firms should consider putting out a catalog:

First, 90 percent of all industrial buyers require printed information before they buy. Buyers use catalogs to check product descriptions, specifications, and performance data. They use it to make intelligent, financially responsible, technically correct decisions. Also, 90 percent won't even consider you if you don't have a catalog, spec sheet, or flier.

Second, 97 percent of all industrial purchases are initiated by the buyer, not the seller. In fact, sellers usually aren't aware of the intended purchase until they get a call. The chances of an ad or salesperson hitting the buyer at the moment the buyer decides to buy are slim. But catalogs, because they are kept as references longer than ads or brochures, have a better chance of being handy when the buyer decides to buy and is searching for suppliers and product data.

Third, your catalog gets in to see prospects your salespeople cannot. No matter how effective your salespeople, they don't call on all prospects. Your catalog provides a way of reaching the prospects salespeople don't meet.

While consumer catalogs tend to stress color and visual appeal, industrial catalogs stress technical information, including completeness, ease of reference, clarity, and comprehensiveness. The industrial catalog may be thought of as a tool the purchasing agent can use to make proper buying decisions. Accordingly, it must:

- Answer questions and provide all the specifications and information needed to select and order the proper product.

- Provide a full selection of products to choose from—all shapes, sizes, models, and options.

- Be thoroughly indexed and cross referenced so the purchaser can quickly locate the items needed.

- Provide tables, drawings, charts, and other devices that guide the purchasing agent in determining exactly which product best meets all needs.

Most catalogs stop here. But this is just a starting point. In addition to serving as an information resource and buying guide, the superior industrial catalog goes beyond these tasks and also functions as a persuasive selling document that convinces the prospect to buy more of what you are selling.

14 Techniques for Improving the Selling Power of Your Industrial Catalog

Here are just a few ideas for improving the persuasiveness of your industrial catalog. Most of these points are illustrated with sample catalog pages taken from the Illustrated Fastener Catalog published by Atlantic Fasteners of West Springfield, MA.

Catalog Technique 1: Use a Title That Implies Value

The full title of Atlantic's catalog (Figure 14.2) is "Illustrated Fastener Catalog and Technical Manual." By calling it a *manual*, the advertiser implies added value of the catalog as a reference tool. Note that the cover also has a price ($19.95) on it. This technique also contributes to the image of higher perceived value. The more valuable your catalog appears to be, the more people will want to get it, read it, and keep it.

Note: Any technique you can use to get the reader to hold on to your catalog gives you a competitive advantage. Research shows that just 3 weeks after a typical catalog is distributed by hand or by mail, there is only a 20 percent chance that it can be found; 80 out of every 100 catalogs have been discarded, misplaced, or misfiled by then. Anything you can do to get your prospect to keep your catalog is a big plus.

Catalog Technique 2: Include a Letter

Add a sales letter on the inside front page of your catalog. The letter provides an ideal opportunity to sell your catalog as a whole or your company as a quality supplier, rather than merely promote individual items. A letter also adds a personal touch to what may otherwise be a rather impersonal, cold book of facts and figures. In the Atlantic Fastener catalog, the letter (Figure 14.3) makes use of several attention-getting sales techniques:

- The headline is in quotation marks (always increases readership).
- The subhead provides a graphic device for bringing attention to a secondary message.
- A picture of the company president personalizes the message and draws the reader's eye to the page.
- A salutation ("Dear Fastener User") identifies the audience.
- The letter is fact-filled and informative. Write it in bullet form for easy scanning.
- A P.S. calls for action.

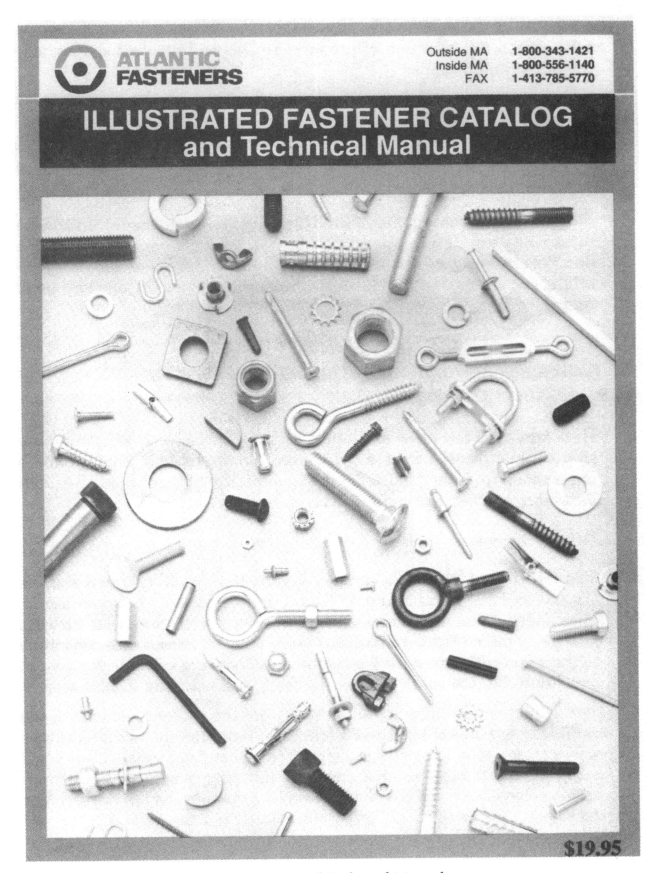

Figure 14.2. Illustrated Fastener Catalog and Technical Manual.

Patrick J. O'Toole
President

"Identify even uncommon fasteners IN SECONDS with our precise, detailed pictures"

Or check-out our fastener measuring guide, anchor comparison table, actual-size rivet chart...and more

Dear Fastener User:

The next time you need fasteners but aren't sure what to ask for, open this catalog.

We've filled it with 264 exact, painstakingly drawn pictures so you can quickly match-up whatever you need.

There are nuts, bolts, machine screws, washers, drill bits, taps, hex keys, threaded inserts — in all 45 categories of fasteners and related products.

Plus, there are pages of helpful fastener information.

■ Our thorough comparison of 15 different anchors, starting on page 35, shows installation instructions, compares pull-out strengths, and recommends when and when *not* to use each.

■ Our handy guide to measuring fasteners on page 27 is packed with easy to follow diagrams and tips, including how to specify shoulder bolts and blind rivets.

■ Our simple to follow "Loctite Problem/Solution Chart" on page 59 shows the products to use for such common maintenance applications as bonding metal or sealing stainless pipe joints.

■ And our easy to understand technical section that starts on page 80 includes such diverse information as washer dimensions and a decimal equivalent chart.

■ Throughout you'll find special "Spotlight Reports" (look for this symbol) on a variety of maintenance products, like Lenox® hole saws and Permatex Color Guard®. We've thoroughly described each, noted superior features, and included helpful tips on using them. Believe me, some of the findings astonished even us.

■ Now, to quickly find what you need, turn to the Index in back. We've listed fasteners by their proper name, like "Socket Head Shoulder Screw"; by nicknames, like "Stripper Bolt"; by category, as under Socket; and by brand names, like Unbrako.

This catalog took 6 1/2 months to complete. We spent countless hours deciding which common fasteners and technical information to include that would interest you.

But, we also stock *thousands* of odd and non-standard fastener varieties that we haven't shown. So, just because you can't find a nut or bolt in here, doesn't mean we don't stock it. Call us for any fastener you need!

Sincerely,

Patrick J. O'Toole

Patrick J. O'Toole
President

P.S. Got a friend who'd like this catalog? Or, do you have some ideas for improving it? Then, please fill-out and mail the post cards in back. Thank you.

Figure 14.3. Attention-getting sales techniques.

Catalog Technique 3: Include a Guarantee

A guarantee of performance or delivery is critical. People do not want to order unless they know they will get their money back or receive some other compensation if you don't deliver as promised.

Many marketers object to guarantees, asking, "Doesn't adding a guarantee put into the readers' minds the notion that something can go wrong, alerting them to possible negatives they weren't thinking of?" The answer is no, because today's buyers are not naive. They realize full well the possibility of problems and are comforted by the fact that you are prepared to stand behind your catalog and do something to correct mistakes. Offering a guarantee is critically important.

The guarantee should be highlighted in a separate box to make it stand out, as is done in the Atlantic Fastener catalog in the upper half of Figure 14.4. Atlantic's guarantee is powerful because it is specific—one-minute quotations and next-day delivery or you get a $50 credit. Body copy surrounding the guarantee tells readers why they are unlikely ever to need the guarantee and explains that Atlantic spent $188,600 to ensure reliable delivery.

Catalog Technique 4: Include a Reason-Why Page

This is a page or series of pages that outline in simple, 1-2-3 fashion the advantages the cataloger offers as a supplier. A typical headline is, "9 reasons why you should buy [type of product] from [name of company]." The lower half of Figure 14.4 shows an example. These reasons might include:

- Broad product selection
- Superior product quality
- Products available and in stock
- Fast shipment
- Generous credit terms
- Availability of difficult-to-find items
- Money-back guarantee
- Large inventory
- Good quality inspection program
- Partnership and just-in-time shipping programs
- Lower prices
- Volume discounts
- Better customer service
- Reliability
- Superior reputation
- Specialty and customized items available

Why it's easier to buy fasteners from Atlantic

 What you dislike most, we guarantee against!

Since introducing Just-In-Time Guarantees in Feb. '86, we've averaged fewer than 8 credits for every 10,000 orders we ship.

But it took five years of planning and organizing before we could offer them. We invested $185,000 to computerize our entire business and $3,600 to automate our shipping department. We spent months developing a foolproof system for packaging correctly, then we turned to hiring and training a dedicated warehouse crew. Finally, we negotiated special shipping privileges with our delivery service.

But it didn't stop there.

Daily, we monitor our performance to insure we uphold our promises to you.

> ## Guaranteed!
>
> One minute quoting of in-stock fasteners
>
> Next day delivery of in-stock fasteners when you order by 3 PM
>
> Error-free, shipping and billing
> ...or *you* get a $50 credit

 Test us without buying a thing

Unload surplus fasteners

We'll issue credit, swap, or buy surplus, saleable fasteners that you ordered from someone else.

Free technical advice

Ask our fastener expert, with four years of fastener training and 2 1/2 years of machine shop experience, to solve your fastener problems. Or let our two former Loctite Corp. salesmen answer your questions on adhesives, sealants, gasketing, or coatings. All are available for free in-plant seminars.

Meet our technical representatives (from left to right) Dean Palozej and Pete Mals formerly of Loctite, and fastener expert Dennis Blain. Call them anytime.

 On the shelf, 33,065,500 standard and hard-to-find fasteners

Stop shopping all over. Atlantic stocks an amazing 15,175 fastener varieties in steel, stainless, brass, silicon bronze, aluminum, and nylon — inch and metric. We're an authorized distributor for:

Permatex	**Loctite**
Tri-Flow	**Tapcon**
Shakeproof	**Tapfree**
SPS/Unbrako	**Lenox**
Lake Erie	**Morse**
Bondhus	**Hindley**
E.W. Daniel Co.	**Gesipa**
SPS/Flexloc	**Cherry**
Rockford	**HeliCoil**
Star Expansion	**Durham**
ITW Ramset Red Head	**Nucor**

Figure 14.4. Reasons-why page.

If you can't tell whether a Grade 8 bolt is counterfeit by looking at it, how do you know you're not buying junk?

Atlantic stocks *only* American-made, traceable Grade 8 bolts — 1/4" to 1-1/4" diameter in 339 sizes

Our Grade 8's come in boxes clearly marked 'Made in USA' and stamped with a tracing number direct from the manufacturer. Order some today.

IS your stockroom filled with potentially dangerous, counterfeit Grade 8 hex cap screws that can fail at high temperatures causing expensive property loss, injury — even death?

According to one fastener trade journal, "…in all probability the entire distribution system for Grade 8 fasteners in the U.S. has been contaminated with millions of improperly marked bolts."

The U.S. Defense Industrial Supply Center in Philadelphia found 30 million substandard Grade 8's in their inventory!

And, Peterbilt, the truck manufacturer, Morton Thiokol, Emerson Electric, GTE, and FMC have reported similar problems.

What about you?

Is your fastener supplier selling you Grade 8's from certain Japanese, Korean, Taiwanese, or Polish manufacturers, known to have mismarked Grade 8's?

Please find out, or consider replacing Grade 8's you've purchased for high temperature applications.

Understand — you can't spot a counterfeit by eye.

The only way to tell for certain is by chemical analysis which costs $200 per bolt!

However, you can avoid future worries by buying from us. We stock *only* American-made, Grade 8's traceable to the steel source.

What's a counterfeit Grade 8?

Grade 8 bolts, marked with six radial lines on their head, are made from medium carbon alloy steel tempered at 800°F. (See below)

Counterfeit Grade 8 bolts have the same head markings but are actually mismarked Grade 8.2 bolts made from less expensive low carbon boron steel which is tempered at only 650°F.

Above 500°F, Grade 8.2 bolts lose tensile strength and may relax or stretch, causing assembly failure. Genuine Grade 8's are safe to much higher temperatures.

American importers are to blame

Ironically, greedy American importers are behind counterfeiting, according to government investigators.

They say that since the late 70's some importers, seeking fatter profit margins, have deliberately asked foreign manufacturers to produce less expensive Grade 8.2 bolts and mark them as Grade 8's.

Then they've sold the less expensive, mismarked Grade 8.2 bolts as higher priced Grade 8's to distributors.

It wasn't until the mid 80's that the problem was uncovered.

Japan, a major foreign supplier, immediately agreed to halt counterfeit shipments. But, just one year ago, U.S. Custom inspectors found that 17% of Japanese imports were still bogus.

So the problem persists, even now when the federal government is taking legal action against fastener distributors and importers nationwide.

Our specially marked boxes is your assurance that they're genuine Grade 8's

Don't take chances. Buy *only* American-made Grade 8's from Atlantic.

We stock 339 sizes, plain and plated, in 1/4" to 1 1/4" diameters.

We package them in bright red, white, and blue boxes, marked 'Made in USA'. And, we stamp each box with a tracing number.

So, if you should ever have a problem with our Grade 8's, we'll trace them back to the exact order and steel batch that our American manufacturer used.

| Nucor Fastener Saint Joe, Indiana | Rockford Products Corp. Rockford, Illinois | Lake Erie Corp Cleveland, Ohio |

Why risk costly down-time, injury, or worse with imported Grade 8 hex cap screws? Buy American-made Grade 8's from Atlantic. Look for these head markings.

Figure 14.5. Sample sell copy.

Catalog Technique 5: Use Sell Copy

In a catalog that is mostly tables of specifications or pictures of products, you can devote one or more pages to more sales-oriented information to reinforce your quality message and give the reader something more interesting to read than dimension and weight tables. The Atlantic Fastener catalog uses a series of full-page ads in its catalog, such as the one shown in Figure 14.5. Each is written so persuasively and interestingly that could easily stand alone as a full-page ads in any trade publication.

Catalog Technique 6: Include Selection Guides

Often, people ordering different grades or types of a specific product are not sure which type to order for their application. Or, they may think they know what to order, but are actually not ordering the proper item and so will be dissatisfied when they try to use what you send them.

The solution is to put selection guides in your catalog explaining the various grades, models, or types, what they are used for, which applications you recommend them for, and how to select them. In Figure 14.6, a "Tapping Screw Guide" from the Atlantic Fastener catalog shows the different types of threadforming screws and describes the features and applications of each.

Catalog Technique 7: Add a Sizing Chart

By putting the dimensions of your full product line in a single illustrated table, you enable the reader to see all the sizes available at a glance, thus making size selection easy. Atlantic Fastener's version is illustrated in Figure 14.7.

Catalog Technique 8: Provide a Cross-Reference Table

In many product categories (semiconductors, for example), there are standard sizes or specifications to which all manufacturers conform. The customer can specify any manufacturer's product in a given size or model. This is called *drop-in technology*—one brand can be automatically substituted for another because you can simply remove one brand and drop in another.

Customers need to know which model number of your product to order as a replacement for a specific model number of a competitor's product they are now using. A cross-reference table makes it easy for the customer to see which model numbers of various manufacturers are interchangeable with one another. A cross-reference table from the Atlantic Fastener catalog is shown in Figure 14.8.

You might object, "But couldn't my customers just as easily use my cross-reference table to replace my brand with my competitor's brand?" Yes, they could. But the fact is, customers want this type of information. Providing it says to the customer, "I am not only here to sell my product but also to help you do your job well." This is the real message customers want to hear. If they turn to *your* catalog instead of your competitor's because they know yours contains a cross-reference table and theirs does not, who do you think they are more likely to order from?

Tapping Screw Guide

Thread Forming

Use thread forming screws in materials that can tolerate high internal stresses, such as plywood, or where a high resistance to loosening is desired, as in thin sheet metal.

Type A Point

Has coarse spaced threads and a gimlet point. Use in light, .015 to .050 thick, sheet metal, resin-impregnated plywood, or asbestos composition material. Often used in place of wood screws because it drives quicker, is fully threaded, and has a larger thread profile. Type AB are usually recommended over Type A, especially for new design.

Type AB Point

Combines the gimlet point of Type A with the thread size and pitch of Type B. Use for thin sheet metal, resin-impregnated plywood, asbestos compositions, and non-ferrous castings. Recommended over Type A, especially in brittle materials such as plastics and zinc die castings.

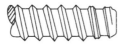

Type B Point

Has a finer thread pitch than Type A and a blunt point. Use in light and heavier sheet metal, .050 to .200 thick, nonferrous castings, plastics, resin-impregnated plywoods, and asbestos compositions. Recommended over Type AB for thicker materials because its point, which has a gradual taper, starts more easily.

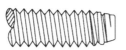

Type C Point

Has a blunt, tapered point and machine screw threads, so it can be replaced with a standard screw in the field. Does not produce chips. Will tap into thicker sections than Type AB, such as heavy sheet metal and die castings. High driving torque required, so as a result, thread rolling screws have frequently been chosen over Type C screws for difficult applications.

Type U Point

Has a pilot point and high helix thread for driving or hammering into sheet metal, castings, fiber, or plastics. Quickly makes permanent assemblies.

Figure 14.6. Sample guide.

Actual Size Rivet Chart

3/32" Rivet Diameter Use in .097 - .100 hole (#41 Drill)	Diam. and Grip	Grip Range		5/32" Rivet Diameter Use in .160 - .164 hole (#20 Drill)	Diam. and Grip	Grip Range
	-32	.063 .125			-56	.251 .375
	-34	.126 .250			-58	.376 .500
	-36	.251 .375			-510	.501 .625

1/8" Rivet Diameter Use in .129 - .133 hole (#30 Drill)	Diam. and Grip	Grip Range		3/16" Rivet Diameter Use in .192 - .196 hole (#11 Drill)	Diam. and Grip	Grip Range
	-41	Up to .062			-62	.063 .125
	-42	.063 .125			-64	.126 .250
	-43	.126 .187			-66	.251 .375
	-44	.188 .250			-68	.376 .500
	-45	.251 .312			-610	.501 .625
	-46	.313 .375			-612	.626 .750
	-47	.376 .437			-614	.751 .875
	-48	.438 .500			-616	.876 1.000
	-49	.501 .562		1/4" Rivet Diameter Use in .257 - .261 hole ("F" Drill)	Diam. and Grip	Grip Range
	-410	.563 .625			-82	.063 .125

5/32" Rivet Diameter Use in .160 - .164 hole (#20 Drill)	Diam. and Grip	Grip Range			-84	.126 .250
	-52	.063 .125			-86	.251 .375
	-54	.126 .250			-88	.376 .500

Figure 14.7. Sample sizing chart.

Actual Size Rivet Chart (con't)

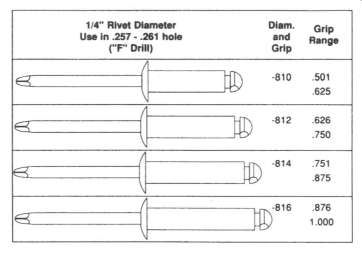

Blind Rivet Cross Reference

Manufacturers' lettering systems. Rivet size "42" is used in all
examples—merely substitute numerical size factors applicable.

PCI	CHERRY	CELUS	AFC	MALCO	MARSON	OSCAR OLYMPIC	GESIPA	SCOVILL	SEMBLEX RIVEX	STAR	USM
AK42A	AAC42	A/A42C	ACA42	AA42K	AC42A		GAMC42A	AA42C	RAK42A	4-2AAC	AK42ABS
AD42ALF	AAL42	A/A42LF	ABA42L	AA42LF	ABL42A	RV633	GAML42A	AA42LF	RAD42ALF	A-2AALF	AD42ABSLF
AD42A	AAP42	A/A42D	ABA42	AA42D	AB42A	RV63042	GAMD42A	AA42D	RAD42A	4-2AAD	AD42ABS
AK42S	BSC42	A/S42C	ACS42	AS42K	AC42		GSMC42A	AS42C	RAK42S	4-2ASC	AK42BS
AD42SLF	BSL42	A/S42LF	ABS42L	AS42LF	ABL42	RV653	GSML42A	AS42LF	RAD42SLF	4-2ASLF	AD42BSLF
AD42S	BSP42	A/S42D	ABS42	AS42D	AB42	RV65042	GSMD42A	AS42D	RAD42S	4-2ASD	AD42BS
SK42S	SSC42	S/S42C	SCS42	SS42K	SC42		GSMC42S	SS42C	RSK42S	4-2SSC	SK42BS
SD42SLF	SSL42	S/S42LF	SBS42L	SS42LF	SBL42		GSML42S	SS42LF	RSD42SLF	4-2SSLF	SD42BSLF
SD42S	SSP42	S/S42D	SBS42	SS42D	SB42	RV67042	GSMD42S	SS42D	RSD42S	4-2SSD	SD42BS
SSD42SS	CCP42	SS/SS42D	FBF42		SSB42S		GSSMD42SS	STST42D	RSSD42SS	4-2STSTD	SSD42SSBS
SSD42S	CSP42	SS/S42D			SSB42		GSMD42SS	STS42D	RSSD42S	4-2STSD	SSD42BS
	MSC42			MS42C							MK419BS
	MSP42			MS42D	MB4-14						MD424BS
CD42S	USP42	C/S42D	CBS42	CS42D	CB42		GSMD42C	CC42D	RCD42S	4-2CCD	CD42BS

Figure 14.8. Sample cross-reference table.

Catalog Technique 9: Include How-To Information

Want your catalog to be perceived as a valuable reference manual rather than just a sales piece? Want it to be cherished, treasured, kept, and referred to often? Then put how-to information into the book. Your buyers want to know: how to install insulation; how to check valves for signs of corrosion; how to select the right size mixer; how to monitor air quality; how to set up a companywide safety program; how to design an office automation system; and so on. Give them how-to information that is genuinely useful and answers the most pressing technical questions they have, and the perceived value of your catalog will double or triple. See Figure 14.9 for an example.

Catalog Technique 10: Use Ordering Guides

Check your body copy. Whenever you can convert long paragraphs of complicated instructions into easy-to-use tables or charts, do it.

Visual tools provide easy-reference guides and make your catalog more useful to the buyer. In Figure 14.10, Atlantic Fasteners has developed a guide the reader can use to quickly determine which type of anchor to order. Whenever you can, put in a table or guide to help the reader order the right type, material, size, or model. *Warning:* If the ordering process is too complicated to explain in the catalog, don't try. Instead, encourage the buyer to call you for help.

Catalog Technique 11: Provide Product Profiles

Specifications are necessary, but a catalog that contains only page after page of numbers and drawings is boring, and readers won't turn its pages any more often than they have to.

Selling is more than just presenting specifications; it's telling the reader all the key facts about your product: features, benefits, strengths, weaknesses, applications, usage tips. So, if you have a 24-page catalog with page after page of specs for three basic types of products, you might devote a full or half a page per product to more descriptive "sell" copy in a product profile. Figure 14.11 shows an example of a full-page product profile on Red Head Chemical Anchors.

Catalog Technique 12: Include Testimonials

Including testimonials is one of the most powerful advertising techniques, yet few catalogs contain them. Testimonials are quotations from satisfied customers saying how good your company, product, or service is.

The best testimonials are those that are not general but address specific advantages of your products or concerns other buyers may have. Some catalogers sprinkle testimonials throughout the catalog, using only one or two per page. Others group them all on one or two pages, as Atlantic Fastener has done in Figure 14.12. The latter technique seems to have more power and impact.

Catalog Technique 13: Use Two Order Forms

A little-known but effective technique is to use not one but two order forms. They are identical except that one is bound into the catalog or printed on one of the regular catalog pages, while the second is loose and is inserted between the front cover and the first page. The loose order form

How to Measure Fasteners

Answers to your most common questions

Screws and Bolts

Q: "Please help. How do you measure the length of a screw or bolt, from head-to-tip or just the amount under the head?"

A: It depends on the head style. For round and pan head, etc., measure under the head. For flat head screws (countersunk), it's the overall length that matters. For oval heads, measure from the tip to where the oval starts.

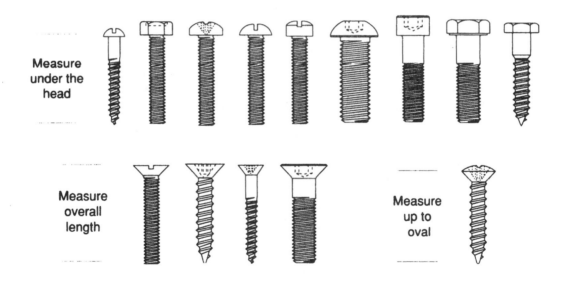

Measure under the head

Measure overall length

Measure up to oval

Hex Cap Screws

Q: "How much of a hex cap screw is threaded and how much is unthreaded?"

A: Here's an easy formula:
• For hex cap screws 6" or shorter, the amount of thread equals twice the diameter + 1/4".
• For hex caps longer than 6", the amount of thread equals twice the diameter + 1/2".

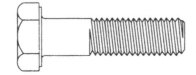

Figure 14.9. Sample how-to information.

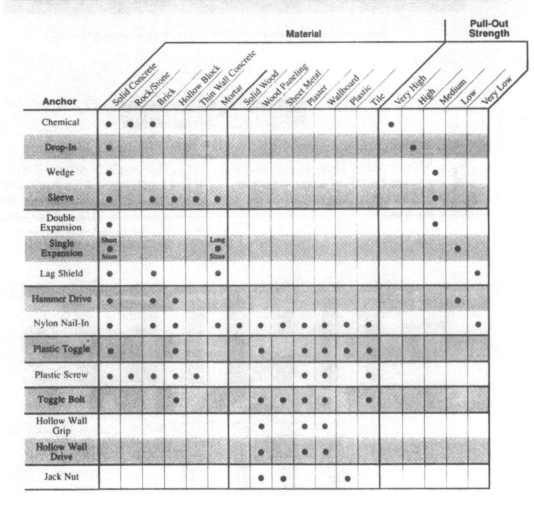

Choosing the Right Anchor

	Material													Pull-Out Strength				
Anchor	Solid Concrete	Rock/Stone	Brick	Hollow Block	Thin Wall Concrete	Mortar	Solid Wood	Wood Paneling	Sheet Metal	Plaster	Wallboard	Plastic	Tile	Very High	High	Medium	Low	Very Low
Chemical	●	●	●											●				
Drop-In	●														●			
Wedge	●															●		
Sleeve	●		●	●	●	●										●		
Double Expansion	●															●		
Single Expansion	● Short Sizes					● Long Sizes											●	
Lag Shield	●		●			●												●
Hammer Drive	●		●													●		
Nylon Nail-In	●		●	●		●	●	●	●	●	●	●						●
Plastic Toggle	●		●				●		●	●	●	●						
Plastic Screw	●	●	●	●	●				●	●	●							
Toggle Bolt			●				●	●	●	●								
Hollow Wall Grip							●		●	●								
Hollow Wall Drive							●		●	●								
Jack Nut							●	●			●							

Need more information?

On the pages shown below, we describe the features/benefits of each anchor, show how to install them, compare pull-out strengths, recommend uses, and warn against misuses.

Figure 14.10. Sample ordering guide.

Red Head Chemical Anchors

Features/Benefits:

■ Heavy-duty, simple two-part anchoring system that consists of a threaded rod anchor and glass chemical capsule.

■ Just drill and clean hole, drop in capsule, and drill threaded rod through capsule to start chemical curing action.

■ Cures to heavy-duty, stress-free, vibration resistant bond that seals out water and moisture.

■ Cures under water.

■ Comes with nuts and washers.

■ Reinforcing bar may be substituted for threaded rod.

Pull-out strength:

As compared to the drop-in, wedge, and sleeve anchors, chemical anchors have the highest pull-out strength. Chemical anchors with carbon steel threaded rods have up to 40% greater pull-out strength than drop-in anchors depending on the diameter used.

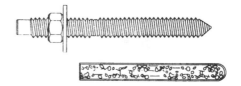

Chemical Anchor

Recommended For:

Ideal for installations where wedge anchors have difficulty gripping such as in hard masonry or rock.

Also recommended for brick, solid block, concrete, and precast.

Use where shock or vibration can loosen sleeve or wedge anchors. Example: anchoring conveyor systems or loading dock bumpers.

Not Recommended For:

Overhead applications or anywhere else that permits the chemical to leak-out such as in hollow blocks or bricks.

Installation Instructions:

1. Refer to box that holds capsules. Select proper carbide tipped drill bit size. Drill hole to recommended embedment depth.

2. Clean all dust from hole.

3. Insert capsule into drilled hole. DO NOT use capsule if cracked or damaged.

4. Assemble two nuts, with a washer between them, onto the anchor rod and tighten together. Place preassembled anchor rod into impact socket and socket adaptor. Insert rod into drilled hole breaking capsule with pointed end of the anchor rod. Turn on drill and drive anchor downward until the recommended embedment depth is attained.

5. Remove impact socket and drill from anchor rod. Remove excess resin from around hole. Avoid disturbing anchor rod until adequate cure time is reached.

6. Install material to be fastened after resin has cured.

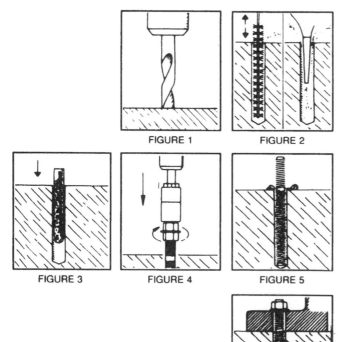

FIGURE 1   FIGURE 2

FIGURE 3   FIGURE 4   FIGURE 5

FIGURE 6

Figure 14.11. Sample full-page product profile.

Customers complain...

"Why can't every supplier be this good?"

We greet you with grins not grunts

"Atlantic Fasteners is the easiest company we deal with. The staff is friendly, courteous, and the most accommodating...We appreciate the attention our account gets."
Terry Veber and Jill Pierpont, Buyers — Mt. Snow

"The staff...is professional and courteous, and makes every effort to assist in our needs."
Scott Aye, Gen. Sup. Plant Eng. — Milton Bradley

"Your personnel are by far the most congenial individuals with which our maintenance department has to deal with..."
Dean LaFond, Main. Sup. — LEGO Systems

"We at Monsanto Co. Saflex have always received exceptional service..."
Keith Korbut, Main. Sup. — Monsanto Co.

Fasteners in every flavor

"I'm forever amazed at the stainless steel variety you have, like the 1 1/4" hex nuts..."
Wayne Avery, Main. Sup. — Sonoco Products Co.

"You always have in your inventory, or can get in a reasonable time, any fastener we need."
Jack Hindle, Tool Room Foreman — Dennison National

From our shelf to yours in one day

"Everybody brags they're the best. But you're the only company I know, besides Federal Express, who makes guarantees and backs them with cash!"
Joe Elias, Owner — A.S.E. Precision

"Atlantic Fasteners has proven that guaranteed next day delivery means next day — not next week."
Ronald Hand, Mfg. Serv. Mgr. — Gloenco-Newport

Hidden savings revealed!

"Switching over to Atlantic Fasteners has allowed me to reduce my in-house inventories, thereby reducing my overhead/stocking costs. Atlantic's prices are also lower than your competitors."
Scott Aye, Gen. Sup. Plant Eng. — Milton Bradley

Returns allowed anytime

"Your take-back policy is great... those hex nuts were just sitting around taking up space for like a year, and you didn't even blink an eye when I returned them."
Dave Falvey, Owner — Tote'Em Trailers

Figure 14.12. Sample testimonial.

falls out when the prospect opens the book, so it gains more attention and encourages immediate ordering. However, if the prospect is not ready to buy now, the loose order form may become lost or get thrown away. When the prospect turns to the catalog later to place an order, the bound-in order form is ready and waiting there.

Tip: Add a line to the bottom of your order form that says, "In a hurry? Simply complete this form and fax to [fax number] for immediate action." Since most businesses have fax machines, this provides prospects with a convenient method of ordering that they will appreciate.

Catalog Technique 14: Make Sure Your Catalog Is Complete

Use the checklist in Figure 14.13 to make sure you have included all necessary information in your catalog. Leaving out a piece of critical information in an industrial or consumer catalog can have a devastatingly negative effect on the number of orders received. Yet the first time you publish your catalog, it's hard to know exactly what should be included, and it's easy to miss an item. Note that most of the items in Figure 14.13 apply equally to consumer and industrial catalogs.

Fig. 14.13. Checklist of catalog contents

Does your catalog contain all of the following?

- Attention-grabbing front cover
- Letter of introduction
- Table of contents
- Index
- Conditions and terms
- Order form
- Reply envelope
- Names of all products
- Physical descriptions
- Photos or illustrations (Is color needed?)
- Features and benefits
- Explanation of how products work
- Weight
- Dimensions, including choice of sizes available
- Other necessary specifications
- Price, including quantity discounts
- Colors
- Shapes
- Styles
- Models

- Applications
- Tips on selection, including cross-reference chart
- Tips on usage
- Packaging and shipping information
- Safety warnings and precautions
- Quality assurance
- Materials of construction
- Efficiency ratings
- Maintenance and repair methods
- Service contracts available
- Cost savings or discounts
- Nearest distributors
- Guarantee or warranty
- Reasons to buy from your company
- How-to articles, product profiles, ads, selection guides, etc.
- Testimonials
- Your company name and address
- Other locations where your products are sold
- Company history, background, philosophy, business mission
- Phone number, including toll-free 800 number if available
- Fax number
- Any additional ordering information required

Chapter

DIRECT MAIL
15

What is direct mail? How does it differ from direct marketing, direct response, and mail order?

Direct mail is unsolicited advertising or promotional material (that is, material the recipient has not requested) sent to an individual or company through the mail. The typical direct mail piece consists of an outer envelope, a letter, a brochure, and a reply form or card. But there are many other formats and combinations. Some companies send a letter only. Others send self-mailers (folded brochures with no envelope or letter).

Direct response is any type of advertising that seeks some sort of reply from the reader. Direct mail is just one form of direct response advertising. Other examples include print ads with reply coupons and television commercials that ask you to call a toll-free number to make an inquiry or place an order.

Direct marketing is basically the same as direct response. It means that the advertising is designed to generate an immediate action on the part of the consumer. This contrasts with general advertising, which aims at building an image or creating awareness of a product or brand over an extended period of time rather than at generating immediate response. Mail order is a way of doing business in which products are sold, ordered, and delivered solely by mail (although orders may be placed via fax or telephone) with no intermediaries such as salespeople, retail outlets, or distributors.

DIRECT MAIL IS GROWING

Because it generates an immediate, tangible response, direct mail is becoming more and more popular in this age of accountability and immediate results. Advertising has always been difficult to sell to top management because such things as image, brand preference, awareness, and communication are difficult to measure. But with direct mail, you can easily point to a stack of inquiry cards or a bundle of checks or charge card orders as tangible proof that your mailing worked.

The accountability factor makes direct mail both appealing and frightening to advertising agencies and advertising managers: appealing because it generates the kind of immediate, tangible results that are easy to sell to management; frightening because it can bring the most arrogant advertising experts quickly to their knees as lofty theories and break-through campaigns are judged by results rather than aesthetics.

Example: A publisher of tax guides for professionals tested a creative versus a traditional direct mail approach to selling its books via mail order. The creative mailing, done by one of the top mail order consultants, was full of high-powered sales talk, made amazing promises, and was creatively conceived and designed. The traditional letter was low key, presenting more honestly the contents of the book in the context of how the book would benefit the reader.

The traditional "dull" letter dramatically outperformed the creative approach. The key point is that you don't know what the result will be until you test your concept in the mail. As veteran copywriter Milt Pierce observes, "After twenty-five years of writing direct mail copy, I can easily spot a mailing that will bomb. But I can rarely predict a winner."

E-mail, fax, and the Internet have not yet made direct mail obsolete. According to an article in *Direct Marketing* magazine (May 1996), 87 percent of executives in firms with revenues of $1 to $10 million use first class mail once a day or more, and 75 percent of executives read mail as soon as they receive it. A survey from the U.S. Postal Service shows that a surprisingly small minority of consumers—only 14.7 percent—say they discard advertising mail without opening it.

A recent Gallup poll shows that direct mail is the most popular communications medium among marketing directors and vice presidents at large and mid-sized U.S. companies, with 77 percent of them using direct mail. On average, direct mail accounts for 22 percent of the marketing communications budget. Eighty-nine percent of these firms use direct mail to generate leads and 48 percent use the medium to generate orders.

A Business Marketing Association survey shows that six out of ten direct marketing messages are delivered via direct mail. Of the $6.3 billion spent on direct marketing in 1997, $3.8 billion was for direct mail, $779 million for telemarketing, and $287 for direct response print ads.

The U.S. Postal Service says it delivers direct mail to every address and post office box in the United States—118 million total. There are 330,000 post office locations where you can drop off your mailings. In 1993, the Post Office moved 171 billion pieces of mail across the United States. According to the Post Office, direct mail generated sales of $333 billion for marketers in 1994. "Direct mail is still one of the most appealing ways to get a message to a buyer," says Jay Lewis, an economist for the Postal Service (memo to mailers, April 1997, p. 4). Four out of ten households surveyed rate direct mail as "useful." Fifty-nine percent of the mail in America's mail boxes is advertising matter.

In a speech at the Semaine du Marketing Direct (Direct Marketing Week) given in Paris in January, 1986, David Ogilvy—founder of Ogilvy & Mather—discussed the philosophical differences between general advertising and direct marketing or direct mail:

> There is a yawning chasm between you Generalists and us Directs. We Directs belong to a different world. Your gods are not our gods.
>
> You Generalists pride yourselves on being "creative"—whatever that awful word means. You cultivate the mystique of "creativity." Your ambition is to win awards. You are the glamour boys and girls of the advertising community. You regard advertising as an art form and expect your clients to finance expressions of your genius.
>
> We humble people who work in Direct do not regard advertising as an art form. Our clients don't give a damn whether we win awards. They pay us to sell their products. We sell—or else. When you Generalists write an advertisement or commercial, you want everybody to congratulate you on your "creativity." When we write an advertisement or a direct mail package, we want people to order the product.
>
> When your commercials appear on television, you have no means of knowing whether they sell anything. There are too many other factors in the marketing mix. When sales go up, you claim the credit for it. When sales go down, you blame the product. We in Direct Response know exactly, to the penny, how many products we sell.
>
> We do everything differently. You Generalists use short copy. We use long copy. Experience has taught us that short copy does not sell.
>
> In our headlines, we promise the consumer a benefit. You Generalists don't think that it is "creative."
>
> You Generalists never give consumers any information about the product. We pack our letters with information about the product. We have found we have to—if we want to sell.
>
> Are you aware that Direct Response is growing twice as fast as general advertising? It is exploding. Soon it will become the tail wagging the dog.

Copywriter Richard Armstrong added his thoughts on this theme in an article in *Advertising Age*:

> Did anyone hear the keynote speech at Direct Marketing Day in New York this year? Can someone please tell me why we direct marketers always invite these clowns from Madison Avenue to be the principal speakers at our conventions? The speaker gave the usual condescending and ignorant performance that we've come to expect from these people. "Direct marketing used to be the ugly stepchild of general advertising, but now it's really come into its own. Aren't we general advertisers smart that we saw the huge potential of direct marketing and got into it when we did? Of course, you in direct mail still have a lot to learn from us, especially when it comes to creating an image for your product and forming emotional bonds with your customers." Blah, blah, blah.
>
> Look, the first sign you're dealing with idiots is when they imply that direct marketing is some kind of a spin-off or stepchild of general advertising. Anybody who says this simply doesn't know advertising history. Actually, the

exact opposite is true. In the beginning, virtually all advertising was direct response advertising. General advertising came much, much later.

We direct marketers were here before general advertising, and it looks like we will be here after general advertising is gone, which looks like it may be quite soon. The keynote speaker at DM Day showed a bunch of commercials that were exceedingly creative, often quite moving, beautifully produced, and, as near as I could tell, entirely unconcerned with selling the product. Some of the ads scarcely even mentioned the product.

BASICS OF DIRECT MAIL SUCCESS

According to direct mail copywriter Mike Pavlish, there are seven basic steps in creating a successful direct mail campaign:

1. Pick the Best Mailing Lists

Choose your outside mailing lists with great care, because they can make or break your mailing. Get list recommendations from at least three different mailing list brokers (a list broker is a firm or individual who rents mailing lists). The lists recommended most will probably be the most effective.

The best lists are generally of those people who recently bought something similar to your offering in your price range by direct mail. Test many different mailing lists and test each list on a small scale first. Then you can gradually mail more pieces to the lists that generate the best results. This is the safest and surest way to go.

Mail to your own list of prospects and customers often. These proven interested people are your best prospects and surest profits in direct mail. Mail to your house list regularly; once a month is not too often. Change your envelope for each mailing so prospects do not assume they have already seen this mailing.

2. Use Your Biggest Customer Benefits in Your Headline and First Paragraphs

Readers are asking themselves, "What's in it for me?" and "How will I benefit?" when they see your mailing. If the headline and first paragraph don't immediately pile on all the wonderful customer benefits the reader will get, chances are your mailing will be pitched.

Don't talk about how good your company is. Don't be cute or funny. Instead, start by piling on all the benefits to the reader. Be specific and positive with your customer benefits. Lay them on thick. Of course, if you are writing to professionals, the wealthy, or high-level executives, you should be a little more subdued. If you make a really good offer or offer something free, this should usually be mentioned in the headline or first paragraphs.

3. Use Hard-Selling, Customer-Benefit Copy

Throughout the mailing, continuously pile on the customer benefits readers will realize when they respond. Then prove your benefit claims and overcome objections. But remember, customer benefits are what sell.

Direct mail copy should sell about three times as hard as an in-person sales presentation. Hard-selling, benefit-loaded direct mail copy is necessary because a sales representative is not there in person to use charm, ask or answer questions, or overcome human inertia to get a response.

4. Make It Look Easy to Read

Not many people will read your direct mail if it looks hard to read, if it looks like work, or if it looks boring or monotonous. Make your direct mail look easy to read, fun, and exciting by:

- using subheads,
- indenting a few key paragraphs,
- using short sentences and paragraphs,
- underlining key words, and
- using wide margins.

5. Make a Hard-to-Resist, No-Risk Offer

To get maximum response, develop and make hard-to-resist, no-risk offers for your prospects and customers. The less financial risk a buyer takes, the higher your response will usually be. This is why inexpensive get-acquainted offers, free trials, discounts, and free bonuses work so well in direct mail.

Always try to put a time limit on your offers. The time limit works because it gets people to take immediate action. Try to develop offers that involve no financial risk to the buyer by offering a money-back guarantee.

If your goal is sales leads, offer free printed information: a brochure, report, checklist, etc. The offering of free printed information usually increases the quantity of leads significantly.

6. Close Hard for an Immediate Response

After you've piled on the customer benefits, proven your claims, and made a great no-risk offer, use a strong closing to get an immediate response. Most people naturally put things off. They need to be nudged to take immediate action. Your closing must be strong to get an immediate response or readers will probably not respond, even if they intend to.

Close for immediate action several times—some subtle, some forceful. The main thing is to get the response now. Close by telling readers all the benefits they'll soon enjoy, relating what they'll lose if they don't respond now, using a time limit, and making hard-to-resist, no-risk offers. Use the P.S. of the letter to make an additional hard close.

7. Use Professionals

Businesses that are successful with direct mail view it as an ongoing program, not a one-shot, hit-or-miss attempt. Most hire professional direct mail ad agencies, graphic designers, consultants, or copywriters. The expertise of the professionals can and should return you many times over the fee they charge. Check out professionals. Chances are, using them will pay off.

SAMPLE DIRECT MAIL LETTER

The letter in Figure 15.1 is included not to be copied by you (it is copyrighted by the owner) but to show you an example of how to write a sales letter correctly. Note the short, punchy sentences; friendly, conversational

---

Figure 15.1. Sample direct mail letter.

Thank you for asking about...

...a new way to profit from old prints. A way that many other galleries have discovered. You can, too.

If you're selling original, antique prints now, here's a reliable source. It will strengthen your hold on this booming, very profitable, market.

To get started, just complete and mail the form enclosed. We'll phone to discuss your needs.

Then, we'll send a package of prints for your no-risk review: about $1,500 at trade prices.

You'll find hand-colored botanicals. Charming animals. Architecturals. Topographicals. Most are from the 18th and 19th centuries. No reproductions or restrikes. All originals. And guaranteed to be so.

And if the news weeklies of the 19th century—such as Harper's—appeal to you, you'll tap a substantial inventory. Local reviews. Occupations. Genre scenes. Civil War events. Sports subjects. And much more.

Just review the prints. Pick what you want. And return the rest. It's as simple as that.

You can request a package as often as you like. Once a year. Every three months. Whenever there's a need. Lots of galleries make their selections and then say "Send another package, at once!" But it's entirely up to you.

And there's no minimum order required. No obligation. But you'll always find something special in every shipment. You'll invest your time wisely when you look through a package from Cobble Hill.

You have more questions, of course. So I've enclosed the answers to those most frequently asked.

But, really, the best way is to review an actual package. That will tell you all you want to know, quickly.

So discover this new way to profit from old prints, won't you? Please complete and mail the form enclosed. We'll phone you soon.

Cordially,
Florence Rosenblum, President
Cobble Hill Prints

P.S. Even if you're not interested, may I ask you to return the form anyway? There's a stamped, addressed envelope enclosed. Thank you.

style; helpful attitude; attention to detail and inclusion of specific factual product information; and the use of an offer, as suggested by Mike Pavlish. (Note: This letter is mailed to prospects who respond to the firm's ad in *Decor* magazine.)

POSTAGE CONSIDERATIONS

Should you mail your direct mail pieces first class or third class? First class delivery is speedier than third class. In fact, third class is notoriously slow. Further, some mail carriers treat third class mail with indifference and contempt. There have been reports of third class mail being dumped (illegally) by mail carriers rather than delivered. In fact, 11 percent of third class mail is never delivered, according to an analysis of a huge, ongoing mail tracking study conducted by the Mailing List Users and Suppliers Association. The mail that was delivered took an average of 9.2 days to reach its destination.

The main reason to use third class mail is cost savings. A one-ounce letter mailed first class requires 32 cents postage; a one-ounce letter mailed third class bulk rate costs 19.8 cents to mail. This is a difference of $122 per thousand pieces mailed, which on a 100,000-piece mailing comes to a cost savings of $12,200. Most advertisers are happy to have the mail take 9.2 days to arrive rather than one or two days if they can save $12,200 in the process.

Further savings can be realized on third class mail through sorting of mail. Third class mail sorted by five-digit zip codes qualifies for a discount rate of 16.5 cents per letter, provided you sort by zip code and have 200 or more pieces per zip code. Mail sorted by carrier route (the route each mail carrier walks or drives to deliver the mail within a zip code) qualifies for an additional carrier presort discount, enabling you to mail for 13.1 cents per letter.

Third class bulk rate mail must be sorted and prepared in accordance with strict Post Office requirements. If you plan to do it yourself, go to your local Post Office and get a copy of the instruction manual for Third Class Bulk Preparation Requirements. If it is unclear to you, ask your postmaster for clarification.

Most mailers do not prepare third class mail in-house but use outside services called letter shops. A letter shop is a direct mail service firm that prepares mailings. You provide the printed pieces—the necessary quantities of outer envelopes, letters, brochures, and reply cards—to your letter shop. They will fold your material, insert it into envelopes, seal the envelopes, affix mailing labels, meter the envelopes or affix stamps, sort and bundle mail according to Post Office regulations, and deliver the mailings to the Post Office. Some letter shops also do printing and will even design your mailing for you. See Appendix H for a summary of postal rates and regulations.

WHAT DOES DIRECT MAIL COST?

There are two basic cost elements to direct mail. The first are one-time charges for creating, writing, and designing the piece. The second are the repeat costs of mailing that are incurred every time you print and mail the piece. They include printing, postage, letter shop costs, and mailing list rental.

Most direct mail professionals express the cost of doing a mailing as a cost per 1,000 pieces mailed. When calculating this, they add up the printing, postage, list rental, and letter shop costs, multiply by 1,000, and divide by the number of pieces mailed. The one-time creative costs are usually not included in this calculation and are considered advertising overhead. The formula for cost per 1,000 is expressed as:

$$CPM = (L_1 + L_2 + P_1 + P_2) \times 1{,}000/N$$

where: CPM = cost per thousand
L_1 = total letter shop charge
L_2 = total mailing list rental costs
P_1 = postage
P_2 = printing
N = number of pieces mailed

For most mailings, cost ranges from $600 to $900 or more per 1,000 pieces mailed, depending on quantity, format, and elaborateness of the piece. The $600 to $900 per 1,000 cost is for a package consisting of a number 10 outer envelope, a two-page letter, a small circular or folder, and a reply card, all printed in two colors in quantities of 10,000 or so.

THE IMPORTANCE OF OUTER ENVELOPES

Your prospects' involvement with your mailing piece begins when they see or pick up the envelope. The envelope forms an impression. It either attracts interest or is a turn-off The outer envelope design must not be accidental. It must be thought out and planned carefully.

In business-to-business direct mail, a common strategy is to make the envelope resemble a regular business letter. This is done by sending the mailing in a plain number 10 business envelope with no advertising message or graphics (teasers) on the outer envelope. The recipient's name and address are typed directly on the envelope to make it resemble a personally typed letter rather than a typical direct mail piece with a label affixed.

In Publishers Clearing House and other sweepstakes-type mailings, the opposite approach is used. The envelopes are made as flashy, promotional, and hard-sell as possible. Apparently, the approach works.

An article in *Journal of Direct Marketing* reports the results of a survey of 520 people who were asked why they open direct mail (as reported in *Metal Working Marketer*, January 1994, p. 7):

- 83 percent say they open an envelope that looks like a bill. (The survey did not ask how they felt about being tricked after opening the envelope.)
- 72 percent say they open handwritten envelopes.
- 69 percent say that envelopes with at least one window entice them to see what's inside.
- 58 percent feel that an official-looking envelope stands a good chance of being opened.
- 51 percent say that an envelope in a color will be opened.
- Only 18 percent say they are enticed to open an envelope that looks like a sweepstakes entry.

Although it is difficult to say with certainty what approach will work best in your mailing, here are three observations that are fairly well supported by hard test data.

Observation 1: Outer Envelopes Do Matter

How you design the outer envelope is important. It can make a big difference. One envelope size, one headline, one color used instead of another can all alter response by as much as 25 percent. I have seen dramatic differences in split versions of three packages that were totally identical in every way, except that each had different teaser copy. The envelope is not an afterthought, but should be given primary consideration when it comes to copy, design, and method of production.

Observation 2: A Good Teaser Can Increase Response Rates

A good teaser will do the trick, but a bad teaser can actually reduce response rates. In split tests, blank or blind envelopes—those with no teaser copy or graphics—pulled up to 35 percent higher response rates than envelopes with teasers. In other tests, teasers outperformed blank envelopes by the same margin. A good rule of thumb is: If you are skilled at writing teasers or have come up with a great teaser concept that seems a natural to you, by all means use it.

A good teaser can be powerful. A book club sent me a direct mail package selling classic works of literature and great contemporary books. The outer envelope dramatized the convenience of membership with this clever teaser: "Imprisonment. Excommunication. Torture. Execution. Writing the Great Books required some sacrifices. Reading them is a lot easier."

If you don't feel competent at writing teasers, or nothing comes to mind, use a blank envelope. Don't force a teaser onto the envelope for the sake of having one. The wrong teaser, a dull teaser, or a teaser that is inappropriate can actually hurt response rates.

Observation 3: A Change in Envelope Can Increase Response Rates

It has been proven in renewal letters, billing letters, credit letters, and other repeat mailing series that varying the envelope size, design, and color from mailing to mailing increases response rates.

The reason usually given is that, if you use the same outer envelope, readers come to believe that they have already received your mailing and, therefore, don't bother to open any further letters from you. Russell Fuchs, president of Retrieval-Masters Creditors' Bureau, observes that in collection letters a change in letterhead and, therefore, in the outer envelope will increase returns almost every time.

Even a seemingly trivial envelope change can make a different. "Put postage stamps on at an angle," advises direct marketing expert Don Libey. "When you angle the stamp on the envelope, it looks like a human licked it and stuck it on and that improves the response because it increases opening of the envelope." Other Libey ideas include using commemorative stamps and old postage stamps. Another idea is to put the postage on the envelope using smaller denomination stamps, so there are lots of stamps on the envelope. This is unusual and is visually arresting.

Royal Forgues, CEO of Fasprint, says hand-addressed outer envelopes—or those that appear hand-addressed—can increase response rates because they look so personal. He says one of his tests generated 28 percent inquiries from handwritten envelopes versus only 3.2 percent from a labeled version.

TEN WAYS TO ADD INTEREST TO YOUR OUTER ENVELOPES

Here are some additional envelope ideas, many of them reprinted courtesy of the Transo Envelope Company:

1. Use an Odd-Sized Envelope

Most direct mail envelopes are similar in size ranging from 6 x 9 to a standard number 10. Something that looks a little different from the rest is an odd-sized envelope, perhaps with an odd-sized letterhead. One example is a greeting card envelope. Another is the number 11 envelope, which is the same shape as a number 10 but slightly oversize.

2. Use Colored Envelopes

Rather than always sending out the same white envelope, have a series of different colors and sizes so your package doesn't always look the same and people don't throw it out saying, "Oh, I already got this one." Using colored envelopes isn't expensive. All you have to do is order your envelopes with color or paper changes.

3. Use a Textured Paper Stock

Unusual paper stocks can add high style, but are also very expensive and often hard to get. A good way to simulate various textures is through overprinting grains such as leather, woodgrain, marble, stucco, and granite.

Ask your printer if he or she has leftover envelopes from other jobs. They may sell you fancy remainder envelopes for less than you would pay if you ordered them from the paper supplier, simply because they are sitting around taking up space in the print shop.

4. State a "Do Not Open Until" Date.

A surefire way to get people to disobey your instructions and consequently to open the envelope is to print copy on the envelope that says, "Do not open until [date]." The tie-in copy might be something about the fact that this is a special offer not available for the general public until such and such a time. However, since the reader cheated and looked anyway, you'll tell him or her the story and make the special offer.

5. Use a Bulk Rate Stamp

Most third class bulk rate mailings have indicia (printed marks in the upper right corner bearing the postal permit number of the sender or letter shop) or are metered using a postage meter. If the choice is between indicia and meters, choose metering, even if your letter shop charges a slight premium. Indicia have the look and feel of third class mail, but metered marks make your pieces look like first class mail.

However, there is a third option: bulk rate stamps. These are available from the Post Office in coils and, although they don't have quite the same impact as first class stamps, they still make your mailing resemble a first class mailing and should generate a higher response rate or at least result in fewer people throwing it away. Many letter shops have automated machinery for affixing these stamps at reasonable cost.

Please note that if you mail first class, you should request that your letter shop affix first class stamps rather than meter the mail. You might also want to stamp each letter First Class, so recipients know they are getting a first class letter rather than a third class direct mail advertising piece.

6. Giftwrap Your Package

Many people enjoy shopping by mail because when the package arrives, it's like a birthday or Christmas. The way to capitalize on this is to decorate the outgoing envelope like a giftwrapped box, with printed ribbons wrapped around the corner. It's hard for anybody to throw away something that looks like a present.

7. Simulate Urgent or Express Mail

One way to get attention is to use envelopes that resemble Express Mail, Federal Express, telegrams, and other urgent or overnight communications. If you choose this approach, be sure to get written approval from your local postmaster for your outer envelope before you mail. The Post Office has strict rules about what is acceptable practice and what is not when it comes to envelopes that deliberately masquerade as urgent, express, or other speedy formats.

8. Use Seals

Foil seals, affixed to the outer envelope, can help emphasize an offer or other special message (e.g., a tenth company anniversary) and draw attention to your mailing piece.

9. Send Bulky Mailings

Another surefire gambit is to put something inside the envelope that adds weight or is three dimensional. People find bulky envelopes irresistible and must open them to see what is inside. A product sample or inexpensive premium makes an ideal mailing stuffer. Teaser copy can further arouse curiosity (e.g., "Your **free** [name of gift] enclosed!").

10. Simulate an Interoffice Envelope

This is an unusual format and not terribly expensive. It uses brown kraft paper stock with six punched holes in it so the yellow paper inside shows through, and it appears as if it's an interoffice memo. Because of the novelty of the device, people tend to open it.

REPLY CARDS

Every mailing should contain at least three elements: the sales letter, the outer envelope, and a reply card or form. You can also add other elements, such as a brochure, reply envelope, and other inserts, but the outer envelope, letter, and reply device are mandatory.

A simple reply card:

- Has a headline that repeats the offer or main selling proposition in a positive way and in the reader's voice (first person), for example, "Yes, I'd like to reduce my printing costs by 30 percent or more!"

- Enables the reader to order or request more information by checking off the appropriate boxed items (e.g., ❑ "Yes, please send me a free copy of your brochure" or ❑ "Yes, please enter my one-year subscription to *Kick Boxing* today").

- In a lead-generating response device, you should offer both a hard and a soft option. A hard option requires personal contact between seller and prospect (e.g., "Yes, please have a salesperson call me"). A soft option typically involves the sending of more information with no personal contact mentioned (e.g., "Please send me more information and sample wall fabrics").

- In a mail order reply device, be sure to include complete details on price, guarantees, terms, conditions, and instructions on how to order. Spell out all order options. Give complete instructions.

- If no salesperson is going to follow up by telephone, put on the reply card the following copy: "No salesperson will call." This will increase response rates.

- If making an inquiry or asking for a sample does not obligate the prospect to make a commitment or buy the product, add the phrase, "No obligation, of course."

- Personalizing the response device, either by affixing a label with the prospect's name and address or by imprinting the reply card with the prospect's name and address using a laser or ink-jet system, makes it easier for the prospect to respond and thus will usually increase response rates.

- In the section of the card where you require the prospect to fill in name, address, and other personal information, leave plenty of room to write in the information.

- Instead of "Name" on the first line of this section of the reply card, put "Mr./Mrs./Ms./Miss." According to Bob Jurik, chairman of Fala Direct Marketing, 80 percent of prospects circle the appropriate prefix. As a result, you find out whether your customers are predominantly male or female, and you can tailor your direct mail accordingly. You also capture information for your customer database, enabling you to correctly address future mailings to these prospects as well as to tailor separate male and female versions of your sales letters, if appropriate.

- Use a business reply card instead of asking the prospect to supply postage. This increases response rates in consumer mailings and makes you look more professional to business prospects.

- Instead of printing your reply cards on plain white stock, use a bright color such as blue, yellow, salmon, canary, gold, or green. Using a different color makes the reply card stand out from the letter and other elements, increasing response rates. In one recent test, Scott Paper found that a blue reply card outperformed a white reply card (identical in every other respect but color) by approximately 30 percent.

THE IMPORTANCE OF TESTING

Because direct mail results can be easily and precisely measured, you can test various approaches, formats, and packages to determine what works best.

Nothing is guaranteed to work; only a test will tell whether a particular mailing is better or worse than other mailings you've done. A case in point is the Scott Paper test: It is one thing to theorize that colored reply cards will outpull white; only a test gives you true and meaningful results.

One important factor to test in mail order promotions is price. One firm selling a cassette album tested three prices:

1. $79.95
2. $89.95
3. $99.95

Which do you think was the winner? Surprisingly, the lowest price is not always the best, because price affects people's perception of the product and its value. After all, which brain surgeon would you want to go to—the one who charges $3,000 for an operation or the one who says the bill is $30?

For the cassette album, 2 was the winner. The $99.95 price did not pull any orders. But the $89.95 price beat the $79.95 price by a 5 to 3 ratio.

This same advertiser performed another interesting test. In its mailings, it illustrated its letters with photos in the upper right corner of page one. The question: Was it better to show a picture of the cassette album itself or of the speaker or writer or producer of the program? The firm tested two packages, one with a picture of the album and one with the speaker's picture. The mailing with the picture of the cassette album produced 40 percent more sales than the mailing with the speaker's picture (and he is goodlooking). The conclusion: It is best to picture the item being sold, not the seller.

Another firm, a newsletter publisher, tested a variety of mailing formats including direct response postcards, double postcards (a small self-mailer consisting of two attached postcards, one of which can be detached and mailed as a business reply card), and traditional number 10 direct mail packages. They found that on postcard deck mailings, the best offer was a free sample issue with the option to write "cancel" on the invoice if not satisfied. Thirty percent of respondents canceled but the low cost of postcard decks made the medium cost-effective.

Although double postcards are being hyped as the new supermedium in direct mail, they were not clear winners and did not outperform conventional number 10 envelopes, either on a total sales or on a cost-per-order basis.

It is important to keep in mind that tests don't instantly result in ironclad rules. Unlike physics, where universal laws hold true throughout the entire universe, test results are valid only for the product, offer, and time period during which they were obtained. What this means is that you can use the test results of others only as a guideline, not as an absolute dictum. Only the test results for your own mailings tell you what works—and what doesn't—for you.

THE FOUR RULES OF TESTING

Rule 1: Key Code

Key coding means adding a key to the mailing label so you can identify which test cell (group of test mailings) a particular response has come from. The list broker renting lists of names to you can key code labels for a slight extra charge, usually $1 or $2 per 1,000 labels.

For key coding to work, you have to make sure you put the right labels on the right mailing pieces. For example, if you are testing two letters with the same reply card, affix labels with key code A on those reply cards going into envelopes containing letter A; affix B labels to package B reply cards.

Another obvious but sometimes overlooked fact is that if you want to count responses by key code, you must design your mailing so that the label comes back with the reply card. For instance, in a lead-generating direct mail package, affix the label directly to the reply card, which shows through a window on the outer envelope.

You can also key code telephone responses. For instance, you can add copy after the phone number that says "ask for Andy" or "ask for extension 222." "Andy" could be a key code for mailing piece A, "Extension 222" could be a key code for mailing piece B, and so on.

Rule 2: The Single Variable Rule

To find out the effect of changing a variable in the mailing, your test can alter only one variable at a time. For instance, if you want to test whether a colored reply card increases response rates, the color of the reply card should be the only element that is changed between package A and package B. They should be identical in all other respects. If package B also has a different brochure or offers the product at a different price or has any other different variables, then you cannot come to any valid conclusion about the effect of changing the reply card color.

Rule 3: The 2,000-Name Rule

How many pieces must you test to get a statistically valid response? Several books, including the *Complete Direct Mail List Book* and *The Basics of Testing*, present statistical tables used to determine how many pieces you must mail, based on the degree of accuracy of results desired and the anticipated response rate.

Without going into the details, a safe rule of thumb is that you should mail 2,000 pieces in each test cell to consider the results statistically valid. If you are testing package A against package B, you need to mail 2,000 As and 2,000 Bs.

Rule 4: The Roll-Out Rule

Let's say you have a list of 2 million names and a test of 2,000 proves your mailing works. Can you predict that the same results will hold true for the entire list based on that small sampling and roll out, or send your test package, to the full list at once? No.

A safe rule of thumb to follow is that your roll-out should be no more than ten times the size of your test cell. Thus, if you test 2,000 names and get a good result, you can roll-out to 20,000. If you then mail 20,000, and the results hold steady, you can safely go to 200,000, and then to 2 million.

CHOOSING MAILING LISTS

According to Steve Roberts, president of Edith Roman Associates, a mailing list broker, there are approximately 30,000 different mailing lists available for rental representing a combined database of some one billion names. "There are few persons in the United States whose names are not on at least one of these mailing lists." Most lists are provided as Cheshire labels, a format that letter shops can easily affix to envelopes using automated equipment designed for that purpose.

Lists are also available on pressure-sensitive labels, but these should not be ordered since they are not easily affixed by machinery and most letter shops charge extra for handling them. The only time to use pressure-sensitive labels is in small mailings you are assembling by hand in-house.

If you are going to computer personalize your mailing, you can order your list from the list broker on magnetic tape or floppy disk instead of labels. Letter shops can personalize using three basic methods: ink-jet, impact, and laser. An ink-jet printer literally sprays the recipient's name and address onto the envelope, letter, or reply element. Although it is the least expensive method, it least resembles a personally typed letter.

Impact letters are formed by striking an inked ribbon that leaves ink on the paper, just like a typewriter or dot-matrix printer. Impact printing can be costly and slow, but is frequently used for mailings requiring an urgent or telegram-like appearance.

Laser printers use an electromagnetic process. Charged particles adhere to the entire sheet, and the computer determines which stay on and which stay off. Lasers are the fastest method, provide the maximum flexibility in type style (and can even reproduce handwritten signatures on letters), and look most like a professional, hand-typed letter.

If you want to measure the response to your mailings, you should either affix the Cheshire label or ink-jet or laser the recipient's name and address onto the reply form, so you get the label back when the reader uses the reply element to respond. Be sure to tell the list broker to add a key code to the label. The key code tells you which mailing list the label is from, so you can compare relative response rates generated by the different mailing lists you are testing.

Mailing lists should always be tested, particularly if you are a consumer marketer mailing large volumes. Experience proves that a mailing piece sent to the best-performing list can generate over ten times the response rate as the same mailing piece sent to the worst-performing list. But you cannot predict which list will be best or worst. You can guess, but you can't know for sure except by testing.

If you mail large volumes, you should test 2,000 to 5,000 names per list on those lists you think are likely candidates. Then, evaluate the results and mail only to those lists that proved profitable in testing. The initial test mailing itself is unlikely to prove profitable, but you will find that one or two lists in the test are productive. You then mail the bulk of your pieces to these lists only, to have an overall profitable program.

How many lists to test? The more, the better. Direct marketing consultant Ken Morris advises clients to test a minimum of five lists and preferably eight lists, along with one or two postcard decks. If you are conducting a test program, do not forget to have the list broker key code your reply cards.

What do lists cost to rent? It depends on the type of list. Compiled lists, or lists taken from various published sources (Yellow Pages, industry directories, etc.) are least expensive, costing around $50 per thousand. Response lists are lists of people who have responded to previous mailings from other companies and purchased products through direct mail. These lists are more expensive, ranging from $75 to $125 per thousand or more. Adding key coding results in a small additional charge, usually only $1 or $2 per thousand.

Which type of list is best for you? It depends. Compiled lists are best when you want to ensure complete coverage of prospects fitting a certain description; for example, if you want to reach all accountants and lawyers in Michigan and Florida, only a compiled list can accomplish that.

However, if you are asking for the order directly from your package (i.e., selling by mail as opposed to trying for leads), response lists are the best choice. Compiled lists rarely work for mail order offers, because research shows that one-third of Americans do not buy via mail. Thus, there is tremendous waste on compiled lists for mail order marketers. Response lists usually promise that 95 percent or more of the people on the list are direct mail buyers. (Look for the phrase "95 percent direct mail generated" in the data card or spec sheet describing the list.)

Mike Pavlish points out that in mail order selling, the best prospect is someone who has bought something similar to what you are selling, at a similar price, and done so recently. Thus, if you are promoting a $795 seminar on Effective Direct Marketing, look for lists of people who have attended other high-priced seminars in your geographic region on advertising and marketing topics.

Sometimes you don't want to mail to an entire list, but only to a portion of it (for example, women only, men only, managers and not workers, people over 50, people under 30). Check the data card (the brochure or flier giving a description of the list) to see what selection factors are available. There is usually a $5 per thousand charge for each selection factor chosen. But experience proves that making intelligent selections usually more than pays back this extra cost.

If you target geographically, you must tell the list broker which ZIP codes you want to select. You cannot simply say, "Names within 50 miles of Rochester, NY," you must provide the correct ZIP codes; the broker will not do it for you. For this reason, you need a good ZIP code map showing the five-digit ZIP codes for every region of the United States.

One proven method for reducing mailing lists is called merge/purge, which means the lists you order are run through a computer to eliminate duplicate names. For instance, if a name appears on three of your five lists, and you don't do a merge and purge, you will get the name on three labels, and that person will receive three copies of your package. If you do a merge and purge, two of the three labels having that person's name will be eliminated and he or she will get only one package.

When should you merge and purge? Consultant Art Yates says that the duplication factor runs 10 to 25 percent for business lists and up to 40 percent for consumer lists, and that merge/purge pays when mailing to 50,000 names or more. Minimum processing charges for a merge/purge are around $1,000, says Yates.

DAVID YALE'S TIPS FOR GETTING BETTER RESULTS FROM YOUR MAILING LISTS

The following is reprinted from *DM News* with the author's permission:

> Managing list selection had always been a problem for our small, lean and mean newsletter publishing operation. Time was always at a premium, we didn't have adequate tools for tracking and analyzing list performance, and we had no mechanism in place for avoiding re-use of the same names across product lines.
>
> The broker we were using did not address any of these problems, despite our healthy volume of five to seven million names annually.
>
> Even worse, their recommendations were usually limited to lists they managed themselves. Some of their recos were for lists that hadn't been updated for a year or more.
>
> We decided to ask for more, and started discussions with a small boutique broker who was very interested in meeting our needs—and suggesting additional ways she could serve our account. The resulting changes in how we select and track lists have had a major impact.
>
> Here are the six critical services we are getting from our new list broker—and the positive changes that have resulted from them.
>
> **1. List Performance Histories:** We had excellent data for individual list performance on a promotion-by-promotion basis. But we didn't have the staff to compile and analyze the data on an ongoing basis. Now that our list broker maintains list performance histories for us, we know the overall profitability of a list historically, and whether its performance is holding steady, rising, or falling. These measurements are in net income as well as response and break-even rates. They've helped us pinpoint and end a problem we had with continuations of marginally profitable lists.
>
> **2. List Usage Histories:** We didn't have an adequate system to track list usage, so we weren't catching reuse of the same names for more than one product within a short time frame. Since we work with a small—and contracting—universe, we strongly suspected that overmailing to the same names was depressing response rates. Our list broker now tracks the use of all of our rent-

ed lists across our entire product line, and warns our product managers before overmailing happens. We are now able to make sure that no names are mailed more than two promotions a month.

3. Long-Term Point of View: Because our new list broker views our relationship as a long-term partnership, she doesn't recommend lists that will mean a quick profit for her but poor results for us. She makes sure that all her recos are for lists that have been updated and cleaned within the past year. Because she is continually monitoring the results of our promotions, she is learning what works—and why.

4. Really Knowing Our Product Line: We insisted that our new list broker had to read our publications—all of them. The response was enthusiastic, and judging by the substantive questions she asks about them, the interest is genuine. Needless to say, her understanding of our product line helps her make recos that are right on target.

5. Net Name Arrangements: Our new broker suggested we pursue net name arrangements, something we had not done because we didn't have the staff to administer it. She made the process remarkably simple and handles it herself, based on our merge and purge reports. Since our typical dupe name rate is 20 percent on rented lists, that's a substantial savings on lists for which net name arrangements are possible.

6. Split Commissions: The proposal from our new broker included split commissions, which means that she gives us part of her 20 percent broker's commission as a credit against our invoices, based on volume. Combining this credit with net name arrangements, the savings are substantial. In fact, we've determined that even though we had been getting a 20 percent broker's commission on many of the lists we rent (we are, in fact, brokers, with a stable of lists we rent out widely), we came out ahead by foregoing the 20 percent commission and taking advantage of the commission split and the net name arrangements.

Of course it is critical that we supply our broker with timely information in order to make this partnership work. We have made sure our product managers fax our broker list performance spreadsheets, merge and purge reports, and interlist duplication reports the moment they're received. We've added our list broker to the comp list for all our publications.

Our broker's help has slashed our list reco time from days to hours, and turned an unpleasant and uncertain task into a simple one.

In addition to the obvious—and immediate—bottom-line results, our new broker is able to search the Internet for new lists, and she contacts owners of lists that aren't on the market. As a result, we are getting recos for lists we've never heard of, which helps us test beyond our traditional marketplace.

TIPS ON DESIGNING DIRECT MAIL BROCHURES

Not all direct mail packages require a brochure; often a letter alone can be extremely effective. When do you need a brochure? The old saying in direct mail is, "The letter sells; the brochure tells." Letters are used to make a strong sales pitch and get a response. Brochures play a supporting role, providing information, facts, and photos and drawings that back up the claims made in the letter.

According to the Petty Co., a direct mail printer:

Brochures receive their impact from a combination of strong four-color art and clever folding techniques. When striving for a luxury look for a deluxe product, use a four-color process on coated stock. Using special metallic inks can deliver impact that provides a rate of response that will pay for itself.

Attention-getting design is required when you are planning to execute a deluxe brochure. Graphic images that are overlapping keep the prospect moving through your piece.

Strategic overlapping of folds leads the reader to each element of your sales story, while building excitement and enhancing the offer as the person reads.

In photographs, have models demonstrate the product in a way that a standard product shot cannot. Photo sequence action shots provide a good way to build action or excitement into your brochure and save money on separations if the shots are all the same size. Photographs should also be prominent to achieve maximum attention-getting power.

Check out the feasibility of any fold running the full depth of the piece. Ask the printer if the stock selected can take the number of folds you want without cracking on the fold mark.

Exciting die-cut edges in provocative shapes on the opening edge can achieve interest in a brochure because they attract attention.

By far the most expensive investment is in the printing. It should be noted that the most cost-intensive part of printing is the paper. For instance, on the printing of a 22-1/2 × 35" four-color brochure, the cost of the paper is $7,500 out of a total cost of $14,000, or 54 percent of the cost.

The cost of stock absorbs from 36 percent to over 50 percent of the job. The kind of stock you select for your printing will have the most influence on your final printing costs.

Request samples of paper of varying styles (dull versus gloss coated), different opacities, and varying weights. Match them against one another. Ascertain their availability on roll-out quantities. Ask your printer how the stock prints. Test-run a sample if you can, or examine other printed samples.

GETTING PAST THE SECRETARY

In business-to-business direct mail, a special concern is getting past the secretary. The problem is that many secretaries screen mail for their bosses and throw away items they judge unimportant. Thus, a direct mail envelope design that might intrigue a consumer or even a business executive has the unfortunate effect of tagging your mailing piece as junk mail, which secretaries safely assume they have the authority and responsibility to eliminate from the bosses' mail piles.

According to a research study from Ogilvy & Mather Direct, most executives do not open their own mail. Fifty-eight percent of top executives and 51 percent of middle managers have their secretaries open their mail for them. Half of the executives who have secretaries open mail also have secretaries screen mail. Therefore, it is important to devise ways to ensure that your mailing will survive this screening. The Ogilvy & Mather study is based on a survey of 500 business executives.

Richard Kerndt, president of the Richmark Group, conducted his own study by interviewing 53 secretaries of presidents or general managers in divisions of large corporations. He found that 87 percent of the secretaries see themselves as the gatekeepers of all mail flowing into the executive suite. To be successful in surviving this screening process, mailers should follow these key rules:

- Acknowledge that the secretary or administrative assistant is the initial audience.
- Use a design that connotes image and quality, rather than the consumer hard-sell approach.
- Create mailings that are short, simple, and easy to understand.
- Use personalization.
- Use accurate mailing lists so the right mailings are sent to the right audience.

As a rule of thumb, the higher the executive is on the corporate ladder, the more the mailing should look like a personally typed business letter and the less promotional in nature it should be. The lower you go on the corporate ladder, the more you can use nonpersonalized mail and a more promotional approach.

Tip: One way to force your way past the secretarial gatekeeper is to send the executive something that the secretary feels she or he cannot pass judgment on or does not have the authority to discard without first showing it to the boss. One company accomplished this by mailing videocassettes presenting a motion picture version of their brochure on tape. Another put their message on audio cassette and mailed it to CEOs with a Sony Walkman tape player included in the package. Another tactic is to mail a book, a special report, or a nice premium personalized with the recipient's name.

HOW TO GET MORE LEADS FROM YOUR MAILINGS

If you are trying to generate leads from your direct mail rather than sell via mail order, these tips from Mike Pavlish can help you generate more inquiries:

- Get your special offer high up in the letter. Everyone is tempted by a good offer. Make sure they see it fast, especially if it's a free offer. (See the checklist in Figure 15.2 for ideas on free offers.)
- If offering something free, state that on the outside envelope.

- Offer printed information—a booklet or pamphlet. The offer of free printed information hikes response rates.
- Put a time limit on your offer.
- Use involvement devices on your reply card. Check-off boxes work well.
- Use a hard-selling P.S. Feature a big benefit and call for immediate action.
- Use testimonials from satisfied customers.
- Use at least a two-page letter. It will almost always outpull a one-page letter because more sales copy can be used to convince the reader.
- Don't put your company name on the envelope if you regularly mail to the same people. Vary the appearance of your envelopes. Otherwise, people will know what's inside and pitch them.
- Try a blank envelope with no teaser copy. It often works better than using envelope copy. Curiosity makes the recipient open it.
- Close hard for a response right **now**. Tell readers why they should respond today. Tell them what they lose if they don't, because 95 percent of readers won't respond "later," even if they intend to. It's now or never.
- Don't talk about your company unless a customer benefit is in the same or next sentence. Readers don't care that you're the biggest company, unless it means they get better service.
- List **all** the benefits. Stress the most important one, but also list the others. The one extra benefit in your list might be what gets a reader to respond.
- Tell the reader how popular your product is. People like popular, proven things.
- Tell your prospects what they care about most: how much money they'll make. The potential for extra profits is a surefire, never-fails benefit. Be specific.
- If your prospects don't think they need your product, develop the problem they have first, then give the solution. If they don't perceive a problem, they won't be open to your solution.
- Say that there is no obligation to buy. Even if readers assume it, they are more likely to respond if you stress it.
- Include your telephone number. Many people prefer to call rather than write, especially those with an immediate need.
- Always use a separate, detached reply card.

TEN DIRECT MAIL COPYWRITING TIPS

Here are ten techniques guaranteed to make your next mailing more profitable:

1. Talk about the reader's needs. Too many mailings are manufacturer-oriented. They talk about the sellers' pet interests rather than the readers' problems and needs. But readers are more concerned with what's on their minds than with what is on yours. Here's the opening of a letter mailed to creative directors, ad managers, and editors:

> "International Stock Photography Ltd. is a quality stock house serving the advertising, corporate and editorial markets. Our files contain some of the finest images available..."

This lead is advertiser-oriented. It boasts about the advertiser's firm, but fails to tell readers why they should care or how the service can solve their business problems.

Compare this with the following letter from a company selling beach property:

> "If you love the city...but long for cool ocean breezes and quiet moonlit beaches, then you should know that your dreams can come true with your own ocean-front vacation home."

This letter succeeds because it addresses a need—the reader's need to get away from the city on vacation. It is also effective because it promises a reward ("your dreams can come true"), paints a picture of the reward ("cool ocean breezes and quiet moonlit beaches"), and gets right to the point (you can own an oceanfront home).

2. Start off with a strong lead. Experienced direct mail marketers know that the average reader scans a letter for just five seconds before deciding whether to read it or throw it away. If your opening doesn't hook readers within five seconds, you've lost them.

It pays to put your strongest sales argument right up front. Don't "warm up" with chit-chat or secondary sales arguments. Don't hold back the most important point for the "big finish." If you do, most readers will never get to it.

For example, if your new heating system cuts fuel costs by 50 percent, don't start off with, "Good morning. I'd like to spend a few minutes chatting with you about an important subject. It's a vital piece of equipment that's keeping your toes toasty even when we speak...but one that's costing you much more money than it should."

Instead, get right to the point:

> "Now you can cut your fuel bills by 30%, 40%, even 50% or more. The enclosed Technical Bulletin tells you how it's done..."

3. State the offer up front. Many sales letters focus on getting the reader to send for free literature. The reader is told, "To receive a free copy of our new product bulletin, just complete and mail the enclosed business reply card."

This offer is usually made in the letter's last paragraph. You can increase response rates by stating the offer in the opening of the letter as well as at the end. Many people will only glance at the lead paragraph of a direct mail letter and then throw the letter away. You can get some of these people to respond by putting the offer up front, as in this sales letter offering life insurance policies for children:

> "There's no gift more meaningful...for the children you love, than the one discussed in a new free pamphlet. It is yours with my compliments if you'll just mail the enclosed card."

The offer is repeated twice more, once in the fourth paragraph and again in the last paragraph.

4. Get personal. A letter, unlike an ad or a TV commercial, is a personal communication, and that's how it should sound—like one person talking to another. A formal, stiff, corporate tone is inappropriate for direct mail. Pompous writing alienates readers; friendly, conversational writing wins them over.

You can't fool readers into thinking direct mail is personal mail. But if you write warmly, sincerely, and naturally, readers will react as if you had sent a personally written letter...even though they know you haven't.

Personal pronouns help make writing sound like natural conversation. So do contractions and an occasional colloquial or slang expression. Here's a sample of appropriate copy style for direct mail, from a letter selling mail order booklets on telephone techniques:

> I wish you could meet Helen...She's the woman who wrote "Your Telephone Personality," our special training program to improve the way people handle their telephone calls. She's so warm, perceptive, and pleasant, you couldn't help but be favorably impressed.

This mailing comes alive, because it deals with a flesh-and-blood person and not just sales talk, statistics, and product specifications.

5. Narrow the focus. The most powerful reason for turning to direct mail is that it lets you target your message to select groups of special interest readers. Yet a surprising number of industrial marketers fail to exploit this opportunity.

Aim your mailing at a narrow audience and highlight the solutions your product offers for its specific problems. The same product may offer different benefits to different groups of users. Take microcomputers, for example. Freelance writers are interested primarily in word processing capability and reasonable cost. A small business might be more concerned with service and customized software. A large corporation would want to know if the microcomputer is compatible with current equipment and if multiple micros can be linked in a network.

A single mailing that attempted to cover all these points would have far less impact than separate mailings tailored to the three distinct audiences. Which of the two lead sentences printed below, for example, would have more appeal to freelance writers?

Focused: "I'm going to tell you how you can make a lot more money writing...without spending any more time on your work."

General: "XYZ Technology, Inc. proudly introduces the latest in personal computers—the XYZ PC-160."

6. Know how much to tell. A client asked me to prepare a mailing to generate inquiries about a new evaporator. The people on his mailing list were engineers already familiar with evaporators. The mailings, which consisted of a short letter and a reply card, focused on the specific advantage of the client's evaporator over all others.

A month later, this same client wanted to do a mailing on a new type of inspection and maintenance service for waste treatment equipment. Because such a service was unique and had never been offered by any manufacturer, readers needed to be educated from scratch. The mailing consisted of a letter and a reply card plus an additional element—a pamphlet explaining how the program worked. More complete information was needed because readers were unfamiliar with what was being offered.

Here are some guidelines for determining how much information to include in your mailings:

- If you are offering a product through mail order (office supplies, machine parts, books, courses), give the full story.

- If you are offering free literature, describe the highlights of what the reader will learn from the brochure and offer key benefits of the product it describes. Your letter should whet the reader's appetite for the information you are offering.

- If you are selling a familiar concept, stress its one or two strongest advantages over similar products or services. If your concept is unique, you need to educate readers—let them know what it's all about.

- If you want a large number of leads, keep it short. If you want fewer but more qualified leads, give more information—complete technical details, prices, specifications.

7. Try the simplest format first. The most basic direct mail package is a letter and reply card mailed in a number 10 envelope. This format is both effective and inexpensive—printing costs run about $140 per thousand. Add a pop-up, a premium, a color brochure, photographs, diagrams, special envelopes, or other extras, and costs quickly skyrocket.

Does this mean creative mailers and gimmicks should be shunned? Not at all. But you should try the basic letter before any other format. Remember, the most profitable mailing is the one that generates the best response rate at the lowest cost. A gussied-up, four-color mailing may tickle everyone's fancy, but it is a waste if it pulls the same 5 percent response rate as the plain but powerful one-page letter.

Start with a plain old letter. Then add a new element—a second color, a photograph, a see-through envelope, a circular, a product sample. If the response rate goes up enough to justify the cost, great! If it doesn't, go back to the tried and proven letter.

8. What gimmicks work? Which ones don't? Here's a partial list of popular direct mail techniques along with an evaluation of their effectiveness in business-to-business selling.

- *Three-D.* A solid object enclosed with the mailing can boost response rates dramatically, because people almost always open an envelope that feels bulky. But even a cheap enclosure can increase mailing costs by 50 cents to $1 a piece or more.

- *Product sample.* When mailable, these add considerably to the selling power of direct mail. But beware: If the product is too intriguing or fun to play with, it may distract your audience from your sales message.

- *Personalized letters.* Personalization can increase response rates if it looks authentic. In business mailing, word processors are used to generate computerized letters that look identical to hand-typed ones. The old-style ink-jet mailings—the gaudy letters with the person's name noticeably inserted into a form letter—don't work in business-to-business direct mail.

- *Circulars and self-mailers.* Mailings without letters—circulars, broadsides, and self-mailers—are usually not as effective as mailings that include a letter. The exception is when you regularly mail sales notices and special offers to your list of current customers.

- *Postcard packs.* These produce a large number of leads at low cost. But because recipients request free literature based on reading a minimum of copy, the quality of the leads is questionable.

- *Premium.* If you offer a free gift (a book, calendar, key ring, coffee mug, pen set), you will be flooded with responses. But most of them simply want your freebie and have little interest in your product. Premiums should only be offered in mailings aimed at lists of highly qualified buyers.

- *Teaser copy.* With the right message, teaser copy, printed only on the outer envelope, can arouse curiosity and get more people to open your mailing. On the other hand, the danger of teaser copy is that it alerts readers with the message, "This is junk mail. You can save time by throwing it away." Many people do just that.

9. Make it painless to respond. The easier it is to respond to your mailing, the more responses you'll get. This is why many trade magazines now use peel-off address labels that can be attached to a reader service card. The label saves readers the trouble of writing in their names and addresses on the card.

Always include a reply card with your mailing—preferably a postage-paid business reply card. Leaving out the card says to the reader, "Don't bother responding to this letter."

Most readers just want to receive a brochure and won't respond if they think they'll be called by a salesperson. If you plan to follow up with a phone call or personal visit, don't mention that in your mailing.

Some mailers include detailed spec sheets or questionnaires for the reader to fill out and return. The information provided by the reader helps the manufacturer quote a price or size the product. However, many prospects—even those who want to buy—don't want to bother filling in a detailed questionnaire. If you use a spec sheet, also include a reply card the reader can mail to request a brochure. Then, when you follow up on the lead, you can get the information you need in person or over the phone.

Many high-tech marketers targeting a sophisticated audience eliminate paper reply forms and just substitute Web site or E-mail addresses for response. Experience indicates it may be better to offer E-mail and Web site response *in addition* to a reply card, phone call, or fax response, but not *instead* of them. A software marketer that has always used only phone, fax, or E-mail as the reply options to direct mail recently added an order card as another option to use in making an inquiry. "We were surprised to receive more replies by mail than by any of the other methods," says the marketer. "Even supposedly sophisticated users of high-tech products prefer mail when they respond" (as reported in *Micro Software Marketing*, June 1997, p. 3).

10. Choose the right mailing list. A skilled copywriter can produce a mailer that pulls two to three times the number of responses of the previous mailing. But selecting the best list over the worst list can increase response rates tenfold.

The best list names buyers with proven interest in what you're selling—your list of current customers and people who inquired about your company or its products through advertising, publicity, trade shows, or contact with salespeople and distributors.

Second best is a list of people who are proven buyers of the type of product you're selling. For example, if you're selling a lubricating oil, mail to a list of people who have purchased lubricating oil within the past six months. This list is far more valuable than a list of people who merely have the "right credentials," (i.e., people who have a particular job title or who fall under a certain Standard Industrial Classification).

Figure 15.2. Checklist of basic direct mail offers.

❏ Free brochure

❏ Free booklet

❏ Free catalog

❏ Free special report

❏ Free newsletter

❏ Free information kit

❏ Free seminar (invitation to attend)

❏ Free information

❏ More information

❏ Free trial

❏ Free use of product

❏ Free product sample

❏ Free gift certificate

❏ Free coupon

❏ Use of toll-free hotline

❏ Free advice

❏ Free consultation

❏ Free survey

❏ Free analysis

❏ Free estimate

❏ Free problem evaluation

❏ Free product demonstration

❏ Have a technical representative call

❏ Have a salesperson call

❏ Add my name to your mailing list

❏ Not interested right now because: (Please give reason; thank you.)

❏ Not interested right now. Try me again (month/year).

❏ Free audiocassette

❏ Free videotape or film

❏ Free gift (with your inquiry)

❏ Free gift (enclosed with mailing)

❏ Free gift (for providing the names and addresses of friends or colleagues who might be interested in our offer)

❏ Free sample issue

❏ Free information to qualified prospects only—others pay X dollars

❏ Free information if requested on your company letterhead

Sample One-page sales letter.

CONSULTING SERVICES
BOX 2722 CONROE, TX 77305

"OIL & GAS WELL DRILLING & COMPLETION PATENTS"
"COILED TUBING PATENTS"

11/7/99

Mr. Dale Fain
25714 Mill Pond Lane
Spring, TX 77373-3144

Dear Mr. Fain:

Now it is easy for you to stay current with the latest engineering developments concerning oil well drilling and completion. At the present time, the U.S. Patent Office issues between 40 and 80 of these types of patents each month. Now you can know about the new industry developments that will affect your business.

The Monthly Patent News enables you to study and understand the patent drawings and information on a continuing and timely basis. This research, if provided to only one company, would cost hundreds of dollars a month. With our services you stay current for about a $1.00 a patent.

I want you to understand the actual type of information you will receive. Please see the enclosed sheet that shows a patent. Note that summary text and usually one drawing are included for each patent. We do offer a service to provide complete copies for those subjects that are of interest to you. With our quick and easy patent presentation format, it is simple to start your own patent library.

Of course the patent information is important to engineers. Also, in most organizations, both marketing and management groups find that this is a quick way to stay up to date with the industry's new directions.

We invite you to evaluate our publication, "Oil & Gas Well Drilling & Completion Patents" without any financial risk. Just fill out the attached Order Form and send it to us with your company Check or Purchase Order. With our **MONEY-BACK GUARANTEE**, we will send you the next issue and if you are not completely satisfied, notify us in writing and a full refund or credit will be issued. This offer is good for three weeks after the first issue is mailed to you. It is important to us to have you as a continuing satisfied customer.

Very truly yours,

J.B. Saunders
Publisher

P.S. Subscribe now and receive a FREE copy of our latest publication "Coiled Tubing Patents." This valuable $74.95 book is included with all subscriptions for a limited time. See the enclosed information for details. This offer is good through December 31, 1999.

PHONE 409-273-1289; FAX 409-273-3159

Chapter

POSTCARD 16 DECKS

AN INTRODUCTION TO POSTCARD DECKS

A postcard deck is a group of direct response postcards mailed to a list of prospects. A direct response postcard is a postcard that combines an ad and a response vehicle on a 3 1/2" × 5 1/2" (piece of stiff paper.

Typically the front of the card, known as the mailing side, contains the mailing address of the advertiser and is designed so that the card will be mailed back to the advertiser when it is dropped in the mail box. The mailing side is typically a business reply card, although some advertisers require the prospect to affix a stamp.

The back of the card is the advertising side. It contains a small ad or sales pitch for the product, typically a headline, a small picture, and a few lines of copy.

A third element is a coupon area where the prospect can fill in a name and address to place an order or receive more information. The coupon can be located either on the mailing side (in the upper left corner of the card) or on the advertising side (usually at the bottom of the panel).

As an advertiser, you have two choices when it comes to doing postcard deck advertising: You can pay to insert your card in one of the many decks that accept advertising, or you can create your own postcard pack containing numerous postcards for the various products you offer. The latter option will work only if you sell a line of related products.

According to Ed Werz, a consultant specializing in postcard deck advertising, the use of direct response postcards is on the upswing. "A decade ago, only a handful of decks existed. Today, one can count nearly seven hundred postcard decks, with new publications added every month."

The average deck, says Werz, is published three times a year with a circulation of 75,000. "As a medium, postcard decks are low-cost, highly responsive, quick to react, and extremely measurable," adds Werz. "No wonder thousands of advertisers are adding card decks to their media schedules each year."

Robert Luedtke, coauthor of *Merchandising Through Card Decks* (Solar Press), says inquiry cards occasionally generate up to a 2 percent response rate per card in a pack of 60 to 70 cards. Bill Norcutt, author of *Secrets of Successful Response Deck Advertising*, says that the cost per lead for inquiries generated from card decks is generally $2 to $20 and can be as low as 50 cents. This compares favorably with $15 to $30 per lead generated by a full-scale direct mail package and $80 per lead from an industrial ad in a trade journal.

"A top, top card (information request) could pull one percent of the total deck circulation," says Norcutt. "I have heard of some offers pulling two percent, and in some very specialized decks as much as five percent, but these are exceptions, not the rule." Norcutt says the average to expect would probably be around one-half of one percent. Business-to-Business, Inc., a postcard deck publisher, says that a typical response rate to a postcard is between one-quarter of one percent and one percent of the deck's circulation.

Numbers of responses and percentage response rates depend, to a large extent, on your product. If you are selling a low-priced product that is frequently ordered by prospects, such as supplies, response rates may be higher than if you are selling an expensive piece of capital equipment that few prospects are likely to need or can afford.

Other factors affecting response rates are newness and uniqueness. If you make an offer that has been overdone in the decks, your response rate may be disappointing. However, if you run a card for a new, unusual offer with strong appeal and interest, the response rate will be higher.

14 WAYS CARD DECKS CAN BUILD YOUR BUSINESS

According to Ed Werz, here are 14 ways you can use postcard decks to generate more business:

1. Sell product. Product can be sold right from the card. Items that sell for $100 or less are most effective. Bill Norcutt says that if you offer a "bill-me" option, 50 percent of those who order in response to a postcard will pay your bill, 30 percent will return the merchandise, frequently in unsalable condition, and 20 percent will not pay at all.

2. Generate sales leads. Use the card to create interest in products or services. Qualify prospects with questions about the immediacy of their needs. Don't forget to ask for a phone number so the sales force can make contact.

3. Distribute literature. Use postcard decks to generate inquiries for literature or catalogs. Show a picture of your company's new catalog. Tell how many new products are featured. Offer both a toll-free number and an order coupon.

4. Offer free samples. Ask the prospect to send for a free sample or actually insert the sample in the deck. Consultant Ken Morris, who specializes in direct marketing of high-tech products, says postcard decks are an ideal medium for generating interest in software via the offer of a free demo diskette.

5. Prospect for new customers. Use postcards to get new buyers at little or no cost. Offer a loss leader (an item advertised at a low price in order to attract buyers whose names can be added to your customer list) or heavily discounted items. The sales will offset the advertising cost. You can also use postcards to offer self-liquidators (premiums or samples having a cost fully covered by the purchase price).

6. Introduce new products and services. Get the jump on the competition. Blitz the marketplace through card deck advertising before anyone can make a counter move.

7. Test copy, price, design, or offer. Many decks will let you run an A-B split (e.g., test the headline "Saves Money" against "Easy to Install"). It's an inexpensive way to test price points, headlines, or other elements. Often, the information gained can lead to more successful direct mail efforts.

Robert Luedtke, director of marketing for a firm serving the medical markets, tells how he split-tested five headlines for a seminar titled Management & Marketing Essentials for the Dental Practitioner. The five headlines were:

a. Build Effective Team Leadership

b. Big Marketing Results from a Small Budget

c. Increase Referrals

d. Creating a Unique Practice Image

e. Increase Patient Flow

Can you guess which was the winner? The headline "Increase Patient Flow" generated twice as many inquiries as the others. Apparently, dentists want patients more than they want to build team leadership, get big marketing results, create an image, or even increase referrals.

8. Test mailing lists at low cost. Before renting a list for direct mail, run a postcard in the owner's card deck, if the owner has one. A small investment will provide a good indication of the list responsiveness.

9. Test new markets. Place a card in a vertical market deck before trying direct mail, or test a few markets for the cost of testing one market via direct mail or space advertising.

10. Reduce excess inventory. Overstocked or discontinued items can be liquidated easily via postcard ads.

11. Build a list. Run a free sample, free demo diskette, free catalog, or free brochure offer to bring in new names.

12. Research inexpensively. A survey card placed in card decks can help you acquire valuable information about customers, products, and markets.

13. Build corporate awareness. Card decks can be a low-cost means of distributing news about a company.

14. Support telemarketing. Card decks can quickly generate fresh names for telemarketing reps or salespeople to telephone.

HOW TO DEVELOP A CARD PACK TEST CAMPAIGN

Let's say you want to spend a portion of your marketing communications budget on postcard decks to support print advertising, direct mail, and other activities. Robert Al Degaetano, writing in the newsletter of the Direct Marketing Club of New York, outlined the steps to take:

First, consult an expert. Card packs represent a unique vehicle with special features, warns Degaetano. Many ad agencies, copywriters, and consultants who know direct mail or print advertising may not be familiar with postcard decks or how to use them.

Second, identify target markets and media. In addition to your primary markets, make a list of secondary markets. Because of the low cost per thousand of card decks as opposed to other media, you can afford to advertise in secondary market card decks even if you can't afford to run ads in those industry magazines or do solo mailings to their mailing lists.

Identify specific decks in these markets. Find out the source of the names (where the card deck mailer gets the mailing lists and which ones are used), the packaging used, and the names of some of the regular advertisers. If your competitors repeatedly run postcards in the deck, that's a good sign the deck would work for you.

Third, develop several different offers. Test price, payment terms, headline, copy, place stamp here versus business reply mail, etc.

Note that some publishers may try to get you to use their card packs with a per-inquiry offer, such that you pay a fee per lead or order generated. One of the largest of these publishers, Select Information Exchange, charges advertisers 45 cents per sales lead. The benefit is that there is no risk: If the card pack doesn't perform, you don't pay.

Fourth, locate a control. A control is the deck that will perform best for your offer. The best deck is probably a card pack that mails to a list you have used successfully or goes to the subscriber list of the top trade magazine in which you advertise.

When using this pack, design your postcard so it closely resembles your most successful solo mailing or trade ad. The card deck response rates will give you a correlation factor between mediums. By comparing the cost per inquiry between the space ads in the publication, sending a direct mail piece to its subscriber list, and running a postcard in its card pack, you will be able to determine which medium (space, direct mail, cards) is most cost effective.

Fifth, split-test the control deck. Create different variations on your basic card and test them in the control pack. For example, you might test three sales appeals expressed in three different headlines (e.g., Saves Money, Increases Productivity, Reduces Maintenance Costs) to see which appeal generates the highest response rate. Or, you might test a postcard featuring the product (New Zinger Widget Gives Better Performance) against a postcard that stresses a free literature offer (Free Zinger Widget Catalog).

Split tests generally result in an extra insertion cost of from 60 cents to $2.25 per thousand names, which on a 75,000-name deck runs from $40 to $168.65. (The base cost can be anywhere from $800 to $1,600 or more.) Says Robert Degaetano, "A great deal of information can be obtained using split testing at a very modest cost."

Sixth, once you have tested cards, test decks. Run your most successful card in a number of decks. Depending on your testing budget, it is often wise to test one or two card packs in each market. Remember, card packs can prove profitable in markets you never before considered possible.

Seventh, develop a campaign. Schedule postcard insertions in good card decks three or four times a year to ensure a steady flow of responses. Be prepared to change your schedule depending on performance.

Card decks offer the benefit of rapid responses that can easily be measured and analyzed. Unlike space advertising, brochures, and mail, the only purpose of a postcard deck is to generate direct response. A card is good or not good depending on how many responses it pulls relative to other cards. If something is not working, change it or drop it.

12 SECRETS OF CARD PACK ADVERTISING SUCCESS

1. Use Card Decks As Part of an Overall Campaign

Although card decks are amazingly inexpensive, responsive, and cost-effective, there are not enough card deck mailings going to your prospects to allow you to rely solely on card deck advertising to promote your product or service.

"Don't use packs as an isolated medium," advises Don Rappaport, chairman of the American List Council. Make them part of your overall advertising strategy. Use ads to build image, direct mail to educate prospects and make them understand your new technology, and postcard decks to generate a large quantity of inquiries at low cost.

2. Use Postcards to Qualify Your Prospects

"Many industrial advertisers have learned that direct-response cards can generate a lower-cost inquiry than almost any other medium," observes Jim Alexander, president of Alexander Marketing Services. "But postcards offer another opportunity that few seem to have learned."

The difference between an ad and a postcard, notes Alexander, is that to respond to a trade ad the prospect merely circles a number on a reader service card or makes a phone call, telling you nothing about himself or herself. With a postcard, on the other hand, the prospect must fill in a name and address to respond.

"What a perfect opportunity to ask for a simple declaration to qualify the prospect's interest," says Alexander. "Like, 'I may have an application involving _____ gallons per minute at _____ pounds per square inch and _____ degrees Celsius.' Readers who fill this out—and a surprising number will—have identified a current need and deserve priority follow-up from the field. That's how our clients make their postcards more productive and how you can, too."

3. Convert Proven Postcards into Successful Ads

Jim Alexander says he frequently takes fractional ads created for magazines and converts them into postcard format by adding lines for the respondent's name and address. "We do it for our clients all the time," he notes.

Jim Morris, senior account executive for the Kingswood Group, takes the opposite approach. If a postcard pulls well, Morris converts it to a black and white, quarter-page ad for placement in trade publications. "This provides a cost-effective 'second tier' to a larger space campaign."

4. Design Tiny Billboards

The key to improving the impact of postcards is to treat them as if they were tiny billboards, says Jim Morris. "Use provocative headlines and graphic devices that focus in on essential benefits and on the offer, call for action, or a toll-free number," he writes.

5. Use Horizontal versus Vertical Cards

Most people looking through decks hold them horizontally, and most cards are designed horizontally. Some advertisers design their cards vertically, hoping to be different and stand out from the crowd. Does it work?

No, according to Bill Norcutt, who says that horizontal cards pull better than vertical cards. The problem with a vertical format, says Norcutt, is that it forces the reader to turn the card to read the message—and most won't do this as they quickly flip through a pile of cards.

Of course, in decks where most cards are printed vertically, the standard vertical card pulls better because it fits the format of the pack.

6. Remember the Rule of One Second

Think about how you go through card packs: You rip open the deck and immediately flip through the cards, glancing at each card about one second before deciding whether to toss it in the trash or put it aside for more serious consideration.

"I hypothesize that card scanners do not fully read the cards of interest as they scan but put them aside for later scrutiny," writes consultant Wayne Hepburn. "There is a subtle self-induced pressure to go through the entire pack and react to each card before getting serious about any of them. This is the exact opposite of magazine reading."

For this reason, you have only one second to grab the prospect's attention. Clarity and directness are the keys to doing this. Your offer must be immediately clear. Your sales proposition must literally pop off the card and grab the reader's eye. Cards that do not instantly communicate are trashed without a second thought. As Don Rappaport points out: "Card packs are 100 percent advertising. There's no reason to read them."

7. Recognize the Importance of the Headline

All the card pack experts agree that the headline is important, and most agree that it is the single most important element determining the success or failure of a direct response postcard.

"The headline should name the product, service, or major benefit," says Ed Werz. "The fewer words, the better."

"The headline will make or break the card," adds Robert Luedtke. His advice? "Sell the key benefit. Make it grab the prospect's attention. The headline must be big, bold, and obvious."

Here are examples of postcard headlines stressing benefits:

Your investment can grow from $7,500 to $20,000	(Federal Mailers)
Up to 75 percent discount on commissions when you trade with Charles Schwab...	(Charles Schwab)
How to save money on office supplies	(Quill)

An equally effective tactic is to put a free offer in the postcard headline:

Write for free book: "How to Win at Commodities"	(Murlas)
Amazing free offer—*Think & Grow Rich*	(SMI)
Free penny stock market report	(Stuart James)

Asking a question, a technique proven effective in print ads, also works well with postcards:

How long must you keep important papers?	(Destroy-it)
Applying address labels by hand?	(Heyer, Inc.)
Moving your offices?	(Relocation Management Systems)

Postcards are an action-oriented medium, so command headlines are a natural for postcard deck advertising:

Protect your company's valuable assets	(Seton)
Be a printer...without a press	(Norco)
Earn insured tax-free income	(Clayton Brown)

If your product or idea is news, stress the news aspect in your headline. You can do this by using such words as *new, discover, announcing, now, it's here, at last*, and *just arrived*:

Discover new ways to schedule personnel	(Methods Research)
New anti-slip PVC Buckboard	(Tepromark)
At last! Overnight shipping at 50 percent savings	(Air Shippers)

8. Highlight the Offer

In a direct mail package, you first entice readers with a powerful promise...then outline all the benefits of your product...and only then, once they're hooked and interested, do you make the offer and let price rear its ugly head.

A postcard is different. The space for copy measures only 3 1/2 × 5 1/2 inches, and some of that is taken up by the headline, a photo or illustration, and a coupon. You don't have space for conventional copy. You have to get your message across quickly in concise, almost telegraphic language.

Remember the one-second rule? The reader glancing at your card has to get a complete sense of what you're talking about, right away. As Herschell Lewis points out, "Your offer must be identifiable instantly." This means simple, uncomplicated offers that can be easily explained in a few words. Some examples:

100 full-color business cards only $53.50	(Southern Color)
Rechargeable aerosol spray can! $29.95 each Includes 5 nozzles at no extra charge	(Abbeon Cal)
16-cent custom tote bags. Fast delivery. Low quantities. For trade shows, meetings, promotion, retail—any occasion.	(Art Poly Bags)

9. Stress Benefits, Not Features

Highlight the benefits of what you are selling. For example, if you are selling a machine that folds sheets of paper into booklets, don't say, "Stainless steel hopper, 12" wide." Say, "Makes up to 600 booklets per hour." As Joe Doyle, president of Federal Mailers, points out, "On a 3 × 5-inch card, there is no room to discuss features. Stress benefits."

10. Use Business Reply versus Place Stamp Here

The standard is to design the mailing side (front) of the card as a business reply card. All the prospect does is drop the card in the mail and it is delivered to the advertiser. No need to add a stamp.

To avoid paying the cost of reply mail, some advertisers omit the business reply permit and instead put a "place stamp here" box in the upper right corner of the card. Unfortunately, this will decrease response rates. Some experts recommend using "place stamp here" as a way of qualifying prospects. But when you're after inquiries using postcards, you should go for all you can get. True, asking for a stamp discourages some "brochure collectors." But it may also discourage some legitimate prospects. Don't do it.

11. Does Position Matter?

Bill Norcutt says that top card positions (being one of the first few cards prospects see when they flip through the deck) can increase orders by 14 percent. Robert Luedtke says that in his experience the first card in the deck does get a higher response rate than the same card positioned somewhere in the middle. If you can get the premium position, do so. It may be worth paying extra for the top position if the card deck publisher charges for it.

12. Simple Visuals Work Best

On a 3 × 5-inch card, you have a space about 2 inches wide by 1 inch high to fit your visual. Elaborate or detailed drawings or photos will lose all their detail and become fuzzy when reduced to this size. The best visual approaches are:

- a straightforward product shot in a card focusing on the product, or
- a picture of your booklet, catalog, or literature when offering free information.

RESOURCES

The Direct Marketing Association's Card Pack Council is a good place to start if you are looking for a qualified card pack broker, consultant, or agency. For information contact: Direct Marketing Association, Card Pack Council, 11 West 42nd Street, New York, NY 10036, 212-768-7277.

There are several directories listing the various card decks and card deck publishers. They include:

- *Card Deck Rates and Data*, Standard Rate and Data Service, 3004 Glenview Road, Wilmette, IL 60091-9970, 800-323-4588 or 312-256-8333. Lists over 700 business and consumer card decks plus hundreds of insert and co-op mailing programs. One-year subscription price: $95.
- *Card Pack Directory*, Solar Press, 1120 Frontenac Road, Naperville, IL 60563-1799, 708-983-1400. Published annually. Call for price and availability.
- *The Response Deck List*, Thinkbank Publishers, PO Box 1166, Arlington, TX 76010, 817-265-1793. Includes information on over 400 response decks.

Chapter

TELEMARKETING 17

If you have a negative reaction to the idea of telemarketing, you're not alone. As consumers on the receiving end of telemarketing calls, many of us find them annoying and disruptive. But telemarketing can be effective when conducted properly. Telemarketing encompasses not only outgoing sales calls but incoming calls from prospects as well. An article in *Target Marketing* (September 1996, p. 14) reports that advertisers spent $54.1 billion on telephone marketing in 1995, which resulted in sales of more than $350 billion.

The American Telemarketing Association (ATA) defines telemarketing as "the planned, professional use of the telephone to advertise, market, or provide service functions." The ATA points out that telemarketing provides both profit and not-for-profit businesses a cost-effective method to communicate quickly with a large segment of their targeted prospect population. For two-income couples with little time to shop, homebound individuals, and busy executives who don't have time to see a salesperson, telemarketing can be a valuable service.

WHY USE TELEMARKETING?

Telemarketing is similar to mass media in that it can reach a lot of prospects quickly. The goal of telemarketing is to provide economical, convenient access to products and services. By talking to the prospect directly, telemarketers can overcome individual objections and adjust their sales approach immediately. In effect, telemarketing combines sales and research.

Because sales costs are frequently reduced through telemarketing, consumers and business buyers alike may benefit from lower long-term product and service prices. Telemarketing provides an opportunity for prospects to learn about products and services on a personalized, interactive level.

Other advantages of telemarketing are:

1. It allows the prospect to ask questions, provide information, give opinions, and react to your message.

2. Telemarketing offers total market penetration. The telephone can reach virtually every business and over 90 percent of the households in North America.

3. The telephone receives priority—the prospect answers the phone when other mediums get put aside or ignored.

4. Telemarketing allows you to pick the best time to contact your prospect or customer. You have time control. With experience, you learn the best time to reach your audience.

5. The telephone is economical and efficient. Telemarketing allows you to service those customers you can't afford to sell any other way.

6. Telemarketing is convenient for your prospects and customers. A telephone call takes less time than a personal visit.

7. Telemarketing is not affected by the elements, the weather, or other factors that can upset an outside sales force.

8. Telemarketing allows you to make a high volume of prospect or customer contacts:

	Consumer	Business
Dial spins per hour:	40 to 60	20 to 40
Completed presentations per hour:	9 to 15	5 to 9

In a standard 8-hour day, the street sales rep makes 4 to 12 calls, whereas an experienced telemarketer talks to 30 to 90 people.

9. Telemarketing reduces the costs of the field force while increasing sales. Lead generation and qualification decrease expenses while providing the outside sales rep with only qualified people to talk to.

10. Telemarketing gives you instant feedback, flexibility, and measurement of your results against objectives.

Not only does telemarketing give you instant feedback as to how effective your sales message is, it gives you a chance to find out why response is or isn't good. That's a distinct advantage over other media such as advertising, direct mail, or public relations, which allow you to measure results only.

Telemarketing is also useful in servicing both major product or market segments where you do a minor volume of your business and minor product or market segments where you do a major volume of business. An example of the first type of market is a specialty product with a good profit margin but a small volume. Telemarketing can reach this small volume of customers more efficiently than field sales calls. An example of the minor market segment that generates a major volume of business is selling outside your normal geographic territory where sales are profitable but customers are few. It would be expensive to send a salesperson to cover this out-of-the-way territory, but telemarketing is an ideal alternative.

TELEMARKETING APPLICATIONS

Telemarketing is not just a convenient tool for soliciting orders or fund-raising. It can be used for:

- Sales support (including scheduling appointments for sales personnel)
- Market research
- Consumer surveys
- Lead generation
- Lead qualification
- Information hotlines
- Reservations service
- Technical support
- Customer service
- Direct mail or advertising follow-up
- Customer satisfaction surveys
- Account management
- Order taking
- Catalog sales
- Fund-raising
- Subscription sales
- Renewals
- Product announcements
- Special promotions
- Generating referrals
- Soliciting trade show attendance

Generally, telemarketing supplements other advertising and marketing channels. It can be used to maximize response to a mailing by preparing prospects to receive the mailing or following up with them afterward. Businesses can use telemarketing to obtain more accurate, up-to-date marketing information, broader market bases, and lower business costs. As Mike Johnson, vice president of the telemarketing agency Mardex, Inc., observes, "Telemarketing is an inexpensive insurance policy guaranteeing success for your efforts in other media."

Telemarketing costs more than direct mail, which typically runs between a half dollar and a few dollars per pieces mailed, but it costs considerably less than making an in-person sales call. According to TeleCross Corporation, a telemarketing agency in Waterloo, IA, the cost of a telemarketing call falls in the $3 to $7 range, while a personal sales call costs close to $200. Of course, the true measure of success is not the cost of the medium up front, but the results the medium generates.

SETTING UP AN EFFECTIVE TELEMARKETING PROGRAM

First you must decide on the goal of your telemarketing program. You should have a clear definition of its purpose and make sure your objectives are in measurable terms. For instance, do you want ten new orders a day? Do you want to double the number of inquiries you are currently receiving?

The next step is finding and keeping good telemarketers. You may decide to train and staff an in-house department for this purpose or hire an outside telemarketing firm. An outside telemarketing firm can also be hired to help you set up an in-house telemarketing center. The operators you hire should have a chance to see, hold, and touch your product if possible, so that they are familiar with it and can answer questions about it from prospects. Probably the most important quality to look for in a good telemarketer is a clear, cheerful, expressive voice and correct pronunciation and grammar. Unlike a salesperson in the field, telemarketers cannot rely on facial and body gestures to augment their message. Telemarketing trainer Mary Anne Weinstein points out, "The voice becomes the sole representative of your company. There is no fancy clothing, no cologne or perfume, no adornment in hairstyle or makeup. The voice is your only marketing tool."

You will also need to prepare a telephone script that is flexible enough to handle a variety of individual responses to your calls, yet is structured with options to anticipate 90 percent of the issues and objections raised by prospects. See the sample script reprinted at the end of this chapter.

Here are some other tips on developing an effective telemarketing program:

- Use a conversational approach in your script; allow dialogue and interaction.

- Listen to what your prospect has to say and respond accordingly. You may have received telemarketing calls that began, "How are you today" and when you say "Fine," the person on the other end automatically replies, "I'm fine, too. Thank you for asking." Don't let your staff blindly follow a script while ignoring the prospect's responses.

- Better yet, don't ask "How are you" or "How are you doing" when you don't even know the person you're calling. It lacks sincerity and annoys most people.

- Make sure the contact list you are using is up to date and accurate. Just as with any other type of marketing, your prospect list is a top priority. The telephone costs too much to waste time on inappropriate calls.

- Never let the phone ring more than six times.

- If you hire telemarketers, hire the best and pay them well.

- Have a control form or some kind of summary record to keep track of your calls and the results, including customer information and specific objections to the sales message.

- Before you begin the calls, make sure you know as much as possible about who you are calling and why.

- Know exactly what you want the person you're calling to do, and make it clear to him or her what you're asking.

- Be sure you have the right person on the telephone before you begin your presentation. Ask for him or her by first and last name.

- Make sure the prospect is free to talk to you. If not, ask when might be a good time to call back.

- Build into your script an opening hook or question, a reason for listening to you. The goal is to get your prospect to agree with you. Present your product or offer's key benefits immediately, concentrating on those that are proven to be key motivators in the buying decision.

- State your offer and its terms clearly, making sure the prospect knows what he or she stands to gain from it.

- Choose two products or services to promote. One is primary, the other is secondary. Each should offer different advantages. Offer the secondary product or service only if the primary one does not interest your buyer.

- Do not assume the prospect understands you. Make certain you are getting through with the message by repeating it and asking questions if you feel there is any confusion.

- React to what prospects say. Feed back key words or phrases they use, showing that you have listened and are picking up on what is important to them.

- Never argue with prospects or tell them they are wrong. Be cheerful, bright, and sincere in your conversation.

- Answer a prospect's question with a question, to keep you in control and out of a defensive position. This technique will also help you qualify the prospect further, since you will be getting additional information.

- Have a strong series of closes ready. Ask for the order. Says Milt Pierce, a New York–based direct mail copywriter and author of several special reports on telephone sales, "This is the salesperson's toughest job. After the pitch has been delivered, the objections have been raised and answered, it is time to produce the order. Be sure your salespeople are trained in closing and verifying the sale."

- Keep it simple. Use short words, simple phrases, "you" language, and make easy-to-understand points. Speak slowly and distinctly, but don't waste the prospect's time. Get to the point quickly.

- Refine your techniques based on prospect responses before you make hundreds or thousands of calls. One of the benefits of telemarketing is its usefulness in testing different sales approaches and markets. Results can be gathered in a few days, changes can be made quickly, and valid tests cost much less than they would with direct mail or space advertising.

A business call requires more give and take and a less rigid approach than a call to consumers. According to Ray Jutkins of Nelson Panullo Jutkins Direct Marketing, only 20 percent of all telephone calls result in a sale within the first few minutes. Eighty percent of orders are achieved because the telemarketing consultant can handle rebuttals, answer questions, and provide details. In fact, most successful closers ask for the order seven times.

Still, if the prospect is really not interested after a couple of requests for the order, the telemarketer should either politely end the call or set a call-back time, if the prospect is agreeable. If an order is taken, be sure to confirm it at the end of the conversation, restating purchase and delivery information and other details. Make sure your staff ends every conversation politely so as to preserve your company's reputation and keep the door open for future calls or follow-up.

IN-HOUSE OR AGENCY?

Should you set up your own in-house telemarketing staff or hire an outside agency to do your telemarketing for you? If you plan a heavy and frequent volume of telemarketing, the most cost-effective option may be to work with an outside agency on setting up your own operation in-house. You'll have more control over personnel and the way they handle calls, as well as the capability to handle technically complex calls.

The advantage of working with a telemarketing agency is that the company is likely to be experienced and knowledgeable in areas that you are not. Unless you hire a staff person with telemarketing know-how, that outside expertise can save you time and money in the long run. An agency can write and test a script based on information you provide, offer a trained staff of telemarketing operators or help you train your own people, coordinate a telemarketing campaign with other departments (such as data processing, shipping, sales, and advertising), advise you on finding or putting together a telephone-responsive call list, and offer suggestions on how and when to best use telemarketing.

The agency you hire should invite you to participate in all phases of telemarketing development, including script development, training, strategic planning, and monitoring of calls. Even before you hire a firm, ask if you can observe the operators making calls to see how courteous they are, how natural they sound on the phone, and how well they handle problems and objections. This will also give you a chance to observe the supervisor and how well he or she motivates the telecommunicators.

If you plan to conduct telemarketing campaigns only occasionally, it will probably be cheaper to hire a telemarketing agency to handle the work for you on an as-needed basis. Otherwise, you must consider whether your operators and phone and computer equipment will be sitting idle when you aren't doing outbound telemarketing. Outbound operators often have a different personality and different aptitudes than customer-service operators who take inbound calls, so having them double as both types of operators may not work out.

Another reason to hire an outside agency is that they can often provide round-the-clock telephone service for inbound calls. By combining your call volume with that of other clients, they can afford to have operators in place 24 hours a day. Outside agencies are also better equipped to handle the flood of calls generated by broadcast advertising, since they have multiple phone lines and a large staff. Finally, they can probably set up both an inbound and an outbound telemarketing campaign faster than you can, since the operators and equipment are already in place.

Most agencies bill by the hour or on a per-call basis. To determine the cost-effectiveness of your telemarketing, calculate the sales revenue per hour and subtract the agency's fee from that. It is generally a good idea to test telemarketing by using an agency before you commit to the cost of setting up an in-house center.

Stewart Cross, president of TeleCross Corporation, offers this advice: "With most of our clients, we recommend they test the telemarketing concept before making a final commitment. It must pay for itself on a small scale before it can pay as a full-size operation."

TELEMARKETING ETHICS

To be successful, telemarketing programs must follow certain guidelines of etiquette, courtesy, and professional ethical behavior. The American Telemarketing Association suggests the following guidelines:

1. Callers should always identify themselves and the company.

2. The purpose of the call should be stated efficiently, courteously, and professionally.

3. Repeated calls with the same offer should not be made to the same prospect.

4. All telemarketing offers to the business or consumer public must be legal, legitimate, and have recognized value.

5. Business calls should occur during normal business hours, and consumer calls should only occur between 9 A.M. and 9 P.M., unless further restricted by local or state laws.

6. For outbound calls using automatic dialing equipment, there should be enough staff to ensure that every call recipient will speak to a live person immediately.

7. For inbound calls, the seller should provide sufficient lines to accommodate anticipated call volumes.

8. A telemarketing manager should be on site to provide control and direction. Managers should also regularly monitor the telemarketers' performance by listening to business calls being made or received. This allows performance problems to be detected and addressed so that tele-

marketing quality can be improved. It also protects customers and the employer against possible unethical practices by certain operators.

QUALIFYING LEADS

Each operator's goal should be to spend the shortest time possible getting the maximum number of sales. You will need to screen leads by getting the answers to several questions.

First, find out if the person you are talking to has the authority to purchase.

Second, find out if the prospect has a need for your particular product or service. If not, find out what specific needs you can satisfy.

Third, determine when the prospect plans to purchase such a product or service—within the next few months, or not for a year? If the time frame is more than a few months away, you may wish to call back later.

Fourth, find out if there any other sources for your product or service that the prospect is considering. The answer can provide a good clue as to the seriousness of the prospect. If there is another source the prospect finds more appealing, try to find out why so that you can relay that information back to the telemarketing manager and, ultimately, the sales manager.

In asking these questions, don't assume an adversarial stance. Think of the questions as part of a conversation that builds rapport with the potential customer. Be sensitive to the inflections and tone in your prospect's voice, as well as to what is being said. Be empathetic toward any concerns and problems. This will help establish a mutually beneficial relationship that can turn a cool prospect into a hot one, if not immediately then perhaps in the future.

WRITING THE TELEMARKETING SCRIPT

Although there are as many different sales pitches as there are telemarketers, most sales presentations fall into one of these four basic categories or types:

1. Benefit/advantage
2. Survey/question (fact-finding)
3. Dialogue/back and forth (rapport-building)
4. Direct

Let's take a look at each type and how to put them together for maximum effectiveness.

Benefit/Advantage

According to psychologists and sales trainers, people's actions are designed to accomplish either one of two objectives: gain reward or avoid punishment. To put it another way, people act either out of desire or out of fear.

Traditional selling is based on appealing to the prospect's desire to gain reward. Therefore, salespeople are taught, "Stress the benefits of what you are selling, not the features." In other words, don't sell insurance; sell financial security and protection from financial disaster.

In benefit/advantage telemarketing, the telemarketer rarely mentions the product feature or fact without tying a benefit to it. Therefore, instead of saying, "The X-900 is the most compact copier in our home office line," you would say, "The X-900 is the most compact copier in our line, which means it's ideal for home offices with limited space."

Why does your prospect want to buy your product? What advantages does it offer? What problems does it solve? How is it superior and different than other solutions the prospect could buy? Write down these key benefits and advantages. Work them into your presentation script or call guidelines.

Be careful not to overdo it. Use benefit/advantage selling selectively. Don't attach a benefit to every single statement you make. If you do, you'll sound like a salesperson making a pitch, which isn't the effect you want. Speak naturally. If something rings phony to you, don't say it just because you think you must add a benefit. If you come on too hard, too much like a "salesperson," you risk turning the prospect off.

Survey/Question (Fact-Finding)

In this technique, you ask prospects questions to find out what they're interested in. Then you present the features and benefits of your product that address the prospects' concerns, interests, needs, wants, and desires.

For instance, if you are selling copiers, you probably can offer many different models with a wide range of features. Which features do you stress? Which model do you try to sell the customer? When you ask questions, the prospect's answers enable you to hone in on exactly the right model copier and to talk about only those features of concern to that prospect.

PROSPECT: We might need a new copier. But why should we buy from you?

YOU: I don't know that you should. What are you looking for in a copier?

PROSPECT: One thing our old copier doesn't have that I'd love to have is collating. But we can't afford a big fancy collator.

YOU: Our X-900 CopyMaster might fit the bill. It's one of the only home office copiers to have a high-speed, high-capacity collator. The collator is included as part of the machine at no extra cost. And the $1,400 price is well within the budget we discussed earlier.

Many salespeople make the mistake of making a blind sales pitch: They talk incessantly about products, models, and features without really knowing what the customer is looking for or what will generate excitement and interest.

The most successful salespeople find out what the customer wants, then provide it. To know what the customer wants, just ask. The telephone is an ideal medium for asking questions, in that you can get an immediate response and reply in context in the next instant. If the prospect needs a copier that can reduce large pages to letter size, you immediately focus on the models with that feature, stressing their convenience, simplicity, and low cost.

Be an active listener. Most people who sell do it absolutely incorrectly. They go in and tell the prospect what they want to say, reciting a memorized list of product features and benefits. But as copywriter Sig Rosenblum points out, prospects care about their own needs, problems, concerns, fears, desires, goals, and dreams. Successful salespeople tailor their presentations to show how the features of their product or service can give every client what he or she most desires or needs to solve his or her problem.

How do you find out what prospects want or desire? First and foremost, you listen. Prospects who do not hear from you what they want to hear from you will tell you so. Often these statements are in the form of objections.

You may think, "I always listen to prospects and clients." But do you? Be honest. Aren't there times when the prospect is talking and you're not really listening, but instead planning what you want to say next? When a prospect says something that you don't agree with or don't want to hear, aren't you immediately planning your rebuttal rather than listening to find out whether the complaint or statement has merit?

Here are some tips for more effective listening:

- *Focus.* When you are listening and doing something else at the same time, you aren't really listening. When prospects speak, give them 100 percent of your concentration. If, for instance, you're talking with a prospect over the phone, don't go through your mail at the same time. Follow the advice of poet May Sarton, who said, "Do each thing with absolute concentration." Listening is an active process, not a passive one, and it requires your full attention.

- *Take notes.* There are several benefits to this. First, you can jot down questions as they occur to you, so you don't forget to ask them later on. Second, you can quickly and easily prepare a good proposal or follow-up letter based on the notes. When you take notes, your follow-up documents will be full of good, specific material prospects want to see, because you recorded their requests and preferences.

- *Respond verbally.* Say things that indicate to prospects that you are listening and have empathy for what they are saying. One simple, effective communication technique for demonstrating your understanding is simply to say, "I understand".

PROSPECT: We're looking for a contractor who can handle the job from start to finish. I don't want to have to coordinate and deal with half a dozen or more different vendors. We want one firm to do the whole job.

YOU: I understand.

Another technique is to rephrase the prospect's statement and repeat it back:

PROSPECT: We're looking for a contractor who can handle the job from start to finish. I don't want to have to coordinate and deal with half a dozen or more different vendors. We want one firm to do the whole job.

YOU: So what you're saying is you want a contractor who can coordinate all the pieces and provide single-source responsibility for getting your system designed and installed?

PROSPECT: Yes, that's correct.

Equally effective is to rephrase the prospect's statement and repeat it back as a question to which he or she will answer affirmatively. This gets the prospect agreeing to things you say, which eventually leads to a close:

PROSPECT: We really need an ad campaign that will penetrate the under-thirty market for this product.

YOU: So would you be interested specifically in dealing with an ad agency with a proven track record in selling to the under-thirty market?

PROSPECT: Yes, that's what we're looking for.

Some salespeople are more aggressive, phrasing questions so that the answers indicate a tentative (if small) commitment on the part of the prospect:

PROSPECT: We would need seminars to train one hundred DP staff members no later than February first.

YOU: So if we could train your total staff of one hundred by the first of February, you'd be interested in going ahead, wouldn't you?

Why is the survey mode so effective in selling? Because questions demonstrate your concern for the prospect's problems. Asking questions puts the focus of the phone call where it should be—on the prospect's needs, not on your products, services, or company.

The survey mode enables you to determine the prospect's requirements so you can tailor your products and services to address those requirements. "In the first meeting with prospective clients, focus on what they really need to make their problem go away," says marketing consultant Howard Shenson. "Don't waste the prospect's time providing a verbal résumé. If prospects need information on your skills, abilities, and experience, they will certainly ask."

Here are some other questions you may find helpful in getting prospects to open up and tell you how you can help them:

"How can I help you?"

"Tell me a little bit about your current situation."

"What specifically do you need me to do for you?"

"What are you looking to accomplish in [name their specific area of interest]?"

"That's interesting. Tell me more."

At times, prospects are unable to articulate their requirements and just go on and on without getting to the point. I help them get back on track by interrupting and saying, "I understand. But what exactly is it that you would like me to do for you?" This usually helps them focus on why they called me in the first place.

If a prospect and I are having a conversation and I decide to inter-ject a question, I don't jump in and immediately ask it. I pause for a sec-ond, then say, "May I ask you a question?" This interruption forces prospects to stop talking, prepares them to listen, and puts them in a receptive, thoughtful state, ensuring that they will hear my question and provide an answer to it. It also conveys, "I think this is so important that I want us to stop and question what we're talking about so we can proceed on an accurate basis." Use "May I ask you a question?" It works!

Of course, the point of the call is not to ask endless questions or gather infinite information. Each question is designed to clarify and diag-nose the prospect's requirements, so that you get, as quickly as possible, to the point where you can outline the prospect's project requirements, your proposed plan of action, and your fee.

Dialogue/Back and Forth (Rapport-Building)

Like it or not, personal chemistry is a major factor in determining whether prospects buy from you. It's really quite simple: People buy from people whom they like and feel comfortable with. They avoid doing business with people they dislike, or are afraid of, or who make them uncomfortable.

In certain instances, a strong reaction between two personalities cannot be avoided or controlled. One person will, for a myriad of reasons, take an instant and overwhelming liking or disliking to another person.

But in most cases, you can create good chemistry—or at least create behavior that allows good chemistry to grow and flourish. For instance, if you have a big ego, be aware that most people don't like braggarts and ego-maniacs. No matter how smart, right, or good you are, many people won't hire you because they can't stand the way you behave.

Suzanne Ramos, a manager at American Express, says she occa-sionally sees salespeople who violate what she considers the unwritten rule that "the client is always right." They talk too much or come across as overconfident, argumentative, even mildly disdainful or arrogant. She is also alert to people who might be difficult to work with. "Life is too short," she says.

In general, people like people who:

- are friendly,
- are warm,
- are courteous,

- are polite,
- are on time,
- are respectful,
- like them,
- share their interests,
- listen to them,
- show an interest in them,
- ask them about themselves,
- treat them well, and
- help them.

In the 1980s, sales trainers and authors introduced the concept of consultative selling. Essentially, the consultative selling theory is that clients and customers want you to solve problems for them, not sell them. Good salespeople aren't peddlers or hucksters; they're sales consultants who work closely with clients, helping them fulfill their needs.

Suddenly salespeople in all fields stopped referring to themselves as salespeople and began calling themselves consultants. People who sold financial services, for example, began putting such impressive-sounding titles as "financial planner" or "financial counselor" on their business cards. The consultative salespeople even developed a slogan—"Solve, don't sell"—to push their approach to sales.

Much of the consultative approach to selling is valid and can be applied effectively to the selling of your products and services. However, in one respect, the consultative selling gurus and disciples went overboard: Some did so much free "consulting" before they were retained by the prospect that they ended up giving away their services for free, removing the need for the prospect to hire them.

The successful salesperson today practices what I call modified consultative selling. That is, we selectively consult with prospects on their problem during the initial calls. We give enough information to convince prospects that we are experts who can help them, without giving away so much that they can solve the problem themselves and don't need our help anymore.

For instance, let's say you run a graphic design studio. A prospect asks, "Is there any way to design a brochure that features all six products but could easily be updated if one of the products changes?" Because you know the answer, your tendency might be to dash off a sketch or fold together a dummy out of scrap paper to show how it's done. Have you sold effectively? No, because the prospect now knows the answer and can take your solution to his or her current graphic designer or staff artist—or, if the prospect is cheap, directly to a printer.

Instead, you should say, "Yes, that's a requirement we've handled in the past for other clients, and when we're further into the design process, we'll present some options that would work with your particular product."

This answer indicates that you are the designer who understands and can solve the problem, but makes it necessary for the prospect to hire you (and not someone else) to get this solution.

That's the essence of modified consultative selling. Consultative selling gurus said, "Act like the problem-solving genius at the initial meeting, do everything you can for prospects, and they will hire you out of gratitude and because you're so impressive."

Modified consultative selling proponents, on the other hand, say, "Act like the knowledgeable problem solver at the initial meeting. Do and say things that convince clients that you indeed do know the answers, but don't give the answers away right then and there. Instead, disclose just enough information so that clients perceive that they need to hire you to get the solution or results they desire."

Be a consultant, by all means, but don't give away the store. Say and do things that demonstrate your abilities and create (rather than eliminate) the need for your products and services.

Should your basic presentation be planned? Of course. But be willing and able to change course in midstream if the prospect takes the conversation in a direction in which you didn't intend to go.

Recently we had a general contractor come to our home to give an estimate on adding a family room. The contractor, a creative and talented professional, had his vision of what a family room should be. Unfortunately, it conflicted with the family room I had dreamed of having.

Mike insisted that at the rear of the room, there should be sliding glass doors leading onto a deck. I, however, do not like sliding glass doors. I don't like the temptation and easy entry they offer burglars, nor do I like the heat loss in winter.

I explained this to Mike. He countered with an explanation of what a wonderful view the doors would give me. I told him a window would do just as nicely. He countered with an explanation of how a rear door adds value to the home. After going back and forth a few times, it should have been clear to Mike that I didn't want sliding glass doors.

At that point, he should have rearranged his presentation to meet my needs. For instance, he might have suggested a fireplace or a wood-burning stove or wall-to-wall built-in bookcases for the kind of cozy family room I envisioned. But he was inflexible. He wanted to design a family room with sliding glass doors and one of his famous decks, and nothing else would do for me.

After fifteen minutes I became impatient, ended the conversation, and showed Mike the door. It's possible I may still give him the job—I like him and his work—but his sales presentation actually decreased the probability of this happening.

That's the risk in being inflexible. If you refuse to listen to prospects, to acknowledge their ideas and wishes, and to tailor your presentation to show that you understand and want to meet their needs—in short, if you insist on doing it your way and your way only—your sales presentation not only won't get you a go-ahead but may actually make prospects less inclined to buy from you than they were before you started. Yes, an ineffective or negative conversation with a prospect can actually unsell you and your products!

Direct

In the direct sales mode, you spend most of your time qualifying the prospect, selling benefits, and pushing toward a close. Aggressive financial services sellers promoting stocks over the phone often take this no-nonsense approach.

One question that arises is: How honest should you be about your products and the results you expect to achieve for the prospects? The position I advise you to take is to present yourself and your products in the most favorable light possible without misrepresenting yourself.

Financial services marketing expert Denny LeBarron advises, "Don't make any commitments or claims you can't live up to." I agree. But at the same time, remember that your competitors are puffing their own abilities and making themselves sound good. They stretch the truth and exaggerate. Some just plain lie.

You should not lie, but in the face of all this hype, it doesn't pay to be overly modest either. Management consultant Gary Blake gives this advice: "Present yourself as about 10 percent better than you really are." My feeling is that you shouldn't lie or exaggerate, but you should present yourself as the very best you can be and have been.

As the song says, "Accentuate the positive." Tell all the good things about your product line. Highlight your successes. Don't go out of your way to tell prospects about your weaknesses and failures. Your competitors will gladly do that for you. Present yourself in the most favorable light possible while maintaining complete honesty and integrity. Prospects want to hire people who are successful, not mediocre. Position yourself as such.

When going for the close, use a preference sell with a limited range of options or choices. In a preference sell, you do not ask the prospect, "Do you want a hair replacement system?"—a close that risks a "no" answer in response. Instead, you ask for the prospect's preference: "Do you want the Poly-Fuse hair replacement system or would you prefer the Poly-Fix?" Notice that "no" is not a logical answer to this question.

"Don't give your clients too many choices," advises direct marketing consultant Joan Harris. "This either confuses them if they're the decision makers, or slows down the process if lots of people have to see the options."

An old trick of clothing salespeople can easily be applied to selling most products and services. The clothes salesperson knows that if a customer is confronted with rack after rack of ties to choose from, he or she will become overwhelmed and unable to make a decision. Instead, the salesperson begins narrowing the choices: "Do you want silk or polyester?" You say silk. The polyester ties are removed from the counter. "Do you want plain or patterns?" You say patterns. Solid color ties are removed from the counter. "Stripes or polka dots?" You say stripes. Polka dot ties are taken away. "Do you prefer bright colors or pastels?" This continues until two or three ties remain. Then the close: "Do you want this one, this one, this one, or will you be taking all three?"

Limit the number of choices. The point is not to overwhelm prospects with lots of choices to make. Remember, they are looking to you for guidance. If they seem unsure, say, "We could do it this way or this way. Which do you prefer?" By all means, give prospects choices. Prospects resent being told what to do and like to make their own decisions. But in reality, you control the presentation, presenting enough options to enable choice without causing confusion.

Another key ingredient in the direct sales approach (or any of the other presentation modes discussed in this chapter) is enthusiasm. You must be genuinely enthusiastic about your service and about the prospect's proposed project or assignment. If you're indifferent, disdainful, or even just plain bored, you are unlikely to close the deal.

How do you show enthusiasm? For once, there's no technique for you to learn, because if you are enthusiastic, it will naturally show through in your voice, attitude, manner, and presentation. By the same token, any lack of enthusiasm will also become apparent to the prospect. Just be yourself.

Many novice salespeople stumble painfully through sales presentations because they haven't planned in advance what they are going to say. Planning means not only having a well-practiced presentation, but also knowing what to say in reply to prospect comments, questions, and objections.

The key to being polished and smooth is to anticipate what prospects will say and prepare sensible answers in advance. Then, when prospects say, "But I can get it cheaper from the printer around the corner," instead of saying "Uhh...well...ummm," you launch immediately into a confident, clear explanation of why you should print the brochure even though you cost a bit more.

When you are prepared, you feel confident speaking with prospects and clients. When you are not prepared, you are nervous, because you're afraid they'll state an objection or ask a question to which you have no answer. The more prepared you are, the less likely this is to occur.

In the movie *The Verdict*, Jack Warden tells Paul Newman, "Never ask a witness a question to which you don't know the answer." The ideal in selling is to be so well prepared that prospects never ask you a question to which you don't know the answer.

TOLL-FREE NUMBERS INCREASE RESPONSE RATES

Providing a toll-free 800 number to customers and prospects for receiving orders and inquiries can boost the number of responses to your offer substantially. The consumer mail order industry has discovered that as much as 80 percent of their total business is done over the telephone when they offer an 800 number. Ray Jutkins of Nelson Panullo Jutkins Direct Marketing points out that it is not unusual to increase orders by 20 percent through the addition of an 800 number in your promotions.

Once a prospect is encouraged to call an 800 number, your company gets an extra opportunity to cross-sell or increase the sale. Toll-free numbers also can provide a way to track media, determining which ones are working best. Make sure your 800 number is prominently featured in all catalogs, ads, press releases, and other promotions you send out.

The same common sense rules that apply to direct marketing apply to telemarketing. Don't plan a major telemarketing push to begin right before Christmas or on another major holiday. Either the phone lines will be tied up by people making calls, such as when one advertiser started an inbound call campaign on Mother's Day, or everyone will be too busy with other plans to place an order or listen to a sales pitch.

One other caveat regarding 800 numbers as well as toll lines: You should have enough incoming lines to handle your normal volume of calls, as well as provision for expected overflow if you mount a major promotional campaign. If you have your own telemarketing center, some outside telemarketing agencies can arrange a temporary link-up with your phone lines so that calls and orders will not be lost during peak periods.

GETTING BACK LAPSED CUSTOMERS

Season Subscribers to the Opera

This sample telemarketing script is reprinted with permission from *Words for Telemarketing* by Steve Isaac (Asher-Gallant Press). It is designed to get people who once bought opera tickets but did not renew to resubscribe.

Hello, M_____? This is_____ from the Albany Opera. I'm calling you tonight to find out where we went wrong. You were a subscriber to the Opera last season, but have not renewed your subscription for the current season.

Since we always try to present the best in sophisticated entertainment, we're disturbed when our subscribers are not pleased.

It would be most helpful to us if you could tell me what it was that made you decide not to renew.

Listen in an interested manner to whatever the prospect says. Answer objections or, if a problem surfaces, say:

I'm sorry that happened. Try as we may, we don't always satisfy everyone. However, it would be a shame for you to lose your priority seating privileges based on one disappointment.

How about this? Let's renew your subscription tonight, so that you're sure of getting the seats you want. If you're unhappy after attending the first performance, you can cancel and will only be charged for the one performance.

And, though we certainly couldn't make up for what happened, I'd like to have you be our guest at a performance of the ABT here at the Opera House this week or next. How does that sound to you, M_____?

If the prospect is pleased, proceed. If the prospect is still unhappy and uninterested, politely terminate the call.

Great. I'll hold a ticket in your name at the box office for any evening this week or next. Just be sure to pick it up by 7:30 or you may not be able to be seated for the performance you've chosen.

In the meantime, I'll get your tickets out to you first thing tomorrow for the opera season and notify the box office to hold your seat.

If the problem was the position of the seating in the first place, say you'll notify the box office to change the seat to the prospect's area of preference if at all possible.

Now, M_____, we take American Express, Visa, or MasterCard. Which would you prefer to put this on?

Take the credit card information. If the prospect wants to pay by check, indicate that you can only hold the seat until one week from tonight.

Now, let me make sure I have your correct address. It's_____, correct? Welcome back, M_____, and enjoy our spectacular 1988 season.

Objection responses

It Just Costs Too Much

Yes, our costs have certainly gone up in the past few seasons, and we're forced to pass those on to ticket purchasers. It costs a lot to put on quality productions. However, it would be a shame for you to miss it at any price.

Let's see, your subscription last year was_____. I do have some seats available at_____. They're not as good as the ones you had, but they are still very good seats. I can reserve for you at _____, or I can still offer you your old seats. Which would you prefer?

To Almost Any Objection

Do you plan to attend any operas this season at all?

If yes:

Well, then, it would really be a shame for someone who has such feeling for the opera and a priority privilege to lose it.

I Want to Think about It

Well, certainly, you can think about it, M_____; however, we won't be able to give you priority seating after tonight. Our computer is about to process all the seating requests of the renewing subscribers before we add the general public.

17 TIPS FOR MORE EFFECTIVE TELEMARKETING

Here are some of the more common mistakes to avoid when planning and implementing a telemarketing campaign:

1. Choosing the Wrong Team

When you're assembling your own management team to control your telemarketing activity, you'll need a strong leader with companywide access, plus the authority to make fast command decisions. The most successful telemarketing directors are front-line generals who stay in direct touch with every phase of operations and keep their lines of communication wide open.

If you plan to conduct all your telemarketing operations in-house, you'll need to find people with the right kind of experience. Telephone experience is not enough. You need to know what kind of telephone work applicants are trained for. A good inbound operator has a far different personality from a successful outbound caller.

It's a mistake to divert your regular Customer Service telephone people to telemarketing activities. It's an entirely different discipline. They won't be able to adapt quickly, and diverting them cuts deeply into your ongoing Customer Service program.

If you elect to bring in an independent telemarketing company for your operations, be as careful as you would in hiring a new key executive in your company. Demand references from current and past clients. Dig deep, but respect your gut feelings; good chemistry is essential, because you're going to be working closely together.

There are about a dozen or so telemarketing firms who can be called top pros, and if you choose one of us you'll get plenty of help in avoiding the other 16, possibly fatal, mistakes you might make.

Getting the right people to represent you out front on the telephone is vital. They need to be experienced enough to appreciate your company image and adopt it, then trained to be as knowledgeable about your products as your regular person-to-person salespeople.

2. Conflicting Chain of Command

Success in telemarketing is driven by the fast, intelligent interchange of information between all the members of your team—your telemarketing company or group, your marketing people, and your operating departments. It's a job for a well-coordinated, fast-acting team. There's no time for congressional delays. If you want to stay in tune with the marketplace and capitalize on the opportunities as quickly as they pop up, you need to be ready and able to modify your program, and improve your media buys on a daily (or hourly) basis.

The chain of command that works the best (with the least cost, least waste, and least confusion) is directly from your chief of telemarketing to the people on the front line. Availability of the chief by phone and in person is the essential key. If your chief is absent on a business trip or tied up in meetings or surrounded by a fence of secretaries, your telemarketing system can't function and perform the way you want it to.

3. Neglecting Your Front-Line People

Like any salespeople, your telemarketing operators need tender loving care.

It's a mistake to turn them loose without sufficient training. In any effective telemarketing company, operator training doesn't begin and end with a brief session on a canned pitch. Operators are given the chance to learn your product inside out so they can handle any questions thrown at them, overcome any objections, and move smoothly into closing the sale. That's only step one.

Step two is to get them in harmony with your company's image and approach to the marketplace, so whether they make a sale or not, they preserve and build up your good relationship with customers and prospects.

Step three is maintaining energy and enthusiasm for the project they're involved in. All the rules of inspired sales management apply. Participate in the design of the training sessions for your own projects. Telemarketing at its best is interactive long before anyone picks up the telephone on your behalf.

All sales jobs are emotionally demanding, but in telemarketing the demand is intensified. Imagine what it feels like to make 30 to 60 calls a day, face the inevitable turndowns, listen politely to the really tough customers who sometimes pop up, keep a smile in your voice as you handle their problems, and then look cheerfully ahead to the next call.

Unlike the field salesperson who gets a breather between calls, your telemarketing agent has very little relief. The front-line action is just about as fast and demanding as a hockey game.

Like any salespeople, your telemarketing phone agents can go stale and even torpedo a program if they're forgotten. Team leaders and coaches shouldn't just sit on the sidelines. They're circulating in the middle of the action, encouraging the team, solving their problems, fielding any difficult questions that crop up, and boosting everyone's performance.

With the right incentive program, your telephone salespeople are going to produce more. The operative word is "right." If you give them incentives that are too enticing, they may push too hard, oversell, and generate phantom sales you can't close or collect on later. Get your telemarketing company's advice on designing a sales incentive program appropriate for the project you have in mind.

4. Calling in the Experts Too Late

Which comes first, the chicken or the egg? If you choose incorrectly, you could hatch a turkey.

Call in your telemarketing company before you start to work out the details of any plans. You'll get all the benefits of their experience in engineering your program from the bottom up. Some telemarketing companies provide this service at no cost, so there's really no good reason not to take advantage of it. Look at your telemarketing firm as a (free) consultant, not just a supplier, and you'll have a much better chance of avoiding mistakes.

For example, one marketer of women's products recently launched a heavy TV sampling program, waiting until the last minute to connect with the telemarketing firm. In the scramble to get started, the program was planned for inbound 800 operators to collect names and addresses—but not telephone numbers.

The marketer forgot to mention that he needed respondents' phone numbers for a follow-up callback effort. The audience was urban women (80% with unlisted numbers) and there was no way to recapture them.

You can stay out of traps like this one by bringing your telemarketing company in on your plans early enough so they can make constructive suggestions.

5. Buying on Price

Inbound 800 service is sometimes bought on price. That's false economy. The few pennies you save up front can cost you hundreds, even thousands of leads and sales lost by a poor quality or underequipped service.

Ask a leading telemarketing company to quote, and you'll know what the fair market price should be for answering all your calls, giving you valid names and addresses, and providing reliable reports. Beware of a company that undercuts the going market price. They're probably hungry because they can't keep their clients. Or maybe they're latecomers to the industry, hoping to get you to finance their education.

Outbound telemarketing is a totally different story. It's a mistake to buy it simply on the basis of the quoted hourly rate. Outbound should be bought on performance, as measured in a test. You can quickly determine your cost-per-order and cost-per-sale. Those are the criteria that make the difference between winning and losing.

Your telemarketing company should be willing to test and contract for 100 hours, for example. Evaluate results daily, and if the test is not paying out, cut it short to save the client's money. Don't string a losing test out to 100 hours. Instead, work toward successful rollouts.

The only way to buy outbound service is on quality. So how do you judge quality before you commit? Visit the telemarketing operational facility. Meet the front-line people who will be on the phone for you. Sit in on training sessions. Although most training sessions and operations are closed to outsiders for client security reasons, we have some clients who are willing to allow noncompetitive observers. Ask for an appointment.

6. Leaving Out Contingency Planning

On the surface, it looks easy enough to hook telemarketing onto your ongoing marketing program. It may turn out to be simple, but don't count on it!

The impact of telemarketing can hit almost every department inside a company, with surprising consequences for every operational system. To plan safely you need to examine all the "what if's" They're easy enough to anticipate and make contingency plans for if you tap into the experience of a telemarketing company that's been around the tracks so many times they know where the pitfalls are.

For example, what if your telemarketing effort is dramatically successful? Suppose you get three or four or ten times the response you expected. Could your data processing department handle it? Most can't absorb a sudden flood of orders without planning well in advance. Will your IS department need to set up a separate data entry screen for telemarketing? Can they accommodate a magnetic tape or on-line transmission from us? If not, how quickly can they install the system to do it? (Hint: Ask them for their best guess and triple it!)

Look and you'll find most departments are not geared to cope with a sudden surprise success, if it happens.

Do you have the product inventory to fulfill the demand?

What will happen in your shipping room?

Do you have the personnel and packaging supplies needed?

Would a big response tie up all your sales force or delivery system so they can't service your regular customers?

Can you get enough product to supply your customers' regular demands after your telemarketing campaign has emptied your warehouse?

Make sure you have plenty of product literature and other fulfillment materials appropriate for the telemarketing job.

Recently one manufacturer with a warehouse full of literature discovered—too late!—that the brochure copy said "Thanks for responding to our mailing" (instead of "our television campaign") and the Service Department 800 number shown in the brochure was outdated. Reprinting under panic conditions is the costly way to go!

Don't skip any departments when you're making plans—the surprise consequences can explode in some of the most unexpected places.

7. Muddling the Marketing

It's a big mistake to think of telemarketing as an add-on to your ongoing marketing program—an orphan you're going to adopt and see how it behaves before you integrate it into the family.

Well coordinated, your telemarketing efforts can work wonders. (See mistake number 17, Overlooking Opportunities.) Lacking coordination, telemarketing can cause confusion inside your company among departments, and outside among your customers and prospects.

Everyone in the marketing chain from top to bottom needs to be primed and ready to cooperate. A few years ago, in a recruiting campaign for one of the armed services, follow-up letters to TV leads arrived 18 months (!) after the names first came in. Someone forgot to alert the recruiters in the field and get their coordinated cooperation on the campaign.

The offer you make on the phone shouldn't conflict with the offer your prospect gets through other media. Prices, benefits, and the way you present them ought to match—unless you want to test offers and you're able to isolate your test markets positively, so conflicting offers in the mail and on the phone don't land on the same prospects at the same time.

Company management may wonder what effect telemarketing will have on the company's image. There's no cause for alarm if you're careful to coordinate. Telemarketing has come of age; many of the country's most distinguished corporations are using it positively to build company image while they generate leads and sales. (See mistake number 8, Putting Your Ad Agency in Charge.) Working in harmony with your other efforts, telemarketing can act as a variable tap you can turn on and off at will to generate leads or sales precisely as you need them.

8. Putting Your General Advertising Agency in Charge

Nobody could dispute the success of advertising agencies in doing what they do best—building images and changing minds through a broad spectrum of traditional media. Telemarketing is not one of these.

Telemarketing is direct marketing, interactive and fast moving, with a completely different set of rules (some of which are directly contrary to traditional advertising practice).

As a noncommissionable medium, telemarketing is a maverick, grown up independently and largely ignored by advertising agencies (with rare exceptions)—sad but true. But there's light at the end of the tunnel for agencies who'd like to carve out a role for themselves in our $13 billion industry.

If you're the boss of an advertising agency, please accept our standing invitation to discover telemarketing's place in your plans. You could be miles ahead of your competition just by calling a telemarketing firm to ask for a presentation and planning help on a proposed project for one of your clients.

Meanwhile, it can be a serious mistake to place your ad agency in a controlling role between you and your telemarketing company. Only direct response pros and the very few ad agencies who understand telemarketing are qualified to play an active role in it.

Just this year a major package goods company let its ad agency mastermind a new product introduction into oblivion. The idea was to give away free samples of the new product to prospects who called an 800 number for a coupon. The agency, not understanding direct response TV, bought maximum reach spots, with limited frequency. The result was sudden avalanches of phone requests that nobody could hope to handle, instead of a steady flow the company could cope with. The TV media buy was so out of balance that the product introduction had to be scrapped and started over. Beware of instant expertise in telemarketing.

If an agency is truly experienced in telemarketing, they won't want to get into the middle of program planning or day-to-day operations at all. There's nothing to be gained, since telemarketing is noncommissionable. But there's everything to lose, since telemarketing must move much faster than an ad agency can function.

The solution: Ask your agency to act in an advisory role to make sure that your image-building efforts are going to be enhanced by your telemarketing activities, but keep the agency out of the day-to-day decisions.

If they insist on a controlling role, ask to see a presentation on their previous telemarketing experience.

9. Using the Wrong Creative Approach

Whether you're creating a print or broadcast program, don't be shy with your 800 number. More than half of the so-called response ads published bury the 800 number. Why? Some agencies, clients, and art directors put their ideas of quality design ahead of sensible direct marketing technique. Make up your mind—do you want to amaze your audience with a beautiful ad, or do you want to sell product?

If you're going for telephone response, make it impossible for the reader to overlook your number. Make it prominent in print ads above the coupon. Show it and say it several times in your TV spot. Repeat it at least three times in a radio commercial. Put your 800 number somewhere on every page of your catalog, and on every piece in your direct mail package, so prospects who are ready to buy don't have to hunt for the number.

It's a mistake to hope that telemarketing is going to act like a magic wand and turn a losing product or poor deal into a good one for the consumer. Today's audience is smart and getting smarter every day, so it doesn't pay to persuade them to buy with exaggerated claims. All that will get you is a warehouse full of returned merchandise and unpaid invoices.

Out on the telephone front-line, the scripts are put together as a team effort. It's a mistake to come to your telemarketing organization with a firm script in hand and demand that they use it. The only scripts that ever work out are worked out in action.

We start with a fact sheet from the client, of course, plus any other materials available such as product sales sheets, literature, and direct mail pieces. We first write a preliminary script, review it with our best telephone agents to see how they think it will work, and then try it out in action. Give the script a live test on the phone, test and improve, test and change, and finally arrive at the verbal presentation you know is working. No guesswork involved.

The client is fully involved in script development, so we can be sure we're presenting the product and the deal correctly, and are working in harmony with the company image. It's a team effort, and the client is a vital member of the team.

10. Failing to Test Thoroughly

Before you dive headlong into the mysterious water, poke a stick in it. In fact, poke a few sticks here and there. The more you poke, the more you'll learn.

The advantage telemarketing has over other testing media is threefold. First, it's unbelievably fast—you get results you can work with in just a few hours, and complete results in days.

Second, it's flexible. You can change your appeal in five minutes by changing the script. Telemarketing is a dynamic dialog between you and your markets, giving you the maximum opportunity to create the right combinations for success.

Third, it's economical. Valid tests can be structured and tried out for little money, compared to the big bucks you have to invest in preproduction costs for a test in direct mail and other media.

Telemarketing is the ideal medium for testing the full spectrum of variables: price, product, benefits, selling platform, the relative effects of direct mail packages. It's ideal for testing a list or the viability of a new market, or testing to see why a list is unresponsive or why it doesn't pay out. The testing possibilities are endless. It's a shame to waste the opportunity.

11. Falling for Bargain Media or Lists

Most of the apparently good deals in media (especially in broadcast media) involve a Catch 22—you have to commit to the full, predetermined schedule to get the low bargain rate. Deals like this lock you into a program you can't change easily or quickly, but rapid media modification is the heart and soul of profitable direct response TV. The pro's analyze their media daily and buy time only where and when the cost is clearly going to be justified by income. Where can you get this kind of media buying expertise?

The first place to look is in the direct response agencies that can demonstrate a substantial track record in TV. This kind of help is also available from the few independent media buying services that specialize in direct response. The last place to look is in the media department of your general ad agency. The criteria they use so successfully for image building are all wrong for direct response TV.

When the salesperson from your favorite TV station comes around with the latest best deal, don't buy a schedule that can't be altered or canceled in the light of hard results.

Beware of bargain mailing lists, too. Some of these don't include up-to-date telephone numbers, and some lists carry restrictions against "dual use" with the telephone and mail, or require an extra charge for it. There goes your bargain!

Lists for sale as mail responsive (if they're good) are generally telephone responsive, as well.

12. Overlooking the Obvious

Believe it or not, many people who are trying telemarketing for the first time overlook the obvious fact that all the common sense rules of direct marketing apply.

For example, one long-distance telephone company recently bought itself a Christmas turkey by ignoring the well-known rules of seasonality. Its direct mail campaign was scheduled to land just three days before Christmas! The hopeful intention was to stimulate calls to an 800 number for closing the sales. Naturally, at this time of year everyone is distracted by the holiday. The phones were painfully silent, and this major national effort bombed.

By way of ridiculous contrast, another advertiser we heard of planned an inbound campaign when all the phone lines in the country are completely tied up and nobody could get through—on Mother's Day!

How about publishing the wrong 800 number? What? How could this happen to any sensible marketer?

It can happen. We've seen it happen repeatedly over the years. It's happening now, even to some very sophisticated marketers. It can be a disaster of major proportions. But if you understand how it happens, you can easily avoid it. It happens in one of two ways:

1. You publish a number that's not really yours. In a rush to produce your TV or print ads, you call your telemarketing company and take the number down over the phone and send it to your typographer. It turns out that you didn't hear the number correctly, or somebody else garbled it. **Wait** for the number to be confirmed in writing before you stick your production neck out.

If you're getting your 800 service directly from AT&T, don't publish the number until after the line is installed and working and you've test-called it yourself. Not until then is the number safe to publish.

2. The most common reason for publishing a wrong number is that copy may be typed, revised, and retyped half a dozen times before it goes to the typesetter or TV producer. Every typing is a fresh opportunity to make a mistake. If you proofread against the prior previous typing, and that carried a wrong number, you are likely to repeat the error.

There's one absolutely surefire way to stay out of this pitfall. Never believe the phone number you read until you pick up the phone and call it yourself. Make it a habit to do this at every stage of production, and ask everyone in the chain—the copywriter, art director, producer, production manager, and account executive—to make this a routine habit before they sign off on any copy or assembly. The last stage is the most vital—checking the engraver's or press proof, or the final art in the studio for TV production.

Calling to check the number at that critical point-of-no-return has saved thousands of dollars (and thousands of lost leads and sales) for our clients who use this simple system.

Here are two free extra tips on 800 numbers:

- Don't assume your national 800 number covers Hawaii, Alaska, or your home state. It doesn't, unless you make special arrangements.

- If you want an appealing 800 number—one that's easy to recall—you have a better chance of getting one from your telemarketing company than if you went directly to your rep at the phone company. Clout makes the difference.

13. Celebrating Too Soon

Sometimes early test success can fool you. The orders your telephone people are piling up may not be convertible into real sales and collectable invoices.

Remember the old saying, "The sale's not made until the money's in the bank"? It's doubly true in telemarketing. Don't commit a full budget until you have good evidence that the early orders you're generating are real and will pay out. An experienced telemarketing firm has ways of guaranteeing confirmation of sales in advance so you can avoid disappointment later.

14. Holding Back Too Long

When the fish are biting is no time to dig for worms! Strike while the iron is hot! When you do have a clearly successful test, it's a mistake to hold back too long before rollout. Grab the momentum you've stimulated. The rich market you uncovered may disappear if you let it languish while committees analyze, re-analyze, and chew over the results. Here's where you need a telemarketing manager with clout inside the company . . . enough clout to roll out and capitalize on success when all the marketing signals are "go."

15. Accepting Sketchy Reports

Telemarketing is marketing in action, sometimes as fast and dramatic as a hockey game, and information is the puck.

Being a live, interactive medium, telemarketing offers a unique opportunity to gather marketing data that is 100 percent accurate and 100 percent current. Plan from the start to seize this opportunity by designing a reporting system ahead of time that allows you to capture, organize, and manipulate the information in useful, understandable ways. This will translate directly into day-to-day improvements you can make and long-term marketing plans for the future. It's a mistake to pass up the possibilities.

The reports and tracking system you set up need to be fully compatible with your current systems, of course. But since you can gather so much more valuable data at very low cost via telemarketing, you may want to expand or modify your data handling systems in advance to accept and process the additional data you can capture.

Once a campaign's underway, it's usually too late to improve the built-in reporting system, so it pays to plan imaginatively from the start. Ask your telemarketing company for creative suggestions.

16. Falling in Love with the Hardware

There are all kinds of low-, medium-, and high-tech hardware for telemarketing. Put it all together and it makes a very enticing package. Some normally clear-thinking executives lose their perspective over it. They think the more hardware and the higher the technology, the better the program is going to work out. That's not necessarily so. Focus should be on the cost-to-benefit ratio and not on gee-whiz gadgetry for its own sake.

At the core of every telemarketing program there's a plain telephone with one person on each end of the line. It's a human encounter: personal and warm.

The cost of maintaining a computer terminal on the phone agent's desk is justified by performance in some applications, but not in others. For example, a customer service rep who can instantly call up sale records and check stock availability on a computer terminal can offer much better service. On the other hand, a well-trained sales agent who is permitted to focus attention on the customer's answers and develop a personal, natural dialog will always outproduce the agent who is locked into a verbatim script on a CRT.

If something is going to cost more...and require people to run it...and take up space...and occasionally break down.... You get the idea.

When you're planning a campaign, don't let high-tech hardware distract you. Use it only when it's appropriate.

17. Overlooking Opportunities

If you use inbound 800 service simply to collect leads or orders, you're missing some valuable opportunities.

Look at it this way. You've already spent your media money to attract the call in the first place. Now that you've made your big investment, why not make it pay extra dividends?

You know your prospects are in a receptive frame of mind—that's why they initiated the calls to you. They're curious and ready to talk. That golden moment is the time to:

- Reinforce the sale. Many prospects who call may be on the fence and need a little more convincing to order (and pay promptly when you bill them later). The golden moment to firm up the sale is now, on the first incoming call.

- Upsell to a more profitable product or package. A well-trained telephone agent can present a decision tree with a number of alternatives for the prospect to consider and buy. The answers a prospect gives to the operator's questions lead to different scripts for different products.

- Cross-sell related items. Once the prospect is committed, the operator can suggest companion purchases, accessories, and supplies.

- Get telephone numbers and arrange callbacks. Inbound calls are your most inexpensive source for accurate, current numbers (some of which may be unlisted and otherwise difficult or impossible to retrieve).

- Solicit applications for your own charge card or credit plan (vs. checks or standard credit cards).

- Ask for referral names of friends or family who might want a catalog, a subscription, information, or a callback. At the golden moment many people want to share their discovery of your product with others, so they're usually happy to give you referral names, especially if you offer a premium for the names.

The possibilities for using inbound service have not been exhausted, and strangely enough, most marketers overlook the golden moment.

Outbound telemarketing, on the other hand, is well known to be a goldmine with its surface barely scratched. Everywhere you look there's another opportunity to use the telephone creatively. The mother lode, naturally, is in marketing and sales.

First ask yourself two questions: How can telemarketing augment the sales activities we're conducting now? Could we use telemarketing as a total selling system?

How could the telephone work to help your sales force before the sale?

- With calls to identify consumer (or dealer) needs?
- With survey calls to test different sales approaches?
- With calls to target and pinpoint your markets?
- By qualifying dealers or retailers?
- By generating leads?
- By qualifying leads from media prior to direct sales?
- By setting up appointments?
- By scheduled follow-up calls leading to the sale?

How could telemarketing help during the sale?

- By supplying answers to customer questions?
- By taking requests for literature?
- By controlling the flow of sales to match the capacity of your delivery and installation departments?
- By confirming orders and payment arrangements?
- By upgrading the customer from a basic unit to a more profitable sale?

There are all kinds of ways telemarketing can work actively to take the burden off the shoulders of your salespeople and your customer service department and maximize their efficiency.

How can you put telemarketing to work after the sale?

- With goodwill calls after delivery?
- Prospecting calls for add-ons?
- Prospecting for referrals?

Surveys over the years show that a company's best prospects are friends and acquaintances of recent buyers and new customers. What an opportunity for creative telephone marketing! But hardly anyone is taking advantage of it, yet. Ask us for suggestions.

If your company sells supplies or accessories for your product, how about putting telemarketing to work to generate orders on a regular basis?

Don't overlook the service department when you're searching for opportunities.

- How about prospecting by phone for service contracts?
- Or goodwill calls to confirm customer satisfaction?

Look for telemarketing opportunities in promotion and advertising and you'll see that they're unlimited. Think multimedia, using the telephone in harmony with your direct mail, print or broadcast, and other promotional activities, as well as publicity.

- Prepare prospects to expect your mailing piece and read it.
- Stimulate response after the mailing has landed. (Remember that telemarketing will increase the response from a mailing, and can often transform a marginal list into a profitable one.)
- Hype your new ad campaign in print or broadcast.
- Solicit attendance at your trade show booth or party.

Telemarketing fits right into almost any kind of promotional activity. It's an inexpensive insurance policy guaranteeing success for your efforts in the other media.

In marketing research, telemarketing is underused. But it's the proven way to get preliminary results without spending a bundle, and to get some pretty conclusive information rapidly, before you spend heavily on R&D dollars.

- Think of testing proposed product changes or improvements.
- Think of testing new product concepts or names.
- Think of getting customer reaction to proposed product benefits or copy platform.

Again, think multimedia, using the telephone in partnership with your direct mail research effort. The combination is unbeatable for getting reliable information, fast and at low cost.

Chapter

18

PUBLICITY, PUBLIC RELATIONS, AND PRESS RELEASES

Publicity and public relations are terms that are used interchangeably by most professionals in the field, although *Crain's Dictionary of Advertising Terms* gives the following definitions:

- Publicity—information regarding a person, corporation, product, and the like released on his or its behalf for non-paid use by media.
- Public relations—activities of persons or organizations intended to promote understanding of and goodwill toward themselves or their products or services.

Professional publicist Stephen Berg defines public relations as "positioning through journalism." Most of us in the field think of it as "free advertising." Essentially, we write copy about our products, send it to the media, and try to persuade them to give us coverage in their publications or on their radio and TV programs. As an article in *Parade Magazine* (November 2, 1997, p.18) advised: "Make a little noise and be sure they spell your name right."

O'Dwyers' PR Services Report found that the public relations departments of Fortune 500 firms go by the following names: corporate communications, public relations, public affairs, communications, corporate public relations, public relations and advertising, and corporate affairs. According to *O'Dwyers'*, 439 of the Fortune 500 have internal departments dedicated to communications or PR.

A survey by *Business Marketing* magazine of business-to-business marketing communications managers suggests that the main purpose of public relations is to promote products and services. Of the executives surveyed, 85 percent say they use public relations programs for marketing and product support purposes. Only 19 percent said they used it to build corporate image.

Which public relations tools are most effective? Of those surveyed by *Business Marketing*, 77 percent said new product press releases. Sending out press releases to announce changes in personnel (promotions, new hires, etc.) was considered the least effective activity. The results of the survey are summarized in Table 18.1.

Table 18.1. The public relations activities top marketers consider most beneficial.

Public Relations Activity	*Percentage*
New product releases	77%
Technical articles	64%
Case histories	39%
Trade show press kits	22%
Newsletters	20%
Editorial tours	19%
Financial/business publicity	15%
Newspaper publicity	10%
Personnel releases	4%
Other	3%

Note: The total response adds to more than 100 percent due to multiple mentions.

HOW TO USE PRESS RELEASES EFFECTIVELY

"A press release is used to tell the media about your particular story or business in the hopes the media will then tell the public," writes Carol Marden, president of Great Stuff Studio, Raleigh, NC.

"The way you reach your 'public' through public relations is by persuading the media to tell your story in their pages or on their airtime," adds Alison Davis. "Public relations thus becomes a matter of adapting your message to fit the editorial needs of the media you target."

"The successful publicist thinks like an editor," says Richard M. Ezequelle, publisher of *Clinical Lab Products*. "This person submits news releases that fit the magazine, that require few or no changes, that are welcome in the editor's mailbox...[and that] present uncolored, factual news and supply specific details about operation features and benefits. If the product has news value, it will get into print."

In a booklet titled "How to Get Your Publicity into Print," the editors of *Powder and Bulk Solids Magazine* explain the criteria by which they judge the suitability of a press release for their magazine: "The item must be brand new to the trade. And, it must be considered of prime importance to our reading audience. Our editors are on the lookout for only the very latest product innovations to meet our readers' ever-changing needs."

Press releases are standard, mass-distributed stories sent to multiple editors and publications simultaneously with the idea that a percentage of those editors will run an article favorable to your company based on the material.

Press releases do work. When the *Columbia Journalism Review* surveyed an issue of the *Wall Street Journal* to find out how many of the stories were generated by press releases, they found that 111 stories on the inside were taken from press releases either word for word or in paraphrased form. In only 30 percent of these stories did reporters put in additional facts not contained in the original release. One professional in the PR field estimates that 80 percent of all published newspaper and magazine stories either have their basis in a press release or at least use material from press releases.

Bob Kalian, a master of publicity, recently got the *National Enquirer* to run an article publicizing his book, *A Few Thousand of the Best Free Things in America*. His release offered a sample from the book in exchange for a self-addressed stamped envelope (SASE). He received more than 10,000 requests from that one article.

Although the standard format press releases—new product releases, personnel changes, address changes, new catalog releases—do work and can be extremely effective, the best way to profit from press releases is to be different and innovative.

How do you do this? Carol Marden says, "Your press release must reflect some newsworthy event." The problem is, few events dealing with your company are, in themselves, newsworthy. The solution? Create news or newsworthy events.

The standard approach to doing press releases is to look around for interesting things to write about and, finding none, try to write up press releases that make the usual happenings seem exciting. A better approach is to create something that is exciting, new, interesting, or newsworthy, then promote it with a press release.

CASE STUDY 1: PR HOTLINE

Alan Caruba, a New Jersey PR counselor, wanted to gain some publicity for his business. The challenge: Caruba is one of hundreds of independent PR counselors and there is nothing newsworthy about being in the PR business per se.

Alan's solution? Create a "PR Hotline" through which he can offer his consulting service on an hourly basis via telephone to smaller firms that either need quick advice or cannot afford to pay the traditional large monthly retainer most PR firms charge. Another interesting quirk: Alan accepts MasterCard and Visa, which is an unusual way to charge for professional services. His release on the topic, which gained wide publication and generated many inquiries to the hotline, is reproduced in Figure 18.1.

Figure 18.1. Sample press release—PR hotline.

```
THE CARUBA ORGANIZATION
Box 40
Maplewood, NJ 07040
201-763-6392

For Immediate Release

CHARGE PR ADVICE TO YOUR CREDIT CARD
"PR HOTLINE"—NEW BUSINESS SERVICE

Maplewood, NJ—Mike Wallace of "60 Minutes" is at the door with a
camera crew! What do you do now?

"Most public relations does not involve a crisis," says PR coun-
selor Alan Caruba of Maplewood, NJ. "In fact, good PR can avert
such problems while helping to promote products, services, and
causes of every description."

Caruba notes that "many business and professional people neither
need, nor want, to retain a full-time public relations agency or
counselor. What they need is good advice from time to time."
That's why Caruba created the "PR Hotline," a telephone service
(201-763-6392) that allows anyone with a PR question or problem
to call. One can charge the service to either a MasterCard or
Visa account.

At $50 for the first 40 minutes or $75 for up to a full hour, "a
lot of very specific analysis and advice can be provided," says
Caruba. "Public relations can be local, regional, or national in
scope. It can represent a single project or a long-term program."

Caruba has been dispensing advice and service to corporations,
associations, small business operations, and individuals for more
than twenty years. He is a member of the Counselors Academy of
the Public Relations Society of America and frequently lectures
and writes on the subject.

END
```

CASE STUDY 2:
LETTERS THAT WORK

Joan Harris is one of the top writers of sales letters in the country. But she is expensive. To make her services more affordable to smaller firms, she created "LETTERSthatWORK," a program of offering a series of custom-written sales letters to firms at reduced cost. Her release is reproduced in Figure 18.2.

Figure 18.2. Sample press release—Joan Harris.

```
PRESS RELEASE

For Immediate Release

From: Joan Harris
Contact: Connie Murphy
616-333-4444

NEW SERVICE OFFERED TO BUSINESSES—LETTERSthatWORK
```

Joan Harris, president of Joan Harris Direct Response, has just announced a new service. It's called LETTERSthatWORK and offers a custom-written series of individually created sales and customer service letters for only $1,760 (a $2,600 value if done separately).

These letters are written to be used, with modifications, over and over by an entire staff. All are expressly written to achieve results. The series offers five separate letters that can sell a service or product, actuate inactive accounts, welcome new customers, introduce a new product, request important information, collect overdue bills, announce new personnel, and much more.

They're created expressly for each client after an in-depth meeting to assess the company's particular needs, style, and goals. Along with this custom-written series comes a "satisfaction" guarantee and a FREE follow-up meeting for "fine-tuning."

The author of *Modern Business Letters* (now in its third edition) and *Selling with Words* (both from Asher Gallant Press), Ms. Harris is a copywriter/consultant specializing in business-to-business direct mail. She says she developed this concept because most of her clients ask her to write their sales and service letters after she's created a direct mail campaign for them.

"I get calls every day that start off, 'Joan, I need a letter to...,'" she says. "Strong, results-oriented letters are very important for every company—just as important as a talented sales staff. Often, a company will put lots of money into their product, their collateral material, their sales training, and then send out unprofessional, ineffective, poorly written letters. Your letters represent you and should be treated that way. They can be a key step in getting ... and keeping ... customers. That's certainly a worthwhile investment."

For more information about LETTERSthatWORK, call Joan Harris or Connie Murphy at 516-829-5452.

```
END
```

SIX HOOKS THAT WORK BEST IN PRESS RELEASES

There are numerous ways to construct a press release that has the characteristics just discussed. Here are six types of press release that have proven successful time and time again:

1. Free booklet or report
2. Special or timely event
3. Telephone hotline
4. New product or service
5. New literature
6. Tie-in with current trend, fad, or news issue

Let's take a look at some examples of press releases in these categories. When writing your own release, you can closely copy the format and style of these releases, substituting details specific to your topic. For example, I've used the format for a free booklet press release to promote numerous products and services, always with substantial results.

1. Free Booklet Press Release

This is my secret weapon in PR and the single most effective type of release I know of. It works as follows: You write a free booklet, report, or tip sheet on a topic relating to your product or service. For example, if you are selling seeds by mail, write up some gardening instructions and offer them as a free reprint. You then send out a release that 1) announces the publication of your new booklet or report, 2) describes some of the useful information it contains, and 3) offers it free to readers of the publication or to the audience of the radio or TV show.

All three elements are critical. Editors are primarily interested in what's new, so if you are offering a new booklet on a topic, your headline should always begin New Free Booklet..., followed by a description of the topic or issue the information addresses.

Next, your press release should repeat (either word for word or edited) some of the key points highlighted in the booklet or report. This is done so the editor can run your release as a mini feature article on the topic. Just saying you have a booklet available might get you a small mention. But if you allow editors to reprint some of its contents by putting such material in the release you send, they'll run longer, more in-depth pieces featuring all the useful information you've provided.

"But if all of the information in my booklet is revealed in the article, then people will have no reason to send for my booklet!" you might protest. That sounds like a logical objection. But experience proves the opposite is true: The more the article describes the contents of your booklet, the more people will read the article and send for the booklet. "The more you tell, the more you sell" is an old saying favored by mail order ad copywriters, but it also applies to free booklet press releases.

Experience has shown that even if the entire text of a booklet is reprinted in an article (or an ad), people still want to get that text in booklet form. Why? Perhaps people don't like to tear out an ad or article, and find booklets and reports are a more permanent medium. Remember, *put excerpts from your booklet into your release.*

Do not assume that the editor will read your booklet and pull out pertinent material for an article. The press release should be a self-contained mini-article ready to use as is, without the editor having to refer to any enclosures or other materials.

Finally, your free booklet release must call for action. In the last paragraph you say, "For a free copy of [title of booklet], call or write [your company name, address, phone]."

Many editors will include that contact information and a call to action when running your releases, and you will get many requests. Some editors will not print such contact information. You have no control over that. However, if you do not put in contact information and a call to action, *no* editors will tell their readers how or where they can request your booklet, and without such information, no one will contact you. So always close with the call to action.

Should you include a copy of your free booklet with the press releases you mail? Including a sample of the booklet may be desirable, but it is not necessary. I have had great success mailing press releases that did not include a sample copy of the booklet or report being offered.

The main benefit of leaving out the sample booklet is cost savings: Including a sample booklet can add another 10 to 70 cents or more per release being mailed, depending on the cost to print the booklet and the weight of the booklet (which increases postage costs). For example, a tip sheet or slim pamphlet will add less cost than a bulky special report, book, or manual.

If the extra 10 cents to 70 cents per piece is significant to you, omit the sample booklet and pocket the savings.

Be sure to put a line after the close of your release that says, "Editor: Review copy of [title of booklet] available upon request. Call Joe Jones at XXX-XXX-XXXX." Some editors may insist on seeing a copy before they'll promote it in their publication, so you should offer to send a copy free to any editor who requests it. Make the information available to the editor instantly via fax or E-mail.

If your free booklet is slim and inexpensive, or if cost is not a factor, include a sample copy with each release you mail. It certainly can't hurt. Some editors may pay extra attention when they open the envelope and see your report or pamphlet.

Several sample new booklet press releases follow.

Sample Release: Free Tip Sheet on How to Market Software

Your free booklet need not be an actual booklet with cover and staples; you can offer a free report, fact sheet, audiocassette, or other free information in your release.

A release I sent out offering a free tip sheet on how to market and sell software follows. The purpose was to get publicity, establish myself as an authority in software marketing, and get leads from potential clients for my copywriting and consulting services.

The tip sheet was an 8 1/2 by 11-inch sheet of paper printed on two sides; each side contained a reprint of a brief how-to article I wrote on the topic of selling and marketing software. The press release was sent to 50 advertising and marketing trade journals and several hundred computer magazines and journals. It was picked up as a story by eight or nine of these publications, generating hundreds of inquiries and resulting in two new clients and consulting assignments.

The cost of printing and mailing the release was less than $200 including postage, and the initial assignments generated amounted to more than $9,000 in revenue from copywriting and consulting fees. In addition, a number of people requesting the tip sheet ordered more of my tip sheets, books, and reports, resulting in hundreds of dollars in product sales.

FROM: Bob Bly, 174 Holland Avenue, New Milford, NJ 07646
CONTACT: Fern Dickey, 201-385-1220

For immediate release

NEW TIP SHEET SHOWS ESTABLISHED AND START-UP SOFTWARE PRODUCERS HOW TO MARKET AND PROMOTE THEIR PRODUCTS EFFECTIVELY

New Milford, NJ—With the glut of software products flooding the marketplace, it's essential to produce mailings, brochures, ads, and other printed materials that quickly, clearly, and dramatically communicate the key functions and benefits of your software to potential buyers.

That's the opinion of Robert W. Bly, a New Milford, NJ–based consultant specializing in software marketing and promotion. He is also the author of a new tip sheet, "How to Sell Software," which presents advice on how both established and start-up software producers can effectively advertise, promote, and market software for PC's, mainframes, and minicomputers.

One of the most difficult marketing decisions facing software sellers, says Bly, is whether to use a one-step or two-step marketing approach—that is, whether to sell the product via mail order directly from the ad or direct mail piece, or instead to generate a sales lead that is followed up by mailing a brochure or sending a salesperson for a face-to-face meeting.

"PC software products in the $50 to $299 price range are good candidates for one-step mail order selling," advises Bly. "In the $399 to $899 price range, you may want to test a one-step versus a two-step approach and see which works best." And at $1,000 and up, says Bly, the two-step lead generating method is best. "Few people will send payment for a $1,999 software package without some extra convincing by a salesperson, free trial, or demo diskette," he notes.

(continued on next page)

Some additional software marketing tips from the fact sheet:

- Early in your ad copy, tell the prospective purchaser what type or category of software you are selling. "People are usually in the market for a product to handle one of the known, identifiable, major applications—project management, word processing, accounts payable," says Bly.

- Talk in terms the reader can visualize. Instead of writing "56 KBPS modem," say "The SuperSpeedy modem transmits data at a rate of 56,000 bits per second—about a third of a second for a full page of text."

- The headline or teaser copy should select the right audience for the ad or mailer. For example, if you are selling C compilers, the teaser copy might read "Attention C programmers."

- Product specifications should be scaled down to numbers the reader can relate to. "Stores a mailing list of 50,000 prospects" is better than "Stores 5 million characters" because people have an easier time grasping the smaller number, says Bly.

- Include testimonials from satisfied users and excerpts from favorable third-party reviews.

One of Bly's all-time favorite headlines is from a small, black and white display ad for Winterhalter Incorporated, a manufacturer of coax boards and controllers that enable micro-to-mainframe communication. The headline reads, "LINK 8 PCs TO YOUR MAINFRAME—ONLY $2,395." Says Bly, "Computer magazines are filled with 'clever' ad headlines that give the reader no idea whatsoever what the product is or who it is for. This headline tells you *exactly* what the product will do for you and what it will cost."

For a copy of Bly's software marketing tip sheet, "How to Sell Software," send $1 and a self-addressed, stamped number 10 envelope to: Bob Bly, Dept. 105, 174 Holland Avenue, New Milford, NJ 07646.

END

Here I requested $1 and a self-addressed stamped envelope from the reader. This was done not to qualify the prospect (I don't believe asking for money does this, except if you're selling mail order information) but to eliminate the labor of addressing envelopes and to cover my costs (I'm a small-time operator on a limited budget).

If I were doing a similar PR mailing for a corporate client or entrepreneur, I'd probably advise them not to require a self-addressed stamped envelope and to send the tip sheet free of charge—unless they were strapped for cash and needed a self-liquidating promotion (one that pays its own cost in revenue generated).

Note in the last paragraph of the release my key code, Dept. 105, in my address. By counting the number of requests for this tip sheet addressed to Department 105, I know exactly how many responses were generated as a result of this PR mailing.

Some practitioners take this a step further and put a different key code on each individual press release; the key code indicates the publication the release was sent to. Therefore the press release on my tip sheet going to *Computer Decisions* would have been key coded "Dept.

CD," while the next copy, being mailed to *InfoWorld*, would have been key coded "IW."

The advantage of individual coding of releases keyed to publications is that it lets you know how many responses were generated from each media outlet; you can target those that generate a high level of response for extra promotion or special attention when doing subsequent PR mailings. The major disadvantage of key coding each release with a different key is that it's time consuming: You have to track it one release at a time. I personally don't think it's worth the time and trouble, but do whatever seems best for you.

Sample Release: Recession-Fighting Business Strategies Booklet

This was one of my more successful new booklet releases, and I think it's a good model for anyone offering free information via a press release: The format is easily adapted to any information offer and has worked for everyone who has tried it.

This press release was mailed to 300 business magazines, 50 advertising and marketing magazines, 80 syndicated newspaper columnists who write on business topics, business editors at the nation's 500 largest daily newspapers, and a few other publications. Because I included a sample booklet with the release, total cost for mailing approximately 950 releases was a bit under $1,000.

The release generated dozens of pickups, ranging from brief mentions to magazines that reprinted almost the entire text word for word. I do not know the specific number of pickups since I did not use a clipping service to keep track of all the placements.

Virtually every pickup included information on how the reader could order the booklet. From this press release alone, I sold well over 3,000 booklets at $7 each, for a gross of $21,000. The follow-up sales included several consulting assignments, half a dozen speaking engagements, and additional sales of other booklets and reports.

The release works for two reasons: first, because the topic was timely—the release was issued during the worst of the recession of the early 1990s, so it was a hot topic with inherent media appeal; and second, because it precisely follows the three-part formula of a) announcing the availability of a new booklet, b) excerpting highlights so editors could run a minifeature article on the subject, and c) providing contact information and a call to action.

The only way in which it violates the formula for the free booklet release is that the reader must pay $7. I did this because my primary motivation was to make money selling this booklet as well as a line of related booklets and reports I offer, and I felt the need for the booklet was so great that charging $7 would not prevent people from ordering.

For a client selling a consulting or advisory service, however, I would probably make the booklet free or ask for a nominal sum if the objective was to generate sales leads for the service.

FROM: Bob Bly, 174 Holland Avenue, New Milford, NJ 07646
CONTACT: Bob Bly, phone 201-385-1220

For immediate release

NEW BOOKLET REVEALS 14 PROVEN STRATEGIES FOR KEEPING BUSINESSES
BOOMING IN A BUST ECONOMY

New Milford, NJ—While some companies struggle to survive in today's sluggish business environment, many are doing better than ever–largely because they have mastered the proven but
little-known strategies of "recession marketing."

That's the opinion of Bob Bly, an independent marketing consultant and author of the just-
published booklet, "Recession-Proof Business Strategies: 14 Winning Methods to Sell Any
Product or Service in a Down Economy."

"Many businesspeople fear a recession or soft economy, because when the economy is weak,
their clients and customers cut back on spending," says Bly. "To survive in such a marketplace,
you need to develop recession marketing strategies that help you retain your current accounts
and keep those customers buying. You also need to master marketing techniques that will win
you *new* clients or customers to replace any business you may have lost because of the
increased competition that is typical of a recession."

Among the recession-fighting business strategies Bly outlines in his new booklet:

- *Reactivate dormant accounts.* An easy way to get more business is simply to call past clients
  or customers—people you served at one time but are not actively working for now—to
  remind them of your existence. According to Bly, a properly scripted telephone call to a list
  of past buyers will generate approximately one order for every ten calls.

- *Quote reasonable, affordable fees and prices in competitive bid situations.* While you need
  not reduce your rates or prices, in competitive bid situations you will win by bidding toward
  the low or middle end of your price range rather than at the high end. Bly says that during
  a recession, your bids should be 15 to 20 percent lower than you would normally charge in a
  healthy economy.

- *Give your existing clients and customers a superior level of service.* In a recession, Bly advises businesses to do everything they can to hold onto their existing clients or customers—
  their "bread-and-butter" accounts. "The best way to hold onto your clients or customers is to
  please them," says Bly, "and the best way to please them is through better customer service.
  Now is an ideal time to provide that little bit of extra service or courtesy that can mean the
  difference between dazzling the client or customer vs. merely satisfying them."

- *Reactivate old leads.* Most businesses give up on sales leads too early, says Bly. He cites a
  study from Thomas Publishing that found that although 80 percent of sales to businesses
  are made on the fifth call, only one out of ten salespeople calls beyond three times.
  Concludes Bly: "You have probably not followed up on leads diligently enough, and the new
  business you need may already be right in your prospect." He says repeated follow-up
  should convert 10 percent of prospects to buyers.

- *Repackage your product line or service to accommodate smaller clients or customers on
  reduced budgets.* Manufacturers and other product sellers can offer compact models, economy sizes, no-frills versions, easy payment plans, extended credit, special discounts, incentives, and smaller minimum orders to appeal to prospects with reduced spending power.
  Service providers can be more flexible by selling their services and time in smaller, less
  costly increments.

(continued on next page)

- *Keep busy with ancillary assignments.* Another recession survival strategy is to take an ancillary assignment to fill gaps in your schedule. For example, a carpenter who normally handled only large, lucrative home remodeling jobs took on lots of smaller jobs and "handyman" work to keep the money coming when his home renovation work fell off.

- *Add value to your existing product or service.* While prospects may seem reluctant to spend money in a soft economy, their real concern, says Bly, is making sure they get the best value for their dollars. You can retain existing accounts and win business by offering more value than your competition. For instance, says Bly, a firm selling industrial components added value by computerizing its inventory system so it could give customers faster telephone quotations on the availability and pricing of needed parts.

- *Help existing clients or customers create new sales for you.* Bly advises businesses to call their existing accounts with new ideas that will benefit the client or customer while requiring them to buy more of what the vendor is selling. "It's a win-win situation," says Bly. "They get your ideas, suggestions, and solutions to their problems at no charge, while you sell more of your product or service to help them implement the idea you suggested."

To receive a copy of Bly's booklet, "Recession-Proof Business Strategies," send $8 ($7 plus $1 shipping and handling) to: Bob Bly, Dept. 109, 174 Holland Avenue, New Milford, NJ 07646. Cash, money orders, and checks (payable to "Bob Bly") accepted. (Add $1 for Canadian orders.)

ABOUT THE AUTHOR: Bob Bly, an independent copywriter and consultant based in New Milford, NJ, specializes in business-to-business, high tech, and direct-response marketing. He is the author of 30 books including HOW TO PROMOTE YOUR OWN BUSINESS (New American Library) and SELLING YOUR SERVICES (Henry Holt). A frequent speaker and seminar leader, Mr. Bly speaks nationwide on the topic of how to market successfully in a recession or soft economy.

END

Sample Release: Free Article Reprint

Here's another variation on the free booklet theme. This company published an article on its specialty, collections, in a trade journal. It made reprints of the article and offered it as a "free special report" in a press release sent to other publications within the same industry. Interestingly, many of these publications used the release, and not one voiced an objection to printing what was essentially an offer to send an article reprint from a competitor's publication.

From this I learned that *any* published article can be offered as a reprint through a free booklet press release and that other magazines will run the offer. You can print somewhere on the booklet cover at the bottom of the tip sheet that the article was "reprinted with permission from Vol. 5, No. 10 of XYZ Magazine" without fear that this will turn off rival magazines from using it.

In the release, however, call your reprint a "special report" if it's a lengthy article, a "monograph" if it's a scholarly or scientific article, or a "tip sheet" if it's a short (one- or two-page) article. Any of these terms sound more important than an article reprint, so more readers will write to or call you to get it.

FROM: RMCB, 1261 Broadway, New York, NY 10001
CONTACT: Russell Fuchs, 800 542-5025

For immediate release

FREE REPORT FOR DIRECT MARKETERS PRESENTS 12 NEW WAYS TO COLLECT OLD BILLS

New York, NY, January—A new special report, published by Retrieval-Masters Creditors Bureau (RMCB), a nationwide agency specializing in the collection of low dollar amount, high-volume accounts receivable, reveals 12 key strategies for using an outside collection agency to turn past-due accounts into paid-up customers.

The 8-page report, "How an Outside Collection Agency Can Improve Your Conversions," is available free of charge to circulation directors, publishers, direct marketers, business executives, advertising professionals, entrepreneurs, and students. The cost to the general public is $5.

Although the report originally was written to show circulation directors how to improve subscription collections, Russell Fuchs, president of RMCB, says the information is applicable to direct marketers selling virtually any product or service through the mail—including publishers, book clubs, mail order firms, continuity plans, and catalog marketers.

Why should direct marketers, whose invoices typically reflect a low dollar balance, be interested in working with collection agencies to improve collection results? "Whenever you extend credit to the customer and allow him or her to say 'bill me,' you typically have a nonpayment rate ranging from 5 to 35 percent or more," says Fuchs. "Experience shows that a competent collection agency can convert 21 to 25 percent of those delinquent accounts into paid-up customers."

Here are some of RMCB's suggestions on how to use a collection agency to improve collection results:

- *Vary the letterhead.* Fuchs says that sending a dunning letter on a third-party letterhead—either in an internal billing series or the collection agency's billing cycle—lifts response virtually every time.

- *Vary the dunning cycle.* To extend the billing series and increase net recovery rates, collection agencies vary the timing between efforts, typically from 14 to 28 days. "This is a proven response-booster," says Fuchs.

- *Make sure "white mail" is given special handling.* "Promptly acknowledge and resolve every nonpayment and partial payment response," warns Fuchs. "Your collection agency should have a special 'correspondence response department' whose job it is to communicate with customers who dispute invoices, make partial payments, or have other responses out of the ordinary."

- *Be aware of the legal requirements for dunning.* For example, the Fair Debt Collection Practices Act requires that specific disclosure copy notifying consumers of their rights appears on each letter sent by any collection agency. (RMCB's report includes the proper wording for this disclosure.)

To receive a free copy of "How an Outside Collection Agency Can Improve Your Conversions," contact: Retrieval-Masters Creditors Bureau, 1261 Broadway Dept. CM1, New York, NY 10001, phone 800-843-8097, ATT: Ruth Malone.

For a free, no-obligation telephone consultation with expert Russell Fuchs about your direct marketing collection problems, telephone RMCB's "Collections Hotline" at 800-542-5025.

END

2. Special Event, Gimmick, or Timely Issue

The press is always looking for a story that captures the public's imagination. Therefore, if you have a special event, timely issue, or unusual human interest story, or can add some sort of hook or angle to your release, you'll have a better chance of gaining coverage.

Editors are interested in stories that are substantial and of value yet have an unusual twist or gimmick to them. If you can be a bit different (albeit in a relevant way), you will get noticed.

Sample Press Release: Empire State Building Location

Here's a perfect example. This company rents mailboxes—a pretty mundane business. But the angle for this story was the unusual, prestigious location of their mailbox address: the Empire State Building.

Mentioning that the Empire State Building is one of the few buildings in the country with its own private zip code and post office is a nice added touch, as some editors like to include a bit of trivia or little-known information in their articles.

FROM: Empire State Communications
350 Fifth Ave.
New York, NY 10118
CONTACT: Arthur Goodman, phone 800-447-0099

For immediate release

NOW BUSINESSES NATIONWIDE CAN ESTABLISH A BRANCH OFFICE IN NEW YORK CITY'S PRESTIGIOUS EMPIRE STATE BUILDING—FOR AS LITTLE AS $35 PER MONTH

New York, NY—Want to give your company added prestige and impress your customers? NYC-based entrepreneur Arthur Goodman has a suggestion: a "branch office" in New York's most distinguished and memorable location: the Empire State Building.

Goodman's company, Empire State Communications, provides mail receiving, fax, telex, and telephone service for businesses nationwide that want to establish a branch address in New York without physically having an office there. And the price is right: Empire's service starts at $35 per month.

"Our service allows firms nationwide to immediately and inexpensively establish a New York presence at one of Manhattan's most memorable—and impressive—addresses," says Goodman. "The Empire State Building is a status symbol worldwide. And the address is easy for your prospects to remember; no multidigit P.O. box number is necessary."

What types of companies use Goodman's Empire State service? " It's for small out-of-town companies that want to convey an image of a larger, more substantial firm through a prestigious New York City address, as well as large corporations that feel they should have a New York City location but don't want the expense of renting costly office space," he says.

How does Goodman's service work? For a small monthly fee, Goodman's clients obtain the right to use his Empire State Building address as their own in letterhead, business cards, and advertisements. "We act as their New York office," says Goodman. "They can receive mail, phone calls, telexes, and fax transmissions, just as if they were physically located in New York.

"In fact, your prospects and customers will have no way of telling that you don't actually have a big, fancy office in the Empire State Building," he adds.

(continued on next page)

Mail received at the Empire State location is forwarded daily by Goodman to any location his clients specify—usually their headquarters' corporate mailroom. According to Goodman, the Empire State Building is one of the few buildings in the United States with its own post office branch and private zip code (10118), which results in faster delivery of his clients' mail. Phone calls, telexes, and fax transmissions received are also forwarded immediately, either by mail, phone, fax, or computer modem.

Goodman, in business since 1953, is no newcomer to the mailbox industry. One of his other companies, Goodman Communications, offers mail receiving and branch office service in three additional Manhattan locations: midtown, downtown, and the Upper East Side.

"This is the first time that the mailing address of the Empire State Building has been made commercially available to businesses of all sizes here and overseas," says Goodman, who adds that Empire State Communications is the only company offering mail receiving service at that address.

For a limited time only, Goodman is making a special offer to entice out-of-town companies to try his Empire State location: one month's service free to people who contact him within the next 30 days.

To receive a free brochure outlining the services offered by Goodman at his Empire State location, call or write to: Arthur Goodman, Empire State Communications, 350 Fifth Avenue, Dept. EPR-2, New York, NY 10118, 800-447-0099.

END

Sample Press Release: Entrepreneur Seminar

A special event such as a convention, sale, grand opening, trade show, or seminar, is also a good topic for a press release because it's timely. When Gary Blake and I decided to hold a seminar on the topic of being an entrepreneur, we sent out the release on p. 409 to local and national business magazines.

Although this release was not wildly successful, it did catch the attention of a reporter at *Nation's Business*, who featured us prominently in a cover story on entrepreneurs in the United States.

3. Telephone Hotline Press Release

Telephone hotlines—numbers people can call to get free advice and information from a live operator, tape recording, or voice mail system—are extremely popular with consumers and therefore with editors. People like the convenience of being able to dial a phone number and order a product, ask a question, or get free assistance or advice. There are telephone hotlines on every conceivable topic, from cancer and lawn care to gambling and auto safety.

While some hotlines are nonprofit, many are sponsored by companies that use them as a way of generating leads, sales, inquiries, visibility, and publicity.

One of the best ways to promote such a hotline is through a press release. Editors will print short blurbs and articles announcing your hotline, describing the information available to callers, and giving the phone number. Such announcements can generate hundreds or thousands of phone calls, plus lots of media coverage.

FROM: The Communication Workshop, 217 E. 85th St.,
New York, NY 10028
CONTACT: Gary Blake, 718-575-8000

For immediate release

NEW NYC SEMINAR SHOWS "ORDINARY PEOPLE" HOW TO BECOME SUCCESSFUL
ENTREPRENEURS—WITHOUT SPENDING BIG MONEY OR TAKING BIG RISKS

NEW YORK, NY, October 30th—Computer whiz kids, chocolate-chip-cookie bakers, and other young hotshot millionaire success stories have become media darlings. But what if you're a regular guy or gal, not looking to make a million but just wanting to make a go of a modest, small business of your own?

Take heart. Two local entrepreneurs, Gary Blake and Bob Bly, co-authors of the new book OUT ON YOUR OWN: FROM CORPORATE TO SELF-EMPLOYMENT (New York: John Wiley & Sons), have created a new one-day seminar on BECOMING AN ENTREPRENEUR.

The seminar teaches would-be entrepreneurs that you don't have to be a Ted Turner or a Victor Kiam to start your own business. Anybody can do it—and succeed—without a lot of money, without being a genius, and without taking big risks.

Says Bly, "Although I always disliked corporate life, I was the person people would have voted 'Least Likely to Take a Risk.' But by following a few simple principles, I successfully made the transition from a 9-to-5 job to self-employment. I didn't have any money in the bank or a great new product. Yet I quadrupled my corporate salary within three years."

Adds Blake, 42, director of the Communication Workshop, a management consulting firm, "It's traumatic to leave the world of weekly paychecks; we know because we've done it. Our seminar on BECOMING AN ENTREPRENEUR helps people progress from just dreaming about quitting to realistically assessing their options, making plans, and then acting on those plans."

The first BECOMING AN ENTREPRENEUR seminar, which costs $85 per participant, will be presented in midtown Manhattan on January 25th. The seminar is aimed at people who are not satisfied with corporate life but may not have the impetus, self-confidence, or focus to break loose. BECOMING AN ENTREPRENEUR gives a blueprint for entrepreneurial success, guiding each participant toward confronting the positive and negative aspects of being your own boss.

The course explores such issues as discovering your values, focusing on what you want to do for a living, weighing the pros and cons of corporate security vs. entrepreneurial freedom, dealing with self-doubt and the criticism of others, coping with solitude, finding a partner, setting fees, setting up a company, getting your first client, managing time, and marketing and advertising for the small business. It also gives special strategies for making a smooth, painless transition from corporate employment to self-employment.

For more information on the BECOMING AN ENTREPRENEUR seminar, phone or write to the Communication Workshop, 217 E. 85th Street, Suite 442, New York, NY 10028, 212-794-1144.

END

Sample Press Release: The Advertising Hotline

Years ago I wanted to promote myself as an authority in advertising. Unlike the big ad agencies, however, I knew that merely sending a release announcing my latest projects or clients would not be effective. The business of J. Walter Thompson is of interest to the trade press; the business of a lone freelance copywriter is not.

When I asked myself, "How can I create something newsworthy and thus get publicity for myself?" the Advertising Hotline was the answer. The idea is simple: a nationwide telephone hotline businesspeople can call to get quick tips and advice on how to improve their marketing.

To implement the idea was even easier: just set up a phone line in my basement and attach an answering machine with a long outgoing message. Hotline callers were treated to a 2-minute prerecorded "miniseminar on tape" on a different topic each week. Here is my release:

FROM: The Advertising Hotline, 174 Holland Ave., New Milford, NJ 07646
CONTACT: Amy Sprecher, 201-385-1220

For immediate release

NEW NATIONAL TELEPHONE HOTLINE PROVIDES FREE ADVERTISING AND MARKETING TIPS TO AD AGENCIES, CORPORATIONS, AND SMALL BUSINESSES

New Milford, NJ, December 4th—The Advertising Hotline, a new nationwide telephone hotline, has been established to provide free advice, information, and tips on advertising, direct mail, publicity, and other forms of promotion to ad agencies, PR firms, large corporations, and small businesses. The Hotline number is XXX-XXX-XXXX.

"Clients and their agencies today need solid, reliable information on what works in advertising—and what doesn't," says Bob Bly, the hotline's director. "As a freelance copywriter, I have hundreds of people calling me and asking questions such as: 'How can I get more inquiries from my quarter-page trade ad? How can I write a direct mail package that will get a good response?' I set up the Advertising Hotline to give these folks some of the answers."

Unlike many other information sources, Bly points out, the Advertising Hotline is free. "A lot of companies can't afford to hire consultants, and it takes time to read a book, listen to an audiocassette, or attend a seminar," notes Bly. "The Hotline is free and takes only five minutes of the caller's time."

In the months to come, callers who phone the Advertising Hotline at XXX-XXX-XXXX can listen to taped "miniseminars" on a variety of subjects. Scheduled topics include: "10 Ways to Stretch Your Advertising Budget," "How to Write Winning Sales Letters," "12 Questions to Ask *Before* You Create Your Next Advertising Campaign," "New Ideas for Your Corporate Newsletter," and "Selling Financial Services by Mail." The current topic can be heard right now by calling the hotline at XXX-XXX-XXXX.

The hotline can be reached from any telephone in the world, 24 hours a day, 7 days a week. The taped message usually runs between 3 and 5 minutes in length. The message is changed approximately once a week.

END

I sent the release to 50 trade publications covering advertising, public relations, promotion, marketing, and sales. Attractively printed Advertising Hotline Rolodex cards were mailed with releases to give editors the impression that the Ad Hotline was a real and ongoing activity.

Eighteen publications ran stories based on the release. At least five ran almost the entire release, practically word for word. This publicity generated thousands of phone calls to the hotline within 12 months.

Note that it is not necessary to have a hotline number that is a toll-free 800, 888, or 877 number or spells out a word (such as 800 AUTO-SAFETY). You can be successful using an ordinary toll number that is staffed by employees or that uses electronic voice mail or an answering machine to deliver its message.

This same type of release can be used to promote your Web site, but the editorial pick-up probably won't be as significant. That's because there are relatively few telephone hotlines being promoted compared with the huge number of Web sites. The more common something is, the less the media is interested.

4. New Product Release

The most popular type of press release is the new product release. This is simply the announcement of a new product. The product need not actually be brand new to qualify for a new product release. Enhancements, upgrades, new models, new features, new options, new accessories, new grades, new sizes and styles, and new applications can all form the basis for a release of this type.

New product releases are typically featured in the new product sections of publications. Editors run short two-or three-paragraph descriptions of the products along with a photo or drawing, if provided along with the release. This type of coverage, while routine in nature, provides additional exposure for your product, builds awareness, and can generate numerous inquiries at low cost.

Here's a typical new product release:

NEWS RELEASE KOCH ENGINEERING COMPANY, INC.
CONTACT: Bob Bly or Mike Mutsakis, 212-682-5755

For immediate release

KOCH ENGINEERING DEVELOPS DRY SO_2 SCRUBBING SYSTEM

Koch Engineering Company, Inc., of Wichita, Kansas and New York City, has developed a dry SO_2 scrubbing system for cleaning flue gas in coal-fired boilers.

The system uses a line-based dryer and a baghouse for SO_2 and particulate removal. To design dry scrubbing systems tailored to individual applications, Koch Engineering has a fully integrated dry scrubbing pilot plant available for test and evaluation of customer coal and chemicals.

"Koch Engineering is the only manufacturer in the dry scrubbing business that has a dry SO_2 scrubbing pilot plant operating off a dedicated pulverized coal-fired boiler, a large-scale semiworks spray dryer, and a commercial-scale system now in operation," says David H. Koch, president of Koch Engineering. "No company is better equipped to design, scale up, fabricate, and install complete dry scrubbing systems for industrial boilers."

The Koch dry SO_2 scrubbing system, he added, uses a two-fluid nozzle in the spray dryer rather than a rotary or centrifugal atomizer. This results in increased reliability, simpler maintenance, and reduced initial investment.

END

This release was picked up in more than 35 trade journals; many ran the entire three-page release word for word. Result: 2,500 inquiries generated within 6 months. Total promotion cost: under $500.

Here's another new product release, this one for a software product:

FROM: PLATO Software, 401 Development Court, Kingston, NY 12401
CONTACT: Richard Rosen or Brian Rifkin, phone 914-246-6648

For immediate release

UNIQUE ACCOUNTING SOFTWARE PACKAGE CAN BE EASILY MODIFIED BY USERS TO FIT THEIR BUSINESS PROCEDURES—WITH NO PROGRAMMING!

Kingston, NY—PLATO Software recently released an upgraded version of its modifiable business and accounting software package, P&L-Pro Version 6.0.

What makes P&L-Pro unique is that it's the only affordably priced accounting software that can be modified by the user with no programming required, claims Richard Rosen, president, PLATO Software.

"Most low-end, off-the-shelf business software forces you to adjust your business procedures to accommodate the limitations of the program," says Rosen. "As a result, you cannot get the software to do things your way. Some high-end business software packages are designed to be modifiable, but these start at $10,000 to $25,000 and up for a complete system."

P&L-Pro, by comparison, is a complete and affordably priced business and accounting software package that can be modified by users, even nonprogrammers, to precisely fit their procedures and operations. Base price starts at approximately $100 per module.

How P&L-Pro works:

Most business software, according to Rosen, is created using complex programming languages, and therefore can only be altered by computer programmers.

P&L-Pro, however, was built using Alpha Four, an easy-to-use database management system. As a result, users can add functions to or modify their copies of P&L-Pro directly, without help from a programmer or software consultant.

The new version, P&L-Pro 6.0, features faster and simpler bank reconciliation, check entry, application of payments to invoices, screen entry, and statement preparation. It also includes two new modules, Payroll and Inventory Control, which, added to the existing modules of General Ledger, Accounts Receivable, and Accounts Payable, make P&L-Pro a complete business and accounting software package that is fully modifiable by the user.

The Payroll module includes all state and federal tax tables and features multiple pay types, unlimited deduction types, and time card entry. It is completely interfaced with the P&L-Pro

General Ledger module. A special feature enables the user to print checks for the new year while still being able to print W-2 forms for the prior year.

The Inventory Control module generates an unlimited number of sales and inventory reports. These reports give the user an up-to-the-minute picture of inventory by product, stock number, location, or any other criteria selected. The module handles purchase order entry, receiving, sales order entry, and shipping. And it can be easily customized to fit any method of inventory management and control.

A new feature, history screens, displays all key data about any given customer or vendor at a glance. This eliminates the time and effort of retrieving customer and vendor data from multiple screens located throughout the program. The customer history screen, for example, includes all products purchased, orders placed, invoices sent, payments received, missed or late payments, and balances due.

P&L-Pro 2.0 with all five modules sells for $495. Plato Software can install the software, set up the company's chart of accounts, and customize the screens, reports, and menus for an additional fee. For more information contact: PLATO Software, 401 Development Court, Kingston, NY 12401, phone 800-SWPLATO (800-797-5286), fax 914-246-7597.

END

5. New Literature Release

The new literature release is used to announce the publication of a new product brochure, capabilities brochure, data sheet, catalog, or any other literature on a product or service. When you come out with a new product, you can send out a new product release first, then follow up a month or so later with a new literature release (announcing publication of the product brochure or data sheet). In this way, you get two PR opportunities for each new product instead of just one. If your literature contains how-to or reference information—for example, it tells how to specify a product, select the proper grade, install the right attachment, or the like—your release should highlight that fact.

Here's a sample new literature release:

NEW CATALOG AND REFERENCE MANUAL OFFERS WIDGET BUYERS GUIDANCE IN PROPER SELECTION, INSTALLATION OF WIDGETS

ANYTOWN, USA—Smith Widget Co. announced today the publication of its new 32-page widget catalog and buyer's guide.

The catalog, available free, contains complete specifications for more than 400 grades and models of widgets for standard and custom industrial applications.

It also contains charts, graphs, cross-reference tables, and other technical data enabling engineers to correctly specify, order, and install the right widget for their application, said Joe Smith, president of Smith Widgets.

[List some of the highlights of features of the catalog here.]

For a free copy of the Smith Widget catalog, call or write to: Smith Widget, Dept. PRC-1, Anytown, USA, XXX-XXX-XXXX.

END

6. Tie-In with Current Fad, Event, or News

Although not always easy to do, if you can tie in your release with a fad, current event, news story, or trend, you will maximize your publicity pick-ups.

In 1997, virtual pets became popular, and I sent out the release below. Within three days of mailing it, six newspapers had called me for an interview; one sent a photographer and reporter to my home and did a front-page story.

FROM: Microchip Gardens, 174 Holland Avenue, New Milford, NJ 07646
CONTACT: Bob Bly, phone 201-385-1220

For immediate release

MICROCHIP GARDENS, WORLD'S FIRST "GIGAPET CEMETERY," OPENS IN NORTHERN NJ

When 7-year-old Alex Bly's gigapet died after he dropped it in the toilet, he couldn't find a place to bury it. So his father, NJ-based entrepreneur Bob Bly, created Microchip Gardens—the world's first gigapet cemetery—in the family's suburban backyard.

Now if your child's gigapet dies and can't be revived, instead of unceremoniously tossing it in the trash, you can give it a proper burial in a beautiful, tree-lined resting place.

For fees starting at $5, based on plot location and method of interment (burial, mausoleum, cremation), Bly will give your dearly departed gigapet an eternal resting place in Microchip Gardens, complete with funeral service and burial certificate.

"Even gigapets don't last forever," said Bly. "There are pet cemeteries for dogs and cats; now gigapets have one too."

To help owners get the most pleasure from gigapet ownership, Bly—author of 35 published books including *The "I Hate Kathie Lee Gifford" Book* (Kensington) and *The Ultimate Unauthorized Star Trek Quiz Book* (HarperCollins)—has written an informative new booklet, "Raising Your Gigapet." The booklet covers such topics as purchasing your first gigapet; taking the pet home; care and feeding; and play and discipline. Gigapet burial rituals and the origins of Microchip Gardens are also covered.

To get your copy of "Raising Your Gigapet," which includes complete information on the Microchip Gardens gigapet cemetery, send $4 to: CTC, 22 E. Quackenbush Avenue, Dumont, NJ 07628.

END

HOW TO PREPARE A PRESS RELEASE

Preparing a press release is simple and straightforward. Just type your copy double-spaced on standard (8 1/2 × 11-inch) sheets of paper.

Press releases can be duplicated by offset at a local quick-copy printshop or run off on your office copier if the quality of reproduction is good. You can reproduce them on plain paper, business stationery, or special PR letterhead with the words NEWS RELEASE or PRESS RELEASE printed across the top; however, special paper is not necessary, and plain paper is fine.

Follow the format of the samples presented in this chapter. At the top of the first page, put FROM: or SOURCE: followed by the name and address of your company. Underneath this type CONTACT:, followed by your name and telephone number.

Note: If you use a public relations agency, it will list its own name and address (under FROM: or CONTACT:) followed by the name and address of you, the client (preceded by the word CLIENT:).

Below this, type "For immediate release." This tells editors that your story is timely, but it doesn't date the release so if you want to keep a supply on hand and send them out to editors as the opportunity arises, you can. If the release is tied to an event that takes place on a specific date, type "For release: Monday, August 22, 1997" (substituting the actual date) instead of "For immediate release."

Underneath this comes the headline. It is typed in all caps and can be as short as one line or as long as three lines. Two lines are typical.

Leave some extra space between the headline and the first paragraph of the story. The first paragraph may begin with a dateline, such as "New York, NY, October, 1997—" with the first sentence of the first paragraph coming immediately after the dash.

There are two basic leads for press releases: news and feature.

The news lead is the prototypical "who, what, when, where, why, and how" opening of a straight news story as taught in Journalism 101. The advantage of using the news lead is that, even if the editor chops the rest of your story and prints only the first paragraph, as is frequently done, the gist of your story still gets across.

The sample press release for the Advertising Hotline is an example of a straight news lead. To see more examples of news leads, pick up today's *The New York Times* and study the first paragraphs of the stories running on page one.

The other type of lead is the feature lead. The feature lead is written in an entertaining, attention-getting fashion similar to the opening of a magazine feature article. The purpose is to grab the editor's attention by being clever, startling, or dramatic, so that more editors read and use your release.

The press release for the Becoming an Entrepreneur seminar is a good example of a feature lead. To see more examples of feature leads, pick up any issue of *Glamour* or *Cosmopolitan* magazine and read the first paragraph of each of the major articles listed on the contents page.

After the lead comes the body of the story. If you are coming to the end of the page and it looks as if the paragraph will have to continue on the next page, move the entire paragraph to that page. Do not divide paragraphs between two pages.

Why not? Some editors may want literally to cut up your release into paragraphs with scissors, then tape it together in a different order. (This is how some editors edit.) For the same reason, releases are always printed on one side of a sheet of paper, never on two sides.

You may say at this point, "But I don't want the editor to edit my story. I want it to run as is!" This is an understandable attitude, but it is self-defeating. In pubic relations, the editor is in clear control. The editor is the customer for your stories, and you must meet the editor's needs and standards first if you are to have any chance of reaching your final audience—readers.

If editors want to edit, make it easy, not difficult. If they want a new angle on your story, don't protest—help them find it. The more you cooperate with editors and give them what they need, the more publicity you will get.

The last paragraph of your press release contains the response information, including name, address, and telephone number. For example, "To get Smith Widget Company's new 32-page Widget catalog, contact: Smith Widget Company, Anytown, USA, XXX-XXX-XXXX."

At the end of the story, you can simply type "END" or "XXX" or "-30-". All three symbols let the editor know that this is the end of the story.

FIVE WAYS TO GET YOUR PUBLICITY RELEASES PUBLISHED MORE OFTEN

Copywriter Mike Pavlish offers the following checklist for making sure your press releases get published:

1. Is it important to the publication's readers? If you were the editor and you had dozens of releases but could only publish a few, would you honestly publish your release? Is the information and story in your release really important—not to your business, but to the publication's readers? If not, forget it and look for a new angle.

2. Is it really news or just an advertisement in disguise? Editors are not in the business of publishing advertising. Almost all will immediately discard publicity that is really advertising in disguise. Of course, most publicity has some advertising value or purpose, but write your publicity to give news or helpful information only.

3. Is it written so the publication's readers benefit from it? Your publicity will get published more often if there is important news in it that will benefit the publication's readers. This could be new technology the readers will be interested in, helpful information, or a new trend that is emerging.

4. Is it short and to the point? Editorial space is very limited, and busy editors don't have the time to sort through irrelevant copy and cut it down to the main points. Write clear and crisp sentences, using only the important, relevant information.

5. Does it include what the editor wants? That is, facts to back up your statements, plus who, what, when, where, how, and why details?

16 ADDITIONAL TIPS FOR IMPROVING YOUR PRESS RELEASES

Don Levin, president of Levin Public Relations, offers these additional tips and tactics on improving press releases:

1. Shorten them. Tighten the writing. Keep paragraphs and sentences concise. Avoid jargon and repetition. Use strong verbs. Create lively but accurate text.

2. Use subheads in longer stories, at least one per page. Help the editor grasp the entire story. Trim sections or put text in sidebars.

3. Consider adding a fact sheet for details that would clutter your release. For example, a New York City restaurant, when sending out a press release announcing their grand opening, included a separate sheet listing their five most special dishes along with the ingredients and recipes.

4. Make the release stand on its own. Do not use a cover letter.

5. Get all the facts and establish perspective before starting to write. Adding and rewriting later cost both time and money.

6. Keep the news up front, not behind the interpretation or buried in paragraphs of analysis.

7. Cut out puffery; stick to newsworthy information.

8. Put opinion and interpretation in an executive's quotation.

9. Forget the cute headline that forces an editor to dig through a paragraph or two to discover the who, what, when, where, and why. The headline should summarize the release so an editor quickly understands your point.

10. Leave plenty of white space, especially at the top of page one, because editors like to have room to edit. Double space and leave wide margins. Never use the back of a page.

11. Write for a specific editorial department (e.g., up-front news, financial, new products). Similarly, provide separate story slants—in separate releases—for different categories of magazines.

12. Create separate, shorter releases for radio and, at minimum, color slides and scripts for television.

13. End releases with a boilerplate paragraph that explains the organization or division.

14. Consider editing the news release copy for product bulletins, internal publications, and other uses.

15. Write to gain respect for your organization and your next release.

16. Streamline the clearance process so only two or three executives approve each release. This saves time and minimizes the chances to muddy the text. As Ford Kanzler points out, "The newsworthiness of a news release is inversely proportional to the number of persons on the approval cycle."

HOW TO DETERMINE WHERE TO DISTRIBUTE YOUR PRESS RELEASE

Your press release should be sent to every publication that could conceivably have an interest in publishing it and whose readers (even a small portion of them) might be prospects for your product or service.

This is the opposite of advertising media selection, in which you focus on those few publications that are most targeted toward your market. Why the difference? In advertising, each publication you add to your schedule can cost thousands or tens of thousands of dollars. But to add a given publication to your press release distribution list costs only a first-class stamp for mailing the release; for this reason, it makes sense to be all-encompassing rather than selective.

For example, if you have a release appropriate to computer publications, don't go through your publicity director and spend time agonizing over which magazines should get the release and which should not. Instead, just send it to all the publications in the computer and data processing category automatically. This actually saves time by eliminating a selection process and incurs minimal additional incremental cost ($32 postage per additional one hundred releases mailed).

USING *BACON'S PUBLICITY CHECKER*

There are many competing directories and services for press release distribution. One of the best-organized, most complete, and easiest to use is *Bacon's Publicity Checker*. There are three volumes—newspapers, magazines, and radio—listing thousands of publicity outlets. Listings are organized by category for magazines and geographically for newspapers, with each listing giving names, addresses, and phone numbers of appropriate contacts.

You have three choices for distributing a release via *Bacon's*. The first is to buy or borrow the books and mail out the releases yourself. This involves typing addresses on envelopes, duplicating releases, and stuffing releases into envelopes. It's time-consuming and difficult to get releases out in a timely manner this way unless you have a secretary with time to spare. One way to save time is to enter the publicity outlets once into a computer program, then print labels or envelopes automatically for each subsequent mailing.

The second alternative is to order the names and addresses from *Bacon's PR Service* on gummed labels. The cost as of this writing is 25 cents per label, which is only $25 for a hundred labels. This eliminates the need to type them yourself. The drawback is that you have to order a fresh set of labels each time you do a mailing.

The third alternative is to send the release to *Bacon's* and let them do it. *Bacon's* has a publicity distribution service that, for a fee, will duplicate and mail your release to publications in select categories from their list. This is the easiest, most convenient option. All you do is mail them one copy of your release. They handle the printing and mailing.

COMPILING YOUR MEDIA LIST

If you are an active mailer of press releases, you may decide to create your own customized media mailing list rather than simply send your release to be mailed by *Bacon's* to their standard distribution list in a given category.

For convenience, put your list on the computer using a database or simple mailing list program capable of generating mailing labels automatically. You do not need word processing capability since the press releases themselves will not be personalized; all you need is mailing labels.

Start by checking the directories and putting into your list all the editors at publications and broadcast media relevant to your markets.

Next, add all the editors who have ever interviewed you or written about you in the past. Because they already know you, these editors will be more receptive to material from you than editors who don't know you.

Then, add any specialized publications or other publicity outlets not listed in the directories. These can include industry newsletters, trade association newsletters, local ad club bulletins, and other specialized outlets too small to make it into the big directories. Even though they are small, they are highly targeted, and these often-overlooked outlets may be your most productive publicity sources.

Because editors move and publications fold, you must clean your mailing list frequently. Update it whenever you get a change of address or the name of a new editor. Once a year, have your secretary go through it, call all the publications, and verify that you have the current information.

PR PHOTOS

Press releases do not have to be mailed with photos. Interesting releases will be picked up and used without an accompanying photograph, so photos are not necessary. On the other hand, if your press release lends itself to photographic treatment, an accompanying photo can only add interest to the article when it is published.

Carol Marden says that a PR photo should be black and white, glossy, have sharp contrast, and measure either 5" × 7" or 8" × 10". Len Kirsch, president of Kirsch Communications, says that black and white photos are "a must for product stories, good if you can swing them for other items."

"If your photograph is important to you, don't just book an appointment and expect professional results," writes consultant Pete Silver in his newsletter, *The Marketing Communications Report*. "Tell the photographer about the ways you intend to use the photo. This allows the photographer to plan the shooting more effectively by selecting the right backdrops, etc."

Photo captions should be typed on a separate sheet of paper and taped to the back of the photo. Do not type or write with ballpoint pen directly on the back of a photo; the impression will come through and show up in reproduction.

Don Levin does not like taped-on captions. "Instead, have the photo duplicator strip in a caption in an expanded border below the photo, and duplicate that," says Levin. He also advises you to have the photographer give you all negatives and contact sheets, and to make sure you control ownership by buying all rights. Do not do business with photographers who say they are selling you only limited rights for a specific use; make it clear in your contracts that your fee permanently covers all rights.

Tip: You may want to check with your attorney to ensure that your contracts with freelancers transfer permanent ownership of all rights to creative work (writing, photos, drawings) to your firm. New legislation enacted in the late 1980s favors the writer, photographer, or creative artist over the corporate client as the owner of creative work in case of a dispute.

FOLLOW-UP

Many experts advocate including a return postcard with your press release to increase editor response and find out whether editors intend to use your material. These postcards typically have check-off boxes similar to the following:

EDITOR: *Please check your response below and mail this card today. Thank you!*

❑ We will use your press release in a story to appear in our publication on (date):
_____

❑ We may use your information but are not certain at this point.

❑ We do not intend to use your release at this time.

❑ We would like to interview you; please call to arrange it.

❑ Please send a black and white photo.

❑ Please send us further information, including: _____

_____

I personally do not recommend use of reply cards in press release mailings. Editors work on tight deadlines. If one is interested in doing a story on you and needs more information, he or she will pick up the phone and call you, not mail a reply card.

In addition, if editors are planning to use your material but have no questions, they may resent your asking them to do the extra work of notifying you of their intent. Their job is to put out a magazine or newspaper, not to let you know that your PR is working. One editor at a magazine told me he hates it when publicists send him a reply card to fill out—and that he never does it.

Returned reply cards indicating editors are unsure as to whether they will use your release or are definitely *not* going to use it can be of some benefit. By phoning these editors, you can find out what the problem is or what they're looking for. You can answer their questions or give the information they need, and in doing so, you may turn a no into a maybe, or a maybe into a yes.

However, I do not use reply cards, because the risk of alienating editors by asking them to do this paperwork outweighs the benefit of a response, in my opinion.

Generally, it is impractical to follow up on all the press releases mailed because of the time and expense of telephoning. If you have mailed your press release to 100 to 300 publications, you probably want to follow up on just the 10 or 12 most important ones.

How do you follow up? First, telephone the editor within a week after mailing the release. Say: "We sent you a release about a week ago concerning [topic of release]. Did you get it?" At this point, the editor will probably say she or he did not get it or doesn't remember it. That's only natural, because there are so many releases flooding the desk. (Pamela Clark, editor-in-chief of *Popular Computing*, says she gets 2,000 releases per month.)

You reply by explaining briefly what the release is about and then offering to send it again. Most editors will say yes to this offer out of politeness. Mail or fax the release to them (be sure to get their fax number before you end the call, and ask permission first before faxing), then follow up again, asking if they got it and read it. This time, the answer will be yes.

Your next question is, "Does this seem of interest to your readers?" If the editor answers yes, ask when he or she thinks the release might run. If you get an issue date, great! If the editor has no immediate plans or isn't sure, ask what questions you can answer or what additional information you can supply, and supply it. Or provide even more information that would make the editor interested in the story.

What happens if the editor is not interested? Find out why not. Say, "Gee, I'm surprised. I thought [topic of release] would be of great interest to your readers because [reason your product or service is newsworthy]." The editor will probably rethink the position if your argument makes sense.

If not, at least you learn why your item is not of interest to this editor or this publication and you can tailor your next one to better meet their real interests. Sometimes, in telling you why your current release is unusable, editors reveal the nature of the real story they are looking for, and if you can help them get that story, favorable publicity may result.

Don Levin offers the following additional tips for working with editors:

1. Develop good relationships with people in the media.
2. Call reporters before or after sending them a release, depending upon circumstances and individual preference.

3. Become a resource. Make yourself available. Visit editors. Steer them to news. Understand their needs.

4. If you can't answer questions, explain why.

5. Keep reporters and editors informed ahead of time when possible. Make yourself fully informed before you talk to the media.

6. Know SEC regulations if your company is publicly held.

7. Ask editors for advice. Ask how you could better serve them. Learn their pet peeves.

8. Cultivate a long-term reputation with key editors and staff members so you're called to be included or quoted in round-ups, staff-written features, and commentary. Remember that reporters move up to managing editors and change jobs to more prestigious publications.

WHAT IF THE PRESS RELEASE GETS YOU AN INTERVIEW?

Occasionally editors who receive your press release will call you up to interview you. This is sometimes done to clarify a point or to get you to expand on the information contained in the release; other times it's done for the purpose of writing a lengthier article about you.

Giving an interview to reporters and writers should take priority over everything except the most important work you are doing for your customers or clients. Journalists are deadline-pressured, fickle, and have lots of other good story material to choose from. When they call, answer!

When editors or their writers express interest in talking with you, be accessible, pleasant, and cooperative. Don't put them off or moan about how busy or pressed for time you are. Instead, act as if the article they are writing is the most important thing in world, and that it is your job to help them complete it—whatever that takes. Be a helpful source of information and editors will come back to you, again and again.

Be as open and forthcoming in the interview as possible. Don't hold back—tell editors everything they want to know about your topic, and answer all questions succinctly but fully.

Businesspeople giving interviews worry too much about making mistakes or accidentally giving away their trade secrets; but if you're too tight-lipped and not forthcoming with a free flow of good information, editors may decide there's not enough there to do a story.

About a year ago, a columnist for *USA Today* called to interview me as part of a feature she was writing on careers, job seeking, and unemployment. She called me because she had read a book I'd written on careers, *Creative Careers* (John Wiley & Sons).

Unfortunately, I'm not a career authority, don't consult in the field, and had written two books on the topic long ago but hadn't kept up. I knew I wasn't giving her what she was looking for when she interviewed me over the phone, and when the article came out, my comments were not included. I was crushed. Don't make the same mistake.

After the interview, thank editors or reporters for their time. You can politely inquire when the piece will be published, but do *not* ask to be sent a copy. "Can you send me a copy of the finished article?" is an imposition and an annoyance to media people. If you want to see a copy, go out and buy the newspaper or magazine with your story in it. (Of course, if the interviewer *volunteers* to send you a copy, accept graciously.)

Another mistake businesspeople make is telling a writer, "Please send me a draft so I can review it before the article is published." Do not make this request; it can cause writers to delete you from a story in which you would otherwise be included.

Why don't writers want to give you a draft to review? Several reasons:

1. They're facing a deadline and don't have time to mail you a draft, get your comments, and incorporate them.

2. They view themselves as journalists and believe that journalists don't show copy to sources. (Woodward and Bernstein, for instance, didn't show Nixon a draft before they printed their story on the Watergate break-in.)

3. Some are not overly concerned with accuracy.

4. Some believe that you will try to make them take out the good stuff (even though you said it) and replace it with safer, blander copy.

    This fear is probably justified. Many people, seeing their words quoted back to them in a story, do not believe they actually said the things they did, and will start rewriting their own quotes.

5. Showing drafts to sources adds to the workload of the already overburdened writer or reporter. It's time-consuming and labor-intensive.

6. They do not want an outside review to hold up a timely piece.

On the other hand, many clients want to see a draft of the story before it is printed because:

*   It is corporate policy to run any copy through layers of management approval before it is printed.

*   They fear the writer will get facts wrong and want to review to correct mistakes and ensure accuracy.

*   They might have said something they didn't want or mean to say, and want a chance to change it.

I know many writers and reporters (and have been in this role myself) and can tell you, from firsthand experience, that most are not willing (or at least not eager) to run their copy by an interview source for correction and approval.

If you insist on approval rights, or even just that you get a draft copy, editors or writers may decide against going ahead with the story. Therefore, if you want to be sure of getting the story printed, it's best *not* to ask to see a draft. If writers or reporters *volunteer* to show one to you, thank them and say you will review it promptly.

Limit your comments to corrections of factual material. Keep changes to a minimum. If you insist on extensive revisions or start correcting for tone or style, you will turn off writers, and the story will probably be killed.

"Too many businesspeople see reports as either a free form of good publicity or an expensive form of bad publicity," writes David Harris in an article for *Inside Business*. "It's probably more helpful to see them as the hunters and gatherers of the information age. Good reporters are looking for ideas, people, and events that explain the world in a way their readers hadn't considered before. Find a way to help them do that, and you'll likely get your story in the paper."

COPING WITH PROBLEM SITUATIONS

Sometimes public relations is used not to promote the good news but to overcome negative perceptions about a company. The most difficult crisis situations arise not when you are following up your press releases but during a crisis or other times when the press calls you rather than you calling them. Public relations counselor Art Stevens offers the following guidelines for handling the press, especially during a crisis:

1. Never speculate. Do not engage in guesswork or speculate about any aspect of the crisis or about company policy. All reports to the media must be based on verified fact. If a specialist is needed to explain a technological context, make it clear that the specialist is providing background, not reporting on the crisis.

2. Be open. Withholding information is almost certain to backfire. Reporters are expert at discovering what is going on. When withheld information comes to light, the company looks like it was deliberately hiding information to cover up some degree of malfeasance.

Exception 1: If releasing information may cause unnecessary pain, hold it back. Divulging the name of a victim of a fatality before the family is properly notified is a clear example.

Exception 2: Do not release information if doing so exceeds the scope of your authority. For instance, stating the cause of death is a doctor's or coroner's responsibility, not a public relations manager's. Even if excellent evidence exists and the media response group is confident it knows the answers to such questions, the questions should be referred to those authorized to make the official determinations.

3. Respond to all media inquiries. Avoid appearing to dodge any media requests. Maintain a log of all inquiries so that every request can be honored. Avoid "no comment" responses. It is far better to say something like, "We don't have a verifiable answer to your questions at this time, but when we do you'll get it." Or, "We're trying to get that information, and we'll give it to you as soon as we have it." Or, "All we know at present is …", and spell out what has been verified.

Always convey the impression that your company is working diligently to be the best source of information available and that it is determined to provide reliable, factual coverage.

4. Establish and convey clear corporate policies. One of the most significant tools available in handling crisis news consists of stating company policies in unambiguous terms. Doing so prevents or lessens the development of resentment, fear, anger, and hostility.

5. Provide media access to top executives. In dealing with a serious crisis, it is effective to have a top executive talk to the media. A press briefing is an acceptable forum, but individual interviews can also prove useful. The words of a top executive, especially those of a policymaker, carry far more import than the same statements from a professional spokesperson. It is usually well worth the executive's time.

6. Allow the story to fade away. All news stories have a life of their own. It is important to handle bad news while it is live. After it fades from public view, let it rest in peace. Sometimes companies feel a need to counteract the effects of bad news in a way that resurrects it. Doing so is a mistake. Once it is out of the public awareness, it is usually best left alone.

PR RESOURCES

For information on buying directories, ordering labels, or the PR distribution service, contact:

- Bacon's PR Service, 332 South Michigan Avenue, Chicago, IL 60604, 800-621-0561.

- Gebbie Press *ALL-IN-ONE Directory*, Box 1000, New Paltz, NY 12561, 914-255-7960. This directory lists more than 21,000 publicity outlets, combining newspapers, radio stations, TV stations, consumer magazines, business journals, and news syndicates in a single volume. Cost is $78. Also available on floppy disk.

- Public Relations Plus, Inc., Post Office Drawer 1197, New Milford, CT 06776, 203-354-9361 or 800-999-8448. Publishes five publicity directories: *New York Publicity Outlets, Metro California Media, All TV Publicity Outlets Nationwide, National Radio Publicity Outlets*, and *The Family Page Directory*. The big advantage of these directories is that they list more editors for each publication, allowing you to better target your release to the proper department and person. Call for free catalog.

- PR DATA SYSTEMS, Inc., 19 Oakwood Avenue, Norwalk, CT 06850, 800-227-7409. PR Data provides targeted media mailing lists, release and photo reproduction, and press kit assembly and mailing. A routine one-page press release mailed to 200 publications costs approximately $96 plus postage. Call for free brochure.

- *Directory of Experts, Authorities, & Spokespersons: The Talk Show Guest Directory*, Broadcast Interview Source, 2233 Wisconsin Avenue, N.W., Washington, D.C. 20007, 202-333-4904. This directory is distributed annually to more than 6,500 newspaper editors, columnists, TV assignment editors, radio talk shows, wire services, and others in the media who use it to locate experts to interview and use as sources for stories. To get your company listed, call or write.

- *The Top 200+ TV News Interview Shows*, Ad-Lib Publications, P.O. Box 1102, Fairfield, IA 52556, 800-669-0773. This report lists 160 television shows that are syndicated or broadcast nationally, including all the major network and cable shows and talk shows. It includes the addresses, phone numbers, and names of producers and information on the topics they are interested in. Cost: $30.

- *Print Media Editorial Calendars*, SRDS Circulation Dept., 3004 Glenview Road, Wilmette, IL 60091, 800-323-4588. One effective way of increasing release pick-up is to target releases at specific issues of magazines covering your topic. *Print Media Editorial Calendars* lists the editorial schedules of 4,200 business magazines, 1,700 newspapers, 1,500 consumer magazines, and 400 farm publications, enabling you to target your release to the right special issues at the right time.

Chapter 19

PLACING THE PLANTED
FEATURE STORY

A planted, or placed, feature story is an article written and submitted to a publication by a corporation, entrepreneur, or business professional either directly by the business or on their behalf by their PR firm or consultant. Unlike a freelance writer who writes articles for creative expression or to earn money from them, the company submitting a feature article has a different purpose: to gain publicity and exposure for the firm, its ideas, or its products and services.

Placing feature articles with appropriate trade, consumer, or business publications is one of the most powerful and effective of all marketing techniques:

- You can get one, two, three or more pages devoted to your product or service without paying for the space (a paid ad of that length could run you $3,000 to $20,000 or more).

- Your message has far more credibility as editorial material than as a sponsored advertisement.

- The publication of the article results in prestige for the author and recognition for the company.

- Reprints make excellent, low-cost sales literature.

Getting an article published in a trade journal or local business magazine is not difficult—if you know how. While editors are quick to reject inferior material or "puff" pieces, they are hungry for good, solid news and information to offer their readers. Unlike newspapers, whose reporters are investigative and frequently antagonistic and adversarial toward business, trade journal editors represent a friendlier audience, and are more willing to work with you to get your information to their readers.

If there is a key mistake novices make in placing feature articles, it's giving up too soon. Your article is probably not going to be accepted by the first editor who sees it, or even the second. But keep trying. Consultant Jeff Davidson, a widely published author, says that to get 400 articles published, he was rejected 8,000 times.

COMING UP WITH IDEAS FOR ARTICLES

Aside from case histories, which we will discuss later in this chapter, most planted feature articles are of the how-to variety, aimed at either executives, managers, professionals, or technicians in a given field. In addition to case histories and how-to material, editors are also interested in stories on new products, developments, or trends in their industry.

One way to come up with article ideas is to make a list of the ads you would run (and the magazines in which you would run them) if you had an unlimited ad budget, then write articles based on topics related to those ads and place them in those magazines.

For example, if you wanted to advertise your new wood chip stacking system in *Pulp & Paper* magazine, but didn't have the budget for it, consider writing an article on "A new way to stack and inventory wood chips more efficiently" for that magazine. You will find it is cost effective to write and place articles in magazines and for secondary markets in which print advertising is unprofitable or beyond your budget.

Many trade journals will send a sample issue and set of editorial guidelines to prospective authors upon request. These can provide valuable clues as to style, format, and appropriate topics. They often tell how to contact the magazine, give hints on writing an article, describe the manuscript review process, and discuss any payment or reprint arrangements.

SELECTING THE RIGHT MAGAZINE

Aside from *Bacon's Publicity Checker*, the best source for learning more about magazines and their editorial requirements is a book called *Writer's Market*, published annually by Writer's Digest Books, 1507 Dana Avenue, Cincinnati, OH 45207, 513-531-2222. *Writer's Market* lists more than 4,000 consumer, general, business, and trade publications that accept articles from outside sources. Listings give detailed descriptions of what editors are looking for, along with names, addresses, phone numbers, and other contact information.

The best magazines to target are the ones you are getting now. This is because you read them, are familiar with their editorial slant and style, and are aware of what articles related to your topic have been run recently. However, there may be many magazines in your industry that you don't get and are not familiar with; you can find them in *Bacon's* or *Writer's Market*. Contact each magazine and ask for a sample issue and editorial guidelines.

When the sample issue comes, study it to gain familiarity with the publication. This is a key step in getting your article published. The quickest way to turn off an editor is to offer an idea that has nothing to do with his or her magazine.

"My pet peeve with people calling or writing to pitch an idea is that they often haven't studied the magazine," says Rick Dunn, editor of *Plant Engineering*. "If they haven't read several issues and gotten a handle on who we are and who our audience is, they won't be able to pitch an idea effectively."

"There's no substitute for knowing the audience and the various departments within a magazine," adds Jim Russo, editor of *Packaging*. "I'm more impressed by someone who has an idea for a particular section than by someone who obviously doesn't know anything about our format."

Tip: Media kits from most publications contain editorial calendars that list the editorial focus for the year's planned special issues. If you can offer an article that ties in with the editorial theme of a special issue, you can increase your chances of making a placement.

Timing is important. For a monthly magazine, an article to appear in a special issue should probably be proposed to the editor three to six months in advance of the publication date.

AVOID PUFFERY

Impartiality is a must with many editors. Remember, they're not there to praise your company's products, although publishing your article can have the same effect. The editor's job is to give readers an objective overview of the goings-on in their industry. Editors can be particularly sticky about dealing with public relations personnel.

"We're certainly not prejudiced against articles from PR firms," says Mark Rosenzweig, editor of *Chemical Engineering*. "We just generally have to make more revisions to eliminate their tendency toward one-sidedness. We want all the disadvantages spelled out, as well as the advantages." Adds Rick Dunn, editor of *Plant Engineering*: "If an article is about storage methods, we want to see all fifteen methods discussed, not just the ones used by the writer's company or client."

Another concern for editors is exclusivity. You should never submit the same idea or story to more than one competing magazine at a time. Only if the idea is rejected should you approach another editor. The majority of editors want exclusive material, especially for feature articles.

If a story is particularly timely or newsworthy and has run in a magazine not directly competing with the one you're approaching, you may be able to get around the problem by working with the editor to expand or rewrite the piece. But be up-front about it or you risk losing the editor's confidence and goodwill.

"I'd like everything to be exclusive," says Jim Russo, editor of *Packaging*. "That increases its value to us and can sway us toward acceptance if it's a 'borderline' story."

"Exclusivity is a quality consideration for a feature article," adds Dunn. "Editors don't want their readers to pick up their magazine and see something they've already read elsewhere."

MAKING THE INITIAL CONTACT

Should you call or write the editor? Most editors won't object to either method of pitching an idea, but they usually have a preference for one or the other. It's simply a matter of personal choice and time constraints. If you don't know how a particular editor feels on the subject, call and ask. An appropriate opening might be: "This is Joe Jones from XYZ Corporation, and I have a story idea you might be interested in. Do you have time to spend a few minutes over the phone discussing it, or would you prefer that I sent you an outline?"

An editor who prefers to get it in writing will tell you so. Editors who prefer a quick description over the phone will appreciate your respect for their time, whether they listen to your pitch on the spot or ask you to phone back later.

But even those editors who will listen to your idea over the phone will also want something in writing. "With a phone call, I can tell right away whether someone's on the right track," says Mark Rosenzweig, editor of *Chemical Engineering*. "If I like the idea, I'll then request a detailed outline describing the proposed article." Adds Rick Dunn: "A phone call is all right, but I can't make an editorial decision until I see a query letter."

WRITING THE QUERY LETTER

The best way to communicate an article idea in writing is to send a query letter. A query letter is a mini-proposal in which you propose to the editor that you write an article on a particular topic to be published in the magazine.

A query letter is, in essence, a sales letter. The prospect is the editor. The product you want to sell to the editor is the article you want to write for the magazine.

Here are a few basic facts about query letters.

1. Editors look for professionalism in query letters. This means no typos, no misspellings. Address the letter to a specific editor by name, and spell his or her name correctly.

2. Editors look for familiarity with their magazine. Don't suggest an article on hunting elk to the newsletter for the ASPCA. Sounds obvious, but such things happen every day; for example, PR firms proposing how-to articles to magazines that don't do how-to. Study the market before you send your query.

3. Editors look for good writing. If you can, write the first paragraph or two of your query so it could be used, as is, as the lead for your article.

This shows the editor that you know how to begin a piece and get the reader's attention.

4. Editors hate lazy writers—those who want to see their byline in a magazine but refuse to do research or get their facts straight. Put a lot of hard nuts-and-bolts information—facts, figures, statistics—in your letter to show the editor that you know your subject. Most query letters (and articles) are too light on content.

5. Credentials impress editors. Tell editors why they should trust you to write the article. If you are an expert on the subject, say so. If not, describe your sources. Tell which experts you will interview, which studies you will cite, which references you will consult. Highlight the breakthrough research your company has done to become a leader in its field. List your previous publishing credentials, if any, especially books and articles in well-known magazines.

6. Editors hate to take risks. The more fully developed your idea, the better. If you spell out everything—your topic, your approach, an outline, your sources—then editors know what they will get when they give you the go-ahead to write the piece. The more complete your query, the better your chance for a sale.

Freelance writer Constance Hallinan Lagan advises that if a magazine states "query only" in its guidelines, you should send a query letter, not the completed article. Always enclose a self-addressed, stamped envelope.

On the following pages are sample query letters. All were successful and resulted in assignments to write articles.

Sample Query Letter: A Travel Article for Newspapers

Writer Carol Andrus had enormous success with this simple, direct query letter. It sold one article on India to 65 newspapers throughout the U.S., Canada, Australia, New Zealand, and even some in India.

```
Mr. Larry Townsend
Travel Editor
The Chicago Tribune
1801 Michigan Avenue
Chicago, IL 30344

Dear Mr. Townsend:

Three summers ago, I decided to explore India by
myself.

The prospect of being all alone on the other side of
Planet Earth unnerved me, so I devised a method to have
a ready-made roster of "friends" and "family" waiting
for me.

The results were truly astounding! I have now just
returned from my SECOND trip to India, where I was the
guest of honor at two weddings ... just two of the many
friendships that I made that unforgettable summer.
```

I have an article on this "experiment in travel." It's a good read, has lots of human interest, and offers generic travel advice. It's just over 2,000 words, and photos are available.

If this sounds interesting, drop the enclosed SASE in the mail.

Very truly yours,

Carol Andrus

Sample Query Letter: Multiple Article Ideas

Although writers usually present one idea per query, Tony Seideman and others have been successful using queries to pitch multiple ideas (usually no more than two or three) to an editor simultaneously, then letting the editor pick one for you to develop into a story. The query gives the writer's qualifications; the article ideas are summarized on separate sheets. Tony said he eventually talked with the editor and sold him one idea immediately while setting the groundwork for a longer-term relationship.

Mr. Paul A. Holmes
Editor
Inside PR and Reputation Management
235 W. 48th St., #34B
New York, NY 10036

Dear Paul:

PR people are among the world's most overworked, under-credited professionals. I know. I've been causing them grief for almost 20 years as a writer for publications ranging from Rolling Stone and Family Circle to Multimedia World and Computer Entertainment News.

As a longtime journalist, I understand how important PR people are to the newsgathering process. I also respect them for putting up with one of the most stressful careers in existence. And I'd like to work with you to do stories that would help make their lives easier. For more than 15 years, I've made the complex comprehensible, specializing in telling businesspeople about the tools, techniques, and strategies they can use to win in an increasingly challenging marketplace.

Topics on which I have exceptional expertise include:

• Business history and achievement
• Multimedia and the Internet
• Electronic commerce and telecommunications
• Cable and broadcast television and the print media
• High-tech databases and direct mail
• Customer service and satisfaction.

Enclosed are copies of my work that deal with the tools PR people can use and some reputations I've helped man-

```
age. If you'd like, I'll be glad to send some story
ideas once I get a better idea of what you're looking
for. Thanks again for your interest. I'll call next
week to see how we can work together further.

Sincerely,

Tony Seideman
```

Sample Query Letter: With Article Outline Attached

If the article requires more description than can comfortably fit in a brief query letter, consider summarizing the key article points or discussing the details in an outline written on a separate sheet and enclosed with the query letter. That's what I did to sell a how-to article on technical writing to a trade journal for chemical engineers. This query sold because it took a general topic (technical writing) and slanted it toward the specific audience reading the magazine (chemical engineers).

```
Mr. Kenneth J. McNaughton
Associate Editor
CHEMICAL ENGINEERING
McGraw-Hill Building
1221 Avenue of the Americas
New York, NY 10020

Dear Mr. McNaughton:

When a chemical engineer can't write a coherent report,
the true value of his investigation or study may be
distorted or unrecognized. His productivity vanishes.
And his chances for career advancement diminish.

As an associate editor of CHEMICAL ENGINEERING, you know
that many chemical engineers could use some help in
improving their technical writing skills. I'd like to
provide that help by writing an article that gives your
reader "Ten Tips for Better Business Writing."

An outline of the article is attached. This 2,000-word
piece would provide 10 helpful tips—each less than 200
words—to help chemical engineers write better letters,
reports, proposals, and articles.

Tip number 3, for example, instructs writers to be more
concise. Too many engineers would write about an "accumu-
lation of particulate matter about the peripheral interi-
or surface of the vessel" when they're describing solids
build-up. And how many managers would use the phrase
"until such time as" when they simply mean "until"?

My book, TECHNICAL WRITING: STRUCTURE, STANDARDS, AND
STYLE, will be published by the McGraw-Hill Book Company
in November. While the book speaks to a wide range of
technical disciplines, my article will draw its examples
from the chemical engineering literature.
```

```
I hold a B.S. in chemical engineering from the
University of Rochester, and am a member of the
American Institute of Chemical Engineers. Until this
past January, I was manager of marketing communications
for Koch Engineering, a manufacturer of chemical process
equipment. Now, I'm an independent copywriter specializ-
ing in industrial advertising.

Ken, I'd like to write "Ten Tips for Better Technical
Writing" for your "You and Your Job" section.

How does this sound?

Sincerely,

Bob Bly
```

Article Outline

TEN TIPS FOR BETTER TECHNICAL WRITING
by Robert W. Bly

1. *Know your readers.*
   Are you writing for engineers? managers? laypeople?

2. *Write in a clear, conversational style.*
   Write to express—not to impress.

3. *Be concise.*
   Avoid wordiness. Omit words that do not add to your meaning.

4. *Be consistent...*
   ...especially in the use of numbers, symbols, and abbreviations.

5. *Use jargon sparingly.*
   Use technical terms only when there are no simpler words that can bet-ter communicate your thoughts.

6. *Avoid big words.*
   Do not write "utilize" when "use" will do just as well.

7. *Prefer the specific to the general.*
   Technical readers are interested in solid technical information and not in generalities. Be specific.

8. *Break the writing up into short sections.*
   Short sections, paragraphs, and sentences are easier to read than long ones.

9. *Use visuals.*
   Graphs, tables, photos, and drawings can help get your message across.

10. *Use the active voice.*
    Write "John performed the experiment," not "The experiment was per-formed by John." The active voice adds vigor to writing.

Sample Query Letter: *Writer's Digest*

If you've ever wanted to write an article for *Writer's Digest*, take a look at this query letter. It sold an article that became a cover story and was reprinted several times in *Writer's Digest* special issues. The acronym SASE in the last paragraph stands for self-addressed stamped envelope.

```
Mr. William Brohaugh
Editor
WRITER'S DIGEST
9933 Alliance Road
Cincinnati, Ohio 45242

Dear Mr. Brohaugh:

John Frances Tighe, a soft-spoken, bearded gentleman,
modestly refers to himself as "the world's second-most
successful freelance direct mail copywriter."

John's fee for writing a direct mail package? $15,000.

But that's peanuts compared to the $40,000 Henry Cowan
charges. According to WHO'S MAILING WHAT!, a newsletter
covering the direct mail industry, Cowan is the highest
paid copywriter in the world. DIRECT MARKETING magazine
reports that his income on the Publisher's Clearing
House mailing alone (for which he receives a royalty)
was $900,000 in a recent year.

Next to the movies and best-selling novels, direct mail
is one of the highest paid markets for freelance writers.
Although it's surprisingly easy to break into, most free-
lancers don't even know about it, and direct mail writing
is dominated by a few dozen writers who earn lush, six-
figure incomes writing only a few days a week.

I'd like to write a 3,000-word article on "Making Money
as a Direct Mail Writer." The article would tell your
readers everything they need to know to start getting
assignments in this lucrative but little-known specialty.

Here are the topics I would cover:

1. THE SECRET WORLD OF DIRECT MAIL. What is direct
   mail? Who is writing direct mail—and how much are
   they earning? Why has this market been a secret
   until now? I would interview some old pros as well
   as some new writers to get their perspectives.
2. A LOOK AT THE MARKET. What are the various uses of
   direct mail (mail order, fund-raising, lead genera-
   tion, cordial contact)?
3. GETTING STARTED. Learning about direct mail. Study
   the market. Building your swipe files. Getting your
   first assignments.
```

4. HOW TO WRITE DIRECT MAIL COPY THAT SELLS. Understanding the mission of direct mail. Tips for writing copy that will get results. How to present your copy to clients. Graphics and layouts for direct mail copy. Differences in sales copy (direct mail) vs. editorial copy (magazine writing).

5. MARKETING YOUR SERVICES. Getting and keeping clients. How to market your services using: Portfolios. Meetings. Telephone calls. Letters. Advertising. Publicity techniques.

6. FEES. How to set fees. Table of typical fees. What others charge.

7. KEEPING UP WITH THE FIELD. Books. Publications. Professional organizations. Courses. Seminars.

This article will draw both from my own experience as a successful direct mail copywriter (clients include Prentice Hall, New York Telephone, Hearst, Chase Manhattan, Edith Roman Associates) and from interviews with top pros in the field—including Milt Pierce, Sig Rosenblum, Richard Armstrong, Don Hauptman, Andrew Linick, and others. I know these people personally, so getting the interviews is no problem.

Also, I am a member of the Direct Marketing Club of New York and author of the forthcoming book, DIRECT MAIL PROFITS (Asher-Gallant Press).

May I proceed with the article as outlined?

A SASE is enclosed. Thanks for your consideration.

Regards,

Bob Bly

Sample Query Letter: *Amtrak Express*

Amtrak Express is an "in-train" magazine, similar in style and content to the in-flight magazines you read on airplanes. Here's a query letter that sold a business article to them.

Mr. James A. Frank, Editor
AMTRAK EXPRESS
34 East 51st Street
New York, NY 10022

Dear Mr. Frank:

Is this letter a waste of paper?

Yes—if it fails to get the desired result.

In business, most letters and memos are written to generate a specific response—close a sale, set up a meeting, get a job interview, make a contact. Many of these letters fail to do their job.

Part of the problem is that business executives and support staff don't know how to write persuasively. The solution is a formula first discovered by advertising copywriters—a formula called AIDA. AIDA stands for Attention, Interest, Desire, Action.

First, the letter gets Attention ... with a hard-hitting lead paragraph that goes straight to the point, or offers an element of intrigue.

Then, the letter hooks the reader's Interest. The hook is often a clear statement of the reader's problem, needs, desires. If you are writing to a customer who received damaged goods, state the problem. Then promise a solution.

Next, create Desire. You are offering something—a service, a product, an agreement, a contract, a compromise, a consultation. Tell readers the benefit they'll receive from your offering. Create a demand for your product.

Finally, call for Action. Ask for the order, the signature, the check, the assignment.

I'd like to give you a 1,500-word article on "How to Write Letters That Get Results." The piece will illustrate the AIDA formula with a variety of actual letters and memos from insurance companies, banks, manufacturers, and other organizations.

This letter, too, was written to get a specific result—an article assignment from the editor of AMTRAK EXPRESS.

Did it succeed?

Regards,

Bob Bly

P.S. By way of introduction, I'm an advertising consultant and the author of five books including TECHNICAL WRITING: STRUCTURE, STANDARDS, AND STYLE (McGraw-Hill).

Sample Query Letter: New Assignment from Current Editor

Once you know an editor, your queries for repeat assignments can be a little less formal...and you know the editor is already familiar with your work and reputation.

You may wonder why I gave my background in the P.S. when the editor has already done business with me. She had only bought one previous article and didn't know me all that well, so I felt it would be beneficial to remind her of why I was exceptionally well qualified to write this particular article for her. It couldn't have hurt, because I got the assignment.

Ms. Kimberly A. Welsh
Editor
CIRCULATION MANAGEMENT
859 Willamette Street
Eugene, Oregon 97401-2910

Dear Kimberly:

Thanks for publishing the article on mailing lists so
quickly. I hope you get good reader response to it.

I'm writing because I have another idea that might be
right for CIRCULATION MANAGEMENT.

How about an article—"Do Premiums Work?"

Background: As you know, response rates are down all
over. In an attempt to combat this, publications are
offering more and more expensive premiums to attract
first-time subscribers. SPORTS ILLUSTRATED, for example,
is offering a videocassette on great sports flubs. TIME
recently offered a camera. And then there's NEWSWEEK's
successful free telephone offer.

Questions: Is there some point at which a premium ceas-
es to be an added inducement and actually becomes a
bribe, overshadowing the primary offer and becoming the
key reason why people respond to a mailing? If so, how
does that affect the quality of the subscriber base
that circulation is delivering to the publication's
advertisers?

This would be the basis of my article, which would
attempt to answer these specific questions:

Do premiums still work? Are they still profitable? Or
is their effectiveness declining as more and more publications jump into premium offers?

Is there any limit to premium cost in relation to the
cost of a one-year subscription? What is this limit?
What's the average premium cost in publishing today?

What works best—an information premium (printed report or
book) or a tangible item (telephone, clock-radio, etc.)?

Must the premium be related to the publication, the
market, or the theme of the mailing? Or do totally
unrelated premiums work well as long as they have high
perceived value?

Once a subscriber is sold through a premium offer, must
renewals also offer a premium?

How do advertising managers feel about subscribers generated through premium offers? Is there a perception
that a subscriber generated through a premium offer is
worth less to an advertiser than someone who buys the
magazine without such a bribe? Any proof to back up
this feeling?

```
To get the answers to these questions, I will interview
circulation directors, advertising managers, direct
response agencies, DM consultants, and freelancers
responsible for creating and testing premium-based pack-
ages. I see this as a feature article running 3,000+
words.

Kimberly, may I proceed with this article as outlined?

Thanks for your consideration. A SASE is enclosed.

Regards,

Bob Bly

P.S. By way of background: I'm a freelance copywriter
specializing primarily in business-to-business direct
mail. Publishing clients include Thomas Publishing,
Hearst, Prentice- Hall, and EBSCO. My most recent book
is DIRECT MAIL PROFITS: HOW TO GET MORE LEADS AND SALES
BY MAIL (Asher-Gallant Press). Magazine credits include
contributions to DIRECT MARKETING, WRITER'S DIGEST, COS-
MOPOLITAN, COMPUTER DECISIONS, and NEW JERSEY MONTHLY.
```

FOLLOWING UP ON YOUR QUERY

One of three things will happen after you mail your query letter:

1. The editor will accept your article "on spec" (on speculation). This means the editor is interested and wants to see the completed manuscript, but is not making a firm commitment to publish. This is the most positive response you are likely to get, and unless the article you write is terrible, there is a better than 50 percent chance it will get published.

2. The editor will reject your query. The next step is to send the query to the next editor and magazine on your list.

3. The third and most likely alternative is that you will not hear one way or the other. There are several reasons for this. The editor may not have gotten around to your query. Or, the editor has read it but has not made a decision. Or, the editor didn't receive your query or lost it.

GETTING THE GO-AHEAD

Your editor is interested. Hurrah! You've passed the first step. Now the real work begins.

Once you've gotten your idea accepted, you'll need to know the length and deadline requirements. If the editor doesn't volunteer this information, ask. The answers may avoid misunderstanding later on.

As a rule, be generous with length. Include everything you think is relevant, and don't skimp on examples. Editors would rather delete material than have to request more.

While a few magazines are flexible on length, most give authors specific word lengths to shoot for. Ask your editor how long your article should be. To translate this to typed pages, every 500 words is equivalent to two double-spaced typewritten manuscript pages. In its final printed form, a solid page of magazine copy (no headlines, photos, or white space) is approximately 800 to 1,000 words. The first page, which has to leave room for a headline and byline, is approximately 700 words. Use Table 19.1 to calculate how much to write to meet your editor's space requirements.

Table 19.1. Guide to article length.

Number of Words	Number of Magazine Pages	Number of Manuscript Pages
800 to 1,000	1	3 to 4
1,500	2	6
2,000	2 to 2 1/2	8
2,500	3	10
3,000	3 1/2 to 4	12

Deadlines, too, can vary considerably among journals. Some don't like to impose any deadlines at all, especially if they work far enough in advance that they are not pressed for material. But if the article is intended for publication in a special issue, the editor will probably want the finished manuscript at least two months before publication. This allows time for revisions, assembling photos or illustrations, and production.

Don't put an editor's patience to the test. Missing a deadline may result in automatic rejection and waste the effort of making the placement and writing the article. Hand in every article on the deadline date, or sooner. If you cannot, advise the editor well in advance and request a reasonable extension. Editors dislike late copy, but they hate surprises.

THE PITCH LETTER

An alternate method of getting feature story placement is to get stories written about you and your product rather than placing stories written by you.

How do you get the press to write about you? Sending press releases, as described in Chapter 18, is one method. An editor who receives a release related to an article he or she is planning may contact you to interview people in your company, even if the material in the release isn't exactly what is needed.

Tip: Whenever editors respond to a press release or query, or call to interview someone in your company, put them on your media list to ensure they receive all future news you issue.

Another way to get articles written about you—or at least get your company mentioned in articles—is to send a pitch letter. Unlike the query letter, which proposes that you write a specific article, the pitch letter simply offers your company as an expert source for interviewing purposes.

Figure 19.4 displays a typical pitch letter prepared by a public relations firm on behalf of its client.

Figure 19.4. Sample pitch letter.

```
Dear :

Compact disc (CD) sales are booming. In fact, some
music industry executives are projecting disc sales will
surpass album sales by the end of the year.

The first "compact disc only" retail store, Compact Disc
Warehouse, in Huntington Beach, California, opened in
November, 1984. It grossed nearly $1 million in sales
in just 18 months operating out of a 1,200 square foot
store.

Now, Compact Disc Warehouse, Inc. is launching the first
CD franchise offering to meet the national demand for
the hottest home entertainment product in the music
industry today.

Edward Dempsey, president of CD Warehouse, is an expert
on why CD's are changing an industry that has been dom-
inated by record albums for decades and how the retail
world is gearing up to meet the CD demand.

If you would like to arrange an interview, please call
our offices.

Sincerely,

Mitch Robinson, Account Executive
S&S Public Relations, Inc.
```

Sending pitch letters is effective because editors and reporters are constantly on the lookout for accessible sources of expert information they can call to get a quote or fill in a missing fact for a story when they're working on a deadline.

It pays to include a Rolodex™ card with your query letter that the reporter or editor can file under the appropriate category. That way, a reporter who is working on a story on "CDs" turns to the card file, finds Edward Dempsey's name, calls Edward Dempsey for a quote, and quotes Edward Dempsey in the story. Edward Dempsey, then, and not his competition, becomes known as the industry leader because he is constantly quoted in the press.

You probably have noticed that within your own industry the same spokespeople are quoted again and again. Well, it's not by accident. Diligent public relations efforts—not fate—ensure that one person or company becomes publicized while others wallow in obscurity.

HOW TO MAKE YOUR PLANTED ARTICLES
GENERATE DIRECT RESPONSE

In addition to building image, increasing visibility, and serving as low-cost article reprints, planted feature stories can also be turned into direct response tools. How is this done? With a resource box.

A resource box—a term invented by Dr. Jeffrey Lant—is a box that appears at the end of your article. Instead of the usual brief author bio (e.g., "Jan Doe is a consultant whose articles frequently appear in *Business Marketing*), the resource box gives complete information on who you are, what your company offers, and how readers of the article can reach you. Figure 19.5 shows a typical resource box.

Figure 19.5. Resource box.

John Doe is a freelance copywriter specializing in business-to-business and direct response advertising. He writes ads, brochures, direct mail packages, and sales letters for more than 75 clients nationwide, including Prentice Hall, Grumman Corporation, Sony, On-Line Software, Philadelphia National Bank, and Associated Air Freight. He is also the author of 17 books including THE COPYWRITER'S HANDBOOK. Mr. Doe can be reached at...

Dr. Lant explains his approach:

I swap the articles I write in return for resource boxes in those publications. Publications run the article. I get the resource box.

Some of these publications swap for outright ad space—that is, they will not let my resource box run along with the article. One publication, with a readership of over 75,000 financial planners, gives me both the resource box and an ad. I therefore have a very good sense of which draws better.

The resource box **always** wins. There are several reasons for this. First, the article acts as a qualifying device. If you're not interested in copywriting, you probably won't read an article on the subject. If you're interested, you may have a need. And if you have a need, you'll be more receptive to filling it.

Second, the article plus the resource box are several times larger than the ad.

Third, the article gives the product credibility. The buyer reasons that the publication wouldn't publish the article—and as a result "recommend" the product—if it wasn't good. The article and the resource box lessen the buyer's suspicion.

Fourth, the words, "resource box" are far superior to "ad." This helps sales. The resource box looks like a public service, which, of course, it is. For these reasons, the resource box always draws substantially better than the same product or service featured in an ad, no matter how well-written and complete the advertisement.

How do you get a resource box printed with your article? Don't ask the editor outright. Instead, simply type in the resource box at the end of your manuscript and submit it along with your article. Editors will print it as is without questioning you 10 to 20 percent of the time. Another 10 to 20 percent of editors will object initially but relent after some discussion.

The remainder will refuse you, because they see the resource box as too blatantly promotional and somehow compromising their standards of journalistic integrity. But with my method you will have resource boxes running with at least 10 percent and up to 30 or 40 percent of all feature stories you place, significantly increasing the effectiveness of these articles.

HOW TO RECYCLE YOUR PUBLISHED ARTICLES

Don Hauptman, a New York City–based direct marketing copywriter and consultant, says that just publishing any article once does not take advantage of its full potential as a marketing tool. "Most professionals who write for publication stop at this point," says Hauptman. "But for the aggressive, savvy self-marketer, the first publication of the article is only the beginning."

Why recycle your article? Because, as Hauptman notes, "The life-span of any magazine, newsletter, or newspaper is limited. You want to get as much mileage as possible out of your effort." Here are his suggestions:

1. When you sell the article initially, make sure the publication gets one-time publication rights (known as first rights only). You, the author, retain all other rights. Ideally, try to have a copyright line printed at the end of your article (e.g., "copyright 1990 Jan Doe"). The reasoning behind this is that you have plans for the article, and you don't want to have to beg for permission to use your own work.

2. Be sure to get several copies of the issue as soon as it's off the press. When you receive them, cut apart one copy and paste it up for duplication.

3. For its new incarnation, the article may require some creative rearrangement. You will probably want to delete surrounding ads. The publication's logo can be cut from the cover, masthead, or contents page and placed at the top. This step is important—it gives your words the imprimatur of a known (and presumably respected) medium. At the end, tack on your firm's name, address, and phone number, easily obtainable from your letterhead or business card.

4. Send the resultant mechanical or paste-up to a quick-print shop or simply run it through your office copier. Watch out for problems that might make your new publicity piece appear unattractive or unprofessional: dirt, skewed paragraphs, or cut marks (stray lines created by the edge of the pasted-up article; they'll disappear with the help of typewriter correction tape or fluid).

5. For maximum readability, print the article in black ink on white or light-colored paper. Your name or your firm's name can be highlighted using a second color ink. Or, save the extra expense and instead circle your name or byline on each printed copy with a contrasting color fiber-tip pen.

6. Distribute copies of reprints to current, past, and potential clients. Include the reprints in your literature package or press kit, leave them in your reception area or lobby, hand them out at conferences and speaking engagements, and enclose them in direct mail packages. The possibilities are endless.

7. Because you own all rights to the article, you are free to publish it elsewhere. Other publications might want to run the article in its entirety, or excerpt or quote from it. An editor may ask you to revise the article for a particular publication, but such adaptation is usually easy; the hard work has been done. You can even use the article as part of a book, either your own or perhaps an anthology edited by someone else.

CASE HISTORIES

Aside from the how-to feature article, case histories (also known as case studies or user stories) are the most popular type of planted article. A case history is a product success story. It tells how a customer saved money, solved problems, or improved his or her life by using a product or service.

In an editorial in *Design News*, Lars Soderholm suggests the following six-step outline for case histories:

1. *Background material:* The nature of the problem—How it came about, why it exists, what causes it to exist.

2. *Negative consequences of the problem:* Why is it so bad? How does it harm us?

3. *The method, product, service, or technique used to solve the problem:* What is it? Describe.

4. *Details:* How the solution was implemented. Specifics.

5. *Results:* How things have changed as a result of the solution.

6. *Benefits:* What are the consequences? How much time, money, energy was saved? By what percentage were productivity, efficiency, profits increased?

Consultant Ryle Miller gives a similar structure in an article in *Chemical Engineering* magazine:

1. The situation: What's the background?
2. The problem: What was wrong?
3. The resolution: The answer to the problem.
4. Information: The details of the resolution.

Karen Kramer, editor of *Chemical Processing* magazine, also uses a problem–solution–results format in the 12 to 22 case histories her magazine publishes monthly. Says Kramer: "In addition to the name and location of the plant using the equipment, the date of installation, and the type of equipment involved, we also like to point out the single most important benefit of the installation and what advantages have been gained, such as reductions in maintenance and downtime, increased production, or higher product quality."

Chapter

TRADE SHOWS

Promoting your company's products and services at a trade show can be an effective adjunct to your other marketing activities. As one industry analyst observes, "Marketing directors find that if strategic planning and administration are employed, the trade show is the most cost-effective means to get direct contact—getting to prospects and developing qualified leads that result in sales."

More than 10,000 industrial and consumer trade shows are held each year in the United States. An article in the February 1997 issue of *Business Marketing* states that of the total $51.7 billion spent on business-to-business marketing annually, $5.5 billion, or 10.7 percent, is spent on trade shows.

ADVANTAGES OF TRADE SHOWS

Why are trade shows so popular? According to an article in *Industry Week*:

> For the manufacturer, trade shows are an opportunity to personally meet prospects as well as a speedy way to get a product—especially a new, high-tech one—introduced to a target audience. For the sales force, they're a motivator. For the customer, they're a quick, convenient way to see and compare competing products.

Moreover, many of those who attend trade shows are buyers, not just browsers. The Trade Show Bureau, an informational and educational organization based in East Orleans, MA, has conducted research revealing that 86 percent of all show visitors represent an important buying influence (i.e., they can recommend, specify, or purchase the product or service being exhibited). Exhibit Surveys, Inc., a major trade show organization, reports that 60 percent of trade show audiences nationwide had buying plans when they attended shows in 1987. A report published by the Trade Show Bureau shows no follow-up calls were required to close 54 percent of exposition leads, with just one call required to close another 16 percent of leads. On average, less than one sales call is required to convert a trade

445

show lead into an order, compared with the 5.1 sales calls needed to close the average industrial sale.

A recent study by Incomm International revealed the following reasons why people attend trade shows:

- To find solutions to known problems.
- To decide on or familiarize vendor selection for post-show purchases.
- To identify new methods.
- To meet with technical experts.
- To assess industry directions.

For the exhibitor, trade shows provide a way to reach people who are not ordinarily contacted by or accessible to a salesperson. According to *Exhibit Surveys*, 88 percent of the average show audience in 1986 had not been visited by a salesperson from the exhibitor in the preceding 12 months. Exhibitors reach new people each time they participate in a show; on average, one-third of attendees are paying a first-time visit to every show, so exhibiting is a good way to meet new potential buyers, find out about new companies, and keep up to date on what the competition is doing.

Used in tandem with other marketing activities, trade shows provide an opportunity to accelerate the buying process. You may be able to accomplish in two or three days what would normally take weeks or months of account prospecting work. Depending on the dollar amount your company spends on its exhibit, personnel, hotel, meals, and other expenses, and the number of people its exhibit reaches, trade shows are often a cost-effective sales vehicle. A 1985 study by the McGraw-Hill Laboratory of Advertising Performance showed that the average cost for obtaining a qualified sales lead at a trade show was $106.89, in comparison to the cost for a conventional industrial sales call, which was $229.70. With the rising costs of sales calls in the field, more companies are finding that attending trade shows, especially regional shows, is an increasingly attractive and cost-efficient alternative.

Trade shows also allow you to control the environment in which you present your product and the way in which it is demonstrated. Your sales force can give prospects information on solving their problems and get direct feedback on the product. The average time spent by an attendee at an exhibit in 1986 was about 15 minutes, so your presentation or demonstration should be no longer than 10 minutes at the most.

Before you participate in a trade show, you should decide upon your primary objective. Unless you have a good idea of what you wish to achieve, you have no way of evaluating a particular show, no guidelines for deciding what you should show and how you should show it, and no way to determine whether or not your investment was worthwhile. Yet only 46 percent of exhibitors set objectives for their trade show programs, according to a 1988 study by Exhibit Surveys. The Trade Show Bureau estimates less than half of that 46 percent sets truly quantifiable objectives and then measures the results.

Your primary objective might be any of the following:

- To make sales.
- To maintain an image and continue contact with customers.
- To create an image or initiate contact with potential customers.
- To introduce a new product.
- To demonstrate nonportable equipment.
- To offer an opportunity for customers to discuss their technical problems and get solutions.
- To identify new applications for an existing or projected product by obtaining feedback from visitors.
- To build the morale of your local sales force and of dealers.
- To relate to competition.
- To conduct market research.
- To recruit personnel or attract new dealers.
- To demonstrate interest in and support of the sponsoring association or industry.

Whenever possible, your objective should be stated numerically—in terms of number of appointments, new names for your mailing list, how many orders to bring back, recruiting so many new wholesalers, and so on. Clear-cut objectives will help you measure your return on investment once the show is over.

SELECTING THE RIGHT KIND OF SHOW

The key to making a trade show exhibit worthwhile is to select a show that will deliver the kind of audience you want to reach. The size and composition of that audience (i.e., attendees' titles, responsibilities as decision makers and purchasers, and whether their firms are located in your company's primary market area) are among the most important factors to consider. Location of both the show and your display area within the show are also important.

To check out audience quality, attendance, and competitors who will be exhibiting (or have exhibited) at a particular trade show, you can request literature and a prospectus from the sponsor. Since this literature is promotional in nature, it will present the show in its best light. But most shows also issue detailed breakdowns of attendance that list the industries and geographic locations represented by visitors. One of the best sources of information is the list of exhibitors at previous shows, whose names you may find in the promotional material or which can be obtained from show management.

An even better idea is to send a company representative to check out shows in person the year before you plan to exhibit, or to ask other exhibitors what they thought of the effectiveness of the shows. Ask them about costs and whether they encountered any problems. The subjects of seminars held in conjunction with the show can also provide clues to who will be attending and what their interests are.

Location of the show and nearby facilities are also important. How well does your market fit—educationally, technically, socially—with the location of the show? Are there entertainment and cultural activities available for spouses and attendees to enjoy after the show? How attractive are the hotel and restaurant choices? How easy is it to get to the show and to register? All of these factors play into how effective a particular show will be in reaching your target market.

REGIONAL VERSUS NATIONAL TRADE SHOWS

The trend throughout the past decade has been toward more and more regional, specialized, and vertical trade shows (i.e., shows that concentrate on a range of products used throughout a single industry, rather than horizontal trade shows that deal with the applications of a particular kind of product in a wide variety of industries). Some experts predict that the big national shows are in trouble because they are too diversified. Regional shows have caught on because they are targeting more specific geographic audiences with very little buyer overlap.

Trade Show Bureau president William Mee says, "Regional shows reach a technical audience that would otherwise not be reached. Vertical segmentation is occurring as marketers understand the importance of identifying and meeting the needs of specific market niches or segments."

For the advertising manager, this means more shows to choose from, greater specialization of audiences, and, for national companies, more shows to attend to cover all the target markets. But it also means it's easier to target specific audience segments in "smaller bites."

Data released by the Trade Show Bureau show that over 50 percent of the audience at a regional exposition travel fewer than 100 miles to attend. At national expositions, 64 percent of the visitors come from at least 400 miles away. So the proliferation of regional shows helps smaller companies reach local markets more efficiently. No longer do small firms with limited resources have to travel hundreds of miles to large metropolitan areas in order to try to reach the appropriate geographic segment of their markets. By securing a presence in local shows, smaller firms can target their regional audiences cost-effectively and still compete with their larger competitors.

EXHIBIT LOCATION AS A FACTOR IN ATTRACTING PROSPECTS

The importance of exhibit location within a show in attracting prospects is a subject of debate. While it's true that you should advertise your participation in the show ahead of time to prospects and customers so as not to rely solely on walk-by traffic, a survey of 607 trade show participants revealed display location was one of the "most important" criteria in deciding whether to enter a show.

Those findings suggest that "it is highly desirable for a booth to be located in a high-density area with good 'intercepting' qualities," write John M. Browning and Ronald J. Adams. "For the small firm with limited resources, this would point to the desirability of locating along major aisles or between major exhibits that are capable of generating traffic."

On the other hand, booth location is not as important for large companies, that tend to be sought out by more visitors and often have larger and more dramatic exhibits anyway. Various studies have shown that what really counts is exhibit size: the larger the better, especially as the size of the show increases.

The Trade Show Bureau, which has conducted studies on the effect of booth location on exhibition performance and impact, claims exhibit location is neither a positive or negative factor. The Bureau conducted studies at two well-known exhibit facilities and determined that being located at the front and center of the hall is not, as is commonly believed, an advantageous location in terms of booth traffic. The report states, "When size of an exhibit is eliminated as a factor in creating impact by adjusting or weighting recall scores for the size factor, there are absolutely no statistically significant differences in impact for exhibits in any area of the hall or complex."

What does all this mean to you, the exhibitor? For your company's exhibit (and products) to be remembered, you should place the most emphasis on creating a large, well-designed exhibit, staffed by well-trained personnel and featuring demonstrations targeted to the show audience. As a safeguard, you should avoid locations in temporary structures, separate facilities requiring transportation to visit, or small rooms and hard-to-find locations within the main facility. Such locations do register lower traffic and make it harder for prospects to find you.

HOW MUCH SPACE WILL YOU NEED?

Once you have located a show that will help you reach your marketing objectives, you need to decide how big your exhibit should be. The most common unit of space is a 10' × 10' booth, although some shows offer smaller units. There is sometimes a space differential depending on location. If space is available, you can get as many booths as you want. A larger exhibit can help both to attract more prospects to your booth and to aid visitors in remembering your company. But how do you determine how much space you really need?

First, make an estimate of how many people visiting the show are logical prospects. You can base this on a study of the attendance reports, counting the number of visitors with meaningful titles, job responsibilities, and so on. You won't be able to reach all of them, but you should be able to get half of them to your booth.

Divide this number by the total number of hours the show will be open. This will give you the average number of visitors per hour. (However, attendance at a show tends to be greatest during the middle days, less on the first and last days. Typically, the second and third days of a four-day show attract the greatest number of visitors, followed by the first day. Attendance tends to drop off substantially on the last day of the show.) The nature of your product determines how many people your sales rep can handle per hour, but 15 is an average. Divide the hourly visitor rate by 15, and you'll get the average number of sales representatives you should have on hand to handle the number of people you expect.

Experience shows that two people talking need about 50 square feet of space. With less space than this, the visitor gets a feeling of being crowded and is unwilling to stop. If there is more space, visitors become unwilling to intrude and hesitate to step into the display area. Multiply the number of sales reps you come up with by 50, and you'll get an approximation of how much space (in square feet) you should have to reach your objective. Add to that the space occupied by your demonstration equipment, furniture, and displays, and that's how much space you need. (In the standard 10' × 10' booth, two reps can usually work easily.) More than that could be a waste of money; less, and you will probably reach fewer than your original audience estimate.

DESIGNING YOUR EXHIBIT

Designing an exhibit is best done by professionals. It's likely more people will see your booth in a few days than see your office or store in months or years, so aim to make a good impression. In planning the design of an exhibit, keep two factors in mind:

1. Your goal is to select, from all those attending, those who are good prospects for whatever you are showing. The most visible part of your display must act like a headline in a good ad—it must attract the attention of the right people in the few seconds it takes them to walk past your booth. Avoid long graphics on signs, since people won't bother to read them.

2. You should use the unique advantages of the medium, which means that you should show your product in action, fully and three-dimensionally, so your prospect can see and touch and handle it.

Something that is in motion and three-dimensional, such as a display of your product in action, is a good attention-grabber. A live presenter demonstrating your product will also help draw prospects, as will interactive exhibits that involve the customer. You might even consider renting a separate conference room or theater in the convention hall to stage a special presentation, demonstration, or performance for your target audience. This way, you get the decision makers to concentrate on your message without exhibit hall distractions for a specific period of time.

There are three types of exhibits:

1. *The custom exhibit.* This is a one-of-a-kind, specially designed exhibit, usually for use at a major show.

2. *The modular exhibit.* Produced in quantity, this type of exhibit can be either a custom modular or an off-the-shelf modular display. Usually they come in 4- or 5-foot sections and are assembled in a row to make a linear exhibit, or in other configurations to make a walkaround or a series of linear arrangements. They have interchangeable story features, so that panels that tell a selling story can be removed and changed inexpensively. These are lightweight, easy to set up, and comparatively inexpensive.

3. *The erector set.* This is an off-the-shelf, suitcase kind of exhibit that can fit in the trunk of an automobile. These consist of rods and panels held together by joining members that can hold shelves and graphics. They're easy to set up, lightweight, flexible, and can be carried around and set on a table top. Although not as impressive as the other types, these kits are perfectly adequate for small regional shows. They can be bought directly from manufacturers or through local exhibit designers or producers.

You can also rent a modular system, which may be a good idea if you are just getting started in trade show exhibiting. By renting, you can get a good idea of what works and what doesn't, so that later on you can work with a designer on a custom exhibit that best meets your company's space, staff, product, and display needs.

While flashier custom exhibits are preferred for the big national shows, as the popularity of regional shows grows, the demand for lightweight, modular exhibits that can be inexpensively shipped and easily adapted to fit different audiences will likely increase.

FOLLOW SHOW RULES

When you sign up for space at a trade show, your rental usually includes nothing more than a draped area and a sign with your name on it hung on the rear wall. You can use this space in any way you want, subject to the show rules outlined in the Exhibitor's Kit you will receive. Be sure to read these rules carefully, or get your exhibit designer to go over them with you. They tell you how high you can build your display; how much of the cubic footage of the display area you can use; how to order electricity, lights, furniture, and the like; and what you can and can't do. The exhibitor's manual also tells you when you can get into the exhibit hall and when you have to be out of it, and includes order blanks for labor and equipment.

The exhibit house can help estimate the hours needed to set up and tear down your booth. Most trade show operations are covered by union and management rules, which vary from city to city. All of this union labor is available to the exhibitor by advance order, which can save your company time and money. In fact, many exhibit services give 15 percent discounts for advance orders. Exhibitors who do not order in advance receive furnishings and labor on a first come, first served basis only after the other orders have been filled. Usually, the exhibitor's responsibilities in setting up the booth are restricted to arranging company products and literature and conducting demonstrations. If you have any problems with receiving or installing your display, seek help from the exhibitor service center, usually set up on the edge of the hall. A work pass or exhibitor badge can be obtained at the show's registration desk to give you access to your booth during setup.

BUDGETING FOR THE TRADE SHOW

Trade show participants commonly allocate between 5 and 20 percent of their marketing budgets to trade shows, with the average being 10 to 12 percent. Typical trade show costs range from $10,000 for a 100 square foot booth to $150,000 to $750,000 for a 5,000 square foot booth at a large show. Budgets for small regional shows are commonly only one or two thousand dollars, or even less. Expenditures for international shows by large companies can run into the millions of dollars. Such things as laser lighting, computer-generated graphics, professional performers, special effects, and original music will add substantially to your tab.

Before your enter a show, know your budget as well as your objectives. Exhibit costs depend not only on the size of the show and how much space you rent, but on the type of exhibit you buy (or rent); on its weight and size, which affect shipping and handling charges; and on how many different parts must be assembled. Costs for readily available 10-foot, professionally designed portable or modular exhibit units equipped with custom graphics range from $2,500 to $5,000. For a custom-designed unit, figure on $800 per linear foot, including graphics. New signs and photography for refurbishing a booth can cost from $500 to $1,000.

Another consideration is drayage, the cost of moving materials from the loading dock to your booth space, storing crates during the show, and reversing the process afterward. Do not ship materials directly to the hotel or convention center. The exhibitor kit will specify the warehouse and shipping instructions. Pricing for drayage is by hundred weight (CWT)—the cost per 100 pounds—with minimums for small cartons. First-time exhibitors may be surprised at the cost; often, prices are above $30 per 100 pounds.

Trade show participation begins with advance planning. Make a floor plan and draw sketches of the exhibit setup and decorations. Will you have a floor, carpeting, drapes? What are your electrical and equipment needs? How will your exhibit be shipped and where will it be stored prior to the show? Who will set it up? Many exhibitors arrange for both installation and knockdown of a display under supervision. Although this service usually costs extra, it can save you two days prior to the show and one day following it, so it may be worthwhile to consider.

You also may want to figure in the cost of promotional literature, advertising, direct mail, giveaways, and personnel travel and time away from the office. To figure out personnel time costs, the Trade Show Bureau suggests estimating the average annual compensation for the employees who will work the booth. Add a percentage to cover benefits and office support; many companies estimate 25 to 40 percent. Then divide by 220, the average number of work days in a year. This is the cost per person-day. Multiply that by the number of people days at the exposition to get personnel time costs.

Tradeshow Week's Annual Exhibits Survey reports can give you average dollar costs for per-square-foot space rentals, per-hour costs for drayage, and hourly rates for skilled laborers (plumbers, electricians, carpenters, etc.). Other costs can include such items as furniture and audio-visual equipment rental, janitorial services, installation and dismantling, new construction, and exhibit prep and refurbishing. You may also want to hire a photographer, florist, security guard, and models or performers.

REFURBISHING YOUR BOOTH

When your booth starts to show signs of wear and tear, or when you need to update it for a new show, allow plenty of time for refurbishing. Here are ten points to remember:

1. Refurbishing requires even more planning than a new presentation. Existing properties take up a lot more room on the exhibit house floor because they must be set up in their entirety to complete the revitalization process.

2. Don't expect a firm quotation for refurbishing. The variables of condition, construction, and unforeseen problems in existing properties preclude precise quotations.

3. Don't insist on rejuvenating those parts of your exhibit that won't be visible on the show floor. It's seldom worth the cost to achieve that state of perfection.

4. It's often better to replace a surface than waste time on spot repairs and touch-ups that may detract from your image on the exhibit floor. Ironically, minor touch-ups are particularly noticeable on painted surfaces. Unless completely refinished for minor blemishes, painted surfaces will frequently begin to look cheap after a few shows.

5. Properties can be covered with materials that withstand frequent use and are resistant to breaking, chipping, flaking, and denting. High-pressure laminates such as Formica may cost more on a materials basis, but consider that it can be applied directly over a damaged surface in its entirety or in sections to provide a durable new face.

6. Acrylic sheeting such as Plexiglas or Lexan can provide a sophisticated look for an exhibit, yet even with the best possible care will still collect scratches. It's possible to buff out minor surface blemishes, but not deep scrapes. Acrylic sheeting is easily replaced, so while material costs may be high, labor costs won't be.

7. Metal properties are perhaps the most durable. They have inherent strengths that allow them to last through many shows with only minor touch-ups. However, keep an eye on the weight. Extrusions and various other lightweight metal components that are available usually provide the best of both worlds.

8. Consider soft surfaces, such as carpeting or cloth. Carpeting provides a durable surface that can stand up to heavy use and also help protect properties during shipping. Carpet surfaces, however, can soil. They cannot be wiped down like high pressure laminates or acrylic sheeting, yet depending on the carpet, spot cleaning can frequently be done. Replacing carpet or cloth is easy, requiring little more than cutting and adhering.

9. Choose fasteners such as Velcro that allow easy interchange of graphics and copy panels, thus providing your exhibit with visual consistency along with flexibility to adapt to changing marketing programs and target audiences at different shows. Transparent Plexiglas panels may also be added to cover graphics, protecting them from damage and keeping them clean and attractive.

10. After many uses, shipping cases as well as exhibit materials become so worn, loose, and tired that the best solution is to start anew. Lightweight, reinforced fiber containers provide the protection materials need, and also save shipping costs.

BUILDING TRAFFIC BY PUBLICIZING YOUR PRESENCE

Especially if you'll be exhibiting at a large show, make the most out of your participation by promoting your appearance at the trade show ahead of time to prospects and customers. This will help increase traffic to your booth, both by directing the right audience to your display and by encouraging those who might not attend otherwise to make the trip to see you. Surprisingly, the Trade Show Bureau reports that only one-quarter of trade show exhibitors bother to publicize their presence ahead of time

Here are several ways to "presell" your exhibit:

- *Use direct mail.* Give your audience specific information about what you'll be exhibiting by sending out a mailing six weeks before the show. In addition to using your own customer or prospect list, you may want to ask the exposition manager if he or she sells lists, or perhaps an industry trade publication could provide one.

- *Write to or call current customers.* Let them know you'll be at the show and encourage them to come. You might even suggest a specific time or set up an appointment when you know floor traffic will be slow. Often slow hours are at the start or end of the day, during lunch, or on the final day of the show.

- *Include detailed information in the events schedule.* The trade show's events program includes a list of exhibitors and a description of what products or services they offer along with their listing. Since attendees do read this schedule, make your listing as specific as possible.

- *Prepare promotional material.* Print up posters for your show windows and corporate lobby, add stickers announcing your presence at the show to your correspondence, mention your plans in your magazine ads, even send admission tickets to the show to special customers. The fact that you're participating in a show can build your image in your customers' eyes, even if they don't go to the show and see you.

- *Advertise in special editions of trade magazines.* Trade associations that sponsor a show often publish a special "show issue" of their magazine that includes a guide to exhibitors, speakers, and events. Publications in the field represented by the exposition may promote and report on the show. These and local newspapers are ideal places in which to advertise your participation.

- *Offer special prices.* Many exhibitors offer special show prices on merchandise bought at the show. Make your discount prices known in advance, and they will help to build traffic. Such discounts are particularly effective if your products are not expensive and do not require a large commitment.

- *Hand out advertising specialties.* Some companies use advertising specialties, often called giveaways, to increase the impact of their participation. Specialties are too often passed out indiscriminately, adding to the cost of participating in a show but contributing little to sales. The best specialty appeals almost exclusively to potential users of your products. It should be an item the recipient will keep for a long time. Be sure to check show rules, since not all shows permit distribution of these items.

- *Create targeted special giveaways.* A particularly effective way to use specialties is to help bring specific people to your booth. You can make up a list of the names and addresses of very important prospects whom you are eager to lure to your booth. Then send each of them something like one of a pair of handsome cufflinks or earrings, perhaps designed around your trademark, if you have one. Your cover letter would then promise the other half of the pair when the recipient visits you at the show. If you have selected both your list and the specialty item carefully, you can expect a high proportion of responses. A good specialty advertising counselor can help you develop a creative promotion.

- *Make a new product introduction.* A trade show is an excellent place to introduce a new product. People come to trade shows specifically to see what is new. If you can get the word out that you will have something new at the show, you will develop a valuable list of booth visitors.

- *Give customers and prospects an idea of what you will be showing.* See that advance announcements are sent out to the publications that cover your industry. Most of them run both previews and follow-up articles on important shows. Many need their material eight to ten weeks before a show, but it is worth the special effort to decide early on what you will be showing. At the show, leave press releases in the show press room, and have an extra supply in the booth for editors who stop by.

TRAIN YOUR SALESPEOPLE

The effectiveness of your booth depends largely on the effectiveness of the people working in it. "Exhibiting is a people-to-people medium—people remember other people," writes Mim Goldberg, a trade show consultant, in the *Business to Business Marketer* (October 1997, page 10). "You need a staff who are skilled in working a show."

Studies show that although graphics, exhibit size, and familiarity with a company name or its products draw people to a booth, what prospects remember the most about their visit is what they are told by salespeople. It is a different and sometimes bewildering experience for most sales representatives, who are more used to visiting prospects one at a time in their offices, not having prospects come up and ask for information. Salespeople often feel uncomfortable at an exhibit if their own customers and territories are not well-represented in the audience, so try to use salespeople who serve the area in which the trade show is held.

Your sales team can be made more effective if you hold a special training session before the show that describes the trade show's audience and outlines your company's objectives, selling procedures, any special sales techniques for dealing with booth visitors or handling product demonstrations, and arrival and departure times. Train your sales staff to present sales information in short summaries that encourage questions and comments. The goal in working with trade show prospects is to encourage a dialogue rather than to launch into a long-winded sales pitch.

Booth personnel must be friendly, able to tell good prospects from curiosity-seekers, and able to move quickly toward advancing the sale. You must let your people know what your objectives are so that they can work toward reaching your goal, whether it is setting up appointments, getting literature into the right hands, giving a demonstration, or making a sale. Don't plan to bring enough literature to give to everyone visiting the show; it's too easy for casual lookers to pick up and then dump as soon as they leave. Some companies estimate literature needs based on 5 percent of total attendance.

Arrange to have two teams of salespeople staff the booth during the course of the day, because this kind of selling is hard work. A salesperson can be effective for about four hours a day; then the physical and mental strain starts to show. However, sales can be reduced by as much as 50 percent if too many people rotate booth duty, so alternate two small teams of people instead. This way, your booth will be staffed by people who quickly become familiar and comfortable with the new environment.

When your people are on duty, they should be up front, standing and not sitting, ready to welcome visitors, and not talking in a corner with other salespeople or spending long periods of time talking to current customers. Educate your salespeople that the value of the trade show is in meeting potential new customers at a relatively low cost.

Writing in the *Record* (March 3, 1996), a business etiquette columnist offers the following trips for trade show exhibit personnel:

- Dress up.
- Clean up—make your booth as attractive as you can.
- Welcome people. Stand to greet them. Smile. Be prepared.
- Be interested.
- Eat privately. Keep your drinks inconspicuous.
- Thank visitors for coming.

FOLLOW-UP ON SALES LEADS

Decide before the show how you'll handle sales leads. Find out what your prospects' needs are, get their names, titles, company names and addresses, what product application they are interested in, and when they are looking to buy. Try to ask open-ended questions about the prospect's true interests that will aid in the sales qualification process.

"The most important part of a lead form may well be the remarks section, an area where the salesperson can explain nuances or why the lead was taken," notes Edward Chapman, Jr. "If an order is written for a new customer, try to obtain some credit information for follow-up."

In an interview in *Co.* magazine (January 1998, p. 64), Jenni Hytaa, vice president of marketing for Galaxy Expocard in Frederick, MD, advises exhibit managers to consider the following questions:

- Does your company want to get information from visitors on the show floor or before the show opens?
- Has the company invested enough in office computers and contact management software to be able to use the electronic databases available at many shows?
- How will the exhibit manager get sales leads to the sales staff?

Then, most importantly, do follow-up with a price quote, sales call, literature, whatever. Too many companies fail to follow up on sales-call requests after the show. Yet trade show visitors are ready and able to buy. In a survey of exposition leads taken from 12 different shows, the Trade Show Bureau found that 40 percent of respondents reported they had purchased one or more products of the type exhibited within 4 to 12 weeks after the show. Although 54 percent of the orders placed by companies that exhibited at the 12 shows were closed without follow-up calls, another 36 percent of sales occurred following one or more calls. (The number of calls required to close the remaining 10 percent of sales was not known.)

In measuring response to your trade show, be aware that "two-thirds of all sales aren't achieved until twelve to twenty-four months after a show," states Dr. Allen Konopacki, president of INCOMM International. So if increasing sales was your primary objective in a show, don't cross off the show as a failure if you don't see an immediate jump in orders. Make sure that your sales staff gets a full report on leads following the show and then stays in touch with those prospects.

The most important single measure of booth performance may be how well your display is remembered. In the *Journal of Small Business Management*, Browning and Adams note, "In 1986, about 75 percent of visitors to a sponsor's exhibit were able to recall the visit and the sponsor eight to ten weeks after the show closed. Cases of low memory impact were generally attributed to lack of interpersonal contact during the show and to insufficient follow-up activity at the show's conclusion."

While you should measure how well each particular show you participate in achieves the quantifiable objectives you set, don't forget to compare show results with each other as well. That will provide a track record of performance and help you decide which future shows to enter.

RESOURCES

A good source of trade show information is *Trade Shows Worldwide*, published by Gale Research Inc., Detroit, MI, which lists dates, locations, number of exhibitors, attendees, and other descriptive information for more than 4,500 trade shows and exhibits held in 60 countries each year. The cost is $195. Call 313-961-3707 for details. Another source is the *Trade Show & Exhibits Schedule*, published by Bill Communications, P.O. Box 3078, Southeastern, PA 19398. This annual directory lists all trade shows held in the United States and is available by calling 1-800-253-6708.

One way to locate exhibit design professionals in your area is to contact their trade association, the Exhibit Designers & Producers Association, 611 E. Wells Street, Milwaukee, WI 53202, 414-276-3372. You can also find exhibit designers and suppliers by checking the Yellow Pages under Exhibits or Expositions.

For a complete listing of up-to-date costs, contact the International Exhibitors Association, 5501 Backlick Road, Suite 200, Springfield, VA 22151, 703-941-3725 to order *The Budget Guide*.

Chapter

21
SPEECHES, SLIDE SHOWS, AND PRESENTATIONS

Public speaking—giving speeches, lectures, talks, papers, and presentations at public events, industry meetings, conventions, and conferences—is a marketing technique that is widely used by individual entrepreneurs and small businesses. But many larger companies don't take full advantage of such opportunities.

Why? Because we advertising managers and professionals tend to concentrate on big projects. There's a lot of excitement and glamour in producing a national ad campaign or prize-winning annual report. Most advertising managers don't get excited about helping a company engineer or manager prepare a speech for a local chamber of commerce or business club. Yet, for many firms, that speech can have more impact and generate more immediate business than the ad campaign or annual report.

Why is public speaking so effective as a promotional tool? For many of the same reasons seminars and articles are. When you speak, you are perceived as the expert. If your talk is good, you immediately establish your credibility with the audience so that they want you and your company to work with them and solve their problems.

Unlike an article, which is somewhat impersonal, a speech or talk puts you within hand-shaking distance of your audience. Because in today's fast-paced world more and more activities are taking place remotely via fax, computer modem, and videoconferencing, meeting prospects face to face firmly implants an image of you in their minds. If that meeting takes place in an environment where you are singled out as an expert, as is the case when you speak, the impression is that much more effective and powerful.

WHEN TO USE SPEAKING

Speaking is not ideal for every product or marketing situation. If you are trying to mass-market a new brand of floppy disk on a nationwide basis to all computer users, television and print advertising is likely to be more effective than speaking, which limits the number of people you reach per contact. On the other hand, a wedding consultant whose market is Manhattan would probably profit immensely from a talk on wedding preparation given to engaged couples at a local church.

In *Effective Communication of Ideas*, George Vardman says speaking should generally be used in the following situations:

1. When confidential matters are to be discussed.
2. When warmth and personal qualities are called for.
3. When an atmosphere of openness is desired.
4. When strengthening of feelings, attitudes, and beliefs is needed.
5. When exactitude and precision are not required.
6. When decisions must be communicated quickly or when important deadlines must be met rapidly.
7. When crucial situations dictate maximum understanding.
8. When added impact is needed to sustain the audience's attention and interest or to get them to focus on a topic or issue.
9. When personal authentication of a claim or concept is needed.
10. When social or gregarious needs must be met.

FINDING SPEAKING OPPORTUNITIES

Unless you are sponsoring your own seminar, you will need to find appropriate forums at which your company personnel can be invited to speak. How do you go about it?

First, check your mail and the trade publications you read for announcements of industry meetings and conventions. For instance, if you sell furnaces for steel mills and want to promote a new process, you might want to give a paper on your technique at the annual Iron and Steel Exposition.

Trade journals generally run preview articles and announcements of major shows, expos, and meetings months before the event. Many trade publications also have columns that announce such meetings on both a national and a local level. Make sure you scan these columns in publications aimed at your target market industries.

You should also receive preview announcements in the mail. If you are an advertising manager, professional societies and trade associations will send you direct mail packages inviting your firm to exhibit at their shows. That's fine, but you have another purpose: to find out whether papers, talks, or seminars are being given at the show, and, if so, to get your people on the panels or signed up as speakers. If the show mailing promotion doesn't discuss papers or seminars, call up and ask.

Propose some topics with your company personnel as the speakers. Most conference managers welcome such proposals, because they need speakers to fill time slots. The conference manager or another association executive in charge of the technical sessions (the usual name for the presentation of papers or talks) will request an abstract, or short 100- to 200-word outline of your talk. Work with your speakers to come up with an outline that is enticing, so as to generate maximum attendance, but also reflects accurately what the speaker wants to talk about. After all, it is the speaker's talk, and he or she must be comfortable with it.

Because many advertisers will be pitching speakers and presentations to the conference manager, the earlier you do it, the better. Generally, annual meetings and conventions of major associations begin planning 8 to 12 months in advance; local groups or local chapters of national organizations generally book speakers 3 to 4 months in advance. The earlier you approach them, the more receptive they'll be to your proposal.

If you are not on the mailing list to receive advance notification of meetings and conventions of your industry associations, write to them and request that they place you on such a list. You will find their names and addresses in the *Encyclopedia of Associations*, published by Gale Research and available in your local library.

SCREENING SPEAKING OPPORTUNITIES

On occasion, you may find meeting planners and conference executives calling you up and asking you (or a representative from your firm) to speak at their events, rather than you having to seek them out and ask them.

This is flattering, but beware. Not every opportunity to speak is really worthwhile. Meeting planners and committee executives are primarily concerned with getting someone to stand at the podium, and do not care whether your speaker or your firm will benefit in any way from the exposure. So before you say "yes" to an opportunity to speak, ask the meeting planner the following questions:

- What is the nature of the group?
- Who are the members? What are their job titles and responsibilities? What companies do they work for?
- What is the average attendance at such meetings? How many people does the meeting planner expect will attend your session?
- Do they pay an honorarium, or at least cover expenses?
- What other speakers have they had recently and what firms do these speakers represent?

If the answers indicate that the meeting is not right or worthwhile for your company, or if the meeting chairperson seems unable or unwilling to provide answers, offer your thanks and politely decline the invitation.

PLAN YOUR OBJECTIVE

Of course, your objective is to sell. But be careful. People attending a luncheon or dinner meeting aren't there to be sold. They want to be entertained, informed, educated, made to laugh or smile. Selling your product, service, or company may be your goal, but in public speaking, it has to be secondary to giving a good presentation, and a soft-sell approach works best.

Terry C. Smith, author of *Making Successful Presentations*, lists the following as possible objectives for business presentations:

- Inform or instruct.
- Persuade or sell.
- Make recommendations and gain acceptance.
- Arouse interest.
- Inspire or initiate action.
- Evaluate, interpret, and clarify.
- Set the stage for further action.
- Gather ideas and explore them.
- Entertain.

You could also add "establish credibility" to this list; delivering a good talk can go a long way toward building the image of both the speaker and firm as authorities in the field.

"Perhaps you are aiming for a combination of these," says Smith. "For example, there is nothing wrong with being both informative and entertaining; the two are not mutually exclusive. In fact, the two may complement one another."

Let's say your talk is primarily informational. You could organize it along the following lines: First, an introduction that presents an overview of the topic. Next, the body of the talk, which presents the facts in detail. Finally, a conclusion that sums up for the audience what they have heard.

This repetition is beneficial because in a spoken presentation, unlike an article, the audience cannot flip back to a preceding page or paragraph to refresh their memory or study your material in more detail. For this reason, you must repeat your main point at least three times to make sure it is understood and remembered.

What if your talk is primarily persuasive or sales oriented? In their book, *How to Make Speeches for All Occasions*, Harold and Marjorie Zelko present the following outline for a persuasive talk:

1. Draw attention to the subject.

2. Indicate the problem, need, or situation.

3. Analyze the problem's origin, history, causes, manifestations.

4. Lead toward possible solutions, or mention them.

5. Lead toward most desired solution or action.

6. Offer proof and values of solution proposed.

7. Prove it as better than other solutions. Prove it will eliminate causes of problems, will work, and has value.

8. Lead toward desired response from audience.

9. Show how a desired response can be realized.

10. Conclude with a summary and appeal as appropriate.

Janet Stone and Jane Bachner present a similar outline for a persuasive presentation in their book, *Speaking Up*:

1. Secure attention of audience.

2. State the problem.

3. Prove the existence of the problem.

4. Describe the unfortunate consequences of the problem.

5. State your solution.

6. Show how your solution will benefit the audience.

7. Anticipate and answer objections you know are coming.

8. Invite action.

Many other organizational schemes are available to speakers. For instance, if you're describing a process, your talk can be organized along the natural flow of the process or the sequence of steps involved in completing the process. This would be ideal for a talk on "How to Start Your Own Collection Agency" or "How to Design Mixers for Viscous Fluids."

If you're talking about expanding a communications network worldwide, you might start with the United States, then move on to Asia, then cover Europe. If your topic is vitamins, covering them in alphabetical order, from vitamin A to zinc, seems a sensible approach.

Lyle Surles and W.A. Stanbury, authors of *The Art of Persuasive Talking*, provide the following advice to speakers who want to persuade or sell as well as inform:

- Be sincere.
- Be honest.
- Show conviction.
- Be empathetic.
- Show respect for your audience.

Finally, Albert J. Beveridge, in *The Art of Public Speaking*, advises speakers to follow these rules:

- Speak only when you have something to say.
- Speak only what you believe to be true.
- Prepare thoroughly.
- Be clear.
- Stick to your subject.
- Be fair.
- Be brief.

THE MOST IMPORTANT PART OF YOUR TALK

A talk has three parts: beginning, middle, and end. All are important, but the beginning and ending are more important than the body. Most people can manage to discuss a topic for 15 minutes, give a list of facts, or read from a prepared statement. That's what it takes to deliver the middle part.

The beginning and ending are more difficult. In the beginning, you must immediately engage the audience's attention and establish rapport. Not only must they be made to feel that your topic will be interesting, but they must be drawn to you, or at least not find fault with your personality.

To test this theory, a well-known speaker put aside his usual opening and instead spoke for five minutes about himself, how successful he was, how much money he made, how in demand he was as a speaker, why he was the right choice to address the group. After his talk, he casually asked a member, "What were you thinking when I said that?" The man politely replied, "I was thinking what a blowhard you are."

How do you begin a talk? One easy and proven technique is to get the audience involved by asking them questions. For example, when addressing telecommunications engineers, ask: "How many of you manage a T1 network? How many of you are using 56 K DDS but are thinking about T1? How many of you use fractional T1?"

If you are speaking on a health topic, you might ask, "How many of you exercised today before coming here? How many of you plan to exercise after the meeting tonight? How many of you exercise three or more times a week?"

Asking questions like these has two benefits. First, it provides a quick survey of audience concerns, interests, and level of involvement, allowing you to tailor your talk to their needs on the spot. Second, it forces the audience to become involved immediately.

After all, when you are in the audience and the speaker asks a question, you do one of two things—you either raise your hand or don't raise it, don't you? Either way you are responding, thinking, and getting involved.

While the beginning is important, don't neglect a strong closing, especially if you are there not just for the pleasure of speaking but to help promote your company or its products. As Dorothy Leeds observes in her book, *PowerSpeak*:

> Speakers, as you now know, are also in the selling business, and the conclusion is the time to ask for the order. Nothing will happen if you don't ask. And you ask by telling the audience what you want it to do with the information you've presented and how they can take that action. An effective speaker presenting a central idea ends by pointing out to those in his audience exactly what is needed from them to put that idea to work. For example...if you've been persuading them to give blood, tell them where. And make it sound easy to get there.
>
> Action doesn't always have to be literal. If you simply want the people in your audience to mull over your ideas, tell them this is what you want them to do.
>
> Although you want a great opening that builds rapport and gets people to listen, and an ending that helps close the sale, don't neglect the body or middle of

your talk. It's the meat; it's what your audience came to hear. If your talk is primarily informational, be sure to give inside information on the latest trends, techniques, and product developments. If it's motivational, be enthusiastic and convince your listeners that they can lose weight, make money investing in real estate, or stop smoking.

If your talk is a how-to presentation, make sure you've written it so your audience walks away with lots of practical ideas and suggestions. As actor and toastmaster Georgie Jessel observed, "Above all, the successful speaker is sincerely interested in telling his audience something they want to know."

When speaking to technical audiences, tailor the content to the technical expertise of the listeners. Being too complex can bore a lot of people. But being too simplistic or basic can be even more offensive to an audience of knowledgeable industry experts.

MATTERS OF LENGTH AND TIMING

Talks can vary from a ten-minute workplace presentation to a two-day intensive seminar. How long should yours be? The event and meeting planner often dictate length. Luncheon and after-dinner talks to local groups and local chapters of professional societies and business clubs usually last 20 to 30 minutes, with an additional 5 to 10 minutes allotted for questions and answers.

For technical sessions at major conferences and national expositions, speakers are generally allowed 45 to 75 minutes. For a one-hour time slot, prepare a 45-minute talk. You'll probably start 5 minutes late to allow for late arrivals, and the last 10 minutes can be a more informal question and answer session.

The luckiest speakers are those who get invited to participate in panels. If you are on a panel consisting of three or four experts plus a moderator, it's likely that you'll simply be asked to respond to questions from the moderator or the audience, eliminating the need to prepare a talk.

Richard Armstrong, a freelance corporate speech writer, says most of the speeches he writes are 20 minutes in length. James Welch, author of *The Speech Writing Guide*, says that a typed, double-spaced page of manuscript should take the speaker 2 1/2 minutes to deliver. This means an 8-page double-spaced manuscript, which is about 2,000 words, will take 20 minutes to deliver as a speech.

That's about a hundred words a minute. Some speakers are faster, talking at 120 to 150 words a minute or more, so the 20-minute talk can run anywhere from 8 to 10 typed pages.

PREPARING THE TALK

What is the advertising department's role in arranging and preparing speeches for company executives, managers, and technical professionals?

It varies widely. In some cases, you may be totally unaware that the speech is being given, and you find out only by accident. Some advertising managers are upset by what they consider unauthorized speaking, and insist that every talk funnel its way through the communications department. Some adopt a more liberal policy. Why inhibit speakers or make the process more bureaucratic than it need be?

In other situations, you may be called upon to coordinate the details of the presentation and help with its preparation. This can range from writing the entire talk, to simply coaching the speaker or assisting with production of slides or other visual aids.

Individuals vary as to how much assistance they want or require. As a rule, top executives with severe time constraints have their speeches written, or at least work from an initial draft prepared by the communications department, while most engineers, scientists, and technical managers prefer to prepare their own papers and presentations.

Don't be too quick to volunteer to write everyone's speeches for them. While such activity can get you into the good graces of your clients at your company, it can easily become an overwhelming commitment if you underestimate the amount of work involved. According to *Best Sermons*, a religious magazine, it takes clergy about 7 hours to prepare a 20-minute sermon. You will find that this figure also holds true for business, sales, and technical presentations.

Allow at least one full day for preparation and rehearsal of any new short (20- to 30-minute) talk. Terry Smith says that for every brand new presentation, his ratio is one hour of preparation for every minute he plans to speak. "That is the preparation level at which I feel comfortable that I'm giving my very best," says Smith.

Tip: The trick to reducing preparation time is to have two or three canned (standard) talks which you can offer to various audiences. Even with a canned presentation, you'll need at least several hours to analyze the audience, do some customizing of your talk to better address that particular group, and rehearse once or twice.

Once the presentation is written, check it against the following list, provided by Dorothy Sarnoff in her book, *Speech Can Change Your Life*:

1. Have I honored all the requirements of the talk? (For example, if you submitted an outline or abstract, were all points covered?)
2. Have I researched the topic enough?
3. Have I taken into account the nature of the audience?
4. Have I rechecked to make sure the talk fits the allotted time? (This is done by rehearsing aloud and timing yourself with a stopwatch.)
5. Have I constructed the talk so it has a clear purpose and makes a point at the end?
6. Have I enough strong ideas in the body, and have I developed them sufficiently and arranged them in good order?
7. Have I asked enough questions and used "you" enough?

8. Have I an appropriate introduction and a strong conclusion?

9. Does the talk include enough specifics?

10. Have I used too many statistics?

ONE EXPERT'S ADVICE ON HOW TO GIVE A SPEECH

Professional speaker Rob Gilbert charges $3,000 to $7,000 to give a speech or presentation. Here are 41 of Gilbert's most effective techniques:

1. Write your own introduction and mail it to the sponsoring organization in advance of your appearance. (Also bring a copy with you for the master of ceremonies in case your original was lost.)

2. Establish rapport with the audience early.

3. What you say is not as important as how you say it.

4. Self-effacing humor works best.

5. Ask the audience questions.

6. Don't give a talk—have a conversation.

7. Thirty percent of the people in the audience will never ask the speaker a question.

8. A little bit of nervous tension is probably good for you.

9. Extremely nervous? Use rapport-building, not stress-reduction, techniques.

10. The presentation does not have to be great. Tell your audience that if they get one good idea out of your talk, it will have been worthwhile for them.

11. People want stories, not information.

12. Get the audience involved.

13. People pay more for entertainment than for education. (Proof: The average college professor would have to work ten centuries to earn what Oprah Winfrey makes in a year.)

14. You have to love what you are doing. (Dr. Gilbert has 8,000 cassette tapes of speeches and listens to these tapes three to four hours a day.)

15. The first time you give a particular talk it will not be great.

16. The three hardest audiences to address: engineers, accountants, and high school students.

17. If heckled, you can turn any situation around (verbal aikido).

18. Communicate from the Heart + Have an Important Message = Speaking Success.

19. You can't please everybody, so don't even try. Some will like you and your presentation, and some won't.

20. Ask your audience how you are doing and what they need to hear from you to rate you higher.

21. Be flexible. Play off your audience.

22. Be totally authentic.

23. To announce a break say: "We'll take a five-minute break now, so I'll expect you back in ten minutes." It always gets a laugh.

24. To get people back in the room (if you are the speaker), go out into the hall and shout, "It's starting; it's starting."

25. Courage is to feel the fear and do it anyway. The only way to overcome what you fear is to do it.

26. If panic strikes: Just give the talk and keep your mouth moving. The fear will subside in a minute or two.

27. In speaking, writing, teaching, and marketing, everything you see, read, hear, or do is grist for the mill.

28. Tell touching stories.

29. If the stories are about you, be the goat, not the hero. People like speakers who are humble; audiences hate bragging and braggarts.

30. Join Toastmasters. Take a Dale Carnegie course in public speaking. Join the National Speakers Association.

31. Go hear the great speakers and learn from them.

32. If you borrow stories or techniques from other speakers, adapt this material and use it in your own unique way.

33. Use audiovisual aids, if you wish, but not as a crutch.

34. When presenting a day-long workshop, make the afternoon shorter than the morning.

35. Asking people to perform a simple exercise (stretching, Simon Says, etc.) as an activity during a break can increase their energy level and overcome lethargy.

36. People love storytellers.

37. Today's most popular speaking topic: change (in business, society, lifestyles, etc.) and how to cope with it.

38. There is no failure, just feedback.

39. At the conclusion of your talk, tell your audience that they were a great audience—even if they were not.

40. Ask for applause using this closing: "You've been a wonderful audience. (Pause) Thank you very much."

41. If you want to become a good speaker, give as many talks as you can to as many groups as you can. Dr. Gilbert has some speeches he has given more than 1,000 times.

SLIDE SHOWS

What's the difference between a talk, a speech, and a presentation? A talk is a lecture given for free, while the term *speech* implies that the speaker receives a fee or honorarium. A presentation is a talk accompanied by slides, overheads, or other audiovisual aids.

When I was a marketing trainee at Westinghouse in the late 1970s, slides were all the rage in the corporate world. Nearly every presentation was an audiovisual presentation. Two managers could literally not get together for an informal chat without one pulling out a slide projector and dimming the lights.

Slides are still popular today, as are overhead projectors, but audiovisual aids are not necessary for most presentations. Most corporate presentations are dependent on slides or overheads and they are boring. Most professional speakers—people who earn thousands for a brief talk—do not use audiovisual aids. Today, businesspeople, especially in the corporate world, have become dependent on the visuals and have lost the spontaneity and relaxed manner that come with "having a conversation" rather than "making a presentation."

The problem with the corporate approach to visuals is that the audiovisual aid is seen as something that must run continuously and concurrently with the talk. So, although only 10 percent of the presentation requires visuals, the slide projector runs for 100 percent of the time, and the speaker fills in with stupid "word slides" that are wasteful and silly. For instance, if the speaker is going to talk for 3 or 4 minutes on quality, the word *Quality* appears on the screen in white against a black background. Such a visual adds nothing to the talk and is, in fact, ridiculous.

A better approach is to have visuals you can use when appropriate, then deliver the rest of your talk unaided. You can use flip charts and magic markers, but don't prepare them in advance. Rather, draw as you speak, which adds excitement and motion. It also creates anticipation: The audience becomes curious about what is being created before their eyes.

Slide projectors and overhead projectors are prone to mechanical failure. Errors in presentations, such as difficulty sorting through a pile of overhead transparencies or slides that are upside down or out of order, confuse and embarrass the speaker; they also cause the audience to snicker or lose interest.

Some speakers, interrupted by a jammed slide tray, lose their trains of thought and never fully recover. Errors or mishaps with audiovisual support can be extremely disconcerting, especially when making a good impression is important or the presenter is not comfortable with public speaking in the first place.

At times, high-quality visuals are needed. You may need a visual to demonstrate how a product works, explain a process, show the components or parts of a system, or graphically depict performance. For instance, if you are trying to promote your landscape design practice by giving a talk on "How to Design a Beautiful Front Yard," you want to show pictures of attractive front yards you have designed. In this case you can prepare overhead transparencies, a videotape, flip charts, or similar displays that can be shown for a brief period and then put away. If you use slides, turn the projector off and the lights on when visuals are not in use.

According to a research study done by 3M, it's estimated that we retain only 10 percent of what we hear, but by adding visual aids, the retention rate increases to 50 percent. A report from Matrix Computer Graphics notes that 85 percent of all information stored in the brain is received visually.

22 TIPS FOR IMPROVING SLIDE AND OTHER AUDIOVISUAL PRESENTATIONS

1. Simple is better. Use slide presentations that can be shown using a single projector. Multi-projector presentations, while dazzling, require special equipment and trained personnel to present.

2. The best length for a slide show: 5 to 10 minutes if prerecorded; 10 to 20 minutes if live.

3. The proper pace for a slide show: one slide for each new thought.

4. To test the readability of a slide: Hold the slide at arm's length. If you can't read the text, your audience won't be able to either.

5. Pick a narrow topic. In 20 minutes, you can't cover much ground. If there's more detail, put it in printed handouts your audience can take with them.

6. Slides and overheads are used to show, demonstrate, create excitement. They are not a good medium for transmitting complex detail. Too much detail in a slide or overhead makes it unclear.

7. Use pictures. Keep the use of word slides to a minimum.

8. Make the visuals clear, bold, and simple. For example, a graph should only have one curve and three or four data points. If there's more data to show, break it up into several slides.

9. Write narration for the ear, not the eye. Your talk will be heard, not read. This means shorter sentences, use of sentence fragments, pauses, and conversational tone.

10. To test your talk: Read it aloud. Rewrite portions that sound awkward or that you stumble over.

11. Slides today are an inexpensive medium. Cost per slide ranges from $7.50 to $50 for word slides, simple special effects, charts, graphs, and pictures taken from existing negatives or photos.

12. Resist the temptation to use silly or humorous slides. What one person finds funny and witty strikes another as offensive or juvenile.

13. "Tell them what you're going to tell them. Tell them. Then tell them what you told them." Your presentation should have an introduction, a body, and a recap or summary. According to Matrix Computer Graphics, a manufacturer of presentation and imaging equipment, you should spend approximately 20 percent of your speaking time on the introduction, 70 percent on the body, and 10 percent on the conclusion.

14. Slides with the most visual appeal include people (especially shots of people in the audience), familiar settings (e.g., their workplace), and familiar problems.

15. Before you start, say: "There's no need to take notes. We have hard copies of this presentation for you to take home." This relieves listeners of the burden of note taking, freeing them to concentrate on your talk.

16. The leave-behind can take one of several formats: hard copy of the slides or overheads, brochures, article reprints, or reprints of the narration (with visuals incorporated, if possible).

17. If the slide tray jams, insert a dime into the screw in its center and turn counterclockwise. This will usually release and allow you to remove the jammed slide. Put it aside and go on to the next slide. Do not try to show the jammed slide—it may be damaged.

18. Try to have someone else handle the audiovisual equipment, so you won't be bothered by such problems. If the problem cannot be fixed within 30 seconds, continue talking without your visual aids.

19. When traveling, always carry your slides, lecture notes, and other audiovisual materials with you. Do not pack them with luggage. Luggage gets lost.

20. Arrive early, set up early, and do a dry run in the presentation room. Get there in plenty of time to make sure all equipment, electrical outlets, markers, and other material you requested are there, and to rearrange the room to your liking. The speaker should always check out the lecture room at least one hour before the talk is scheduled to start.

21. The big advantage of slides: They are modular. You can quickly change, rearrange, update, or revise the presentation at virtually no cost.

22. Keep originals or masters under lock and key. Make several duplicate sets available in trays for others in your firm. Also keep copies of individual slides in a light cabinet (illuminated storage rack system) so people can have access to individual visuals as needed.

Chapter 22

PROMOTIONAL VIDEOS

Video, with its mesmerizing effect, has a potentially greater sales impact than print media. Reading takes effort and requires concentration. But few people can resist the impulse to stop and stare at a TV or film screen, which always seems a relaxing pastime.

Computer Video Productions, based in Minneapolis, specializes in "video sales brochures." Craig R. Evans, CVP's marketing director, points out that video (and, for our purposes, film) "is a very intimate medium. It appeals to both the audio and the visual sense. A paper brochure just sits there. With video you can see the product and also hear it. And you have a captive audience. People tend to watch your video brochure from start to finish, in the order you want the information presented."

Granted, a video or film is less convenient to watch than sales literature is to read. It is also surely be more expensive to produce. But it is less likely to be thrown away or easily misplaced. Pallace, Inc., a Maryland-based advertising agency, puts it thus: "In today's junk-mail jungle, a videotape stands out from the pack."

Audiovisual media are also cost-competitive compared to the salary of a full-time salesperson. "And unlike the salesperson," says Craig Evans, "your video never has a bad day."

APPLICATIONS

Videos As Sales Tools

A film or video may be the ideal sales solution for services or high-tech products that are too big to lug around from client to client, or for reaching potential consumers at point of sale locations. Nonbroadcast commercial films can run in department store windows, airport terminals, hotel lobbies, and at trade shows. If you are selling a system of some kind, the audiovisual approach can demonstrate an entire step-by-step process.

New products can be introduced or explained. If a pharmaceutical company is marketing a new drug, a videotape can be distributed to doctors to make them aware of the availability and benefits of the new drug.

Sales videos can be mailed directly to customers or left at their offices during sales calls, for viewing at the prospect's convenience. Most executives welcome the opportunity to turn out the lights and watch a little TV during the course of a day's work.

Using Audiovisuals to Produce Employee Motivation

Audiovisuals can be presented to the sales force at conventions, conferences, seminars, or smaller meetings. These productions can be used to launch new products or kick off promotion campaigns, or to instill team spirit by chronicling company successes. Presentations geared to top management can showcase accomplishments, introduce new concepts, or offer projections for the future.

Video and Film As Training Devices

Audiovisuals can be used to orient new employees or update the skills of your current staff. Big-screen presentations are useful with large groups, and could be used in conjunction with live instruction. Audiovisuals can also be used for recruitment.

Using a Video As a Public Relations Tool

A video could show community service projects or document a pioneering research program behind new product development. It can be sent to civic groups, such as the Rotary Club, Elks, or B'nai B'rith, or to libraries or schools. These films often have educational overtones, but always reflect well on the company. A utility company could distribute audiovisuals on how to clean a furnace, how to conserve energy, or the importance of recycling.

Videos As Tie-Ins

Films or videos can be used as part of a larger presentation, which can include live speakers, multimedia displays, product demonstrations, or supplemental print literature to take home after viewing the film.

Interactive Videos

In this format, instead of sitting passively, the viewer participates directly by responding to the choices presented. Kings Supermarkets provides culinary tips to shoppers via interactive videos. A shopper presses a button to select a choice of video offering helpful kitchen advice, such as how to cook a salmon or carve a turkey.

Interactive videos linked to computers are also used in training such technicians as auto mechanics or hospital personnel. In the latter case, the video simulates an emergency situation, and an on-screen menu gives the trainee a choice of response A, B, or C. If the wrong answer is selected, the video explains why and demonstrates the proper procedure.

FILM OR VIDEO: WHICH IS BEST FOR YOU?

Video is the predominant format of industrial audiovisual presentations. It is an instantaneous technology. On a set, you can see results immediately and mistakes are easier to rectify on the spot. If you didn't get what you wanted on the first take, you can reshoot. With film, you have to wait to see the rushes (unrefined, developed prints), usually the next day; if the results are unsatisfactory, you may have to set up the entire shoot again, which may be impractical, cost prohibitive, or impossible.

Production time for film and video is about equal, but in terms of overall efficiency (especially from the producer or director's standpoint), video clearly has the edge. It is, overall, a more convenient technology.

For viewing, video also has the edge over film. A client is likelier to be equipped with a VCR and TV monitor than a projector and screening room, and this trend will accelerate in the coming years.

Image clarity differs between the two formats. Video tends to look more "live," hence more immediate. But it also looks flat, not fully dimensional. Video lighting often lends a harshness to the image. Film, on the other hand, is richer, softer, and has more depth of field. Film looks permanent, almost timeless. (Music videos, in fact, are often shot on film and then transferred to video.)

Steve Dooms, a Brooklyn-based filmmaker specializing in animation, admits: "I'd be hard-pressed to advocate film production over video for corporate and industrial purposes. Costs for video are getting a lot lower. In terms of aesthetics, film is more intimate, warmer. It requires a lot less glaring, directional light. But video equipment is smaller, and you've got a lot more mobility. And with film, costs are always escalating. If your bottom line matters, you can do better with video on the cheap than with film. But I'd have to say that as bad as a low-budget film looks, cheap video in inexperienced hands looks even worse."

Regardless of which medium you use, it's possible to convert at a later stage. A film can be transferred to video (and vice versa, though there are fewer instances where this would be desirable). There will be some loss of image quality in the process, but if you need to distribute quick copies of a film to clients who only have VCRs, the option is available.

THE KEY QUALITIES OF AUDIOVISUALS

Visual Impact

It's important that pictures tell as much of the story as possible. Clients may have distractions while viewing—phone calls, conversations with colleagues, or surrounding noise. But while their ears or mouths may be otherwise engaged, the eyes are likely to remain fixed on the screen to catch what the ears miss.

Motion

The advantage of a film over print literature or a slide show is movement (although multi-imaging slide shows, using as many as 20 screens at once, almost resemble animation). The medium should be used to its advantage. Keep the action paced for comfortable viewing. Stills may be inserted where motion pictures aren't available, but these images shouldn't linger.

However, the kind of rapid-fire, quick-cut action editing so stylish in rock videos should be avoided, or you may succeed only in confusing the viewer. Quick cuts may be good for an opening or closing, but for product depiction, the viewer should be given time to assimilate the visual.

Length

This will always vary depending on the purpose of the production. Gloria Piliero, of A.D. Venture Video, Fairfield, NJ, gives some indication: "If you have a captive audience that has to watch, the video can be as long as it takes to get the information across. An orientation video for banks to train new tellers can run ten to thirty minutes. But if it's going to run longer than thirty minutes, it should be segmented. People you want to sell services or products to are not going to spend a lot of time with a prolonged commercial. So, make it as short and sweet as you can while still getting the necessary information across—maybe between four and seven minutes. Ten minutes is probably too long, unless the visuals are interesting or it's funny. But just because it's longer doesn't mean it'll prove the point better. As soon as you get the message across—stop!"

Pacing is the key, and when the audience's patience is tested, attention begins to flag. As a general rule, shorter is always better than longer.

Plot

The most engaging productions involve storytelling. A conflict, struggle, or problem is presented and must be resolved. Introduce characters with whom the viewer can identify, either by age, economic status, gender, or profession. Use real people rather than glamorous dreamboats or starlets. Show how the character's problem is resolved, either by using your product or by following the correct procedure.

If the subject is an institution, such as a hospital, corporation, bank, or international agency, never forget that such organizations consist of people. Emphasize these folks doing their jobs. No one can relate to a large bureaucracy, except as an individual working as part of a team.

Language

Your script language will depend on the projected audience and their familiarity with the subject. Unless they are highly trained technicians, it's best to keep the tone conversational. Use familiar but descriptive language, and avoid bureaucratese. Freelance scriptwriter John Baldoni recommends using "words for the ear, not for the eye...active verbs, colorful words and phrases." Never lose sight of the human interest element.

Let the visuals do most of the talking. It isn't necessary to point out everything that's happening on-screen. Keep it tight, and don't meander or throw in gratuitous digressions. In a film or video, narrative should be used for reinforcement or continuity, but rarely for primary information.

Dynamics

Use different elements: voice-over narrative; musical interlude; various on-camera spokespeople; anecdotal material; on-screen text (captions, titles); illustrations (charts, graphs, diagrams); animation; special effects. Keep the production moving, using as much variety as your budget permits.

ESTIMATING THE COST OF YOUR AUDIOVISUAL

The breakeven point between video and film seems to be about 30 seconds in length; cost for either will probably be equal. For longer productions, video is usually cheaper (and most nonbroadcast audiovisual productions are longer than 30 seconds).

However, there is no rule of thumb for film or video costs. Fees vary depending on the following factors:

- sophistication of production,
- editing time,
- script writing,
- music (and whether the score is original or canned),
- director,
- actors,
- voice-over announcers,
- technical assistance,
- props,
- special effects,
- animation (computer or hand-art), and
- travel (and lodging for extended shoots).

Writing in the October 1997 issue of the *Business to Business Marketer*, Dave Williams reported that a high-quality video costs from $1,000 to $10,000 per minute and runs between 10 and 20 minutes. Videos with a simple format, like a company president making an address from the office, would fall into the low range, says Williams, while animation, household-name talent, actors, original music score, and shooting footage on multiple locations all add cost.

A low estimate for a professionally made industrial video is about $7,000. For that price, you can get what looks like a fancy home video. The image will be decent but not top-notch, scripting will be minimal, and there will probably be no voice-over announcer or special effects. Such a budget could cover one day of on-location shooting, relatively little editing, and more than likely no director. You might have only a technician with a videopack and tripod aiming the camera and shooting from a stationary position. Such an approach might be suitable for in-house productions or for short-term usage with restricted distribution. However, a video intended to create an image or be used to market to a broad consumer base will cost much, much more.

One video studio quoted a figure of $13,000 to produce a seven-minute short spotlighting an industrial hire-the-handicapped program. The price included minimal special effects, two days of on-location shooting, a canned (prerecorded, generic) music bed, no voice-over, some direction, and three days of reviewing and editing footage. The video was for a non-profit organization with a limited budget. On the high end, a corporate video could run between $50,000 and $250,000. Not exactly Spielberg, but the result would be an excellent, high-quality production, full of glamour and glitz.

To give an indication of how costly special effects are: one second of computer graphics for a slick video opening costs about $1,000. The entire opening might run for four to seven seconds.

Some of the reasons film costs more than video are explained by Steve Dooms: "A lot of the cost of film is more than just setting up the camera and shooting. You have an entire run of laboratory costs. Titling (adding captions and credits) gets very difficult. With any additions to the raw image, costs multiply geometrically. Video production editing can cost as much as $200 to $300 an hour. But with video, even on the low end, you get a fully assembled tape, with titles and any other weirdness you need for presentation purposes."

The major investment is in producing the master. Regardless of which medium you choose, copies are relatively inexpensive. Cost of duplication varies based on transfer format, number of copies, packaging, and vendor. One copy of a 20-minute, 3/4" master to 1/2" VHS costs between $15 and $25. Per-copy cost for quantities over 25 are between $8 and $15; 100 copies, $7 to $10 each; 500 copies, $6 to $9 each; and 1,000 copies, $3 to $5 each. These are basic duplication costs, including a cardboard sleeve with no fancy labeling or packaging. The field is competitive, however, and comparison shopping is worthwhile.

THE STAGES OF PRODUCTION

Video Production

Original footage is recorded on 1/2" Betacam (a trademarked name used, incorrectly, to refer to portable, on-location video equipment).

Original footage can also be recorded on 3/4" videotape, but 1/2" is more practical and convenient. In the studio, the raw footage is stepped up to 1" tape for the final mix (or if you're budget-conscious, onto 3/4" tape, which is slightly cheaper). This process is called interformat editing. The original footage is referred to as source tape, and the final version is the master. (Jargon varies, however. Some technicians refer to original footage as the master, and the final version as the edited master.)

All copies (called dubs or dupes) are made from this final version. Copies can be made on either 3/4", VHS, or Beta. Beta and VHS are both air tape formats, but the cartridge sizes differ, and they cannot be played on each other's machines. VHS is the more popular for in-house corporate screening; an advantage to VHS is that a client can take your video home for viewing on the family VCR.

Film Production

After ideas have been developed on a storyboard (hand-rendered, panel-by-panel approximation of major sequences of the film) or in a shooting script, raw footage is shot in either 16mm or 35mm film. The 35mm format captures a superior image, but is more expensive. The raw footage is then developed into a work print and a negative. The work print can be scratched (rough cut) to conform to the director's conception of the film. A slop print is a black and white composite of the film, also a work print, that contains the basic soundtrack elements, including dialogue, ambient effects, or off-camera noises. The negative is then conformed to the rough-cut work print, creating a fine cut. The negative at this stage is "married" to the soundtrack mix.

The lab then sends back an answer print, based on all work so far. The director diagnoses the film for necessary color changes, flaws in synchronization, damage to the negative, or other imperfections. After corrections are made to the answer print, the release print is made. This is the version that is distributed to the public.

TIPS ON GETTING WHAT YOU WANT

Preplanning

Know what you want and what you hope to achieve. This applies to the conceptual framework, script, storyboard, mood, and the target audience. Plan. The unexpected will always arise, and though you can't avoid every hindrance or delay, you can thwart Murphy's Law as much as possible with purposeful planning.

"Never write a script without committing to a treatment [outline] first," writes video producer Ron Skotleski in *ADV* (September, 1996, page 10). "Your treatment is your blueprint, your foundation for the video. Changes made here are the least costly."

Editing

Always sit in on editing sessions. This is standard procedure. Editing time is expensive and revisions can be costly. You should be present to steer the edit. If you have a specific direction or cut in mind, the time to talk about it is during the editing process, not later.

Copying

Copies should be made from the edited master. Each step of duplication from the master is called a generation, and there is loss of clarity with each subsequent generation. It may not be noticeable from a second to a third generation, but from the third on, the image will lose sharpness, colors will look flatter, and the soundtrack will build up hiss or distortion. For optimum quality, avoid making copies of copies.

WHERE TO FIND FILM- OR VIDEOMAKERS

There are many elements to video or film production, such as lighting, camerawork, scripting, set design, acting and voice talent, editing, special effects, and duplicating. When contacting video technicians, filmmakers, or studios, inquire whether they offer full production capabilities or merely one specialized aspect of production. If you hire all the separate vendors yourself, you become the producer. The alternative is to hire an independent producer or large production house to take care of the myriad details. Having an experienced professional handle the entire package could save you a lot of headeaches later.

If you see an industrial video or film you like, watch the credits at the end for a contact name or studio.

Referrals

Ask your colleagues or other advertising managers who have worked with videomakers for referrals. As with any creative vendor, artistic vision and experience are never the whole story. When seeking recommendations, inquire about temperament and cooperativeness.

Vendors in related disciplines (e.g., script writing, set design, make-up, music) might be good sources for recommending film- or videomakers with whom they've worked.

Many large corporations use independent video- and filmmakers. Ask their advertising departments for recommendations. Some, such as Prudential Insurance, have their own in-house video departments that can be hired for outside work.

Service Organizations

Most film or video service organizations or unions publish member directories or offer referrals of qualified members. The ITVA (International

Television Association), headquartered in Irving, TX, is one of the largest such associations, with regional chapters around the country. Their phone number is 214-869-1112.

Yellow Pages

Look under Film, Video, Audiovisual, and sometimes under Photography. A few companies do both film and video, but most do either one or the other.

Publications

Magazines (regional and national) that deal with video and film feature advertisements for freelance technicians or production houses are good resources. *Video Systems*, an excellent professional journal, is available from Intertec Publishing, P.O. Box 12901, Overland Park, KS 66282-2901, 913-341-1300. *Backstage*, a tipsheet geared heavily toward the entertainment industry and available at many newsstands, also has listings for commercial and industrial production talent. *Audiovisual Communications Monthly* (Horizons Media, 475 Park Avenue, NY 10016, 212-682-7010) is aimed at corporate in-house media production. *In Motion* (1203 West Street, Annapolis, MD 21401, 410-269-0605) is helpful for professionals working in film or video production and related imaging media.

Knowledge Industry Publications, Inc. (KIPI) offers authoritative books on video graphic design, computer animation, and scriptwriting for corporate productions. Their catalog can be acquired by calling 1-800-800-5474. They also publish the magazine, *AV Video*.

Trade Shows

Keep abreast of creative trade shows and expos in your area. They are sure to include exhibition booths hosted by local producers seeking your business.

Chapter

BILLBOARDS AND SIGNS
23

BILLBOARDS

If you want to expand your advertising reach, consider venturing into the great outdoors. Depending on your company's market and message, you may not have to go too far—just to your local highways or town streets to find the right billboards to advertise your company's services.

Billboard advertising can be effective for small, local firms as well as big consumer companies. It can help you reach prospects, impress customers, build your image as a successful company, attract future employees, even strengthen your position as a creditworthy client at your local lending institution.

Despite the public outcry in recent years over the proliferation of billboards and the subsequent restrictions by local governments in the number and location of signs—or perhaps because of it—billboard advertising is an effective way to get your company's name before prospects and to open doors when the sales staff calls.

According to the Institute of Outdoor Advertising, "Outdoor advertising is ideal for product introductions, store openings, or promotional events where timing is critical. Outdoor advertising bridges the gap between the in-home message from other media and the out-of-home purchase." The Institute reports that in 1996, billboard advertising spending was $1.96 billion—a 7.3 percent increase over the $1.22 billion spent in 1985.

All-Day Selling

The big advantage billboard advertising has over radio, TV, direct mail, and newspaper advertising is that once your message is up, it's there 24 hours a day. John Selix, the owner of an 11-store graphic arts chain in Milwaukee, WI, points out, "Prospects can't shut their eyes when they're driving."

Billboards come in two forms: bulletins, which are most often 14' by 48' and can be painted on or posted with preprinted paper; and poster panels, which are smaller structures that measure 12 1/4' by 24 1/2' and contain either bleed posters or 30-sheet posters.

Bulletins have relatively high circulation compared to poster panels because they are located only on major thoroughfares. However, poster panels are more widely distributed and achieve a broader and faster market reach. While bulletins are bought on an individual unit basis, posters are bought by "showing," which means the intensity with which a number of poster panels covers a market. Common showing sizes are 100, 75, 50, and 25.

For example, a 50 showing delivers 500,000 daily exposures in a market with one million people. A 25 showing would deliver 250,000 people in that same market. An average 50 showing will reach over 80 percent of all adults in one month, and more than half are reached the first week.

In addition, retailers benefit when manufacturers place outdoor advertising close to their stores. In return, they may give the manufacturer prime shelf space and carry higher inventory for the advertiser.

Location Is Critical

As with buying real estate, location is the essential factor to consider when purchasing billboard advertising. Will more prospects see your billboard in town or on a nearby highway? Do you want to target an upscale neighborhood or a commercial district? A distinct advantage of outdoor advertising is that it can offer a more highly targeted placement than other media, since poster panels can be placed in communities of different ethnic backgrounds and levels of income.

After a year and a half of using a rotating bulletin system, Gilbert Thompson, President of Thompson Printing in Belleville, NJ, signed an 18-month contract for a billboard on a busy highway that leads into New York City. "I wanted that location because most of our clients, who are advertising and business people, at one time or another go into New York," explains Thompson. "In fact, about half the population of New Jersey takes that road into New York at one time or another, so it's worth the $2,000-a-month price tag."

But for Bob Fellman, president of five consumer service stores located in four Wisconsin cities, the only good locations are city locations. "Our customers are mostly individuals who live or work close to our shops," he explains, "so I would never use a highway billboard." For five years, Fellman has personally selected every board, and he changes their locations every month to get the broadest exposure possible.

Other important factors to consider include reach (how many people drive by the sign) and frequency (the average number of times an individual has the opportunity to be exposed to an advertising message during a defined period of time); speed and volume of traffic at the site; height and dimensions of the sign (displays that "break above the skyline" are better, as are larger signs); the number of other signs in the area (too much clutter could cut down on the readership your sign receives); and whether the sign is illuminated so it's visible late at night in high-traffic locations. Also, proximity to a stoplight or intersection increases readership.

While outdoor advertising companies provide demographics and traffic circulation statistics on various locations, common sense and personal experience are good guidelines. The president of a Connecticut company chose his bulletin location as a result of his own experience as a commuter on a major highway close to company headquarters. "The billboard was sizeable—about twenty-four square feet—and positioned right before the toll booths, where everyone was slowing down," he says. "You couldn't help but read that sign." Although he had to wait a year before the billboard was available, the results were worth the wait. "I've probably gotten more attention from that billboard and from advertising placards on commuter trains into New York City than from any other promotion I've done in the last ten years," the president of the $12 million company comments. Moreover, the placards, a cousin of billboard advertising, produced more than 30 leads during the two years the company used them for promotion.

Impact on Sales

The Institute of Outdoor Advertising claims that "dollar for dollar, outdoor advertising delivers a greater audience than any of the major media." Table 23.1, taken from *Adweek's Marketer's Guide to Media*, gives cost per thousand comparisons.

Table 23.1. Comparison of Cost per Thousand for Outdoor Advertising to Other Media

Cost per Thousand	Men	Women
Outdoor (50 showing)	$ 1.70	$ 2.15
TV (30 seconds, prime time)	12.90	10.25
Radio (30 seconds)	4.10	3.30
Newspapers (600 lines, black & white)	7.00	6.75
Magazines	7.30	4.60

Outdoor advertising has a unique target ability, in that the outdoor message is the last one potential buyers see on the way to the store. "It's the most local medium, but it can be as national or regional as you want it to be," says Andrea MacDonald, marketing manager for the Institute of Outdoor Advertising. "A lot of advertisers use outdoor as the design basis for their other ads to enforce a one-idea, one-benefit message. But it's also a very flexible, creative medium. One advertiser we know of lit up the headlights on a car featured on his bulletin, which had a dramatic effect at night. Another advertiser uses fiber optics to create simulated lightning on his board."

Currently, there are 260,000 billboard and poster structures in the United States available for leasing. Ten thousand of that number are poster panels, and the rest are billboards.

Tracking sales results from billboard advertising is difficult. In most cases, determining their effectiveness depends largely on getting feedback from customers, salespeople, and business associates. As part of a media campaign, outdoor advertising can strengthen sales results through improved audience delivery, higher frequency, and more gross rating points (the total number of impressions delivered by a media schedule as expressed by a percentage of the population) per dollar. While billboards reach every population strata, Simmons Market Research Bureau (SMRB) shows an above-average performance in the younger, affluent, and working markets.

Thompson notes that "a billboard gives extra punch to our sales force so when they go out, prospects have seen the name and our logo. It opens doors more easily."

Another indication of the bulletins' effectiveness, says Thompson, "is that we're getting many more requests for quotations from people we haven't contacted. More importantly, the quality of the responses has gone up. We're not interested in doing one-time projects; we want high-quality leads that translate into steady business. That's what we're getting from billboards."

To obtain a more accurate analysis of sales impact, Fellman has recently begun tabulating the results of his stores' various advertising efforts through customer reply cards that customers pick up with their orders. Although the cards only ask whether customers have seen the boards, not whether they responded to them, 70 to 75 percent of customers indicate they've seen the poster panels. That places the medium above newspapers and about even with radio in terms of effectiveness for the company.

Not only do billboards reach prospects, but they seem to convince customers that the advertiser is a sizeable and stable company that's good to do business with. Says one company president, "Here's my hundred-and-twenty-five-employee company out there on the billboards side by side with Coca Cola and Dewar's scotch. That gives our buyers a sense of security. And it reinforces the message that we're a pretty big company in this area."

Thompson echoes those sentiments, noting, "We started using billboards when we moved to our present location in 1984, because we thought they would give us great exposure and help build our image. The strategy has surpassed our expectations. Our customers have told us they're impressed with the sign. They know putting up a billboard isn't something you do if you don't have money and aren't interested in growing, and they feel good about doing business with a company that's on the upswing."

Short on Copy, Big on Design

Billboards must state a message clearly and quickly, since the reader is usually in a car going 50 or 60 miles per hour and will only glance at your billboard for a few seconds. All outdoor messages are viewed at distances ranging from 100 to 400 feet. Copy must be kept to a minimum, and the design has to grab attention. In fact, the Institute of Outdoor Advertising tells advertisers, "The fewer the words, the larger the illustration, the bolder the colors, the simpler the background, and the clearer the product identification, the better the outdoor advertisement."

Thomas Lavey, President of Lakeland Outdoor in Manitowoc, WI, offers this advice on design: "Try to come up with a graphic or visual that tells the story. If you have to add copy, use a play on words—it will result in a more memorable message."

The vivid colors that can be used on outdoor displays are a distinct advantage of the medium. Outdoor advertising professionals recommend using colors that are dissimilar in both hue and value, such as yellow and purple. White will work with any dark-value color, and black is ideal for colors of light value.

"Hire a top designer," advises one company president, whose company billboard won an award from the Printing Institute of America. "It will pay off."

Outdoor advertising companies will give you the specifications to contract out the design work, or in some cases, they have art departments that will help you design your billboard. Bulletins are either hand-painted in an artist's studio and then put up in sections on location, or painted directly on-site.

Ninety percent of bulletins today are hand-painted on poster board, but messages can also be applied by posting preprinted paper or using computer-generated painting. Poster panels are lithographed or silk-screened and then shipped to the outdoor company. "The industry is moving toward high-technology, computer-aided design systems," says Lavey. "They speed up the design process and make it easier."

Gannett Outdoor, the nation's largest outdoor advertising company, hopes advertisers will switch to a new material it has developed called Superflex, a combination of canvas and plastic stretched over a billboard frame. A computerized painting system sprays the design directly on the material, eliminating individual variations in execution. The new material costs about 25 percent more than paper, but provides brilliant color and a consistent, high-quality reproduction for advertisers who want to use the same design on more than one billboard.

Purchasing Outdoor Advertising

There are hundreds of outdoor advertising companies in the United States. Once you have selected the markets for outdoor advertising, you can look up those markets in the *Buyer's Guide to Outdoor Advertising*. It will identify the outdoor company in each market and the cost of poster panels and bulletins in those markets. For more information on the *Buyer's Guide*, contact: Leading National Advertisers, 136 Madison Avenue, New York, NY 10016, 212-696-4533. Or, if you're interested in using a particular board, you can usually find the outdoor advertising company's name posted at the bottom. Another option is to look in the Yellow Pages under Advertising: Outdoor.

Contracts generally run for either a 12-, 24- or 36-month period for bulletins, or on a monthly basis for poster panels. You should contact the outdoor advertising company at least 90 days before you would like your ad to appear. While poster production takes from 21 to 45 days, artwork for painted bulletins must be sent to the outdoor company 60 days in advance.

Costs vary tremendously according to region of the country, specific billboard location, number of billboards leased, designer, complexity of the design, whether the sign is illuminated, whether the billboard is a bulletin or a poster panel, and whether the billboard is hand-painted or computer-printed.

Average costs for poster panels are $200 to $400 per month, plus about $80 each to produce. The average cost of a bulletin is typically $1,000 to $3,000 per month, plus about $1,000 each to produce.

You can keep down production costs by agreeing to let the outdoor advertising company rotate the location of your billboard every 60 or 90 days. This kind of agreement allows the outdoor company to take advantage of unrented space. The plus side for the advertiser is that balanced coverage of the market can be achieved with just one billboard. Some companies also give discounts based on volume and length of contract, so that if you rent four or five billboards for a three-, two-, or even one-year period, 10 to 30 percent may be knocked off the price.

Even without such discounts, the cost efficiency of billboard advertising is high. As promotional literature published by the Institute of Outdoor Advertising notes, "Outdoor is seen all day, every day. It cannot be turned off like television, tuned out like radio, or discarded like newspapers and magazines. And the mere size of your ad makes it difficult to ignore."

For more information on outdoor advertising, or to request the File Cabinet information kit that charts cost comparisons between billboards and other media and explains how to buy and design outdoor advertising, contact the Institute of Outdoor Advertising, 12 E. 49th Street, New York, NY 10017, 212-688-3667.

SIGNAGE AS A PROMOTIONAL TOOL

Signs are efficient and effective communications tools. Most businesses depend heavily on signs to help people find them, advertise their business, and present an image of their business. In short, signs tell people who you are and what you are selling.

Signage is such a powerful communication medium that it is difficult to estimate the extent of their influence. Other media require the directed attention of the person receiving the message. Signs, however, can convey a message while creating a mood or feeling of atmosphere. It is not necessary for people to give full attention to your sign in order to derive meaning from its presence.

What Is a Sign?

A sign is the most direct form of visual communication available. In fact, so many people use signs without a second thought that it is easy to overlook their importance. When we cannot talk to other people directly in a given location, we put up signs: wet paint, beware of dog, enter here, garage sale, et cetera. Signs are the only form of mass communication directly available to everyone—they are the people's street communication system.

What Signs Can Do for Your Business

Signs perform three major communication functions for your business:

1. Signs give information about your business and direct people to your business location. Signs index the environment so people can find you. This is especially true for travelers, new members of your community, and impulse shoppers who may be on a journey to purchase the particular goods or services that you sell. Americans are mobile. Each year 40 million of us travel over 1.7 trillion miles by automobile and approximately 19 percent of us change our places of residence. A primary source of customers for your business is the large number of people who are new to your community or who may be just passing through. Your sign is the most effective way of reaching this mobile or transient group of potential customers.

Signs can help correct a poor location by substituting effective communication for poor site characteristics. If your business is located on a site that is not visible or in a building that does not correspond with the goods or services offered, your sign can overcome this disability. For example, most buildings are not built to conform to the design needs of any particular type of tenant. Without an effective sign it is often impossible to determine what type of business is being conducted in a given building. In addition, when your site is located off a busy traffic artery or in an area that is not easily accessible, your sign can communicate to people who are passing on a busy street several blocks away. If you are located off a busy freeway but far from an exit, your sign becomes the main device for directing people to your business. High-rise signs are used when a business is located away from potential customers' normal pathways of travel.

2. Signs are street advertising. Your sign provides an easily recognizable format for the goods or services you are selling. For most businesses, the street is where potential customers are. The message displayed on the street reaches people who are close enough to make a purchase. Street advertising also helps people develop a memory of your business name and the products and services you sell. People tend to buy from businesses they know.

3. Signs build image. Signs can build an image for your business and help you identify with the market segment you are trying to reach.

Through materials and design, a sign can appeal to a given group of potential customers. For example, various firms attempt to capture the youth market, senior citizens, unmarried single people, and so forth. If you wish to attract a particular market segment to your business, your sign can be an important means of bringing these people in.

The Advantages of Signs

On-premise signs are the most effective and efficient means of commercial communication because they are inexpensive, available, practical, easy to use, always on the job, and directly oriented to the trade area of your business.

Your sign is an integral part of your advertising program, along with the other forms of commercial communication such as television, radio, newspapers, magazines, and billboards. There are four basic criteria used to judge the effectiveness of all these advertising media: 1) coverage of the trade area; 2) repetition of a message; 3) readership of a message; 4) cost per thousand exposures of a message. Two other criteria important for the small business owner are 5) availability and 6) ease of use. Here's how signs measure up to these criteria:

1. Signs are oriented to your trade area. Signs do not waste your resources by requiring you to pay for wasted advertising coverage. The people who see your sign are the people who live in your trade area.

2. Signs are always on the job, repeating your message to potential customers. Your on-premise sign communicates to potential customers 24 hours a day, 7 days a week, week after week, month after month, year after year. Every time people pass your business establishment they see your sign. The mere repetition of the message will help them remember your business.

3. Nearly everyone reads signs. Signs are practical to use, for nearly everyone is used to looking at signs and using signs, even small children. Studies have shown that people do read and remember what is on signs. When special items are displayed, sales increase for these particular items within the store.

4. Signs are inexpensive. When compared to the cost of advertising in some other media, the on-premise sign is very inexpensive. Unless your trade area encompasses an entire city or region where you must rely upon broad-based media coverage, there is no better advertising dollar value than your on-premise sign.

5. Signs are available to each and every shopowner. There is no need to schedule the use of your sign. Your sign is available to you whenever you need it and to be used however you please.

6. Signs are easy to use. No special skills or resources are needed to operate a sign once it has been installed. If it is an illuminated sign, all you need to do is flip the switches and even that may not be necessary with timing equipment. Once the initial expenditures are made, no special resources or professional services are needed. You need only operate and maintain your sign.

Checklist for Ordering a Business Sign

Before you select a sign for your business, there are several things you need to consider. A competent sign company in your area can help you with the answers to some of these questions.

1. Who are your customers? Potential customers for your business are people who reside in your trade area. Most of your customers come from the immediate area within a half mile to a mile of your business location. Trade areas come in assorted shapes and sizes depending upon the business. Trade areas may also vary seasonally.

2. How do you get information on potential customers? Plot a dot map of your customers as soon as you begin business. This is easily done by plotting the addresses of people who shop in your store as a dot on a street map of your city. Within a few months you will have a fairly clear idea of the trade area from which you are drawing your customers. You will then be able to decide what type of sign would best meet the needs of the people in that trade area. For example, if your customers can only reach you by automobile or if you are located on a very busy street, the type of sign that you use will be very different from what you would use if you had a shopping center location and people walked to your store from parking lots.

Obtain your street profile from a city traffic engineer. Since your sign communicates to people who pass your business establishment, you can direct your message to potential customers if you know what type of traffic passes your door. Your city traffic engineer can provide information that will tell you: where people begin and end their trips, how people travel, when people travel by time of day, why people travel, and where they park when they reach a destination. Even small cities and towns have traffic volume maps available to tell you how many people pass by your business every day.

Know how many new people move to your area each year. This is a potential market for your business. This type of information can be obtained from any board of realtors, chamber of commerce, or police department.

3. How are you going to communicate with customers? In order to communicate effectively, a sign must be noticeable and readable. After a while a sign becomes part of the landscape. It loses some of its ability to attract attention. By periodically changing some small design element or by using changeable copy, you can continue to attract interest with your sign. Time and temperature devices or rotating and moving parts can be used to maintain interest in a commercial message. Time and temperature displays also provide a much-needed public service.

A sign needs to be large enough to read. How far will people be from your store when they first see your sign, and what is the real speed of traffic on your street? With this information, a competent sign company can calculate the necessary size for your design and build you an effective sign.

4. What are you trying to say? Decide on a message that is clear and simple. First, focus on key words. Choose one or two words that describe your business. Clever or strange names may attract only certain customers.

Second, be brief. The cleaner and clearer the message, the more impact it has. Listings of names or unclear symbols confuse rather than communicate.

5. What image are you trying to portray? The design of your sign is important. Your sign tells people a lot about your business. Stark, simple designs and materials may suggest discount prices and no frills. Elegant and expensive sign materials may suggest luxury goods and services. Two basic design considerations are important when ordering a sign—physical elements and graphic elements.

Physical elements include considerations such as size, placement, materials, and structure. The size of the sign is an important consideration for your business. The biggest sign that you can afford may not necessarily be the best one for your needs. A sign should go with its surroundings. A sign that is either too big or too small will not communicate your message effectively. The number of signs is also important. If there are too many signs in an area, they compete with one another and reduce the effectiveness of your message by presenting an image of confusion to potential customers.

The materials used by your sign determine its appearance and performance. For example, differences in cost, appearance, color, durability, flexibility, and reaction to extreme weather conditions can be found in the many types of plastics available. The structure of a sign also contributes to its effectiveness. Pole covers and cantilevered construction (signs displayed at right angles to a vertical surface) help portray an attractive message.

Graphic elements include layout of the message, colors, lettering, shape, symbolism, harmony, and daytime versus nighttime lighting conditions. If your sign is well designed, it will be easy to read. Legibility means that the letters or characters on the sign are distinct from one another. Certain color combinations of background and letters are much more legible than others. To test your sign's legibility, drive past your business to see if you can read the sign from a distance, both in the daytime and at night. Some signs are difficult to read because of illumination problems such as glare from street lights, signs on nearby business establishments, or shadows caused by buildings. A well-designed sign blends with the environment, has a message impact, and overcomes viewing problems.

6. How much should your sign cost? You should consider several factors when determining the cost of your on-premise sign.

A sign is an investment. Your sign is one of the most permanent parts of your business and is exposed to weather and constant use. The average life span of a sign varies from 5 to 11 years, depending on type of materials used, construction, and other factors. Ask the sign maker how many years of service to expect from your sign. It pays to purchase good materials if you intend to use the sign over a period of years.

Don't forget to budget for maintenance costs. No business can afford to have its signs fall into disrepair. A dilapidated sign tells the public that you are not concerned with your business image or their visual environment. Some types of signs are virtually maintenance-free, while others require more attention. Find out how to replace burnt-out bulbs or tubes in your sign. Determine who is responsible if the wind blows your sign down and someone is injured.

Consider all energy consumption costs. New technological developments now enable some types of signs to achieve energy savings without sacrificing effects. Inquire about new energy-saving bulbs and internal materials.

Decide between owning and leasing. Many sign companies have programs whereby you lease a sign for a given period of time and they maintain it for you. This may be more economical for a new business, especially if there is any chance that logos or names may change in the first few years of operation. Statistics show that if a small business fails, it will happen between the first and second years of operation. Leasing a sign during this period of time might reduce some of the initial capital needed for operating expenses.

Should your sign be custom or standardized? Some large companies offer standardized signs that are less costly than custom designed and constructed signs. Many of the standardized units use ingenious design techniques to enhance creativity and individuality. Often the standardized units can be arranged in different configurations depending on your needs. Some standardized sign units use the highest quality materials and are designed to be relatively maintenance-free. Mass production enables these units to be sold inexpensively.

7. How will your sign affect the community? Signs communicate in a shared environment. A sign's ability to send its message beyond its location requires that you be sensitive to the effects of your message on others. Since you share your space with others, consider their rights and responsibilities, too. They are potential customers.

Consider city or town planning goals and regulations when ordering a sign. Some types of signs are not permitted. Determine what the regulations are in your community before you discuss design with a sign designer. Most sign companies are well aware of the regulations in any given community and can guide you in selecting a sign that is not in violation of the law.

Chapter 24

MARKET RESEARCH

According to *Business Marketing's* Starmark Report, nine out of ten business marketers say that research is important in their communications programs. Market research helps businesses learn more about their customers and prospects, including their needs, wants, likes and dislikes. As defined by the American Marketing Association, market research is "the systematic gathering, recording, and analyzing of data about problems relating to the marketing of goods and services."

"People who think they don't need to understand marketing because they have enough business are courting disaster," warns Dr. Richard Lancioni, professor of marketing at Temple University. "You need to have a longer view of maintaining profitability. Don't assume you know what your customers' needs are. Conduct surveys and audits at least once a year to develop a proactive approach to anticipating those needs."

"Often we don't know the best prospects; we don't know which products or services they'll prefer; we don't know which messages they'll respond to," notes Terry Pranses, president of Pranses Research in Hoboken, NJ. "Market research gives you a competitive advantage and lets you get your advertising right the first time."

While longtime experience and continuing contact with customers will give you an edge in understanding the market, they are not infallible. Information about markets gained from long experience isn't always enough to base selling decisions on. Customers don't always tell you how they really feel or what they really want, even if they are unsatisfied with some aspect of your service or product. That's why market research is a valuable tool for maintaining and increasing your company's market share.

USES OF MARKET RESEARCH

Terry Pranses says market research can help marketers gain the background information on:

- new markets,
- new products and services,
- new applications,
- new or growing competitive threats, and
- consumer reaction to advertising materials.

Market research covers a broad range of topics, including product research, market performance research, copy testing, ad testing, pricing research, distribution channel research, new market research, competitor research, even finding out why a salesperson in one area of the country isn't doing as well as a salesperson in another part of the country. It can be applied specifically to a product problem, sales problem, or corporate situation. Without market research, your ad campaign, TV commercial, direct mail program, or other promotions may "miss the mark" and waste a lot of money.

The goal of market research is to gather facts that will help your business solve problems, avoid problems, allocate funds better, and continue to grow. It provides what you need to:

- reduce business risks;
- spot problems and potential problems in your current market; identify and profit from sales opportunities; and
- get basic facts about your markets to help you make better decisions and set up plans of action.

Obviously, it's much easier to sell people what they do want than what they don't want. Market research is useful in uncovering what's important to your prospects and customers, what products or services are in demand, and what problems your company can help your prospects solve. It can also open doors to new opportunities, whether it's a previously untapped segment of the marketplace, a new application of a product, or the creation of additional products or services to meet a need in your current market.

Even if you think you know your customers and how they perceive your products or services, research may surprise you. One large manufacturer, for example, was surprised to discover that customers highly valued the cleanliness of its plant. A commercial printing shop polled its customers and discovered that they wanted a variety of graphic arts services, so it invested in developing those additional services. A corporate book supplier found that many of its prospects wanted to receive a single detailed invoice instead of many separate invoices addressed to each department that bought books, so that the companies could then issue a single check in payment. The book supplier switched to a new computer program that enabled it to provide the necessary information—and convert more prospects to customers.

WHAT YOU NEED TO KNOW

Judy Bjorling, Managing Director of Bjorling & Associates, a Glenview, IL-based marketing consulting firm, says you can increase useful marketing information inexpensively by asking yourself the following questions at least every six months:

- Who are our customers?
- What do I know about them?
- What do they think they're buying?
- What are we selling?
- What do customers think our strengths and weaknesses are?
- What are our strengths and weaknesses?
- Who are our competitors?
- What do our customers think about them?
- How long has it been since I talked to a salesperson about our customers?
- How long has it been since I talked face-to-face with one of our customers?

Marketing research should also answer such questions as:

- Am I offering the kinds of goods or services customers want, at the best place, best time, and in the right amounts?
- Why have old customers left us?
- What attracts new customers to buy from us?
- Are my prices consistent with what buyers view as the products' values?
- Are my promotional programs working?
- How does my business compare with my competitors'? What are my competitors' strengths, and how can we capitalize on their weaknesses?

Marketing research must be timely, since customers' likes and dislikes shift constantly. It's better to get a little information rapidly than to get too much too late. If you take too long to gather information, it may be out of date by the time you've collected it all.

Researching Your Market, a publication of the Small Business Administration, lists the steps involved in conducting market research as follows:

1. Define the problem.
2. Assess available information.
3. Assess additional information, if required.

   a) Review internal records and files.

   b) Interview employees.

c) Consult secondary sources of information.

d) Interview customers and suppliers.

e) Collect primary data.

4. Organize and interpret data.

5. Make a decision.

6. Watch the results of the decision.

Key market research methodologies are summarized in Table 24-1.

Table 24.1. Key market research methodologies. (Source: Pranses Research)

Type:	Uses and benefits:
Telephone survey	Survey projectable sample to get a feel of where consumer attitudes currently stand.
Mail survey	Survey projectable sample by receiving large numbers of responses while holding down costs.
Mall survey	Have 50+ respondents see ad prototypes or sample products to measure interest.
Tracking study	Measures attitudes and awareness over time. Provides gradation of interest and readings on trends. Can be done by mail or phone.
Fax or E-mail survey	Used when speed is crucial.
Focus groups	Used when ideas and creative solutions are needed. Gives ability to observe and ask questions. Captures the language in which consumers discuss the product and application.
In-depth, one-on-one interviews	Outreach for senior executives, doctors, and other hard-to-reach, high-level consumer audiences. Can uncover their personalities, motivations, and outside buying influences.
Ethnographies	Slides or videos of decision makers in their work or home environment.
Library and on-line secondary research	Get background information at minimal expense. Provides a foundation for new learning.

DEFINING THE MARKETING PROBLEM OR OPPORTUNITY

Before you begin to collect marketing information, know your goal (i.e., what you hope to accomplish with that information). Market research may be exploratory, predictive, or diagnostic.

Examples of exploratory problems include trying to decide what a new market is looking for, whether you can find a new market for an existing product, which acquisition you should make, or which of five new product designs you should implement.

A predictive problem occurs once you have chosen an option and you want to know what it is likely to achieve. How profitable is the option likely to be? Can you sell enough of these widgets to make it a viable product? What progress are you making generally, and how does your progress compare with what your competitors are doing?

Some market research is diagnostic; it attempts to solve a particular problem. For example, the fact that a product is selling in one area but not in another, or that you are losing current customers, is a symptom of a problem, not the cause. You need to come up with a list of possible causes (i.e., a hypothesis) before you begin your marketing research efforts. For starters, you might consider whether there has been:

- A change in the areas your customers traditionally come from.

- A change in customers' tastes.

- Price cutting by a competitor.

- Increasing competition.

- Turnover or reduction in your customer service department that has adversely affected customer relations.

- Decline in product quality.

- A decrease in product distribution efficiency.

- A change in direction or media placement of advertising or promotional materials.

- A change in fulfillment of requests for company literature.

Only when you've formally defined the problem can you assess your ability to solve it. You may realize you have all the information you need to determine if your hypothesis is correct, or solutions to the problem may have become obvious in the process of defining the problem. You may realize you can get the necessary information through secondary research, published or readily available information from various sources outside your company, or that you need more data. Realize that there is a big difference between information you would like to know and information that helps to solve the problem.

Then, you can set a specific objective for your market research. What are you going to use the information for? What will it help you accomplish? If your objective is very important, the information is worth much more than information that applies to a smaller objective. "Reality Based Market Research," a B/PAA white paper, notes that "Some companies have spent a hundred thousand dollars for research on a product whose most optimistic sales would net a profit of no more than ten thousand dollars."

By categorizing the information you need and deciding on your research objective, you can determine the research methodology best suited to your task. If the objectives cannot be met through available secondary research, or if it's too hard for your company to be objective about the information it needs, a market research consultant or firm should be called in.

Market research is also valuable in assessing marketing opportunities. Perhaps you want to find a new application for your product in either the same market you currently sell to or a different one. Based on your product's features and capabilities, you may be able to brainstorm a list of possible new uses for it. But will those uses fill a need in the marketplace? Before you spend thousands or hundreds of thousands of dollars touting that new use, it makes far more sense to spend several thousand dollars or more on market research to find out if the idea has any potential in the marketplace.

Before conducting market research you must determine who should be polled and what questions should be included. For example, if you manufacture lawn mowers and your current customers are mostly men, but you are interested in finding out whether weight and color adaptations in your product would increase sales to women, polling your current customer base would be a waste of time and money. Instead, your ideal group of respondents would be women homeowners, especially heads of households, who live in suburban or rural areas.

ASSESS AVAILABLE INFORMATION

Often, the information you need to solve a marketing problem is available within your company. All you may need to do is go through your files, check with sales staff or marketing staff, or use your company library.

Available information typically includes credit information about your customers that you have on file; sales staff or customer service reports on customers; any recent surveys or studies you have conducted regarding your market, product, or service; recent articles about your industry, competitors, the economy in your selling area, changing demographics in your marketplace, and so on; competitors' literature; customer complaint letters; and records of product sales and returns.

If you have the information you need to solve the identified problem, stop there. Further market research will only be a waste of time and money. However, if you're not sure whether you need more information, you must make a subjective judgment, weighing the cost of more information against its usefulness.

ASSESS ADDITIONAL INFORMATION

If you feel you need additional information, there are several inexpensive routes to consider before undertaking expensive surveys or field experiments or hiring an outside consultant. For example, addresses on cash receipts can tell you where your customers live so that you can cross-reference their geographic areas with the products they purchase. This, in turn, can tell you the effectiveness of your advertising placements.

Another valuable source of customer information is your employees. Either talk to them informally or ask them to fill out a survey revealing their perceptions of customers' likes and dislikes. A good source of information about your competitors is their employees—you can even call anonymously and speak to the receptionist or sales staff about the company's products, new developments, sales, or their competition. The B/PAA report, *Reality-Based Market Research: Factors to Consider*, states "...most confidential information leaks do not come from the hiring of outside consultants that work in your industry. They come from within, from the receptionist or salesperson who is trying to make a sale or a variety of other internal sources."

Another excellent and relatively inexpensive source of information is secondary research. It involves using already-published surveys, books, and magazine articles—especially trade journal articles and their authors—to find information relevant to your industry and customers. Writers are often happy to direct you to their secondary sources of information, which can save you considerable time. Libraries, universities, trade associations, government agencies, newspapers, chambers of commerce, local TV and radio stations, computer database services, and economic development offices are other sources of secondary research information. If your business is concerned only with a local market area, look for local statistics and newspaper articles that report on market potential in your geographic area.

PRIMARY RESEARCH ACTIVITIES

If your internal files and secondary sources of information don't provide the data you need, the next step is to conduct primary research. This can be as simple as asking your customers or suppliers how they feel about your store or service, or as complex as the surveys done by the sophisticated professional marketing research giants.

What kinds of research will help you achieve specific goals? *Business Marketing's* 1986 Starmark Report identifies the most successful market research projects and the goals they help reach:

- Focus groups provide an in-depth view of sales prospect attitudes.
- Key market surveys identify potential markets and clarify the needs of individual accounts.
- Market position studies identify perceptions of a company's product lines.
- Product feasibility studies point out market needs and allow the company to capitalize on them.

The most popular market research studies are listed in Figure 24.1. These primary research activities may be accomplished through direct mail questionnaires, telephone or on-the-street surveys, experiments, panel studies, test marketing, or behavior observation. Primary research can be classified as reactive or nonreactive. Reactive research tends to be the most expensive, consisting of surveys, interviews, and questionnaires. It's best left to marketing research experts, who know what kinds of questions to ask and how to elicit unbiased responses. There's also the danger that either people won't want to hurt your feelings when you ask them their opinions about your business or they'll answer questions the way they think they are expected to answer, rather than the way they really feel.

Figure 24.1. The Top Ten Marketing/Advertising Research Studies Used by Today's Marketers

Study Type	Percent Responding
Market Position Studies	56%
Readership Studies	46%
Customer Attitude Studies	42%
Focus Groups	37%
New Product Feasibility Studies	37%
Competitive Environment Analyses	35%
Brand Preference Studies	33%
Market Potential Studies	31%
Company Image Studies	27%
Prospect Feedback Studies	20%

(Response adds to more than 100% due to multiple mentions.)

Nonreactive research involves observing your customers, specifically how they are dressed, how old they are, how educated they appear to be, and how and when they purchase your products. It may also involve noting:

1. which products and prices appeal to them the most, as determined by comparing sales results, split testing of direct mail and ads, coded business reply cards, or observation of in-store traffic patterns; and

2. where your customers live, through license plate analysis, checking phone numbers on checks and credit slips, or using coded coupons or "tell them Jan sent you" radio and TV advertising.

One unusual example of nonreactive research was conducted by a discount merchandiser who gave away "all the roasted peanuts you can eat" during a three-day promotion. At the end of the third day, he could see which product displays and store aisles attracted the most attention from customers just by looking at the peanut shell trails and heaps that had been left behind.

PURCHASING MARKET RESEARCH SERVICES

At most companies, the marketing manager is responsible for conducting or arranging market research. Other company staff who may be responsible for this activity are the product manager, marketing director, vice president of marketing, sales manager, or advertising manager.

Marketing information can be gathered by an in-house staff or by an outside marketing agency. *Business Marketing's* Starmark Report shows that 61 percent of top marketers use an in-house department for market research activities; 28 percent hire a marketing research firm; 16 percent use magazine publishers; 15 percent rely on an ad agency; and another 15 percent hire a consultant.

Reasons to hire an outside firm include time limitations on your in-house staff; lack of market research expertise within your organization; a sensitive political situation, such as having to advise a company president whose pet product may bomb if you suspect lack of marketplace interest; the need for international market information, which outside consultants are often able to get more easily; or the need to collect information anonymously, such as when contemplating the acquisition of another firm.

In hiring an outside firm, you should consider industry expertise and experience, reputation, price, how capable the firm is at defining measurable and meaningful research objectives, and how quickly the market information can be delivered to you.

Good market research consultants don't have a bias. They are able to look at a situation and help you address what your information needs are, what your goals are, and what's necessary on an objective basis. They can also put concentrated time against a marketing problem when you need information fast and they know where to go to get the best information. Custom research can also reduce your overhead. You don't have to have a market research professional or information source on staff 52 weeks a year for the two or three times during the year that you need market information.

ORGANIZING AND INTERPRETING DATA

Once you have assembled all your information, how do you analyze it? This step requires both keeping an open mind so as not to jump to early conclusions and checking out inconsistencies. You must also be careful to look at all the data, not just selected segments of it.

Writing in the B/PAA *Intelligencer*, Dr. Arnold Diamond, vice president at Harry Helter Research Corp., explains: "Correlation does not mean causation. The classic example is in stating that there is a high correlation between the number of fire engines at a fire and the extent of damage at the fire, suggesting that fire damage can be lessened by limiting the number of fire engines at a fire. Obviously, it is the third variable, 'size of fire,' that is highly correlated with the number of engines present at a fire and the extent of damage that is 'causing' things to happen."

Likewise, if the demographics of your respondent groups are not similar, you may draw incorrect conclusions. Demographic differences in age, income level, education, sex, marital status, and other variables between two groups of respondents can throw off results. For instance, if one ad for a high-priced product appears to generate a great deal more interest than another, it may be simply that those who saw the first ad are in a higher income group. To make a valid assessment of the effectiveness of the two ads, your two groups of respondents must be balanced demographically.

Proper analysis requires looking beyond basic data to a variety of possible correlations that may affect the final conclusions. For example, the fact that Brand A is bought and used by more people may not be related to superior attributes, but rather to the fact that Brand B is not advertised enough, or that its advertising is ineffective.

For a study to be successful, it must discriminate between executions, products, ad concepts, etc. Market research should not only point to revelations about product performance and customer preferences, but to the reasons behind them.

Consistencies in responses, and especially consistencies in the reasons behind those responses, increase the confidence you can place in your findings. But, according to Dr. Diamond, "sometimes it is the inconsistencies in the data that produce the most meaningful results in a study. Inconsistencies may reveal errors in the data, so they must be verified as true before proceeding with an analysis. Then, the inconsistency in the data must be resolved by looking at other measures to try to determine, for instance, why buyers apparently prefer a product but won't purchase it." Possible reasons might include that the preferred product is too expensive, too large, or the wrong color. Armed with that information, you can then make product modifications that will lead to improved sales.

CHOOSING THE RIGHT RESEARCH METHODOLOGY

The type of research methodology you use to gather information depends on several factors, including the purpose of the research, the type of data desired, the nature of the individuals being researched, and timing and cost considerations. In general, research methods fall into either subjective or objective categories.

Subjective research is best suited for the preliminary or early phases of researching a new market: to investigate why products are purchased, how the purchase process occurs, what potential market segments exist, etc. Subjective techniques are appropriate when qualitative information is desired, that is, information related to the *hows* and *whys* of product selection. They are used for generating ideas for new products or promotional strategies, for understanding complex issues or decision processes, and for identifying areas for further research. They are not appropriate for gathering quantitative information (e.g., size of the market, proportion of subscribers in certain job functions). A subjective technique would involve an unstructured interview in which questions are phrased in a conversational context and topics are explored in a flexible fashion.

The objective approach is best suited for the later phases of research, when quantitative information directly tied to decision making must be gathered. Size of the potential market, relative importance of various product features, and extent of interest in various industry segments are all types of information that should be gathered through objective techniques. An objective technique might be a mail survey or questionnaire that permits the interviewer little or no latitude in what is asked or how it is recorded. Telephone surveys as well are often objective, with the interviewer essentially reading from a prearranged script and recording responses in a standard fashion. Personal interviews may also be objective, as in an exit poll in which voters are briefly questioned as they leave the polling place.

TELEPHONE VERSUS MAIL SURVEYS

Mail surveys are often selected over telephone surveys because they are less expensive. The most common reason for choosing telephone surveys is speed. However, the nature of the study, the questionnaire, and the characteristics of the respondents should also be considered.

Longer questionnaires are usually better done by mail since respondents may tire before a long telephone interview is completed. Sensitive or controversial topics are also better covered in a mail format, since talking with a live interviewer may limit respondents' candor or bias their responses. Technical subjects that are difficult to discuss over the phone are also easier to cover by mail. It is difficult to reach people in certain positions or in certain types of companies on the telephone, so a mail survey may be more productive.

Telephone surveying, on the other hand, affords the researcher a great deal more flexibility, which can be essential if not enough is known about the market to cover all bases in an objective format. A well-designed telephone survey can combine both subjective and objective elements.

INEXPENSIVE MARKET RESEARCH TECHNIQUES

Owners and managers of small businesses often have an advantage in conducting market research more efficiently, since they are closer to their customers. They can go out and learn much more quickly and react faster to what their customers like and don't like. For the large firm, market research usually involves hiring experts to sift through their mass markets for clues as to what makes customers buy or not buy. But even large companies can conduct market research inexpensively by following these tips from Judy Bjorling:

1. Make a list of assumptions you, your boss, and others make about your business for which there is little supporting data. The longer the list,

the more likely it is that you need a better system for gathering useful information.

2. Provide incentives to your sales force for accurate and insightful information. Make the sales force aware of the importance you place on up-to-date information and insights about loyal customers, those customers who have recently switched to another firm, new customers, and potential customers who have thus far eluded them.

3. Listen to customers yourself on a regular basis. There is no substitute for direct exposure to customers. Asking their opinions (and actually modifying your products based on their input) makes them increasingly loyal.

4. Form a good customer panel that meets periodically to volunteer information. Be sure that R&D, engineering, and production managers have the opportunity to interact directly with this panel.

5. Make it easy for customers to complain about your product. Resolution of complaints leads to increased loyalty. Complaints provide a legitimate source for product improvement ideas.

6. Attend meetings. Your competitors suffer many of the same problems you do and often will share information and solutions on the trickiest problems.

7. Whenever you realize that an executive from a competitive firm is speaking at a meeting, be sure someone in your company attends the meeting. Executives often reveal future directions for their companies, as well as insights about the industry.

8. Make yourself, or designate someone in your company, the industry expert. Read and subscribe to trade publications, but don't keep the information to yourself. Plan regular meetings to update your associates on trends and new developments.

TIPS FOR CONDUCTING SUCCESSFUL SURVEYS

Surveys are a popular way to gather market research information. They can be used to assess customers' opinions of your product or company, establish a customer profile that tells what common characteristics your customers share, find out what customers want or need from your industry, or solicit their reactions to a new service you are thinking of offering. Richard P. Gorman of Association Management, Inc., Washington, D.C., offers these tips for designing a survey that will increase response rates:

1. Set your goals. Define what you want your survey to accomplish.

2. Identify your sample group and define your boundaries, such as size, type of industry, or whatever.

3. Recognize any particular limitations or problems associated with your survey topic or sample group. For example, do you need the results in a

very short time? Were previous surveys on this subject too difficult to answer?

4. Keep your survey as short as possible.

5. Keep your questions unbiased and unambiguous. Make them easy to answer.

6. Discard questions with obvious answers or those with illegal implications.

7. If you are seeking an answer that is long or complicated, break it up into several simple questions rather than one long question that is difficult to understand.

8. Make as many responses as possible simple check-offs or multiple choice. This makes it easier for respondents to reply and for you to tabulate the final results.

9. Make your survey stand out; dare to be different, but keep it professional looking.

10. Set a deadline for returns.

11. Prepare a cover letter that encourages people to respond.

12. Pretest your survey on a small portion of your sample in order to debug any problem questions.

13. Offer an incentive for reply. For example, explain that respondents will be entered in a drawing for a $100 savings bond.

Chapter

25
Promotional Newsletters and Company Magazines

PROMOTIONAL NEWSLETTERS

One proven promotional tool is the company newsletter. In our age of specialized information, newsletters are popular. There are more than 10,000 newsletters published in the United States. Most of these are paid subscription newsletters, sold for profit by entrepreneurs for whom the newsletter is their primary source of income.

In this chapter, we deal with another kind of newsletter, the promotional newsletter. It is also called the company newsletter or house organ. These are newsletters, magazines, tabloids, or other publications regularly published primarily as promotional tools. They range from simple sheets published in-house to elaborate, four-color company magazines with photography and professional writing that rival newsstand magazines.

The Function of Promotional Newsletters

The main purpose of a promotional newsletter is to establish your image and build your credibility with a select audience (the people who receive the newsletter) over an extended period of time.

Instinctively, most marketers recognize that they should be in touch with their customers and prospects far more often than they actually are. You know, for instance, that there are many people in your life, business and social, who you don't think about, see, or talk to for long periods of time simply because you are busy and not thinking of them.

Your customers and prospects are busy, too. While you may be agonizing over why Jan hasn't placed an order from you recently or called your

505

firm to handle a project, Jan isn't even thinking about you...because there are so many other things to think about.

You know you should be doing something to keep your name in front of Jan. But what? You may want to call or send a letter, but you think this is too pushy; besides, there's no real reason to call, and you don't want to appear to be begging for business.

The newsletter solves this problem. It regularly places your name and activities in front of your customers and prospects, reminding them of your existence, products, and services on a regular basis. You need no "excuse" to make this contact, because the prospect expects to receive a newsletter on a regular basis. The newsletter increases the frequency of message repetition and supplements other forms of communication such as catalogs, print ads, and sales letters.

Frequency and Size

How long should your newsletter be? How often should it be published?

Four pages seems to be the ideal length for a promotional newsletter. Eight pages is too much reading, and two pages seems insubstantial—more like a flier or circular (which is perceived as junk mail) than a newsletter (which is perceived as a useful publication). If you need more than four pages, use six, not eight.

As for frequency, four times a year—once every three months—is ideal. Publish fewer issues, and people aren't aware you are sending them a newsletter per se; they perceive that they're just getting a piece of mail from time to time. Four times per year is enough to establish credibility and awareness. Publishing six times or more per year is unnecessary, because some months you may prefer to make contact with your prospects using other media, such as the telephone, direct mail, or catalogs.

What's more, experience indicates that most companies don't have enough news to fill six or more issues each year. If your schedule is too frequent, you may find yourself putting unnecessary fluff and filler in the newsletter just to get something in the mail. Your readers will be turned off by the lack of quality and poor content, so this approach would hurt rather than help.

Building Your Subscriber List

Who should get your newsletter? Basically, it should go to anyone with whom you want to establish a regular relationship. These people can include:

- current customers;
- past customers;
- current prospects;
- past prospects;
- expired accounts (e.g., past subscribers, expires, etc.);

- employees;
- vendors;
- colleagues;
- consultants, gurus, and other prominent members of your industry;
- trade publication editors, business columnists, and other members of the press who might possibly use material in your newsletter in their own writings.

Here is how to build the subscriber list:

1. First, put all current and past prospects and customers on the list. Don't use names that are too old. For past prospects and customers, for example, you might go back two or three years, but no more than that.

2. Next, get your salespeople to give you all the names of the people they call on regularly. Salespeople have their own favorite prospects, and these people may not be in the advertising inquiry files. Get salespeople to give you names of people who should get the newsletter. You essentially want to convert the dozens of individual Rolodex TM files kept by various salespeople and sales reps into a single, integrated subscriber list for your newsletter.

3. Go to your PR department or agency and add their media list. Get the names of all editors who should receive the newsletter.

4. Make sure all new inquiries and new customers are automatically added to the subscription list.

5. For trade show booths, create a subscription application form and offer a free one-year subscription to anyone who stops by your booth and completes the form.

6. Make sure the subscriber lists contains the names of your immediate supervisors, product and brand managers, sales and marketing managers, CEO, and any other key personnel whose support you need to run an effective advertising department. Company managers enjoy getting the newsletter and often offer ideas for articles and stories you can use. You might also approach your most important colleague and ask her or him to contribute a regular column.

Promoting the Newsletter

In addition to compiling the subscriber list, you can do a number of things to promote the newsletter (and to use the newsletter offer as a promotion):

1. Offer the newsletter as an extra incentive to people who respond to your direct mail. This can be done simply by adding a line to your reply cards with a box that says, "Check here if you would like a free one-year subscription to our quarterly newsletter, [title of newsletter]." Stress the newsletter offer in the P.S. of your sales letter.

2. Offer the newsletter as an extra incentive for responding to your space ads. Again, add an option to the response coupon that says, "Check here for a free one-year subscription to our newsletter, [title of newsletter]."

3. At speeches, seminars, and presentations, your company representatives can use the newsletter offer to get listeners involved in conversations with them. At the end of the talk, the presenter says, "Our quarterly newsletter, [title of newsletter], will give you more information on this topic. Just give me your business card and I'll see to it you get a free one-year subscription to it." The presenter will collect many business cards for follow-up, far more than he or she would get if there were no newsletter offer.

4. Rent a list of names and send them the newsletter for free two or three times. The third or fourth time, send it with a cover letter that says, "We hope you find [title of newsletter] informative and helpful, and we would be happy to continue sending it at no cost. To continue your free subscription, just complete and mail the reply card enclosed." Then continue sending the newsletter only to those who return the reply card, which eliminates the cost of continually renting names.

5. Send out a press release offering a free sample copy of the newsletter to people in your industry.

6. Run small space ads with a picture of the newsletter. Offer a free sample copy to anyone who responds.

Designing Your Newsletter

Newsletters do not have to be elaborate, but the design should be consistent from issue to issue in order to build recognition and awareness. After a time, many recipients will come to welcome your newsletter and even seek it out from the piles of mail in their baskets. But this can only happen if the newsletter has a distinctive, recognizable design that is consistent from issue to issue.

Although many paid subscription newsletters are typewritten, you probably want a design that is a little slicker, so as to enhance your image. Text is generally typeset in two- or three-column format. Paper stock may be white or colored, and the newsletter is usually printed in one or two colors. The key to the design is a distinctive masthead highlighting the name of the publication.

The look, content, and "feel" of the newsletter are usually arrived at after a couple of issues. By the third issue, you know the approximate length of copy, the type of visuals needed, the technical depth of the content, and the types of articles to be featured.

For instance, you might decide that each issue will contain two feature articles, one biographical profile, a regular question-and-answer column on technical issues, one product-related story, three or four short news tidbits, and a box with short previews of the next issue. Your newsletter may be different, of course, but the point is, you'll eventually find a formula that works. When you do, stick with it from issue to issue.

Readers like consistency of format because they know what to look for in each issue. For instance, some people opening the Sunday paper turn to sports first; some go to the comics; others read Dear Abby first. In the same way, some readers might check your technical tips column first, while others will read the profile. Make these features look and read the same in each issue (even position them in the same spot) so readers gain a comfortable familiarity with your publication.

Charging a Fee for Your Newsletter

One common question is, "Since so many newsletters charge hefty subscription fees, what about charging a fee for my newsletter?" Don't do it. A promotional newsletter is not the same as a paid subscription newsletter.

The paid subscription newsletter must deliver unique and valuable editorial material to readers; otherwise, they will not continue to pay a hefty price for it month after month. This material must be useful, informative, new, and special. In short, it must be material the reader cannot easily get elsewhere. The newsletter's purpose is to be the reader's source of critical information in the area covered by the publication.

The promotional newsletter is quite different. Although it should contain helpful and interesting information, readers expect less from a promotional newsletter than from one they pay to receive. As a result, they will accept a blend of how-to and technical information mixed with production information, company news, and sales talk, which is the mix you want to give them. Remember, the ultimate goal of the newsletter is not to educate readers (you are not in the business of educating people for free) but to get them to do business with your firm and buy your products.

Because your newsletter is free, you're entitled to make some subtle (and not-so-subtle) sales pitches. If you were charging a fee, readers would not accept this, so your newsletter should be free. Another reason not to charge is that paid newsletters typically capture only a small percentage of any market as subscribers. If you want to reach a broader base of prospects, you must offer your newsletter for free.

Putting Your Newsletter Together

Putting your newsletter together is not terribly difficult. The first step is to make a list of possible story ideas. (See the checklist of 29 such ideas in the next section.)

The material in your promotional newsletter does not have to be original, nor must it be created solely for the newsletter. In fact, a company newsletter is an ideal medium for recycling material from other sources—speeches, articles, press releases, annual reports, presentations, and so on. This helps you get maximum use out of material you've already created while minimizing the time and expense of writing and producing the newsletter.

The second step is to review your story ideas and select the ones to be featured in the next issue. If you are unsure as to how much room you have, it's better to select one or two extra ideas than to have too few. You can always use the extra material in a future edition.

The third step is to create a file folder for each article and collect the material that will serve as background material for the person who writes the story. Background material typically includes sales brochures (for product stories), press releases (which are edited into short news stories), and reprints of published trade journal articles on a particular topic (which are often combined and compiled into a new article on a similar topic).

The fourth step is to write each story based on this material. Many advertising managers hire freelance writers to write and edit their company newsletters. A few hire their ad agencies to do it. Using freelancers is usually more cost-effective. Besides, while most freelancers relish such assignments, most ad agencies don't like doing company newsletters because they find them unprofitable.

Some articles may require more information than is contained in the background material. In this case, supply the writer with the names and phone numbers of people within your company who can be interviewed to gather the additional necessary information. Call these people ahead of time to let them know a freelance writer will be calling them to do an interview for the newsletter. If they object, find someone else to take their place.

Once you get the copy, the fifth step is to edit it, send it through for review, and make any final changes. The sixth step is to give the final copy to your graphic artist or printer, who will create a mechanical for the newsletter. This should be carefully proofread and reviewed before it is printed. Many companies use desktop publishing systems in-house or hire outside desktop publishing services for newsletter layout and creation.

Once the mechanical is completed and approved, print the newsletter. You may want to order a small run above what you need to mail to the subscribers. These extras can be kept on file for people who request a back issue. If your newsletter is truly perceived as valuable by the subscribers, as is Niagara Lockport's *Tissue Issues*, you can periodically offer back issues as a "bait piece" in your ads and mailings.

If your subscriber list is small, say, only a few hundred names, you can have your computer generate gummed mailing labels and affix them in-house. Once you have a thousand or more subscribers, you might want to use a letter shop, fulfillment house, or similar mailing service to handle the mailing and distribution of your newsletter on a regular basis. This is not terribly expensive.

A Checklist of 29 Newsletter Story Ideas

1. Product stories: new products; improvements to existing products; new models; new accessories; new options; and new applications.

2. News: joint ventures; mergers and acquisitions; new divisions formed; new departments; other company news; also, industry news and analyses of events and trends.

3. Tips: tips on product selection, installation, maintenance, repair, and troubleshooting.

4. How-to articles: similar to tips, but with more detailed instructions. Examples: how to use the product; how to design a system; how to select the right type or model.

5. Previews and reports: write-ups of special events such as trade shows, conferences, sales meetings, seminars, presentations, and press conferences.

6. Case histories: either in-depth or brief, reporting product applications, customer success stories, or examples of outstanding service or support.

7. People: company promotions, new hires, transfers, awards, anniversaries, employee profiles, customer profiles, human interest stories (unusual jobs, hobbies, etc.).

8. Milestones: use of such phrases as "1,000th unit shipped," "sales reach $1 million mark," "division celebrates 10th anniversary," etc.

9. Sales news: new customers; bids accepted; contracts renewed; satisfied customer reports.

10. Research and development: new products; new technologies; new patents; technology awards; inventions; innovations; and breakthroughs.

11. Publications: new brochures available; new ad campaigns; technical papers presented; reprints available; new or updated manuals; announcements of other recently published literature or audiovisual materials.

12. Explanatory articles: how a product works; industry overviews; background information on applications and technologies.

13. Customer stories: interviews with customers; photos; customer news and profiles; guest articles by customers about their industries, applications, and positive experiences with the vendor's product or service.

14. Financial news: quarterly and annual report highlights; presentations to financial analysts; earnings and dividend news; reported sales and profits; etc.

15. Photos with captions: people; facilities; products; events.

16. Columns: president's letter; letters to the editor; guest columns; regular features such as Q&A or Tech Talk.

17. Excerpts, reprints, or condensed versions of: press releases; executive speeches; journal articles; technical papers; company seminars; etc.

18. Quality control stories: quality circles; employee suggestion programs; new quality assurance methods; success rates; case histories.

19. Productivity stories: new programs; methods and systems to cut waste and boost efficiency.

20. Manufacturing stories: SPC/SQC (statistical process control/statistical quality control) stories; CIM (computer-integrated manufacturing) stories; new techniques; new equipment; raw materials; production line successes; detailed explanations of manufacturing processes; etc.

21. Community affairs: fund-raisers; special events; support for the arts; scholarship programs; social responsibility programs; environmental

programs; employee and corporate participation in local, regional, or national events.

22. Data processing stories: new computer hardware and software systems; improved data processing and its benefits to customers; new data processing applications; explanations of how systems serve customers.

23. Overseas activities: reports on the company's international activities; profiles of facilities, subsidiaries, branches, people, markets, etc.

24. Service: background on company service facilities; case histories of outstanding service activities; new services for customers; customer support hotlines; etc.

25. History: articles about company, industry, product, community history.

26. Human resources: company benefit programs; announcement of new benefits and training and how they improve service to customers; explanations of company policies.

27. Interviews: with company key employees, engineers, service personnel, etc.; with customers; with suppliers (to illustrate the quality of materials going into your company's products).

28. Forums: top managers answer customer complaints and concerns; service managers discuss customer needs; customers share their favorable experiences with company products and services.

29. Gimmicks: contests; quizzes; trivia; puzzles; games; cartoons; recipes; computer programs; etc.

COMPANY MAGAZINES

The company magazine, or house organ, is a larger, more ambitious effort than the company newsletter. The term *newsletter* implies a slimmer publication, with simple graphics and short, concise, to-the-point articles. The term *magazine* implies a larger, slicker, more visually oriented publication, with photos, illustrations, more pages, more text, and lengthier, feature-type articles.

There's nothing mysterious about custom-published magazines. Companies, associations and other organizations have been using them for years to promote products and services, bolster sales efforts, and strengthen relationships with customers and members. They come in a variety of shapes and sizes. They may contain outside advertising or only ads for the sponsoring firm. Most rival the publications available on newsstands.

The best custom-published magazines present a positive image of their sponsors while providing helpful and useful information to readers. They may cover several subjects or focus on a single item such as travel, food, health, or finances, much as newsstand magazines do. But custom-published magazines are not aimed at general audiences. They're carefully constructed for the customers and prospects their sponsors want to reach. Their content is designed to support the sponsor's products and services by targeting values and lifestyles.

The first custom-published magazine was developed by DeWitt Wallace at the Webb Company before the turn of the century. Wallace took articles about farming practices and farm life from the pages of other magazines and reproduced them in digest form. Banks purchased them and gave them to customers. Wallace eventually left Webb and founded one of the most successful magazines in the long history of American publishing, *The Reader's Digest*.

The most familiar contemporary custom-published magazines are probably the airline in-flights, magazines tucked into the seat pockets of commercial jets. They combine information a traveler can use (whether it's feature material about vacations or practical tips about business travel) with promotional and advertising information for the airline. There are several custom-published magazines for farm audiences providing information about farm management, progressive farming practices, and other topics focused on today's farm audience—their value systems and lifestyles. Other magazines appeal to insurance purchasers, car owners, brides-to-be, and dozens of other consumer groups.

What Magazines Can Do That Other Media Can't

Custom-published magazines combine the trustworthiness of print, the visual appeal of consumer magazines, and the targetability of direct mail. They cost much less per customer contact than a sales call while providing audience involvement that no television or radio station can hope to match. The pages in these magazines can be read, reread, underlined, torn out, and even mailed back.

With marketing costs increasing, companies are becoming more and more concerned with the effectiveness of their advertising campaigns. No other vehicle provides the same capability for accurate media and marketing research as a magazine. Company-sponsored magazines can include mail-back questionnaires designed for a known audience.

Magazines also build company and product loyalty as nothing else can. They build positive corporate and organization images in addition to selling products and services. More than 3,000 sponsored magazines are published in the United States, a good indication of how popular they are with companies and groups that have made them part of their marketing strategies.

Several strengths of custom-published magazines were outlined in *Marketing & Media Decisions*:

- Ability to target an audience of prospects identified by dealers or company management.
- Total control of the message, free of competitive advertising clutter.
- Elimination of placement problems in general circulation media.
- Ability to stimulate floor traffic at dealerships with coupons and special offers.

- Seasonal timing, which puts the message into customers' hands when they are planning purchases.
- Space to present specific and detailed product information with charts, graphs, etc.
- Penetration of hard-to-reach markets.

    Other strengths include:

- Service to readers through education and updates on product lines.
- Image building in a positive, controlled environment with each issue creating its own environment.
- Direct sales support as part of an overall sales strategy.
- Semi-confidential distribution of the marketing plan.
- Reinforcement after the sale.

Getting Started

The first step in developing a magazine program is to set goals and objectives. How important is it for you to establish regular contact with your customers and top prospects and to encourage customer involvement with your sales and distribution network? Is your first priority to enhance the image of the company, or should direct sales support be the primary objective? Is the company most interested in cross-selling its goods and services, getting feedback from customers, reducing sales costs, lobbying decision makers, retaining customers, or educating consumers? All are worthy goals. However, it's important to establish one or more objectives so the magazine will have a clear focus.

The next step in planning your magazine is the last step of the publishing process: distribution.

Companies and associations have different problems getting their magazines to the right people at the right time. An association can simply use its membership roll to develop a circulation list. A business usually doesn't have members (co-ops and buyers' clubs are exceptions), so it has to develop its own list. This takes time and money, but a good list is invaluable as a sales-lead developer, a market survey tool, and the start of a direct mail program. A confidential customer-prospect list is a recognized business asset.

Here are some good places to start building a circulation list:

- Current customers.
- Respondents to mass media advertising.
- Existing lists, assembled by professional list brokers and rentable.
- Professional association lists, also rentable.
- Dealer-supplied names, available two ways. (The term *dealer* represents the closest-to-consumer level in your distribution network, whether it's dealer, agent, salesperson, or franchisee.) Dealers can supply names to you for computer storage, either in your computer or in

your publisher's. Computer printout labels can then be mechanically affixed to magazines after they are printed. Magazines also can be bulk shipped to dealers, who will distribute them. While this is less satisfactory, it is sometimes necessary because independent dealers often have a stake in keeping their customer lists confidential.

- Dealer imprints. When dealers pay part of the magazine cost, it is often extremely important to them to have their names, addresses, and phone numbers on each issue. This imprint can be as simple as a double computer label with "from" and "to" printed on each part of the label. A more uniform look can be achieved by typesetting the information and imprinting it during the printing process. Finally, you can provide dealers with a full-page ad or allow them to have their own newsletters bound into the magazine.

Ink-jet printing will permit matching of dealers' names on insert cards with the correct labels imprinted on the outside. Sophisticated dealer imprint systems use a specialized computer program that does far more than just produce labels. A well-designed program can provide a treasure of demographic information. It can provide printouts on participation by dealers, districts, regions, ZIP codes, etc. This is particularly important if dealers are billed for their participation in the program.

In any case, if you are selling the program to dealers on a cost-sharing or cost-liquidation basis, you must educate and sell them on the program to ensure participation.

There are other ways to distribute the magazine:

- Point of service: Distribute the magazine when customers purchase products or services.

- Focal point distribution: Place magazines where potential customers gather. Farmers, for example, might receive it at a county fair, stockyard, or grain elevator; teachers might receive it at school in the teachers' lounge.

- Piggyback distribution: The magazine is physically attached to a product in the packing crate or included with a company's annual report so it acts as an incentive as well as a marketing device.

The next step is to decide what kind of magazine to publish, taking into account your marketing objectives, the kind of image you want to project and how these can best be supported by a publication. The elements to consider are size and shape, and editorial and graphic approach.

Size and Shape

Among the basic formats are magazine, tabloid, newsletter, bulletin, booklet, and specialty piece. Magazine format is a clear choice when you want a top-quality marketing publication with four-color photos and illustrations. Usually the page is a press-efficient size, about 8 ×10 3/4". Digest-size magazines (5 3/8 × 8") offer a smaller alternative. Booklet form can be effective for one-time use, partly because it is both unusual and easy for a reader to keep. Newspaper formats—tabloid and broadsheet—offer low cost, but can be messy to handle and have shorter retention rates than magazines.

Specialty pieces are the most expensive pieces to produce, but often are the most impressive custom-published products. Some examples: a fold-out poster that resembles an 8 x 11 3/4" magazine when folded; a circular book; square or other odd-shaped pages (this wastes paper in longer press runs but might make sense in shorter ones); calendar magazines with articles on the backs of pages; or die-cut publications with special ink combinations or unusual paper.

The Editorial and Graphic Approach

The corporate image a publication conveys can be enhanced by the heft, feel, and appearance of the publication as well as by its editorial approach. There are two very basic editorial questions to ask:

* What message should be conveyed?
* What does the selected audience want to read?

The first question really isn't difficult to determine because most companies have been trying to communicate effectively with people for a long time. The second isn't difficult, either. Most companies probably have demographic and psychographic data on their audiences and can list topics that will attract readership. They can select subjects that best support the goals they want to achieve.

For example, a financial institution with a strong community reputation for supporting the arts and a clientele with an upper-income socio-economic base might start a magazine covering the regional arts scene. An airline whose audience consists mostly of businesspeople might produce a magazine that emphasizes business topics and stories featuring destinations on its flight routes.

Success isn't guaranteed by the best editorial approach and a sophisticated corporate message. A custom-published magazine has to be well written and well designed, with a specific readership in mind. Magazines that make it are not overloaded with corporate promotion material. If readers get the idea that a magazine is little more than a monthly sales brochure, they'll throw it out. At the same time, properly presented articles about a company's services and products can be perceived by readers as interesting, useful, and helpful.

Once a planned approach is chosen, it's time to bring in a topflight editor and art director to establish the editorial focus, graphic design, and budget. It is their job to clearly understand marketing objectives and then plan the proper mix of stories, photographs, and illustrations to ensure both good readership and effective reception of the sponsor's message.

Control is a primary concern for any sponsor of a custom-published magazine. If an editor and art director can't or won't take direction and produce what's expected, the sponsor will be unhappy with the final product. How much the sponsor wants to be directly involved with the creative staff depends on time, expertise, and inclination. At the very least, the sponsor should review all copy and layouts before magazine production is so far down the road that changes become expensive.

The keys to properly producing the magazine are communication and control. The sponsor and the creative staff must be on the same wavelength before and throughout production. Be sure to establish checkpoints before production starts. In a typical publishing situation, the sponsor should review work on the magazine at four steps:

1. editorial planning,
2. manuscripts,
3. rough layouts (including photos), and
4. blueprints or color-keys.

This four-point checklist lets the sponsor direct every step, from initial planning through final check. If properly used, this system will not cause costly delays, whether the editor and art director are across the hall or half a continent away.

Superior graphic design ensures magazine readability and creates a distinctive personality for the publication. A conservative financial firm may want a more formal look, for example, than a company selling records and laser discs. The effects of appearance may be subliminal, but if they clash with the desired image and editorial content, the discord will jar readers even though they may not be able to recognize what's wrong.

Good production planning and control are essential, too. In almost any magazine with a circulation of several hundred thousand, the cost of physically producing it exceeds creative costs. Therefore, you can save more money by making excellent production decisions than by cutting creative costs. Because there are many cost-saving options in producing any publication, experienced production managers are invaluable.

A production manager can help answer questions about the most economical way to produce a magazine. For example, does it need to be published with full-color photos throughout or will black and white do? That decision could result in significant savings. Should inserts be slid into the magazine, glued in, or stapled in with the rest of the pages? What are the paper stock alternatives? Which other production options are available? Each decision contributes to the final cost of the magazine.

At the same time, graphic skill can frequently make a one- or two-color publication look as sophisticated as a full-color magazine, and production can be organized so some pages are printed in one color and others in four colors.

If the production manager is on your staff, that person can help decide which printer should be employed. Is the lowest bid the best bid, or is the added experience and capability of a higher-priced printer worth the difference? Are reliability, longevity, and proven ability to meet schedules more important than price? Does a bid cover everything, or are there additional hidden costs? A production manager can help answer these and other questions about the publishing process, as well as review costs and establish an accurate, workable budget.

Costs

Magazines can be expensive or inexpensive depending on the number of copies distributed and the quality of the publication. Because the work that goes into producing a magazine is a substantial part of the cost, the price per copy drops rapidly as the size of the press run grows. Here is a breakdown of the costs involved in publishing a magazine:

Production

Except when dealing with short press runs (less than 30,000, for example), production dollars will dominate all costs. In press runs of several hundred thousand, cost of paper is the biggest item, as much as 60 percent or more of the total budget. As a result, most long-run magazines are printed on standard-size pages to save money.

The cost of large printing jobs varies little among most large, reputable printers. Quoted figures may vary because some printers price items such as stripping and platemaking as options, while others include them as basic costs. Production costs also are influenced by the kind of paper used, the number of pages, size of pages, number of copies, and the number of color separations needed for artwork. Service and quality will also affect cost.

As in most industrial production, the cost per unit for magazines goes down as press runs get longer. At about 500,000 copies, the cost curve becomes almost horizontal. Comparing variable costs versus fixed costs is another way to express volume efficiency. Fixed costs get the first copy of the magazine off the end of the press: creative, administrative, list development, separations, film, stripping, plates, etc. Variable costs are the additional costs of a continued press run, including stitching and mailing.

The fixed cost–variable cost concept is important in certain types of cost sharing. For example, a sponsoring company can pay fixed costs, then charge dealers only variable costs. This helps dealers pay for promotional material while the company controls the content and its own part of the budget.

Postage and Handling

The second largest cost is usually postage (depending on method of distribution), but it is often overlooked in initial plans. Third-class bulk mail, used by the majority of sponsored publications, costs a minimum of 19 cents per magazine at current rates. In addition, it costs another penny to label, tie, sort, and bag for the Post Office.

Creative

In both editorial and art areas, there are two costs: outside purchases and staff production. A large number of custom-published magazines buy some articles, photographs, and artwork from outside suppliers, partly because it is more efficient than producing everything in-house and partly to take advantage of a variety of talents. A typical magazine pays between $200 and $1,000 for an article.

How much creative time does it take to put out a magazine? Again, that depends on the size and quality of the magazine. A 32-page monthly magazine that uses about eight stories with some photos for each, but doesn't get into in-depth, investigative editorial material and whose literary standards are positioned somewhere between the *New Yorker* and your basic club bulletin probably will require a full-time editor and a half-time artist. The ratio would be reversed for magazines with heavy emphasis on graphics. Magazines need research, secretarial, and clerical support, too.

Administrative

This is another cost often overlooked. A custom-published magazine invariably involves administrative time spent by the sponsor. Someone must set marketing direction, monitor editorial material, approve copy through channels, and monitor production.

Miscellaneous Costs

Other costs to be planned for include libel insurance in case someone whose name or photo appears decides to sue. Correspondence generated by the magazine will require substantial administrative and secretarial time, even if it's viewed as a plus for the magazine's image.

Total Cost Guidelines

The way to estimate magazine costs more precisely is to sit down with people whose business it is to do just that. Talk with someone who has extensive publishing experience, especially with custom-published magazines, to find out what all the options and costs are before you begin to figure out the bottom line.

Making the Decision

Are custom-published magazines for everybody? Probably not. Here are some questions to answer before deciding if they're right for your company or organization:

- How important is repeat business to maintain a profitable volume or keep membership levels high?

- How important is it to maintain contact between sales?

- Can your staff locate sources of probable future business or membership for building a mailing list as well as for follow-up calls?

- Can you expect higher sales volume from more frequent calls on potential customers or members?

- Is your company's sales force already overloaded with more customers and prospects than can be served satisfactorily?

- Does your company line include several distinctively different major products as opposed to several similar products? (Special alloys are similar products; sheets, plates, and beams are different products for a steel company.)

- Are your products sold in more markets than you can effectively reach with purchased advertising within your budget?

- Do you have potentially profitable fringe markets whose chief buyers could be contacted for less than it costs to run a standard advertising campaign?

- Does your product line include more minor products than you can afford to advertise adequately in existing publications?

- Could an educational emphasis stimulate your sales volume, using articles on How to Install, How to Apply, How to Service, and so on?

- Do your employees, salespeople, dealers, or jobbers need to be better informed about products and sales methods?

- Does your company sell through exclusive representatives—the kind of people who would appreciate having their names or advertisements appear in a publication going to customers and prospects?

Finding the Money to Launch the Program

New company-sponsored publications, often financed by newly created budgets, sometimes have difficulty getting started because it's hard to justify additional expenditures when corporate belts are being tightened.

A creative manager, however, may discover money is already available in existing budgets. For example, a review of advertising budgets may indicate a magazine should be included as the most efficient, on-target medium for reaching prime customers and prospects without waste.

Public relations budget dollars may be reallocated to sponsor a magazine that functions as the ideal vehicle for corporate image articles, new product and service news, and major personnel changes.

A solid case can be made for using the sales promotion budget for a custom-published magazine, especially when the publication promotes local purchases by identifying local retail outlets with imprints or special promotion inserts at less cost than separate mailings. A high-circulation magazine mailed at bulk rate may cost only a few cents per copy more than a letter mailed first class.

If research is important, the research budget may be tapped for part of the magazine cost. Surveys can be conducted very effectively and economically, either inserted into the magazine or bound with the rest of its pages.

Corporate communications budgets can reasonably be applied to a magazine. An all-important letter from the chief executive officer is especially significant in the company's own magazine.

In other words, your magazine may require no new dollars, but simply a readjustment of existing budgets. There are two other options for financing the magazine: advertising and cost sharing.

When a magazine can help generate floor traffic for a retailer who sells your product or when it is used as a value-added extra to help sales, the cost of publishing the magazine can be shared with dealers. This report has already discussed the hypothetical mechanics of cost sharing in the sections on distribution and costs.

In addition there are many compelling reasons to consider selling advertising in a custom-published magazine, but some equally compelling ones that may mitigate against it. Theoretically, noncompetitive advertising should be beneficial to the sponsored magazine through the revenue generated.

Making a company-sponsored magazine self-liquidating through advertising is a considerable challenge. Consider the high failure rate for ordinary consumer magazines that are designed solely to make money for their publishers, with no mandate to carry a company message. How difficult would it be to sell enough advertising in a magazine designed for something other than pure readership?

It is even more difficult for a custom-published magazine to be competitive because consumer magazines have additional revenue streams including newsstands sales, paid subscriptions, list rental, and book sales to help support the publication.

Remember that sponsored magazines are driven by specific marketing objectives for the sponsoring company. Whether or not some of the costs can be reduced by outside advertising should be a factor in evaluating the overall need for a publication, but not the final decision factor. Even if everything is done correctly to launch a magazine advertising sales program, most advertisers take a wait-and-see attitude on any new publication.

Does this mean advertising in a custom-published magazine should be discouraged? Yes and no. There are some magazines that sell ads successfully. A great deal depends on the circulation and editorial justification. In-flight magazines are just one example of successful, company-sponsored magazines carrying paid advertising.

However, Webb's experience selling advertising in a wide variety of such publications leads us to recommend a very cautious and realistic appraisal of advertising revenue and cost projections before investing dollars in an ad sales program.

Starting an ad sales program is expensive. In the best situation, only about 50 percent of revenue is returned to finance the cost of the magazine. In addition to the cost of retaining an advertising representative firm, sales commissions generally run about 20 percent, ad agencies get 15 percent of the sale, rate cards and promotions claim another 5 percent, and bad debts take another 5 percent.

These considerations will help you decide how to use advertising in your publication:

- Start a company- or association-sponsored magazine only when a clear marketing justification exists.

- In the initial stages, sell paid advertising to your own company's other divisions.

- Establish the publication as a solid marketing tool, obtaining feedback from customers about their interests, level of readership, demographics, etc. Make certain the publication works well for the company before figuring in the costs of selling advertising. Convincing evidence that the publication is proving effective for you is strong sales medicine for outside advertisers.

- Ask potential outside advertisers if they would advertise when the publication is established. Their reactions to page count, frequency, distribution method, and content will help you determine the economic feasibility of outside advertising. Be careful, though. "What-if" commitments are a long, long way from signatures on contracts. It may take ten "what-ifs" to equal one sale.

- Make careful economic projections of cost versus income before deciding to sell outside advertising.

Suppose, after all this, you find your magazine is attractive to advertisers and you are willing to underwrite the costs. How do you capitalize on the potential? Hire an experienced advertising sales manager to lead an internal staff; or contract with one or more reputable advertising rep firms with proven results in your field; or work with an established contract publisher who can supply solid advertising sales experience and results along with the complete professional package of creative and print production.

Doing It In-House

In general, establishing a magazine division within your company or association can cost more in time, money, and headaches than contracting for services. Unless a sponsor already has a need for publishing experts on staff, taking the work to a professional contract publisher is a better choice. There are many capable suppliers that can produce travel publications, health, sports, and general interest magazines. Outside editors are likely to produce a magazine more efficiently and smoothly than in-house editors because of their experience with the subject matter and relationships with freelance writers and photographers.

Still, most decisions are not clear-cut. Internal company politics and policies also enter the picture, but here are some things to consider when making a decision:

- Is the magazine viewed as a long-term commitment? If it's not, you'll have to fire or absorb staff members with skills foreign to the company's other operations when you shut it down. It might be better to contract with an outside supplier until the company is ready to make a firm commitment.

- Do current staffers have magazine experience? Public relations specialists have different skills than magazine editors and publication designers. Producing a magazine will probably require hiring full-time publication specialists or contracting for the services.

- Do you have a realistic estimate of the time necessary to prepare the publication for printing? It always seems to involve a great deal more time than most people think. Editors, for example, assign stories, write them, do research, gather background information, handle editorial correspondence, and coordinate work with art directors and photographers. They also coordinate material with someone responsible for company policy and work with production specialists, printers, and sometimes an advertising manager. Let an experienced magazine professional assess the total requirements before someone is assigned to handle the job in spare time.

- Is it cheaper to buy expertise from outside than develop it within? Hiring one or two people to produce a company magazine negates the opportunity to tap a reservoir of expertise provided by a full-time publisher.

- Do the company's politics indicate that an internal editor would be under pressure in the selection or slanting of editorial content from within the company? An outside supplier, dealing with only one highly placed contact at a company, is free of those pressures.

- Will publishing, if handled internally, coordinate well with regular responsibilities? Starting a new division from scratch to produce a magazine takes an astounding amount of administrative time.

- Is there enough management time to oversee an internal staff? This is a cost not usually considered when you begin to total the financial commitments to an internally produced company-sponsored magazine.

- Do you, or someone you might assign, have experience and time to keep the many facets of a publishing operation moving on schedule? Printers' time is tightly scheduled and missing deadlines can be costly. If magazine material is tied to an advertising or promotional campaign, missed deadlines could ruin the entire effort.

III

PRODUCTION

Chapter

GRAPHIC DESIGN

Chapter 26

A graphic designer can be likened to an orchestra conductor. The job of a conductor is to take individual elements (in this case, musical instruments), and with a particular direction in mind (symphonic score), coordinate them faithfully and imaginatively. The result is a brilliant work of art.

The graphic designer, too, must take individual elements (text, photographs, illustrations, headlines) and coordinate them in a layout to create a stunning work of art. The object, in this case, is to attract attention and sell the goods.

Products can sell on their own inherent quality, but the marketplace is logjammed with meritorious merchandise, and some not so meritorious. Your sales edge comes from advertising and promotion campaigns. What makes these campaigns effective is great design.

As with text and visual elements, design must complement and enhance your product or service. It must also intrigue, excite, or flatter the reader. A direct mail pitch for Rockliff & Bundy Studios expressed its importance thus:

> Your sales media should work as hard as you do. Effective graphic design doesn't punch out at 5 o'clock. It doesn't take three-day weekends or bank holidays. Sick days? Good heavens! It works all the time, or not at all....
>
> You work hard. Good design media may not make your work easier. But it should create more of a demand for it.

Graphic designers (also called graphic artists) may or may not be visual artists themselves, but their job is to work with artists and art. They are involved in the intermediary stage between creation and print production. A B/PAA white paper defines the role as "problem solving. Developing a solution to a particular problem within a given time frame, budget, materials availability and client objectives. If the graphic designer is to be effective, he must be knowledgeable enough to function in many areas."

Imaginative design is an expert mix of art and science that, capably executed, is the invisible partner in a campaign. Everyone praises the copy, admires the illustration, and raves about the product. But it was the graphic designer who brought all these elements together to create the whole package.

WHERE TO FIND GRAPHIC SERVICES

1. Directories. A number of national and regional directories list vendors in the graphic design field, such as the Creative Black Book (New York, NY), RSVP (Brooklyn, NY), and Adweek Portfolio (NY, NY). Artists (arranged by category) pay a fee for inclusion in these annual publications and are usually allotted one page to display a sample of their work. Because of the space limitations, displays tend to be highly specialized rather than indicative of any broad range of design skill. These publications are sold in art stores and distributed to advertising agencies and art directors.

The Graphic Artists' Guild (212-463-7730) and the American Institute of Graphic Artists (212-246-7060) publish member directories. Both organizations have regional chapters around the country.

2. The Yellow Pages. Check under Graphic Design, Graphic Art, Design, or Art. You will find freelancers, design studios, and creative boutiques.

3. Freelancers. Many independent designers compile mailing lists of former and prospective clients. Read and keep on file any direct mailers that cross your desk.

4. Printers. Printers work with graphic designers in the normal course of their business. A printer who does not have a graphic artist on staff can easily recommend local talent.

5. Referrals. Ad agencies, photographers, illustrators, magazines, and newspapers can all recommend freelancers with whom they've worked.

6. Awards Annuals. A number of expensively produced awards annuals are published by graphic arts organizations. These high-visibility volumes exhibit prize-winning designs by the best studios. They are prestigious showcases and, as one envious designer (who wasn't included) said, "You can't buy your way into those books." They include *Typography*, published by the Type Director's Club (New York, 212-983-6042); *Design Annual*, put out by Communications Arts (Palo Alto, CA, 415-326-6040); and, perhaps the most coveted of all, the *Graphics Design Annual*, published in Switzerland, which features international award winners. These books are good sources for locating cutting-edge talent, and probably the most expensive talent as well.

THE STAGES OF GRAPHIC DESIGN

Planning

In the initial phase, you (and your art director, if you have one) should sit down with the graphic designer and explain your needs, which can be artistic (creative input) or technical (executing production). You may have a specific concept in mind, or just broad parameters. Lacking a total overview, you can grant a certain degree of creative freedom to the designer.

What makes a graphic designer's job easier? Clients who know the business, know what they want, and know what to expect. Conversely, a client who is stubborn about ideas but has no concept of the technical aspects was described by one graphic designer as a living nightmare. If you know what you want, but don't know how to achieve it, rely on the graphic designers' advice, and don't tell them how to do their job.

Bill Graef, an applied artist based in New York, also has misgivings about design by committee. "Unfortunately, things are getting more that way. Advertising works like that, and publishing is becoming more that way. Everyone wants to get their fingers in the pie so they can say they had something to do with it. As a result, design either gets very bland and watered down, or the look becomes overly ambitious. It's depressing, but it's a consequence of big business."

Background

In the early design stages, the graphic artist may be required to do some research, to see what's been done on the subject, or to find supportive material or appropriate visuals. The designer may look through a swipe file (a collection of pictures clipped from magazines or miscellaneous illustrations for conceptualizing). These visuals are used for reference, to give an idea of atmosphere, model positioning, or prop placement.

Execution

The graphic artist uses tracing paper and pencil or marker to draw a thumbnail sketch. (A thumbnail isn't as tiny as the name implies; it can be full-size or smaller, perhaps 25 percent of actual size.) Also referred to as a layout or rough comp (short for comprehensive), the point is to visualize the direction of the design. Samples from the swipe file may be Xeroxed or copied on tracing paper and inserted into the rough comp. You can even scan them as a computer file, then modify to suit your tastes. The artist may do three to ten thumbnails for the client's inspection. The client may pick one, or suggest a combination of two or three, or send the designer back to the drawing board.

The graphic artist selects type styles and typefaces. Bill Frederick, a graphic designer for Frederick and Froberg Design Offices in Montville, NJ, estimates that "an ad manager spends a good twenty-five to fifty percent of the time dealing with the 'word' element, having text approved by the product manager, making sure it's proofread. Then it's time to have the designer experiment with typefaces to suit the flavor and, finally, make the type fit the format. Every time ad managers see text, they probably want to change something. Or have to." (In the final phases, however, typefaces are rarely changed, except for size.)

During this stage, the designer also selects colors, borders, and special effects to be achieved during print production. Unless you have expressly relinquished control over these decisions to the designer, you reserve the right to approve each element before final inclusion. In any case, the final product will be your responsibility, so every element should require your approval.

Next, the graphic artist produces a finished sketch, or comp. (Be advised that these terms are used somewhat loosely, depending on who you're talking to. In discussions with a designer, you could be using different jargon while talking about the same thing. A rough can also be called a pencil sketch, and a finished comp a tight comp.) In the finishing stages, you will know exactly what typeface, colors, visuals, and text will be used, and their relative placement. A Xerox study claims that color draws readers up to 80 percent better than black and white and increases memory retention by 78 percent (cited in *QP Today*, Quick Print Industry Study, 1996).

When the comp is approved, a mechanical can be prepared, which involves affixing all the elements to stiff art board, in position and camera ready (ready to be photographed for printing). This process is discussed in greater detail in Chapter 29.

WHAT TO LOOK FOR IN GOOD DESIGN

The newsletter *Communication Briefings* suggests the following method for judging the strength of a layout: "Hold (it) at arm's length and squint at it. The weak elements will disappear, and you'll be able to see the powerful ones that attract and direct the eye." This will also give an overall impression of the layout's balance, contrast, unity, and proportion.

Bill Graef believes "...the most important aspect of good design is refinement. There is no excess. Every detail in a design either serves a purpose, or it's removed." You should also judge your design by the following characteristics.

Originality

Originality was once described by an anonymous wag as "the art of concealing your source." There are standard clichés in any field, and traditional approaches. The most imaginative, adventurous applications are often the product of the more glamorous (and expensive) design studios. But even within a limited budget, it's possible to find talented vendors who aren't satisfied churning out assembly-line design. Even clichés can be played with and twisted.

One designer referred to "...business paranoia, [when] everybody wants to look like everybody else." Just because a design worked for them is no reason to assume it will work for you. It will most likely succeed in making you look like a copycat. If you want your appeal to stand out from the competition, resist the impulse to make it look like everyone else's.

Readability

Having devoted considerable attention to text and headlines, does the typography enhance your message, or obscure it? Do the typefaces complement the overall visual impact of the design? Are type sizes sufficiently large to be read easily and understandably? All text elements should be friendly to the eyes. Unusual type could attract attention but hinder readability. Avoid large blocks of copy set in italics, upper case, or gimmicky typefaces.

Judging a design's readability goes beyond mere words; it should also apply to visuals. Are your illustrations "readable?" Is your product recognizable? Do essential details stand out? Were any details lost in the design process? Does the overall atmosphere convey a favorable impression? Every one of these questions deserves an affirmative answer in judging the effectiveness of design. A single untoward element could handicap an otherwise worthy production.

When type is superimposed over a tint or visual, the reader may get the picture, but lose your words. High contrast between these elements is essential.

Color

Do the colors flatter your design, or cheapen the impact? Do they create interplay with the text, or distract the reader? How pure are the tints? Are they muddy, or so bright they almost blind the reader?

Are colors appropriate for the context? If your product is food, some colors stimulate the appetite, while others, such as brownish-green khakis, are downright unappetizing. Certain colors excite, others soothe. They should be selected and arranged to maximize the intended effect.

White Space

Mark Twain once referred to "the eloquence of silence." Because white space represents "nothing," it is often overlooked as an effective attention-getter. But when competing with "busy" adjacent layouts (in a magazine, for instance), a block of white space may be a startling eye-catcher.

A balance is best, neither too much nor too little, evenly distributed throughout the design. Again, there are no firm rules. Uneven layout can be used to good effect if the intention is to throw the reader off balance.

Consistency

Keeping your design consistent shapes an image. Related elements, used in your campaign over an extended period of time, lend an air of continuity that the audience comes to identify with your company, product, or service.

You've no doubt seen the long-running ad campaign touting *Forbes* magazine as a "Capitalist Tool," illustrated by noted designer Seymour Chwast. *Forbes* is one of the most respected and widely read publications among businesspeople, a community noted for dignified behavior. Yet the

Chwast campaign features coloring-book style cartoons and playful, pun-filled captions. As a result of this offbeat approach, *Forbes* stands distinctively apart from other business publications, appearing bold, unafraid, almost devilish. What years ago must have seemed a daring tactic has evolved into a familiar image on the American publishing scene.

The series of ads for Pallace, Inc. (Figures 26.1, 26.2, and 26.3) demonstrate how several relatively simple elements, slightly reconfigured and reworded, can be used effectively in an ongoing campaign. Each successive ad builds upon the previous, reinforcing Pallace's image as a knowledgeable and common-sense advertising agency.

Roger C. Parker, author of the best-selling book *Looking Good in Print*, offers the following advice for achieving consistent graphic design of marketing materials.

To check whether your print communications are doing a good job of networking, gather samples of a variety of them and hang them on a bulletin board or place them on a large table. Invite your friends and coworkers to analyze them in terms of the following:

- *Logo.* Does the same version of your logo appear on each of your print communications? Does your logo always appear in the same position and at the same relative size on each document?

- *Color.* All of your print communications should be printed in the same colors. Your image is seriously undermined when the colors on your business cards don't match those on your letterhead or in your newsletter.

- *Typography.* Typography refers to the typeface, type size, and alignment used for headlines, body copy, and supporting information (like street and E-mail addresses, phone and fax numbers). If you use a serif typeface (like Times New Roman) for body copy and a sans serif typeface (like Arial Bold) for headlines and subheads in your brochure, you should use the same combination in your newsletters. Likewise, if you use flush left, ragged right body copy in your brochures, use flush left, ragged right body copy in your newsletters.

- *Margins and borders.* Does the same relative amount of white space appear at the edges of your letterheads, brochures, and newsletters? Do the borders surrounding your brochures match those surrounding your letterhead and newsletter?

- *Layout.* Are all of your print communications based on the same layout, or column structure? Your firm's image is seriously weakened when one issue of the newsletter is based on a two-column layout, another on a three-column layout.

- *Spacing.* Does the same amount of white space always appear above and below headlines and subheads?

- *Paper.* Always use the same paper color and texture (i.e., smoothness) even though the weight (i.e., thickness) and stiffness may change depending on how the message is delivered.

High-Tech Marketing Executives

If you want to increase your sales, you must stand above the competition.

Positioning: Determine how your company and its products will be perceived by the marketplace.

Setting yourself apart from and superior to the competition. Building preference for your products and services.

A complex and never-ending job. It involves how you answer the phone, the reliability of your products, the integrity of your people, the quality of your advertising and sales literature, and much more.

At Pallace inc., we can do the research to determine your current position in the market. We can help formulate the strategy to enhance or alter your position.

We can develop the advertising, the literature and the publicity that will help you implement the strategy. And set you above the competition.

To learn more about our services, call Joy McIlwain or Bob Pallace at (301) 622-5100.

Pallace inc.
A High Technology Advertising Agency

11961 Tech Road, Silver Spring, MD 20904
(301) 622-5100

Figure 26.1. Pallace, Inc. ad.

Figure 26.2. Pallace, Inc. ad.

High-Tech Marketing Executives

If you want to increase your sales, you must bring the customers to you.

Response: It has been demonstrated over and over again that advertising actually lowers selling costs.

But this shouldn't surprise anyone. Interview one salesperson who has spent the day cold calling and one salesperson who has spent the day following up qualified leads. Who was more productive?

Making your sales force more productive can begin with a call to Pallace inc.

We can develop direct response programs that will put qualified leads into the hands of your sales force. We have been doing this for over 20 years.

For one client, we generated 17,000 sales leads in one year on a relatively modest budget.

If your sales force needs qualified leads, call Joy McIlwain or Bob Pallace at (301) 622-5100.

Pallace inc.
A High Technology Advertising Agency

11961 Tech Road, Silver Spring, MD 20904
(301) 622-5100

Figure 26.3. Pallace, Inc. ad.

- *Photographs and captions.* If thin rules (or lines) surround some photos, they should surround all photos. Likewise, always set captions in the same typeface and type size and place them in the same position relative to the photograph.

"The consistency in the way you handle these details reflects your approach to business. Consistency communicates professionalism and attention to detail. Drifting standards reflect an unprofessional, devil-may-care attitude that destroys your credibility," says Parker. "Small companies today have the unprecedented ability to create their own communications materials that can help them build rapport with prospects and strengthen relationships with existing customers, both of which result in faster, easier sales."

Like in-person contacts with prospects and clients at meetings, trade shows, and social events, your firm's business cards, brochures, correspondence, and newsletters are powerful networking tools. As you settle at your keyboard, mouse in hand, to create your documents, consider these rules of thumb that will ensure that your paper-based presence has maximum effect.

"Just as your prospects won't recognize you if your voice changes and your height, weight, and hair color are different every time you meet them, prospects won't recognize your print communications unless they project a consistent image," notes Parker. "Each of your print communications should project a strong 'family' resemblance. There should be more similarities than differences between ads, brochures, business cards, correspondence, and newsletters."

DESKTOP PUBLISHING

Computers have brought about a D.I.Y. Revolution, which means Do It Yourself. Jobs that formerly would have been farmed out to studios, agencies, or independent vendors can now be completed in-house at tremendous savings in cost and time.

"Today store shelves are flooded with increasingly affordable products that promise to give businesses graphic design capabilities," writes Anthony Vagnoni in *Co.* magazine (January 1998). "For a sum that runs about 40 percent less than some of the lower-priced professional design firms, you can assemble a fairly sophisticated in-house graphics setup and put a marketing employee in charge of it." Products he recommends include:

- Macintosh computer with 17-inch or larger monitor and 32 MB or more of RAM,
- laser printer,
- flatbed scanner,
- SyQuest or Iomega Zip drive,

- QuarkXPress,
- Adobe Illustrator, and
- Photoshop.

The applications of design software are far-reaching, and can facilitate every aspect of production, from conceptualization to printing. In Chapters 27 to 29, you will see how computers aid photographers, illustrators, and print production houses. They perform miracles no less for graphic designers. Bill Frederick paints the inevitable scenario: "If you don't have a computer within five years, you won't be able to compete (in the design field)."

The name desktop publishing has become generically associated with design software that allows the user to produce any sort of document electronically. (The CRT screen, or monitor, is the "desktop.") You can compose and incorporate all elements, including text, visuals, color, typography, positioning, borders, and special effects. Instead of leaning over a drafting table, the artist punches keys and slides around a mouse (a little box linked to the computer by a thin cable, that affects the on-screen movement of a pointer; instead of typing keys to move a cursor, you slide the mouse, which moves the pointer to the work area, then click a button to execute the application). The on-screen layout is sometimes referred to as an electronic pasteboard.

Like the traditional graphic artist's workshop, design software features a "tool box," consisting of on-screen methods for creating, modifying, and positioning the various elements in a design. Depending on the program, tools are usually represented by symbolic images, such as knife blades (for cutting), pencils (for sketching), paint brushes (for coloring), or boxes (for squaring or enclosing). In addition, many programs include ready-made templates (a standard pattern to form an accurate copy of a shape or sectional arrangement).

Any number of desktop publishing programs are available. The two leading programs for IBM users are Ventura and Aldus PageMaker. IBM systems also use GEM (short for Graphics Environmental Manager) and First Publisher. These programs are updated on a regular basis (usually every six months) as improvements are developed. Each subsequent update is called a *release*.

For Macintosh users, there are QuarkXpress and Ready Set Go! In addition, Aldus PageMaker and Ventura are available to run on Macintosh.

A complete desktop publishing system is linked by component programs, commonly consisting of:

- a personal computer (e.g., a Macintosh, IBM, or IBM clone);
- a graphics or "paint" program, such as McDraw or Adobe Illustrator, for creating visuals;
- a word processing program, such as Microsoft Word or MacWrite for creating text;

- a page-making program, such as Aldus PageMaker or Harvard Publishing's version;
- a laser printer, which reproduces the entire work on paper.

These systems are infinitely flexible. Whatever can be designed by hand can probably be done just as effectively (and more efficiently) on computer. It takes no less artistic skill, though, to execute a fine design. A desktop publishing system is ultimately just a tool kit. What's done with it depends on the person facing the screen.

Some of the materials that can be produced on desktop publishing systems include:

- newsletters;
- press releases;
- business cards;
- proposals;
- announcements;
- menus and price lists;
- reports;
- user manuals;
- small directories and catalogs;
- mailers, including postcards; and
- sales literature.

As you can see, practically any printed material that serves your business needs can be produced on computers. The few (generally larger) jobs they cannot do at present, they will probably be capable of doing with subsequent generations of technology.

These systems, however, are not foolproof. In terms of artistic application, they are capable of anything—including human error. A computerized design system will not turn a careless, unimaginative designer into a genius. Hugh P. Curley of Direct Marketing Consultants, Inc. refers to the final product as WYSIWYG, which stands for What You See Is What You Get. In a mini-report on the state of the art, he notes: "We've seen many examples of newsletters produced by companies using desktop publishing where it was patently obvious that the fine touch of a good graphics artist was sorely lacking . . . (M)any of these in-house productions all have that same 'boxy' appearance that doesn't lend itself to leading readers quickly and easily through the copy. Even the best newsletter we've seen produced via desktop . . . was set up by an outside design team working closely with its editors."

Computer systems are extensions of the human mind and, as such, are only as good as the people who use them. But a top-notch designer accustomed to using traditional means can adapt his or her talents to the electronic pasteboard and create designs that will astonish, delight, turn heads, and sell.

More Desktop Publishing Tips from Roger Parker

Here are twelve additional ideas I found discussed in greater detail in Roger C. Parker's *One-Minute Designer*. Some of the tips are very detailed, because one of the main themes of the *One-Minute Designer* is that details often determine a document's success or failure. Poorly executed, great designs rarely succeed; indeed, the better a document appears, the more important the details become.

1. Determine the hierarchy of ideas before you begin considering design. Successful designs are based on determining the relative importance of the various text and visual elements in your message. Before you can add emphasis through contrast, you have to be able to identify those elements that communicate the most important information. Ask yourself questions like: What is the most important idea I'm trying to communicate? What is the next most important idea? Which ideas are merely supportive or illustrative? One useful technique is to go through your word processed manuscript with a yellow highlighter and highlight the important ideas. These are the ideas that you should emphasize.

2. Design with your computer turned off. Desktop publishing and page layout programs are terrific production tools, but they inhibit your creativity. Use a pencil and paper to create rough sketches of your document before you try to create it on your computer. Use boxes to indicate the size and placement of photographs, pencil in headlines, and use parallel horizontal lines to indicate columns of text. Your creativity and ability to experiment with different page layouts and proportions will flow much more freely when you work with a pencil and paper than when you fuss with menus and software comments.

3. Build white space into the sides of every page. Avoid gray pages. Gray pages are those filled top to bottom and margin to margin with text. Avoid them by adding a deep sink, or pool of white space, at the top of each page. Provide space between headers and footers and adjacent columns of text. Provide white space at the sides of each page. This not only focuses your reader's eyes on the contents of each page, but the margins provide space for their thumbs to hold your document without obscuring any of your message.

4. Exercise restraint when choosing typefaces. The overuse of different typefaces is one of the characteristics of a newcomer to desktop publishing. Use the minimum number of typefaces necessary to separate display type (headlines and subheads) from columns of text and captions. Often just two typeface designs are enough: a sans serif design like Helvetica or Arial for headlines and a serif design like Times Roman for text.

5. Base type size on line length. Avoid long lines of type (wide columns) set in a small type size. Likewise, avoid short lines of text set in a large type size. Long lines of type set in a small type size are extremely difficult to read. It's very easy for readers to get lost at the end of each line. Instead of jumping to the beginning of the next line, they may inadvertently return to the beginning of the same line or (worse) jump down two lines. Short lines of type set in a large type size are equally difficult to read. Short lines of type set in a large type size do not contain enough words for readers to establish a comfortable rhythm, based on two or three left to right eye movements across each line. Short lines of type set in a large type size are frequently characterized by excessive hyphenation.

6. Base line spacing on typeface, type size, and line length. Avoid using your page layout program's default, or automatic, line spacing. Line spacing is as important as type size, and deserves your careful attention. Automatic line spacing generally creates headlines with lines spaced too far apart and columns of text with lines spaced too closely together. In general, increase line spacing as line length increases; the horizontal bands of white help separate each line of type and make the text passage easier to read.

7. Replace white space within headlines with white space around headlines. Always reduce letter spacing in headlines. This is called tracking (when you reduce spacing the same amount of space between each pair of letters) and kerning (when you reduce letter spacing between problem pairs of letters, such as upper case *W*'s next to lower case *a*'s or *o*'s). Likewise, reduce line spacing within headlines so that your headline emerges as a single typographic element, rather than as a series of disconnected lines. Headlines gain impact to the extent that they are surrounded by white space. If you reduce letter and line spacing in headlines, your headlines will look better and be easier to notice and easier to read.

8. Use a condensed, extra heavy typeface for headlines. Don't be content with boldfaced type. Condensed versions of most headline typefaces are available. These permit you to include more letters within a given amount of space. Going from a regular to a condensed typeface often changes a three-line headline into a far easier to read, two-line headline. Search for extra-thick versions of your favorite headline font, typically called Heavy or Black. Condensed heavy typeface designs create a stronger contrast with the adjacent body copy text and make the headlines more noticeable.

9. Avoid unnecessary borders. Don't add a four-sided box around your pages unless you want to communicate a classic or dignified appearance. Boxed borders are often added out of habit, rather than as a deliberate design decision. Experiment with just a pair of thick horizontal rules (lines) to separate header information (publication title and page number) from the text columns. Experiment with rules of different thickness and try using a thicker rule at the bottom of a page to weight the page.

10. Employ a limited color palette whenever possible. The fewer colors you use, the better. Just because you have access to a virtually unlimited selection of colors doesn't mean you should use them all! Choose a few colors carefully and use them consistently throughout your documents. Use a few key colors to create a unique identity, or look, that unifies every ad, brochure, fact sheet, newsletter, and training document you create.

With color, less is usually more. The most striking documents often only employ a second, or accent, color once or twice on a page.

11. Use color with care. Color is often used to draw attention to text, but, paradoxically, color often makes text harder to read. Headlines set in color, for example, often lack the legibility of black against white. Instead of setting headlines or publication titles in color, consider reversing the text out of a colored background. Always strive for maximum legibility. Avoid setting dark blue text against a light blue background, for example. Finally, if you do decide to set text in color, slightly increase its size or use a boldfaced type to compensate for reduced legibility. A final trap to avoid is setting headlines in colors so bright that they attract attention to the detriment of the text they introduce, which defeats the whole purpose of the headlines!

12. Use screened, or tinted, colors with care. Be very careful when running shades of color, percentages like 20, 40, or 60 percent. Often, strong, vibrant colors turn weak when screened. Red turns to pink, for example, and a strong green turns into a slightly seasick shade when screened. Always remember that there is a world of difference between what you see on the monitor and what will emerge from the printing press. Colors on the monitor are projected, whereas colors on printed publications are reflected. What looks good on screen often looks weak when printed.

In conclusion, Roger reminds us that you only get one chance to make a first impression. Just as you wouldn't trust a lawyer or a surgeon who showed up for a serious office visit wearing a pair of ripped Bermuda shorts and a paint-smeared T-shirt, your readers are going to make an immediate read or not read, trust or don't trust decision based on their initial impression of your document. Design integrity, based on restraint and careful attention to detail, isn't a luxury; it's a requirement if your message is going to receive the attention it deserves.

"Desktop publishing design," Parker says, "is as much an art as a science." But, he continues, "It's an art that shouldn't overwhelm the message." He reminds us to always keep the readers, the audience, and the competition in mind when designing your publications, and to train ourselves to exercise consistency and restraint.

Chapter 27

PHOTOGRAPHY

If the purpose of an ad is to introduce a product to a prospective consumer, think of a visual as a handshake. Blocks of copy, on casual glance, look pretty much alike; photographs and illustrations catch immediate attention, welcoming the reader into an ad. Without an attention-getting visual, your target reader may never make it to the first sentence.

Unbroken blocks of text also intimidate readers. Graphic art (and white space) allow a page to breathe, and ultimately they give an ad (and your company) style.

Consequently, much thought should be given to a number of concerns:

- Which is more appropriate: Photo or illustration? Color or black and white?
- How do you judge the impact of a visual?
- Should you create a new visual image or use existing stock?
- Can you do it yourself or should you hire a pro?
- How and where do you find the right technician for the job? What's a fair price?
- What's the step-by-step process in getting your concept accurately materialized in the final image?
- What's your design budget? Often this last factor determines the other variables in the equation. Without exception, color costs more than black and white.

Having decided that visual art is a key part of your campaign, the next decision is: Photograph or illustration? Cost is always a factor, but there is no rule of thumb. An illustration can be rendered at a drafting table less expensively than airlifting a photographer to the polar icecap. On the other hand, a LeRoy Niemann color painting of a racehorse will probably cost more than a color photograph of the same. Budgeting aside, many factors will affect your choice.

THE ADVANTAGES OF PHOTOGRAPHS

Some of the advantages of photos are:

- They are real, hence, more believable. Terry C. Smith, communications manager at Westinghouse, attests: "Nothing beats an actual photograph for adding authenticity."
- Certain products demand it, especially if stylishness is part of their appeal (e.g., cars, sportswear, fine china, jewelry) or if the package is particularly eye-catching.
- If the product is new and unfamiliar to consumers, a photo proves that it exists.
- Before-and-after comparisons are possible.
- Photos depict tangible benefits of a product, such as compactness (laptop PC shown carried by consumer) or design innovations.
- Product use can be demonstrated, especially through a step-by-step photo sequence.

An effective photograph has to accomplish many things:

- It must be eye-catching; it should hook a viewer with something familiar or something strikingly different.
- It should stand out distinctively from its surroundings, including other photographs.
- It should avoid clichés.
- By conveying tone and mood, it must reflect on the product (and your company) in a complimentary fashion. An ad does more than direct sell; it enhances public relations.
- A photo should look professional, not like a high school internship project. It should be crisp, with true colors and appropriate special effects.

Perhaps the ideal negative role model is the proverbial bikini-clad vixen posed alongside, say, a high-pressure containment vessel. Scantily clad females are eye-catching, especially advertising a sauna, wine coolers, or Caribbean resorts; badly used, they can distract from the product, add gratuitous salaciousness to ads that don't require it, and convey a mood ranging from the frivolous to the absurd. So used, they require and demonstrate no imagination on the part of ad designers. Another reason bikini-bait can backfire is that a growing number of business prospects are female, and they resent this sexist approach to advertising.

KNOW THE FIELD

Having decided to go with a photograph, the first step is to study the competition. What do others in your field use in their ads? Are they effective or ineffective by the standards listed in the previous section? Scrutinizing other ads can give you ideas on what to do, what not to do, and how to avoid the obvious and overdone. Positioning yourself distinctively vis-à-vis the competition demands that you be familiar with their approaches.

GET THE PICTURE

There are three ways to acquire photographs:

1. Hire a photographer.
2. Take them yourself.
3. Buy existing prints.

1. Hiring Professionals

This is the most expensive way to acquire photographs, but carries the best assurance of quality. Photographers' fees vary widely, from a hundred dollars per day to several thousand. As with most independently contracted creative services, there are many patterns but few standards.

Price will depend on the level of sophistication you desire as well as the particular level of expertise and fee schedule of the professional you hire. Rates may be negotiable. Day rates are often determined by the target medium, such as the number of different magazines in which an ad will run, or the circulation of a specific periodical in which the ad will appear.

Know what you're getting for your money: Does the fee include expenses (film, props, processing, special effects), or will these be extra? Is travel included? Avoid the shock of last-minute surcharges by asking up front.

Where to locate a photographer? The Yellow Pages, studios, and camera shops are sources for local pros. Newspapers have staff photographers who moonlight, and editors can recommend reliable freelancers. Regional magazines are also good sources of freelance talent; check photo credits of shots you find appealing and call the editors. The fine arts departments of nearby colleges or universities can recommend faculty or qualified students (the latter are a good source of inexpensive, promising talent).

During an interview, examine the photographer's portfolio for craftsmanship. Technical skills are important, as is personal style. Since you'll be paying for both, you should have a good idea what to expect. If your ad photo will be in color, make sure you see color samples. Pay attention to details such as purity of colors, range of tones, and whether the prints are clean and the composition attractive. Note special effects (and overuse of such). If your requirements call for shooting in an industrial setting, is the person behind the lens suited to the task? All photographers have specialties. Some excel at glamour and fashion or meticulously sculpted stills of inanimate objects. Others focus best on nature panoramas or machinery. Some can handle any challenge. Your product, standing alone under the harsh glare of studio lights, may lack dynamic. But, as New York lensman and *Life* magazine contributor Jan Staller explains, "A professional can make a boring subject interesting with good photography."

Ask for references, and don't be afraid to call them. Questions you might ask are: Does this photographer follow instructions and deliver as promised? Is he or she cooperative and easy to work with?

You can describe your ideas to photographers and have them shoot to your specs, or you can allow them a free hand to work their creative magic within certain guidelines. Often, the best result is a combination of the two. But you should know what you want and be able to explain it so the assignment is understood.

Generally, a layout is provided, sketching your (or an art director's) conception of the ad, including size, placement of copy and visuals, color (if any), and graphic parameters. It may help for the artist to talk with the graphic designer about type specs and the particular reproduction process being used. The more a photographer knows about the final application, the better the chances that the final prints will be what you asked for and that no loss of quality will occur in reproduction.

A written agreement or purchase order should be drawn up, specifying fees, obligations, deadlines, and definitions of satisfactory completion of the assignment. This will help you avoid misunderstandings, hidden charges, or your having to pay for substandard work (not to mention inconvenient court appearances).

2. Taking Your Own

Taking your own photos can be an exciting adventure, a risky proposition, or both simultaneously. When you click the shutter yourself, you have greater control over the final product. Consequently, you have no one to blame but yourself if you don't like the results.

If you're fairly proficient with a camera and darkroom techniques (or work closely with someone in a developing lab), you can save a lot of preliminary headhunting and interviewing by getting behind the lens yourself. But if your forte is vacation snapshots with an Instamatic, creating your own ad photo could be iffy. Although modern cameras boast ever simpler operation while eliminating a lot of guesswork, achieving an ad-ready shot isn't as easy as it sounds. Such variables as color, lighting, depth of field, and tonal range require a trained eye. You could waste a lot of time (and money) trying to do it yourself, only to end up having to hire a professional to get it done right.

Legal Note: Shots of people add life to an ad. However, courts have ruled a person's privacy can be violated if a recognizable image—not just a face—appears in an ad without permission. When shooting candids (e.g., at the beach, office, or supermarket) or using old pictures, if you intend to use any people other than hired models in your ad, get them to sign releases. Get their signatures before you shoot, to avoid having to retake the shots if they refuse permission.

3. Licensing Stock Shots

Stock photo houses keep files of photographs by category that they supply for a price. This method is obviously impractical if you intend to depict your own product. But for illustrative effects such as a sunset, a traffic jam, or a clock striking midnight, buying stock photos might be the easiest and least expensive route.

You can also acquire photos for free or at reasonable cost from libraries, newspapers, PR agents, museums, and government agencies. Software companies such as Comstock publish photos in computer format, including vacation, business, household, and technology images.

When using any of the above sources, be aware of possible copyright infringement issues. Inquire whether a particular photo is licensed for commercial use before you use it.

PRODUCING YOUR OWN

Plan Your Shots

Draw up a shoot list. This is an agenda of photos that must be taken, and it should be organized in such a way as to maximize convenience. This will save time, and since many photographers charge by the day, it also saves money.

The shoot list should specify locations (including travel), sets, models' costumes, props, and special effects. Make sure each element is ready (or will be delivered) in time for the shoot, hopefully beforehand to avoid last-minute anxiety when something (or someone) is missing. Shooting at the photographer's own fully equipped studio will always save travel expenses and usually saves time.

If you are traveling, arrange to complete all shots on one location before moving on to the next. Schedule locations in a geographically logical sequence to minimize travel and backtracking. Think ahead: If you envision a long campaign for the same product, have extra shots taken to stockpile for future use. If you're planning a slide presentation of your product line, have the shots taken with slide film, from which prints can easily be made for ads. As long as you've contracted the photographer's services and all the elements are in place, everything may as well be done at once. Get the maximum number of shots possible out of your agreement with the photographer. The greater the volume of material generated (provided quality is not spared), the wider your selection and the greater its possible application.

Preparing the Set

If you watch a professional arrange a set for a shoot, you will notice great attention paid to minute, cosmetic detail. Since many details aren't detectable until viewing a finished print, the advantage of hiring a seasoned pro instead of doing it yourself is obvious.

Cameras do not see what the human eye sees. They magnify certain characteristics and completely miss others. But in the final analysis, your ad photo shouldn't imply: "You had to be there." It either captures the essence or it doesn't. If the shoot is prepped by a knowledgeable professional, the wrinkles, shadows, and stray lint will be instinctively taken care of.

However, if you're doing it yourself, the following is a (necessarily partial) checklist of details to note. Even with a competent professional behind the lens, remember that you are the client and the finished product should reflect your needs, not the photographer's. When you (or your art director) are supervising a session, if something seems amiss or not quite what you wanted, point it out before the shutter clicks.

Framing

This is the actual composition of the photo as seen through the camera's viewfinder. Composition can, of course, be corrected in the darkroom via cropping (editing) and retouching. But while you can easily take away during processing, it's more difficult to add something left out of the original shot. You must guide the photographer, especially regarding the use of props, arrangement of models, color, and lighting. By working closely with the technicians, you can orchestrate an entire tableau to tell a story.

Background

Your background should be harmonious with the objects being photographed. Backgrounds can also clash for dramatic or humorous effect, but they should not distract to the point of upstaging the photo's focal point. Excessive clutter makes a photograph busy, reducing its impact. Any dirt—from stray threads, dust, and fingerprints on windows to bits of tape and exposed clips, perhaps even the odd insect wandering across the set—should be removed.

Unwanted Lettering

Avoid anything that can be read on props. Wall signs, brand names (other than your own), book titles, and newspaper headlines are examples, unless these are conspicuous for deliberate effect.

Sweat

Unless you're advertising athletic shoes or air conditioners, watch for it. Sweat can create glare from a flash or look just plain grungy. Adjust the temperature in the studio, mop the model's brow, or apply pancake powder to avoid unnecessary shine.

Shooting Time

Shooting models early in the day guarantees a fresher look and avoids clothing fatigue (wrinkles and wilted collars).

Colors

Sharp, solid colors, often contrasting with the product or model, add an immediate impact and grab attention. Even if you're shooting in black and white, sharp visual juxtapositions prevent muddiness and highlight important features.

Dates

Unless they are intended for one-time immediate or seasonal use, don't date your shots. Wall calendars, holiday trappings, and soon-to-be-out-of-fashion attire can make photos obsolete by the time they are in print.

Keep in mind at all times that even though there are tried-and-true formulas for successful photos, the most imaginative often break the rules to create the most visual excitement. If you can afford to experiment, don't be afraid to try something different.

Processing

Developing and printing are as important as shooting in the photographic arts. Such techniques as burning in (darkening), dodging (lightening), toning, airbrushing, and screening are available to the darkroom technician. Different grades of paper, lens filters, and enlargements or reductions can all improve the impact of photos. Special effects, such as multiple exposures or silhouetting, can create stunning dreamscapes. Conversely, if done carelessly or artlessly, they can ruin an otherwise effective shot.

Discuss your ideas with the photographer and listen to any suggestions. He or she knows from experience what's possible. When skillfully applied by adept veterans, corrective touch-up is undetectable and can improve a print's impact by as much as 50 percent.

For photo selection, the photographer will supply contact sheets. These are pages of actual size (meaning small, 20 to 35 per page) positives of all negatives from a session. They should be examined with a magnifying glass.

As a photo is enlarged, the sharpness of the image is reduced, and graininess increases. However, if its final destination is a highway billboard, the graininess won't matter because from a distance, the eye automatically reduces the larger-than-life image to a smaller, less-detailed size. Reductions of 8" × 10" prints lose incidental detail and subtle textures. These inevitable consequences should be taken into account during the shooting stage.

Except in rare instances, you will not be accompanying the photographer into the darkroom, so your processing instructions should be carefully explained.

Storage

Negatives, contact sheets, and prints should be stored in protective folders, away from light and high temperatures. When handling negatives, do not touch either surface with your fingers. If you jot down notes on the backs of photos, do not use a sharp ballpoint pen (which will make an impression) or certain indelible markers (which may bleed through). To avoid scratching negatives and prints, don't attach paper clips to them or store them with stapled literature.

28 ILLUSTRATION

THE ADVANTAGES OF ILLUSTRATIONS

Some advantages to using illustrations are:

- Generally speaking (with many exceptions, however) art costs less than photography.

- It's easier to make changes to an illustration. It's usually too impractical (and expensive) to reschedule and re-create an elaborate photo shoot.

- With repeated use, artwork, especially a logo, becomes emblematic of your company's product. You can save money and reinforce an image by recycling illustrations.

- For instructive or data-supportive purposes you can use flow charts, diagrams, maps, and scales. These can be produced inventively and precisely with computer graphics.

- Simple illustrations are good for symbolic shorthand. Think of highway signs that convey important information (steep grade, deer crossing, two-way traffic) via simple drawings that are universally recognizable.

- If your product is unattractive, a drawing can give an impressionistic artist's rendering, softening harsh features.

- If the product doesn't exist yet—a building under construction, design samples, or next year's model—it can be depicted to create anticipation in the reader.

- Cross-sections or exploded views detail the inner workings of appliances or complex technology.

- Because photographs must reflect reality (even if surrealistically staged), the medium has inherent limitations. The wilder the effect, the higher the cost. The more your desired visual is inclined toward the land of make believe, the likelier it can be created by an artist, whose only limitation is the imagination. Cartoons and caricatures, in particular, give ads a fun, mischievous appearance.

With illustrations, more so than with photos, the sky's the limit. A photograph, even one employing spectacular darkroom wizardry, ultimately must capture the real. An illustration can more easily explore the unreal. You can't photograph a unicorn, but you can draw one. The next section describes 11 categories of illustrations.

TYPES OF ILLUSTRATIONS

Drawings

A drawing is a freehand sketch, using any writing utensil: pen and ink, pencil, crayon, felt-tip marker, or chalk. Any of these media can be used for different effects. For a new line of children's jumpsuits, a playfully rendered crayon scribble could catch the attention of parent readers. Drawing tools, skillfully applied, can convey elegance, economy, or stylishness. Cartoons, once considered juvenile, are excellent visual accompaniments for youth-oriented products or for creating a mischievous image. Caricatures can also add flair in the right context.

Paintings

Paintings are easy enough to visualize, ranging from a few abstract splashes of acrylic to Hieronymous Bosch's nightmarish "Garden of Earthly Delights." Hiring painters can be an expensive but classy way to make your ad stand out.

From watercolors and pastels to airbrushed designs, paintings are distinctive and add a touch of sophistication. The only thing they lack is realism; hence, paintings are better suited to creating moods than to depicting products. Many corporations have made effective use of timeless masterpieces from da Vinci to van Gogh; discretion should be used, however, to avoid pretentiousness.

Maps

Maps express location with greater visual impact than words. The phrase "30 outlets nationwide" conveys less than 30 red pinpoints on a map of the United States. Depending on the scope of your sales network, maps can depict towns, states, countries, continents, worlds, or galaxies. They can be rendered by hand or by computer graphics.

Diagrams

Diagrams can visually express how your product, system, or process works. They can consist of a few basic lines and arrows or a complex schematic that may be understood only by technical specialists. Block diagrams show a series of boxes representing related elements in a network or system, with each box separately labeled and connected by arrows. Each box could represent steps on an assembly line, or a mainframe linked to user terminals, or the manufacture-to-marketing process of garden supplies. Flow charts are also used to depict sequential steps.

Cross-Sections or Cutaways

These detail the internal assembly of appliances and machinery, or in-wall or underground installations. Some devices, such as security systems, motors, or high-tech audio circuitry, are best illustrated in use. But they can be difficult to photograph or express in a surface drawing. Cutaways provide a glimpse of what goes on inside. Similar to the cutaway is the exploded view, which depicts a product's component elements pulled apart (exploded) to show how they're put together. Assembly instructions for the home crafter benefit from this type of drawing.

Graphs

A graph depicts a trend or pattern plotted against a web of horizontal (x) and vertical (y) axes. A wavy line, parabola, or series of zigzags illustrate the linear progress or cumulative rating of the x variable charted against the y variable. Such data as fuel efficiency, cost-effectiveness, and sales trends can be easily conveyed via graphs. A number of computer software programs are available to plot graphs. Bar charts convey similar information, but use a series of solid bars (often color-contrasted) to show comparisons in quantities or time frames, with longer bars representing higher values.

Pie Charts

A pie chart is a circle cut into slices to represent proportions and percentages. With the entire circle representing 100 percent, pie charts can reflect population breakdowns, budgetary allocations, or market shares. Often, each pie slice is shaded in a different color. These, too, can be easily and accurately created on a computer.

Tables

Tables are often rows of numbers, or characteristics arranged in columns for logical organization and comparison. Otherwise-dull tables can be dressed up by imaginative use of color or by the inclusion of icons, which are tiny, symbolic drawings (usually silhouettes) that represent units (e.g., cars, chickens. homes).

Symbols

Symbols provide a good way to express broad concepts through simple, familiar visuals. Some can be devised especially for your ad; others are universally recognized. A skull and crossbones on a label says one thing: Poison! Anyone who sees an image of Smokey the Bear knows not to play with matches. If you've ever seen the old *Alfred Hitchcock Hour*, you remember the opening credits superimposed over a few very basic contours, instantly recognizable as the Master's profile. Granted, your product may not be as familiar to the public, so symbols should be intelligently designed to evoke the broadest recognition from readers.

Clip Art

As the name implies, these are small, often thumbnail-size images that can be clipped and pasted onto a layout. Art stores carry inexpensive clip art catalogs that feature thousands of illustrations in color and black and white. Many are cute and campy, some are outrageously loony, others are generic or broadly symbolic. Sometimes you can find just the right clip for your purposes. But bear in mind that because others have equal access to the catalog, your artwork may turn up in someone else's ad.

Computer Graphics

The state of the art of computer graphics is such that almost any form of visual can be created on a computer. An entire generation of illustrators has grown up concurrently with the computer graphics revolution, and they are no less artists simply because they accomplish with a scanner and mouse what previous generations did with a sketchpad and T-square. There's a burgeoning industry of desktop publishers and computerized design studios serving every corner of the business and advertising community.

These highly skilled specialists can save you time and money by executing in 15 minutes what previously took a whole day. Another time-saving advantage is pointed out by Norman Cahn, who trains artists on computer-aided design systems: "Neither clients nor artists ever have to settle for anything they are not completely satisfied with because changes take only minutes," says Cahn. "There is less temptation to 'go with what we've got,' and more incentive to 'go for the best we can do'."

Graphs, pie charts, and perspective grids can be created with microscopic accuracy. As technology advances, the possibilities astonish. Kevin O'Rourke, vice president of Whitman Studios (Clifton, NJ), explains: "An illustration job will come in that the client is not necessarily requesting to be done on a computer. But we look at it and realize it's a natural for this high-tech approach."

Computers will not put traditional artists out of business. A canvas, a sketchpad, and a CRT all serve the same purpose: They are media on which an artist visualizes an idea. Smart illustrators, accustomed to grease pencils and Exacto knives, are learning to use new tools to make their creative concepts materialize.

In addition, computer clip art libraries are available on disk from a number of software publishers. Inexpensive CD-ROM disks, which look and are packaged like musical compact discs, feature high-resolution illustrations in a variety of styles, from a palm tree to a chimpanzee, from cats' paws to Santa Claus. One CD-ROM can hold as much as 500MB of storage space (almost 700 times that of 3.5-inch disk). The advantages are obvious. Larry Orchier of Lawrence Computer Systems (New York) attests: "A clip art library that would have taken up a foot's worth of disks, I now have on one CD-ROM, indexed and easily accessed. There's no deterioration or loss of image. It's always there."

Some clip art sources limit commercial use without permission; others are licensed for unlimited use.

WHAT TO LOOK FOR IN AN ILLUSTRATION

To judge an illustration, you should use many of the same criteria you would use for photography: The design should be clean; the periphery shouldn't distract from the focal point; all elements should complement each other and the ad as a whole (unless shock or humor is intended).

Illustrations create moods, and they should reinforce the image you wish to project for your company and products. Every aspect of an illustration has an effect on the viewer, often subconsciously. Hanks and Belliston, in their book *Rapid Viz* (William Kaufmann Inc., 1980), which teaches techniques for making rapid sketches of ideas, point out:

> People naturally tend to see visual things in common patterns. They have a tendency to read from left to right,...[and] things are usually viewed from top to bottom. If a circular pattern is used, people feel more comfortable seeing it in a clockwise direction.... Horizontal lines suggest a quiet, stable movement.... The vertical line becomes very active, suggesting movement from top to bottom. A diagonal line is dynamic. It feels like it's falling down, and suggests danger and temporariness.

Colors can create tension or alleviate it. Reds are exciting, dark colors foreboding; icy blues are cool, and rainbow patterns look festive. Give careful consideration to every nuance of an illustration before it is used in your campaign. If it is subject to misinterpretation, it could cause reader confusion. If it is offensive, it could lead to consumer backlash. Once it's out there in the world, you can't recall it—all you can do is expend a lot of effort at damage control. Study an illustration's impact from every conceivable angle, and get second opinions.

WHAT TO LOOK FOR IN AN ILLUSTRATOR

An illustrator is not a graphic artist. The latter designs and prepares printed literature for publication (supervising typography, color, layout, and paper selection). There is some overlap between fields, but many graphic artists don't illustrate, and many illustrators know nothing about graphic design. All illustrators have specialties, and you must hire the person with the right qualifications. If you want line art, don't hire a portrait artist. If a caricature is required, look for these skills in an artist's portfolio. If you need graphs and charts, make sure the artist has experience with these formats.

Note the quality and style of previous work, and suitability to the assignment. You should be comfortable with an artist's approach, because it will reflect on your company. What you see is what you're going to get. Personality should also be a factor. Some artists refuse to relinquish creative control, failing to accept the realities of the business and advertising worlds. Such unprofessional attitudes will ultimately drive them from the field or force them to adjust. Make sure the artist you're considering is accustomed to servicing the needs of clients. This will usually be obvious from a brief conversation and a glance at a portfolio, so it isn't necessary to ask.

Locating Illustrators

Many illustrators work as freelancers. Keep in mind that artists are looking for clients, and that requires visibility. They are trying to attract your attention; you only have to know where to look.

Publications. Look for artwork that impresses you in periodicals, either illustrating articles or in ads. Contact the editor, advertiser, agency, or (if signed) the artist directly. Publications that serve the interests of creative professionals often contain display or classified ads for studios or freelancers.

Referrals. Ad agencies, creative consultants, book publishers, and art studios can all recommend available talent. Unions and creative service organizations serve as resource clearinghouses, linking talent with prospective clients. Neighborhood print shops, if they don't have illustrators on staff, may farm out work to reliable independents. Ask your colleagues. Explain your needs, and follow leads. Art schools can also recommend faculty or gifted students.

Directories. National, state, and regional directories are available in a variety of fields. The Yellow Pages are a good place to start. Creative service organizations usually publish member directories that can be purchased or requested for free. Additionally, books such as the Creative Black Book (212-254-1330) or the Adweek/Art Directors' Index (212-529-5500) will be helpful.

Associations. Contact the Society of Illustrators, 128 E. 63rd Street, New York, NY 10021, 212-838-2560.

Working with Illustrators

Know what you want. In discussing concepts, be as specific as possible: color or black and white; painting, line art, or cartoon. How many drawings do you require? If you saw samples in the artist's portfolio that approximate your needs, say so. Point out similar ads that have features you like or don't like.

Without clear instructions, an artist can neither give a reliable cost estimate nor guarantee meeting your needs. Artists are good at visualizing what's in their minds, but they can't read yours. Either your art director or the hired illustrator should produce a thumbnail sketch (so named for its small scale) to indicate positioning of all the ad's elements.

Indicate the final size of the illustration, as well as the target medium (e.g., magazine, billboard, retail display), accompanying text, and type specs. It may be necessary for the artist to consult with the graphic designer about the particular reproduction process, to ensure that the finished work can be compatibly reproduced with as little distortion as possible.

The illustrator should be provided with as much background material as available: product samples, photographs, blueprints, instruction manuals, and examples of the effect you want achieved.

An agreement or purchase order should be drawn up, stating the nature of the work for hire, fees, deadlines, revisions, payment provisions, and a definition of satisfactory completion of assignment.

STAGES OF DEVELOPMENT.

Work should proceed in stages, with incremental review of progress at each stage. The initial thumbnail (or larger) sketch will determine the direction. Once this is agreed upon, work proceeds. Stage two is your review of the half-completed illustration; in stage three, the artist submits the work for final approval. If you review in stages and changes are required, they can be incorporated before the job is finished.

Bear in mind that artwork prepared for publication rarely looks exactly as it will after printing. Reduction, enlargement, screening, and paper stock will all affect the final image. If care is taken during pre-production, you can avoid unforeseen complications.

Upon completion, you are the judge of whether the work is satisfactory. Artwork pasted to a piece of board is reviewed in a less than flattering context, so you'll have to imagine the art as it will appear in the ad. Is it what the artist was hired for? Is it what you paid for? Even if the answer to either of these questions is no, a more important consideration should be: Will it do the job? Does it convey the essence of your product or service? Is it helpful, instructive, and eye-appealing? If you came across this image in a publication, would it grab your attention?

If not, it's back to the drawing board for modifications or to start over again, with the attendant unpleasantness of a dissatisfied client and (probably) a dejected or defensive artist. At that point, there's the matter of your agreement and purchase order, final settlement of which may or may not be in dispute.

ILLUSTRATION IN THE COMPUTER AGE

The rise of computer publishing offers an affordable alternative to retaining illustrators: purchase or rental of computer-based stock illustrations.

Thousands of images are available on disk, on CD-ROM, or even for downloading via the Internet. The quality of many of these computer images is spectacular, although many of them still have a distinct look and feel that identify them as computer-based.

There are many sources for stock computer images on CD-ROM. One of the best is Image Club Graphics, a division of Adobe Systems. For information, call toll-free at 800-387-9193 or visit their Web site at www.imageclub.com. Several sources of stock cartoons are listed in Appendix J.

Chapter

PRINT PRODUCTION

29

Having created text and illustrations for your campaign, the next step is turning these raw materials into a finished, printed product.

In photography, darkroom technique is 50 percent of the artistic process. So it is with print production. These are the last crucial steps before your ad, brochure, or flier is submitted for final approval to your prospective customer. The impression your presentation makes depends on the care and professional expertise of whoever attends to print production. Your photograph may be as dynamic as Avedon's; the text could be clever or rich in metaphor and subtlety; the illustration may be outright gallery-worthy. Yet sloppy, careless, or substandard print production could defuse an otherwise explosive sales pitch.

There are three elements to a printed product: text, photography, and illustration. The first stage after creating the elements is putting together a layout (or mock-up), which in its early form is known as a rough layout or simply a rough. The final layout is called a finished or comprehensive layout (comp, for short). It indicates positioning of text and visuals, and should leave no doubt as to the appearance of the final product.

A mechanical, also known as a paste-up, is the actual assembly of all art and text elements. A mechanical consists of copy and visuals pasted on stiff art board, ready for reproduction. The actual process of reproduction involves a special camera photographing the mechanical. Printing plates are made from the resulting negatives. Finally, the plates are duplicated on the press, and your job is run, hopefully resulting in the final product you envisioned.

With computers playing an increasingly pivotal role in graphic design, the layout and mechanical stages can be streamlined. Razor blades and rubber cement, once the tools of layout specialists, collect cobwebs in many studios as design-oriented software captures a larger share of the graphics market. Just because computers are used is no reason to assume your printed material will look sterile or untouched by human hands. It should, however, turn out closer to your specifications: alignments are scientifically precise, and there is virtually no loss of quality between generations (each time material is duplicated).

Regardless of the process used, care should be exercised in selecting production services, and progress should be monitored at each stage to ensure the quality of the final product.

TEXT

Blocks of text are also known as copy. They comprise the "word" component of your presentation. The printed letters themselves are called type, and they must be processed via typography, which is the art of arranging type for printing. Type must also be set (transcribed into reproducible form) by a typesetter. This is usually done by manual entry from a keyboard.

Typewriters and word processing printers are, in a sense, basic typesetting machines. Many executives still use typewritten documents for presentation purposes. But according to a Boston University study noted in *Communications Briefings*, "[Three hundred] professionals...considered typeset documents to be more credible, persuasive and professional than those turned out on a typewriter or dot-matrix printer." It is invariably worth the extra time and money to have your text typeset.

Any words you read in published material contain the following characteristics, which must be considered during (or preferably before) the typographic stage.

Size

The height and width of the lettering, usually measured in points (72 per inch) or picas (12 points or 1/6 of an inch). For comparison, most newspaper columns are set in 8- or 9-point type; headlines are generally in 18- to 54-point type. Extremely small type is difficult to read, causing eyestrain. Any type smaller than 8 point is likely to be ignored by readers (hence the phrase "fine print," referring to legal details of secondary concern set in tiny type). Type size may depend on the copyfitting requirements, that is, the amount of space allotted for text in the final design.

Font

This is the style of type. Fonts run in families, with upper- and lower-case variants, that evolved from ancient styles of calligraphy (hand-lettering), such as roman and gothic. There are hundreds of styles to choose from, each conveying a different effect. Some look modern; others have an eighteenth-century charm. Through careful selection of fonts, it is possible to convey such qualities as urgency, politeness, or even aristocracy. The tone of your text will, on a subconscious level, be affected by your choice of font. Printers provide catalogs displaying font samples.

Typeface

This refers to particular variations within a font, including boldface (thicker lettering), italics (slanted type), or such special effects as shadowing (ghost letters behind the type) or outlining (the basic configuration of the letter with no internal fill).

Kerning

Kerning is the space between letters in a line of text. Most fonts are computer based, so the kerning is controlled by the computer.

Leading

Pronounced *ledding*, this is the space between lines of type. Space between paragraphs can be different from line spacing, depending on the desired level of readability.

Justification

Type that is justified has a square look, with both column edges being perfectly straight. Unjustified type has a ragged edge, either on the right (left justified), or on the left (right justified), or on both sides. Lines that are justified have corrective spacing between words, either uneven or even (microjustification), depending on the typesetting system. This makes the column edges optically straight.

Column Width

Column width is measured in inches, picas, or characters. Avoid making columns too wide, because a reader's eyes may have difficulty shifting from one line of text to the next.

All the above choices comprise the type specifications (specs, for short). Specs are provided to the typesetter, to set text per your instructions.

COPY PREPARATION

In the old B.C. (before computer) days, copy was sent to the typesetter on standard 8 1/2 × 11-inch bond paper, and a tiny minority of businesses still do it this way.

If you give a printer hard copy to typeset, it should be typed neatly, double-spaced, on one side of each page only. Any corrections should be absolutely clear. Typesetters are not paid to decipher sloppily altered copy, and if they can't make sense of your corrections, time and money will be wasted (probably yours). Before you send copy to the typesetter, have it proofread. Any corrections should be made in ink, not pencil, and indicated directly on the copy, rather than on little scraps of paper stapled or taped to the margins, which can be lost or misunderstood. Any mistakes in spelling or punctuation will not be corrected by the typesetter; they will be set as submitted.

Make certain that the pages are numbered consecutively, and that each page is identified at the top by a helpful title—company name, assignment, or project heading—to avoid a possible mixup if the pages get separated.

After the copy has been typeset, you will receive galleys, which are long sheets of copy to be cut and pasted onto the mechanical (either by the printer or by a graphic artist). Galleys must be proofread, preferably against the original text. Typesetters make mistakes: Words get misspelled, lines are left out, paragraphs become transposed. If mistakes are the fault of the typesetter, indicate corrections on the galleys (usually in blue, nonreproducible pencil) or in the margins. However, if errors appeared in your original document, amending the galleys or asking for major editing may be cost-prohibitive without having the entire job (paragraphs or pages) redone—for an extra charge. That's why you should double check all text before sending it to be typeset.

Typesetting via Computer

The entire process explained above can be done on a computer, particularly with a desktop publishing system with all text entry, editing, and type specs done on-screen. Many programs (such as PageMaker and Aldus FreeHand) are available that allow the user to incorporate visuals for constructing an entire layout on-screen.

You can save a lot of time and money by doing your own typesetting. Any of various Macintosh programs or IBM desktop publishing and design programs allow more immediate control over the typesetting process—including editing, corrections, last-minute revisions, and paste-up. Hundreds of fonts and typefaces are available. If you plan to generate a lot of printed material, you should consider shopping around for your own in-house typesetting system.

If your text was generated on a word processor, you can submit your documents to the printer on disk or over the phone via modem. Check with your printer about the compatibility of your respective software programs. Though there are industry standards (such as ASCII, a common encoding system for binary data), not all computers can communicate with each other directly. However, it is possible to have data converted from one format to another via conversion programs. The advantage to using disk or modem is that it eliminates having a typesetter re-key (enter on a keyboard) the text. The disk (properly converted to a compatible format) is loaded, and the text pops up on the screen. This saves time, reduces production costs, and avoids errors during retyping.

Most printers and graphic design studios can accept a standard file from your computer sent via E-mail as an attached file. Four-color designs and sophisticated page layouts are best transmitted on a Sytek or similar disk.

Optical character scanners are also available that work like fax machines hooked up to a computer instead of to a telephone. A document is fed into the unit, which reads a page of text, recognizes characters (in hundreds of fonts and dozens of languages), and converts the text to any of several standard formats on-screen, at which point the text can be edited.

PHOTOGRAPHY

Graphics arts photography (preparing photos for print) uses much the same technology as creative art photography: cameras, film, negatives, and light-sensitive paper.

The actual processing of the photo will be done by the printer. But an understanding of the process is important so you know what to expect and what can and cannot be done.

Black and White Photos

Before a black and white photo can be printed (for most purposes), it must be screened. This involves converting continuous tones to halftones.

Continuous tones are the broad range of solid and graded images the eye sees when looking at a camera-produced creative photograph. Inks cannot produce graded tones, only solids. In order to print a photograph, a halftone screen breaks a continuous-tone photograph into millions of tiny but clearly defined dots (which can be seen under a magnifying glass). The dots represent solid points having equal spacing and ink density, but different area. This creates the optical illusion of a screened photo that appears to consist of continuous textures, but is actually made up of a broken pattern. The human eye is "fooled" into seeing solid patterns.

Screening is done by a printer. The actual halftone-processed picture is called a felon and can be pasted directly onto a mechanical.

There are different kinds of halftones, such as square, highlight, vignette, and outline, that can be used for impact. Duotones, which are two-color halftones, can make a black and white photo appear to be in color. Ask your printer for samples of each technique.

Color Photos

Color photos must undergo color separation before printing. This can be done by the printer or by a graphic artist. It involves breaking down full-color images into primary color (red, blue, and green) negatives using a camera and filters. A fourth color, black, is added as a color corrector to compensate for imperfections in the process. What appears to the viewer as a full-color reproduction of the original image is actually a collage of microscopic, single-colored dots either next to or overlapping one another.

Thanks to the introduction of laser scanners that use electronic technology, the quality of color reproduction has risen while the cost has dropped. Camera color tends to be more expensive, and though many professionals still swear by camera-quality technology, each new generation of scanners improves the laser possibilities. Ask your printer about the respective advantages of each, depending on the printer's own in-house state of the art.

Regardless of the process used, contrast is important in a photo that is to be reproduced. Calvin York of Danbury Printing laments: "You'd be amazed at the number of people who bring in artwork that has a white product against a white background, or dark against dark. Using monotone colors like pinks and reds doesn't work either." There are also certain combinations that create hallucinatory effects, such as red on green and fluorescents. York adds, "What you spend on good photography, you will save at the printer's. Sharp, well-lit, good contrast pictures, in which you don't have to hunt for the product, are keys to good color printing."

The color of the paper on which the photo is printed will also affect the final image. For the purest color reproduction, a neutral shade of white works best.

Basic Checklist for Preparing Photos

Here are a few things to keep in mind when preparing your photos for printing:

- Protect photographs. Store and ship all photos in protective plastic sleeves, or attach a tissue overlay.

- Don't write on the front or back of photos. If you need to label a photograph for owner identification, placement, or captions, use adhesive labels, and write the information on the label before applying it to the back of the photo. Writing on the back of a photograph with a pen or pencil will leave a welt across the photo surface, and certain inks will bleed through to the front.

- Submit original photos to the printer, rather than reproductions. Each generation loses sharpness in color and tone.

- Specify the degree of reduction or enlargement of the photo. This is expressed in percentages: shot at 50 percent is half-size; at 75 percent is three-quarter size, and so on. A 20 percent reduction means the final image will be 80 percent of the size of the original. Art Service Technical Promotions (Loveland, CO) recommends that you avoid enlarging color prints more than 150 percent, to minimize loss of quality.

- Indicate cropping instructions. Cropping is how photos are edited; any portion of the image you don't want to appear in the final reproduction can be cut. There are three ways to indicate cropping: 1) make a Xerox copy and draw crop lines on the copy; 2) indicate crop instructions on a tissue overlay; or 3) have the picture mounted on a sheet of paper with horizontal and vertical axes (crop marks) indicating the desired cuts.

- Do not paste photos directly onto mechanicals. Though a velox can be inserted into a mechanical, original photos are handled differently. Boxes on the mechanical are labeled by the artist and keyed to visuals, indicating their respective positions, such as Photo A in Box A, and so on. To assure correct keying, apply an adhesive label to the back of a photo and write key references with a felt-tip pen, or attach the photo to a sheet of paper or artboard, and note key match-ups in the margin.

- Mount photos (and illustrations) on stiff artboard, leaving a wide enough margin to accommodate key references or special instructions. However, if laser scanning is to be used, do not mount prints on artboard. They will not be flexible enough to wrap around the cylinders of some scanners.

ILLUSTRATIONS

There are two types of illustrations: line art and continuous tone images. Line art includes simple sketches, diagrams, maps, charts, and most hand drawings. Line art does not have to be screened and can be pasted directly onto a mechanical.

Complex artistic renderings can be continuous tone images. Like photographs, they must be converted to dot-pattern halftones before they can be reproduced. Continuous tone color illustrations must also undergo color separation to create overlay transparencies.

Here again, traditional hands-on methods are giving way to modern means. Through computerized graphic arts systems, images (including continuous tones) can be fed onto magnetic tape, for instance, going directly to separation and other prepress stages without the need to create color transparencies. This eliminates an entire generation in the production process, with virtually no loss of quality. In addition, it's possible to do retouching, repositioning, color control, image enhancement, and layering, all on-screen. Special effects, such as warping (distorting) or reflecting (creating a mirror image) are simple and quick to execute. Nancy Faherty, art director at Graphics One Fifty, a New Jersey–based design studio, attests: "By going directly from the magnetic tape format and eliminating the intervening transparency stage . . . I am experiencing a new stage of design freedom."

CHECKING YOUR MECHANICAL

Before the mechanical, film, or disk goes to the printer, refer to the following checklist:

- It should be clean—not just dirt-free, but free of pencil marks, glue smudges, white-out, and paper clips. The less touch-up the printer has to do, the better.
- Everything should be pasted into final position, including headlines, text, veloxes, line art, captions, and boxes keyed to photos or other visuals to be "picked up" by the printer and inserted.

- Check spelling one last time. An error in copy could cause acute embarrassment if caught by a reader. Triple-check all text, including capitalization. Headlines in particular, the most obvious attention-getters, are sometimes overlooked while small details are checked carefully.

- Check alignment: Is everything cut and positioned squarely?

- Make sure all elements are pasted securely, so they don't slip off on the way to the printer.

- Double-check all key cross-references so their placement is clearly indicated.

- Place a tissue overlay atop the mechanical or put the film in an envelope for protection.

- Include samples of the paper stock to be used, to avoid mistakes.

- Make sure your company name is on every piece of artwork that is sent to the printer, as well as your phone number and the name of the job or purchase order number.

PAPER

Selecting the right paper for your printed material is a major decision, and because of the wide variety available, it's rarely simple. Paper thickness, weight, weave or texture, color, and ink sensitivity are all factors. The importance of good paper is emphasized in *How to Buy Printing and Related Services*, which states: "The cost of taking color pictures and having separations made is so high that these projects should be protected with…good paper to give the color work the best support possible."

Just to give a brief idea of the multitude of factors affecting choice, consider the following examples:

- Color photos always look better on glossy (coated) stock. However, because glossy finishes reflect light, they can affect readability.

- The lifespan of a piece of paper varies: Is your printed material expected to last for years, or for a few days? Permanent documents require a higher grade of paper.

- Will your literature be folded, stapled, or bound? Certain grades of paper are better suited for such use.

- Are illustrations featured? Are they two-color, four-color, or black and white? Tinted stock will affect visuals, regardless of format.

- If you plan to mail your literature, postal costs must be considered in selecting the weight of the paper.

The choices that go into paper selection are limitless, and could (and probably do) fill entire books. Zona Meravi of Printer's Place says they routinely offer advice on paper to clients. "Colors, weights, card stock—there's so much. Certain tints make illustrations stand out better. Different colored inks reproduce better on certain stocks," she says. "We always recommend printing flyers on brightly colored paper to make them more noticeable."

Your printer will, of course, be familiar with the pros and cons of various papers and can steer you toward the right paper for the job. You should also consult your art director for ideas.

FINDING A PRINTER

If you intend to do a lot of printing, it would be in your best interest to develop a solid working rapport with a reputable shop. Allen Glazer, founder of Berkeley House Publishing, recommends: "Of all your business relationships, the relationship with your printer is among the most important. You should plan to devote some time to locating a good one—maybe even a perfect one."

Some good places to find the perfect printer are:

- Those your company has used in the past with success.

- Printers who actively solicit your business, either by phone or mail. Read and file any sales literature that comes across your desk.

- The Yellow Pages. Look under Printing, Copying, Duplication Services, Invitations and Announcements, Artists—Commercial, Advertising Art, Layout and Production Service, or Graphic Designers. Some of these may not offer printing services, but they all work with printers and can probably give you references.

- Industry trade associations. The Printing Industries of America has over 9,000 members (which is fewer than 20 percent of all printers). The PIA has regional offices in many metropolitan areas, and they can recommend printers in your region to meet your exact requirements. The PIA's phone number is 703-519-8100.

- Another printing industry trade group to contact is the National Association of Printers and Lithographers, 201-342-0700.

By shopping around, you will discover quite a range of available technology, some more advanced than others. Depending on your needs and your budget, inquire about the particular services each offers and get several cost estimates before selecting the right one for you. Glazer points out that, "...in most cases, 25 to 75 percent of a direct mail budget will go to the printer. And...you'll discover that prices can vary greatly—often by as much as 30 percent or more."

Besides saving money, a trusted, reliable printer is an adjunct to your business. He or she can offer advice and helpful shortcuts. Printers, like any entrepreneurs, appreciate repeat customers; a shop to which you bring a steady flow of work will go out of its way to deliver exactly to your specifications.

For an in-depth discussion of modern production, see *Pocket Guide to Digital Prepress* (Delmar Publishers, 1996) by Frank J. Romano.

Part **IV**

ELECTRONIC MARKETING

Chapter 30

Fax Marketing

Faxes are, and will continue to be, everywhere. The fact is, more professionals rely on the fax to communicate externally than on any other communications device except the phone. With this much use—and usage is growing exponentially—it's important to use fax technology in the most efficient and productive manner possible.

FAX ON DEMAND (FOD)

Imagine serving your customers—while you sleep. What happens when a potential customer hears about one of your products and wants more information? People are busy these days. The prospects are interested now. If they have to wait until tomorrow, they may never get around to contacting you. But wait, there is a great new solution: fax on demand. Now your customers and potential customers can call your office at any time, day or night, to request information, and your computer will fax them the information they request in seconds—without operator intervention. This is fax on demand, and it serves your customers while you sleep.

FOD automates requests for information. Documents such as price lists, product spec sheets, and order forms are stored in a computer's memory and made available for instant retrieval, via fax, 24 hours a day, 7 days a week. Callers dial an 800 number and are greeted with a welcome message. Voice prompts then direct callers to enter a code for the documents they want, along with their fax numbers, on their touch-tone phones. When the request is complete, the computer searches its memory, locates the requested documents, and transmits them to the prospect's fax machine; 99 percent of all documents are faxed within one minute.

- **Get 'em while they're hot.** You want potential customers to get information on your product now—while they are still thinking about it. If you mail the brochure, they won't get it for two to four days, and may have cooled or be otherwise distracted. A quick response to customer requests for information can mean the difference between making a sale or losing it, between building customer trust or risking it, or between superior customer service and business as usual. With fax on demand, you can deliver accurate, timely documents into the hands of your customers when they need them. Your FOD service is open 24 hours a day, 7 days a week, with no overtime costs. FOD allows you to stretch your business day to accommodate your customers coast to coast and even around the world, without straining your budget.

On the road and need a telephone number or other information from one of your documents? Call your own FOD system.

- **Save time and money.** You can deliver product fliers, price lists, and news releases at the speed of light. With FOD, you save on printing, envelopes, postage, and staff time. Now you do not have to answer the telephone, write down what the customer wants, find the brochures and other documents, stuff them into an envelope, and add the postage. You can spend your time filling orders. With FOD, the response time is faster day or night, at no additional cost for labor, mailing, or printing.

- **Sender or caller may pay to send the documents.** On some FOD systems only one line is required. Callers pay for both their (incoming) call and the return fax because they are calling from the handsets on their own fax machines and the fax information is sent while the line is still open. There is no complicated number-punching for international calls because the open line is used for the return fax. Documents are kept private because the caller is still at the fax machine when the document arrives. You could also offer the service on an 800 number and pay for both the incoming call and the outgoing fax. Most systems give you the choice. The caller can call in from a fax handset or a touch-tone telephone and the sender can send the documents out on the same call (if it's from a fax) or a new one (if it's from a telephone). Some of the systems require two or more lines and will not return the fax on the same incoming call.

- **Collecting money.** Some FOD systems have a module that allows customers to charge the documents they wish to buy to a credit card. They validate card numbers through your mini terminal. Other systems will add this feature soon.

- **How much can you charge?** One firm that tracks bills through a state legislature charges $15 per call and $2 per page after two pages. Requests can be charged to a credit card or to a prepaid account.

- **Is FOD for my company?** If your sales are mostly business-to-business, then FOD should work well because most businesses have fax machines. If most of your sales are to individuals, then FOD may not be successful for you.

Fax on Demand Systems

There are two types of systems. Here are examples of each.

FOD Computer Boards

This system has boards (a voice-processing card and fax card on one or two boards), a speaker, and software that you install in an IBM 486 or Pentium personal computer. If you have to buy a new computer, monitor, and keyboard, you should expect to pay $1,000 to $1,200.

Just load your documents and store them on the hard disk. Connect the computer to a dedicated (new) telephone line.

Contact these suppliers for the latest information on their systems. Specifications and addresses change from time to time. Please send us any corrections you may discover, but please **do not** call us for new numbers.

1. *Fax-It-Back* from Castelle, 800-995-9141, for $995. This is a dedicated FOD system. Requester may call from a fax machine or telephone. You need a 486 or better computer with two half-size slots available and at least a 250MB hard disk, 8MB RAM, MS Windows 95 or higher, and one telephone line.

2. *PhoneOffices* from Comline Systems, 714-641-1235 for $495. This Windows program has call directing, voice mail, and fax on demand. Requires a 386 or better PC.

3. *FactsLine* by Ibex, 800-975-4239, from $6,300 for a basic Windows-based system. *FactsLine* can accept calls from a telephone and includes options as to who pays for the return fax. It also provides voice mail. It requires a 486-66 or faster computer with Windows 3.1 and DOS, 4 MB of RAM, and an 80 MB or larger hard disk.

4. *FaxBack*™ from FaxBack, 800-329-2225, for $8,450 to $13,950. *FaxBack* is a powerful system with a lot of options but is higher priced. There is a software module that will allow you to sell information while you sleep: It will automatically accept and verify credit cards before sending the fax. *FaxBack* requires a Pentium or faster computer.

5. *FaxBack Lite* from FaxBack, 800-329-2225, starting at $2,995, can be managed from a touch-tone phone or fax machine. For minimum installation, it requires a 386 PC, 4MB RAM, 4MB available hard drive space, one available serial port, and Windows 3.1 or higher.

6. *FaxFacts* by Copia, 630-682-8898, from $3,565 for DOS and $4,195 for NT. A voice board, fax board, and software you add to a PC running under MS-DOS or Windows NT. Price are calculated per line. Choice of one-call and call-back methods of fax delivery. *FaxFacts* has a credit card verification option.

7. *Command Fax* from Nuntius, 314-968-1009, from $800, requires base system with between two and six open slots, 8MB memory, color monitor, graphics card, DOS 5.0 or above, and 40MB hard disk. An endless number of applications can be used with *CommandFax*. Multilingual callers can listen to voice messages in their own languages and broadcast fax capabilities are built in.

8. *The Small Business Assistant (SBA) for Windows* from Essential Data, Inc., 800-795-4756, starts at $345 for two-line software and $395 for the two-line Bicom Voice Board. *SBA* runs under Microsoft Windows 3.1 or Windows 95 operating systems with at least 8MB RAM and a 486SX/33 or better processor.

9. *Info-on-Call* by TTC Computer Products, available from Essential Data, 800-795-4756, is a program for building customized interactive voice response systems using a PC with voice or fax modem card. With *Info-on-Call*, your computer can be your telephone operator, voice mail recorder, and automated fax machine all in one. *Info-on-Call* for Windows is priced at $295.

10. *Telepro 2.0* from Essential Data, Inc., 800-795-4756, $345 to $745, is a DOS-based multiline voice mail product that can handle 2 to 24 lines. When using the Bicom, NewVoice, or Dialogic boards, *Telepro* can run in the background under Windows.

11. *VoiceFX* from Orion Telecom, 800-669-8088 or 800-371-1760, is voice mail software that handles up to four phone lines, offers autoattendant capabilities, and provides extensive fax-back and fax on demand features. Fax retrieval can be done either by calling from a touch-tone fax machine or by calling from a touch-tone phone and entering the phone number of the desired fax machine. *VoiceFX* is available in three versions: MS-DOS, Windows, and Windows 95.

12. *Document on Demand* from Trio Community, 800-880-4400 or 919-846-4990, starting at $2,495, is a module providing a set of tools for building your own system for document retrieval. Documents may be either voice messages or fax documents. An easy-to-use Drag and Drop Windows interface lets you create a catalogue of documents that the caller can request and have automatically delivered by fax or voice.

13. *BitWare Plus* 4.0 from Cheyenne Software, 516-465-4000, $199.95, offers a sophisticated fax on demand as well as voice on demand in its standard package.

14. *InfoFast* v.1.0 from Artisoft, 800-233-5564, at $1995, will support two voice lines and one fax line and is scalable to eight voice lines and four fax lines. System and other requirements include a 486-66 MHZ processor or higher, Microsoft Windows 95, 16MB RAM, 34MB hard disk space, 2 slots, and a CD-ROM drive.

15. *Boca Multimedia Modem* with *FaxWorks* 3.0 included is a 14.4 modem available for DOS or Windows for $245.

16. *WinFaxPro* with *TalkWorks*™. Software you install in a computer with a fax voice board.

17. *FAXGenie* stores up to 99 documents. Talking Technology, 1125 Atlantic Avenue, Alameda, CA 94501, 800-395-4884.

18. *SuperVoice Pro*, $149.95, Pacific Image Communications, 2121 W. Mission Rd., Suite 301, Alhambra, CA 91803, 818-457-8880. Fax: 818-

457-8881. E-mail: PaxImage@deltanet.com. If your computer has an 80 MB hard drive, it will store about 2,000 pages of documents.

Self-Contained, Stand-Alone FOD Machine

This is a single box with a computer, voice board, fax board, and software. Just load your documents from a fax machine or PC and store them on the hard disk. Customers may call in from a telephone or fax machine.

1. Brother MFC 6550 from Brother, 800-284-4329, $1,800 suggested retail, is a 6-in-1 fax machine, copier, scanner, FOD system, 600 dpi printer, and voice mail or fax message center.

2. QuadraFax from Brooktrout Technology. The unit costs under $2,600 for four ports and under $2,000 for two ports. You can contact them directly at 410 First Avenue, Needham, MA 02194, 617-449-4100 or 617-433-9553 (sales coordinator). Fax: 617-449-3171. For their FOD demo, call 800-333-5274, or visit them at their Web site: http://brooktrout.com.

How Fax on Demand Works

Make up a menu or table of contents of all the brochures, free reports, short lists, news releases, and other documents you mail free to customers who call for information. Don't mail a heavy package; just fax them this one- or two-page FOD menu. This is much less expensive than mailing all the documents. Customers are not only impressed with your responsiveness, they get the information instantly—when they need it.

Your FOD number and table of contents can be stored in your (small) ads, brochures, letterhead, answering machine recording, direct mail solicitations, and other promotions. Existing and potential customers can call at any time for a current list of free documents. When customers call your FOD number, they are prompted by digitally recorded messages. If they know the number of the document they want, they can punch in the number on the keypad. Otherwise, they can request your complete menu. Once they punch in the numbers of the documents they want, they are asked to press the Start button. The requested documents are received by their fax machine, and they simply hang up the handset.

For a demonstration and to get more information on book promotion, pick up the handset on your fax machine and call Para Publishing, 805-968-8947. Request Document 109 for a list of free documents on book marketing, promoting, and distributing. For demonstrations and to get more information on FOD systems, pick up the handset on your fax machine and call:

- SpectraFax: 800-833-1329

- Brooktrout for information on the QuadraFax: 800-333-5274

- Castelle for details on Fax-It-Back: 800-289-9998 or 415-380-2561

- Comline Systems for details on PhoneOffice: 714-641-1235

- ComArt International for details on Faxcess: 800-FAX-DEMO, Doc 455
- Ibex for details on FactsLine: 800-289-9998
- FaxBack, Inc. for details on FaxBack™ and FaxBack Lite: 800-FAX-BACK (329-2225) or 503-614-5372
- Trio for details on Document on Demand: 919-846-4935
- Novacore Technologies for details on Novafax: 508-371-2424
- Copia for details on FaxFacts: 847-923-3030
- Nuntius Corporation for details on CommandFax: 314-776-7076
- Essential Data for details on Small Business Assistant, InfoOnCall, and Telepro 2.0: 916-692-1221
- Cheyenne for details on BitWare Plus 4.0: 516-465-5979
- Brother International for Brother MFC 6550MC: 800-521-2846

Fax Services

Service bureaus are popping up all over to provide FOD services. Many charge more per month or quarter than a simple FOD system costs. However, if you decide that setting up your own system is too complicated, you may wish to subcontract to a fax service. Contact them for prices and further information.

Auditory Communications Corp.
Steven Draksler
4541 N. Prospect Road, Suite 101
Peoria, IL 61614
Tel: 309-686-7770
Fax: 309-686-7773
E-mail: sdraksler@auditory.com
Web Site: http://www.auditory.com

Epigraphx Automated Fax Services
965 Terminal Way
San Carlos, CA 94070
Tel: 415-802-5858
Fax: 415-802-5850
FOD Demo: 800-959-9908
Web Site: http://www. epigraphx.com

Faxt Telysis, Inc.
11740 Dublin Blvd., Suite 102
Dublin, CA 94658
Tel: 800-551-6970 or 510-829-6390
Fax: 510-829-3995
E-mail: TucherD@rest.com
Web Site: http://www.mast.ent.com

Global Fax Network, Inc.
8885 Rio San Diego Drive, Suite 255
San Diego, CA 92108
Tel: 619-491-2995
Fax: 619-491-2905
E-mail: rlee@glogalfax.com

MCI Fax Reply
800-999-2096

PR Newswire
810 Seventh Avenue, 36th Fl.
New York, NY 10019
Tel: 800-832-5522 or 212-832-9400
Fax: 212-596-1537
Web Site: http://www.prnewswire.com

Prism Group
300B West Main Street
Northboro, MA 01532
Tel: 508-393-1957
Fax: 508-393-0012
E-mail: prism@prism-group.com
Web Site: http://www.prism-group.com

SpectraFax Corp.
3050 N. Horseshoe Drive, Suite 100
Naples, FL 34104
Tel: 941-643-5060
Fax: 941-643-8790
E-mail: sfc@spectrafax.com
Web Site: http://www.spectrafax.com

US West FaxRequest
Tel: 800-603-6000
FOD Demo: 800-864-4433

V*Channel, Inc.
Alan Yatagai
3080 Olcott Street, Suite 135-C
Santa Clara, CA 95054
Tel: 408-908-9999, ext. 102
Fax: 408-492-9999
FOD Demo: 408-492-1234
Web Site: http://www. vchannel.com

Xpedite Systems. Inc.
446 Highway 35
Eatontown, NJ 07724
Tel: 800-546-1541 or 908-544-9595
Fax: 800-989-5154 or 908-542-9436
FOD Demo: 800-853-5879

Modems

Get a 28.8 bps modem, as a minimum speed. Most fax machines operate at 9600 or 14.4 bps, but speeds are improving and you may wish to use the machine to access the Net or the Web. A 28.8 bps modem will cost more, but it will save you time and will save telephone charges when you use it to download programs. Make sure the modem conforms to the new industry standard called V.34. Modems with V.34 transmit at a full 28.8 bps and can handle poorer connections.

If you use a PC, make sure your input/output board's serial port is supported by a 16550 UART chip. Older computers are bottlenecked and transmit data at slower speeds, even with a fast modem.

PC Magazine rated the PC288LCD V.34 modem from Practical Peripherals the very best. At $459, it is in the medium price range. Do not buy a cheap modem; they fail to make connections and rarely run at their rated top speed. Call the Computer Network at 805-685-5040 for price and delivery.

- To load your brochures and other documents onto the hard drive of the FOD system, just plug your fax into the computer and fax them in, load them from a floppy disk, or send them from your computer with a fax board such as WINFAX. Documents loaded from a floppy or sent from a fax board will be a little clearer. Scanned from a fax machine, the documents will be in traditional 200×200 dpi resolution.

- The activity log lets you know the callers' fax numbers, what they requested, and how many of each document they requested. Callers can also leave voice messages if they wish. Now when you arrive at work, you can check your FOD machine to see who has requested what.

- Direct mail advertising. Instead of mailing to everyone in sight and hoping for a 3 percent response, with FOD only the interested potential customers will request your sales information. No more 97 percent waste.

MAGAZINES COVERING FAX ON DEMAND

Voice Processing Magazine
PO Box 6016
Duluth, MN 55806-9792
Tel: 218-723-9200
Fax: 218-723-9437
Controlled circulation; you must be a member of the industry to qualify for a free subscription.

InfoText Magazine (Free subscriptions)
9200 Sunset Blvd., #612
Los Angeles, CA 90069
Tel: 310-724-6448
Fax: 218-723-9477 (Subscription office)

Some people prefer to call this new technology Fax on Request since it sounds softer and more generous. However, the term Fax on Demand is still recognized by more people.

Fax on Demand is revolutionizing the way we do business. It is the customer service machine of the millenium. Customers want to be able to call your company in the middle of the night to get descriptions of your products and services, with prices. If you do not provide FOD, potential customers will wonder if you really are in business.

Fax on Demand will only get better. As people move to plain-paper and 14.4 bps fax machines, FOD will be used even more. As people use telephones more and area codes keep changing, customers will be less and less concerned with the call and connection time charges.

Do not ignore the Internet. All your FOD documents should be on your Web site too. Make up your documents for your FOD system and then transfer them onto your Web site.

Companies are introducing applications that enable Internet browsers to view your Web site and choose information to be faxed back to them. WebPage Fax from FaxBack, Inc., 800-329-2225 and WebFax Gateway from V*Channel, Inc., 408-980-9999 are two companies to contact. Fax on Demand saves you time and money. Now you can truly serve your customers while you sleep.

FOD AND FAX MARKETING TIPS

These tips are from Maury Kauffman, author of *Computer-Based Fax Processing* and fax columnist for *Computer Telephony Magazine*. His articles have appeared in numerous business and trade publications including *DM News, Target Marketing, Information Week, Folio*, and *Voice Processing Asia*. He is active in the direct marketing industry and is a regular speaker at voice and fax marketing conferences worldwide.

According to Kauffman, there are 86 million fax machines installed worldwide and thousands of fax modems sold monthly. A recent survey by his firm showed that 90 percent of the direct marketing professionals surveyed have tested enhanced fax technology. A Gallup poll of large and midsized companies found that 60 percent of daily fax users are faxing more than they did last year.

Just as PCs can be networked through a server, allowing resources to be distributed throughout an organization, a fax server can allow multiple users to share fax equipment efficiently and transparently.

With a LAN fax server, users fax documents created on their PCs. This is the most popular type of fax server. A dedicated fax server, by comparison, uses its own PC and provides fax services to a network. A typical fax server has access to 16 to 24 phone lines and is used when fax volume is high, a thousand pages a day or more. Such systems cost tens of thousands of dollars.

EQUIPMENT

When advertising fax machines, manufacturers tout many must-have features. You don't have to have them all.

1. Transmission speed—Faster speed does not always mean lower telephone costs. A fax's transmission speed drops to the slower rate of the two devices.

2. Memory options—Helpful, but not always necessary. If your machine is typically full of paper and available to receive incoming faxes, memory may be a moot point.

3. Paper trays—A 100-page tray is the minimum you'll want.

4. Feeders—Most machines jam at least some of the time when sending more than a few pages, regardless of feeder capacity.

5. All-in-one machines—Save these for a home office; they're not industrial strength.

6. Price—at $200, they're not going to go any lower.

7. Page rates—Rates or speeds are generally lower than manufacturers' specs.

8. Paper cutters—Make sure they are automatic.

9. Fax/phone switches—They do fail. Get a second line. If you don't, you're not really in business.

10. Gray scales—For most applications, these do not make a significant difference.

11. Resolution—200 × 100 dpi is standard and 200 × 200 dpi is as good as it gets.

12. Electronic cover pages—These have limited usefulness and programming them takes too much time.

13. Speaker phones, copy functions, and auto redial—These are standard on most fax machines.

SAVING MONEY WHEN FAXING

1. Transmit during off-peak hours when telephone rates are lower.

2. When possible, omit a full cover page. Save the paper and the transmission time and use a Post-It™ note instead.

3. Make sure your fax machine is clean. If you're not sure, send a fax to yourself using the copy function. If it comes through with lines or specs, your machine needs cleaning. Try using a hair dryer to blow out the dust.

4. Send as few pages as possible. Use single spacing and cut down on white space in the documents you send by fax.

FAX BROADCASTING

Fax broadcasting allows you to send a personalized document to hundreds, even thousands, of different locations automatically. It's an amazingly effective yet often overlooked marketing tool. To increase response rates, try fax broadcasting, and:

1. Personalize each and every fax: Use data from customer files to communicate.

2. Add a response mechanism to your fax.

3. Broadcast at night when telephone rates are lower, for maximum impact in the morning!

4. Keep the medium in mind: Photos and detailed graphics will not transmit well.

5. Don't overuse the fax or you can lose the sense of urgency.

6. Know the law. Read the Telecommunications Consumer Protection Act.

"I think it is very risky to broadcast fax to cold or new leads, people with whom you have not established a relationship," writes Dan Kennedy (*Marketing Briefing*, issue four, volume six, page 4). "This can and does work; you can make sales; but you will really aggravate a lot of people, and I wonder if doing that is smart, especially in a market you wish to live in for any length of time."

Although regulations change over time, as of this writing the Telephone Consumer Protection Act prohibits the use of telephone facsimile machines to send unsolicited advertisements Section III, Part D.2, Paragraph 54: Facsimile Machines. Kaufman says marketers should use faxes to communicate only with companies with whom they have a prior relationship, and not broadcast fax to cold prospects who don't know you (this is illegal). A "prior relationship" doesn't necessarily mean the people receiving your fax are customers; they may just have made an inquiry at one time, requesting a catalog or brochure.

"Keep an internal Do Not Fax list," advises Kaufman. "Prospects who dislike fax messages or who have communicated that they do not wish to receive faxes should be taken off your fax broadcast database." He also advocates adding the following message to the bottom of all fax broadcasts: "If you wish to be removed from our fax distribution list, call us."

SAVING MONEY WITH FAX BROADCASTING

1. Broadcast at night when telephone rates are lower.

2. Limit graphics; they transmit much more slowly than text.

3. Keep your fax to one page.

COMPILING YOUR FAX LISTS FOR BROADCASTING

1. Request fax numbers on all business reply cards and other response devices.

2. Make sure fax numbers are up to date; verify them periodically.

3. Double postcards should do double duty. Use them to clean your list and update fax numbers.

4. Consider offering an incentive to those who mail or call with updated info.

5. Your sales force should always update fax numbers when they update addresses and phone numbers.

6. Customer service reps should verify fax numbers when customers call in.

EXPANDING YOUR FAX NUMBER LIST

1. Consider an association list; typically most people in your target group belong.

2. If you need fax numbers immediately, use telemarketing to locate and verify them.

3. Once your list is compiled, make sure updates are done on an ongoing basis.

ADDITIONAL FAX ON DEMAND TIPS

1. Promote, promote, and promote some more. Send out press releases to the media and "new birth" announcements to customers and prospect lists.

2. If you want your FOD service to be used, install a dedicated 800 number.

3. Put the FOD service's 800 number on letterhead, cards, catalogs, and DM pieces.

4. Encourage employees to test the system and then recommend it to customers.

5. If you have an auto attendant on your phone system, offer FOD as an option.

6. Make your service user friendly. If your FOD service has too many levels or is confusing or complicated, callers won't call back.

7. If you are selling information, give something else away free.

8. Add coupons and special offers. This will turn first-time callers into repeaters.

9. Promote, promote, and promote—again. Send out another round of mail, faxes, etc. Keep your FOD number in front of your audience.

HIRING SERVICE BUREAUS

Costs for fax broadcasting and fax on demand applications vary depending on the volume, the sophistication of the system, and how you choose to operate the service. Most companies find that it is more cost-efficient to outsource. But how do you choose a service bureau? Here's what to ask:

1. How long have they been in business? You want to make sure that the company has a proven financial track record and will be around when you need them. (Hint: This is a new industry, but not that new. Look for four to five years of experience.)

2. Do they have state-of-the-art equipment? Do they use intelligent fax boards or Class 2 modems?

3. Ask for references and check them.

4. If the service bureau has experience, they may also be able to also provide marketing assistance.

5. Does the service have sufficient ports (phone lines) to transmit your broadcast in a timely fashion (thousands of pages per hour)?

6. Can they handle both fax broadcasting and fax on demand? You don't want to hire two vendors.

7. Price is important but should not be the overriding factor. (You get what you pay for.)

8. Turnaround time for both applications is critical. The service should be able to get a broadcast out in one day, maximum. Fax on Demand can take up to 30 days to set up, for programming, scripting, etc.

LANFAX

LANFAX technology is much like a printer server, allowing multiple users to use one fax line without standing on line. The software stores, prioritizes, and sends out faxes originating from many sources. How do you know if you are ready to consider LANFAX?

1. If you have a high volume of faxes (50 or more a day), consider LAN-FAX.

2. Do you have more than five people sharing one fax machine? Then consider LANFAX.

3. If you rely on your fax to receive incoming orders, consider LANFAX to direct outgoing transmissions.

4. Is your fax machine substituting for the water cooler? That is, are people using it as a meeting place? If that's the case, LANFAX might be right for you.

Chapter

31
MARKETING ON THE INTERNET

Unless you live in a cave or on a deserted island, you've heard a lot about the Internet and how it is revolutionizing the way computer users communicate—and how businesses market their products and services.

In his newsletter, *Publishing Poynters* (FOD #199), consultant and author Dan Poynter reports that 11 percent of the 98.7 million U.S. households are on the Internet. Of these, one out of four visits shopping sites. A study by IntelliQuest found that in the U.S., 35 million Americans—17 percent of all adults 16 or older—have used an on-line service in the past three months. Half of those surveyed said they used the Internet to obtain information for their business or work.

A 1997 survey showed executive use of the Internet varied by job title and function. Marketing, publicity, communications, and Information Systems professionals were the most eager users. Sixty-four percent of managers overall said they used the Internet.

The growth of the Internet has created a new medium for advertisers and their copywriters: Web pages. In the fourth quarter of 1996, Web ad spending in the U.S. totaled $102 million, a healthy 51 percent rise from the previous quarter. This chapter provides tips for creating an effective Web site and writing copy for the Web.

The Web is a powerful tool for generating leads and sales, especially among prospects who are computer literate, technically sophisticated, and early adapters of new products and technologies. Prospects who don't ordinarily respond to print promotions can be enticed to inquire if they know you have a Web site with interesting, relevant content. Surplus Direct, for example, a direct marketer of computer hardware and software, gets almost half its orders directly from its Web site, the other half coming from its more costly print catalog. As one executive of the firm commented: "Putting the catalog on the World Wide Web and having the customer order over the Internet using a credit card is the future of catalog sales."

WHAT THE WEB CAN OFFER YOUR BUSINESS

The World Wide Web offers several marketing advantages over conventional print promotions. It costs you almost nothing to fulfill inquiries by inviting prospects to visit your Web site, and the prospect gets instant gratification—no waiting for a brochure or catalog to arrive in the mail.

You can offer additional information or help to prospects who fill out a registration form on your Web pages, which allows you to instantly and easily qualify leads on-line. You automatically capture the E-mail addresses as well as the usual information about prospects who register, allowing you to build a list for future E-mail promotions.

Unlike mailings and brochures, which must be reprinted to be changed, you can modify your Web pages at any time. Prospects who access your Web site know they are getting the latest information. There is also an excitement and novelty to Internet marketing that print promotion sometimes lacks.

To keep things simple, let's start with a few definitions. The *Internet* is a large network through which virtually every computer in the world can be connected to virtually every other computer in the world.

The *World Wide Web* is a subsegment of the Internet. The Web consists of about a million computers, known as *servers*, that store information designed to be accessible to people who surf the Web. *Surfing*, also known as navigating or browsing, is looking through the information on these computers to find information of particular interest to the user.

The information is divided into segments, each accessible using a different code, known as the *URL* (e.g., http://www.bly.com/). These segments are called *Web sites*. A server containing the text and graphics for one or more Web sites is said to be *hosting* those sites. Poynter reports that there are more than 16 million host servers connected to the World Wide Web.

The first page of the Web site is the *Home Page*. This is always the first thing a Web surfer sees when accessing any given Web site. Think of the Home Page as a table of contents and brief introduction combined into a single concise page. Just as the table of contents in a book leads the reader to other pages, the Home Page leads the Web browser to other pages, known as Web pages. The two main elements of any Web site are the Home Page and Web pages.

A third element are the *hypertext links*. These are electronic links that help browsers immediately find information of interest to them within or between Web sites.

To show how links work, let's compare Web pages to the printed page. In his best-selling book, *Dianetics*, L. Ron Hubbard used a printed version of the hypertext concept. Hubbard believed the only reason people could not understand text was because they didn't know the meaning of one or more of the words. Therefore, in *Dianetics*, each new word or concept is highlighted in **bold**. This signals the reader to look for the definition at the bottom of the page. The highlight is the link that refers the reader to another section of the text.

Hypertext links on the Web work similarly. Any time there is a word the Web browser might want more detailed information on, that word is highlighted by putting it in a different color on the screen and <u>underlining</u> it. To find out more, the Web browser clicks on the underlined word with the mouse. The computer immediately displays a Web page that gives more detailed information on that particular subject.

This explanation is no substitute for actually getting on the Web and surfing it yourself. If you are going to write Web pages, you *must* become familiar with the World Wide Web. The only way to do this is to get on the Web and browse.

Connecting to the Internet is not at all difficult. You need a computer, a modem, a telephone line, an Internet Service Provider (ISP), and browser software such as Netscape or Microsoft Internet Explorer. You can find an ISP by checking ads in the business section of your local paper, looking in the Yellow Pages, or asking your local computer store or consultant. Most ISPs provide the browser free when you subscribe to their service. You can also access the Internet through the major on-line services including America Online and CompuServe.

As this book goes to press, more than 60 million people worldwide use the Internet, and more than 17 million Americans browse the World Wide Web at least once a week. Market research firm Dataquest estimates that by 2001, 268 million computers will be connected to the Internet. Digital Equipment Corporation estimates there are already 100 million Web pages on the Internet, and Helmut Epp, dean of the school of computer science at DePaul University, estimates there are half a million Web masters employed in the U.S. alone (as reported in the *Record*, November 3, 1997).

There are more than 7 million home pages on the World Wide Web. Jeffrey Lant, an Internet marketing consultant, says this number is expected to increase to an incredible 1 billion home pages within a few years. According to an article in *Forbes* (August 25, 1997), 88 percent of professionals surf the Web at least once a week.

To target your Web copy to this special audience, consider their demographics:

- 75 percent of the Web audience is between the ages of 16 and 44.
- 55 percent of Web surfers have incomes over $55,000 a year.
- 54 percent have college degrees, and 26 percent have graduate degrees.
- Seven out of ten business users surf the Web for production information and evaluation.
- Web surfing by business prospects is projected to double by the year 2000.

In an article in *Proof* (April 1997), Peter Eder, president of IM&C International Marketing and Consulting Group (White Plains, NY), said the top reasons corporations adopt Internet technology are as follows:

To communicate with external customers	62%
To improve external customer services	48%
To improve and expand product distribution	41%
To develop an intranet	37%
To communicate with vendors and suppliers	33%
To generate new revenue streams	32%
To create a marketing advantage	28%

The Business Marketing Association surveyed advertisers to find out how involved they are in electronic marketing and communications. Two-thirds included the Internet and other electronic marketing as a budgeted item in their communication plans, with budgets for electronic marketing ranging between $5,000 and $250,000. Twenty-eight percent of the advertisers surveyed had set aside money to create or maintain a Web site. Three out of four expect their budgets for electronic marketing to increase.

TIPS FOR BUILDING AN EFFECTIVE WEB SITE

1. Determine your objective before you begin to write. Marlene Brown, an authority on Internet Marketing, offers this advice as the first step in creating a Web site:

> Before you set up shop on the Internet, determine what your objectives are. Do you want to sell your present products? Launch a new one? Market your programs and services? Build traffic on your home page? Clearly determine your objectives, then establish measurable goals as to what will constitute success.
>
> Define your target audience. Where and who are your best prospects? Do you want to advertise your products generically, or target them? Browse through present bulletin boards, join discussion groups, share ideas on mail lists to enable you to see what is in demand and who wants to buy it.
>
> Surveys are a great way to get information about what Internet people think of your products, especially new ones you may launch, or a series of related products you plan to bundle. Surveys prevent us from wasting time on products for which there is not a big market, and give us ideas on needs.

The Web is, in a sense, a low-cost, electronic version of traditional direct marketing. Like traditional direct marketing, Internet marketing can generate an immediate, tangible, and measurable response. But you can't know whether you are getting a good or bad result unless you establish objectives and then measure your results against those objectives.

In an article in the December 1997 issue of *Intercom* magazine, Theresa A. Wilkinson suggests that the following questions are useful in planning your Web site:

- What are the goals and objectives of the site?
- Who are the intended audience—will there be multiple audiences accessing different information (e.g., dealers, distributors, and resellers vs. end users)?
- What tasks will people come to the site to perform? These might include: obtaining company background, getting product information, viewing recent press releases, downloading documents or software, getting customer support, or finding out about new releases and upgrades.

Roger Parker, in his book, *Web Content and Design* (New York: MIS Press), also suggests asking:

- What types of information are the visitors to your site likely to want?
- What action do you want your Web site visitors to take?
- What information do they need to make a decision or take a step that benefits your firm?

After your Web site is operational for a few months, you'll have a better idea of what you can realistically expect to achieve, and can adjust your objectives accordingly. At the same time, read articles in the business press to find out the results others are getting with their Web sites. This gives you a goal to shoot for.

2. Register a domain name people will look for. The domain name is the key part of the code the Web surfer types to reach your Web site. To reach Bob Bly's Web site, for example, type http://www.bly.com. The domain name is bly.com. Poynter says there are more than 900,000 registered domains.

Your ISP, or whatever firm you select to host your Web site, can register a domain name for you. Choose a domain name that people would be likely to guess was where they could find your home page on the Web. Reason: Although there are many simple-to-use *search engines* (a search engine is a tool you can use to search the Web for home pages of interest to you, according to subject matter and source), many new Web browsers don't know how to use them or don't bother to use them. Therefore, they are more likely to type in a few guesses until they hit upon your real domain name and can access your Web site. For instance, the domain name for the BOC Group, a large industrial manufacturer, is, logically, BOC.com. The domain name for Bob Bly is bly.com. Bob could also have chosen BOBBLY.com.

You should choose a domain name that is either identical to or close to your company name, or one that relates to the category of product or service you provide. For instance, if you are a large freight forwarder, you might select freight.com or ship.com. If your company name is Global Transportation, you might chose global.com or globtrans.com.

Domain names are unique: If your competitor registers a domain name, no one else can use it. However, you can always register a variation of the name, if that domain name is still available. For example, if barbecue.com is taken, perhaps you will want to register BBQ.com or maybe grill.com, all good choices for a manufacturer of barbecue grills.

3. Use a "Web site under construction" sign. Arrange with an ISP or other Web company to give you *server space* for your Web site. Then have them register a domain name for you. Once these things are done, your Web site will be "live," in that someone who types your domain name into their Web browser will be sent to the site. Unfortunately, the site will be blank (empty) because you haven't put anything on it.

How long does it take to build a Web site? A small one- or two-person business can put up a simple Web site with a home page and a few Web pages in a couple of weeks or sooner. If you have a medium-size company, estimate four to ten weeks to create your Web site. We've seen large corporations with multiple companies and divisions take 6 to 12 months to develop their Web sites. The Web sites of large corporations can be so involved that a new job title, *Web Master*, has been created within the corporate world. The Web Master is the manager in charge of the corporate Web.

Because the content of your Web site will lag behind your site becoming operational ("live") by several weeks to several months, you don't want people to seek out your site and find it empty. Here's what to do.

Put some boilerplate copy on the home page about your company and its products and services. Include contact information—phone number, fax number, E-mail address—so people interested in learning more can contact you directly, even though your Web site does not yet have a mechanism for direct response through the Web. (It will soon; see tip number 8.) You can write something custom for the Web site or simply scan or edit existing boilerplate copy from a corporate capabilities brochure, backgrounder press release, or other existing marketing documents.

This noninteractive message puts your company on the World Wide Web until your full Web site is ready, so visits to your site are not wasted. Above this descriptive copy, add a box with text in large, bold letters that says, "Web site under construction." This tells visitors to your site that this is a temporary site, not a permanent one, and so they shouldn't be put off by the lack of functionality, design, and detailed content, all of which are to come.

Interestingly, many ISPs automatically provide 8 megabytes (MB) of server space for you to have a Web site at no extra charge when you use them to provide your Internet access. Our guess is that there are thousands of ISP customers who have, in effect, paid for server space on which they could put a Web site and don't even know it. As of this writing, even CompuServe customers automatically get 1 MB of server space at no charge, yet many CompuServe users don't use the space.

4. Make your copy modular. The Web is a truly modular medium. The information you put on your Web site must be divided into separate pages. These pages are electronically connected, but the Web browser need not go through them sequentially. He or she can skip back and forth, from page to page, looking for information of interest. Write and design your

Web site with this in mind. Break the subject of the Web site up into modules, the way you would break a training course into segments or a manual into chapters.

Make the text within each Web page modular as well. Don't make the page a solid block of text, as in a book. Break it up into four or five sections, each with its own subhead. This is the way Web browsers prefer to digest information—in short, bite-size chunks.

5. Keep it short and simple. Web pages are, in many ways, strikingly similar to regular printed prose. Web pages are written in plain, simple, everyday English; no special language, computer codes, diagrams, or flow charts are used in place of conventional sentences and paragraphs.

The beauty of the World Wide Web is that information can be presented and accessed in layers. This is what enables you to keep your Web pages brief while still offering more detailed information to those who are interested.

Aside from hypertext links, if there is a difference between the printed page and on-line writing, it's that Web page copy must be brief. There is no need to make Web pages longer than a page or two because if more detailed information is available, the Web surfer can be directed to a separate on-line document on that topic (using a hypertext link).

Most of your Web pages should be one to one and a half pages long. If the information will exceed two pages, break it up into two separate subject pages, and connect them via a hypertext link.

Keep paragraphs in Web pages short. Most paragraphs should be no longer than three to four sentences. An occasional longer paragraph is okay, but when in doubt, break long paragraphs into two or more shorter paragraphs.

6. Use internal hypertext links as an on-line index. In a printed book, you turn to the index in the back, look up a subject by name, then turn to the pages where this information is located. In on-line writing, the document itself is its own index. Key words are highlighted and hypertext linked to other sections of the document.

Do not overdo the links. If every other word is underlined, highlighted, and hyperlinked, it will confuse readers and they won't click on anything. Highlight only those key topics that you want the prospect to explore further. As a rule of thumb, if you break up a Web page into sections with subtopics separated by subheadings, you shouldn't have more than one hyperlink per section, or more than four or five per Web page.

7. Use strategic external hyperlinks to increase visits to your Web site. One type of hyperlink connects Web pages within a Web site. But you can also have hyperlinks that instantly transport your prospect to the home pages of other advertisers or organizations. In return, they hyperlink their sites to your home page.

For example, if you sell pet supplies, it would be natural to hyperlink your Web site to the home page of the American Cat Breeders' Association. If you sell desktop publishing software, a link to a Macintosh user's group, such as MacSciTech, makes sense, as would a link to the Apple Computer Web site. You get the idea.

By arranging these strategic hyperlinks, you can increase visits to your own site (by pointing browsers at these other sites to your own home page) as well as improve the usefulness of your site (by helping browsers access related relevant information on other home pages).

These links don't take place automatically. You have to arrange them with related Web sites. Some Web site owners may agree to cross-link their site to yours just for the mutual benefit of increased traffic and leads. Others who don't see an advantage in getting referrals from your site may charge a fee for providing a link from their site to yours.

8. Give people a reason to complete your enrollment page. Every business Web site should have an enrollment page. The enrollment page is a Web page where visitors to your site can register, giving you key information about each prospect, including the person's name, company, title, address, phone and fax numbers, and E-mail address.

You must give people a strong incentive to take the time to register on your enrollment page...or they won't do it. A survey conducted by the Boston Consulting Group and reported in *Micro Software Marketing* (April 1997, p. 2) found that 41 percent of respondents report leaving Web sites when asked to provide registration information. Another 27 percent of respondents provided false personal information on Web site registration forms.

The same issue of *Micro Software Marketing* reported on another survey conducted by Cyber Dialogue, a New York City research firm. The survey found that for 76 percent of Web site visitors, submitting personal information on-line is seen as a positive way for companies to learn about customers. Seventy-seven percent of Web site visitors said they would be willing to participate in short surveys (of course, that result may be skewed, since everyone who responded filled out a short on-line survey to be included in the study). Seventy-three percent will fill out demographic information about themselves to have a site tailor content to their specific needs. Only one-third of those surveyed said registration forms are a waste of time. Cyber Dialogue's director of research Kevin Mabley concludes: "Incorporating registration forms on a site should be optional, nonintrusive, and positioned as a way for customers to receive added value from the site on their next visit."

For the Web advertiser, the enrollment page is nevertheless an extremely valuable tool. It allows you to measure Web response more acurately, provides a vehicle prospects can use to request additional information, and enables you to build a prospecting database that includes, among other things, prospects' E-mail addresses. Once you have this database, you can target E-mail, fax broadcasts, direct mail, and other repeat promotions to those prospects as appropriate.

Getting qualified prospects to register (fill out your enrollment page) isn't difficult. Simply offer them something of value that they cannot gain access to until they have completely filled out an enrollment page. This can be the ability to:

- download or request free literature,
- use an on-line calculator, search engine, or other Web site utility,
- subscribe to an E-mail newsletter or other on-line or printed publication, or
- request a price quotation or get preliminary recommendations.

The principle is similar to that used in printed direct mail that includes a reply card the advertiser wants the reader to fill out and mail back. Direct mail reply cards are filled out and returned only when prospects are given an incentive to do so, such as a free gift, free catalog, free estimate, and so on. Enrollment pages work exactly the same way: Give your site visitors a compelling reason to register, and they will.

9. Add functionality, not just information. Because Web pages are computer files that run on computer systems, they can go beyond the regular printed page to offer degrees of functionality that conventional sales literature cannot match. For instance, on the home page for Studebaker-Worthington, a nationwide computer leasing company, there is a handy Quick Quote calculator. Simply enter the purchase price of the computer system, and the calculator instantly shows you the monthly lease payments.

On the home page for Edith Roman Associates, a large mailing list broker, a Quick Count calculator can be used to get instant list counts. You enter the type of market you want to reach; the program instantly displays the names of the available mailing lists, the quantity of names on each list, and the list rental cost. This is a convenient feature for marketing managers who are planning campaigns and need to get a quick idea of the size of potential markets.

If your product or service lends itself to this type of calculator, add it to your Web site and make it accessible from your home page. You don't need to make it elaborate or to have many of them. But adding a useful utility makes your Web site more interesting and useful, so more of your prospects will visit it more often.

10. Change the content periodically and make it clear that you do so. Another big difference between printed brochures and on-line marketing documents is that on-line marketing documents can easily be updated, at any time, at virtually no cost. Brochures, by comparison, cannot be updated once they are printed. If you have new information, you either have to reprint the brochure and throw out the old copies, or add an insert sheet or other supplement highlighting the new information (which doesn't delete any dated or wrong information in the old brochure).

Advertisers with Web sites find its ease of updating to be both a blessing and a burden. The blessing is that on-line marketing documents can always be up to date and don't cost anything to revise. The burden is that you're always going back into your Web site and making changes, revisions, and corrections as new information becomes available.

Because the content of your Web site is continually being changed and upgraded, prospects have a reason to periodically revisit the Web site to obtain the latest, most accurate information. Let them know this. Put a message on your home page that says, "Information changes rapidly and the XYZ Company Web Site is continually updated. Visit us often to get the most current data."

Another technique is to have a separate section (Web page) dedicated specifically to news and announcements. This bulletin can change monthly, weekly, or even daily. The more often it changes and the more important the information, the more frequently prospects will visit your site. If you have such an announcements page, feature it on your Home page with a hypertext link, and encourage browsers to visit it on every trip to your site.

11. Use a FAQ. A FAQ is a unique type of Web page containing frequently asked questions. These pages are extremely important, very popular, and nearly always read. A FAQ page is a way to convey information simply, easily, and quickly. If it weren't for FAQ pages, E-mail systems would be jammed with people asking the same questions over and over again.

Having a FAQ on your Web site can be highly valuable. When people ask you questions, refer them to your FAQ. When people want to know more about what you do, point to your FAQ. When you receive E-mail requests for your brochure, E-mail them your FAQ. Since the FAQ is a separate Web page, Web surfers can easily download it and even print it for permanent reference.

Joe Vitale, an authority on Internet writing, offers these suggestions for writing effective FAQs:

- **Use the Q&A format.** FAQs rely on the tried-and-true question and answer format because that is the simplest way to get information across. If you've been around for a while, you've heard the same questions asked numerous times. These are the questions to include in your FAQ. Naturally, include your succinct answers too.

- **Be brief.** By now you know that everything you write on-line should be as brief and to the point as possible. There's simply too much happening on-line and too many other posts to read for anyone to spend a great deal of time on your material. Write a clear question, give a direct answer, and move on to the next question. Ten lines of text is a wise target maximum for each of your answers.

- **Be lively.** FAQs that simply give information can be boring. Spice up your writing. Add eye-opening statistics, engaging stories, and stimulating quotes. Make reading your FAQ a delight. Say something that surprises your readers. Add a fact that makes them say, "I didn't know that!"

- **Give resources.** Although you aren't writing a term paper or dissertation, your FAQ is a resource for people. Make it a complete one by including details on how to get more information. If you have a list of books, articles, or tapes, include it. If you have a directory of people or places to contact for more information, include it. Remember to add your own name, address, phone and fax numbers, and E-mail address.

- **List questions up front.** It's common practice to list all the questions being answered in your FAQ at the beginning of the FAQ. This way anyone wanting to know the answer to a particular question can tell at a glance whether you cover it or not.

12. Cross-promote. Once you have a Web site, promote it heavily. In your ads, mailings, and company newsletter, encourage prospects and customers to visit your Web site. Put your Web site address (e.g., http://www.bly.com) on every marketing and business document you produce, including letterhead and business cards.

In marketing communications, mention a benefit to the prospect, an incentive for going to your Web site. For instance, list special information that is only available on the Web site and not in other media, or post special sales and discounts on the Web site that are only available there. Studebaker-Worthington Leasing Corporation offers cash incentives and merchandise gifts to computer resellers who use their leasing services. They now offer special gifts only available on the Web site, which increases traffic.

13. Use selective Web publishing. A basic Web site has a home page and several brief (one-page) Web pages. But you have a lot more information about your products and services than can fit in these formats. What do you do?

You have two choices. As discussed in tip number 8, you can include an enrollment page people who browse your Web site register. On this enrollment page, you can offer additional materials that can be sent to prospects via E-mail, fax, or *snail mail* (the Internet user's derogatory term for regular Post Office mail). The second alternative is to engage in Web publishing. *Web publishing* is converting marketing and informational documents to electronic form, and placing these electronic files on your Web server. The documents can then be read on-line and instantly downloaded, or even printed out, by browsers visiting your Web site.

Enrollment page response offers and Web publishing are not mutually exclusive. We recommend you put your most important marketing documents—those containing information most relevant and interesting to prospects—directly on your server, so interested prospects can download them right from the Web.

But if you include all your documents, you can clutter up your site and eat up your server space. So documents of secondary importance can be listed or described within the Web site and offered on the enrollment page. As a rule of thumb, the 10 percent most important marketing documents should be published on the Web site, with other relevant documents offered on the site through the enrollment page, E-mail, or other means.

14. Keep graphics to a minimum. Says Joe Vitale, "Don't overdo the graphics. Not everyone can see graphics on-line. Even those who can usually don't have the patience to download large graphics files. If users have slow modems, waiting for a graphic to appear on the screen might take several minutes...time that some are being charged for by their access provider or long-distance phone company. Use graphics selectively. Don't get fancy."

"Graphics slow systems down," Larry Kacyon points out in an article in *Metalworking Marketer* (August, 1997, p. 4). "Most people want to access information as quickly as possible. When possible, keep graphics small and minimize file size. Some users prefer text-only Web surfing. Offer a text-only equivalent with hypertext links and menus."

An article in *Board Report for Graphics Artists* states that 20 percent of Web site visitors surveyed say speed of transfer is the most important factor for a Web site, and 65 percent rate information content as the most important factor. Only 5 percent rate graphics as most important. "If your site has a lot of graphics, try to build in a bypass button that downloads text only," the survey concludes.

Graphics add interest, but words communicate the bulk of the information on the Internet, so keep your Web site simple. "Ease of communication and clarity of use should be your targets," says Vitale. "Always aim for simplicity. If your copywriting isn't compelling, few will buy. True, online browsers certainly want information, but don't feed it to them in dry chunks. The more you can add emotional excitement to your words, the better your chances of being read, being remembered, and having your services bought."

Vary what you write. Some people create their own paperless documents, such as e-zines, or electronic magazines, and design them for home page use. There are far too many diversions for readers in cyberspace, so don't bore anybody. With one click they can leave your site and never return.

Keep what you say interesting. Always think of your readers and give them what they want, not what you want. A good rule of thumb in writing any marketing piece is, "Get out of your ego and into the reader's ego." Write what would keep them interested. As Howard Gossage, a famous ad executive, once said, "People read whatever interests them, and sometimes it's an ad." Make your on-line text interesting and they just might read what you write.

Be sure to place your name, address, phone and fax numbers, and E-mail address on every page of your Web site documents. You never know when a reader will suddenly want to contact you. Don't make that person backtrack through several layers of hyperlinks just to find out your phone number. Put your contact information at the top of every page.

WEB SITE DESIGN TIPS FROM ROGER C. PARKER

In search of design tips for advertising managers venturing onto the Web for the first time, I asked Roger C. Parker, author of *Roger C. Parker's*

Guide to Web Content and Design: 8 Steps to Success (New York: MIS Press, 1997, 1-55828-553-9) for some tips. Roger came back with ten important ideas:

1. Design for the lowest common denominator of Web browser hardware and software. Don't become seduced by the latest technology. (And don't let outside designers and consultants talk you into it!) Although technology is advancing at a rapid rate, visitors to your Web site are likely to be using older, slower computers and earlier versions of software than you are. It's very easy to get so excited by the latest software bells and whistles features that you end up designing a Web site that can be accessed only by those with the latest hardware and software. This seriously limits the delivery of your message. Accordingly, keep your Web site as simple as possible and test it on a variety of computers and Web browsers before posting it. Pay attention to visitor complaints and watch for signs that your design is encouraging visitors to move on to other sites.

2. Design for speed. Keep graphics as simple as possible. Employ as much live text as possible. Restrict the use of formatted text that has been stored as graphics and must be downloaded as graphic images to an absolute minimum. Keep complex illustrations and scanned images as small as possible. Better yet, include thumbnails of them that visitors to your Web site can click on if they want to wait until the graphic downloads so they can view it at larger size.

3. Provide Alt tags. Alt tags consist of text that describes the contents of a text or graphics file before it downloads. Remember that many of the visitors to your Web site may be surfing the Web with their graphics card turned off. Unless you provide a text description of a headline or graphic, they won't know what they're missing.

4. Always use Web-safe colors. Although your computer may be equipped with a graphics card and sufficient memory to display millions of colors, most of your visitors aren't so lucky. In order to make sure that your Web site will look good to the broadest range of visitors, restrict your color choices to the 216 colors that reproduce equally well on most computers running the Apple Macintosh, Microsoft Windows, or Unix operating systems. If you use colors outside of the 216 Web-safe colors, the colors are apt to dither, or appear very grainy, when displayed on the vast majority of computers in use.

5. Don't use design as a substitute for content. Remember that visitors to your Web site aren't as interested in jazzy graphics or special effects as they are in information that can help them save time, save money, or work more efficiently. Keep the design of your Web site as simple as possible so your message will emerge as quickly and clearly as possible.

6. Avoid bright or heavily textured backgrounds. Respect your visitors' eyes! Provide soft, restful backgrounds. Bright backgrounds can be very fatiguing, contributing to eyestrain that encourages visitors to your Web site to move on. Textured backgrounds can easily overwhelm your message by distracting visitors. Often, background elements make text hard to read by appearing to be connected to the text.

7. Avoid long lines of text. Avoid columns of text that extend in an unbroken line from the left edge of the screen to the right. These are extremely difficult to read. Reduce line length by using either tables, frames, or the HTML Block Quote feature to add white space outside the left and right margins of each text column.

8. Provide plenty of subheads. Reading from a computer screen is much harder than reading from a printed piece of paper, so it's much harder for you to keep your reader's interest. One of the ways you can encourage readers to continue reading is to include plenty of subheads in your text columns. Each subhead summarizes, or presells, the information that follows and presents an additional entry point into the material.

9. Avoid false clues. False clues are words or graphic elements (like bullets) that appear to be links, but aren't. Often a second color is used for emphasis, but because the color is different from adjacent text, the colored text appears to be a link to another section of the Web site. Frustration is certain to result when readers click on a text or graphic element and nothing happens.

10. Encourage involvement. Provide numerous ways for visitors to your Web site to do more than passively read your Web site. Invite them to submit questions or comments and provide an incentive for those who register. Ask visitors which parts of the Web site they found the most or least useful and attempt to find out how they located your Web site (e.g., referral from another Web site, an advertisement, word of mouth, etc.) Likewise, encourage Web site visitors to prequalify their needs and provide them with content based on their responses. For example, on your home page, ask visitors to rate their knowledge of your product or service and provide content tailored to newcomers, intermediate users, and advanced users. This helps you to offer meaningful advice to newcomers without boring those who already know the basics.

Roger concluded by reminding us that the Web is both similar to and entirely different from any other advertising medium. The Web resembles traditional advertising media to the extent that the site has a goal and satisfies the Web site visitor's needs. It also communicates meaningful information as simply and quickly as possible. The Web is totally different from traditional media in that you can employ color, photographs, and sound and include as much information as desired without incurring increased printing or postage expenses.

"But," Parker says, "Web site visitors are selfish. They're as selfish as readers. Like readers of traditional media, Web site visitors are constantly asking themselves: 'What's in it for me?' Visitors will only remain at your Web site as long as you provide them information that will help them make better informed buying decisions. Web site visitors are not looking for entertainment—they can turn on the TV for that. Web site visitors are not looking for brag-and-boast claims. Rather, Web site visitors are looking for meaningful content that will enrich their lives."

For more information, visit Roger C. Parker's Meaningful Content Web site at http://www.rcparker.com .

LEAD GENERATION AND TRACKING ON THE WEB

Interactive Web sites are the future of Internet marketing. Guest books, surveys, order forms, catalogs, dynamic FAQs, demographic capture, data push, inquiry fulfillment, lead tracking, shopping carts, and other neat stuff yet undreamed of, can transform a Web site from a simple billboard approach into a truly dynamic, two-way communication medium for true interactive marketing.

- *Guest books*. Capture complete information on people who visit your Web site by asking them to fill in an on-screen guest book, similar to one you might sign in a church you are visiting or to get on the mailing list of a store from which you've just made a purchase. You can motivate qualified prospects to complete the guest book by giving them more in-depth access to information on your Web site in return, access that people who do not fill in the guest book do not get. For example, if you offer technical papers, you might only allow people to read and download them if they sign into your guest book.

- *Customer surveys*. Market research and other prospect and customer surveys can be put right on your Web site. Again, you can offer an incentive such as better information access, as a reward for completing the survey. Web surfers who complete the survey and indicate by their answers that they are qualified prospects can be treated as sales leads.

- *Order forms*. Your Web site can include a form the customer fills out to order a product. Products can be sold on credit, or to reduce payment risk you can require the buyer to provide credit card information. There are a number of on-line services, such as AT&T SecureBuy, that enable you to accept credit card orders over your Web site while keeping credit card numbers completely confidential. Shoppers can preregister their credit card information with AT&T, eliminating the need to re-enter it each time they visit your site.

- *Catalogs*. A number of companies have put their catalogs on CD-ROM. If you have sufficient server space, a CD-ROM catalog can be placed on your Web site and accessed over the Internet by prospects and customers.

- *Dynamic FAQs*. We've already discussed FAQs. If you treat your FAQ as a database rather than as a text document, customer service people can enter and answer new questions, adding them to the FAQ list dynamically as they come up. This ensures a FAQ list that covers all bases and is up to date.

- *Demographic captures.* You get demographic information on any hits to your Web site during which the Web surfer registers on the desk book. But you get the Internet addresses of everyone who visits, whether they register or not. Soon demographic capture applications will allow you to enhance these Internet addresses with demographic data, so you will know more about where inquiries are coming from and whether they are leads worth pursuing.

- *Data push.* With data push, marketing documents of interest to specific prospects are automatically E-mailed to those prospects as soon as they are posted on your Web site. For example, a Web site for a restaurant asks customers to register on a guest page in return for discounts or a free glass of wine with dinner. The guest page asks diners to indicate their cuisine preferences. If the Wednesday night special is vegetarian lasagna, that morning the Web site automatically data pushes (E-mails) an announcement and discount coupon for the special to all customers who have indicated they prefer vegetarian cuisine.

- *Inquiry fulfillment (E-mail on demand).* Just as a Fax on Demand (FOD) system automatically sends specific sales literature requested by people who phone an automated system and enter their requests through the telephone key pad, you can set up an E-mail on Demand (EMOD) system that automatically E-mails product information to prospects over the Internet, based on their demographics, interests, needs, or other preferences as captured from their visit to your Web site.

- *Shopping cart.* Shopping cart is a techie term for a Web site on which you can conduct electronic commerce. Think of it as going through a store that's open 24 hours a day, 7 days a week, on the World Wide Web. You pick items to put in your cart. The Web site automatically retrieves the product description, number, price, shipping and handling charges, and availability.

  When you're ready to buy, you go to an electronic checkout counter that adds your purchases and tallies your bill. You can subtract items or even go back into the store and add items before making the transaction final. When you're ready to place the order, you pay by giving credit card information or through some other type of electronic funds transfer.

- *Lead tracking.* The Web site guest page can be integrated with a contact management program to enable precision tracking, reporting, and follow-up on Web-based sales leads.

Implementing these tactics requires the ability to develop database applications and integrate them with your Web site. You can hire a programmer or use a high-level application development tool such as Webfiler, a program that helps Web designers create interactive Web sites quickly and easily. Features to look for in such a tool include a native database engine for rapid development of Web database applications; connectivity to existing databases (Oracle, SQL Server, Access, and other popular database managers); built-in database field rules; high-level or code-based application development; built-in data push capabilities; data file transfer by FTP, E-mail, or HTTP; password-protected multiuser security system; storage of GIF and JPEG images; and browser-based (no client software required), query-by-form, and customized layouts using any popular HTML editor. Even easier, don't do it yourself, but hire a Web designer (see Appendix E). For more information contact Alpha Software at 800-451-1018 or visit their Web site at http://www.Webfiler.com.

INTERNET DIRECT MAIL

Internet direct mail has many advantages over traditional paper direct mail:

- It's faster. The average delivery time from the Post Office for third-class bulk rate mail is 2 1/2 weeks. Internet direct mail can reach its target literally in seconds.

- It's less complicated to produce. Internet direct mailings are typed E-mail messages you create right on your computer screen. It doesn't require a professional graphic designer, Web developer, HTML programmer, or printer.

- It costs less to send. For a paper direct mailing, the cost to send the mailer—including printing, postage, mailing list rental, and production—is typically 60 to 80 cents each. At that rate, mailing 100,000 pieces would cost $60,000 to $80,000. By comparison, you can send your Internet mailing to the same number of prospects for as little as $150.

The profit implications for marketers are staggering. At a cost of $600 per thousand, a typical industry figure, a mailing that generates the standard 2 percent response rate for an offer of a $30 product *will not even make a profit*. On the other hand, an Internet direct mail offer for the same product will turn a profit if the entire mailing produces only one-tenth of a percent response or even less!

Internet direct mail is a marketing revolution. It's the wave of the future, and smart people will send out as many of their marketing communications as possible via E-mail, just as many companies are doing right this minute.

To do direct mail on the Internet, you need an effective E-mail message and a list of E-mail addresses. How do you distribute your message to these prospects? With a list server.

A list server is a software program that sends E-mail messages to Internet mailing lists. When you use a list server you put yourself on the cutting edge of marketing

and give yourself an astonishing competitive advantage. This is easy to understand when you think about how much a business spends to mail or fax its marketing offers versus how little it costs to send the same messages over the Internet.

You can get an adequate list server for a purchase price (actually an annual license fee) of around $200 to $500.

Here are some of the advantages a list server can add to your business' Internet marketing program:

1. A list server enables your Internet mailing list to grow itself. Prospects can place themselves on your Internet mailing list by filling in a reply form on your Web site. You do nothing! They simply click on "submit" and are added to the list. The list server will send a note out to the address that was added, confirming acceptance. It can also attach a separate welcome note, confirming that the prospect subscribed and is now on the list and providing instructions on how to be removed from the list.

2. The list server program removes bad E-mail addresses instantly. If you mail your information out to, say, 5,000 people, the odds are that about 50 addresses will be obsolete, because of people changing their addresses or cancelling their service. The list server handles these bad addresses with no effort on your part. It deletes the bad addresses and sends you a note letting you know which addresses were removed and why.

3. Removing an address from the list server is as easy as putting it on in the first place. Suppose you send out a note to that list of 5,000, and 25 people want to come off the list. If you used a manual bulk E-mail program to send to the list, you would need to look up the addresses and remove them one at a time, which could take over an hour. No need to do this with the list server.

With a list server, people have two ways of removing themselves from your list. They can visit your Web page to remove their addresses or they can send a note to the list server with the word "Remove" in the body of the message. You will have a template ready that requires you to "clip and paste" the address for removal.

The average number of people who are not able to follow instructions and remove themselves from a list of 5,000 names is about 5. It takes about 5 seconds per address to remove them, since the list server only needs the address for removal. It does the look-up and deletion automatically.

4. Posting (sending) a message to your entire list of 5,000 (or whatever quantity you desire) is as quick and easy as sending an individual E-mail to a single person! You simply send a note to the list server and include a special password that tells the program you are posting. The list server understands the password and instantly sends the message to the entire list. Then it E-mails you a confirmation letting you know what the message was and how many people on the list it is being mailed to.

5. You can access and examine your list at any time. Simply send a message to the list server with the same password for posting but including the command "list" and the name of your list. You will instantly receive an E-mail message including all the names on the list. This allows you to monitor the list's growth.

By using a series of simple password-protected commands you can manage a list of 20,000 as easily as 20 via E-mail. There are no fancy UNIX codes or need to connect with the server to remove names from or send messages to the list. List servers are perhaps the most advanced services on the Internet today; they have been around even longer than the World Wide Web and newsgroups.

Using the List Server to Distribute a Promotional Newsletter

Think of the list server as a mini broadcast center you control from your desktop. It builds its own list and takes care of posting, just as a microphone allows a disk jockey to broadcast to listeners of a radio station. You need to figure out what content to send to people so they will keep reading. Remember, it is just as easy to lose an E-mail prospect as it is to gain one, so take the time to craft messages of interest.

Here are some useful guidelines for material content for publishing to your list:

1. Never simply send ads to the list. Even if the purpose of your list is updates, there should always be something in your message that will benefit the audience. There is no faster way to lose readers than to overstuff your message with ads.

2. Assign someone in your organization to produce the content for your message. Some companies, like magazine publishers, have it easy here. They can have one of their editors make up an E-mail newsletter from their print materials. Minimal modification is required to get the material Internet-ready.

Product manufacturers have to do more research. For example, a company that sells ski equipment would add content regarding the latest ski news, resorts, and so on to its message. A hint: Visit some newsgroups and Web sites that are relevant to your business. You would be surprised at how many of these sites have articles and news that you can use for your publication. Just ask for permission to use the information and you will be on your way to publishing your first Internet newsletter.

3. The format of an Internet newsletter is almost as important as the content. Have you ever picked up a book or magazine that didn't have a table of contents? To say that's annoying is an understatement! You must include a few key things in your newsletter to make it work. These include:

- name of the publication,
- date and issue,
- removal information,
- table of contents,
- short intro paragraph,
- publisher's and editor's names, and
- well-defined headers that correspond to the table of contents.

Under each major heading, make sure you include a title and any other relevant information.

Figure 31.1 illustrates how CompuServe begins its monthly newsletter.

Figure 31.1. First page of "All about CompuServe," CSI E-mail newsletter.

"All about CompuServe," Vol.1 Issue 2. Sept. 18, 1997

The Companion Newsletter to CSI's Forum and Communities

From CompuServe Interactive Business Partners and Sysops

ISSUE HIGHLIGHTS

- Finally, Flat-Rate Pricing Is Here!
- H&R Block Announces CompuServe Sale to WorldCom-AOL
- Personalize Your E-mail Address
- Use 5 Megs of Space for Your Web Page
- New Version of Off-Line Navigator: Virtual Access 4.0
- "Kevin and Kell" Cartoons in Funnies Forum
- Microsoft Access Support Live in the Access Forum
- A Handbook for Maturing Hipsters
- Deal with Tough Back-to-School Issues in ADD Forum
- Screen Saver Salutes Princess Diana
- See How Versace Dressed the Supermodels
- Need Help Ferreting Out Those E-mail Addresses?
- Go Winsupport for Windows 95 Patches, Updates on CSI
- Screamin' Guitars in Rock Forum
- Help Is Here for Cranky Electronic Gadgets!
- Headache Support Group Launches in Good Health
- Real Estate Forum
- Can We Talk? Try the Internet Chat Relay Forum

FROM THE EDITOR'S KEYBOARD

Two big decisions last week had us sitting on the edges of our chairs. First, CompuServe announced a landmark decision to let members choose flat-rate pricing if they wished. On its heels came the announcement that telecommunications giant WorldCom agreed to buy CompuServe Inc.—and that a complex swap would allow America Online to assume control....

Order information is also critical to the success of your Internet newsletter. You don't need an order form in the newsletter, because you can simply refer people to a URL or E-mail address.

Purchasing a List Server

Be careful when shopping for a list server. Many companies set a very low monthly or yearly license fee but then charge you for the number of times you use the list server and for the number of names you acquire. This leads to your getting bills every time you mail out to your list. Over the course of a year this can get very expensive, especially as your business grows.

A good list server vendor charges a flat fee and clearly states any extra costs. Expect to pay in the neighborhood of $300 to $600 per year for your own list server.

Why won't a cheaper bulk E-mail program do as well? Bulk E-mail programs are designed to send E-mail to a list of people that you manually input onto the list. Bulk E-mail programs have many major drawbacks:

- E-mail addresses must be manually added or removed. To add subscribers, people must send you their addresses and then you must retype them onto the list. Removal takes more time since you have to perform look-up and then delete commands.

- Bulk E-mail programs offer no way for the person receiving the message you send to get off the list automatically. This leads to administrative problems if you are out of the office and forget to remove half a dozen people. The next time you mail to the list you can expect complaints to your Internet Service Provider that you are *spamming* (sending junk E-mail).

- Bulk mailings to a list are often one-time events and are considered spam. The real purpose of most bulk E-mail programs on the market today is to strip E-mail addresses from newsgroups and Web sites for a single purpose: to send spam!

- The worst part of bulk E-mail is that it is a program used on your local computer. It is not a mail server program and it can only send mail through your ISP's server. Most ISPs are set up so that bulk E-mail programs can't transmit through their mail server. A list server adds the benefit of a high-speed connection to the Internet rather than a 28,000 baud connection from a regular computer modem.

A list server is like a broadcast tool to be used as you see fit for solo Internet E-mail or in coordination with your Web site. It keeps your current customers and prospects updated on your business in a timely manner and costs only pennies a day to maintain. It eliminates administrative tasks, so you do not need to hire a person to handle your Internet marketing.

Internet Direct Mail Formats

One-Shot Direct Mail

This is an E-mail sent to an Internet mailing list you rent or compile. It is clearly promotional. In today's increasingly commercial Internet environment, these mailings work well. Although you may get *flamed* (receive angry E-mail replies), it should be at a reasonable level you can deal with.

```
Sender: FSZone@netwerks.com
Received: from bosshog2.netwerks.com ([ 207.199.6.150]
(may be forged)) by hil-img-9.compuserve.com
(8.8.6/8.8.6/2.5) with ESMTP id WAA25305; Thu, 11 Sep
1997 22:40:30 -0400 (EDT)
```

```
From: FSZone@netwerks.com
Message-Id: 199709120240.WAA25305@hil-img-
9.compuserve.com>
Received: from [207.199.6.150] ([207.199.6.140]) by
bosshog2.netwerks.com (Post.Office MTA v3.1.2 release
(PO205-101c)
ID# 32-34537U100L100S0) with SMTP id AAJ168;

Thu, 11 Sep 1997 14:53:50 -0700
To: FSZone@netwerks.com
Date: Thu, 11 Sep 97 14:44:38 EST
Subject: Fantasy Sports Zone
Reply-To: FSZone@netwerks.com

This is a one-time message. You will not be contacted
again.

Fantasy SportsZone
(http://www.fantasysportszone.com/sports.htm) is the
best FREE Fantasy Sports site on the Internet, featuring
fantasy baseball, golf, basketball, hockey and now the
FREE weekly Fantasy Football game, Pigskin Picks. Sign
up today to win CASH prizes and merchandise, just for
picking the winners of this week's NFL games. It's
FAST, it's FUN and it's totally FREE to play.

Unlike other fantasy games, each Fantasy SportsZone game
is easy to play and doesn't require a lot of your time.
Plus you can get started in the middle of a season and
still have a chance to win weekly and monthly prizes.
For example, if you sign up for Pigskin Picks by
Friday, you'll be eligible for Week Three prizes.

So sign up today and tell your friends, because it's
even more fun when you play a group game.

Sincerely,
Fantasy SportsZone
```

Advertorial

These E-mails are written like a cross between an advertisement and an article. They are similar to what copywriters call "editorial style ads"—copy-heavy print ads designed to look like an article in the magazine or paper rather than a paid message. This is a popular format and works well because it fits in with the Internet's focus on information and news.

```
ARE YOU BEING INVESTIGATED????

Learn the Internet tools that are used to investigate
you, your friends, neighbors, enemies, employees or any-
one else! My huge report "SNOOPING THE INTERNET" of
Internet sites will give you...

Thousands of Internet locations to look up people, cred-
it, Social Security, current or past employment, driving
records, medical information, addresses, phone numbers,
maps to city locations...
```

Every day the media (television, radio, and newspapers) are full of stories about PERSONAL INFORMATION being used, traded, and sold over the Internet... usually without your permission or knowledge.

With my report I show you HOW IT'S DONE!!!

It's amazing...
* Locate a debtor that is hiding, or get help in finding hidden assets.
* Find that old romantic interest.
* Find E-mail, telephone or address information on just about anyone! Unlisted phone numbers can often be found through some of these sites!!

Perhaps you're working on a family "tree" or history. The Internet turns what once was years of work into hours of DISCOVERY & INFORMATION.

* Check birth, death, adoption or Social Security records.

MILITARY
* Check service records of Army, Navy, Air Force or Marine Corps. Find out who's been telling the truth and who's been lying. Perhaps you can uncover the next lying politician!!!

FELLOW EMPLOYEES
* Find out if your fellow employee was jailed on sex charges, or has other "skeletons" in the closet!!

PERFORM BACKGROUND CHECKS
* Check credit, driving or criminal records, verify income or educational claims, find out military history and discipline, previous political affiliations, etc.

YOUR KID'S FRIENDS
* Find out the background of your children's friends & dates.

WHAT'S THE LAW? STOP GUESSING!!
* Look up laws, direct from law libraries around the world. Is that new business plan legal??

NEW JOB? NEW TOWN? NEW LIFE?
* Employment ads from around the world can be found on the Internet. Get a new job and disappear!

The Internet can tell you just about ANYTHING, if you know WHERE to look.

BONUS REPORT!!!!

Check your credit report and use the Internet to force credit bureaus to remove derogatory information. My special BONUS REPORT included as part of the "SNOOPING THE INTERNET" collection reveals all sorts of credit tricks, legal and for "information purposes only," some of the ILLEGAL tricks.

Research YOURSELF first!

What you find will scare you.

If you believe that the information that is compiled on you should be as easily available to you as it is to those who compile it, then...

You want to order the SNOOPING THE INTERNET report I've put together.

This huge report is WHERE YOU START! Once you locate these FREE private, college and government Web sites, you'll find even MORE links to information search engines!

YOU CAN FIND OUT ANYTHING ABOUT ANYBODY ANY TIME using the Internet!!!!

1) WE TAKE: AMERICAN EXPRESS VISA MASTERCARD

TYPE OF CARD AMX/VISA/MC??_____

NAME ON CREDIT CARD_____

CREDIT CARD #_____

BILLING ADDRESS_____

CITY_____

STATE_____ZIP_____

PHONE (INCLUDE AREA CODE)_____

WE WILL BILL 39.95 to your account
SALES TAX (2.90) added for CA residents

Send $39.95 ($42.85 in CA) cash, check or money order to:
CASINO CHICO
Background Investigations Division
305 Nord Ave.
P.O. Box 4191
Chico, CA 95927-4191

2) Send the same above requested credit card information to above address.

3) Fax the same above credit card information to 916-895-8470

4) Call phone # 916-876-4285. This is a 24-hour phone number to place a CREDIT CARD order.

I will RUSH back to you SAME DAY my "SNOOPING THE INTERNET" report!

Log on to the Internet and in moments you will fully understand what information is available—and exact Internet site to get there!

```
2nd BONUS!!!!
```

```
Along with the report we will send a 3 1/2" disk with
sites already "HOT LINKED". No need to type in those
addresses. Simply click on the URL address and "PRESTO"
you are at the Web site!!!
```

```
Personal ads, logs of personal E-mail, mention of indi-
viduals anywhere on the Internet are "yours for the
taking" with this report.
```

```
Lists of resources to find even more information (pri-
vate investigation companies, etc.)
```

```
Order surveillance equipment (if legal in your state)
Send anonymous E-mail
Research companies
Research technology
Locate military records
```

```
FIND INFORMATION ON CRIMINALS
•  Find Wanted fugitives—perhaps even a close associate!
```

```
ABSOLUTE SATISFACTION GUARANTEED:
Your satisfaction is 100 percent guaranteed; just return
the material for a full refund within 30 days if you
aren't 100 percent satisfied.
```

```
Jon Scott Hall Publications
```

Web Site Teaser

This is a short E-mail message, the purpose of which is to entice people to go onto your Web site. Because more detailed instructions are on the site, the E-mail itself can be only a few lines, as long as the copy is intriguing. For example:

```
Subj: Taxes
Date:97-09-12 14:37:25 EDT
From:ann537@hotmail.com
Reply-to:ann537@hotmail.com
To:ann537@hotmail.com

Beat the IRS—pay no taxes! Free report!
```

Story Format

Telling a story in your E-mail instantly engages the reader and creates the perception that the message is from someone you know rather than an unsolicited advertisement.

```
Subj:  Home Computer Operators Needed Now
Date:97-10-22 00:34:54 EDT
From:mnybank@aol.com
To:mnybank@aol.com
Subj:Home Computer Workers Needed Now!
```

I Never Thought I'd Be the One Telling You This: I Actually Read a Piece of E-mail & I'm Going to Europe on the Proceeds!

Hello! My name is Karen Liddell; I'm a 35-year-old mom, wife, and part-time accountant. As a rule, I delete all unsolicited "junk" E-mail and use my account primarily for business. I received what I assumed was this same E-mail countless times and deleted it each time.

About two months ago I received it again and, because of the catchy subject line, I finally read it. Afterwards, I thought , "OK, I give in, I'm going to try this. I can certainly afford to invest $20 and, on the other hand, there's nothing wrong with creating a little excess cash." I promptly mailed four $5 bills and, after receiving the reports, paid a friend of mine a small fee to send out some E-mail advertisements for me. After reading the reports, I also learned how easy it is to bulk E-mail for free!

I was not prepared for the results. Every day for the last six weeks, my P.O. box has been overflowing with $5 bills; many days the excess fills up an extra mail bin and I've had to upgrade to the corporate-size box! I am stunned by all the money that keeps rolling in!

My husband and I have been saving for several years to make a substantial downpayment on a house. Now, not only are we purchasing a house with 40 percent down, we're going to Venice, Italy to celebrate!

I promise you, if you follow the directions in this E-mail and are prepared to eventually set aside about an hour each day to follow up (and count your money!), you will make at least as much money as we did. You don't need to be a wiz at the computer, but I'll bet you already are. If you can open an envelope, remove the money, and send an E-mail message, then you're on your way to the bank. Take the time to read this so you'll understand how easy it is. If I can do this, so can you!

Karen Liddell

The following is a copy of the E-mail I read:
LEGAL MONEY-MAKING PHENOMENON.

PRINT this letter, read the directions, THEN READ IT AGAIN !!!

You are about to embark on the most profitable and unique program you may ever see. Many times over, it has demonstrated and proven its ability to generate large amounts of cash. This program is showing fantastic appeal with a huge and ever-growing on-line population desirous of additional income.

This is a legitimate, LEGAL, money-making opportunity. It does not require you to come in contact with people, do any hard work, and best of all, you never have to leave the house, except to get the mail and go to the bank!

This truly is that lucky break you've been waiting for! Simply follow the easy instructions in this letter, and your financial dreams will come true! When followed correctly, this electronic, multi-level marketing program works perfectly...100 percent EVERY TIME!

Thousands of people have used this program to:

- Raise capital to start their own business
- Pay off debts
- Buy homes, cars, etc.
- Even retire!

This is your chance, so don't pass it up!

OVERVIEW OF THIS EXTRAORDINARY ELECTRONIC MULTI-LEVEL MARKETING PROGRAM

Basically, this is what we do:
We send thousands of people a product for $5.00 that costs next to nothing to produce and E-mail. As with all multi-level businesses, we build our business by recruiting new partners and selling our products. Every state in the U.S. allows you to recruit new multi-level business on-line (via your computer).

The products in this program are a series of four business and financial reports costing $5.00 each. Each order you receive via "snail mail" will include:

- $5.00 cash
- The name and number of the report they are ordering
- The E-mail address where you will E-mail them the report they ordered.

To fill each order, you simply E-mail the product to the buyer.

THAT'S IT!

The $5.00 is yours!

This is the EASIEST electronic multi-level marketing business anywhere!

FOLLOW THE INSTRUCTIONS TO THE LETTER AND BE PREPARED TO REAP THE STAGGERING BENEFITS!

I N S T R U C T I O N S

This is what you MUST do:

1. Order all 4 reports shown on the list below (you can't sell them if you don't order them).

For each report, send $5.00 CASH, the NAME & NUMBER OF THE REPORT YOU ARE ORDERING, YOUR E-MAIL ADDRESS, and YOUR RETURN POSTAL ADDRESS (in case of a problem) to the person whose name appears on the list next to the report.

- When you place your order, make sure you order each of the four reports. You will need all four reports so that you can save them on your computer and resell them.
- Within a few days you will receive, via E-mail, each of the four reports. Save them on your computer so they will be accessible for you to send to the 1,000's of people who will order them from you.

2. IMPORTANT—DO NOT alter the names of the people who are listed next to each report, or their sequence on the list, in any way other than is instructed below in steps "a" through "d" or you will lose out on the majority of your profits. Once you understand the way this works, you'll also see how it doesn't work if you change it. Remember, this method has been tested, and if you alter it, it will not work.

   a. Look below for the listing of available reports.
   b. After you've ordered the four reports, replace the name and address under REPORT #1 with your name and address, moving the one that was there down to REPORT #2.
   c. Move the name and address that was under REPORT #2 down to REPORT #3.
   d. Move the name and address that was under REPORT #3 down to REPORT #4.
   e. The name and address that was under REPORT #4 is removed from the list and has NO DOUBT collected their 50 grand.

Please make sure you copy everyone's name and address ACCURATELY!!!

3. Take this entire letter, including the modified list of names, and save it to your computer. Make NO changes to the instruction portion of this letter.

4. Now you're ready to start an advertising campaign on the WORLDWIDE WEB! Advertising on the WEB is very, very inexpensive, and there are HUNDREDS of FREE places to advertise. Another avenue which you could use for advertising is E-mail lists. You can buy these lists for under $20/2,000 addresses or you can pay someone a minimal charge to take care of it for you. BE SURE TO START YOUR AD CAMPAIGN IMMEDIATELY!

5. For every $5.00 you receive, all you must do is E-mail them the report they ordered. THAT'S IT! ALWAYS

PROVIDE SAME-DAY SERVICE ON ALL ORDERS! This will guarantee that the E-mail THEY send out, with YOUR name and address on it, will be prompt because they can't advertise until they receive the report!

AVAILABLE REPORTS

Order Each REPORT by NUMBER and NAME

Notes:
- ALWAYS SEND $5 CASH FOR EACH REPORT
- ALWAYS SEND YOUR ORDER VIA FIRST CLASS MAIL
- Make sure the cash is concealed by wrapping it in at least two sheets of paper
- On one of those sheets of paper, include: (a) the number & name of the report you are ordering, (b) your E-mail address, and (c) your postal address.

REPORT #1 "HOW TO MAKE $250,000 THROUGH MULTI-LEVEL SALES"

ORDER REPORT #1 FROM:
Edwards Inc
1454 Mt.Ulla Hwy.
Mt.Ulla, NC 28125

REPORT #2 "MAJOR CORPORATIONS AND MULTI-LEVEL SALES"

ORDER REPORT #2 FROM:
Marico
2350 Spring Road #30-194
Smyrna, GA 30080

REPORT #3 "SOURCES FOR THE BEST MAILING LISTS"

ORDER REPORT #3 FROM:
David Noah & Co
514 S. Oxford Valley Rd. # 207
Fairless Hills, PA 19030

REPORT #4 "EVALUATING MULTI-LEVEL SALES PLANS"

ORDER REPORT #4 FROM:
NDZ, Inc.
1579F Monroe Drive
Box 240
Atlanta, GA 30324

HERE'S HOW THIS AMAZING PLAN WILL MAKE YOU $MONEY$

Let's say you decide to start small just to see how well it works. Assume your goal is to get 10 people to participate on your first level. (Placing a lot of FREE ads on the internet will EASILY get a larger response.) Also assume that everyone else in YOUR ORGANIZATION gets ONLY 10 downline members. Follow this example to achieve the STAGGERING results below.

```
1st level—your 10 members with $5          $50
2nd level—10 members from those 10
($5 x 100)                                 $500
3rd level—10 members from those 100
($5 x 1,000)                               $5,000
4th level—10 members from those 1,000
($5 x 10,000)                              $50,000
```

THIS TOTALS $55,550

Remember friends, this assumes that the people who participate only recruit 10 people each. Think for a moment
what would happen if they got 20 people to participate!
Most people get 100's of participants! THINK ABOUT IT!

Your cost to participate in this is practically nothing
(surely you can afford $20). You obviously already have
an internet connection and E-mail is FREE!!! REPORT#3
shows you the most productive methods for bulk E-mailing
and purchasing E-mail lists. Some list & bulk E-mail
vendors even work on trade!

About 50,000 new people get online every month!

TIPS FOR SUCCESS
• TREAT THIS AS YOUR BUSINESS! Be prompt, professional, and follow the directions accurately.
• Send for the four reports IMMEDIATELY so you will
  have them when the orders start coming in because:

When you receive a $5 order, you MUST send out the
requested product/report to comply with the U.S. Postal
& Lottery Laws, Title 18, Sections 1302 and 1341 or
Title 18, Section 3005 in the U.S. Code, also Code of
Federal Regs. vol. 16, Sections 255 and 436, which
state that "a product or service must be exchanged for
money received."

• ALWAYS PROVIDE SAME-DAY SERVICE ON THE ORDERS YOU
  RECEIVE.
• Be patient and persistent with this program. If you
  follow the instructions exactly, the results WILL
  undoubtedly be SUCCESSFUL!
• ABOVE ALL, HAVE FAITH IN YOURSELF AND KNOW YOU WILL
  SUCCEED!

YOUR SUCCESS GUIDELINE
Follow these guidelines to guarantee your success:
If you don't receive 10 to 20 orders for REPORT #1
within two weeks, continue advertising until you do.
Then, a couple of weeks later you should receive at
least 100 orders for REPORT #2. If you don't, continue
advertising until you do. Once you have received 100 or
more orders for REPORT #2, YOU CAN RELAX, because the
system is already working for you, and the cash will
continue to roll in!

THIS IS IMPORTANT TO REMEMBER:
Every time your name is moved down on the list, you are placed in front of a DIFFERENT report. You can KEEP TRACK of your PROGRESS by watching which report people are ordering from you. If you want to generate more income, send another batch of E-mails and start the whole process again! There is no limit to the income you will generate from this business!

NOTE: If you need help with starting a business, registering a business name, how income tax is handled, etc., contact your local office of the Small Business Administration (a Federal agency) for free help and answers to questions. Also, the Internal Revenue Service offers free help via telephone and free seminars about business taxes.

T E S T I M O N I A L S

This program does work, but you must follow it EXACTLY! Especially the rule of not trying to place your name in a different position. It won't work and you'll lose a lot of potential income. I'm living proof that it works. It really is a great opportunity to make relatively easy money, with little cost to you. If you do choose to participate, follow the program exactly, and you'll be on your way to financial security.
Sean McLaughlin, Jackson, MS

My name is Frank. My wife, Doris, and I live in Bel-Air, MD. I am a cost accountant with a major U.S. corporation and I make pretty good money. When I received the program I grumbled to Doris about receiving "junk mail." I made fun of the whole thing, spouting my knowledge of the population and percentages involved. I "knew" it wouldn't work. Doris totally ignored my supposed intelligence and jumped in with both feet. I made merciless fun of her, and was ready to lay the old "I told you so" on her when the thing didn't work... well, the laugh was on me! Within two weeks she had received over 50 responses. Within 45 days she had received over $147,200 in $5 bills! I was shocked! I was sure that I had it all figured and that it wouldn't work. I AM a believer now. I have joined Doris in her "hobby." I did have seven more years until retirement, but I think of the "rat race" and it's not for me. We owe it all to MLM.
Frank T., Bel-Air, MD

I just want to pass along my best wishes and encouragement to you. Any doubts you have will vanish when your first orders come in. I even checked with the U.S. Post Office to verify that the plan was legal. It definitely is! IT WORKS!!!
Paul Johnson, Raleigh, NC

The main reason for this letter is to convince you that this system is honest, lawful, extremely profitable, and is a way to get a large amount of money in a short time. I was approached several times before I checked this out. I joined just to see what one could expect in return for the minimal effort and money required. To my astonishment, I received $36,470.00 in the first 14 weeks, with money still coming in.
Sincerely yours, Phillip A. Brown, Esq.

Not being the gambling type, it took me several weeks to make up my mind to participate in this plan. But conservative that I am, I decided that the initial investment was so little that there was just no way that I wouldn't get enough orders to at least get my money back. Boy, was I surprised when I found my medium-size post office box crammed with orders! For awhile, it got so overloaded that I had to start picking up my mail at the window. I'll make more money this year than any 10 years of my life before. The nice thing about this deal is that it doesn't matter where in the U.S. the people live. There simply isn't a better investment with a faster return.
Mary Rockland, Lansing, MI

I had received this program before. I deleted it, but later I wondered if I shouldn't have given it a try. Of course, I had no idea who to contact to get another copy, so I had to wait until I was E-mailed another program...11 months passed then it came...I didn't delete this one!...I made more than $41,000 on the first try!!
D. Wilburn, Muncie, IN

This is my third time to participate in this plan. We have quit our jobs, and will soon buy a home on the beach and live off the interest on our money. The only way on earth that this plan will work for you is if you do it. For your sake, and for your family's sake don't pass up this golden opportunity. Good luck and happy spending!
Charles Fairchild, Spokane, WA

ORDER YOUR REPORTS TODAY AND GET STARTED ON YOUR ROAD TO FINANCIAL FREEDOM!!!

Chapter

32
ELECTRONIC
COLLATERAL

CD-ROMs are the way of the future. Not only do they turn your computer into a super-high-powered knowledge and entertainment machine, they can also make a lot of money for you, if you have vision and the willingness to try some new things.

A CD-ROM is basically a compact disk (like the kind music comes on) that can be used in a computer. *CD* stands for Compact Disk, and *ROM* stands for Read-Only Memory (which means your computer can read what's on the CD, but it can't write new information to it).

In order to use a CD-ROM on your computer, you must have a CD-ROM unit, much like a disk drive, installed in your system. The CD-ROM unit can either be internal (installed inside the computer case) or external (hooked to the computer by a cable). Note: Most CD-ROM units can also play regular music CDs, as well as the new Kodak Photo CDS.

Why would anyone want a CD-ROM unit? Well, for one thing, a CD-ROM can hold tons more information and programming than a regular computer disk, almost 400 times as much, to be exact. Entire encyclopedias fit on only one or two CD-ROMs! These aren't just plain, boring encyclopedias, either. The large amount of storage on a CD-ROM allows full-motion video, digitized sound, and other special effects to be included. For example, if you look up the first moon landing, you might see an actual short video of Neil Armstrong stepping onto the moon and hear him deliver his famous "one small step" speech!

Games on CD-ROM are incredible! Many CD-ROM games are ultrarealistic, with real actors, real speech, and thousands of possibilities. Desktop publishers love CD-ROMs, too. There are CD-ROMs available that hold thousands of typestyles and clip art graphics. Why not add these exciting graphics and interactivity to your marketing documents? You can when you have them on CD ROM.

The ability to use CD-ROMs is almost essential these days if you have a Web site. There are dozens of CD-ROMs available that contain hundreds of shareware programs each. Visitors to your Web site can download these programs to their computers and use them. With a few of these, you can have the largest downloadable file base of any Web site in your industry literally overnight!

Major software companies are jumping onto the CD-ROM catalog bandwagon. Some companies are now putting all their programs onto a CD-ROM. The programs may be hindered in some ways from functioning 100 percent effectively (for example, a word processing program may not be able to save what you've typed). Companies do this so you can try the program to see if it's what you want. If you like the program, you call and give them your credit card number; they charge you for the cost of the program, send you the manuals, and give you a code you can type in to make the program fully functional. Companies are discovering that it is very cost-effective to operate this way. Also, people are able to try more software, and potentially purchase more.

To appreciate CD-ROMs and understand how to use them, there is no substitute for using them firsthand. Immerse yourself in the world of CDs. If you don't already have a CD-ROM unit, spring for one. Here are two sources for low-priced CD-ROM units: Crazy Bob's (yes, that's the actual name of the place), 50 New Salem St., Wakefield, MA 01880, 800-776-5685 (an excellent source for CD-ROM units starting at $259, plus tons of CDs at low prices; call for their catalog); and Corporate Sysytems Center, 1294 Hammerwood Ave., Sunnyvale, CA 94089, 408-734-3475 (new and refurbished CD-ROM units from $149).

Be careful about renting CDs, though. If you're dealing with CDs that contain programs that can be copied, such as graphics, make sure the contents of the CD aren't protected by copyright. If they are, they are only intended to be used by the original purchaser of the CD. If they are in the public domain, then you may rent them as many times as you want.

I hope you can see the profit potential locked inside CD-ROMs. They are not a fad, but a coming wave. Look at how CDs revolutionized music: They **will** do the same for computers. Establish yourself as a source of quality product information on CDs. Customers will perceive you as state of the art, and you will have added a powerful marketing tool to your arsenal.

Thomas Publishing offers these additional tips for putting your product catalog on CD-ROM:

The basic principles of good layout design remain the same, whether you're creating a print catalog or an electronic one. The most important consideration is content—making sure you provide buyers with all the information they need in order to buy from you. The layout must be organized so the buyer can quickly access needed information. Keep your basic design and color scheme consistent throughout the catalog.

When you make it easy for buyers to find what they need, you invite them toward your information—away from the competition—and you increase your chances of making a sale.

- **Design your screens from the user's point of view.** Always present the broadest, most general information first. Then invite users deeper into your catalog by providing navigation (scroll bars, icons, etc.) to lead them into more specific and detailed information.

- **Your main index should be very general in nature.** Buyers are more likely to explore your catalog if you start out with a friendly, generalized index, which leads to more and more specific and detailed information.

- **Make sure the text is readable.** Remember, the way your catalog appears on the user's screen depends to a great extent on the kind of computer and monitor being used. Smaller monitors tend to make type appear smaller on the screen. The rule of thumb is to always design your electronic catalogs so that the smallest type used is at least a 10-point type size.

- **Always provide the user with an easy way to get back to your main index.** Electronic catalog users typically "drill down" through material looking for specific information. If they pursue a path that doesn't yield the needed information, they'll want a quick way to get back to your main index. There you'll have another chance to interest them in one of your products or services. Most Internet browsers automatically provide this kind of navigation. If you're designing a CD-ROM catalog, it's up to you to provide the navigation.

- **Use photography judiciously.** Photos can add to the esthetic appeal of your electronic catalog, but there are some trade-offs, particularly on the Internet. Photos can take a long time to appear on the screen for Internet users. Any kind of delay will cause some users to lose patience and leave your site. Some companies give users the option of either waiting for the photos to appear or reading a text-only document. Other companies use art (which is quick to download) instead of photographs. CD-ROM catalogs, however, don't have the same limitations. So go ahead and use photography when it will enhance your CD-ROM presentation.

- **Provide the navigation necessary to help users find the information they need.** Scroll bars help users move up, down, and across several screens in order to access all your information. Icons are also used to transport users to new locations within your catalog.

AUDIO CASSETTES

Direct marketers expend a lot of creative thought and effort trying to find the ideal gimmick to make their mailings stand out from the crowd. One such attention-getter is a familiar, everyday object: the audiocassette.

By adding an audiocassette to your outgoing direct mail or inquiry fulfillment packages, you can dramatically increase readership, response rates, and the time people spend with your message.

There are several reasons for the effectiveness of audiocassettes:

- They are bulky. "One of the major challenges of designing direct mail packages is to get them opened," says Paul Cook, advertising manager of Eva Tone, a large cassette duplicator. "The cassette is dimensional, so the package gets opened."

- They are tangible. Your prospect is flooded with paper mailings. A cassette stands out from the rest of the package. Prospects notice it.

- They are not overused. Personalized sales letters, laser-addressed envelopes, yes-no-maybe stickers, 800 numbers, buck slips, lift letters, and other attention and involvement devices are all overused to some degree. But not one direct mail or inquiry fulfillment package in a thousand contains an audiocassette. This uniqueness adds to the cassette's attention-grabbing powers.

- They have high perceived value. The retail price of a single C-60 spoken-word cassette ranges from $10 to $15. Because their perceived value is higher than that of a paper brochure or sales letter, secretaries are less likely to screen out mail containing cassettes and prospects are less likely to throw them away.

- They address the time problem. Business prospects complain of overflowing in-baskets and having too much to read. A cassette can be listened to when the prospect has nothing else to do—in the car on the way home from the office, or while taking a walk with a Walkman radio.

- They address the reading problem. We're told that the young entrepreneurs and executives of today's generation, brought up on TV, don't like to read long copy, but they do listen to cassettes. By including a tape with your letter and brochure, you can reach prospects who don't read direct mail as well as those who do.

Cassettes can be used by business-to-business advertisers in two types of mailings: outgoing direct mail and inquiry fulfillment.

A single C-60 or C-90 cassette in a soft poly box with label adds about two ounces to each outgoing direct mail package. A one-ounce letter and reply card that costs 32 cents to mail first class would go up to 75 cents for first class postage (the current rate for a three-ounce, first class letter) when you add a cassette to the package. If mailed third class bulk rate, the three-ounce package would cost 23.3 cents.

Because of the postage costs involved, some business mailers prefer to use cassettes in inquiry fulfillment packages rather than in cold prospecting mail. The cassettes still add two ounces to the packages, but in a large, heavy inquiry fulfillment package that costs $1 to $2 more in postage, the additional weight and cost are negligible.

Another advantage of audiocassettes is their low production costs.

One small, independent video producer in New York quoted a package price of $12,000 to produce a professional quality, eight-minute promotional video. Many video producers charge similar or higher fees, with the cost of producing a finished video ranging from $1,000 to $3,000 per minute.

An audiocassette can be produced on an extremely low budget. Professional studio recording and editing aren't as necessary for audio as they are for video; excellent results can be achieved by renting a good quality tape recorder and narrating your own program in your office, or recording a live presentation at a meeting or seminar.

Purists in the audio business will argue that such a method is amateurish and produces low-quality tapes that present a poor image of the advertiser. I disagree. There is something vibrant and energetic about most live recordings of seminars and speeches that is in pleasant contrast to the stilted dullness and lack of enthusiasm found in many professional, "slick" audio productions. I have gotten excellent sales results using live recordings of presentations, seminars, demos, and similar events as inserts.

Audiocassettes are also less expensive to duplicate than videos. They have a lower cost per unit than videos and, unlike printed materials, can be duplicated economically in small quantities.

For example, I recently produced a 16-page booklet to be mailed in a number 10 envelope. Although the cost per unit was low (only 39 cents each), to make the promotion economical I had to print a minimum of 1,000 booklets.

By comparison, for a series of 90-minute audiocassettes I use as promotional items, the duplication cost—including cassette, label, and soft poly box—is abut $1.25 per cassette. But there is no minimum order: I pay this price whether I order 5 or 50.

Formats That Work

- *Message from the CEO.* One way to gain the prospect's attention is to have someone important talk to him or her on the tape. Have the message narrated by your CEO or another executive who is at an equal or higher level than the prospect. If you're selling a technical product to a technical buyer, have the message presented by a credible technical expert the listener will respect.

- *Commercials.* A number of direct marketers use cassettes to present short commercials. Essentially, they take the promotional copy from their letter or brochure, condense it, and present it as a sales pitch on tape.

- *Explanation.* When the message is complex, it can sometimes be made more palatable if presented on tape. People who are intimidated by a prospectus or detailed information are more open to the same material if it is clearly explained by a narrator.

- *Demonstration.* An audiocassette can be used to demonstrate products, especially those with an audio component. For instance, if you sell enclosures designed to dampen the clatter of noisy computer printers, your tape can present the sound of a printer both before and after.

  One music publisher selling musical arrangements includes a demo cassette in his mailings. School and church music directors can hear arrangements played with a full orchestra or sung by a full choir before they buy.

- *Information.* An overlooked approach, and perhaps the easiest to implement, is to send the prospect a tape whose content is informational rather than promotional. This works well for service firms, manufacturers, and any other business-to-business marketer selling to an audience that seeks solutions to problems, answers to questions, or just more information.

Audiocassettes can be your secret weapon in boosting direct response rates. In a mail campaign to sell disaster recovery services, U.S. West used an audio tape to dramatize what would happen to the prospect's company if they were unprepared for a communications disaster. The mailing series pulled a 50 percent response rate, generated millions in sales, and won the DMA's Gold Echo Award.

Chapter 33

DATABASE MARKETING

AN OVERVIEW OF DATABASE MARKETING

A *prospecting database* contains names and addresses of as many people as you can identify who are potential customers for your products and services. The prospecting database is created by identifying appropriate lists, merging these lists, and eliminating duplicate names.

A *customer database* contains the names and addresses of your existing customers, including those who have bought recently and those who are inactive.

An *integrated marketing database* contains the names and addresses of both customers and prospects. You can select names by choosing prospect versus customer, active versus inactive buyer, and whatever other selection criteria you build into the database and can gather on the names in your possession.

While the lists are important, the driving force in reaching your best prospects is the ability to manipulate your prospect universe in a database environment. This lets you market to those who are the best responders, and you can accurately target specialized mailings to address the needs of different subsegments of this universe. That's the advantage a prospect database gives you.

Databases also contain phone numbers, fax numbers, and E-mail addresses. Maury Kauffman, a fax marketing consultant, offers the following tips for keeping fax numbers in your database up to date (these work equally well for other elements of the database, including address, phone number, and E-mail address):

1. Request fax numbers on all business reply cards and other response devices.

2. Make double postcards do double duty. Use them to clean your list and update fax numbers. Offer an incentive to those who mail back the card.

3. If you have a sales force or customer service department, make sure they collect and update fax numbers each time there is a customer contact.

4. Look at renting or trading an association list. These are typically up to date, due to their need to keep accurate member records.

5. Consider renting a magazine circulation list. These too tend to have accurate information, and in some cases, magazines can be productive marketing partners.

6. If you need fax numbers or E-mail addresses immediately, consider implementing a telemarketing effort to locate and verify these numbers and addresses.

7. Once the database is compiled, make sure updates are made on an ongoing basis, so the file is ready when the need to use it arises.

Implementing a database marketing program means that your company builds, maintains, and runs a relational database, or outsources these tasks to a third-party vendor. Tasks related to database marketing include creating direct mail marketing plans, negotiation with list owners, administering updates, file restructuring, statistical modeling and reporting, and training.

To create mail plans, for example, you or your consultant might use advanced statistical response models to study lifetime value, RFM (recency, frequency, money), product affinity, and market penetration to determine how to allocate marketing funds for maximum return on investment. This allows you to target prospects who are most likely to respond and purchase, maximizing the profitability of your direct marketing efforts.

ORGANIZING YOUR DATABASE

A list of customers who have previously bought from you is your most important asset. These are the customers who will come to you for return business, which is more profitable than the first sale. But are you getting the most from your customer list? There are some secrets you should know, so you can squeeze the most benefits out of your mailing list.

Most business' customer lists consist of this information: Name, Address, City, State, Zip. That's it. Unfortunately, this mailing list is almost worthless. You need to have more information in your files than just that. I have 32 information fields in my customer database! You should be able to set these up in your computer's database, or, if you don't use a computer (you really should), all this information should fit on a large index card in a card file.

For the mail order business I run, the Marketing Resource Guide (we sell books, reports, videos, and audiocassettes on marketing and sales topics direct to businesspeople), here are the fields I have in my customer database:

Product Code
Publication
Issue Purchase
Last Name of Customer
First Name of Customer
Address 1
Address 2/ POBox
City; State; Zip
Amount Paid
Ship Date
Phone Number 1
Phone Number 2
Phone Number 3
InqDate
ReferSource
Followup 1
Followup 2
SubDate
SubAmount
RenewDate
Purch 1
Purch 2
Purch 3
Tot Amount
Comments
Cust #

Almost any address possible can be put into my database without having to leave out information or abbreviate. The next three fields are for phone numbers. You **must** have your customer's phone number to be able to follow up quickly and efficiently. Making one phone call can mean the difference between a big sale or no sale.

The InqDate field is where I record the date the customer first inquired about my products and services, and the date I sent the information, since it's always the same day. (There's no excuse not to follow up your inquiries on the same day you receive them.)

This information, coupled with the ReferSource field, tells me when my ads are hitting, and how quickly people are responding to them. If I see that inquiries are coming in slowly, or long after the ad was placed, I know that I need more action incentives in my next ad. The ReferSource field is where I enter the "key" from my ad. I use a letter code after my street address to indicate which publication and issue the inquiry comes from. I also code my mailings, for the same reason.

I enter a date into the two Follow-up fields to indicate when I want to send follow-up literature to customers who don't order on the first try. I usually put a date two weeks from the InqDate in FollowUp1, and one two weeks later than that in FollowUp2. Then, every day, I run a search on these two fields to pull up any records that have today's date as a follow-up date. I can then print labels and put them on the envelopes and literature I have ready for follow-ups.

I use the next three fields (SubDate, SubAmount, Renew Date) for the newsletter I publish. These have the date I receive the subscription, the amount paid (I sometimes run special prices), and the date I want to send subscription renewal information (usually 10 1/2 months from the SubDate). I can then print labels in the same manner as I do for the FollowUp fields.

Next come the Purchase fields. I have three sets of purchase fields, one for each purchase the customer makes. In the Purch 1 field, I enter a code for the product purchased. The other two fields get the date and amount of the purchase, respectively. The second and third sets of fields get the same information for the customer's second and third purchases. The best customers to mail offers to are the ones who have purchased within the last 90 days, so I don't have to worry about many customers making more than three purchases during that time period (though I hope they will!). If someone does make a fourth purchase, I move the second and third sets of data up to the first and second lines, and enter the new purchase information in the third data set.

These fields are extremely important. I can instantly pull up a list of customers who have purchased within the past 90 days, or 60 days, or 30 days, or even 15 days. When you rent out your house mailing list, like I do, this information is vital. The rental amount you can charge increases as the amount of time since the customer's last purchase decreases.

The TotAmount field contains the total dollar amount of sales to the customer from the last three purchases.

The Comments field is used to store any miscellaneous information about the customer that I think its important to know.

I use the Cust# field for a specially coded customer number that I assign each customer. I use this code to identify the recipient of any commissions I may pay to customers who have brought business my way.

That's a lot of information, and you may be wondering why I would need all of that. I've already told you how I use the purchase data fields for identifying the age of the customers. I can also use the TotAmount field to compile a list of customers who have bought more than a certain amount from me. Together, these field searches can be used to produce a customized mailing list of, for example, customers who have spent more than $50 in the past 30 days. These would be the most responsive people to mail to, and would render the highest rental rate.

I can use certain mailing list fields to identify people who should be dropped from my list. For example, I can search for customers with FollowUp2 dates that are four weeks past today's date, and TotAmounts of zero. These customers could be erased from my list or left on file with a word or two in the Comments field reminding me not to mail anything else to them, in case they inquire again. This saves me the cost of mailing something to someone who probably won't respond.

Finally, if a customer has returned too many orders or has defrauded me in some way, I can put that information in the Comments field. Then, if the customer orders again, I will see the history when the file comes up and can use extra caution.

As you can see, if you use foresight when initially setting up your customer list, you will have a valuable tool that you can use to increase your order potential, increase your income through specialized list rental, and decrease your mailing cost by eliminating deadwood from your list. These are the most important methods you can use to increase your chances of success.

RENTING YOUR CUSTOMER LIST TO OTHER MARKETERS FOR A FEE

A *mailing list manager* is an individual or firm that markets your house mailing list or database of customers and prospects on the open market. They promote your list to mailers, agencies, list brokers, consultants, and others looking to rent mailing lists. A list manager represents one or more specific lists and gets a management fee every time the list is rented. A list broker, by comparison, arranges the rental of any list the customer wants, and gets a commission regardless of which recommended lists are rented.

If you have a house list of customers and prospects that you are currently renting to other marketers, a list manager may be able to help you reduce the administrative work of list management while increasing your list rental revenues. If you don't currently rent your house list but are thinking of doing so, the list manager can help you evaluate the list's marketability and profit potential, and then market and promote your list to generate additional income.

Mailing lists rent from $75 to $200 per thousand names and more. As the list owner, you get this income minus the commission fees that go to the list manager, broker, or ad agency. A well-managed list can generate $1 to $3 per name per year or more in revenue.

Therefore, if you put your house list of 50,000 names on the market, you can make an additional $50,000 to $100,000 or more in income with virtually no extra work or involvement on your part. In addition, you can have mailers renting your list return the undeliverable addresses to you. This way, you continually update your mailing list, with your list renters paying the cost of the postage.

John Ganis, director of List Management, Edith Roman Associates (Pearl River, NY) offers the following tips to help list owners and managers work together to maximize list rental income and put more money in the owner's pocket:

- *Keep the base price reasonable.* Many mailers want to charge fees above average, but relatively few own above-average lists. If you want to get extra income from your lists without putting a price on the data card that causes sticker shock, keep the base price affordable and charge a slight premium for selects.

  Key coding can be $1 or $2 per thosuand. The home versus business address select can run from $5 to $10. Selections by job function, industry, and products recommended or specified can run $10 to $20. List renters are more accepting of a slightly higher select fee, but prefer that the base price be reasonable.

  An unusually high base price is flattering to the list owner's ego but may be harmful to sales. The exceptions are truly unique lists reaching desirable markets; here price is not as much of a barrier to sale.

- *Actively market to list brokers.* List owners and managers like doing creative selling to list users, but you'll get better sales results by concentrating a good part of your effort targeting list brokers. Approximately 80 percent of list orders are generated by brokers; only 20 percent are generated by list users directly.

  Marketing to both list users and their brokers can be effective, but be sure to respect broker–client relationships. Don't try to circumvent brokers; instead, include them in the sales process.

- *Do test-and-continuation promotional mailings.* Whenever a list user rents your list, send a letter thanking them for their business and encouraging a reorder. If list users are deciding whether to test your list, send them a list usage report showing tests and continuations to demonstrate that your list is working for other mailers.

- *Broaden the potential renter base.* The natural tendency is to market lists to a narrow base of potential users; software buyer lists, for example, are heavily marketed to mail order software firms. You have a good chance of making a sale and having a mailing success when you do this, but you also limit your potential market. Many lists can work for products and offers that, at first glance, don't seem directly related.

If you own a list of subscribers to a computer magazine, for example, you might think to offer it only to other computer magazines (for subscription promotion) and maybe for software. But such lists have worked for a wide variety of offers including seminars, gift merchandise, consumer electronics, books, record clubs, and more.

In marketing your list, think of the character of the buyer. A list of software programmers is a natural for a software offer, but what these people have in common (aside from software knowledge) is that they are do-it-yourselfers who aren't afraid of tackling challenging projects. Such a list might pull well with a test mailing for a set of how-to home repair books or videos, or for a mail order tool and gadget catalog.

- *Go beyond the data card.* List brokers want to feel they are making the right recommendations to their clients. List users want assurance of the quality, responsiveness, and relevancy of the list to their target audiences. A data card communicates some of this information, but the more proof you send, the more you give the list renters a good feel for the nature and unique character of your list.

  If you own a list of magazine or newletter subscribers, for example, provide your list manager with copies of your publication and media kits they can give to potential renters. If you have a seminar attendee list, give the list managers copies of your seminar brochure. If yours is a mail order buyer list, provide the list manager with copies of your catalog for distribution to their clients.

- *Promote your list on the World Wide Web.* If you have a Web site, add information on your mailing list and how it can be rented. Ask your list manager whether they can promote your list on the Internet. Direct marketers planning direct mail campaigns often need fast, last-minute access to counts, prices, selects, and other list data. The Internet is a quick and easy way for them to get it.

- *Use demographic overlays.* Enriching mailing lists with overlays can add data and selections, making the lists more marketable. An effective strategy is to enhance a response or compiled list by adding such demographics as age, income, SIC code, or number of employees. Your list manager can help you here.

- *Consider database participation.* Many list owners are hesitant to let their lists be incorporated into custom prospecting databases, fearing they will lose control over usage and proper compensation. On the other hand, having your list incorporated into these databases can generate significant incremental revenue for you with no additional effort. It's up to you.

- *Keep the list accurate.* According to an article in the *Information Marketing Report* (December 1993, p. 4), databases deteriorate at the rate of approximately 20 percent a year. Almost 47 percent of the population do not live at the same address they lived at five years ago.

  Since 40 million Americans move each year, NCOA (National Change of Address) processing should be performed on your list quarterly or semiannually. Many list managers can also clean list files for their clients. The NCOA program makes change of address information available to reduce undeliverable or duplicate mailing pieces. By updating address information, NCOA processing can improve mailing results and increase continuations.

Database Marketing Case History: Non-Profit Fundraiser

One advantage of building a customer database is that it enables you to market to your customer base continually in an organized fashion. By tracking results, you can determine the lifetime value of the customer—the amount of revenue customers generate, on average, during their tenure as buyers of your goods and services.

Once you know the lifetime value of a customer, you can make a sensible determination of what you can reasonably afford to spend to acquire a new customer. This gives you an edge over your competitors who don't know customer lifetime value and therefore base their returns on marketing dollars on the revenue from the initial sale only instead of on the lifetime revenue from that customer.

This principle, which works in both the profit and non-profit worlds, is not well understood by the press, the general public, or even many marketing professionals. For example, charities are often criticized because they spend a lot of money on direct mail to get a modest donation. What the critics don't realize is the non-profit's return is not just the initial donation; it is the sum value of the multiple donations the donor will make over the years.

Bruce Eberle, an expert in fund-raising, gives the following example of the value of a database in marketing:

> List brokers are understandably eager and willing to rent any and all lists in as large a quantity as possible. After all, prospecting for a non-profit is all about building that donor file up to its largest imaginable size so that subsequent house appeals will raise a maximum of net income for the organization. But have you ever stopped to consider just what a new donor to your organization is really worth? Should you spend scarce dollars to acquire new donors or should you insist on no-loss prospecting?

> Prospecting at a loss is tough to swallow, especially if you can't be confident that you will cover the loss from the donors generated. Of course, you must show a worthwhile net return in the long haul.

After nearly three decades of intimate involvement with direct mail fund-raising programs, Eberle makes this observation with a great deal of confidence: The organization that chooses to insist on generating net income from its prospecting program, or even operating on a breakeven basis, is probably cutting off its nose to spite its face.

The numbers don't lie. The giving history on your house file will tell you a number of things, such as: 1) Donor life, i.e., how long will that donor continue giving to your organization? 2) Giving amount, i.e., what average gift will you receive from your house donors? 3) Response rate, i.e., each time you send a direct mail solicitation to your house list, what average response rate can you expect? With this information in hand you can determine exactly what a new donor to your organization is worth and how much, if anything, you should spend to acquire new donors.

Obviously, the answer is not the same for every organization. That's why you need to understand the giving patterns of your donor file and establish standards for your prospecting effort that will maximize the net income available for your projects and programs. If you don't take the time to do this analysis, you may be denying yourself access to the maximum revenue available for your cause.

For nearly two decades Eberle has worked with a non-profit that has generated the bulk of its operating income through direct mail. It's own analysis shows that it can count on a $10-plus donor making 1.3 additional donations in the 12 months following the original gift. Equally important, a good number of such donors will most certainly continue giving to the organization on a repeat basis in the years that follow. Utilizing this information, let's conduct a test analysis using the following example:

Prospect Mailing Parameters

Quantity	100,000
Percent response ($10+ donors)	1.4%
Number of donors	1,400
Package cost	$.33 ea.
Total cost	$33,000
Average size of gift	$19.50
Total revenue	$27,300
Dollar in/dollar out	$.83/$1.00
Profit (loss) on investment	($5,700)

Using this example the question is: Can the $5,700 prospecting loss be recaptured from the 1,400-donor pool and, if so, how quickly? This is what you must know before you can decide how much you should spend (if anything) to acquire new donors for your organization. Let's take a further look at the mailing program of this particular non-profit organization.

House Mailing Parameters

Number of appeals (6 mos.)	7
Avg. response rate	9.5%
Donor quantity/mailing	1,400
Contributors per appeal	133
Avg. gift size	$20.75
Gross revenue per appeal	$2,760
Total gross revenue (7 appeals)	$19,320
Package Cost	$.98 ea.
Cost per appeal	$1,372
Total cost (7 appeals)	$9,604
Net per house appeal	$1,388
Net per package mailed	$.99
Net revenue (7 appeals)	$9,716
Prospecting loss (investment)	$5,700
Net after-prospect investment	$4,016

As you can see, in less than six months that $5,700 loss on the prospecting side has turned into a net of more than $4,000 for this organization. In fact, in just five months, it has covered the prospecting investment made to acquire those 1,400 donors and by the sixth month it is realizing net income. And this is just the beginning!

This organization will make even more net income from that donor pool in the years to come. In order to estimate net income in future years we must first factor in an anticipated attrition rate. A typical pool of new donors will begin declining in number in the sixth month after their original gift. In the months that follow, that donor pool will continue to contract at a rate of approximately 4 percent per month.

While some of those donors may continue giving for five years or more, let's see what net revenue this non-profit can expect from these same donors over a three-year period. The following table utilizes the same parameters as the original projection, but factors in a 4 percent attrition rate beginning in the seventh month.

3-Year Net Revenue Projection

Net revenue year one	$18,266
Net revenue year two	$13,882
Net revenue year three	$10,550
Three-year net	$42,698
Original prospecting investment	$5,700
Available net to organization	$36,998

There you have it. At the end of just three years, that prospecting investment of $5,700 has turned into more than $35,000 of net income for this organization! Obviously your results could be somewhat more or somewhat less depending on the parameters of your house and prospect mailings. Regardless, you can see that when you analyze the numbers and you have established results, spending scarce dollars to acquire additional donors can make those dollars less scarce.

The bottom line is that you should carefully analyze your house and prospect results in order to make certain that you are maximizing net income from your direct mail program. That way you can make an intelligent decision in regard to the price you are willing to pay to acquire new donors (or, if you are a commercial enterprise, new customers). When you implement that strategy, the result will be more net income for your cause.

V

ADVERTISING MANAGEMENT

Chapter

34
CHOOSING AND WORKING WITH AD AGENCIES, PR FIRMS, AND FREELANCERS

GETTING HELP

If you are like most advertising managers, you will need to use many outside vendors to get your ad campaign created and implemented. Although some companies have complete in-house advertising departments or even in-house ad agencies, the trend today is to downsize or reduce internal staff and buy most of what is needed on the outside. Even firms with large internal resources buy a lot of services on the outside.

Companies go outside for a number of reasons. First, most of the services required are used only on an occasional basis, for example, photography or illustration. It doesn't make sense to have a full-time person on staff.

Second, as freelancer Eugene A. Hosansky observes, advertising and public relations have a "crisis-lull-crisis" rhythm. Things can be slow, then suddenly get busy. During peak periods, the internal staff becomes overloaded and freelancers are needed to handle the extra work.

Third, outsiders offer the benefit of a fresh point of view. While staff members gain a superior knowledge of the product and familiarity with the company and its procedures, these can in fact become drawbacks to doing good work. People who do the same thing repeatedly for years tend to repeat themselves eventually. Outsiders bring fresh thinking to marketing problems.

Fourth, certain skills are rewarded so handsomely that a corporation cannot afford to keep such people on staff. A top direct mail copywriter, for example, can earn upward of $200,000 a year as a freelancer; few copywriting staff jobs pay nearly that amount. Thus, the best talent is sometimes available only at an agency or from freelance resources.

This chapter will help you select and work with ad agencies, PR firms, and freelancers.

IS AN AD AGENCY RIGHT FOR YOU?

You probably need an ad agency if:

- You place a lot of newspaper and magazine ads or run a lot of TV and radio commercials.
- Your firm is marketing-driven and needs strategic direction as well as creative implementation of marketing communications ideas.
- You market to several different niche industries or to a broad consumer marketplace.
- You advertise and market aggressively, on a continuous basis, and spend at least $50,000 to $100,000 a year on marketing communications.
- You have a small or nonexistent internal advertising staff and need an outside firm to manage and coordinate advertising activities for you.

You probably don't need an ad agency if:

- You run few or no ads or commercials.
- Most of what you do in marketing consists of producing brochures, data sheets, price lists, and other collateral materials.
- Your management is not marketing-oriented, does not view marketing as an activity that needs to be planned strategically, and prefers a straightforward rather than a creative approach to marketing communications.
- You market to only one or two narrow vertical markets that are small and easy to reach and that you approach mainly through a single vertical publication or a group or association.
- You spend less than $50,000 a year on marketing communications.
- You have a well-staffed advertising department or an in-house advertising agency with both professional and administrative or clerical staff capable of handling the planning as well as the day-to-day paperwork of implementing and managing an advertising program.

Some Observations about Ad Agencies

These random observations may be helpful to you in selecting, working with, and understanding the mentality of advertising agencies.

- Agencies come in all shapes and sizes, but most are small, ranging from one or two employees to 40 or 50. Most agencies in suburban locations near local industry have between 5 and 15 employees.

- Many people who work for ad agencies do so because they perceive the business to be both creative and glamorous. While the owners and upper managers often understand and appreciate the marketing objectives behind your ad campaign, some of the writers and artists may have as their primary objective the creation of work that is creative, clever, aesthetically pleasing, stylish, and capable of winning awards. They are not likely to enjoy working for a client who wants pedestrian advertising or otherwise puts limits on their creative expression.

- Agencies, unlike freelancers and other vendors, provide a single-source service, handling each project from concept to finish. This is a big advantage. It ensures single-source responsibility for getting the project done on time and within budget. The agency, not you, acts as project manager and coordinator. This greatly reduces the administrative and clerical work associated with advertising management, freeing you to concentrate on more creative aspects. With an agency, you're a sort of quality control supervisor. When you use freelancers, you take on heavy administrative, coordination, and project management burdens.

- Agencies are not oriented toward project work. Most want to handle all of the advertising for your company, division, product line, or product—not just a brochure here or an ad there. Their reasoning is that it takes so long for them to familiarize themselves with the product and the market that they cannot make a profit handling just one job. Many agencies today, in fact, will do a single project only to allow a potential client to sample their services before assigning an entire account to them. If you tend to have project work rather than ongoing ad campaigns, freelancers might be better for you.

- Agencies are set up primarily to do major ad campaigns, both print and broadcast. For the agency to be enthusiastic about handling your account, at least half of the work you give them should involve preparing and running print ads for magazines and newspapers or commercials for radio and television. Agencies know this work well and are skilled at it. They will probably do a good job for you, giving you a fresh, original approach that is different and more arresting than you would have thought of on your own. Because they make money placing the ads or buying air time on your behalf, their fees for the actual production work—copy, design, photography—will be reasonable (though not inexpensive).

- Agencies are not oriented toward other marketing communications. Their writers and artists are unenthusiastic about producing your brochure, catalog, manual, or data sheet. The accounting and billing procedures used by agencies make having such materials produced by them an expensive proposition. Many clients routinely have their collateral materials produced by agencies when it would be more cost-effective and better for all parties concerned to use internal resources or freelancers.

- As with most professional service providers, advertising agencies are paid on the basis of materials produced, not results achieved. This system encourages advertising agencies to advise their clients to do more advertising, regardless of whether this is in fact the most profitable course of action for the client. An independent marketing consultant, on the other hand, gets paid to render objective advice, not to run or create ads. Such a consultant may, at times, give you a more realistic appraisal of the efficiency of your marketing communications, actually advising you to do less space advertising rather than more. That's a recommendation you'll rarely get from an agency.

- Agencies would rather do big jobs than little jobs. They would rather run ads in *Newsweek* than in *Sludge Journal*; and they prefer to create four-color, one- and two-page ads rather than tiny, black and white fractional ads. When an agency gets a 15 percent commission every time an ad or commercial runs, the tendency is to tell the client to run lots of ads and commercials and to run a full-page ad that costs $10,000 ($1,500 commission) rather than a quarter-page ad that costs $3,000 ($450 commission).

- What about getting help with strategy and planning? Agencies are more oriented to handling this type of work than they were a decade or so ago. In years past, the agency was simply a place where ads were created, type was set, and insertion orders were typed up. Today, many agencies seek and can offer a more active role in helping clients plan marketing and advertising strategy. Yet too few clients take advantage of these services or see their agencies in the role of advisor. If you need strategic guidance and not just implementation, it's probably better to retain an agency or consultant than to rely solely on freelancers and other vendors.

A Seven-Point Checklist for Ad Agency Selection

Stan Merritt, president of Stan Merritt Advertising, New York, provides the following advice on selecting an ad agency:

1. First and foremost, look at your needs and budget. What do you want an agency to accomplish? How much do you have to spend? When you've determined the services you really need—after eliminating the obvious fluff and ego-building departments you'll probably never use—get a firm grip on your actual promotion dollars (not the funds you hope you'll get but probably won't). Look at your company through the eyes of the potential agency.

With what you have to spend, will your account be significant to the agency? For example, if you choose an agency with $300 million in billings, and you have $3 million to spend, you'll get 3/300th or 1 percent of the agency's creativity, effort, and concentration. That $3 million may look big to you, but how will it be viewed by a potential agency? What happens if you only have a million dollars to spend, or even half a million or less?

It's just not in the cards for a small account in a large agency to expect more than a sliver of the time of the expensive management of that agency. What a small account receives is a wafer-thin slice of a creative person, a few minutes from a marketing person, a quick hello from the $125,000 creative director, and a quicker, but firmer, handshake from the $200,000-a-year president. In sum, a million-dollar account doesn't belong in a $50 million agency, no matter what the agency promises in any presentation. It just doesn't make dollars and sense.

2. Look carefully at the agencies whose billings would get a significant boost from your business. See how much compatibility really exists between you and the people you'd be working with on a day-to-day basis.

After an initial meeting, seriously analyze the personalities involved and, above all, trust your gut reaction. Remember, you met them on their best behavior—they won't get any better as time goes on. Unless you can honestly say, "I can live with those people," keep looking elsewhere.

3. Ask yourself, "Will I be paying for services I don't need?" Branch offices are terrific, but if they don't help you, you shouldn't be paying for services that benefit another account. It's difficult enough to justify the services you do require.

4. If you decide that a smaller agency meets your needs and budget, is the agency small because the principals like the intimacy of a smaller group and the chance to work closely with clients? Or is the agency small because it's staffed by small people with small aspirations?

5. Analyze the agency's clients. Is the quality of their business and service comparable to yours? When your product is a quality one and the agency's clients are shocked, do you want to be in their company?

6. Check for conflicts, accounts that would directly compete with yours. Check the agency's financial stability, duration of business, and likelihood of staying in business for at least the next five years.

7. Once you've winnowed the choice of agencies to a possible one, pay for a look at the kind of work they do. Ask for and pay for a campaign that will show how the agency copes with your company's situation. The work they did for others may give you a vague feeling of reassurance, but they'll probably never show you the ads that failed, only those that worked, or at least look good even if they didn't work.

If you think the agency might be right for you, spend a little money and have your assumptions confirmed before you make a major commitment.

There are also some don'ts to keep in mind in agency selection. Avoid these reasons for choosing an agency:

- Don't pick an agency as a crutch or to boost you or your superior's ego. The potted palms, gorgeous secretaries, and innovative decor have nothing to do with the effectiveness of the advertising.

- Don't forget that the buck stops with you. The agency will perform only as well as you let it.

The best thing for any businessperson's ego is to see the company's profits soar. The right agency can make a real contribution to the cause. The wrong one will provide an incredible financial and emotional drain, benefiting you little if at all.

As a marketing person, you should look at every decision analytically, not emotionally. That goes for selecting an advertising agency too.

More Tips on Ad Agency Selection

In addition to Stan Merritt's comments, here are a few more thoughts on selecting an ad agency:

- Examine their portfolio carefully. Take a close look at the work. Most agencies quickly flip through portfolio cases showing samples at their presentation. Ask them to send you copies (photocopies are fine) of some of the more interesting pieces so you can read them at your leisure and get a feel for their copy style and creative approach. The work should be studied carefully, not casually, as is usually done.

- Select an agency whose style and creative approach are in sync with yours. That is, you should like their work and feel it's the type of work you'd like to get. Don't pick an agency whose style doesn't fit yours, or whose approach you don't like, thinking that they can simply create work in any style you specify. Agencies all have styles and cannot easily switch on command. For instance, an agency that does hard-sell mail order copy is not the right agency to handle your high-class, image-oriented corporate ad campaign. When you see an agency's work, realize that the work they do for you will have a quality and flavor similar to the materials already in their portfolio.

- If you need strategic assistance or marketing planning or want an agency that is more of an advisor than just an ad maker, select an agency with experience and expertise in your industry. There's much debate over whether it's better to hire a general agency or an agency that specializes in direct response, financial services, industrial advertising, high-tech, fashion, or whatever. Both the general and the specialized agency can probably turn out first-rate work on your account. But the specialized agency can get up to speed faster, because they work in your industry on a daily basis and they know the market, the competition, and the media. Also, the specialized agency is more likely to be able to provide marketing advice and guidance based on a thorough knowledge of your business. A general agency has to learn from you, rather than teach you. On the flip side, general agencies may offer a fresh approach, while specialized agencies may be giving you versions of campaigns done for past clients (not necessarily a negative if the campaign works).

- Many agencies today push desktop publishing, computer graphics, and other in-house computer capabilities as a competitive advantage. Are they? It depends. If your primary need is for print ad campaigns and

TV commercials, having computers in-house is a nice plus but hardly a major reason to choose the agency. On the other hand, if you produce a lot of printed materials—data sheets, price lists, manuals—then it may be important that your agency have a desktop publishing system or at least a computer system compatible with your own computers.

- As Stan Merritt observed, personal chemistry is important. You should meet not only with the agency president and account executive but with all the people you (and your staff) will deal with on a daily basis. If the copywriter is a snob who hates talking to clients and your advertising is copy-driven, you're going to have problems.

- Make a list of services you require from an agency and check to see whether the agency currently provides these services to its clients. The agency you choose should already offer these services as standard; beware of the agency that says, "We don't do it but if you give us the account, we'll get someone who can." You want to hire an agency with all the services, equipment, staff, and procedures you need already in place.

- Small agencies can be good, but that does not always mean that a large agency always treats small accounts with minimal service. Some large agencies have divisions or subsidiaries created specifically for smaller accounts. Others are set up to handle such accounts profitably and welcome the smaller advertiser.

- On the flip side, a small agency may not have the resources to handle a large account. They may lack computer resources, media buying clout, specialized departments, staff, office space, secretarial support, and even the cash flow required to lay out money for art, printing, production, and media. Don't pick an agency that would be overwhelmed by the size and complexity of your account.

- Do not ask agencies to do speculative campaigns. Typically, an advertiser picks a number of agencies and says, "It's between you and three other agencies. Do a campaign for us and show us how you work, and..." [and this part sometimes goes unspoken] "...we don't expect to pay you for this effort." Because advertising is such a competitive business and many agencies are desperate for work, you can probably get them to do these spec campaigns for you. Don't. Instead, do as Stan Merritt advises: Pick one agency you like, have them do a campaign (or initial test project), and pay their full fee for the work. This is the only fair test. Spec campaigns usually produce work that is colorful, wildly creative, and—because the agencies have no access to the proper information and are not being compensated to do the careful planning and research that normally precedes ad preparation—totally off base. A reputable agency may meet with you and prepare a cost estimate or proposal at no charge, but it will not engage in spec work.

- Contrary to conventional industry practices, there's no reason why you have to give your account to any agency you feel you'd like to work with. Instead give them a few projects or put them to work on a special assignment or a portion of your account. Or retain them, but for a 6- or 12-month trial period. Test them out. Sample their work, and the working relationship. This is the best way to see if things will work out.

How to Locate Advertising Agencies

Finding advertising agencies is not at all difficult. If you are the advertising manager of a sizable firm, you undoubtedly get many phone calls, mailing pieces, and other solicitations from local ad agencies seeking your business. If you don't, you can ask colleagues, competitors, and space representatives from the media to recommend some agencies. Consult the local Yellow Pages or the *Standard Directory of Advertising Agencies* (see the Resource section at the end of this chapter). This book lists 4,400 advertising agencies in alphabetical order and is indexed by city and state. Each listing gives the agency's name, address, phone number, specialties (if any), number of employees, year founded, billings (gross income), breakdown of billings by media, key personnel, and major accounts.

Working with Your Agency

Who's responsible for the up-front planning of the marketing campaign? According to a special report published by Starmark, Inc. and Business Marketing, only 20 percent of companies rely on their advertising agencies to assist with the internal planning function. Yet many of these marketers say they would like the agency to be more involved with planning.

Why aren't agencies more involved in planning? According to the survey, some 40 percent of top marketers regard their agency's planning expertise to be only fair to poor. Other areas ranked fair to poor include account service, cost control, and the match of the size of the agency to the size of the client.

Most of these answers agree with common-sense observation. As stated earlier, while there is an ongoing debate between whether to select a general or specialized ad agency, one-fifth of the clients surveyed clearly feel their agencies do not have enough experience in their specialized industries.

Table 34.1. Clients' complaints about ad agency performance.

According to the Starmark report, the most common complaints marketers had about ad agencies:	Percent
Lack of industry experience	20%
High costs/lack of structure	15%
Inability to listen	8%
Tendency to overact	6%
Slow response	4%
Unqualified employees	2%
Undefined objectives	1%

Also not surprising is that cost is the second-biggest complaint. Unfortunately, professional advertising services are expensive, yet many clients are not sophisticated enough, knowledgeable enough, or operationally able to track advertising results and link them to sales and profits. As a result, many business executives feel they are spending a huge amount of money with their ad agencies and getting no tangible results in return.

Slow response is a not a big problem, cited by only 4 percent of the clients surveyed. This too is not surprising. Whatever their faults, agencies are known for their willingness to jump through hoops and meet impossible client deadlines. However, agencies may be mistaken in being willing to do so. Good work takes time to conceive and create. Rushing the agency usually produces a mediocre result, puts a strain on their employees, and results in substantial overtime charges for the client from printers and other vendors. The shame of this is that it's unnecessary: Most client deadlines are artificial, and there's no reason why due dates can't be set to allow the agency the time it needs to do the job right.

The survey also revealed that clients wanted to see the following from their agencies:

- Stronger creative skills, adapted to specific selling strategies.
- More in-depth media review and more integration of media strategies with planning objectives.
- More market research services tailored to specific client needs.
- Increased telemarketing and direct mail services.
- Stronger inquiry qualification methods and more creative solutions to inquiry follow-up.
- More in-house capabilities such as photography and typesetting as means of improved cost control.
- More cost flexibility, such as more modestly priced services for smaller projects.

Additional Tips on Working with Your Agency

Account Executives

Your agency will assign an account executive to handle your account and to serve as liaison between you and the rest of the agency's staff. Matters of planning, scheduling, coordination, and administration should always be dealt with through your account executive; the creative director or media buyer is not authorized to give cost estimates or agree to delivery dates. However, make clear that you welcome direct contact from agency staff on matters pertaining to the work at hand (for example, the copywriter who needs more information about the product can call you directly).

The account executive function was created to prevent chaos and to provide a smooth, efficient mechanism for a client to communicate with its agency. For the most part, it works; but don't be ruled by it. In situations when direct contact between you and people within the agency would be more efficient, encourage that direct contact. Let the copywriter, media planner, traffic manager, and art director know they can contact you directly.

Make Experts Accessible

Others within your company will have to function as sources of information for your agency. Product managers, engineers, quality control managers, designers, research scientists, and others have firsthand knowledge of facts that may be vital to the success of the ad campaign.

Whenever possible, encourage these people to have direct communication with the agency. The briefing will be more accurate and take less time. If the information is passed on from the engineer to you, from you to the account executive, from the account executive to the creative director, and from the creative director to the copywriter, much will be lost in the translation. Far better to have your engineer and the copywriter speak directly.

Responsiveness

You and the account executive must establish how rapidly you expect the agency to respond to requests and problems. Some veteran account executives feel they should always get back to the client within one hour, regardless of whether they are in the office, traveling on business, or on vacation. It is reasonable to expect someone from the agency to return and acknowledge your call within a few hours. This is part of the extra service you're paying agency rates for.

Conference Reports

Conference reports are reports written by the account executive and distributed to the client and agency staff after each client–agency meeting. The report summarizes what was said in the meeting and what actions, plans, and projects were initiated, if any.

Most agencies generate such reports not for the benefit of the client but to create a written record and protect themselves if a misunderstanding or disagreement arises later on about what was said. If you're an agency and you have reason to need such protection, conference reports are probably a good idea. If you're a client, unless you really read and like getting call reports, they're a waste of paper and money (even if you aren't billed directly for them, the account executive's time is valuable, and believe me, you're paying for it in your overall monthly bill). If you don't read the call reports, save time and money by instructing your agency not to issue them.

Meetings

Meetings can take place in the agency's offices or the client's. Account executives typically travel to the client's office to meet with the advertising manager and his or her staff to discuss ongoing business once a week or less frequently. New campaigns can be presented either at the agency or client offices, depending on the preferences of the parties.

Although many agencies don't submit a bill for the account executive's time spent in meetings and travel with you, this cost is factored into the overall fees you pay. You can do business more efficiently by reducing the number of meetings and doing more by phone and fax. The agency will likely pass some of the savings on to you and keep some as profit. Even the latter is beneficial, since the more profit the agency is making on your account, the better the treatment you'll get.

Cost Estimates

Let your agency know that small, incidental items, such as getting prints of a photograph or reprinting 500 copies of a price list, can be done without the need for you to approve the fee or review a cost estimate. Making the agency do a written cost estimate or proposal and get approval for mundane tasks that they'd rather not handle, make little or no profit on, and do for you only as a service is counterproductive to the relationship. If you're uncomfortable giving your agency a blank check, establish a minimum expenditure above which they must get your approval. This could be $1,000 or $3,000 or any figure you're comfortable with.

For projects that are still routine but more expensive—say, producing a new ad or mailer—tell the agency you want to approve the cost estimate before they proceed. This will prevent unpleasant surprises. The estimate can be oral or in writing.

For major projects that require management approval—a new brochure, catalog, or trade show booth—get a detailed estimate in writing that you can circulate to the appropriate executives for their okay.

Establish with the agency how precise you expect estimates to be. Keep in mind that in the early stages, before the project has been conceptualized and formulated, it's difficult for the agency to provide a firm, to-the-penny projection of what the job will cost. For instance, how can the agency tell you a brochure will cost $35,890 when you don't know what size it will be, or how many colors, pages, or photographs it will contain?

One common solution is to get estimates with a contingency, typically 10 percent. This means that the estimate is accurate, plus or minus 10 percent. Thus, a $20,000 job with a 10 percent contingency can cost anywhere from $18,000 to $22,000. Keep in mind that jobs estimated on a contingency basis usually end up costing the top fee and sometimes the middle fee, but almost never come in below the original estimate. Agencies tend to estimate on the low side because they're afraid a high estimate will prevent them from getting the job (which is often true).

Haggling

A common tendency of smaller clients or clients with limited budgets is to haggle. That is, when the agency presents an estimate for a job, the client protests it's too expensive and they can't afford it, in the hope that the agency will lower the price.

Occasionally, you may think a fee is more than you can or should be asked to pay; by all means, raise the issue with your account executive. But don't become a chronic haggler. Agencies dislike such clients and cannot make a profit on them. They may keep you as a client, but a minimum of time will be spent on your account.

Many clients think they're smart because they consistently get ad agencies, printers, electricians, and service providers of all types to lower their prices. But that's not smart. A smart client knows that the ad agency (or any other service firm) will only serve enthusiastically and happily if they are making a profit. Smart clients go out of their way to make sure agencies, vendors, freelancers, and others are making a decent profit. They know that the vendor who is getting paid well gives the best effort.

If the price is too high, don't try to get your agency to do the same work for a lower fee. Instead, redesign the project so it costs less. For instance, instead of a four-color, twelve-page brochure, do a two-color, eight-page brochure; instead of five new ads, do three ads; and so on.

Compensation

Most agencies charge a 15 percent commission for placing ads and get an additional fee for the preparation of TV commercials, print ads, brochures, and other materials. Many agencies have hourly rates established for each function at each level (e.g., different hourly rates for account supervisors versus account managers, media planners versus media buyers, copy supervisors versus copywriters, etc.) and can supply you with a copy of the rate schedule. Other agencies maintain detailed job cost records on computer, which yield averages of what clients can expect to pay for color ads, black and white ads, direct mail pieces, and other common assignments. Make a list of typical projects and ask your agency to give you a rough range (not an exact cost estimate) for each category.

Payment

Prompt payment of agency invoices can rapidly put you at the top of their "favorite client" list. Slow payments from clients cause severe cash flow problems, especially in smaller agencies, and have even put some agencies out of business. Agencies are expert in finding creative solutions to marketing problems, yet their corporate clients—who, for the most part, are far wealthier, with far greater cash reserves—expect the poor agencies to act as their bankers. When your agency lays out $100,000 to the media and you take six months to pay their invoices, you're asking them to give you an interest-free loan for six months. Once they pay overhead and salaries, the commissions they get hardly justify the effort.

The agency business is such that most agencies shell out a tremendous amount of money up front—or incur large indebtedness on behalf of their clients—to printers, typesetters, media, and other vendors. Pay your bills promptly, or consider paying the media and other vendors directly. Do not use ad agency cash floats to your advantage. It's wrong and unethical.

Conflicts of Opinion

Because the creation and approval of advertising campaigns hinge on subjective judgment, there are bound to be conflicts of opinion between clients and agencies. This is natural. As Brian Cohen, CEO of Technology Solutions notes, "When clients and agencies meet, it's to discuss important things, and so there are going to be strong opinions and differences." How you handle these differences sets the tone for the client–agency relationship.

In an ideal world, agencies are the total experts on advertising and clients always defer to agency judgment because the agency is always right. Sadly, in the real world, such is not the case. Be prepared to work at resolving the differences that will inevitably arise.

Nonadvertising Tasks

Use your advertising agency when you need advertising. Don't have them print business cards, design letterhead, get folders produced, or typeset price lists. Printers, freelance graphic artists, and other vendors should be used to handle more routine tasks that do not require great creativity or ingenuity and would therefore be inappropriate as agency assignments. As one advertising executive put it, "Don't use a machine gun when the job calls for a water pistol." Agencies are geared toward handling major advertising projects and should not be assigned routine work that's more efficiently and less expensively done elsewhere.

Rights

When you pay an agency for an ad or photograph, do you own the rights to the work for all time? You'd think so, but there's some debate here. Photographers, for example, will tell you that when you hire them to take a photograph for your new ad or catalog, you're buying rights to use that picture in a specific medium aimed at a particular market for a specified period of time. You're not getting all the rights or the photo itself. So when you want to put that picture in next year's catalog, you may find yourself facing a photographer who wants to bill you (or your agency) a hefty fee for the additional usage.

In the same way, there has been a recent debate in the copywriting field about whether clients or freelance writers own the copyright to a work. You would think that if a client pays a freelancer $5,000 to write a direct mail package, the client owns the rights. But articles in *Who's Mailing What?* and other industry publications say the copyright may very well belong to the writer.

As a client, you want to make sure you're buying all rights. You might have the agency sign a blanket agreement to this effect or put this wording in all your purchase orders; consult your attorney for details. The key point is to make it clear that you are buying all rights to the work. This is what most clients think they are getting when they hire an agency or a freelancer, and this is what they should get. Make sure you do.

Improving the Client–Agency Relationship

Why is it important to have a good working relationship with your ad agency? Because advertising, unlike dentistry, medicine, or home repair, is a team effort. Your dentist doesn't need your help in filling your cavity. But your ad agency does require your cooperation to create good advertising for you. Not only do they depend on you for all the background information needed to write and design the ad, but they cannot proceed without your approval at every step.

How do you improve the agency–client relationship? Here are four suggestions.

First, determine what you're looking for in an agency. This refers to quality of work and service, prices, philosophy, and attitude. Do you want an agency that will simply comply with your orders, meekly accepting all your dictates? Or do you want fighters who will stand up for what is right, even if it means risking your wrath? (You may have reason to want the former or the latter. The important thing is to choose one or the other.)

Next, choose the right ad agency—one whose work is in sync with what you're looking for, and whose employees are people you can get along with. Most problems occur because the relationship should not have been established in the first place.

Third, provide leadership that encourages excellence and allows for intelligent risk-taking. Don't impose unnecessary restrictions, unworkable budgets, unrealistic deadlines, or rules that prevent effective work from being created. Give your agency the freedom to do good work, but be clear enough about what you want so they don't waste your money creating unrealistic materials that won't be approved or run.

Finally, use the most potent phrase in the motivational manager's vocabulary: Thank you. Make sure everyone on the agency team receives your personal thanks from time to time for jobs exceptionally well done. Creative people thrive on praise, but seldom receive it. Most client communications are to request revisions or voice complaints, things that demotivate rather than motivate. A simple thank you is a profitable investment in a good agency–client relationship.

The Myth of Full Service

The term *full service* is used to designate an advertising agency that provides a broad gamut of advertising services, as opposed to design studios, freelancers, creative boutiques, and other vendors offering limited or specialized services. Typically, a full-service advertising agency provides all of the services you need under one roof—marketing, planning, copy, art, photography, illustration, production, media buying, account management, market research. The advantage to the advertiser is that the agency manages the project, eliminating the need for the advertising manager to hire multiple vendors and manage their various activities.

If you want a full-service ad agency, by all means hire one. But don't get too caught up with the idea of full service. Many agencies that promote themselves as full service don't perform all those activities in-house; they hire freelancers and other vendors to do things like write copy, take pictures, or set type. Some agencies make it clear to clients that is what they're doing; others attempt to conceal the use of subcontractors.

But with the trend toward downsizing and the proliferation of independent contractors in all business service areas, few so-called full-service agencies really are. For instance, even the biggest agencies buy much of their printing in-house, and virtually all hire freelance directors to direct national TV commercials for their major clients. Full service doesn't really mean that the agency has all the capabilities in-house anymore; it means the agency will provide a total package to the client, encompassing all of the services required.

As the years go by, your needs may change. For instance, when you first hired your agency, you didn't think desktop publishing was important; now you do. Should you fire the agency and get a new one, simply because your current agency does not do desktop publishing? Probably not. Keep in mind that the services your agency does not provide in-house can easily be purchased by them or by you from independent contractors. Don't insist that they have a capability, piece of equipment, or specialized employee in-house unless it's clearly in your and their best interest to do so. (Let them be the judge of this.)

Agency Reviews

Some advertisers periodically hold agency reviews. This consists of asking the current agency plus four or five potential new agencies to make a pitch for the business based on a new campaign, often prepared on a speculative or low-pay basis. The message to the current agency is that they must produce better work or lose the account. The lure to the new agencies is that if they do a superior job, they will replace the current agency.

Do not conduct agency reviews. If your current agency is not performing to your satisfaction and you wish to continue the relationship, explain precisely what is wrong. Outline the changes you want (be specific) and give them an opportunity to make those corrections. If the relationship is beyond saving, fire the agency and get a new one according to the procedures described earlier.

Do not hold agency reviews. They're unfair to the new agencies, because the new agencies rarely have a fair chance to win the business and are thus being exploited. Agency reviews are also insulting to the existing agency—if they have your business, they have your business, and they don't want to compete for an account that's already theirs. Even if they win, the agency review is likely to leave a bitter taste that sours the relationship.

HANDLING PUBLIC RELATIONS

The first question to answer is, "Should public relations (PR) and advertising be handled by separate agencies?" The answer depends on several factors:

1. Do you handle both advertising and PR, or is PR handled by another manager within your firm? If you are responsible for both, you may want to buy both services from a single source. If PR is a separate func-

tion, it's likely that the PR manager will choose the agency best suited for that job, which may or may not be your ad agency.

2. Does your ad agency also do PR? Some do and some don't. If yours offers PR services, you can certainly put them on your list of potential PR firms. If they don't, go elsewhere. Don't ask an ad agency to do something they're not set up to do.

3. How important is it to you to get advertising and PR from a single source? The advantage of getting both from one vendor is that it eliminates the need to brief and deal with multiple suppliers. If you use separate firms, you have to spend a lot of time educating both your PR and your advertising account executives about your business, strategies, products, technology, and so forth.

On the other hand, many ad agencies offer PR services but are not as expert and are not comparable to firms that specialize in PR. Having a separate PR firm may be worth the extra effort if they get better results.

Finding a PR Firm

As with advertising agencies, finding a PR firm is not at all difficult. If you're an advertising manager at a sizable firm, many PR firms will approach you each month seeking your business. You can also consult colleagues and the Yellow Pages, or look up local PR firms in directories such as *O'Dwyer's Directory of Public Relations Firms* (see the Resources section at the end of this chapter). This book lists approximately 1,700 PR firms, including their addresses, phone numbers, key executives, number of employees, and areas of specialization.

Selecting a PR Firm

Here are 10 questions to consider when selecting a PR firm. (Reprinted with permission from *The Ten Most Commonly Asked Questions about Public Relations*, Smith & Shows, Menlo Park, CA.)

1. What can public relations do for me and my company? Professional and well-programmed public relations creates market awareness; establishes a position; and builds and reinforces credibility for a company, its management, and its products over an agreed-upon and predetermined period of time.

The public relations professional accomplishes these objectives by talking to your intended marketplace through the media—newspapers, business and trade publications, and various broadcast avenues. The PR firm sets strategic goals and controlled, consistent program objectives.

2. How much will a good PR program cost? Typically, a public relations budget for a manufacturing company runs about 20 percent of the established advertising budget, but that rule may vary depending on the tasks to be accomplished.

One rule of thumb is that the broader the company's marketing objectives (the broader the product lines or types of messages—recruitment, investor, original equipment manufacturers, dealers, consumers), the more costly the program.

Using a PR firm simply to introduce a product, for example, will cost between $8,000 and $40,000 depending on the size of the press community to be addressed and the nature of the product to be introduced.

3. What am I paying for? Time, contacts, and results are all any PR agency has to sell. The more important the project or marketing problem you have to solve, the more time and contacts are required to produce results. An agency's time will be used to create a plan of action, consult with you about each step of the process, write materials, and contact the many reporters and editors of newspapers, magazines, trade publications, broadcast outlets, and your own target audiences directly as well. Time is required to gather approvals from your management, groom spokespeople, take descriptive photographs, analyze editorial opportunities, and so on. Because the business of public relations is a fairly technical process, your PR firm should be experienced and comfortable with all the segments of that process.

4. How can I measure results? While there are very formal procedures for measuring communication program results—awareness studies, publication studies, secondary research data, and so on—the results of PR programs are evident without incurring such expense.

You must be prepared to track and monitor leads that come into the company. Many of them are inspired by an article or news announcement. Beyond that, read the publications pertaining to your market to see if you're included in them. Listen to your market, your employees, your investors, your prospective employees and customers. What are they saying about you? If a trend is reported to be developing, your PR program is working. If the message is negative, your PR program needs to be strengthened or more strategically directed.

5. How can I tell if I'm getting my money's worth? If you've set clear objectives with your PR firm, you will know in approximately four months whether your program is giving you value.

If the objective was to determine a position for your company and a positioning study and consultation have taken place and an appropriate, acceptable position has been agreed upon, your objective has been met.

If the objective was to be visible in three key publications that speak to your prospective customers, and your message was carried in those publications in a given time period, that objective has been met.

If your objective was to educate an audience about a particular feature of your product through a sales seminar, and that seminar took place with good attendance and feedback, that objective was met.

Objectives must be targeted realistically. *Business Week*, for example, is one of the most difficult publications to penetrate and has very specific information criteria that interest the editors. Achieving the objective of appearing in that particular publication requires both strong news and plenty of time to develop a relationship between your company, its story and growth, and the publication editors.

After six months or a year, you can review your PR plan to determine how many of the objectives set out in the plan have been met.

6. Should I use an outside agency or an in-house PR person? The broader and more complex your program objectives, the better chance you'll have of accomplishing them if you use an agency with extensive contacts and the system in place to produce your press materials.

Many companies use an in-house PR person to write or handle the voluminous details and coordination work required in a good PR program, leaving the press contact up to an outside PR firm. Because the PR firm has multiple clients and multiple reasons to talk with members of the press every day, that relationship can be leveraged for each client, providing many more opportunities for press exposure.

Whether you determine to use an in-house professional, an outside agency, or a combination of both, it is important to realize that creating and following a strong strategic PR plan as your company emerges and grows is essential. A good PR plan begins the day your company opens its doors and drives the visibility campaign on a consistent basis ever afterward.

7. If I use an outside agency, will I have the attention of top agency management? You should make certain your relationship with the agency gives you access to principals or top management when necessary. Typically, an account is managed by an account manager or account executive. Upper management is called in during the strategic planning phases of the program, and for the extensive personal press contacts that may not be available to less experienced PR professionals. Conversely, the more mechanical day-to-day functions such as production or event coordination may be assigned to an agency support person, or an assistant.

8. How will I know what kind of program is best for me? A general session with your agency will help you focus on the market challenges and opportunities to be addressed in your PR program. A plan will be designed with specific objectives based on those realities.

9. How should I select an agency? Do some homework first in order to cut down on the number of agencies you want to see. Talk with your peers, your competitors, and most importantly, the press. If you think a particular company of your size has a good PR program, find out what PR firm they are using.

Prospective agencies should have experience in reaching your markets and understanding your types of products, and have a good solid reputation with the press.

Select up to five agencies to meet with. Any more than that will prove confusing to you. Look for strategic planning, strong press contacts, and a sense of a well-managed company in the first meeting. Select two finalists and meet with them at their offices. Meet the people who will be working on your account, particularly the account manager in charge of it. Look for creativity, leadership ability, and chemistry between yourself and the account team. If you don't have a sense of confidence in your account team, you'll never be comfortable that the agency is doing the best job for you, no matter how good its reputation or results may be.

10. How can I, as a client, make sure the PR program is successful? It's critical that you understand that PR is a deadline-driven business—daily and hourly deadlines as well as weekly and monthly. Respecting that reality is a key to making your PR program work.

Here are some very simple rules:

- Trust your agency's advice and recommendations.

- Give your account team all the information they require and the time to develop a solid program and press materials for you.

- Keep the agency informed about all new or changing situations. They should know as quickly as you do about production schedule changes, new management additions, etc.

- Be realistic. *Business Week* really isn't for everyone. Don't insist that your PR firm "get you in" the *Wall Street Journal* when a) there's nothing about your company that would interest the *Wall Street Journal*, b) getting in the *Wall Street Journal* really wouldn't benefit your company all that much, and c) you want to reach chemical engineers and so the right publications for you are *Chemical Engineering* and *Chemical Engineering Progress*.

- Be accessible. Many valuable opportunities are lost because executives don't bother to return phone calls and publication deadlines pass by.

- If you have a concern, call your account supervisor as quickly as you recognize the concern. Allowing the situation to wait may mean it will never get resolved.

- Pay your bills promptly. Few agencies are large enough to exist on 60- to 90-day pay cycles. Work might be halted just as a big break is developing because your accounts payable department has assumed the PR agency's bill isn't that important.

Don Levin, president of Levin Public Relations, offers the following additional tips: Chances are the first thing you'll do in your search for a firm is ask a few friends for recommendations. Ninety percent of Levin PR's new business clients approach them based on the word of others. But don't rule out the firm that contacts you. Instead, learn from them. Review their materials; save the information that might help you make a decision about their firm. Take them up on a free consultation meeting if you have something to gain from their knowledge. Three excellent client relationships of Levin PR's developed out of one phone call Don made over four years ago.

Paying for PR

The most effective method of paying for PR is with incentives. Motivate the PR firm to give their all. The worst arrangement is a flat monthly fee without accountable staff charges or time statements. This invites the PR firm to spend as little time as possible on the account and to generate minimal acceptable results.

The best method of payment is a minimum monthly fee against time and action statements plus the incentive for additional productive work through additional payments. The PR firm will then be driven to pursue more useful work. Be sure to indicate a ceiling beyond which written consent is required for additional work and payment. This will protect you against excessive charges and ensure that the ongoing work is well under control before your firm creates new projects.

Managing PR Services

Expect a flow of exciting ideas. Ensure continual access to top management and feedback from them. Make sure your PR firm is operating according to your own agenda, not their own. Pat them on the back when they deserve it.

Test them. Make a little mistake on purpose to see if they pick it up. Be sure they offer constructive advice and criticism and don't just yes you to death.

Choosing between Big and Small

Use a big firm when you need instant national and international service or a wide variety of highly experienced specialists (e.g., in SEC regulation or environmental law). Large firms have the most diverse resources.

When you want a general public relations program on a limited budget, a smaller firm may be better suited to your needs. Remember that regardless of size, you are actually hiring one account manager and some helpers.

Levin reports that one small PR firm is getting frequent projects (some elementary, some sophisticated) from a company that already has a big PR firm. Why? The big firm has a junior account manager coordinating client work who doesn't really know or use the large firm's resources; enormous overhead makes the large firm too costly for small assignments.

FREELANCERS, CONSULTANTS, INDEPENDENT VENDORS, AND SELF-EMPLOYED PROFESSIONALS

From time to time, you may want to hire a variety of self-employed professionals and small service firms who provide services to advertising managers and their companies. These include:

- Copywriters
- Graphic artists
- Photographers
- Illustrators
- Desktop publishers

- Computer service bureaus
- Copy editors
- Proofreaders
- Typesetters
- On-line information researchers
- Market researchers
- Telemarketers
- Printers
- Letter shops (direct mail production houses)
- Slide houses
- Audiovisual production studios
- Marketing consultants
- Advertising and creative consultants
- PR consultants

Why should you, as an advertising manager, turn to outside freelancers and vendors, especially if you already have an ad agency or PR firm? Freelance copywriter Richard Armstrong says there are seven basic reasons:

1. *The advertising department is overloaded.* The staff are busy with other work and they don't have time to do the project, or they could do it, but not by the deadline. The outside vendor is called in to help when your own staff is overloaded.

2. *The advertising department is understaffed or not staffed.* There are busy times and slow times. Rather than overstaff and have people sitting around doing nothing in the off-season, most companies prefer to understaff and hire freelancers during busy periods. Some companies may not have any advertising staff aside from the ad manager, and must depend on outside sources for all their work.

3. *Quality.* In some situations, a freelancer may be able to do a better job on specific assignments. One of the advantages of using outside specialists is that you can pay for top talent on an as-needed basis, choosing the freelancer who is exactly right for that particular job. Joan Lipton, president of Martin & Lipton Advertising Agency, observes: "Freelancers are apt to be even more talented than the permanent staff."

4. *Fresh perspective.* In-house and agency personnel can get bored dealing with the same products and accounts year after year. For this reason, companies turn to independents for renewed enthusiasm, new concepts, a new point of view, and fresh ideas. Freelancers can approach a project with the sense of excitement and vigor that staff and agency personnel may have lost.

5. *The company or ad agency can't do the job themselves.* This occurs when an assignment is outside the company's or agency's regular area of expertise. A corporation that has never used direct mail before would benefit by hiring a graphic artist who knows how to design pieces to comply with postal regulations. An ad agency that specializes in fashion and then acquires an account in telecommunications will probably look for a freelance copywriter specializing in high-tech industries. A fashion writer just doesn't understand the ins and outs of the telecommunications field as thoroughly as a writer who specializes in that field does.

6. *The company is dissatisfied with its current suppliers.* For a variety of reasons, you may become unhappy with the work you are getting from your ad agency or other resources. If your displeasure continues, you may decide to farm out more and more projects to independents until you decide what to do about hiring a new agency.

7. *The independent can do the job cheaper.* Most advertising agencies and PR firms shy away from handling one-shot projects, like a single ad, brochure, or press release. PR firms work on monthly retainers, which usually start at $1,000. Ad agencies expect clients to have an established annual advertising budget, with $50,000 a common minimum figure. For the company with an occasional rather than a steady need for advertising and PR services, freelancers are a cost-effective solution. Most freelancers are available to handle single projects on a fixed-fee or hourly basis, and with their lower overhead, they can charge less than an agency.

Overall, corporate executives are satisfied with outside advertising and creative services, according to a survey conducted by Jenkins & Jenkins Market Research and reported in *Adweek*. Of those surveyed, 62 percent said they use freelance writers and photographers and 67 percent said they would consider using freelance help if the freelancers could provide a service not already provided in-house. Of those who used freelancers, 78 percent said they were satisfied with the work that was produced.

The trend is clearly toward doing less in-house and with agencies, and more through freelancers. Alfred Brown notes that the main advantage to using freelancers over in-house staff or agencies is access to a broad range of specialized talent on an as-needed basis.

"The main idea is to utilize the talents and skills of individuals who are uniquely suited to a particular project," writes Brown. Using freelancers "provides broader, more flexible access to the best creative talent [and] a broader range of ideas than you can get either in-house or through an agency," he maintains. The major advantages of using freelancers are:

- getting access to the best talent;
- getting access to a broader range of talent;
- getting access to highly specialized talent tailored to the project at hand; and
- paying for this talent only when you use it.

The main disadvantage of using freelancers and independents is that the advertising manager must coordinate the activities of many different suppliers who, although they are working on the same project, rarely communicate with one another and certainly are not working as a team. "The danger is lack of control," says Brown. "It's like shopping at ten specialty stores rather than writing one check to Sears." No one vendor on the team takes single-source responsibility for getting the job done right and meeting the deadline, and if there's a slippage, independents can easily blame it on others, citing their own lack of control over the total project.

Elaine Tyson suggests these 12 steps for getting the best work from your freelancers:

1. Avoid prima donnas.

2. Hire the right people.

3. Know how much you're paying (and what you're paying for).

4. Provide enough information.

5. Be prompt with feedback.

6. Critique copy constructively.

7. Streamline the approval process.

8. Build and maintain good relationships.

9. Pay fairly and promptly.

10. Be cooperative. Get freelancers the information they ask for promptly, and answer all questions as soon as possible.

11. Don't waste their time.

12. Give everyone several printed samples of the finished job. Discuss results.

Finding Freelancers and Other Vendors

As with ad agencies and PR firms, finding a freelancer, consultant, or other specialist is usually not difficult. Most likely, they will contact you by phone or mail, asking for work. Save the mailings and request résumés, then save them in a file for future reference.

If you need a specialist and don't know one in that field, call friends, colleagues, and competitors for a recommendation. Your ad agency or PR firm account executive is also a good source for names. Many freelancers and independents also advertise in the classified sections of magazines such as *Adweek* and *Advertising Age*. You can also find them listed in the *Creative Black Book* (see the Resources section at the end of this chapter) which lists audiovisual producers, typographers, retouchers, graphic designers, photographers, printers, engravers, and many other professionals.

Unlike advertising agencies and PR firms, which tend to be generalists, freelancers and self-employed professionals today are specialists. You can find someone to handle whatever you need, whether it's setting up a telemarketing operation and writing telephone scripts, or creating a computer system to track leads and sales, or building a three-dimensional model for your trade show exhibit. Do not settle for a generalist; look for a vendor with expertise in what you need, whether it's PR or direct mail or brochure writing.

Hiring Freelancers and Independent Vendors

Here are ten steps to finding and hiring independent service providers.

1. Ask around. Need to find a writer, artist, or photographer? The best way is through referrals. As discussed, ask friends, colleagues, and acquaintances to recommend names to you. The people most likely to know the names of independent advertising professionals include:

- local advertising and PR firms;
- magazine space reps and editors;
- printers, typesetters, and design studios;
- advertising managers of local companies; and
- other independent advertising professionals.

2. Choose someone with experience in your industry. When you use people who are already knowledgeable about your business, you spend less time briefing them and bringing them up to speed in your technology and your markets.

Because they speak your industry lingo, they'll have an easier time communicating with engineers, product managers, and others within your firm, and their superior knowledge of your markets and industry will enable them to critique your ads, make suggestions on strategies, and come up with new ideas based on their experience working with clients whose products are similar to yours.

3. Hire someone at the right level. In every business, there are beginners and old pros, those with average skills and those with superior talent. The best costs more, but you may not need the top pro for every job.

Matching the right freelancer or vendor to the right assignment ensures a competent job at reasonable cost. Don't hire a $2,500-a-day fashion photographer to shoot routine black and white photos of the company picnic. Not every project justifies top-dollar talent. Know which ones do, and choose freelance talent accordingly.

4. Use service providers whose style is in sync with your own. Freelancers and independents are mercenaries. The term freelance comes from *free lance*, a system in which knights and warriors served as lances for hire to the highest bidder.

Freelancers can do a good job and provide the talent and expertise you can't get elsewhere, but they're not going to change your corporate culture for you. The relationship is too brief, too tenuous, and too temporary. Management is not going to change its style of advertising dramatically because a freelance guru suggests it. More likely, they'll reject the work and ask for something similar to "what we did in the last ad."

You will be most successful if you choose freelancers and independents whose styles are in sync with your own. The work done by freelancers should complement, not revolutionize, what was done previously. Only a large ad agency with a multimillion-dollar budget can create a brand new image or campaign with any hope of getting it approved and implemented. Freelancers can't.

5. Get their information. Most freelancers and independents have brochures, checklists, article reprints, samples, resumes, bios, and a variety of other information they'll happily send you. Ask for it, get it, read it, and keep it. You'll get a good idea of who's available, what they charge, and what jobs you can use them for. You may also get some good free marketing advice by studying their articles, booklets, and samples.

Start a file labeled Freelancers and save all this material. From experience, I've learned that the best time to evaluate a freelancer is at your leisure, not when a project deadline comes crashing around the corner. That way, when you need someone with specialized expertise, you'll know who to call and have their phone number handy.

6. Don't try to get something for nothing. It's human nature to want to get something for nothing; few people volunteer to pay for something if they feel they can get it for free.

Many prospective clients take this attitude with freelancers. They call up the freelancer and promise all sorts of lucrative work, but say they just want to ask a few questions and then proceed to pump the freelancer for all the free advertising advice he or she is giving out that day.

Even if you can get away with this, don't do it. Your interviewing of the freelancer should be solely to ascertain whether the freelancer is the right person for the job and what it will cost, not to get free advice, service, or consultation that you should be paying for.

One of the biggest gray areas in rendering freelance service is when to stop talking for free and when to start charging the client. If you are a client, points out consultant Howard Shenson, it's really in your best interest for you to disclose to the freelancer whether you intend to pay for an initial meeting or conversation. Why? Simple: If the freelancer and you both expect money to change hands, the freelancer will be much more forthcoming with ideas, strategies, and useful suggestions. In short, he or she will be working with you to solve your problem.

On the other hand, if you expect to pay for the initial consultation but the freelancer doesn't know this and thinks it's a free, sales-type meeting, he or she won't be forthcoming with ideas, suggestions, and strategies. The freelancer will be holding back the good stuff for when you sign on the dotted line. You'll eventually be disappointed unless you've agreed that this initial meeting is really just a sales call during which you're looking the freelancer over and making a decision about whether to hire him or her.

Don't try to get free advice, and communicate to the vendor when you expect to begin paying for advice and service.

7. Discuss fees up front. Get an exact estimate for the project, and get it in writing. To make this estimate, the freelancer needs as much information from you as possible about the job. For example, if it's a brochure, what's the topic? How many pages? How many words? What size? How many colors? How many drawings? How many photos? What research is required? Will there be original photography or illustration or will you use existing materials? What background information can you provide? Will travel be required? To what and how many locations?

If you can't provide detailed job specifications, then ask the freelancer to give you a fee schedule or an explanation of how jobs are billed and what the charges are. Does the service provider charge by the project, by the hour, or by the day? How much per hour? How much per day? If charges are by the project, ask for typical fees or a range of fees for projects similar to what you need. Most independent firms have a written fee schedule explaining rates, charges, terms, and conditions in detail.

Terms and conditions are also important. Does the freelancer require a purchase order, or will you be asked to sign a standard agreement or contract? Can you review a copy of the agreement or contract in advance? What are the terms and conditions? Is payment due upon completion, or is an advance retainer required? If advance payment is required, how much? What happens if you want changes? How are revisions handled? What happens if you are not satisfied?

8. Provide complete background information. The more background information and the more complete job specifications you provide, the more accurately the freelancer can estimate the cost of the job. If you are vague or uncertain about the parameters of the job, the freelancer will be flying blind, not knowing how much work is really involved, and the high estimate will reflect this degree of uncertainty.

You'll get the best price by giving the freelancer whatever information is required to make an informed, accurate estimate of what the job will cost.

9. Get it in writing. Put the fee, terms, deadlines, and a description of the assignment in a purchase order or letter and send it to the vendor.

A written agreement eliminates confusion and spells out what you are buying and what the vendor is selling. Too many buyers and sellers in all fields of business have gone to court because they made their deals orally. Don't make that same mistake.

When you write the job description as you see it and send it out as a purchase order or letter, that becomes the understanding and agreement unless the vendor notifies you otherwise in writing. A written agreement protects you, so don't just shake on it. Put it in writing.

10. Stand back. Once you've hired vendors, stand back and let them do their jobs. Don't interfere, don't ask to "take a look at the first few pages," don't badger them with constant "How's it going?" calls. You've hired professionals, so let the professionals do their jobs. You'll get your work by the deadline date, or sooner. If you've hired the right person, you'll get quality work.

RESOURCES

An aid in locating an advertising agency: *The Standard Directory of Advertising Agencies*, published by Reed Reference Publishing Company, 121 Chanlon Rd., New Providence, NJ 07974, 800-521-8110.

A directory to help you find a PR firm: *O'Dwyer's Directory of Public Relations Firms*, published by J.R. O'Dwyer and Company, Inc., 271 Madison Avenue, New York, NY 10016, 212-679-2471.

A resource to help you find freelancers, consultants, or other specialists: *The Creative Black Book*, published by Friendly Press, 401 Park Avenue South, New York, NY 10016, 212-870-2586.

Chapter 35

INQUIRY HANDLING AND FULFILLMENT

For many advertisers, a prime objective of advertising and promotion is to generate inquiries and sales. Indeed, American business spends billions of dollars each year to generate, track, and follow up on sales leads.

For some companies, the sales lead program represents a tremendous investment in time and money. For instance, a marketing communications manager at Digital Equipment once reported that the company processed 120,000 inquiries per year. A survey conducted by *Business Marketing* magazine found that nine out of ten marketers believe proper handling of inquiries is important. (Tables 35.1 through 35.4 are from this survey.) The responses are summarized in Table 35.1.

The survey also found that counting leads generated was one of the two methods of advertising measurement most favored by successful marketers, the other being measures that relate advertising to sales or profits. The results are shown in Table 35.2.

Interestingly, these concrete measures—leads, sales, and profits—were the only ones advertising managers really valued. They do not put much faith in ad benchmark studies, readership studies, company awareness research, and other soft methods of measuring communications effectiveness. Nor do they value feedback from the sales force, although this may reflect an unfortunate animosity toward salespeople rather than logic.

Despite the importance placed on inquiry handling, only three out of ten of these marketers use a computerized system for inquiry fulfillment, and nearly as many (27 percent) have no inquiry handling system at all.

Table 35.1. How top marketers rate the importance of inquiry handling.

Extremely important	59%
Very important	21%
Relatively important	11%
Not important	4%
No answer	5%

Table 35.2. Preferred methods of measuring advertising progress.

Relating communications activities to sales and profits	39%
Number of leads generated	28%
Ad benchmark/readership studies	13%
Company awareness research	12%
Sales force feedback	12%

WHAT'S IMPORTANT IN INQUIRY HANDLING

The key to successful inquiry handling is speed. Experience proves that the value of a sales lead decreases almost exponentially in proportion to the delay in responding to it. You should try to fulfill all inquiries within 48 hours of receipt of the lead. Prospects will not wait to receive your material before seeking proposals from other vendors or making purchases. Instead, they will consider only those vendors who respond promptly. Even prior to when the sales rep gets the lead, some means of acknowledging the prospect's inquiry is effective.

Some marketers mistakenly believe there's some benefit to being the last to respond to an inquiry. They reason that the prospect is more likely to remember the last brochure received and will already have forgotten the first ones by that time.

Unfortunately, this isn't true. The best strategy is to respond quickly, then follow up several times to keep your name in front of the prospect. Delaying response is inappropriate. Many prospects reason, "If they're this slow in sending a brochure, I can imagine how unresponsive they'll be when we order from them!" First impressions are important, and a slow response to the initial inquiry is a poor first impression indeed.

Advertisers spend billions of dollars to generate inquiries annually, but then are slipshod in their handling of leads. An article in *Business Marketing* (May 1997) reports that 37 percent of inquiries sent to 405 trade advertisers that were monitored in a study were never responded to. Of those that were answered, the average response time was a miserable 38 days; 25 percent of the responses didn't include a cover letter, 69 percent didn't include a reply card, and 34 percent had mistakes in the recipient's address. In a study reported in *Metalworking Marketer* (May 1997), Performark replied to 7,000 advertisements placed by thousands of advertisers in 200 trade publications. They found that 21 percent of their inquiries were not fulfilled. Forty-five percent of the companies took 60 days or more to respond.

Aside from speed in responding to inquiries, qualifying the sales leads—that is, making sure you turn over only quality leads to the salespeople—is the second key function of inquiry handling.

What is a qualified lead? It's a response from someone who has the money, authority, and desire to buy your product or service and is interested in what you are offering. It is not the person who says, "I just want a brochure for my files; don't call me—leave me alone!"

Either the initial marketing communication (ad, letter, mailer) or the follow-up material must qualify the prospect so that leads turned over to salespeople are of good quality and serious intent. You can use an automated system like the one Dun & Bradstreet offers, providing on-line access to their data files. When a response comes in, you key in the name of that company and the computer sorts through four or five million names and prints out for you all the data Dun & Bradstreet has on that company—size, number of years in business, type of business, location, and so on.

Qualification of leads can also be done over the phone by support staff or telemarketing representatives. Some typical qualifying questions include:

What is your specific application?

When do you think you will be making a buying decision? Within three months? Six months? One year?

What size (capacity, volume, power) unit do you require?

Who else in your company will be involved in making this purchasing decision?

What is your budget for solving this problem or handling this application? Under $1,000? Under $10,000? Under $50,000? Under $100,000? Under $1 million?

Do you currently use this type of service or product? Who is your current supplier?

Table 35.3 lists the elements marketers consider most important in an inquiry follow-up and handling program. *Business Marketing* also asked marketers what improvements they were likely to make to their inquiry handling systems. Half said they were thinking about computerizing their inquiry handling systems (remember, only three out of ten cur-

Table 35.3. The elements marketers consider part of a successful inquiry program (responses total more than 100 percent due to multiple mentions).

Fast turnaround	80%
Qualification process	53%
Relation to sales process	47%
Use with telemarketing and research	23%
Reporting methods	18%
Economy	15%
Flexibility	15%
Customization	15%

Table 35.4. Inquiry handling improvements marketers would consider (responses total more than 100 percent due to multiple mentions).

Computerized handling	52%
Telemarketing	49%
Dial-in reader service	27%
Multiple prospect mailings	27%
Electronic mail	17%
Dial-in computer service	16%
Other	3%

rently use a computer to handle inquiries). Table 35.4 shows the other potential upgrades and improvements marketers said they would consider making to their inquiry handling systems.

DESIGNING THE INQUIRY HANDLING SYSTEM

Whether computerized or manual, an effective inquiry handling system must perform the following functions:

- Record all necessary information about each lead.
- Respond to the inquiry in the appropriate fashion.
- Pass the lead information on to salespeople and others who require it.
- Provide a mechanism for future follow-up and promotion.
- Track the buying decisions of each lead.
- Report on inquiry and sales results.

   Let's look at these functions one at a time.

RECORD ALL NECESSARY INFORMATION ABOUT EACH LEAD

You should design your system so that a computer operator, secretary, or other member of your support staff records into the inquiry handling system all necessary information about the prospect. This can include (but is not limited to):

- Name of prospect
- Title
- Company
- Address
- City
- State
- ZIP code

- Daytime phone number
- Evening phone number
- Fax number
- Date of inquiry
- Source of inquiry
- Method of response (reader service card, letter, phone call)
- Nature of prospect's business
- Type of application
- Timeframe of need (immediate, three months, six months, one year, no immediate need, etc.)
- Quality and urgency of lead (i.e., whether the prospect has an urgent need, a less urgent need, or is just collecting brochures for future reference)
- Date literature was sent
- Dates and summary of follow-up contacts
- Salesperson's opinion as to the probability of closing the sale (can be ranked from 1 to 10)
- Comments

When designing your inquiry handling system, make a complete list of the information you think you need, then show it to salespeople, product managers, and others. They may want to add additional information to the inquiry records.

It's important to do this analysis carefully. Especially with computer databases, it's much easier to take time at the beginning to design it right, and much more difficult to go back and change the database once you've been using it.

Think about any specific information not on the above list that would be important to your sales and marketing efforts. For example, if in ad coupons and direct mail reply cards you ask prospects to indicate whether they have life insurance, it would make sense to add this information to your prospect database. If you've captured the information, you can analyze leads by type of business, size of business, geography, census information, income information, or ZIP code. You can also analyze where where you get your best results from, in any type of direct mail program. If you received a 4 percent response to a particular program from, say, the southern half of Atlanta, look at other prospects in the southern half of Atlanta because that seems to be where you're getting the best response.

RESPOND TO THE INQUIRY IN THE APPROPRIATE FASHION

Of course, every company should respond to inquiries promptly and by sending the appropriate materials. These materials include the specific catalog, brochure, or other information the prospect asked for along with any other materials you think would help sell the prospect on using your product or service.

Will the Internet make paper inquiry fulfillment obsolete? "Vendors who plan to cut down the distribution of printed documents once their Web sites are up and running soon find that the demand for non-Web distribution remains strong," states an article in *Micro Software Marketing* (May 1997, p. 8). The article recommends creating inquiry fulfillment materials in two formats: one for the Web and the other as text files that can be converted into E-mail or hard copy, concluding: "Despite all the attention paid to the Web, the Web is not as commonly used as much of the hype indicates."

Inquiry Fulfillment Package

An effective inquiry fulfillment package typically consists of the following elements:

Outer Envelope

The outer envelope should be imprinted or stamped with a teaser, in large bold letters, that proclaims, "Here is the information you requested." Otherwise, prospects or their secretaries might not remember asking for the material, will think it's unsolicited direct mail, and are more likely to throw it away. When you remind prospects that they asked for the material, they're more likely to at least open and look at it.

Brochure or Other Information the Prospect Requested

The most important element in the package is the brochure or other sales literature the prospect asked you to send. Ideally, the brochure should be about the specific topic featured in the ad or mailing to which the prospect responded.

For instance, if you did an ad offering information on Circular Widgets, the most effective response is a brochure specifically about circular widgets, not a general all-line widget brochure. If you must send a general all-line piece, clip the appropriate pages with a paper clip and attach a note to the cover that says, "The information you asked for on circular widgets appears on pages XX to YY."

Additional Brochures and Sales Literature

Without overwhelming the prospect by sending too much literature, selectively include additional materials you feel would be effective in selling the prospect on your product or service. These pieces can include user stories, case histories, testimonial sheets, article reprints, technical papers, applications bulletins, and corporate capabilities brochures.

You can often cross-sell a prospect interested in one product or service on other products or services by including a statement of your full capabilities, either as a page in a larger brochure or as a separate piece. For instance, if you are responding to an inquiry about floppy disks, the prospect would also be likely to buy computer paper, printer ribbons, and other PC supplies. Sending a catalog or full-line brochure could quite possibly stimulate additional sales.

Sales Letter

Your inquiry fulfillment package should be accompanied by a persuasive sales letter that thanks prospects for their interest, explains a little more about your products or services, tells them what you've sent in the package, and encourages them to take the next step in the buying process.

The letter can be personalized or nonpersonalized. A form letter works well and eliminates the need to run off a personalized letter on the computer for each prospect. The letter can be long or short. In some situations, it's better to be brief and let your brochure do the selling. If your literature doesn't do the whole selling job, you can turn the letter itself into your main selling tool.

Dealer List

If inquiries are fulfilled from a central location rather than by the local rep or regional office responsible for sales in the prospect's territory, include a mechanism in your inquiry fulfillment package that gives the prospect the name, address, and phone number of a contact or salesperson to call for more information or to arrange an appointment.

This can be done in the sales letter; the computer can pull the appropriate salesperson or dealer's name and insert text that says, "The salesperson handling your account is (name, address, phone)." If you use a form letter, you can staple or clip the appropriate sales representative's card to the letter and include a line that says, "For more information, contact the dealer [or sales rep] whose card is attached to this letter. Or call us directly at the corporate office at [phone number]." The latter is in case the card becomes detached or lost.

An alternate method is to enclose a typeset list of your dealers, agents, or sales offices nationwide and check or circle the appropriate name for the prospect to contact. Copy in the form letter would say, "The name and phone number of the dealer (or agent or sales rep) assigned to your account is indicated on the attached Dealer List (or agent or sales rep list)."

The important thing is to give the prospect access to the name and number of a local contact. All else being equal, prospects would rather buy from someone local than from someone far away. If you have a branch office, dealer, outlet, rep, or field salesperson in the prospect's territory, it's a competitive advantage and should be pointed out in the inquiry fulfillment package.

Reply Form

It's important not only to tell the prospect what the next step is, but also to make it easy for him or her to take it. For this reason, you should include some sort of reply element in every inquiry fulfillment package you send. The reply element can be a survey form, questionnaire, specification sheet, or order form. Encourage prospects to fill it in and return it to you by mail or fax as the next step in getting more information on how you can help them solve their problems.

One strategy is to print the reply element on a brightly colored piece of paper, usually gold, yellow, blue, pink, or green. In your inquiry fulfillment letter, say, "To order (or to get more information), just complete and mail the pink [or blue, etc.] form today." The prospect's eyes immediately locate the response form because it's a different color from the rest of the package.

Business Card

Always include your business card or the business card of the salesperson or representative handling the prospect's territory. This personalizes the package and many people routinely keep and file business cards.

Tip: If you sell a product or service the prospect is likely to need later instead of now, and if it's the type of product or service that is bought on an as-needed basis (e.g., printing, office supplies, mailing lists, etc.), you can increase the likelihood of your prospect contacting you when in need by enclosing a Rolodex™ card with your company name, phone number, and a description of what you offer. Business cards printed to fit in Rolodex card files have become increasingly popular in recent years; many, many prospects automatically remove such cards from mailings and put them in the Rolodex, even if they have no pressing need for the product or service advertised.

Keep in mind that the dual goals of the inquiry fulfillment package are a) to promptly provide the prospect with the information requested— that is, the data the prospect wants and needs to make a decision about buying your product or service, and b) to actually sell the product or service by including additional material that will capture attention and persuade the prospect to take action favorable to you.

PASS THE LEAD INFORMATION ON TO SALESPEOPLE AND OTHERS WHO REQUIRE IT

The next function of the inquiry handling system is to distribute information about the lead to salespeople. This is typically done by geographic region (territory) or by product line, depending on how your sales force is organized.

With a manual inquiry handling system, you can use a carbon form so that as mailing labels are typed or leads are recorded, duplicates are created; the copies are routed to the appropriate salespeople. Or, you can simply photocopy the sheet or ledger on which you record leads and distribute copies to salespeople. A computerized system can generate a listing of the leads (with complete information on each) assigned to each salesperson to follow up on.

How quickly should salespeople or telemarketing staff make the first follow-up call? For consumers at home addresses, allow one week after you mail the inquiry fulfillment material. For business prospects at corporations, one and a half to two weeks seems about right (this allows enough time for delivery by the post office and corporate mailrooms and assumes the material will sit in the prospect's in-basket a few days before it is read).

PROVIDE A MECHANISM FOR FUTURE FOLLOW-UP AND PROMOTION

Marketers who want to convert more leads to sales realize they must follow up, again and again, to overcome inertia and get prospects to take action.

How often should you follow up? Keep making follow-up phone calls and mailings until the latest mailing or call in the series doesn't at least pay for itself. How much is this in practice? Author Jeffrey Lant says seven follow-ups in 18 months are needed to get prospects to take action. Consultant Robert Sieghardt reports that if you send an inquiry fulfillment package and follow up with a series of three mailings, approximately 55 percent of prospects will respond.

The inquiry handling system should make prospect names easily accessible for follow-up and should be organized so you can determine which prospects should be followed up this week, next week, next month, and so on.

A computerized inquiry handling system can be designed to generate reports that list leads according to original date of inquiry as well as date of last contact, so you can easily get a list of those who are due for a friendly follow-up phone call or letter.

A manual inquiry handling system can be organized in a notebook with 12 sections, each for a different month. The prospects in section one all get called in January, the prospects in section two get called in February, and so on. This is cumbersome but it can work.

TRACK THE BUYING DECISIONS OF EACH LEAD

Another desirable feature of the inquiry handling system is the ability to track the status of each lead. For instance, one service firm uses direct mail to generate leads. All leads are mailed a brochure, then followed up by telephone. Those who are interested get a more in-depth discussion of their specific need, then receive a price quotation and proposal to do the work discussed. Some sign the proposal and buy the service; others who receive proposals do nothing.

The firm's in-house inquiry handling system identifies each lead according to these categories:

- Inquiry—The person has requested a brochure but has not talked with a salesperson.

- Open quote—The person has talked with a salesperson and has been sent a proposal and cost estimate for work to be performed.

- Sale—The person has accepted the price quotation and bought the service.

- Dead lead—After six months, those who received a proposal and did not buy are no longer considered potential customers and go in a dead file.

The inquiry handling system can print a report showing the status of each lead. For this level of sophistication, you need to computerize your inquiry handling; it's nearly impossible to keep track of this information accurately using a manual system.

When should a lead be considered dead? Your own experience will determine this. Selling cycles vary by industry and by product. In general, the more costly the product, the longer it takes the prospect to make a buying decision.

In my copywriting and consulting business, I find that many prospects who request my information do so for future reference; only a minority who call have an immediate project they are ready to assign on the spot.

Of those who say they have a future need, the ones who end up hiring me generally do so within 12 months after making the initial inquiry (and most do so within 2 to 6 months). If they don't contact me after 12 months, then they are not sufficiently motivated or genuinely interested in my service, and I move them from the active to the dead file.

You must observe your own prospects' buying patterns and make a decision as to when leads should be moved from active to inactive status.

REPORT ON INQUIRY AND SALES RESULTS

In addition to tracking individual leads, you also want to get a picture of the success of your advertising and sales programs. How many leads did your last ad produce? Of those, how many just wanted a brochure and how many were really interested and requested a proposal? This tells you whether your ad is generating leads of good quality or poor quality. Of those who requested a proposal, how many actually became customers? This tells you how effective your sales program is in converting leads to sales. Of those who bought, what were the total sales and average sale per order? This tells you how profitable your ad was.

Here is some (but not necessarily all) of the information you will want your lead handling system to be able to produce for you:

- Name and source of promotion (e.g., January mailing to *Forbes* list).
- Total cost of promotion (in dollars).
- Total number of leads generated.
- Cost per lead (divide total cost of promotion by total number of leads generated).
- Number of leads who requested a proposal or sales presentation or took some other action step.
- Percentage of leads that took the above step (divide number of leads taking action by total number of leads, then multiply by 100).
- Cost per qualified lead (a qualified lead is someone who took the above step; to calculate, divide total cost of promotion by number of leads who took the action step).

- Number of orders generated.
- Cost per order (divide total cost of promotion by number of orders generated).
- Percentage of leads converted to orders (divide number of orders by number of leads, then multiply by 100).
- Total sales generated.
- Ratio of total sales to cost of promotion (this tells you if the promotion was profitable or not; to calculate, divide total sales in dollars by cost of promotion).

Without this information, you have no way to tell if your advertising is making money for you, and no way to rationally judge the effectiveness of any promotional effort you produce.

This level of sophistication is generally available only in computerized inquiry handling systems. You can track it manually if you receive a small quantity of leads (up to a few hundred per month).

MANUAL INQUIRY HANDLING SYSTEMS

Let's look at how one small marketer uses a manual inquiry handling system to track leads using a simple form (Figure 35.1)

Figure 35.1. Lead sheet for manual inquiry handling system.

Date_____ Source of inquiry_____   Response via_____

NAME _____   TITLE _____

COMPANY _____

PHONE _____   FAX _____

ADDRESS _____   ROOM _____

CITY _____   STATE _____   ZIP _____

Type of business:

Type of projects: ❏ marketing assistance ❏ marketing plan ❏ ad
❏ direct mail package ❏ sales letter ❏ brochure ❏ feature article
❏ press release ❏ newsletter ❏ other:
FOR: ❏ immediate project ❏ project within _____weeks/months ❏ future reference

STATUS:
❏ Sent package on (date):
❏ Enclosed these samples:
❏ Next step is to:
❏ Probability of assignment:
❏ Comments:

CONTACT RECORD:
Date: Summary:

The date at the top of the form is the date the prospect contacted you. Source of inquiry tells whether it's a referral, ad, mailing, and the exact source. Response via indicates whether the prospect wrote or called (those who call are usually better leads for me because they have taken a more aggressive role and have actually spoken to me).

Fill in the name, title, company, phone, fax, and mailing information completely. Knowing the type of business prospects are in and the type of projects they face will help you tailor your inquiry fulfillment package. Ask whether a prospect has an immediate project, has a project coming up soon, or is calling to get material for file reference.

Under Status, list the date you sent the package, what you sent, what you think the next step is (Did the prospect ask you to call on a specific date or to be added to a mailing list?), the probability you will get work from them (rated on a scale of 1 to 10), and any miscellaneous comments you feel are important (for example, "Need this in a hurry" or "A small company, don't have much money"). Under Contact Record, record the date of each follow-up call and brief notes on what was said.

Keep leads for the past 12 months in a binder in chronological order, with the most recent lead first. When a lead becomes older than 12 months without buying from you, put it in an inactive file organized alphabetically by company name. When prospects buy from you, their sheets go into a Clients notebook, again organized alphabetically by company name. Thus you have three notebooks: one for leads you hope to sell to, one for clients (current, ongoing, and past), and one for old leads (people who asked for information but never bought).

COMPUTERIZED INQUIRY HANDLING SYSTEMS

The following eight criteria are the building blocks on which an effective computerized inquiry handling system is built:

1. The system should be easily understood and accepted by staff and sales force. It should also be planned and sponsored by top management to assure cooperation and compliance.

2. It should be relevant and timely, providing requested materials while inquirer interest is still high and forwarding qualified leads to the sales force without delay.

3. It should be qualification-oriented with a facility to determine the best candidates for sales force follow-up.

4. It should be oriented to follow-up with the ability to determine the level of sales force participation as well as inquirer action.

5. It should be measurable and accountable.

6. It should provide information with which management can properly evaluate both the advertising program and the communication system.

7. It should be accurate, efficient, and disciplined, recording all data correctly and consistently. It should not become a self-defeating ocean of paper.

8. Finally, it should be flexible and accessible. It should be able to handle hundreds or thousands of inquiries per month and provide needed information in a reasonable time frame.

What are the pros and cons of handling inquiries in-house? Advantages of processing leads internally include shorter lines of communication and the potential to develop reports with greater detail. Disadvantages include the high cost of initial software development (or purchase), lack of access to company computer because of low priority (solvable if the advertising department has a dedicated micro- or minicomputer), and the extra cost of inquiry handling personnel and supervisors.

Some advantages of using an outside computerized sales inquiry service are:

- guaranteed turnaround time for literature fulfillment and reports;

- fixed cost per inquiry—often lower than what a company would incur internally; and

- more sophisticated system reporting, such as field sales tracking and prospect follow-up.

Disadvantages of using outside services include problems in communications, the high cost of customization of special programs for your company (if required), and the hesitancy of management to release information to an outside service for what is traditionally an inside operation.

The greatest cost internally for an inquiry handling system is labor. The cost to stuff envelopes and type labels, including fringe benefits, runs somewhere between $13,000 and $16,000 or more annually per clerk. Assuming an individual worker can do 10,000 fulfillments a year (that's 40 per day or 5 per hour), the per-inquiry cost is $1.30 to $1.60 or more in labor alone. If the cost for labor in your area is greater, adjust these figures accordingly.

In addition, postage and literature costs can range from $1 to $4 per inquiry package, More elaborate packages can top $5 apiece or more! Space is also a consideration. Some companies that are dealing with 30,000 to 35,000 leads a year use considerable cubic foot area. If three to four or more people are employed to handle leads and you employ a supervisor, the cost could easily be an additional $20,000 to $25,000 a year.

CASE STUDY:
HOW IBM CREATED ITS LEAD PROCESSING SYSTEM

Here is how IBM computerized its inquiry handling, as explained by a sales program administrator in the IBM National Marketing Division:

About two years ago, IBM found that the need for mass marketing was rapidly growing. McGraw-Hill says that it costs about $137 (1980 figure) just to have a salesperson make a call. With that, we actively moved into the area of mass marketing. We found we could identify our prospects very easily using direct mail, advertising, and business shows, but what made sales was the lead processing, getting those leads out to the salespeople in the most timely way. Our problem was not being able to turn those leads around quickly enough, which resulted in the loss of the money we'd invested to find the prospects. We wanted a system that would meet several objectives.

The first objective was to reduce the number of lost leads. Second, because we support over 200 locations across the country, leads must get to our branch offices quickly. Third, we needed to track the progress and the results of each of our different campaigns, so we had to record the result of each lead. Did the prospect buy? If so, what was bought? If not, why not? Finally, we wanted to build a database for future mailings to prospects who indicated interest, those who may not buy at the present time but may buy later or when we introduce a new product.

We considered using outside services, both the pros and the cons. We had only 90 days to put a system in place, so we decided to develop our own system because we had in-house expertise. The key question was whether to use one of our own large systems or a small commercial business computer. Because of the short time frame and lack of access to a large system, the answer to our problem was a small business computer. We installed our own, with several key functions.

The first function is lead capture: the name, the address, and any key qualifying data to transmit to the salesperson. The next function is lead distribution—taking it from when it comes into our headquarters in Atlanta and distributing it to the appropriate location, one of 200, so that it reaches the right marketing rep in the field.

We also wanted to relieve the field personnel of the burden of literature fulfillment, so we automated fulfillment. Of course, the next step is tracking leads once they're fulfilled and sent to the salesperson, recording the final result and how much business we actually generated.

The last function is lead management. If a prospect doesn't buy, can we keep the prospect in our system, using a different series of mailings or a different means of contact—possibly telephone prospecting or salesperson follow-up—based on the prospect's interest?

What are the results of our new system? We've developed several ways of getting reports, so that we can actually analyze the time it takes to get a decision made as well as recording what the decision is. Then we can analyze what is the best offer. We can also analyze what the cost of closing the order is, which is a key factor considering how much money is spent on marketing.

We get good field participation, and that was probably the most difficult hurdle. How do we get nearly 1,800 salespeople across the country participating in this program? We devised our own internal direct mail and advertising campaign. We sent each rep a simple, preaddressed check-off form to be put into our internal mail system and sent back to us. We explained that they would get better prospects in the future because we would know what mailings were better campaigns and resulted in better ways of qualifying prospects. So far our response rates have increased and our sales force is achieving higher and higher closing rates. Now, with the total mass marketing program, they're beginning to rely more and more on our lead generation.

I think we took the right route, and that the in-house system fit us best, with the expertise and assistance we had on hand and the number of people we had to handle.

To Computerize or Not to Computerize?

Most of the companies involved in lead generation either via direct mail specifically or via space ads and other direct response promotions are not Fortune 500 companies. Many more companies have gotten into direct mail and direct response as the primary vehicles for the sales of their products. It will take in-house analysis to determine whether to computerize, but the decision to automate any type of system basically depends on the quantity of whatever you're processing. If you process 100 or 200 leads a month, it's probably not worth the expense to automate the system.

QUALIFIED LEADS VERSUS COUPON CLIPPERS AND BROCHURE COLLECTORS

It's one thing to generate responses. You might mail a promotion that includes either giveaways or special triggers and generates a 4 percent response rate. But if your field sales force can only sell a small percentage of the leads you've generated, you haven't generated a 4 percent sales response.

Look at it from this standpoint: "We received responses of X, we made presentations of Y, and that resulted in a sales factor of Z." Of course, sales closed is the bottom line. Generating responses doesn't do a whole lot for you or the company unless you're able to close on those responses.

Coupon clippers are people who respond to get a free brochure but are not genuine prospects. Your inquiry handling system should rank leads, distinguishing between hot leads and coupon clippers.

Leads can be separated into five preselected categories of qualified leads. The first category includes prospects who come to a trade show and say they want to see a sales representative. The second category are direct mail campaign prospects who check off a box that says, "Yes, I would like to see a sales representative."

The third category are phone inquiries; any telephone call that comes in from a prospect is considered a qualified lead. Letter writers, the fourth category, are also considered qualified lead. The fifth category are people who clip a coupon from an ad and check a box indicating they would like a salesperson to call. These are the primary categories for sending a sales lead notice on to the sales force. Salespeople will get fewer leads, but the leads they do get will be fairly well qualified.

To fill salespeople in on all the activity in a territory, generate a monthly report listing all prospects who inquired or requested literature to supplement the leads. Now the salespeople have the opportunity to go over a master register and decide whether any individual secondary lead warrants a telephone call. There are no gaps in the information. The salespeople get their hot leads on a daily or weekly basis, and they also get a monthly report outlining in detail all the prospects in their areas.

CASE HISTORY:
COMPUTERIZING THE PRIORITY OF LEADS

One industrial advertising manager reported:

We have evolved from assigning lead processing to any secretary who had the time available, to using a computerized service and assigning a high level of priority to specific sales leads. We identified what we required in a lead processing system and went through several stages of development.

First, we formalized a manual system and operated it for about one year. It was satisfactory, even though it didn't allow us to get all of the information we could get from all the names that we were spending hard marketing dollars to generate. It was sufficient to fulfill a prospect's request, to gauge quantities, and to assign a priority to the lead. As far as getting other marketing information, it was insufficient.

We then looked at the computer as a solution to all of our problems and found somebody with a system who thought it could do what we wanted. But the service was not completely debugged. It was a mail list maintenance program designed to do one thing, and we were trying to make it do something else. This proved fatal. Retrieving information from the system was almost as difficult as it was with a manual system. Throughout the manual stage and the first computer stage, we were fulfilling all requests on a timely basis and notifying the field on a timely basis. It's primarily in the area of getting additional information, or getting the names back out for other promotions, where we had difficulties.

We decided that the major features we wanted in a new computerized system were timely fulfillment of the inquirer's request, timely reporting to field sales, and timely reporting to management, with the addition of being able to draw data from the system for other promotions, like direct mail, trade shows, and special campaigns.

We identified the type of service we wanted now, and identified future service needs, based on a given lead quantity that we expect to be generating many years hence. We wanted a versatile system that would give us the information we wanted now, with the option of adding several different types of reporting that would be valuable to marketing as the company became used to a more sophisticated database and to using the information available from the database.

We now fulfill inquiries within 48 hours after they are received. We send notifications of every lead to our field salespeople at the time of fulfillment. On a monthly basis, we send a status report of all leads in a given territory to the field sales offices as well as to the regional managers' offices. We also have a quarterly status report of all the leads broken down by sales territory, by the lead type source (whether it be direct mail, advertising, or trade shows), and by specific medium. It also totals the leads generated and the cost per inquiry.

Other types of reports are also available to us. We've used this computerized inquiry system for one year and we think we can now use additional reporting and additional data to make our promotions and our field sales follow-up still more efficient.

Follow-up mailings to a prospect can be extremely valuable. If a manufacturer is paying anywhere from $10 to, in some cases, $200 for an industrial sales lead, plus from $3 to $7 for the package of literature, plus the postage and the labor required to get that material out, and the prospect does not respond, why drop that prospect right then and there? Reinvest another 30 or 40 cents and contact prospects a month later. Ask them basically the same set of questions. There may be a very good reason why they didn't respond the first time. If you don't hear from them this time, try it again a month later. Try two more comparatively inexpensive mailings over a two-month period to see if you can get a prospect to say, "Yes, I'm ready to see a sales representative now."

In some cases two follow-up mailings have generated a 125 percent increase in qualified leads over the original bounce-back card [reply card] in the five categories of prequalified leads [mentioned in the previous section].

With an inquiry database, you own a ready-made list of people who were interested in your product earlier. There are opportunities for using those names again, for example, to reawaken interest when you have new products, a change in terms and conditions, or new prices. That's a major announcement to someone who hit a stumbling block in making a decision to buy from you before.

Each new contact will increase your response rate by some percentage. Names you get from any type of direct mail program are precious to you. It's so much more valuable than going to a compiled list and buying 200,000 raw names that previous analysis has indicated should be prime prospects. Responses you receive are people you know are definitely prime prospects. The overwhelming majority of them will be qualified prospects for you, so you should continue to work that list just as frequently as you can allocate the money or as long as response rates continue to justify it.

The list of names can be used for other promotions, such as product newsletters and special offer direct mailings for the individual product of interest to the prospects. These names are also a valuable source of market information for market research surveys.

The list can also be a source of revenue for a firm because there is an increasing amount of rental and usage of response names to noncompeting sellers. A firm may have a file of 50,000 or 100,000 companies or individuals who have responded to a certain type of offer. Someone else may be looking for a similar list for an offer they are promoting. Renting the list can be a profitable source of revenue.

Note: The revenue from list rentals can be from 50 cents to $3 per name per year. If you have 100,000 names and earn $1 a year from renting them, that's an additional $100,000 per year in revenue. This is significant because the list rental revenues can help finance (or in some cases totally pay for) the inquiry handling system.

SEVEN STEPS TO COMPUTERIZING YOUR INQUIRY HANDLING

1. *Analyze your problem.* Is it volume? Is it lack of information? Determine your key problem, because that's the area that should be your priority in addressing the use of the computer.

2. *Pursue the proper solution.* How can you handle the problem? Is it ability to process more leads, or is it reports that you need? Investigate the financial cost. Often it's quite easy to justify either an in-house or out-

side service, because you're talking about handling an asset, something of real value.

3. *Select the right system.* It has to fit into your business. Consider ease of use and ability to solve your problems.

4. *Develop a plan.* How are you going to go about installing this computer system in your company?

5. *Start a training program for your people.* Include salespeople, administrative people, and the management team.

6. *Prepare accurate data.* Take what you currently have and put it into the system.

7. *Look at what you have to do in the future.* Will you have growth capability? Design a system (or ask your service bureau to design a system) that's going to address your future needs as well as your current ones without going through a complete redesign.

THE LITERATURE FULFILLMENT CENTER

If you decide to handle inquiry processing in-house, then in addition to the computer system you will also need a literature center—a separate work area dedicated to the physical storage, assembly, and mailing of inquiry fulfillment materials.

The literature center can be a separate room or the corner of an office. Depending on the number of inquiries you receive, it might require the services of a single worker or a staff of several employees stuffing envelopes, entering leads into the computer, and distributing lead reports.

The important thing is to make the distribution and management of literature a separate function, not something your secretary does when he or she has some extra time. If lead handling is given a priority below other routine tasks, these routine tasks will fill the secretary's day and the inquiries will not get fulfilled on time.

Here are ten additional points to keep in mind when setting up your literature center:

1. The best setup is to have a completely separate room or area set aside for literature storage and distribution. Don't ask secretaries to do the job in their normal work space. They will quickly run out of room and become overwhelmed. Handling and mailing multiple pieces of literature, and storing the leads, requires space.

2. Equip the literature center with shelves for stocking an ample supply of brochures. The best shelves are the metal type found in warehouses; shelf height can easily be adjusted. Shelving allows workers to quickly find and pull the material they need. Do not store your working supply of brochures in boxes; this makes the material hard to get at.

3. Shelving, of course, holds a limited supply and must be restocked at intervals. The rest of the brochures are best stored in the original card-

board boxes in which they arrived from the printer. Be sure the literature center has enough room to stock these boxes. Stacking boxes in a
large, open room is best because it allows easy access. Piling boxes atop
one another in a cramped closet discourages people from looking for the
materials they need.

4. When estimating space requirements for your literature center, consider all the things you'll need. These include workstations for each secretary or clerk; room for the computer system; shelves to hold the literature; space for one or more postage meters; file cabinets to hold lead
reports, forms, and other materials; and a place to keep outgoing mail
(which may be substantial in volume) until the mailroom pick-up person or mail carrier arrives.

5. The literature center should be dry, well-lit, and kept at normal room
temperature. Excess humidity and extreme temperature changes can
cause printed material to wrinkle and fade, creating a poor impression.

6. Put in a few extra work areas in the literature room to accommodate
temporary help you may need to hire if the volume of leads suddenly
increases. It's better to hire extra help and keep current rather than
save money on labor and fall behind on fulfillment (which can cost you
orders).

7. Set up the literature center as a pleasant, efficient workplace. Workers
should have everything they need within easy reach. If, for example, literature is to be bound into spiral or hard-spine covers, keep the binding machine on a table in the literature room with ample space for people to spread out and work. Make sure people can complete the steps
involved (collecting materials, assembling packages, typing labels, keying computer data, putting materials in envelopes, affixing postage)
with minimal movement and travel.

8. Stock the literature center with an ample supply of all essential items.
In addition to an inventory of sales literature, this can include:
envelopes, stamps, postage meters, cardboard backings, paper clips,
rubber bands, mail bags, address labels, rubber stamps, ink pads, form
letters, notebooks, forms, pencils, pens, and computer supplies.

9. Since there will be a steady flow of mail into and out of your literature
center, try to locate it near your mailroom or near where the mailroom
clerk comes by with a cart to pick up the mail each day. Don't force literature center employees to drag or cart heavy bundles of outgoing literature to a distant location for sorting and mailing.

10. Ideally, one or more employees should work in the literature center full
time. If workers complain that this is boring, you could rotate assignment to the literature center among available clerical personnel.

The main idea is to process leads and get the literature into the
mail quickly and efficiently. Hot leads can cool off quickly, and the longer
you sit on your inquiries, the more business you lose. Speed is of the
essence when it comes to turning leads into sales.

COMPUTERIZED INQUIRY HANDLING VENDORS

The following companies offer either software or complete computer systems for handling of inquiries, leads, and prospect and customer databases.

Applied Information Group
720 King Georges Road
Fords, NJ 08863
Phone 908-738-8444
Product: Advertiser Response System

Brock Control Systems
2859 Paces Ferry Road
Suite 1000
Atlanta, GA 30339
Phone 404-431-1200
Product: Brock Activity Manager

Claritas Corporation
201 N. Union Street, Suite 200
Alexandria, VA 22314-2645
Phone 703-683-8300
Product: COMPASS

CoLinear Systems, Inc.
2814 New Spring Road,
Suite 217
Atlanta, GA 30339
Phone 404-578-0000
Product: Response

Compusearch Market and Social Research Ltd.
16 Madison Avenue
Toronto, Ontario M5R 2S1
Phone 416-348-9180
Product: Compusearch

Data Absolute
PO Box 784
Nevada City, CA 95959
Phone 916-265-4779
Product: TeleMOM

Donnelley Marketing Information Services
70 Seaview Avenue
PO Box 10250
Stamford, CT 06904
Phone 203-353-7261
Product: CONQUEST

Richard L. Fleischer & Associates
135 Village Road
Roslyn Heights, NY 11577-1522
Phone 516-621-2826
Product: Zip + 4 Coding and Mailing System

Geographic Data Technology, Inc.
13 Dartmouth College Highway
Lyme, NH 03768
Phone 603-795-2183
Product: GeoSpreadSheet ZIP Code

Group I Software
Washington Capital Office Park
6404 Ivy Lane, Suite 500
Greenbelt, MD 20770-1400
Phone 301-982-2000
Products: List Conversion Management System, Accu-Mail, ArcList

Inquiry Plus
814 Eagle Drive
Bensenville, IL 60106
Phone 708-595-5059
Product: Inquiry Management Software

Inter Active Micro, Inc.
PO Box 478
Bradford, NH 03221
Phone 603-938-2127
Product: The Front Office

Key Systems, Inc.
512 Executive Park
Louisville, KY 40207
Phone 502-897-3332
Product: Prospecting, Accountability

LEADtrack Services
595 Colonial Park Drive, Suite 302
Roswell, GA 30075
Phone 404-587-0412
Product: LEADtrack

Market Power Computer Innovations
101 Providence Mine Road #104
Nevada City, CA 95959
Phone 916-265-5000
Product: The Sales Manager

Nashbar Associates, Inc.
4141 Simon Road
Boardman, OH 44512
Phone 216-788-9000
Product: Quick Order Processor

PER Software, Inc.
38109 87th Street
Burlington, WI 53105
Phone 414-537-4131
Product: Direct Marketing/400

INQUIRY HANDLING SERVICES

If you prefer not to handle inquiries in-house, here are some outside inquiry handling service bureaus that can help you:

Epsilon Data Management, Inc.
24 New England Executive Park
Burlington, MA 01803
Phone 617-273-0250

Fala Direct Marketing Inc.
70 Marcus Drive
Melville, NY 11747-4278
Phone 516-694-1919

LCS Industries, Inc.
120 Brighton Road
Clifton, NJ 07012
Phone 201-778-5588

McGraw-Hill
The Qualified Lead System
1221 Avenue of the Americas
New York, NY 10020
Phone 212-512-2000

FULFILLMENT HOUSES

If you don't want the hassle of setting up a literature center, or don't have room in your office to store all your brochures, fulfillment centers can help. They'll fulfill inquiries, sending the literature you specify, and some can even maintain your customer database for you on computer. There are hundreds of fulfillment houses nationwide; here is just a sampling:

Controlled Distribution
1100 Boston Avenue
Bridgeport, CT 06610
Phone 203-334-4060

FalaDirect Marketing, Inc.
70 Marcus Drive
Melville, NY 11747-4278
Phone 516-694-1919

Four Star Associates, Inc.
1560 Fifth Avenue
Bay Shore, NY 11706
Phone 516-968-4100

Fulfillco Fulfillment Center
90 Dayton Avenue
Passaic, NJ 07055
Phone 201-471-5980

Mailco, Inc.
150 S. Main St.
Woodridge, NJ 07075
Phone 201-777-9500

Progress Distribution Services, Inc.
5505 36th St. S.E.
Grand Rapids, MI 49512
Phone 616-957-5900

White Mountain Fulfillment Services
2625 S. Roosevelt Ave.
Tempe, AZ 85282
Phone 602-894-9618

Part **VI**
APPENDICES

Appendix A
BIBLIOGRAPHY

BOOKS

Bly, Robert, *The Copywriter's Handbook: A Step-by-Step Guide to Writing Copy That Sells* (New York: Henry Holt & Co., 1990). How to write effective copy.

Bly, Robert, *Power-Packed Direct Mail* (New York: Henry Holt & Co., 1995). A guide to planning, writing, designing, and producing direct mail promotions.

Bly, Robert, *Selling Your Services* (New York: Henry Holt & Co., 1994). Selling skills for service providers.

Bly, Robert, *Targeted Public Relations* (New York: Henry Holt & Co., 1996). A handbook on how to do public relations.

Bly, Robert, *The Perfect Sales Piece* (New York: John Wiley & Sons, 1993). Guide to creating effective brochures, catalogs, and other sales literature.

Caples, John, *Tested Advertising Methods* (Englewood Cliffs, NJ: Prentice Hall, 1974). Secrets of writing effective space ads.

Cates, Bill, *Unlimited Referrals* (Wheaton, MD: Thunder Hill Press, 1996). How to get lots of referral leads.

Floyd, Elaine, *Marketing with Newsletters* (St. Louis, MO: Newsletter Resources, 1994). How to create effective promotional newsletters.

Harris, Godfrey with Harris, J., *Generate Word of Mouth Advertising: 101 Easy and Inexpensive Ways to Promote Your Business* (Los Angeles, CA: The Americas Group, 1995). Interesting, innovative, low-cost promotions for yourself and your clients.

Kauffman, Maury, *Computer-Based Fax Processing: The Complete Guide to Designing and Building Fax Applications* (New York: Telecom Books).

Lant, Jeffrey, *No More Cold Calls* (Cambridge, MA: JLA Publications, 1994). How to generate leads for your service business.

Muldoon, Katie, *How to Profit Through Catalog Marketing* (Lincolnwood, IL: NTC Business Books, 1996). Recommended for anyone writing catalog copy.

Ogilvy, David, *Ogilvy on Advertising* (New York: Crown, 1989). Required reading for every copywriter writing print ads.

Reeves, Rosser, *Reality in Advertising* (New York: Alfred A. Knopf, 1985). Excellent book on how to increase advertising effectiveness.

Romano, Frank, *Pocket Guide to Digital Prepress* (Albany, NY: Delmar Publishers, 1996). Comprehensive yet readable guide to digital prepress.

Sayles, Sarah, *Creative Direct Mail Design* (Rockport, MA: Rockport Publishers). How to illustrate and design direct mail pieces.

Smith, Terry, *Making Successful Presentations* (New York: John Wiley & Sons, 1984). Excellent guide to writing and delivering workplace, instructional, and sales and marketing presentations.

Stone, Bob, *Successful Direct Marketing Methods* (Chicago, IL: NTC Business Books). Everything you need to know about direct marketing.

Vitale, Joe, *CyberWriting: How to Promote Your Product or Service Online* (New York: AMACOM, 1997). How to write copy for the Internet.

Wheildon, Colin, *Type & Layout* (Berkeley, CA: Strathmoor Press, 1995). Best guide ever written on designing print materials that are clear and readable.

Wunderman, Lester, *Being Direct* (New York: Random House, 1996). Great information on direct response advertising and direct mail, with insights into Internet, electronic, database, and other emerging marketing technologies.

PERIODICALS

Advertising Age
740 N. Rush Street
Chicago, IL 60611
(312) 649-5200

Adweek Magazine
49 E. 21st Street
New York, NY 10010
(212) 529-5500

American Demographics
PO Box 68
Ithaca, NY 14851-0068
(607) 273-6343

The Art of Self Promotion
PO Box 23
Hoboken, NJ 07030
(201) 653-0783

Business Marketing Magazine
740 North Rush Street
Chicago, IL 60611
(312) 649-5260

Catalog Age
911 Hope Street
Six River Bend Center
Stamford, CT 06907
(203) 358-9900

Commerce Business Daily
Government Printing Office
Washington, D.C.
(202) 512-0000

Direct Marketing Magazine
Hoke Communications
224 Seventh Street
Garden City, NY 11530
(516) 746-6700

DM News
Mill Hollow
19 W. 21st Street
New York, NY 10010
(212) 741-2095

Exhibitor Magazine
206 S. Broadway, Suite 745
Rochester, MN 55904
(507) 289-6556

Industrial Marketing Practitioner
1661 Valley Forge Road, #245
Lansdale, PA 19446
(215) 362-7200

Public Relations Journal
33 Irving Place
New York, NY 10003
(212) 998-2230

Sales and Marketing Management
633 Third Avenue
New York, NY 10017
(212) 986-4800

Target Marketing Magazine
North American Publishing Co.
401 N. Broad Street
Philadelphia, PA 19108
(215) 238-5300

Telemarketing Magazine
One Technology Plaza
Norwalk, CT 06854
(800) 243-6002

DIRECTORIES

All-In-One Directory
Gebbie Press
PO Box 1000
New Paltz, NY 12561
(914) 255-7560
Media directory

Bacon's Publicity Checklist
332 S. Michigan Avenue
Chicago, IL 60604
(800) 621-0561
Media lists for mailing press releases

Bradley's Top Talk Shows
Bradley Communications Corp.
135 E. Plumstead Avenue
Box 126
Lansdowne, PA 19050
(800) 989-1400

Co-op Advertising Programs Sourcebook
National Register Publishing Company
121 Chanlon Road
New Providence, NJ 07974
(800) 521-8110
Descriptions of some 6,000 co-op advertising programs

The Encyclopedia of Associations
Gale Research
Book Tower
Detroit, MI 48226
(313) 961-2242
Associations to whose membership lists you can target promotions

Exhibitors Resource Directory
206 S. Broadway, Suite 745
Rochester, MN 55904
(507) 289-6556
A directory of trade show suppliers

The Interactive Multimedia Sourcebook
R.R. Bowker
121 Chanlon Road
New Providence, NJ 07974
(908) 464-6800
Sourcebook for marketers interested in Internet promotion

The Information Catalog
Find/SVP
625 Avenue of the Americas
New York, NY 10011
(800) 346-3005
Catalog of market research studies

National Directory of Mailing Lists
Oxbridge Communications
150 Fifth Avenue
New York, NY 10114-0235
(800) 955-0231
Directory containing descriptions and contact information for 15,000 mailing lists

New Jersey Source
Calsun Inc.
PO Box 327
Ramsey, NJ 07446
(201) 236-9099
Directory of NJ area ad agencies, photographers, illustrators, and other creative services

O'Dwyer's Directory of Public Relations Firms
J.R. O'Dwyer & Company, Inc.
271 Madison Avenue
New York, NY 10016
(212) 679-2471
Directory of public relations firms

Standard Directory of Advertising Agencies
R.R. Bowker
121 Chanlon Road
New Providence, NJ 07974
(908) 464-6800
Directory of advertising agencies

Standard Rate and Data Service
1700 Higgins Road
Des Plaines, IL 60018-5605
(847) 375-5000
Comprehensive directory of publications that accept advertising

Thomas Register
Thomas Publishing Company
One Penn Plaza
New York, NY 10019
(212) 290-7200

The Yearbook of Expert Authorities and Spokespersons
Broadcast Interview Resource
2233 Wisconsin Avenue NW, Suite 540
Washington, D.C. 20007
(202) 333-4904

Appendix

SOFTWARE

BUSINESS PLANNING

BuzPlan Builder Interactive
Jian Co.
800-440-5426

Business Plan Pro
Palo Alto Software
800-229-7526

Plan Write
Business Resource Software
800-423-1228

MasterPlan Professional
MAUS Business Systems
509-663-9523

LEAD TRACKING AND CONTACT MANAGEMENT

Act
Symantech
(800) 441-7234

FastTrack
Fastech and Gelco Information Network
400 Parkway Dr.
Broomall, PA 19008
(610) 359-9200

LPS
Simplified Office Systems
16025 Van Aken Blvd., Suite 102
Cleveland, OH 44120
(216) 572-1050

MailEasy
Applied Information Group
720 King Georges Road
Fords, NJ 08863
(908) 738-8444

GoldMine
GoldMine Software
(800) 654-3526

Mail Order Manager (MOM)
Dydacomp Development Corporation
150 River Road, Suite N-1
Montville, NJ 07045
(201) 335-1256

Marketing Professional's InfoCenter / Smart Marketing Suite
Group One Software
4200 Parliament Place, Suite 600
Lanham, MD 20706
(301) 918-0721

Maximizer 97is
Maximizer Technologies
(800) 804-6299

MSM
Marketing Information Services
1840 Oak Avenue
Suite 400
Evanston, IL 60201
(847) 491-0682

Order Power!
Computer Solutions, Inc.
6187 NW 167th Street, Unit H33
Miami, FL 33015
(305) 558-7000

Postalsoft
439 Mormon Coulsee Road
LaCross, WI 54601
(608) 788-8700

Pro-Mail
Software Marketing Associates
2080 Silas Deane Highway
Rocky Hill, CT 06067-2341
(860) 721-8929

Profit Smart
Digital Arts LLC
1551 Valley Forge Road, Suite 259
Lansdale, PA 19446-5459
(215) 361-2650

Telemagic
(800) 835-MAGIC

C FORMS

RECORDING DATA ON SALES LEADS

Date _____ Source of inquiry _____ Response via _____

Name _____ Title _____

Company _____ Phone _____

Address _____ Room/floor _____

City _____ State _____ Zip _____

Type of business:

Type of accounts (if an ad agency):

Type of projects:

For: [ ] immediate project   [ ] future reference

[ ] project to be started in:_____
                                                        (month/year)

STATUS:

[ ] Sent package on (date):

[ ] Enclosed these samples:

[ ] Next step is to:

[ ] Probability of assignment:

[ ] COMMENTS: _____

_____

_____

CONTACT RECORD:

Date: _____ Summary: _____

_____

TRACKING PR RESULTS

Name of Media Source	Contact Person	Title	Address	Telephone	Someone I Know Who Knows Contact	Date of First Contact

TRACKING AD RESPONSE

Month _____   **Year** _____

Ad or mailing _____   **Key code** _____

Product _____   **Offer** _____

Total cost _____   **Total sales** _____

Day	# Inquiries	Total inquiries to date	Day's sales	Total sales to date
1				
2				
3				
4				
5				
6				
7				
8				
9				
10				
11				
12				
13				
14				
15				
16				
17				
18				
19				
20				
21				
22				
23				
24				
25				
26				
27				
28				
29				
30				
31				

INSERTION ORDER

Use this insertion order form to place lead-generating classified and space ads in appropriate media. By establishing yourself as an agency, you will often be granted the 15 percent ad agency commission. This saves you 15 percent on the cost of the ad space. When copying the form, insert your own company name and address at the top.

ADVERTISING INSERTION ORDER

From:

ABC Ad Agency
Anytown, USA
Phone XXX-XXX-XXXX

Date:

Advertiser:

Product:

To:

Publication in which ad is to run:_____

Date of insertion:_____

Size of ad:_____

Instructions:_____

_____

Rate:_____

Less frequency discount _____%

Less agency commission _____% on gross

Less cash discount _____% on net

Net amount on this insertion order:_____

Insertion order placed by:_____

TELEMARKETING CALL SHEETS

Date_____   Telemarketer Name_____

ABC Moving Company
Prospect Data Sheet

Name _____

Title _____

Company _____

Street Address _____

City, State, Zip _____

Phone _____

Fax _____

E-Mail _____

Call Attempts:

Date_____ Time_____   Date_____ Time_____

Date_____ Time_____   Date_____ Time_____

Contact:

[ ] Prospect Busy. Call Back on _____ at _____ (Day, Time)
      Best Time to Call _____ (Time of Day)

[ ] Long-Term. Call Back During _____ of _____ (Month, Year)

[ ] Phone Presentation Made an _____ (Month, Day, Year)

[ ] Left Message to Return Call

Action:

[ ] Appointment Set for _____ at _____ (Month, Day, Time)

[ ] Referral Given: _____

_____

[ ] Not Interested. Reason:_____

_____

Current Company Information:

Number of Employees _____

Number of Anticipated Moves Per Year _____

Types of Services Needed:

[ ] Office Moves

[ ] Industrial Moves

[ ] Household Moves

[ ] Computer/Electronic Moves

[ ] Storage

Optional Information:

Current Moving Contract Expires _____ (Month, Year)

Date_____   Telemarketer Name_____

**ABC Moving Company
Daily Activity Sheet**

Outbound Calls

# of Dials _____

# of Busy Signals_____

# of Voice Mail Messages _____

# of Call Backs Scheduled _____

# of Presentations _____

Literature Sent_____

of Appts Booked _____

No Interest_____

Referrals Given_____

Inbound Calls

# of Query Calls _____

# of Presentations _____

Literature Sent_____

of Appts Booked _____

BUDGETING WORKSHEET FOR NEWSLETTER OR OTHER PRINTED PROMOTION

			Budgeting Worksheet		
Option 1: Size: # Colors:		Paper	Qty:	Freq:	Other:
Option 2: Size: # Colors:		Paper:	Qty:	Freq:	Other:
Option 3: Size: # Colors:		Paper:	Qty:	Freq:	Other:
Description	**Set-up Cost**	**Cost** *Option 1*	**Cost** *Option 2*	**Cost** *Option 3*	
Design					
Research & Writing					
Editing					
Proofreading					
Typesetting & Layout					
Imagesetting/Laser Printing					
Printing					
Mailing List Set-up & Printing					
Labeling & Sorting					
Postage					

Miscellaneous Expenses
    Labels
    Art Supplies
    Courier services
    Long-distance phone calls
    Fax fees
    Mileage
    Shipping charges					

Other					
Total:					
Total Cost/Year:					

PROJECT SCHEDULE

Client: _____

Project:_____

Task	Assigned To	Time Needed	Begin Date	Proof Date	Final Deadline
Finalize Content					
Approval from Client					
Collect Information					
Write Articles					
Find/Create Graphics					
Edit Articles					
Approval from Client					
Layout					
Proofread					
Camera-Ready Output					
Approval from Client					
Print					
Run Mailing Labels					
Mail/Distribute					
Follow-up					
Other:					

PRINT PURCHASE AGREEMENT

Company name & address

Job#:_____

Representative:_____

Date:_____

__Please note that failure to notify us of any delays 3 days prior to this due date will void this agreement.__

Due:_____

Printer: _____

Address: _____

Phone #:_____   Payment Terms: _____

Project Name: _____

❏ Mock-up included

❏ Confirmed price: _____

❏ Quantity*:_____   *This is the minimum needed; underruns are not allowed and overruns not billable.

❏ Size   ❏ 8 1/2 x 11   ❏ 8 1/2 x 14   ❏ 11 x 17

❏ # Pages: ❏ front only   ❏ front & back   ❏ 4-page   ❏ ___ pages

❏ Fold: Fold____times down to_____(dimensions)

❏ Perforations: As marked on markup copy

❏ Paper: ❏ weight: ❏ name: ❏ color: ❏ finish:

❏ Ink Color: ❏ black   ❏ PMS#____   ❏ PMS#____   ❏ other:____

❏ Photos: ❏ scanned in ❏ need___halftones

❏ Screens: ❏ on artwork ❏ need____cut

❏ Artwork: ❏ camera-ready
             ❏ copy on disk, printer to typeset & lay out
             ❏ layout on disk; printer to image set

❏ Blue line or other proof required

❏ Press check required: Call_____at_____when ready for press

❏ Packaging required: ❏ in boxes ready to ship   ❏ shrinkwrapped in_____s

❏ Shipping: ❏ customer pick up   ❏ deliver to mailhouse at:
        ❏ deliver ❏ samples to client at:
        ❏ deliver ❏ samples to address above
        ❏ deliver ❏ balance to address above

❏ Ship via:

❏ Special instructions file cs PPA:

PROJECT EXPENSE RECORD
(ESTIMATED VS. ACTUAL)

Project _____ Amount Budgeted $_____

Line Number	Estimate	Actual	Variation	Running Total
1				
2				
3				
4				
5				
6				
7				
8				
9				
10				
11				
12				
13				
14				
15				
16				
17				
18				
19				
20				
21				
22				
23				
24				
25				
26				
27				
28				
29				
30				

Appendix D

ORGANIZATIONS AND CONFERENCES

Advertising Club of New York
235 Park Avenue South, 6th Floor
New York, NY 10003
(212) 533-8080

Advertising Council
261 Madison Avenue, 11th Floor
New York, NY 10017-2303
(212) 922-1500

Advertising Research Foundation
641 Lexington Avenue
New York, NY 10022
(212) 751-5656

American Advertising Federation
1101 Vermont Avenue NW, Suite
  500
Washington, D.C. 20005
(212) 898-0089

*American Association of
  Advertising Agencies*
405 Lexington Avenue, 18th Floor
New York, NY 10174-1801
(212) 682-2500

*American Council of Highway
  Advertisers*
PO Box 388
Shady Side, MD 20764
(301) 261-9197

*Association of Independent
  Commercial Producers*
11 E. 22nd Street, 4th Floor
New York, NY 10010
(212) 475-2600

Association of National Advertisers
155 E. 44th St.
New York, NY 10017-4270
(212) 697-5950

Business Marketing Association
150 North Wacker Drive
Suite 1760
Chicago, IL 60606
(312) 409-4262

*Business to Business Direct
  Marketing Conference*
Box 4232
Stamford, CT 06907-0232
(203) 358-9900

Cable Television Advertising Bureau
757 Third Avenue
New York, NY 10017
(212) 751-7770

Center for Business Intelligence
500 West Cummings Park, Suite 5100
Woburn, MA 01801
(781) 270-6201
Conferences and research on marketing to
  children

Direct Marketing Association
1120 Avenue of the Americas
New York, NY 10036-6700
(212) 768-7277

Direct Marketing to Business
Target Conference Corporation
90 Grove Street
Ridgefield, CT 06877
(203) 438-6602

Newspaper Association of America
400 N. Michigan Avenue
Chicago, IL 60611
(312) 902-1600

Outdoor Advertising Association of
  America
12 E. 49th Street, 22nd Floor
New York, NY 10017
(212) 688-3667

Point of Purchase Advertising Institute
1660 L St. NW, 10th Floor
Englewood, NJ 07631
(202) 530-3000

Promotion Products Association
  International
3125 Skyway Cir.
N. Irving, TX 75038-3526
(214) 252-0404

Radio Advertising Bureau
261 Madison Avenue, 23rd Floor
New York, NY 10016
(212) 681-7200

Retail Advertising and Marketing
  Association
333 N. Michigan Ave., Suite 3000
Chicago, IL 60611
(312) 251-7262

Television Bureau of Advertising
850 Third Avenue, 10th Floor
New York, NY 10022
(212) 486-1111

Trade Show Exhibitors Association
5501 Backlick Road, Suite 105
Springfield, VA 22151
(703) 941-3725

RECOMMENDED VENDORS

To accomplish some of the tasks outlined in this book, you may want to work with outside vendors. This list is by no means comprehensive; it simply lists the vendors I recommend in each category right now. A recommendation doesn't guarantee your satisfaction, so you should check out vendors thoroughly before hiring them.

AUDIO TAPING
Mr. Mike Moe
Moe Company
133 Deerfield Road
Sayreville, NJ 08872
908-257-3760

BUSINESS PLANS
Lisa Hines
Business Plan Concepts
134 Oklyn Terrace
Lawrenceville, NJ 08648
609-530-0719

CARTOONS
The Cartoon Bank
A Division of *New Yorker Magazine*
382 Warburton Avenue
Hastings on Hudson, NY 10706
800-897-8666 or 914-478-5527
Web site: www.cartoonbank.com

Ted Goff
PO Box 22679
Kansas City, MO 64113
816-822-7370

e-mail: tgoff@tedgoff.com
Web site: www.tedgoff.com

CUSTOM CALENDARS
Ms. Judith Roth
Judith Roth Studios
Stone House Road
Mendham, NJ 07945
201-543-4455

DATABASE MARKETING
Tito DeFilipo
Database Direct
Blue Hill Plaza, 16th Floor
PO Box 1556
Pearl River, NY 10965-8556
914-735-3200

Ernie Schell
Communications Center
538 Street Road
Southampton, PA 18966
215-396-0610

DIRECT MAIL GRAPHIC DESIGN
David Bsales
David Bsales Design
16 W. Palisade Ave. #206
Englewood, NJ 07631
201-567-1474

Lucien Cohen
New York City
212-685-7455

Mr. Harry Moshier
Moshier Communications
15 East 12th Street, 2nd Floor
New York, NY 10003
212-645-7554

Ms. Elaine Tannenbaum
Elaine Tannenbaum Design
310 West 106th Street, Apt. 16D
New York, NY 10025
212-769-2096

FAX MARKETING
Sarah E. Stambler
Marketing with Technology
370 Central Park West #210
New York, NY 10025-6517
212-222-1713

Maury S. Kauffman
The Kauffman Group
324 Windsor Drive
Cherry Hill, NJ 08002-2426
609-482-8288

GRAPHIC DESIGN, BROCHURES
Paul Spadafora
Park Ridge Marketing
1776 On the Green
67 Park Place
Morristown, NJ 07960
201-984-2622

Mr. Steve Brown
Brown & Company
138 Joralemon Street #4R
Brooklyn, NY 11201
718-875-0674

LETTER SHOP
Mr. Jerry Lake
Jerry Lake Mailing Service
Airport Industrial Park
620 Frelinghuysen Avenue
Newark, NJ 07114
201-967-5644

Mitch Hisiger
Fala Direct Marketing
70 Marcus Drive
Melville, NY 11747
516-694-1919

USA Direct
2901 Blackbridge Road
York, PA 17402-9708
800-441-1850

LIBRARY RESEARCH
Mr. John Maddux
2665 Leda Court
Cincinnati, OH 45211
513-662-9176

Bob Concoby
Box 754
Kent, OH 44240
330-494-5504, ext. 814, 330-677-8085

MAILING SYSTEMS
Mr. Steve Roberts
Edith Roman
253 West 35th Street
New York, NY 10001
800-223-2194

Ralph Drybrough
Direct Media
200 Pemberwick Road
Greenwich, CT 06830
203-532-1000

Mr. Ken Morris
Morris Direct Marketing
300 West 55th Street #19D
New York, NY 10019
212-757-7711

MARKET RESEARCH
Terrence J. Pranses
Pranses Research Services
40 Willow Terrace
Hoboken, NJ 07030-2813
201-659-2475

Peter Fondulas
Taylor Research & Consulting
6 Glenville St.
Greenwich, CT 06831
203-532-0202

MEDIA BUYING SERVICES
Direct Marketing Concepts
23 Anderson Drive
PO Box 3353
Wayne, NJ 07470
201-790-6427

Linick Media
7 Putter Lane
Middle Island, NY 11953
516-924-8555

Novus Marketing
601 Lakeshore Parkway, Suite 900
Minneapolis, MN 55305
612-476-7700

ON-HOLD ADVERTISING MESSAGES
Fred Guarino
Tikki
186 Glen Cove Avenue
Glen Cove, NY 11542
516-671-4555

PAPER
Paper Direct
100 Plaza Drive
Secaucus, NJ 07094-3606
800-A-PAPERS

PHOTOGRAPHERS
Mr. Edward Parker
RE Parker Photography
78 Washington Avenue
Dumont, NJ 07628
201-384-7052

Jonathan Clymer
Jonathan Clymer Photography
180-F Central Avenue
Englewood, NJ 07631
201-568-1760

Phil Degginger
Degginger Photography
9 Evans Farm Road
Morristown, NJ 07960
201-455-1733

Bruce Goldsmith
Bruce Goldsmith Photography
1 Clayton Court
Park Ridge, NJ 07656
201-391-4946

POCKET FOLDERS & BINDERS
Mr. Jeff Becker
Clients First
90 Elm Street
Westfield, NJ 07090
908-232-1200

POWERPOINT PRESENTATIONS
Prime Time Staffing
1250 E. Ridgewood Avenue
Ridgewood, NJ 07450
201-612-0303

Ms. Bonnie Blake and Mary Cicitta
Design on Disk
400 River Road, 2nd Floor
New Milford, NJ 07646
516-694-1919

PREMIUMS AND INCENTIVES
American Slide Chart Corporation
25 W. 550 Geneva Road
Wheaton, IL 60187
708-665-3333

Perrygraf Slide Charts
19365 Business Center Drive
Northridge, CA 91324-3552
800-423-5329

PRINTERS
Leesburg Printing Co.
1100 North Blvd. East
Leesburg, FL 34748
800-828-3348
Booklets and newsletters

Rapidocolor
705 E. Union Street
West Chester, PA 19382
800-872-7436
Full-color printing

U.S. Press
PO Box 640
Valdosta, GA 31603-0640
800-227-7377
Full-color printing

PROJECT AND TRAFFIC MANAGEMENT
Mr. Grant Faurot
92 Glendale Street
Nutley, NJ 07110
201-661-5074

PUBLIC RELATIONS AGENCIES
Mr. Mark Bruce
GHB Marketing Communications
1177 High Ridge Road
Stamford, CT 06905
203-321-1242

Mr. Don Levin
Levin Public Relations
30 Glenn Street
White Plains, NY 10603
914-993-0900

RADIO COMMERCIALS
Chuck Hengel
Marketing Architects
14550 Excelsior Blvd.
Minneapolis, MN 55345
612-936-7500

STOCK ILLUSTRATIONS
Stock Illustration Source
16 W. 18th Street
New York, NY 10011
212-691-6400
Web site: www.sisstock.com

TELEMARKETING
Frank Stetz
240 E. 82 St., 20th Floor
New York, NY 10028
212-439-1777

Grace Software Marketing
3091 Mayfield Road
Cleveland, OH 44118
216-321-2000

Mariann Weinstein
MAW Associates
115 N. 10th Street
New Hyde Park, NY 11040
516-437-0529

TRANSLATIONS
Harvard Translations
137 Newbury Street
Boston, MA 02116
617-424-9291

WEB PAGE DESIGN
Mr. Jason Petefish
Silver Star Productions
21 Wilwood Road
Katonah, NY 10536
914-232-5363

Kent Martin
Network Creative
104 Mountain Avenue
Gilette, NJ 07930
908-903-9090

Barry Fox
FoxTek
49 West Street
Northport, NY 11768
516-754-4304

Appendix

SAMPLE DOCUMENTS

SAMPLE LEAD-GENERATING LETTER:
IN-HOUSE CORPORATE TRAINING SEMINAR

Important news for every systems professional who has ever felt like telling an end user, "Go to hell...."

Dear IS Manager:

It's ironic.

Today's users demand to be treated as *customers* of IS.

Yet many systems professionals don't have the customer service skills to make the relationship work.

Our training program, "Interpersonal Skills for IS Professionals," solves that problem...by giving IS staff the skills they need to deal effectively with end users and top management in today's service-oriented corporate environment.

Presented jointly by the Center for Technical Communication and the Communication Workshop—two leaders in teaching soft skills to technical professionals—"Interpersonal Skills for IS Professionals" quickly brings your team to a new level in listening, negotiating, teamwork, customer service, and other vital skills for communicating complex systems ideas and technical processes to managers and end users.

Many leading companies ... including IBM, AT&T, Symbol Technologies, Price Waterhouse, Cigna, American Airlines, Lever Brothers, Barnett Technologies, First Union, and Turner Broadcasting ... count on us to help their technical professionals communicate more effectively and work more productively. You can too.

For more information, including an outline of our "Interpersonal Skills for IS Professionals" program, just complete and mail the enclosed reply card. Or call (516) 767-9590. You'll be glad you did.

Sincerely,

Gary Blake, Ph.D., Director

P.S. Reply now and we'll also send you a FREE copy of our new tip sheet, "The IS Professional's Guide to Improving Listening Skills." It will help everyone in your department gain a quicker, more accurate understanding of what users want, while helping to transform your customers from uninitiated end users into educated consumers who are easier and more reasonable to deal with.

[reply card]

YES, I'm interested in learning more about your on-site seminars in:

[ ] "Interpersonal Skills for IS Professionals"
[ ] "Technical Writing for Systems Professionals"

Name_____   Title_____

Company_____   Phone_____

Address_____

City_____   State_____   Zip_____

[ ] Call me now. *Number of people requiring training:* _____
[ ] Call me in _____

                                          (month/year)

For immediate information, call 516-767-9590 or fax this card to 516-883-4006.

SAMPLE LEAD-GENERATING LETTER: CONSULTING SERVICES

Dear Marketing Professional:

"It's hard to find a copywriter who can handle industrial and high-tech accounts," a prospect told me over the phone today, "especially for brochures, direct mail, and other long-copy assignments."

Do you have that same problem?

If so, please complete and mail the enclosed reply card, and I'll send you a free information kit describing a service that can help.

As a freelance copywriter specializing in business-to-business marketing, I've written hundreds of successful ads, sales letters, direct mail packages, brochures, data sheets, annual reports, feature articles, press releases, newsletters, and audiovisual scripts for clients all over the country.

But my information kit will give you the full story.

You'll receive a comprehensive "WELCOME" letter that tells all about my copywriting service—who I work for, what I can do for you, how we can work together.

You'll also get my client list (I've written copy for more than 100 corporations and agencies) ... client testimonials ... biographical background ... samples of work I've done in your field ... a fee schedule listing what I charge for ads, brochures, and other assignments ... helpful article reprints on copywriting and advertising ... even an order form you can use to put me to work for you.

Whether you have an immediate project, a future need, or are just curious, I urge you to send for this information kit. It's free ... there's no obligation ... and you'll like having a proven copywriting resource on file—someone you can call on whenever you need him.

From experience, I've learned that the best time to evaluate a copywriter and take a look at his work is before you need him, not when a project deadline comes crashing around the corner. You want to feel comfortable about a writer and his capabilities in advance ... so when a project does come up, you know who to call.

Why not mail back the reply card TODAY, while it is still handy? I'll rush your free information kit as soon as I hear from you.

Regards,

Bob Bly

P.S. Need an immediate quote on a copywriting project? Call me at (201) 385-1220. There is no charge for a cost estimate, and no obligation to buy.

SAMPLE LEAD-GENERATING LETTER OFFERING A PREMIUM

TO: Newsletter publishers
FROM: Ilise Benun
RE: Copywriting for DM packages

Dear Newsletter Publisher:

On April 8, 1997, copywriter and consultant Bob Bly gave a talk on creating effective newsletter DM packages at the luncheon meeting of the NPA NYC chapter.

For a limited time only, you can get this presentation, "6 Keys to Creating a Successful DM Package to Sell Newsletter Subscriptions," on audiocassette—absolutely FREE!

To get your copy, just call me at (201) 653-0783. I'll have the tape sent to you at no cost via first-class mail.

By the way, Bob is a first-rate DM copywriter who has written packages for such publishers as Marketing & Publishing Associates, Agora, Phillips, WEKA, Brownstone, Medical Economics, Bureau of Business Practice, Economics Press, Institutional Investor Journals, Reed Reference Publishing, McGraw-Hill, John Wiley & Sons, and Prentice Hall.

Bill Bonner of Agora Publishing (Target Marketing's "Direct Marketer of the Year") says, "Bly's writing is clear, direct, and well organized. He's a pleasure to read."

One of Bob's recent DM packages, for a financial advisory service, outpulled the control almost 3:1.

If you would like to discuss the possibility of having Bob Bly write a direct mail package for you, call me at (201) 653-0783. Or mail the enclosed reply card.

P.S. For a free information kit on Bob Bly's DM copywriting services for newsletter publishers, complete and mail the enclosed reply card. Your kit will include sample DM packages, a client list, fee schedule, and the free audiocassette, "6 Keys to Creating a Successful DM Package to Sell Newsletter Subscriptions."

SAMPLE TELEMARKETING SCRIPT WITH INSTRUCTIONS FOR TELEMARKETERS

ABC Moving Company
Instructions to Telemarketers

1. Complete a **Prospect Data Sheet** for each company called (or for each incoming call that qualifies as a prospect). Some of the information can be entered prior to the phone call as part of your research on (targeting) companies.

2. The **Daily Activity Sheet** helps you keep track of how many calls are made and how productive the calls are. This helps to evaluate the telemarketing effort, in general.

3. You should confirm appointments 24 hours before the designated time. It will save time in the long run even though you may lose prospects occasionally because they changed their mind about seeing a sales rep.

4. There will be some people who won't want to see a sales rep but will want you to send literature. Send the literature and call them back a week later. You'll hit some of them when they need your company's services.

5. You should use the **script** as a dialogue guide. At the beginning, use the script and **objection-response guide** verbatim. After you feel comfortable with both, feel free to ad lib. However, make

sure that you...

- Introduce yourself.

- State the purpose of your call.

- Probe in some way to get the prospect to talk and "buy in" to the conversation.

- Present features and benefits.

- Do a trial close during your presentation ("How does that sound?", "Is that OK?", etc.) to get a reading on how you are doing.

- Close (get some sort of commitment from the prospect) even if it isn't an appointment (e.g., agreement to a call back, send literature, etc.).

- Try to get a referral if you cannot close an appointment.

- Reassure prospects that they have made a wise choice in meeting with a sale rep.

6. The **objection response guide** should help to overcome 95% of the objections and questions raised. If someone asks you a question you cannot answer, say that you will get back with the answer. MAKE SURE YOU DO CALL BACK.

7. No instructions are given after the objection responses. That is because you do not know when the objection will be raised during the script presentation. In those cases, respond to the objection and then return to where you left off in the script.

8. Although completing forms is boring work, it is very important that you do so. Write comments in the margins of the **Prospect Data Sheet**. Finish completing this form after each phone call, if possible. Only then will you have a complete record of each prospect. Only by filling in the **Daily Activity Sheet** with tick marks after each call will you know how well you are doing overall.

ABC Moving Company
Outbound Telemarketing Script

Locator:

Good morning/afternoon. This is (FULL NAME). Could you please tell me the name of the person in charge of (COMPANY NAME'S) moving and storage and their extension, please? Thank you.

Introduction:

Good morning/afternoon, Mr./Ms. _____. This is (FULL NAME) calling from ABC Moving Company.

The reason for my call is to set up a time when our vice president, John Doe, could stop by for about 10 to 15 minutes...introduce himself...and drop off a FREE copy of our publication, *How to Make a Move* Effortlessly. It lists helpful information you can use to make sure each one of your moves goes smoothly. RESPOND TO OBJECTIONS.

Probe:

Mr./Ms. _____, how many employees does (COMPANY NAME) have? What types of moving and storage do you normally handle for (COMPANY NAME)? About how many moves per year is that?

Features and Benefits:

Mr./Ms. _____, ABC Moving Company is a full-service, licensed interstate carrier. ABC has been in business for the past 75 years.

- Our rates are 35% lower than those of most other major movers...and we are members of the International Brotherhood of Teamsters, Local 666.

- We offer a special discount program for office and commercial moving and free estimates and consulting.

- ABC Moving Company has one of the lowest average costs per claim records among the leading providers of shipping services.

Close:

Mr. Doe will be in the (COMPANY'S CITY LOCATION) area next week. When would be a good time for him to come by, introduce himself, and drop off a FREE copy of *How to Make a Move Effortlessly*? RECORD DATE AND TIME.

That's great. He'll only take a few minutes of your time...to learn about your needs...and to briefly outline the services ABC can help you with.

IF PROSPECT SAYS "NO," GET REASON WHY AND SAY:

Well, I can understand your decision. Is there anyone else within (COMPANY NAME) that could use ABC's services?

RECORD NAME, TITLE, AND PHONE NUMBER.

Thank you for your time, Mr./Ms. _____.

ABC Moving Company
Outbound Telemarketing Script
Objection-Response Guide

GENERAL OBJECTIONS/QUESTIONS

How Did You Get My Name?

The telephone operator was kind enough to connect me.

I Don't Have Time to Talk/Too Busy/Call Back Later.

When would be a good time for us to talk, Mr./Ms. _____? RECORD CALL BACK DATE AND TIME.

Call Back in 3-to-6 Months.

I can do that, Mr./Ms. _____. But why wait until then? Mr. Doe would like just 10 to 15 minutes of your time to introduce himself, learn about your shipping needs, and drop off a FREE copy of our publication, *How to Make a Move Effortlessly*.

Let Me Think About It and Get Back to You.

We can do that...or I can set up a time right now...and I'll call you the day before...to verify your appointment with Mr. Doe.

You'd Be Wasting Your Time/Resistance to Setting Up an Appointment.

Well, Mr./Ms. _____, may I send you some information on ABC Moving Company? Once you've had a chance to look over the material I send, I'll call you back to set up a time for Mr. Doe to stop by and introduce himself. OK?

SPECIFIC OBJECTIONS/QUESTIONS

Who's ABC Moving Company? I Never Heard of You.

ABC Moving Company is a full-service, licensed interstate carrier. We've been in business for 75 years. We are also registered agents for Athena Van Lines...one of the three carriers preferred by most corporate shippers.

How Long Will the Appointment Take?

Our vice president, John Doe, would like no more than 10 to 15 minutes of your time...to introduce himself and learn about your shipping needs.

Must Ask Boss.

By all means, Mr./Ms. _____. Why don't you invite him/her to join you and Mr. Doe when Mr. Doe briefly outlines the services ABC can help you with?

Send Information.

I can do that, Mr./Ms. _____. And once you've had a chance to look over the information I send you, I can call to set up a time for Mr. Doe to stop by to introduce himself, learn about your shipping needs, and drop off a FREE copy of our publication, *How to Make a Move Effortlessly*. OK? VERIFY NAME AND ADDRESS. SEND LITERATURE. RECORD CALL BACK DATE.

MOVING-RELATED OBJECTIONS/QUESTIONS

I'm Not in Charge of Moving.

Could you tell me who is, Mr./Ms. _____? And their extension, please? RECORD NAME AND PHONE NUMBER.

We Already Have a Moving and Storage Company. Call Me When My Contract with Our Current Supplier Expires.

I can do that, Mr./Ms. _____. But why wait until then? Mr. Doe would like just 10 to 15 minutes of your time to introduce himself and briefly outline the services ABC can help you with. IF RESISTANT, FIND OUT WHEN CONTRACT EXPIRES AND MAKE A NOTE TO CALL 3 TO 6 MONTHS PRIOR TO EXPIRATION.

I'm Satisfied with the Moving Company We Use.

Well, good, Mr./Ms. _____. May I send you some literature for you to keep on hand...just in case your situation should change? IF YES, VERIFY NAME AND ADDRESS. SEND LITERATURE.

I Use a Moving Company So Infrequently/No Need/No Interest.

I understand, Mr./Ms. _____. But when you do need shipping help, you'll want to have the information and the name of a contact person at your fingertips. Let me send you some information on ABC Moving Company. Once you've had a chance to look over the material I send you, I'll call you back to set up a time for Mr. Doe to stop by and introduce himself. OK?

What Would You Charge for _____?

I'd like to be able to quote you a price over the phone, but as you know, it's based on a number of different things. What don't you ask Mr. Doe when he stops by to introduce himself?

Tell Me Your Rates...Over the Phone...Not in Person.

I'd like to be able to quote you prices over the phone, but as you know, they're based on a number of different things. That's why I'd like to set up a time when Mr. Doe can stop by and introduce himself. He'll be able to give you all the information you need.

Who Are Some of Your Corporate Clients?

Our corporate clients include...[Company Name], [Company Name], [Company Name], [Company Name], and [Company Name]...to name a few. Mr. Doe would be happy to show you testimonials and letters of reference from these companies when he stops by.

We're a Small Business/No Need.

I understand, Mr./Ms. _____. But when you do need shipping help, you'll want to have the information and the name of a contact person at your fingertips. Let me send you some information on ABC Moving Company. Once you've had a chance to look over the material I send, I'll call you back to set up a time for Mr. Doe to stop by and introduce himself. OK?

MARKET RESEARCH QUESTIONS FOR A FOCUS GROUP STUDY

Date:
Courtesy:
Pranses Research Services

Investor Group
Discussion Guide for Focus Groups

Introductions
(15 Minutes)

- Independent Market Researcher
- Focus Group Background & Rules
    - Speak individually and clearly
    - Not all respondents on all questions
- Respondent Introductions
    - First name

    - Former/current occupation
    - How long have you owned individual issues of stock?

Investment Objectives and Decision Making
(20 minutes)

1. What are your investment goals? Specifically for your investments in individual issues of common stock?
    - Short term? Specifics—increased income, new house, new car(s), travel, other?
    - Long term?
        - Education for children/grandchildren
        - Retirement
        - Safety net for health/emergencies
        - Longer term higher standard of living
        - Other?

2. Now I'd like to hear about the role of the people you rely upon.
    - How many of you utilize/have utilized the services of a personal financial advisor?
        - How and when did that relationship start?
        - What have been the benefits?
        - Any shortcomings?
    - Is this advisor your primary resource in the buying/selling of common stocks?

3. How many of you utilize a full-service broker to provide advice in your buying/selling of stock?
    - Has that broker been a good source of information?
        - Why/why not?
    - Does your broker provide you with reading material?
        - Is that useful/not useful?

4. How many of you utilize a discount broker to buy and sell stock?
    - Do you look to that discount broker for advice on specific stocks and/or timing?

5. Do any of you belong to investor clubs or groups?
    - How did you initially get involved? What was the attraction?
    - Have they been useful to you? How so/not so?

6. What media help provide you with financial information?
    - TV/radio shows?
        - Which and why?

- Are any of you tracking your investments via the Internet?
    - What are the pros and cons of that?
- Newspapers/financial columns?
    - Which ones and why?
    - Everyday or periodic?
- Magazines
    - Which ones and why?
    - Every issue or periodic?
- Financial advice newsletters
    - How many do you get/review?
    - How did you initially subscribe/buy?
    - Have those newsletters lived up to your expectations?

7. How do you rank these different sources of information?
    - Is your broker or advisor your main source?
    - Or the media?
        - Which ones, specifically?

Review of Positionings
(50 minutes)

8. During this next section, we're going to distribute several descriptions of a portfolio management service. We call each of these "concept descriptions."
    - Not advertising; not finished or polished.
    - Just an idea, a way of presenting this new publication.

After you read each one, I'd like you to take a moment and fill out this form. Please do this individually and without discussion.
    - The letter given each concept.
    - Bullet-point its top strengths and weaknesses.
    - A rating for this concept on a scale of 1 (no interest) to 5 (very high interest).

Then we'll discuss each in depth.

9. Now let's discuss how you reacted to this concept statement. PROBE, for each concept:
    - Key strengths
    - Key weaknesses
    - Overall ratings

Now keep your copy of this concept statement. But pass back the concept rating form.

10. (After individual discussion of all concepts:) Now quickly review the concepts you have in front of you. I'd like you, on that last rating form, to jot down the letter of your favorite of all of them.
    - How many said (show of hands):
        A?
        B?
        C?
        D?
        E?
        F?
- Why is ____ your favorite? Anything else?
- ____ came in second overall. Which of you ranked that one the highest? Why was that? Why else?

Distribute/Discuss Sample Copies of an Investment Newsletter
(15 minutes)

11. Here are some copies of an investment newsletter that would go to customers of this portfolio management company. Please take a few minutes to review it. (Allow 3 to 5 minutes.)
    - Is this the type of information/advice you expected to see? Why/why not?
    - Now that you've looked it over:
        - What do you think are its big strengths? Any others?
        - How might those be useful/relevant to you?
        - What do you see as weaknesses?
    - What might you suggest to fix the shortcomings? Any other suggestions?

12. What, beyond this informative newsletter, are the other things a portfolio management firm might do to help upscale investors, such as yourself, be satisfied clients? (Capture on easel.) Any others?
    - Which of these are your favorites? (Capture counts.)
    - Why?
    - How can this portfolio management company make its offering more unique? More competitive?

Wrap-Up

We appreciate your input. We've certainly learned a great deal about investor interests and needs with you today!

MARKET RESEARCH CONCEPT RATING FORM

Concept Letter: _____

After reading this concept to yourself, please jot down a few words that summarize how you feel about it.

Major Strengths: _____

_____

_____

Major Weaknesses: _____

_____

_____

Then rate it, overall, on the following scale.
(Circle most appropriate answer.)

1	2	3	4	5
No interest	Of some/moderate interest	Would definitely consider		Very interested

SPECIFICATION SHEET

KOCH static mixing unit specification sheet
(To be filled out to facilitate Koch Engineering Co. in preparing design and quotation)

Name _____ Title _____ Tel. _____

Company _____ Street _____

City _____ State _____ Zip _____

Date _____ Date Quotation Required _____

I. PROCESS DATA

Component	1	2	3	4	Mixture
Fluid					
Flow Rate (gpm or #/hr)					
Viscosity (cp)					
Density (#/ft3)					
Temperature (o F)					
Pressure (psig)					

Maximum pressure drop available across static mixing unit _____ psi.

Desired degree of homogeneity (δ x) _____
(δ x of 0.05 is usually adequate for industrial applications)

II. MECHANICAL DESIGN DATA

Design Pressure _____ Design Temperature _____

Existing or Preferred Pipe Diameter _____ Maximum Length Available _____

Removable Elements Required? Yes _____ No _____

Housing Schedule Required? 40 _____ 80 _____ Other _____

(If metal or PVC)
Is Lined Pipe Required? Yes _____ No _____ Lining Material _____

End Connections: Plain _____ If Flanged, Rating _____

Threaded _____ Type _____
Flanged _____

III. MATERIAL OF CONSTRUCTION

	Elements	Pipe	Flanges		Elements	Pipe	Flanges
Carbon Steel	___	___	___	Titanium	___	___	___
304 SS	___	___	___	PVC(1)	___	___	___
316 SS	___	___	___	Polypropylene (1)(2)	___	(3)	(3)
316L SS	___	___	___	Kynar (1)(2)	___	(3)	(3)
Monel	___	___	___	Teflon (1)(2)	___	(3)	(3)
Alloy 20	___	___	___	FRP	___	___	___
Hastelloy B	___	___	___		___	___	___
Hastelloy C	___	___	___		___	___	___

(1) Smallest diameter available is 2-inch. (2) Elements are glass reinforced. (3) Available only as a lining on carbon steel.

The Koch static mixing unit can be made of almost any material of construction. If you desire a material not listed above, please explain:

_____

_____

_____

IV. MIXING APPLICATION

Indicate type of mixing operation taking place (check one):

❑ Turbulent mixing of miscible low-viscosity liquids
❑ Laminar mixing of miscible high-viscosity liquids
❑ Gas-gas mixing
❑ Gas-liquid contacting
❑ Liquid-liquid dispersion (immiscible liquids)
❑ Mixing of liquids of extreme viscosity ratio
❑ Other. Please explain:_____

MAIL TO: Koch Engineering Company, Inc.   Koch Engineering Company, Inc.
            Static Mixing Product Group   Static Mixing Product Group
            P.O. Box 8127   161 East 42nd Street
            Wichita, Kansas 67208   New York, New York 10017
            (316) 832-5110   (212) 682-5755

SAMPLE PRESS RELEASE

```
FROM: Bob Bly, 174 Holland Avenue, New Milford, NJ
07646
CONTACT: Bob Bly (201) 385-1220

For immediate release

NEW BOOKLET REVEALS 14 PROVEN STRATEGIES FOR KEEPING
BUSINESSES BOOMING IN A BUST ECONOMY

New Milford, NJ—While some companies struggle to sur-
vive in today's sluggish business environment, many are
doing better than ever largely because they have mas-
tered the proven but little known strategies of
"recession marketing."

That's the opinion of Bob Bly, an independent marketing
consultant and author of the just published booklet,
"Recession-Proof Business Strategies: 14 Winning Methods
to Sell Any Product or Service in a Down Economy."

"Many businesspeople fear a recession or soft economy,
because when the economy is weak, their clients and
customers cut back on spending," says Bly. "To survive
in such a marketplace, you need to develop recession
marketing strategies that help you retain your current
accounts and keep those customers buying. You also need
to master marketing techniques that will win you new
clients or customers to replace any business you may
have lost because of the increased competition that is
typical of a recession."

Among the recession-fighting business strategies Bly
outlines in his new booklet:

•    Reactivate dormant accounts. An easy way to get more
     business is to simply call past clients or cus-
```

tomers—people you served at one time but are not actively working for now—to remind them of your existence. According to Bly, a properly scripted telephone call to a list of past buyers will generate approximately one order for every ten calls.

- Quote reasonable, affordable fees and prices in competitive bid situations. While you need not reduce your rates or prices, in competitive bid situations you will win by bidding toward the low end or middle of your price range rather than at the high end. Bly says that during a recession, your bids should be 15 to 20 percent lower than you would normally charge in a healthy economy.

- Give your existing clients and customers a superior level of service. In a recession, Bly advises businesses to do everything they can to hold onto their existing clients or customers, their "bread-and-butter" accounts. "The best way to hold onto your clients or customers is to please them," says Bly, "and the best way to please them is through better customer service. Now is an ideal time to provide that little by of extra service or courtesy that can mean the difference between dazzling the client or customer and merely satisfying them."

- Reactivate old leads. Most businesses give up on sales leads too early, says Bly. He cites a study from Thomas Publishing which found that although 80 percent of sales to businesses are made on the fifth can, only one out of ten salespeople cans beyond three times. Concludes Bly: "You have probably not followed up on leads diligently enough, and the new business you need may already be right in your prospect files." He says repeated follow-up should convert 10 percent of prospects to buyers.

To receive a copy of Bly's booklet, "Recession-Proof Business Strategies," send $8 ($7 plus $1 shipping and handling) to: Bob Bly, Dept. 109, 174 Holland Avenue, New Milford, NJ 07646. Cash, money orders, and checks (payable to "Bob Bly") accepted. (Add $1 for Canadian orders.)

Bob Bly, an independent copywriter and consultant based in New Milford, NJ, specializes in business-to-business, high-tech, and direct response marketing. He is the author of 18 books, including How to Promote Your Own Business (New American Library) and The Copywriter's Handbook (Henry Holt). A frequent speaker and seminar leader, Mr. Bly speaks nationwide on the topic of how to market successfully in a recession or soft economy.

SAMPLE PRESS RELEASE

NEW TELEPHONE HOTLINE PROVIDES FIRST-TIME HOME BUYERS WITH FREE INFORMATION, TIPS, AND MONEY-SAVING ADVICE

WEST HEMPSTEAD, N.Y., April 7 /PRNewswire/—Potential home buyers may want to call the non-profit First-Time Home Buyers' HelpLine (TM). This new telephone hotline provides Queens and Long Island home shoppers with free advice, information, and tips on how to buy a home.

"Live" real estate experts answer the phones and answer buyers' questions on a wide variety of topics ranging from how to figure out their budget, choose a neighborhood, make an offer, or obtain favorable financing.

"Buying a home for the first time can be an overwhelming experience," according to HelpLine founder "Uncle" Ira Freireich, a certified financial planner and licensed real estate broker. "Many new buyers feel a need to be walked through the process and coached on the various financial aspects. And of course, every buyer has that fear of paying too much for the house or buying a lemon."

According to Freireich, the HelpLine provides the type of information buyers can't always get from their real estate agents. "Since the real estate broker usually represents the seller, it's sometimes hard for a buyer to get objective advice."

"For example, one gentleman I spoke to was considering buying a house that was situated on a banked curve. I pointed out to him that because of where the home was situated, the headlights from cars passing at night would shine right into his bedroom. This is the type of information a buyer would not receive from the seller's agent. In fact, volunteering this type of info could be considered a breach of ethics on the agent's part."

Buyers calling the HelpLine can also request a free 16-page booklet entitled 13 Common Mistakes to Avoid When Buying a Home.

According to the booklet, one of the biggest mistakes home buyers can make is to be deceived by appearance. As Freireich explains it, "Savvy sellers know how to conceal a home's flaws by painting and sprucing up. One good way of judging the true condition of a home is to look at the window frames. Their condition will tell you if the homeowner really took care of the property or just did a little fixing up before putting it on the market."

The First-Time Home Buyers' HelpLine can be reached by calling 800-682-8937, ext. 102. If no one is available to answer the question, an expert will return the call within 24 hours.

```
NOTE TO EDITORS: Photos, interviews, review copies
available.

CONTACT: Roger Dextor of Blitz Media Direct, 516-924-
8555, or 24-hour fax, 516-924-3890.
```

SAMPLE ARTICLE QUERY LETTER

You can promote yourself by publishing how-to and informational articles related to commercial writing in trade and business magazines read by your potential clients. To propose an article to an editor, use a query letter. The sample query below got me an assignment to write an article on letter-writing for Amtrak Express magazine—they even paid me $400!

```
Mr. James A. Frank, Editor
AMTRAK EXPRESS
34 East 51st St.
New York, NY 10022

Dear Mr. Frank:

Is this letter a waste of paper?

Yes—if it fails to get the desired result.

In business, most letters and memos are written to gen-
erate a specific response: close a sale, set up a meet-
ing, get a job interview, make a contact. Many of these
letters fail to do the job.

Part of the problem is that business executives and
support staff don't know how to write persuasively. The
solution is a formula first discovered by advertising
copywriters, a formula called AIDA. AIDA stands for
Attention, Interest, Desire, Action.

First, the letter gets attention . . . with a hard-hit-
ting lead paragraph that goes straight to the point, or
offers an element of intrigue.

Then, the letter hooks the reader's interest. The hook
is often a clear statement of the reader's problems,
his needs, his concerns. If you are writing to a cus-
tomer who received damaged goods, state the problem. And
then promise a solution.

Next, create desire. You are offering something—a ser-
vice, a product, an agreement, a contract, a compromise,
a consultation. Tell the reader the benefit he'll receive
from your offering. Create a desire for your product.

Finally, call for action. Ask for the order, the signa-
ture, the check, the assignment.
```

I'd like to write a 1,500 word article on "How to Write Letters That Get Results." The piece will illustrate the AIDA formula with a variety of actual letters and memos from insurance companies, banks, manufacturers, and other organizations.

This letter, too, was written to get a specific result: an article assignment from the editor of <u>Amtrak Express</u>.

Did it succeed?

Regards,

Bob Bly

P.S. By way of introduction, I'm an advertising consultant and the author of five books including <u>Technical Writing: Structure, Standards, and Style</u> (McGraw-Hill).

SAMPLE SHORT-FORM RESOURCE BOX

BOB BLY, an independent copywriter and consultant, has written copy for more than 100 companies including IBM, AT&T, Agora Publishing, Hyperion Software, and Allied Signal. He is the author of over 35 books, including <u>The Advertising Manager's Handbook</u> (Prentice Hall), <u>Business-to-Business Direct Marketing</u> (NTC Business Books), and <u>The Copywriter's Handbook</u> (Henry Holt & Co.).

Bob writes sales letters, direct mail packages, ads, brochures, articles, press releases, newsletters, scripts, and other marketing materials clients need to sell their products and services to businesses. He also consults with clients on marketing strategy, mail order selling, and lead generation programs.

For more information contact: Bob Bly, 22 E. Quackenbush Avenue, Dumont, NJ 07628, phone 201-385-1220.

SAMPLE PITCH LETTER TO GET SPEAKING ENGAGEMENTS

Another excellent way to market yourself is by giving talks and speeches to groups of advertising and marketing professionals. Here's a model query letter you can use to generate such engagements.

Ms. Jane Smiley
Program Director
Women in Engineering
Big City, USA

Dear Ms. Smiley:

Did you know that, according to a recent survey in <u>Engineering Today</u>, the ability to write clearly and concisely can mean $100,000 extra in earnings over the lifetime of an engineer's career?

For this reason, I think your members might enjoy a presentation I have given to several business organizations around town, "10 Ways to Improve Your Technical Writing."

As the director of Plain Language, Inc., a company that specializes in technical documentation, I have worked with hundreds of engineers to help them improve their writing. My presentation highlights the 10 most common writing mistakes engineers make, and gives strategies for self-improvement.

Does this sound like the type of presentation that might fit well into your winter program schedule? I'd be delighted to speak before your group. Please phone or write so we can set a date.

Regards,

Blake Garibaldi, Director
Plain Language, Inc.

SAMPLE CLASSIFIED AND SMALL DISPLAY ADS

You can run ads promoting your consulting services in local business magazines, association newsletters, advertising trade publications, and other media. Classified or small (1- or 2-inch) classified display ads work best. Here are some of the more successful ads I have run over the years.

I Write Ads!

Over 75 corporations and ad agencies count on my crisp, accurate, hard-sell copy for ads, brochures, direct mail, PR, and A/V scripts. High-tech, industrial, and Business-to-Business advertising my specialty. Call or write for free information kit: Bob Bly, 22 E. Quackenbush Avenue, Dumont, NJ 07628, (201) 385-1220.

Call the High-Tech Copy Pro

I specialize in industrial and high-tech copy: computers, electronics, chemicals, software, telecommunications, heavy equipment, banking, health care, corporate, many other products and services. To receive full details by mail, call today. Bob Bly (201) 385-1220.

Improve Your DM Results!
Send for Free Report . . .

I specialize in writing lead-getting sales letters, DM packages, and ads for high-tech and business-to-business clients and agencies. For FREE report, "23 Tips for Creating Business-to-Business Mailings That Work," phone or write: Bob Bly, 22 E. Quackenbush Avenue, Dumont, NJ 07628, (201) 385-1220. Also ask for a free information kit on my copywriting services.

SAMPLE FULL-PAGE LEAD-GENERATING ADS

NOW YOU CAN FREE YOURSELF FROM THE MOST COSTLY (AND TIME-CONSUMING) PART OF DOING BUSINESS OVERSEAS...

THE PAPERWORK.

For most companies, filling out Customs forms, calculating Value Added Tax, revaluating assets and liabilities, and coping with the myriad rules and regulations of doing business overseas is an administrative nightmare. But now there's a software system that can help you get through it.

Presenting the International Business System from Digital Linguistix Corporation.

The International Business System is an international accounting and distribution software system with true foreign currency translation and revaluation capabilities.

Now, thanks to IBS, multinational corporations, import/export firms, and other companies conducting business domestically and abroad can enhance the efficiency of their operations, saving countless hours of labor and gaining total control of their financial picture.

Revaluates Your Assets and Liabilities in Every Country on Demand, Instantly.

Only IBS automates the tedious task of adjusting your books to account for fluctuations in foreign exchange rates—a capability other financial packages do not offer. At the touch of a key, IBS automatically revaluates your balance-sheet items on-line, at any time, calculating and posting the unrealized and realized gain or loss.

If you do business in multiple currencies, this unique revaluation feature will give you an instant, to-the-penny picture of your financial position—by currency and by country—in strict accordance with FASB 52. (It will also save your accounting staff hundreds of hours of paperwork every month.)

What's more, IBS also assists you with the preparation of all necessary international customs documents—and ensures that you conform to the statutory reporting requirements of foreign countries.

A Total Multilingual, Multinational Business Package.

IBS is a fully integrated financial and business software package, with modules for accounts receivable, accounts payable, general ledger, financial report writer, invoicing, order entry, purchasing, inventory, international currency control, and more.

And, IBS is a multilingual package that speaks English, Spanish, French, German, Dutch, or whatever language you choose. Invoices, financial statements, forms, screens, and reports are generated in all languages and currencies from a single common database—with no duplication of files or records. IBS runs on IBM 9370, IBM PC, DEC VAX, Honeywell, and Tandem hardware.

Get the Facts—FREE.

For more information on the International Business System from Digital Linguistix Corporation, fill in the coupon below and return it to us by mail or FAX today.

Digital Linguistix
CORPORATION

30 CHAPIN ROAD, PO BOX 609
PINE BROOK, NEW JERSEY 07058
PHONE (201) 882-3630 FAX: (201) 882-3505

Digital Linguistix Corporation is a dealer for the Ultimate Corporation. The International Business System software can be run on DEC, IBM, Honeywell, and Tandem hardware through the powerful relational database management tools of the Ultimate/PICK operating system.

YES, I'd like to know more about the International Business System from Digital Linguistix Corporation.

☐ Please send me a free copy of your fact-filled brochure.

☐ Have a sales representative call.

Name _____ Title _____

Company _____ Phone _____

Address _____

City _____ State _____ Zip _____

Country _____

Mail to: Digital Linguistix, 30 Chapin Road, PO Box 609, Pine Brook, NJ 07058
FOR FASTER SERVICE, TEAR OUT AND FAX TO: (201) 882-3505

SM001

Circle Reader Service No. 24

SAMPLE FULL-PAGE ADS FOR GENERATING VISITS TO WEB SITES

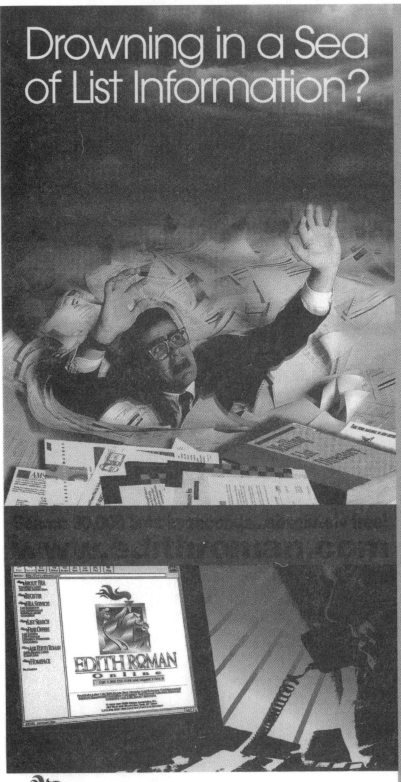

LETTER REQUESTING REFERRALS

One of the best sources of sales leads is referrals from existing clients. If your clients aren't giving you as many referrals as you want, here's a letter you can use to ask for more.

```
Ms. Joan Zipkin
Acme Retail Outlets
Anytown, USA

Dear Joan:

I'm glad you liked the Spring catalog I recently com-
pleted for you. Like you, I'm always on the lookout for
new business. So I have a favor to ask. Could you jot
down, on the back of this letter, the names, addresses,
and phone numbers of a few of your colleagues who might
benefit from knowing more about my services?

(Naturally, I don't want anyone whose product line com-
petes with your own.)

Then, just mail the letter back to me in the enclosed
reply envelope.

I may want to mention your name when contacting these
people. Let me know if there's any problem with that.

Thanks for the favor!

Regards,

Sam Tate
```

LETTER FOR SOLICITING TESTIMONIALS FROM CLIENTS

After completing a job successfully, you can use this letter to solicit a testimonial from the client. A sheet of paper filled with testimonials is a very powerful addition to a promotional package and convinces prospects you are good at what you do. I always send a self-addressed, stamped envelope and two copies of the letter. This way the recipient doesn't have to make a copy of the letter or address and stamp an envelope.

```
Mr. Andrew Specher, President
Hazardous Waste Management, Inc.
Anywhere, USA

Dear Andrew:

I have a favor to ask of you.

I'm in the process of putting together a list of testi-
monials, a collection of comments about my services from
satisfied clients like yourself.

Would you take a few minutes to give me your opinion of
my writing services? No need to dictate a letter—just
```

jot your comments on the back of this letter, sign
below, and return to me in the enclosed envelope. (The
second copy is for your files.) I look forward to
learning what you like about my service . . . but I
also welcome any suggestions or criticisms, too.

Many thanks, Andrew.

Regards,

Bob Bly

YOU HAVE MY PERMISSION TO QUOTE FROM MY COMMENTS, AND
USE THESE QUOTATIONS IN ADS, BROCHURES, MAIL, AND OTHER
PROMOTIONS USED TO MARKET YOUR FREELANCE WRITING SER-
VICES.

Signature_____   Date_____

LETTER REQUESTING PERMISSION TO USE EXISTING TESTIMONIAL

Some clients will send you letters of testimonial unsolicited. Before you use
them in your promotions, get their permission in writing, using this form
letter.

Mr. Mike Hernandez
Advertising Manager
Technilogic, Inc.
Anytown, USA

Dear Mike:

I never did get around to thanking you for your letter
of 2/15/87 (copy attached). So . . . thanks!

I'd like to quote from this letter in the ads,
brochures, direct mail packages, and other promotions I
use to market my writing services—with your permission,
of course. If this is okay with you, would you please
sign the bottom of this letter and send it back to me
in the enclosed envelope? (The second copy is for your
files.)

Many thanks, Mike.

Regards,

Bob Bly

YOU HAVE MY PERMISSION TO QUOTE FROM THE ATTACHED LET-
TER IN ADS, BROCHURES, MAIL, AND OTHER PROMOTIONS USED
TO MARKET YOUR FREELANCE WRITING SERVICES.

Signature_____   Date_____

SAMPLE NEEDS ASSESSMENT FORM

Bob Bly's
Business-to-Business
Marketing Communications Audit

In today's economy, it pays to make every marketing communication count.

This simple audit is designed to help you identify your most pressing marketing communications challenges—and to find ways to solve problems, communicate with your target markets more effectively, and get better results from every dollar spent on advertising and promotion.

Step One: Identify Your Areas of Need

Check all items that are of concern to you right now:

❑ Creating a marketing or advertising plan

❑ Generating more inquiries from my print advertising

❑ Improving overall effectiveness and persuasiveness of print ads

❑ Determining which vertical industries or narrow target markets to pursue

❑ How to effectively market and promote our product or service on a limited advertising budget to these target audiences

❑ Producing effective sales brochures, catalogs, and other marketing literature

❑ How to get good case histories and user stories written and published

❑ Getting articles by company personnel written and published in industry trade journals

❑ Getting editors to write about our company, product, or activities

❑ Getting more editors to run our press releases

❑ Planning and implementing a direct mail campaign or program

❑ Increasing direct mail response rates

❑ Generating low-cost but qualified leads using postcard decks

❑ How to make all our marketing communications more responsive and accountable

❑ Designing, writing, and producing a company newsletter

❑ Creating an effective company or capabilities brochure

❑ Developing strategies for responding to and following up on inquiries

❑ Creating effective inquiry fulfillment packages

❑ Producing and using a video or audio tape to promote our product or service

❑ Writing and publishing a book, booklet, or special report that can be used to promote our company or product

❑ Choosing an appropriate premium or advertising specialty as a customer giveaway

❑ Getting reviews and critiques of existing or in-progress copy for ads, mailings, brochures, and other promotions

❑ How to promote our product or service using free or paid seminars

❑ How to market our product or organization by having our people speak or present papers at conventions, trade shows, meetings, and other industry events

❑ Training our staff with an in-house seminar in:

_____
(indicate topic)

❑ Learning proven strategies for marketing our product or service in a recession or soft economy

❑ Other (describe): _____

_____

_____

Marketing Communications Audit

Step Two: Provide a Rough Indication of Your Budget

Amount of money you are prepared to commit to the solution of the problems checked off on page one of this form:

❑ under $500 ❑ under $1,000 ❑ under $2,500

❑ under $5,000 ❑ other: _____

Step Three: Fill in Your Name, Address, and Phone Number Below

Name _____ Title _____

Company _____ Phone _____

Address _____

City _____ State _____ Zip _____

Step Four: Mail or Fax Your Completed Form Today

Mail: Bob Bly, 174 Holland Avenue, New Milford, NJ 07646

FAX: (201) 599-2276

Phone: (201) 599-2277

If you wish, send me your current ads, brochures, mailing pieces, press releases, and any other material that will give me a good idea of the products or services you are responsible for promoting. I will review your audit and materials and provide a free 20-minute consultation by telephone with specific recommendations on how to solve your marketing problems, implement programs, and effectively address your key areas of concern. To schedule a specific date and time for your free, no-obligation phone consultation, indicate your preferred date and time below:

Preferred date and time_____

Alternate date and time_____

Mail your audit form today. There's no cost. And no obligation.

Bob Bly • Copywriter/Consultant • 174 Holland Avenue • New Milford, NJ 07646

SAMPLE CAPABILITIES BROCHURE

THE CENTER FOR TECHNICAL COMMUNICATION

Technical and business writing seminars for corporations

In-house training programs

Public seminars

Conferences

Publications

The Technical Writing Hotline™

Fax Critique service

Train-the-trainer programs

Contract technical writing services

CTC Trainers Bureau

The Center for Technical Marketing

Everything you need to train your employees to write better and faster, boost productivity, and enhance the quality of your organization's written communications.

WHAT IS THE CENTER FOR TECHNICAL COMMUNICATION?

The Center for Technical Communication (CTC) is a company that specializes in improving the writing skills of corporate employees and the quality of written communications within your organization.

CTC's primary service is conducting in-house workshops in technical and business writing for corporate clients nationwide. Our on-site writing seminars give your employees the skills and confidence to write better, faster, and more productively.

CTC also offers public seminars, conferences, and publications covering all aspects of technical and business communication. Other services designed to improve the quality of communication in your organization include our telephone hotline, fax critique service, contract technical writing services, and more.

IN-HOUSE WRITING WORKSHOPS

CTC offers the following in-house training seminars for corporations and associations:

Effective Technical Writing

A 1 or 2-day workshop on how to write clear, correct, technically accurate reports, manuals, documentation, specs, proposals, papers, and other technical documents. This program is designed to improve the writing skills of engineers, scientists, systems analysts, technicians, technical writers, technical editors, and others whose writing deals with technical or semi-technical subject matter.

Effective Business Writing

A 1 or 2-day workshop on how to write clear, concise, persuasive letters, memos, reports, proposals, and other business documents. This program's focus is on improving the writing skills of executives, managers, professionals, and support staff.

Our instructors know technical writing because they are technicians and technical writers.

What sets CTC apart from other training firms is that our instructors are not only skilled and entertaining trainers but are also *recognized authorities* in their fields. Our technical writing seminars, for example, are taught by instructors who hold technical degrees, have worked as full-time professional technical writers for large corporations, and have taught technical writing at the university level. In-depth experience and technical background not only improve the quality of instruction but also break down barriers between the instructor and the audience: Your technical trainees become more receptive when they realize the instructor is a "techie" like them.

PUBLIC SEMINARS AND CONFERENCES

Although CTC gives priority to meeting the in-house training needs of our corporate clients, we occasionally sponsor public seminars and conferences on technical and business writing. Companies with six or more people requiring training, however, will probably find an in-house program more cost-effective.

TRAIN-THE-TRAINER PROGRAM

Some companies do not have the budget to send as many of their employees as they'd like through our technical writing workshops. As a cost-effective alternative to on-site training, we offer a train-the-trainer program in which CTC licenses its course materials, including outlines and hand-outs, to you for use within your organization. We also coach your trainers in how to present our program effectively.

PUBLICATIONS

CTC offers books, special reports, monographs, and audio cassettes on a variety of topics including technical writing, marketing communications, and business communications.

THE TECHNICAL WRITING HOTLINE ™

This unique telephone hotline gives you instant access to technical writing experts who can provide immediate answers to questions concerning grammar, punctuation, spelling, usage, word choice, format, and style.

FAX CRITIQUE SERVICE

Clients can fax drafts to CTC for immediate review and editing. A qualified CTC technical editor reads the document, edits, provides further suggestions for improvement, and returns the original with corrections and comments to the client via fax.

CONTRACT TECHNICAL WRITING SERVICES

CTC maintains a large database of qualified technical writers with varied backgrounds and hourly rates. If your staff is overloaded and you need a technical writer, call CTC. We'll provide technical writers to work at your place or theirs on a project, hourly, or per diem basis. Should you wish to hire the writer full-time, CTC can arrange this through our Executive Search and Placement Division.

CTC TRAINERS BUREAU

In addition to staff instructors specializing in technical and business writing, CTC operates a trainers bureau providing trainers who fit your budget and can speak on such topics as:

- Business writing
- Technical writing
- Copywriting
- Persuasive writing for salespeople
- English as a second language
- Presentation skills
- Selling
- Direct mail/direct marketing
- Client service
- And many others.

THE CENTER FOR TECHNICAL MARKETING

The Center for Technical Marketing (CTM) is a division of CTC specializing in business-to-business, industrial, high-tech, and direct response marketing.

CTM creates award-winning, result-getting direct mail, packages, sales letters, brochures, ads, press releases, newsletters, data sheets, and other marketing documents for more than 100 clients nationwide.

CLIENTS (A PARTIAL LIST) *

Airco
Associated Distribution Logistics
Atech Software
Brooklyn Union Gas
Cambridge Scientific Abstracts
Chemical Bank
The Conference Board
Convergent Solutions
CoreStates Financial Corporation
Creative Group, Inc.
Crest Ultrasonics
Dow Chemical
Drake Beam Morin
EBI Medical Systems
Executive Enterprises
Fala Direct Marketing
Fielder's Choice
Grey Advertising
Howard Lanin Productions
IBM
IEEE
ITT
International Tile Exposition
The Institute of Management Accountants
JMW Consultants
J. Walter Thompson
Leviton Manufacturing
Metrum Instruments
Midlantic
M & T Chemicals
On-Line Software
Optical Data Corporation
Prentice Hall
PSE&G
Reed Travel Group
Sony
Siemens
Specialty Steel & Forge
Thompson Professional Publishing
Timeplex
Union Camp
Value Rent-a-Car
Wallace & Tiernan
Wolfram Research
And many, many others...

* The firms and associations listed have retained the seminar, training, writing, or consulting services of CTC, Bob Bly, or The Center for Technical Marketing.

WHAT CLIENTS AND ATTENDEES SAY ABOUT CTC SEMINARS AND SERVICES...

" Thanks for the seminar. Besides clarifying technical points, you gave me insight into my position, and my abilities, as a writer. And observing you in action was excellent training. "

— Mike Goldscheitter, technical writer
Loveland Controls

" Thanks again for joining us in Atlantic City. I, and the entire group, found your thoughts insightful and right on target."

— Edward H. Moore, editor
communication briefings

" Your presentation for our seminar was sparkling, enthusiastic, and informative. The audience response was wonderful to see and hear. Our group benefited greatly and were quite vocal in their praise of you."

— Wendy Ward, program chair
Women in Communications

" The first issue of the spinal newsletter is enclosed. The sales force was very receptive to the newsletter and its contents. Thank you for helping us launch this important project. "

— Mary Ellen Coleman, product manager
EBI Medical Systems

" I just wanted to thank you personally for the energy and effort you put into your two days with us. We are now far better equipped to do direct mail for our clients and ourselves that will have a greater impact and get measurable results. "

— Greta Bolger, account executive
Sefton Associates Inc.

" I just finished reading the copy for our CERTIN-COAT system brochure and I was very happy with it. You did an excellent job of editing a large amount of information, much of it extraneous, into a strong, cohesive selling message."

— Len Lavenda, advertising manager
M&T Chemicals Inc.

" I found the seminar helpful and noticed a definite greater awareness of style afterwards. Your presentation was lively, and kept the participants' attention well into the afternoon and longer than I had expected beforehand."

— J.E. Koschei, editorial director
Thompson Professional Publishing

ABOUT CTC'S DIRECTOR

Bob Bly, director of the Center for Technical Communication, has been a technical writer and technical writing instructor full-time since 1979.

He taught technical writing at New York University and has presented training sessions to such groups as the American Chemical Society, the American Marketing Association, and the American Institute of Chemical Engineers.

Mr. Bly is the author of 25 books including *Technical Writing: Structure, Standards, and Style* (McGraw-Hill), *The Copywriter's Handbook* (Henry Holt), and *The Elements of Business Writing* (Macmillan).

Bob Bly has worked as a staff technical writer for the Westinghouse Electric Corporation and also as an independent technical writer handling projects for dozens of firms including Brooklyn Union Gas, Crest Ultrasonics, On-Line Software, and M&T Chemicals.

Mr. Bly holds a B.S. in engineering from the University of Rochester. He is a member of the Society for Technical Communication, American Institute of Chemical Engineers, and the American Society for Training and Development.

THE NEXT STEP

For more information on any of the services described in this brochure, or to discuss scheduling a technical writing or business writing seminar for your organization, call CTC at (201) 385-1220. Or write us today.

THE CENTER FOR TECHNICAL COMMUNICATION
22 E. Quackenbush Avenue
Dumont, NJ 07628
phone (201) 385-1220
fax (201) 385-1138

SAMPLE INQUIRY FULFILLMENT LETTER

Thanks for your interest in my copywriting services....

Now, maybe you asked for this information kit out of curiosity. Some folks do—especially those who never hired a freelance copywriter before.

But, more likely, you need a good business-to-business copywriter—someone who combines writing skill and sales ability with technical know-how and product knowledge.

Whatever your reason for calling or writing, you want to know more about a writer before you hire him. If we were sitting face to face, chatting in your office, you'd ask me questions. Let me try to answer a few of those questions right here.

"WHAT ARE YOUR QUALIFICATIONS AS A COPYWRITER?"

As a freelancer, I've written copy for more than 100 agencies and advertisers. And, I'm the author of 25 books including The Copywriters Handbook (Henry Holt & Co.), The Perfect Sales Piece (John Wiley), and Direct Mail Profits (Asher-Gallant Press).

I've given seminars on copywriting and direct marketing for numerous corporations and associations. I have also taught copywriting at New York University.

Before becoming a freelancer, I was advertising manager for Koch Engineering (an industrial manufacturer) and a staff writer for Westinghouse. The attached material will give you the full story.

"DO YOU HAVE A TECHNICAL BACKGROUND?"

I have a Bachelor's degree in engineering from the University of Rochester. And 95 percent of the work I do is in industrial, high-tech, business-to-business, and direct response.

I've written copy on computers, chemicals, pulp and paper, mining, construction, electronics, engineering, pollution control, medical equipment, industrial equipment, marine products, software, banking, financial services, health care, publishing, seminars, training, telecommunications, consulting, corporate, and many other areas. In the computer field, for example, I'm the author of five computer books including A Dictionary of Computer Words, published by Dell/Banbury.

Most important to you, I'm a business-to-business, direct-response copy specialist.

Writing business-to-business copy isn't something I do to pass the time between TV commercials. Rather, it's my bread and butter. So I put all my skill, knack, and know-how into every piece of business-to-business copy I write. And, after writing hundreds of ads, articles, brochures, and sales letters for people like you, I've learned how to sell to corporate executives, entrepreneurs managers, purchasing agents, technicians, engineers, professionals, and other business and technical buyers.

"DO YOU HAVE EXPERIENCE IN MY FIELD?"

If you sell to business, industry, professionals, or through direct response, chances are I already have experience dealing with your type of product or service— or something very similar.

Take a look at my writing samples enclosed with this letter. Do they seem "right up your alley"? If not, give me a call, and I'll send additional samples that are closer to your area of interest.

"WHAT KINDS OF ASSIGNMENTS DO YOU HANDLE?"

I cover the spectrum. About 80 percent of my business is writing direct mail and sales brochures for business, industrial, and high-tech clients. The rest involves creating a wide assortment of marketing communications materials, including ads, feature articles, slide presentations, film and videotape scripts, press releases, newsletters, catalogs, case histories, annual reports, product guides, manuals, and speeches.

My specialty is my ability to write clear, credible, persuasive copy about a wide range of business products and services, from the simple to the highly technical.

I am able to quickly grasp complex marketing problems and understand sophisticated technologies. Clients appreciate the fact that I can sit down with engineers, scientists, systems professionals, and other specialists, ask intelligent questions, and speak their language.

What's more, my copy gets <u>results</u>. One ad, written for a manufacturer of pollution control equipment, was the number-one inquiry producer in four consecutive issues of <u>Chemical Engineering</u> magazine.

Another piece of copy, a direct mail campaign I wrote for a telephone company, won the Direct Marketing Association's Gold Echo Award...and generated a 50 percent response rate (and $5.7 million in revenue) for the client.

I can't predict how many responses my ad, mailer, or literature package will pull for you. But I can guarantee your satisfaction with the copy you receive from me.

"WHY DOES YOUR LETTERHEAD SAY 'COPYWRITER/CONSULTANT'?"

In addition to writing copy, I also work with many of my clients as a consultant, helping them plan marketing campaigns that generate maximum response. They're pleased to get on-target advice that works—at an affordable fee—and they like the fact that I don't charge a monthly retainer.

YOUR FEE SCHEDULE LISTS A PRICE FOR A COPY CRITIQUE—WHAT'S THAT?

A copy critique provides an objective review of an ado, sales letter, brochure, or direct mail package. You can have me critique either an existing piece or a draft of copy in progress. It's up to you.

When you order a Copy Critique, you get a written report of two or more single-spaced typed pages that analyzes your copy in detail. I tell you what's good about it and what works, what doesn't work, what should be changed ... and how. My critique covers copy, design, strategy, and offer. It also includes specific directions for revisions and rewriting, although I do not write or rewrite copy for you under this arrangement.

A copy critique is ideal for clients who want a "second opinion" on a piece of copy, or who need new ideas to inject life into an existing package that's no longer working. It also enables you to sample my services at far less than you'd pay to have me write your copy from scratch.

"SPEAKING OF MONEY, WHAT DOES IT COST TO HIRE YOU FOR A PROJECT?"

For any copywriting assignment—a direct mail package, a sales letter, an ad, a brochure, a feature article, an A/V script—just let me know what you have in mind and I'll quote you a price. The enclosed Schedule of Estimated Fees gives typical prices for a variety of different projects.

"WHO ARE YOUR CLIENTS AND WHAT DO THEY SAY ABOUT YOUR COPY AND COUNSEL?"

"Working with Bob Bly was easy," reports Robert Jurick, CEO of Fala Direct Marketing. "Bob Bly is more than a copywriter; he becomes part of the client and writes with understanding and sense. His copy resulted in several projects from some of our big accounts."

Andrew Frothingham, former ad manager of Timeplex, comments: "When I was the ad manager at Timeplex, I used Bob Bly a lot, because he has the best understanding of any writer I found of the issues in the world of high technology."

"I would like to express my thanks for your assistance in helping us develop a marketing program via the mass media," writes Stan Stevens, president, Personal Health Profile. "I was impressed with your professionalism, knowledge of the field, willingness to extend yourself, and your eagerness to help us succeed. It was a real pleasure working with you."

"HOW LONG WILL IT TAKE YOU TO WRITE MY COPY?"

Ideally I like to have 2 to 3 weeks to work on your copy. That gives me the time to polish, edit and revise until I'm happy with every word.

However, I realize you can't always wait that long. So if the job is a rush, just indicate the date by which you must receive the copy on the enclosed order from. If I take on the job, I guarantee that you will have the copy on your desk by this deadline date—or sooner.

No matter what the deadline, the copy I submit to you will be right. You can depend on it.

"WHAT HAPPENS IF WE WANT YOU TO REVISE THE COPY?"

Just tell me what you want improved and what the changes are, and I'll make them—fast. There is no charge for rewriting. Revisions are included in the flat fee we've agreed to for the assignment provided they are assigned within 30 days of your receipt of the copy and are not based on a change in the assignment after copy has been submitted.

Most clients are pleased and enthusiastic about my copy when they receive it. But if you are not 100 percent satisfied, I will revise the copy according to your specific guidelines... and at my expense.

"HOW DO I ORDER FROM YOU?"

Putting me to work for you is easy. First, just tell me what you're selling and who you're selling it to. Send me your brochure, catalog, or any other literature that will give me the background information I need to write your copy. Use the enclosed order form as a guideline. But don't worry about organizing anything—I'll do that. If I have any questions, I'll pick up the phone and ask.

If you'd like to get together to go over the job in person, we can do that, too. I'd be delighted to meet with you, wherever and whenever you wish.

When you give me the go-ahead, I'll write the assignment for you. You will receive your copy on or before the deadline date. And remember, it is *guaranteed* to please you.

Dozens of firms—including Wallace & Tiernan, Medical Economics, Philadelphia National Bank, Digital

Linguistix, Prentice Hall, GE Solid State, IEM, F&W Publishing, Alloy Technology, Ascom Timeplex, Allied Signal Aerospace, and Edith Roman Associates—have found my copy ideal for promoting business, industrial, and high-tech products and services and direct-response offers.

So... why not try my service for your next sales letter, direct mail package, feature article, press release, ad, or brochure? I promise you'll be delighted with the results.

PS If you have an immediate need call me right now at (201) 385-1220 or fax me the details on my dedicated fax line: (201) 385-1138. There is no charge to discuss your job with you and give you a cost estimate. And no obligation to buy.

SAMPLE LETTER PROPOSING A SWAP OF LISTS OR CUSTOMER DATABASES WITH A VENDOR OF PRODUCTS AIMED AT MARKETS SIMILAR TO YOURS

Mr. John Jones
President
ABC Collectibles
123 Main Street
Anywhere, New York

Dear Mr. Jones:

If you want to increase the profit from your "Princess Diana" mailings, you might consider testing our growing lists and letting us test yours.

You've heard of the Society for the Preservation of History. Well, right now, we're running with the winner: The Princess Diana "Queen of Hearts" Porcelain Figure.

It's a Limited Edition collectible. And has received high praise from press, public and collectible watchers everywhere.

I enclose a current ad so that you can judge for yourself.

We think a test and exchange of lists makes good sense. So, if you'd like to test our hotline names, we'd be glad to work with you.

To get the ball rolling, please complete the form enclosed and send it along with an ad or mailing about your own Diana project. And we'll take if from there.

If you prefer, give me a call at 602-948-4336.

This can be an exciting, win-win situation for us both. So, I hope you'll complete and mail the form today!

Cordially,

[Reply Form]

Yes, we're interested in exploring a list exchange program with you. Please phone me at

(_____)_____
Area code Phone number

For your comments: _____

_____

_____

Print your name _____   Title _____

Firm_____

Address _____

City _____   State _____   Zip Code _____

[Footline]

PLEASE COMPLETE THIS FORM AND MAIL IT WITH YOUR OWN "PRINCESS DIANA" PROMOTION OR AD TO THE SOCIETY FOR THE PRESERVATION OF HISTORY, 4461 112TH STREET, URBANDALE, IA 50322-2083.

SAMPLE CONFIDENTIALITY AGREEMENT

NONDISCLOSURE AGREEMENT

This nondisclosure agreement (the "Agreement") is made by and between Robert W. Bly, having a principal place of business at 22 East Quackenbush Avenue, 3rd floor, Dumont, New Jersey 07628 ("Contractor"), and ABC Technologies, Inc., having a principal place of business at 1505 Ocean Street #1, Santa Cruz, California 95018 ("ABC").

RECITALS:

A. Contractor desires to provide ABC consulting services.

B. In the course of dealings between Contractor and ABC, Contractor has and will have access to or have disclosed to it information relating to ABC which is of a confidential nature as that terms defined in this Agreements.

C. ABC desires to establish and set forth Contractor's obligations with respect to ABC's confidential information.

AGREEMENT:

In consideration of the foregoing, Contractor and ABC mutually agree as follows:

1. "Confidential Information" as used in this Agreement shall mean any and all technical and nontechnical information including patent, copyright, trade secret, and proprietary information, techniques, sketches, drawings, models, inventions, knowhow, processes, apparatus, equipment, algorithms, software programs, software source documents, and formulae related to the current, future and proposed products and services of ABC, and includes, without limitation, its respective information concerning research, experimental work, development, design details and specifications, engineering, financial information, procurement requirements, purchasing, manufacturing, customer lists, business forecasts, sales and merchandising, and marketing plans and information.

2. Contractor agrees that it will not make use of, disseminate, or in any way circulate within its own organization any Confidential Information of ABC which is supplied to or obtained by it in writing, orally or by observation, except to the extent necessary for negotiations, discussions, and consultants with personnel or authorized representatives of ABC and any purpose ABC may hereafter authorize in writing.

3. Contractor agrees that it shall disclose Confidential Information of ABC only to those of its employees who need to know such information and certifies that such employees have previously agreed, either as a condition of employment or in order to obtain the Confidential Information, to be bound by the terms and conditions of this Agreement.

4. Contractor agrees that it shall treat all Confidential Information of ABC with the same degree of care as it accords to its own confidential information of the same or similar nature, and Contractor represents that it exercises reasonable care to protect its own confidential information.

5. Contractor further agrees that it shall not publish, copy or disclose any Confidential Information of ABC to any third party and that it shall use best efforts to prevent inadvertent disclosure of such Confidential Information to any third party.

6. Contractor's obligations under Paragraphs 2, 3, 4 and 5 with respect to any portion of ABC's Confidential Information shall terminate when Contractor can document that:

(a) it was in the public domain at the time it was communicated to Contractor by ABC;

(b) it entered the public domain subsequent to the time it was communicated to Contractor by ABC through no fault of Contractor;

(c) it was rightfully communicated to Contractor free of any obligation of confidence to the time it was communicated to Contractor by ABC;

(d) it was in Contractor's possession free of any obligation of confidence at the time it was communicated to contractor by ABC;

(e) it was developed by employees or agent of Contractor independently of and without reference to any information communicated to Contractor by ABC;

(f) it was communicated by ABC to an unaffiliated third party free of any obligation or confidence; or

(g) the communication was in response to a valid order by a court or other governmental body, was otherwise required by law, or was necessary to establish the rights of either party under this Agreement.

7. All materials (including, without limitation, documents, drawings, models, apparatus, sketches, designs, customer lists or any other proprietary data) furnished to Contractor by ABC shall remain the property of ABC and shall be returned to ABC promptly at its request, together with any and all copies thereof, including those stored in electronic form.

8. All work product resulting from this contract (including, without limitation, procedures, documents, drawings, models, apparatus, sketches, designs, or any other proprietary or confidential information) created by Contractor independently or with the assistance with ABC shall become the property of ABC.

9. Contractor will not communicate any information to ABC in violation of the proprietary rights of any third party.

10. Since unauthorized disclosure of Confidential Information will diminish the value to ABC of the proprietary interests that are the subject of the Agreement, if Contractor breaches any of its obligations hereunder, ABC shall be entitled to equitable relief to protect its interests therein, including but not limited to injunctive relief, as well as money damages.

11. This Agreement shall govern all communications between the parties made during the period on the date of contract award to Contractor by ABC until contract completion. Contractor's obligation under Paragraph 2, 3, 4 and 5 with respect to Confidential Information of ABC shall continue in perpetuity unless terminated pursuant to Paragraph 6.

12. This Agreement shall be construed in accordance with the laws of the State of California, without giving effect to principles of conflict of laws.

13. This Agreement is the complete and exclusive statement of the agreement between the parties and supersedes all prior or contemporaneous written and oral communications and agreements relating to the subject matter hereof.

14. Any notice required to be given under this Agreement shall be deemed received upon personal delivery or three (3) days after mailing if sent by registered or certified mail to the addresses of the parties set forth below, or to such other address as either of the parities shall have furnished to the other in writing.

15. In the event of invalidity of any provision of this Agreement, the parties agree that such invalidity shall not affect the validity of the remaining portions of this Agreement.

IN WITNESS WHEREOF, the parties have executed this Agreement as of the date first written below.

CONTRACTOR   ABC TECHNOLOGIES, INC.

By:_____   By:_____
       Robert W. Bly   Chris Knudsen

Title: Principal   Title: VP Marketing
Date_____   Date:_____

Appendix

PRECOPYWRITING CHECKLIST

Here's a four-step checklist I use to get the information I need to write persuasive, fact-filled copy for my clients. This technique should be helpful to copywriters, account executives, and ad managers alike.

STEP #1: GET ALL PREVIOUSLY PUBLISHED MATERIAL ON THE PRODUCT.

For an existing product, there's a mountain of literature you can send to the copywriter as background information. This material includes:

- Tearsheets of previous ads
- Brochures
- Catalogs
- Article reprints
- Technical papers
- Copies of speeches
- Audiovisual scripts
- Press kits
- Swipe files of competitors' ads and literature

Did I hear someone say they can't send me printed material because their product is new? Nonsense. The birth of every new product is accompanied by mounds of paperwork you can give the copywriter. These papers include:

- Internal memos
- Letters of technical information

- Product specifications
- Engineering drawings
- Business and marketing plans
- Reports
- Proposals

By studying this material, the copywriter should have 80 percent of the information needed to write the copy. The other 20 percent can be gotten by picking up the phone and asking questions. Steps #2 to #4 outline the questions that should be asked about the product, the audience, and the objective of the copy.

STEP #2: ASK QUESTIONS ABOUT THE PRODUCT.

- What are its features and benefits? (Make a complete list.)
- Which benefit is the most important?
- How is the product different from the competition's? (Which features are exclusive? Which are better than the competition's?)
- If the product isn't different, what attributes can be stressed that haven't been stressed by the competition?
- What technologies does the product compete against?
- What are the applications of the product?
- What industries can use the product?
- What problems does the product solve in the marketplace?
- How is the product positioned in the marketplace?
- How does the product work?
- How reliable is the product?
- How efficient?
- How economical?
- Who has bought the product and what do they say about it?
- What materials, sizes, and models is the product available in?
- How quickly does the manufacturer deliver the product?
- What service and support does the manufacturer offer?
- Is the product guaranteed?

STEP #3: ASK QUESTIONS ABOUT YOUR AUDIENCE.

- Who will buy the product? (What markets is it sold to?)
- What is the customer's main concern? (Price, delivery, performance, reliability, service maintenance, quality efficiency.)
- What is the character of the buyer?
- What motivates the buyer?

- How many different buying influences must the copy appeal to? Two tips on getting to know your audience:
- If you are writing an ad, read issues of the magazine in which the ad will appear.
- If you are writing direct mail, find out what mailing lists will be used and study the list descriptions.

STEP #4: DETERMINE THE OBJECTIVE OF YOUR COPY.

This objective may be one or more of the following:

- To generate inquiries
- To get appointments
- To qualify prospects
- To transmit product information
- To build brand recognition and preference
- To increase visits to your Web site

Before you write copy, study the product—its features, benefits, past performance, applications, and markets. Digging for the facts will pay off, because in business-to-business advertising, specifics sell.

POSTAL RATES

Postal Rates

Sort	First Class		Standard Mail(A)		Standard Mail (A) BMC		Standard Mail (A) SCF	
Level:	Letters*	Card	Letters	Flat	Letters	Flat	Letters	Flat
Basic	32.0	20.0	25.6	30.6	24.3	29.3	23.8	28.8
Basic Barcode (100%)	26.1	16.6	18.3	27.7	17.0	26.4	16.5	25.9
3/5 Digit Presort	29.5	18.0	20.9	22.5	19.6	21.2	19.1	20.7
3-Digit Barcode (100%)	25.4	15.9	17.5	18.9	16.2	17.6	15.7	17.1
5-Digit Barcode (100%)	23.8	14.3	15.5	18.9	14.2	17.6	13.7	17.1
Carrier-Route	N/A	N/A	15.0	15.5	13.7	14.2	13.2	13.7
Carrier-Route Barcode (100%)	23.0	14.0	14.6	N/A	13.3	N/A	12.8	N/A

*FIRST CLASS—.0625 lb. (UP TO 1 oz.). Each additional oz. Charge .23. Max. Wt. 11 oz.
FIRST CLASS NONSTANDARD SURCHARGES = BASIC .11/each. PRESORT and CARRIER ROUTE
.05/each.

STANDARD MAIL (A) = .2068 lb. (3.3087 oz.) or less.
STANDARD MAIL (A) CARRIER ROUTE - .2066 lb. (3.3062 oz.) or less.

Reprinted with permission of The Fala Group
Fala Direct Marketing, Inc., Fala CCG. Inc., Fala Sorting Services, Inc., FalaRx
Corporate Headquarters: 70 Marcus Drive, Melville, NY 11747-4278 Phone (516) 694-1919, Fax (516) 691-7493

Additional Charges

First Class/Standard Mail (A)
LETTERS
- Must be between 5" and 11.5"
  in length, 3.5" and 6.125" in height.
- When length is divided by height, the
resulting ratio must range from 1.3" to 2.5".
- Must be between .007" and .25"
  in thickness.

First Class nonstandard surcharge applicable
when above ratios are not met.

ADDITIONAL RATES FOR STANDARD MAIL
- ENHANCED CARRIER ROUTE (NEW)

	LETTERS	BMC	SCF	DDU
High	14.2	12.9	12.4	11.9
Density	13.3	12.0	11.5	11.0
Saturation				

FLATS
- Must be between 6" and 15" in length and 6" and 12" in height.
- Must be between .25" and .75" in thickness.

	FLATS	BMC	SCF	DDU
High	14.7	13.4	12.9	12.4
Density	13.7	12.4	11.9	11.4
Saturation				

POSTCARDS (FIRST CLASS)
- Must be between 5" and 6" in length and 3.5" and 4.25" in height.
- Must be between .007" and .0095" thick.

Business Reply Mail (Rates in cents per piece)

BUSINESS REPLY LETTERS (Up to 1 oz.)	Surcharge	Single place rate	Rates	BUSINESS REPLY CARDS (max. size 4.25" X 6")	Surcharge	Single place rate	Rates
With BRAMAS Approval	.02	.32	.34	With BRAMAS Approval	.02	.20	.22
Without BRAMAS Approval	.10	.32	.42	Without BRAMAS Approval	.10	.20	.30
Without Advanced Approval	.44	.32	.76	Without Advanced Approval	.44	.20	.64

Annual Permit Fee $85.00. Annual Accounting Fee $205.00

WEB SITES

American Association of Advertising Agencies
www.commercepark.com

Advertising Media Center
www.amic.com

Advertising Professionals Online
www.webcom.com

American Marketing Association
www.ama.org

Bob Bly
www.bly.com
Articles and resources on copywriting, direct mail, and related topics

Creative Freelancers
www.freelancers.com

Direct Marketing Association
www.the-dma.org

Direct Marketing Club of New York
www.dmcny.org

Direct Response
www.direct-response.com

Dun & Bradstreet
www.dnbmdd.com
Information on business prospects available by company

Edith Roman Associates
www.edithroman.com
Online mailing lists, counts, and data cards

FIND/SVP
www.findsvp.com
Market research studies and services

Freelance Online
www.FreelanceOnline.com

IBM
www.ibm.com/patents
Online patent searches

Jeffrey Lant Associates
www.worldprofit.com
Sophisticated, practical, proven advice and ideas to enhance your Web marketing

Newspaper Advertising Association
www.naa.org

Public Relations Society of America
www.prsa.org

Radio Advertising Bureau
www.rab.com

U.S. Post Office
www.usps.gov

Writers for Hire
www.mindspring.com/~lhill

ADVERTISING TO SALES RATIOS BY INDUSTRY

1997 Advertising-to-Sales Ratios for the 200 Largest Ad Spending Industries

Industry	Ad dollars as percent of sales	Industry	Ad dollars as percent of sales
Accident & health insurance	0.5	Lab analytical instruments	2.0
Advertising	2.4	Lawn, garden tractors, equip	5.5
Agriculture chemicals	3.8	Leather & leather products	6.4
Agriculture production-crops	1.5	Lumber & other bldg matl-retl	0.8
Air cond, heating, refrig eq	1.5	Lumber & wood pds, ex fum	0.3
Air courier services	1.4	Machine tools, metal cutting	0.9
Air transport, scheduled	1.1	Magnetc, optic recording media	1.7
Apparel & other finished pds	5.8	Malt beverages	10.2
Apparel & accessory stores	2.3	Management services	1.2
Auto & home supply	1.4	Meas & controlling dev, nec	2.7
Auto dealers, gas stations	0.8	Meat packing plants	5.9
Auto rent & lease, no drivers	2.8	Men, yth, boys fmsh, wrk clthg	2.6
Bakery products	2.7	Metalworking machinery & eq	3.6
Beverages	7.6	Misc amusement & rec service	2.9
Biological pds, ex diagnstics	0.9	Misc business services	1.6
Bldg matl, hardwr, & garden-retl	3.9	Misc elec machy, eq, supplies	0.4
Books: pubg, pubg & printing	10.7	Misc fabricated metal prods	0.7
Brdwoven fabric mill, cotton	1.3	Misc food preps, kindred pds	2.9
Btld & can soft drinks, water	5.0	Misc furniture and fixtures	1.0
Cable & other pay TV svcs	0.8	Misc general mdse stores	3.6
Calculate, acct. mach, ex cmp	1.3	Misc manufacturing industries	3.9
Can fruit, veg, presrv, jam, jel	1.7	Misc mondurable goods-whsl	3.6
Can, froznpresrv fruit & veg	4.4	Misc shopping goods stores	2.6
Catalog, mail-order houses	9.0	Misc transportation equip	4.8

Industry	Ad dollars as percent of sales	Industry	Ad dollars as percent of sales
Chemicals & allied pds-whsl	3.1	Miscellaneous publishing	2.5
Chemicals & allied prods	7.8	Miscellaneous retail	1.3
Cigarettes	5.9	Mortgage bankers & loan corr	3.4
Cmp & cmp software stores	0.7	Motion pic, videotape prodtn	7.4
Cmp integrated sys design	1.5	Motion pict, videotape distr	6.4
Cmp processing, data prep svc	1.1	Motion picture theaters	3.4
Cmp programming, data process	6.0	Motor homes	1.8
Commercial printing	6.0	Motor veh supply, new pts-whsl	0.4
Communications equip, nec	3.5	Motor vehicle part, accessory	0.7
Computer & office equipment	1.3	Motor vehicles & car bodies	2.4
Computer communication equip	1.8	Motorcycles, bicycles & parts	1.8
Computer peripheral eq, nec	2.6	Newspaper, pubg, pubg & print	4.8
Computer storage devices	1.4	Office machines, nec	0.4
Construction machinery & eq	0.3	Operative builders	1.2
Construction-special trade	7.5	Ophthalmic goods	8.3
Convrt papr, paprbrd, ex boxes	3.7	Optical instruments & lenses	2.8
Cookies & crackers	2.7	Ortho, prosth, surg appl, suply	2.2
Cutlery, hankd tools, gen rdwr	11.4	Paints, varnishes, lacquers	2.3
Dairy products	2.0	Paper mills	2.2
Dental equipment & supplies	1.7	Patent owners and lessors	11.0
Department stores	3.6	Pens, pencils, oth office matl	3.5
Dolls & stuffed toys	15.3	Perfume, cosmetic, toilet prep	8.5
Drug & proprietary stores	1.2	Periodical, pubg, pubg & print	5.5
Eating & drinking places	4.1	Personal credit institutions	1.2
Eating places	4.0	Personal services	3.3
Educational services	7.7	Petroleum refining	1.1
Elec meas & test instruments	3.3	Pharmaceutical preparations	5.2
Electr, oth elec eq. ex cmp	1.4	Phone comm ex radiotelephone	2.1
Electric housewares & fans	4.1	Phone recrds, audiotape, disc	10.5
Electric lighting, wiring eq	3.4	Photofinishing laboratories	8.3
Electrical indl apparatus	1.1	Photographic equip & suppl	3.3
Electomedical apparatus	0.8	Plastic matl, synthetic resin	1.2
Electronic components, nec	1.3	Plastics products, nec	3.9
Electronic computers	1.7	Plastics, resins, elastomers	0.9
Electronic parts, eq-whsl, nec	3.3	Pottery & related products	4.7
Engines & turbines	1.7	Poultry slaughter & process	3.8
Equip rental & leasing, nec	2.2	Prepackaged software	3.6
Fabricated plate work	1.8	Printing trades machy, equip	2.6
Family clothing stores	2.6	Racing, include track operations	3.0
Farm machinery & equipment	1.0	Radio broadcasting stations	5.8
Fire, marine, casualty ins	0.8	Radio, TV broadcast, comm eq	0.9
Food & kindred products	7.8	Radio, TV, cons electr stores	3.4
Food stores	3.9	Radiotelephone communication	4.4
Footwear, ex rubber	3.5	Real estate investment trust	2.8
Furniture stores	7.6	Refrig & service ind machine	2.1
Games, toys, chld veh, ex dolls	13.1	Retail stores	2.8

Industry	Ad dollars as percent of sales	Industry	Ad dollars as percent of sales
Gen med & surgical hospitals	0.9	Rubber & plastics footwear	8.1
General indl mach & eq. nec	0.8	Sausage, oth prepared meat pd	6.1
Glass, glasswr-pressed, blown	1.2	Securities brokers & dealers	1.8
Grain mill products	8.3	Semiconductor, related device	2.3
Greeting cards	2.8	Ship & boat bldg & repairing	1.7
Groceries & related pds-whsl	6.3	Shoe stores	2.4
Grocery stores	1.0	Skilled nursing care fac	2.9
Gskets, hose, bltng-rubr, plstc	1.1	Soap, detergent, toilet preps	9.7
Hardwr, plumb, heat eq-whsl	2.4	Spec outpatient facility, nec	0.9
Heating eq, plumbing fixture	4.3	Special clean, polish preps	12.5
Help supply services	0.7	Special industry machinery	2.0
Hobby, toy & game shops	4.5	Sporting & athletic gds, nec	6.3
Home furniture & equip store	2.9	Steel works & blast furnaces	0.3
Hospitals & medical svc plans	0.9	Structural clay products	1.2
Hospitals	2.5	Subdivid, develop, ex cemetery	4.5
Hotels, motels, tourist courts	3.2	Sugar & confectionery prods	17.4
Household appliances	2.4	Surgical, med instr, apparatus	1.5
Household audio & video eq	3.3	Svcs to dwellings, oth bldgs	1.7
Household furniture	4.6	Tele & telegraph apparatus	0.7
Ice cream & frozen desserts	5.1	TV broadcast station	1.7
In vitro, in vivo diagnostics	1.9	Tires & inner tubes	1.9
Indl inorganic chemicals	1.1	Tobacco products	4.2
Indl trucks, tractors, trailrs	1.5	Unsupp plastics film & sheet	4.6
Industrial measurement instr	0.8	Variety stores	1.7
Ins agents, brokers & service	1.3	Watches, clocks & parts	15.9
Investment advice	5.7	Water transportation	4.8
Jewelry stores	4.3	Wmn's miss, chld, infnt, undgmnt	6.5
Jewelry, precious metal	4.8	Women's clothing stores	2.0
Knit outerwear mills	3.1	Women's, misses, jrs outerwear	4.3
Knitting mills	2.3	Wood hshld furn, ex upholsrd	3.2

INDEX